D1031965

THE WINE REGIONS of AUSTRALIA

THE WINE REGIONS of AUSTRALIA

JOHN BEESTON

ALLEN&UNWIN

To my dear wife Lynn, for her patience and loving support
during the completion of this book

This edition published in 2002

Copyright © John Beeston 2002
Maps by Mapgraphics Pty Ltd

All rights reserved. No part of this book may be reproduced or transmitted in
any form or by any means, electronic or mechanical, including photocopying,
recording or by any information storage and retrieval system, without prior
permission in writing from the publisher. *The Australian Copyright Act* 1968
(the Act) allows a maximum of one chapter or 10% of this book, whichever is
the greater, to be photocopied by any educational institution for its educational
purposes provided that the educational institution (or body that administers it) has
given a remuneration notice to Copyright Agency Limited (CAL) under the Act.

Allen & Unwin
83 Alexander Street, Crows Nest NSW 2065 Australia
Phone: (61 2) 8425 0100
Fax: (61 2) 9906 2218
Email: info@allenandunwin.com
Web: www.allenandunwin.com

National Library of Australia
Cataloguing-in-Publication entry:

Beeston, John.
  The wine regions of Australia.

  2nd ed.
  Bibliography.
  Includes index.
  ISBN 1 86508 677 0.

  1. Wine and wine making – Australia. 2. Wine and wine
  making – Australia – Directories. 3. Wine industry –
  Australia. I. Title.

641.220994

Set in 10/12 pt Goudy by Midland Typesetters
Printed and bound by Shannon Books
10 9 8 7 6 5 4 3 2 1

❧ CONTENTS

PART II   TASMANIA

PART III   SOUTH AUSTRALIA

❦ PREFACE TO THE SECOND EDITION

Since the publication of the first edition in November 1999, many more wine regions and sub-regions have been registered throughout Australia. Their names and boundaries have not avoided local controversy and so many important areas remain unregistered. Such a process is very reliant not only on differences in soil and climate, but also on the 'marketability' of the name chosen. Has the wine consumer heard of the name? What expectations does he or she have of it? Such considerations must be carefully considered before a name is rushed forward for registration. Since November 1999, the law has intervened and has changed the boundaries of what is arguably Australia's most famous region, Coonawarra. This judgement may, in turn, lead to the resolution of difficulties in other regions. It is to be hoped that the Australian wine industry itself will be enriched by such decisions and not just the pockets of a few lawyers.

❧ PREFACE TO THE FIRST EDITION

Australia's wine boom, for such it has been since the re-awakening of our export markets in the mid 1980s, has produced a surge of new vineyard areas in addition to our traditional winegrowing areas. For the first time in our vinous history, treaty obligations have made it necessary to define wine zones, regions and sub-regions, converting once vague areas into strictly delineated locations. Such boundary definition, together with the Label Integrity Program instituted some years ago, should ensure the authenticity of origin of our wines and be of great assistance to the discerning consumer of Australian whites and reds.

Over 60 maps of zones, regions, sub-regions and other areas, which will in the course of time achieve regional or sub-regional status, have been included. The maps of zones, regions and sub-regions are based, subject to changes of scale to accommodate the pages of this book, on the official maps used to delineate the boundaries of such areas.

The approach to defining these areas has been interesting. Wine zones have been delineated purely according to 'political' boundaries. Some wine zones in remote parts of Australia presently possess no vines and probably never will. These zones say nothing about the suitability of their vast expanses of territory for vines. The smaller wine regions, however, do make certain statements about Australian wine and the sub-regions even more. It is only natural that all winegrowing areas have sought to encompass and involve all the growers and makers within their 'region'. Thus it is quite understandable that some regional winegrowing associations have adopted a 'political' approach merely following municipal boundaries. Others, however, have looked more deeply into regionality regarding altitude as an important unifying factor. Thus both altitude and municipal limits have been taken into account. None as yet (even Coonawarra, and it has not yet been granted final regional status) has relied solely on uniqueness of soil type as the basis of extent of their region or sub-region. However, even as I write, this consideration is arising in many sub-regions and will surely arise more often in the future.

Thus I have dealt with every wine region and sub-region registered, or in the process of being registered, as at 31 March 1999. I have largely excluded reviews of individual wines, as there is no place for them in a book of this kind, but a very few have been included as being typical of their particular regional style. There are many vineyards and wineries included, both huge and minute, but I can make no claim to be all-inclusive. No writer, however assiduous, ever can. There are winegrowers and makers who wish to keep their activities entirely to themselves, making no response to letters, faxes or phone calls. They are entitled to their privacy, however frustrating it may be to an intrusive author. What I hope I have achieved is not only a valuable vineyard guide for those wine enthusiasts who love to travel to both our new and old vineyard areas to appreciate the great variety of wines found there. I also hope this work will be of some interest to those who may one day, in however large or small a way, become winegrowers themselves and also to those enthusiastic wine and vine explorers who have already become vignerons within the vast and still largely unknown vineland that is Australia.

❧ LIST OF MAPS

❧ A note on the maps

Wineries and vineyards shown on the maps have cellar door sales outlets open during hours specified or by appointment, or they are vineyards of importance. Wineries or vineyards not shown on the maps either do not have cellar door sales or have chosen not to be included in this edition.

❧ INTRODUCTION: APPELLATION AUSTRALIA AND GEOGRAPHIC INDICATIONS

In the mid-1980s, Australia's wine exports showed the first signs of awakening from a 40-year slumber. As a result, they began to attract the unfavourable attention of European Commission regulators who were keen to protect depressed and oversupplied local markets from foreign competition and to help drain an already flooded European wine lake. They were only too anxious to erect tariff barriers as Australia's winemaking practices differed in a number of technical respects from those of the Europeans.

In 1987, Australia therefore began—at first informally through the sole efforts of Professor Terry Lee, at that time of the Australian Wine Research Institute—what proved to be far-sighted negotiations with the European Commission. They were far-sighted because the European Commission now represents over 350 million people and only the year before (30 June 1986) Australia's wine exports had exceeded 10 million litres for the first time since 1946/47 and were to increase twelvefold in the ensuing eight years. The talks soon became formalised as bilateral Australia–EC negotiations. After nearly six years of complex discussions in both Canberra and Brussels concerning wine and food law, trade practices, trademarks, the Australian Constitution and the Treaty of Rome, the Agreement was initialled in late 1992 and came into effect on 1 March 1994.

The major provisions of the Agreement can be summarised as follows. Australia agreed to protect all European geographical indications and traditional expressions as set out in Annex II of the Agreement except for a few geographic and traditional expressions which Australia either agreed to phase out by certain dates or negotiate a phase-out period by 31 December 1997. This was a very real concession because Australian winemakers and marketers relied quite heavily on generic styles such as 'Chablis' to describe cheap white blends. In return for this concession:

1 The EC provided exemptions from EC wine law for the following winemaking practices for wines originating in Australia:
   a the addition of erythorbate
   b the minimum acidity level
   c botrytised and late harvest wines with a total alcohol content higher than 15%
   d maximum limits for the addition of several specified processing aids
   e the extent to which the initial acidity can be raised by acid addition
   f a five-year exemption on the use of cation exchange
2 The number of analyses required for the VI-1 certificate (a certificate stating that non-EC wines comply with EC wine regulations and which must accompany non-EC wines into the EC) decreased from eight to three—alcohol, titratable acidity and sulfur dioxide—and for red wines malvidin diglucoside.

3 The EC allowed an Australian wine to name up to five grape varieties on one label and to be a blend of wines from up to three geographical indications. (Previously an Australian wine had to come from a single geographical indication and could be described with no more than two varieties on the label from which the wine had to be entirely made.)

4 Australian geographical indications and traditional expressions were to be protected within the EC.

Because of difficulties encountered with the National Food Authority in the revision of the Wine Standards P4 and P6 (winemaking standards and codes of practice), in which the negotiating team had hoped to embody the provisions of the EC Agreement, the team was obliged to suggest to the Government that the *Australian Wine and Brandy Corporation Act 1980* be amended in such a way as to give effect to the provisions of the Agreement.

The amendments which came into force on 1 January 1994:

1 provided for the implementation of the Agreement
2 defined 'wine'
3 established the Register of Protected Names
4 established the Geographical Indications Committee
5 enabled the Australian Wine and Brandy Corporation (AWBC) to write regulations in respect of the labelling of wine and oenological practices and processes.

As a result, Australia's wine law as to the manufacture and labelling of wine in Australia and for export is now embodied in the AWBC Act and Regulations while other relevant sections of wine law are contained in the Food Acts of the states and territories, in particular Standard A16—processing aids, Standard P4—wine, sparkling wine and fortified wine, Standard P5—alcoholic beverages not elsewhere standardised, Standard P6—wine products and Standard S1—miscellaneous foods. Embodied in the Register were all the geographical indications for wine of the European Union as listed in Annex II of the Agreement and as regards Australia the terms 'Australia', 'Australian' and the names of each state and internal territory. In January 1994, as a result of these amendments, the Geographical Indications Committee was constituted and later that year commenced the formulation of the first official wine map of Australia.

Issued on 7 February 1995, the first of the Committee's 'final determinations' consisted of the geographical indication South Eastern Australia (an indication that includes most of the cheaper mass blends of Australian red and white wines) and officially delimited the wine 'zones' of Victoria and New South Wales. Since then the whole of Australia has been divided into wine zones as follows:

1 Victoria: Gippsland; Central Victoria; North East Victoria; North West Victoria; Port Phillip and Western Victoria
2 New South Wales: Big Rivers; Western Plains; Northern Slopes; Northern Rivers; Hunter Valley; South Coast; Central Ranges and Southern New South Wales
3 Tasmania (whole of state)
4 Northern Territory (whole of territory)

AUSTRALIAN WINE ZONES

WINE ZONES

1 Western Victoria
2 Central Victoria
3 Port Phillip
4 Gippsland
5 North East Victoria
6 North West Victoria
7 Barossa
8 Limestone Coast
9 Fleurieu
10 The Peninsulas
11 Lower Murray
12 Mount Lofty Ranges
13 Far North
14 Eastern Plains, Inland and
   North of Western Australia
15 West Australian South
   East Coastal
16 South West Australia
17 Central Western Australia
18 Greater Perth
19 Big Rivers
20 Central Ranges
21 Hunter Valley
22 South Coast
23 Southern New South Wales
24 Northern Rivers
25 Northern Slopes
26 Western Plains
27 Queensland
28 Northern Territory

Southeast Australia

NORTHERN TERRITORY 28

QUEENSLAND 27

WESTERN AUSTRALIA 14

SOUTH AUSTRALIA 13

NEW SOUTH WALES 26

VICTORIA

TASMANIA

Darwin

Brisbane

Sydney

Canberra

Melbourne

Adelaide

Perth

Hobart

0   400
Kilometres

5   Queensland (whole of state)
6   Western Australia: Eastern Plains, Inland and North of Western Australia; Western Australia South East Coastal; South Western Australia; Central Western Australia and Greater Perth
7   South Australia: Adelaide, a Superzone which includes the zones Mount Lofty Ranges, Barossa and Fleurieu and suburban Adelaide and the Adelaide Plains: Limestone Coast; Lower Murray; Far North; The Peninsulas (York and Eyre); Mount Lofty Ranges; Barossa; Fleurieu. Winemakers from any of the zones constituting the Superzone may use the name Adelaide instead of their local zonal name, if they so wish.

Regionalisation and sub-regionalisation will continue as Australia discovers and explores its special wine areas in the years to come.

MANDATORY RECORD KEEPING

Soon after the commencement of the negotiations for the EC/Australia Wine Agreement, the Australian wine industry in consultation with the AWBC, introduced its Label Integrity Program to come into force from vintage 1990. LIP, as it became known, was designed to put teeth into wine laws which, though uniform among the Australian states, had been previously left to the individual states to enforce. Importantly, verification of compliance with and enforcement of LIP was to be vested in the AWBC.

The earlier laws had concerned grape variety, area of origin and vintage. In brief, they required that, if the label of a wine included any allusion to grape variety, locality of growth or year of vintage, the wine must contain at least 80% of that variety and must be at least 80% from that locality and 95% of the year of vintage. (From vintage 1994, in line with the EC/Australia Wine Agreement, the percentages for grape varieties and localities were increased to 85% and lowered to 85% in respect of vintage content.)

Thus authorised, the AWBC now insists on the keeping of standard winery records and may audit, at any time, claims made relating to grape variety, area of origin and vintage. It can do this by checking winery records made at four key points in the wine-making and sales process. These are the winery weighbridge where grapes are bought and received; the cellar where the grapes are converted into wine; the sales desk where inter-company sales and purchases take place; and the wholesale desk where finished wine leaves the cellar as a product. The product has either a label stating a grape variety or varieties, the region of origin and year of vintage or an invoice stating those details if the wine has been sold in bulk. Such records must be made within three months of the occurrence of any of these events.

The standard system of record keeping, or 'universal recording system' as it is known by the AWBC, insists that weighbridge records show year of vintage, location of vineyard (origin), grape variety, tonnage and name of grower. In the winery itself, records must indicate the identity of the wine produced from those grapes identified at the weighbridge, the volume of wine made from them, consolidations of identical wines, blendings of non-identical wines, identity of ensuing products and records of release of the finished wine. In this way, the wine retains its official identity acquired at the weighbridge, which it can lose if it is destined to be a generic (such as chablis) or a style (such as dry red). It should be noted that such 'generics' are being phased out because of the EC/Australia Wine Agreement. If the wine is required to be sold in bulk or in unlabelled bottles (cleanskin) in an inter-company transaction, the records must specify the identity, volume and purchaser of such bulk or cleanskin wine and the source, identity and volume of wines brought in from other wineries to form the whole or part of any wine with a vintage, varietal or region of origin claim. Finally, if the wine is destined for the retail market, when bottled, labelled and packaged, its records must show the total production of a wine carrying vintage, variety and region of origin claims, stocks of wine carrying such claims and sales of all such wines.

Thus it has become possible for an auditor not only to check the legitimacy of all vintage, variety and region of origin claims made by winemakers but to go further and check the wines of any company or group of companies, or even the varietal wines of any particular region. Needless to say there are substantial penalties for infraction, not the least of which, in a time of buoyant export sales, is the cancellation of export approvals and the subsequent recall of offending wines.

AUSTRALIAN REGION OF ORIGIN

The Australian wine industry has had few wine scandals. In the past the industry was never important enough in national economic terms. Now, as its economic worth increases, it has realised that it cannot afford them. The occasional infractions of winemaking regulations have been dealt with according to law, the offenders punished and the industry has returned to normality. Though the recent amendments to Australian wine law have considerably extended the control of the Australian Wine and Brandy Corporation, it remains a self-policing industry and takes pride not only in its adherence to existing legal standards but also in its levels of quality, which have always been well above ordinary legal requirements.

This has not always been the case in Europe, where periodic wine scandals led to the scheme Appellation d'Origine Controlée (AOC) being introduced to French law during the first three decades of the twentieth century. This has resulted in governmental control of virtually every aspect of the French industry, from the soil in which the vines are planted, the types of vines that may be planted, the manner of pruning them, maximum grape yields, minimum alcoholic strengths and even the manner in which the finished wines are invoiced to clients. Similar legislation has followed in all the leading wine-producing countries of the European Union. As a result, wine fraud in Europe is now much more difficult, but it has occurred as recently as 1974 in Bordeaux. In some cases, appellation control is therefore equated mistakenly with a guarantee of the quality of a wine, whereas it is often merely a guarantee of origin and of conformity with the standards set out for its appellation. Though tasting does occur in some regions of Europe before a wine can be granted a controlled appellation, what the tasters are seeking is not necessarily quality but typicity—that it has the regional and varietal characters of the other wines of its appellation in that year, be they good or bad. The rules have resulted in a general conservatism pervading the European industry and have accounted in part for the marketing success of Australian and other New World (i.e. non-European) wines in Europe in the past decade.

Not surprisingly, Australian winemakers regard the European system as stultifying and as stifling individual initiative and have been firmly against the introduction of similar schemes to Australia—a view that is now being supported by many younger European winemakers. Due therefore to the quality of New World wines and the strength of their marketing, European wine authorities have been forced to recognise the existence of 'international' grape varieties, such as cabernet sauvignon and chardonnay, and to allow their inclusion on wine labels which were previously blessed only with the name of an obscure village or region. It must, however, be admitted that in most areas of Australia wines are not tasted unless they are intended for export and then only on the basic levels of soundness and marketability. Australian wine legislators have wisely left wine quality to be determined by its winemakers and its acceptance or otherwise to be decided by the wine drinkers of the world.

Definitions of zones, regions and sub-regions

Zone: an area of land that (a) may comprise one or more regions, or (b) may reasonably be regarded as a zone.

Region: an area within a zone or zones consisting of a minimum of five vineyards of at least five hectares each without common ownership and producing at least 500 tonnes.

Sub-region: an area within a region of a minimum of five vineyards of at least five hectares each without common ownership and producing at least 500 tonnes. There must also of course be a factor or factors common to the sub-region which distinguish it from the rest of the region.

These definitions are not intended to encourage over-production, which an average of 20 tonnes per hectare might otherwise suggest, but to ensure 'critical mass' and the economic survival of the region and/or sub-region.

Within the above formulae, the identification of regions and sub-regions has been largely (and wisely) left to the winegrowers themselves. Their various professional organisations have adopted differing approaches to these boundaries. Some quite conservatively have adopted municipal boundaries or, in the case of Margaret River, a line of longitude. Others more imaginatively, and relevantly, have used contours of altitude, above or below which the most favoured vine sites for the characteristic wines of their region or sub-region have been proved to exist, for example, the region of Sunbury and the sub-region of Broke-Fordwich. Of course this approach is only possible where there has been historical experience of the quality of certain wines. The more conservative approach is understandable where the wine region is comparatively new and unproved. As for sub-regions, many more common denominators of altitudes and soil types will need to be seen before their existence can be positively justified, although the importance of soils as constituting the limits of regions or sub-regions is very much recognised in the case of the Coonawarra Region (recently much in dispute and referred to the Administrative Appeals Tribunal) and the proposed Victorian region or sub-region of Heathcote.

SOME COMPULSORY VITICULTURE

Climate is of course critical to the success or failure of viticulture in any region. Yet prior to the work of RE Smart and PR Dry (*Viticulture*, vol. II), climate as a factor in determining the suitability of a region for viticulture had been defined in little more than degree days which, though useful indicators of heat, do not give a full picture of climate. Smart and Dry chose to paint climate in much greater detail and broader colour, delimiting four important climatic factors: temperature, aridity, relative humidity and sunshine hours. In his own state of Western Australia, John Gladstones, another eminent research scientist, has also made fundamental contributions to viti-cultural knowledge in the past 35 years. Gladstones' *Viticulture and Environment* is essential reading for any viticultural professional today. In the last decade the whole climatic picture has become much clearer and the whole Australian wine industry owes a considerable debt of gratitude to these researchers.

Throughout this book climatic details of regions are coded as follows. These are basically as defined by Dry and Smart in Chapter 2 of *Viticulture* (edited by Coome and Dry).

MJT (Mean January Temperature) is the mean temperature of Australia's warmest month, which correlates well with degree days.

MAR (Mean Annual Range) is the difference between the Mean January Temperature and the Mean July Temperature (the coldest month). It is a measure of 'continentality' of a region and, if it is higher than another region with the same MJT, means that spring and autumn temperatures will be lower, signifying slower development in spring and ripening in autumn.

HDD (Heat Degree Days) are calculated by taking the mean temperature of months during the growing season in degrees Celsius, subtracting 10°C (below which the vine does not grow) and multiplying by the number of days in the months of the growing season. The growing season is usually October to April in cooler areas, but there seems no good reason why, in warmer areas, that period should not be September to March or—as occasionally happens in benign maritime regions such as Margaret River—July to April.

AR (Annual Rainfall) is given in millimetres and where such data are available the October–April growing season rainfall is listed. If another period applies, that period is specified in the particular regional details given.

RH (Relative Humidity) is the measure of the dryness or dampness of the climate taken (by Smart and Dry) as at 9am approximating the daily mean figure of relative humidity in January or over the growing season. Low humidity accelerates the loss of water from the vine by evapo-transpiration while high humidity slows this process but increases the incidence of some fungal diseases. (Gladstones' relative humidity takes this figure at 3pm, when humidity is likely to be at its lowest for any particular day.)

AI (Aridity Index). It is acknowledged that mature vineyards lose moisture at about half the rate as measured by a Class A pan evaporimeter. Irrigation water requirements can therefore be calculated from month to month by subtracting the millimetres of natural rainfall from half of the millimetres of Class A pan evaporation and totalling the result during the growing season. Dry and Smart specify the season as being from October to March but it can be extended over a longer, slower growing season if necessary.

SH (Sunshine Hours) are the number of bright sunshine hours averaged daily, again from October to March or such longer period of the growing season.

Gladstones (in *Viticulture and Environment* p. 8), however, considers the most important factor in ripening in practice is the mean temperature of the ripening month. He lists three key elements of ripening: (a) loss of malic acid, (b) accumulation of sugar, and (c) the most critical of all, but not necessarily happening at the same time as the preceding two elements—'physiological' or 'flavour' ripening. For high quality table wines, his research points to a mean temperature of just 20°C, as the optimum for 'flavour' ripening, as indeed it seems to be for vine growth, bud formation, flowering and early fruit development.

CLIMATE, SOILS AND VITICULTURE

If local climatic conditions are too cold, too hot, too wet or too arid, the vine will not thrive. So before soil and viticulture are examined, it is necessary to discuss climate. The French use their word *climat* in two senses. They use it to refer to climate as it is understood in English. They also use it as an extension of the word to mean vineyard, which includes the whole raft of factors that influence the growth of the vine and the ripening of its grapes—for they contend that the great difference between the best wines of France and those of the rest of the world, especially the New World, is that their best wines enjoy incomparable *climats*.

Australian viticultural history is short by world standards. Our early settlers often brought grapevines merely to plant as an alternative crop on land they had never even seen. They certainly had little time to study the optimal climate for the varieties planted. They simply learnt day by day, as the vines did or did not flourish. Today the situation is entirely different. There are meteorological records going back many years for many areas. Even a century ago, a Victorian Royal Commission divided that state, then a colony, into three viticultural areas based primarily on climate. About 50 years ago, two eminent Californian viticulturists, Amerine and Winkler, evolved a system of classifying Californian vineyard areas into five regions based on temperature summation through their growing season (April to October). Such summation is measured in degree days and is at best only a general measure of the suitability of an area for any particular grape varieties or indeed wine styles. This system is now considered too simplistic as it neglects many other important meteorological factors which influence a vineyard and the ripening of its fruit, such as frost risk, frequency of rainfall, totality of sunshine hours, prevailing winds at critical times of the season and so on.

Continentality

'Continentality' is often considered a high quality wine factor in that it seems to encourage delicate aromas, fine fruit flavours and the retention of natural acidity, as espoused by Smart and Dry. However, some viticulturists are not convinced, stating that, although continental-type climates have great potential for quality, such potential is often not realised because 'continental' vintages are 'notoriously variable'. As Gladstones points out, Burgundy certainly has a 'continental' climate and its best vintages are characterised by two crucial factors—'a warm, sunny spring' to encourage early development and 'high mid-summer temperatures and sunshine hours'. The next most important factor is sunshine in August and to a lesser extent thereafter. Temperatures during the ripening period, commonly August to September, whether high or low, had virtually no relationship to the quality of the vintage.

Continentality, however, has its advantages. It increases winter dormancy in vines with a correspondingly longer pruning season. In some maritime Australian vineyard sites, such as Margaret River, budburst sometimes occurs in July, resulting in a far longer and therefore more risky development period for the vine and dominance by a cane's terminal shoots with little intermediate budburst. Such canes—often of 'continental' varieties such as traminer, riesling and chardonnay—are very prone to damage by high winds and heavy rain. Continentality on the other hand, with its more sudden onset of warmer weather, results in a more even budburst and subsequent cane development. Continentality and its extreme summer heat can also reduce berry size. This can give a high skin to pulp ratio with attendant better colour extraction and flavour concentration although, as Gladstones suggests, there are maritime viticultural areas which often have summers hot enough to achieve this. Of course, smaller berry size may come at the price of less quantity, though perhaps higher quality, in wine.

Casual temperature variability

If continentality (MAR) is a function of the difference between Mean January Temperature and Mean July Temperature, then, beyond the range of anticipated seasonal fluctuations, casual temperature variability can also cause severe problems. At its coolest, in 'continental' vineyards, it can cause a failure of budburst in spring or a failure to ripen the crop in autumn. It can also cause frosts which, if severe enough in winter (though rarely ever in Australia), can cause the death of vines. Spring frosts can cause havoc in young shoots and their potential crop, whereas frosts in autumn will certainly 'freeze' the ripening. Even in maritime areas where vineyards are within 5 kilometres of the sea, the still, cold nights following a dry spell can cause a damaging frost.

At its warmest and accompanied by high winds and low relative humidity, temperature variability can cause bushfires with attendant severe damage to vineyards. Even if a bushfire does not occur, bunches and berries, especially of red varieties at the time of veraison, may be exposed to sun damage. Wine made from such fruit may suffer from 'off' aromas and flavours. Whether it be heat or cold, the chemistry of the vine prefers equability of temperature.

Sunshine hours

These of course are an index of solar radiation, referring to the number of sunshine hours and not the total of their warmth. Their effects vary according to the season. In spring it is acknowledged that sufficiently warm, still, calm, sunny conditions will aid budburst and later promote growth, pollination and fruit-set. The warming of the soil also promotes cytokinin (see glossary) development in the roots of the vine, while local heating and the spectral quality of direct sunlight may help the bud by reducing its sensitivity to gibberellins (see glossary). During ripening, sunshine will also assist fruit-bearing canes to obtain a more rapid sugar accumulation in the berries. This has been found to be extremely important in the establishment of winegrape quality at or soon after veraison. Gladstones contends that, though numerous—perhaps even unlimited—sunshine hours are desirable for viticulture in theory, in practice the issue is more complex. Very sunny climates tend to be quite variable in temperature and to have low relative humidities, which are usually detrimental to viticulture. He concludes that sunshine hours have a positive benefit for both yield and quality in winegrapes, 'but only if temperature variability and relative humidity remain favourable' (*Viticulture and Environment* p. 21).

The following can be concluded from the relationship between sunshine hours and degree days:

- Vines in warm climates require a greater number of sunshine hours to achieve a given fullness of wine body and style than those in cool climates. This is logical since the consumption of nutrition by the vine increases as temperature increases, whereas nutrition production by photosynthesis stabilises at intermediate temperatures.
- Temperature not sunshine is the primary limiting factor and determinant of wine style in cool climates (no more than 1450 biologically effective degree days). Temperature summation decrees whether particular varieties will ripen at all and, if so, when and on average at what temperatures and total of sunshine hours.
- Differences in sunshine hours over a growing season still influence sugar levels and therefore the formation of aroma and flavour at given physiological ripening stages in cool climates. Flavour development, however, is limited chiefly by the degree of physiological ripeness achieved—as a direct result of temperature. Thus sunshine hours contribute to physiological ripeness but only through their effects on temperature.

Light

Light and its wavelength and colour composition (spectral quality) have recently been shown to be of great viticultural significance. Research has indicated that varying degrees of spectral quality within the vine canopy influence the physiology and perhaps also the fruit quality of the vine. As Gladstones points out (*Viticulture and*

Environment p. 26), red wavelengths and sunlight of normal spectral quality are well recognised to cause leafy, stocky growth, vigorous branching, fruitfulness, dark green leaf colour and generous production of pigments, analogous to the supply of ample cytokinins from the roots (see also the comments on red soils on p. 14).

Rainfall

Australia is one of the driest countries in the world. Yet until 30 years ago, except in areas which were the subject of state irrigation schemes, irrigation was a dirty word. Dryland viticulture was de rigueur. It was commonly thought that drought stress was good for vines and even that the ensuing wines, being products of drought years, were somehow superior. Since then, attitudes have undergone a vast change as viticulturists have pointed out the damage that moisture stress, whether too little or too much, can do to vines. These days, drip irrigation is to be seen in virtually all new vineyards. Such irrigation depends on capacious surface dams and is often programmed (by virtue of electronic probes) to cut in when the vineyard shows the merest signs of drought stress. Yet these dams have to be filled and more often than not the only source of good quality water is natural rainfall. Although such rainfall is barely relevant in irrigated areas, except for the direct damage it may cause, it is of utmost importance in vineyards that are non-irrigated or reliant on trickle irrigation from smaller surface dams, which may dry up at critical times during the growing season.

Two of those critical times are flowering and berry-set, when too much or too little moisture can have a tremendous effect on potential crop quantity. Moisture stress in late spring can also affect the differentiation of fruitful buds on new shoots. Equally, too much rain can physically disrupt flowering, upsetting pollination, and the concomitant effects of lack of sunshine and photosynthesis also interfere with fruitful bud differentiation. Heavy rain in spring also promotes heavy vegetative growth, which shades lower leaves and new buds, absorbs excessive amounts of nutrition and produces the vine hormones, auxins (see glossary) and gibberellins, which counteract the fruit-flavouring cytokinins.

After bud differentiation and just before veraison, vines and their young berries seem well able to bear moisture stress. Indeed at this time, in cooler climates, some moisture stress may actually be desirable, (a) to discourage further vegetative growth so that nutrition and cytokinins are diverted to the fruit not the vegetation, and (b) to harden existing vegetative growth so that any consequent stresses during the ripening period are tolerated.

If the period around veraison is subject to moisture stress and to higher temperatures, then the vine will require sufficient moisture for development of full berry size if this is desired. If not, continued (mild) moisture stress at this time will limit berry size but augment berry colour and flavour. A reduction of quantity but increased quality should result. Severe moisture stress at this time is not desirable (if it is ever desirable), as it may interfere with the flow of sugar to the berries.

From the time just after veraison through the weeks to harvest, it is critical that enough moisture is continuously available to maintain the vines in a healthy state and to bring the crop to full maturity. Root growth and the cytokinins ascending through the roots must be uninterrupted to prevent stress and premature ageing. At this stage, healthy vines bearing a full crop need no moisture stress, since the bunches have to be the sole focus of the vine's endeavours to provide nutrients and growth hormones.

Such is the situation in cooler climates. In those that are hotter, moisture stress may cause leaf drop and thereby expose the bunches to direct sunlight. This can be catastrophic if the berries are not fully ripe since they can ripen no further and will only shrivel. Even if leaf drop does not occur, photosynthesis will be reduced with the consequence of reduced sugar supply to the berries and perhaps increased potassium, which can lead to unbalanced musts. Even after maturity and indeed picking, it is necessary to maintain an adequate supply of moisture until normal leaf fall so that the canes mature properly and store sufficient nutrients to ensure a healthy start to budburst in the ensuing spring.

So far this discussion has been concerned with a deficiency of moisture, but what of excess? During winter, the vine is normally dormant, so it has little need for moisture, be it a trickle or a flood. If the former, the subsoil may become excessively dry and will therefore need irrigation on budburst. If the latter, the vigneron must look to the suitability of the natural drainage of the soil to avoid waterlogging and consequent damage to roots. In Mediterranean-type climates, in spring, sufficient rain is necessary if only to fill surface dams for the moisture demands of the ensuing growing season. If the vineyard is unirrigated, it is essential to provide enough subsoil moisture to carry the vine through without stress to the vintage. Important factors here are soil depth and moisture-holding capacity. But whenever excess rain occurs in whatever type of climate, the vigneron will hope that it will not be at flowering. Nor should excess rain occur in the few weeks before ripening as moisture take-up may increase pH and decrease total acidity, even if it does not bloat the berries, making them liable to splitting and thereby susceptible to bunch rot. Nor indeed in any climate should there be hail at this stage. Hail can be devastating at any time during the growing season, but at vintage a year's work can disappear in a flash.

Relative humidity and saturation deficit

What is saturation deficit and how is it relevant to the Australian vineyard? Briefly, it is the difference between the actual water vapour content of a given air body and what it could contain if it were vapour-saturated (100%) at the same temperature. Its value is that it is a direct indicator of the evaporative power of air and therefore very relevant to potential moisture stress in vines. Research has shown that in arid climates, even fully irrigated vines cannot take up water fast enough to meet the evapotranspirational demands of the leaves. The result is that photosynthesis ceases in mid- to late morning as the leaf pores (stomata) close to preserve moisture. The greater the saturation deficit in hot, arid climates, the more moisture is transpired by the leaves per unit of carbon dioxide taken in through the stomata with the consequence that growth and yield per unit of water are reduced (see Gladstones, *Viticulture and Environment* p. 29). Another effect of saturation deficit is an increase in potassium absorption by vines and subsequently by their fruit which leads to a higher potassium content in grape musts. Excess potassium in turn leads to loss of tartaric acid (reduced natural acidity) and an increase in pH through its precipitation as potassium bi-tartrate. The wine consequences of this are detrimental, leading to a loss of flavour freshness and a greater risk of oxidation and perhaps microbial spoilage. As a remedy, the winemaker will add appropriate amounts of tartaric acid or use ion exchange but it is better of course in all cases to start off with a well-balanced must. On the other hand, high relative humidities and high temperatures encourage fungal diseases and rot. The prospective winegrower should therefore find a vineyard site with as high a relative humidity as possible in a cool area, but not so cool as to put at risk the ripening of the grapes. An optimal relative humidity in cool to mild climates seems to be about 55% in early afternoon, a compromise between quality and potential fungal problems. Such sites occur more commonly near our southern and south-western coasts. Coastal or near-coastal climates elsewhere seem either too hot or too wet or both. (Gladstones takes his relative humidities at 3pm as opposed to Smart and Dry who use 9am. Gladstones prefers 3pm because he believes that saturation stress is at its most marked from midday to early afternoon whereas Smart and Dry support 9am as it approximates the daily mean figure.)

Wind

Like rain, wind can be both beneficial and detrimental. Air circulation is important in spring, helping to keep temperatures equable and thereby preventing frosts. Later in the growing season it forestalls excessive humidity and perhaps prevents mildews and rots. Just as importantly it moves the leaves, thereby allowing the entry of sunlight into the canopy to improve photosynthesis.

On the debit side, strong winds may cause direct damage to exposed vineyards at flowering time and later to fruiting canes, sometimes blowing off whole bunches of partially ripe fruit. In maritime areas, strong sea breezes may also carry salt spray, which can seriously interfere with flowering buds. Inland, strong winds are often accompanied by extremely hot weather and such conditions rapidly dehydrate vines, closing down photosynthesis with consequent interruption to the ripening process and perhaps even a reduced yield. Measures to counteract the damaging effects of wind are the planting of quick-growing windbreaks, the use of established forest land, planting on east-facing slopes—usually subject to least wind effect in Australia—or planting on reverse slopes and allowing the brow of the hill to break the force of the prevailing wind, thereby protecting the vines naturally.

Soils

Aspect, soil and climate are all essential ingredients of *climat*. When noble grape types, selected by centuries of winemaking experience and wine history, are added to *climat*, it is easy to see why the French believed their appellation controlée wines to be the best in the world. That many such wines were successfully challenged in the marketplaces of the Old World by the superior technology (and cheaper price) of the wines of the New is now history, but it alters very little. It only underlines the fact that the winemakers of Australia need to know much more about their own *climats*, especially their soils. As Louis Jacquelin and Rene Poulain wrote many years ago in *Wines and Vineyards of France* (p. 39), 'the whole art of the wine grower rests in knowing his [sic] soil, supplementing it wisely, growing only suitable varieties and maintaining a judicious balance between vine and soil in order to achieve the best wine and a reasonable yield'.

So what are the physical properties of soil that will achieve the best wine? Certainly not 'the most fertile and best manured soils' (Busby, *Treatise on the Culture of the Vine*, 1825 p. 7)—although such soils will grow a most luxuriant plant, the resultant wine will probably be unripe and green-tasting. Shallow soils are also unsuitable as the vine roots quickly become waterlogged and, in times of drought, drought-stressed. Nor are thick, clayey soils suitable. Again in Busby's words, 'their firmness prevents the dissemination of the minute fibres of the roots and their coldness is prejudicial to the plant'. As well as this their impermeability prevents the initial absorption of moisture and heat and later the evaporation of any moisture that has managed to penetrate to the roots. Heavy, clay soils therefore conduct heat, air and moisture badly. This leads either to insufficient plant moisture if the surface is impermeable or excessive moisture (waterlogging) if the moisture cannot be evaporated.

Busby recommends soils for the vine that are 'dry, light and free', preferring in general those that are sandy, volcanic in origin, calcareous (limestone) or of a decomposed granite nature which, he says, possess certain wine attributes: '. . . sandy soil will, in general, produce a delicate wine . . . calcareous soil a spirituous wine and decomposed granite a brisk wine'. Another point stressed by Busby and virtually all the French authorities of the nineteenth century is the importance in soil of a 'mixture of stones', even in soils otherwise dry, light and porous. Stony, pebbly soils allow easy root penetration, restrict evaporation of moisture where such stones are on the surface and allow the infiltration of moisture. At the same time they absorb heat which is later re-radiated to the vine canopy and the fruit within it. In the nineteenth century, even the colour of the soil was thought to be important. Reddish soils were thought to increase quality in red wines, while grey or yellow soils were favoured for white. Gladstones (in *Viticulture and Environment* p. 33) points out that the spectral quality of light offers an alternative reason for these widely-held beliefs: reflection of white, yellow or especially orange or reddish light into the lower vine canopy and bunch area might be a factor in raising the ratio of red to far-red wavelengths there and so tip the balance in all grape varieties towards cytokinins and fruitfulness.

Even today, the pragmatic observations of the nineteenth century retain their importance in dry-land viticulture, though most Australian vineyards are now irrigated by one means or another. Yet soil requirements have not changed markedly. What has changed is the capacity to manage water supply, so the extremes of over- and under-supply are avoided and this in turn allows for a wider tolerance of different soils. What is sought in a soil is balance—soils of sufficient organic and inorganic elements and of good enough structure—yet with comparatively poor fertility to allow the vine to develop a successful root system, which will penetrate to sufficient depth to allow use of all available moisture and nutrition.

It is advantageous also to know as much about the chemical properties of a vineyard soil as possible. Is the soil acid, alkaline or neutral? Each type has a varying cation exchange capacity (cec). Soils with low cec have a hydrogen predominance and are acid. Those with a high cec have a predominance of the metal ions calcium, magnesium, potassium and sodium and are alkaline. The cec values for neutral soils lie in between. Thus, in general, when similar soils are compared, acid soils have low nutrient element reserves, neutral soils have adequate reserves and alkaline soils have high reserves.

There are delicate balances in soils of either an acid or alkaline nature. Balances in acid soils can be easily disturbed by overcropping or by continued applications of the same fertiliser and such treatment results in imbalances of other nutrient elements. Alkaline soils containing a great deal of calcium carbonate (such as calcareous earths) may also be upset by heavy phosphate fertiliser applications, causing, for example, a zinc deficiency.

Nutrient elements

Plant growth generally requires a whole larder of nutrient elements. About sixteen are commonly listed: carbon, hydrogen, oxygen, nitrogen, phosphorus, potassium, sulphur, calcium; and the trace elements, boron, chlorine, cobalt, copper, iron, manganese, molybdenum and zinc. The first three are easily found—green plants absorb carbon from the air, while hydrogen and oxygen are obtained from water. The rest are obtained from the soil.

Nitrogen and organic matter in soils are generally provided by decomposing plant remains and soil organisms. Nitrogen can also be fixed by organisms forming nodules on the roots of leguminous plants. Usually all nitrogenous compounds in soil are oxidised by soil organisms to form nitrates, in which form plants will readily accept them. Most Australian grape-growing soil is moderate to low in nitrogen which is a very mobile element in soil and can be readily leached from it. Shallow soils, leached acid soils and sand soils are frequently low in nitrogen. Low soil nitrogen levels also mean low fertility and while vineyard soils need not be highly fertile, soil fertility and with it vine vigour can be improved by the growth of self-regenerating subterranean clover during winter and early spring. The clover can be slashed or turned in before it competes with the budding vines for moisture. Another reason for turning in such crops before budburst is, of course, frost minimisation in frost-prone areas. Production of nitrogen with minimum cultivation has the added advantages of avoiding soil compaction and less destruction of earthworms.

Besides their nitrogen deficit, Australian soils are also deficient in phosphorus. Like nitrogen, phosphorus deficiency in soils can be remedied by legume-rich green-manuring (the growing and turning-in of legumes). As phosphorus is comparatively immobile in soil it is important that it is placed close to the root zone of vines so as to be available. A similar observation applies to the use of superphosphate.

The presence of the metal potassium varies quite widely in our vineyard soils, in both its total and exchangeable forms. (Total potassium includes all potassium present while exchangeable potassium is that part associated with the clay minerals.) In this latter form it is most readily available to plants. Low exchangeable potassium content is usually associated with acid soils, while alkaline soils have higher content and some alkaline soils may indeed be over-supplied.

While sulphur deficiency can exist in acid soils, it is presently rare in vineyard soils. In the past, the widespread use of superphosphate (which contains about 11% sulphur) and the use of sulphur in fungicide sprays have prevented such a deficiency.

Magnesium deficiency is also rare in Australian vineyard soils, though it has been shown to have been induced in Europe by the excessive use of potassium fertiliser.

Iron deficiency is more commonly present, taking the form of chlorosis associated with high pH, and is usually linked with high lime content or with poor soil drainage. In either case iron is made unavailable to the grapevine. Water-induced chlorosis may disappear when the soil dries out. Chlorosis induced by lime is naturally common in high lime soils and other alkaline soils and is particularly evident in spring when the vineyard soils are cold and wet. Again, warmer weather that dries out the soil will reduce the effect of this chlorosis.

Boron deficiency is rare in Australian vineyards and has been recorded only in Stanthorpe in acidic, sandy soils. Excessive boron is more common, existing in Murray River irrigation areas, and can be leached from such soils by irrigation water, provided they are adequately drained.

Deficiency in manganese occurs largely in alkaline soils and soils with thick lime-stone subsola (calcareous earths). The intake of manganese becomes restricted when soil pH exceeds 6.5. Manganese supply is usually adequate in acid soils, except for highly leached sands and some leached ironstone soils. It has also been shown that the application of lime to acid soils where the resulting pH surpasses 6.5 will induce manganese deficiency.

Of all the trace elements, zinc is most important in its effect on grapevines. Even a mild deficiency can affect yields and zinc deficiency does occur in some of our major irrigation areas where there are alkaline soils. A zinc deficiency has been found in such soils in Riverland, Sunraysia and the Murrumbidgee Irrigation Area. It has also been recorded in acid soils in Western Australia, especially those subject to sub-surface waterlogging.

Copper deficiency, as with sulphur, is rare in Australia, having been recorded only once, over 50 years ago. Applications of copper in various vineyard sprays will ensure that there is no recurrence.

The remaining trace elements—cobalt, molybdenum and chlorine—seem to be required more by legumes than by higher plants, such as grapevines. In any event, deficiencies in trace elements seem fairly easy to remedy with foliar sprays.

Topography and aspect

In addition to soil, topography and aspect are two other crucial but intertwined factors in the appreciation of *climat*. Altitude too may be important. Is the vineyard on flat land? Or hillside? Or on a high plateau? The virtues of stony soils have been discussed and these often occur on lower hillsides and valley slopes. Such soils are usually well-drained and often reasonably deep. If there is also a free movement of air along this hillside or valley slope (thus reducing frost risk) then, subject to its aspect and temperatures, it may make an excellent vineyard site. Based on the European experience, Gladstones (*Viticulture and Enrivonment* p. 41) states that the very best vineyard sites usually have at least two of the following features:

- they are situated on slopes with excellent air drainage above the fog level
- the very best are usually on the slopes of projecting or isolated hills

- even in hot areas, they usually face the sun during some part of the day at least—part-easterly and southerly [for Australian conditions, read northerly] aspects are common
- if the sites are inland, they are usually close to a large body of water (a lake or a major river).

Many French examples readily spring to mind, such as the hill of Hermitage, the hill of Corton, the east and south-east facing slopes of the Côte de Nuits and the Côte de Beaune. Australian examples are more difficult to find, especially those involving large bodies of inland water—Lake George perhaps, and Lake Alexandrina immediately south of the Langhorne Creek Region may also be a case in point, though it could be argued that it is virtually an estuary. We do, however, have significant hills. Over a century ago, Hubert de Castella discoursed on the three notable hills of the Yarra Valley. Other examples of Australian hills influencing local viticulture are Brokenback Range in the lower Hunter Valley, the Strathbogie Ranges in Victoria, the north–south hills forming part of the eastern slope of the Clare Valley and, of course, the Adelaide Hills as a more elevated and very suitable hilly area.

Another important factor is the 'thermal zone', the warm nocturnal air on the middle and lower slopes of hills, sitting above the 'inversion' or fog layer which, in turn, clothes the dense cold air at the valley bottom or on the flats. In the absence of any new chilled air from above, such thermal zones are quite stable in temperature. When temperatures are less variable, the vineyard warms and consequently ripens more quickly. The identification of such sites is critical in very cool climates as it often means the difference in any given grape variety between full and effective ripening on the one hand and incomplete and inferior ripening on the other.

It is a truism that the further north we go towards our tropical areas the warmer the climate becomes and, if table wine grapes are to be grown with any chance of success, then suitable cooler sites must be those that are higher. Several emerging vineyard areas are located over 600 metres in altitude (for example, the South Queensland Granite Belt and Orange in the Central Ranges of New South Wales) and other recently developed areas are only slightly lower at more than 500 metres (such as the Adelaide Hills and the Canberra and District regions). Altitude, however, does have its disadvantages. One is low relative humidity, which has already been discussed. Another is a lower concentration of carbon dioxide.

As Gladstones points out (*Viticulture and Environment*, p. 45) altitude leads to lower concentrations of carbon dioxide in the air, reducing the potential photosynthetic rates of the vine. This may in fact be counteracted by the vine developing more breathing pores (stomata) per unit of leaf area, thus maintaining a normal rate of carbon dioxide intake, but this has its own price—the greater evaporation of water from the leaves for each unit of carbon dioxide absorbed. This in turn may mean a higher rate of potassium accumulation to sugar production in the leaves, then to the berries, then to higher pH in the grapes, musts and wines and a consequent reduction in quality. Moreover, these detrimental effects may be cumulative.

WINE GRAPE VARIETIES: MATURITY AND SUITABILITY FOR VARIOUS REGIONS

It is commonsense to grow grape varieties in regions most suitable for them. Yet in Australia, this has rarely been the case. Our warmer grape-growing areas have mostly happened by happy accident. Grapes were an alternative crop which grew well. There was a market for fresh fruit and wine. Such sites were generally close to inhabited areas (cities, towns or mining regions) or had access to transport to such areas, usually by water and later by rail.

The wine industry, like any other, is subject to fashions. The current preference among consumers for table wines has only really been with us for 25 years and may simply be a longer-lasting fashion, which in time may pass. Consider the trend (though on a much smaller scale of consumption) away from lighter table wines to stronger reds and fortifieds in the late nineteenth century. If certain regions today were restricted to making the wine styles most suitable for their climates, then pity the regions that would be compelled to make only fortified wines. Their economic survival would be gravely imperilled. So in such areas, which are usually very warm, white and red table wines made from varieties not suited to the region will often be found.

What of new areas, where *vitis vinifera* has not previously been attempted in Australia? How are suitable sites selected? It is useful to follow Gladstones' approach. Employing available climatic data, the viticulturist must be able to forecast maturity dates for any given grape variety. Further, as grape varieties mature at different times in any environment, they can be classified into groups with similar maturity times and can be interrelated by being described as ripening a certain number of days before or after another group. Maturity in this context can have differing meanings because of differences in the wine style intended to be made, but it is usually taken to mean the time most suitable for making a dry wine. There may of course be other factors affecting grape maturity. For example, late pruning, leading to correspondingly later budburst, may retard maturity for several weeks or the maturity of a second crop will be delayed after frost damage. Variations in altitude and slight variations in temperature between the site of the weather station and that of the vineyard may mean a hastening or a delaying of maturity by a few days. Soil type also may have an influence.

Having taken all of this into consideration, Gladstones assumes that temperature is the chief element affecting vine phenology. However, he contends that the following three modifications should be made to raw temperature data:

1 A cut-off mean temperature of 19°C for the warmest months, beyond which, he argues, there is 'no further increase in the rate of phenological development'.

2 A day-length/latitude adjustment. This is an additional adjustment for day-length at latitudes over/under 40 degrees for each month of the growing season, where 40 degrees is the approximate mean latitude for world viticulture. Temperatures (less 10°C) in latitudes above 40 degrees were adjusted upwards, temperatures (less 10°C) in latitudes below 40 degrees were adjusted downwards.

3   Adjustment for diurnal temperature range. He suggests that low night temperatures have a retarding effect on budburst and subsequent growth in areas with a widely varying diurnal range of spring temperatures and, consequently, a later than

Degree days required for wine grape varieties in commercial use, Australia

Degree days	White/rosé wine variety	Red wine variety**
1050*	—	—
1100	chasselas, pinot gris, pinot noir, meunier, muller-thurgau	—
1150	gewurztraminer, sylvaner, chardonnay, sauvignon blanc, frontignac, melon, verdelho, sultana, pedro ximenes	pinot noir, meunier, gamay, dolcetto, bastardo, tinta amarella
1200	semillon, riesling, cabernet franc	malbec, durif, zinfandel, tinta madeira
1250	chenin blanc, crouchen, marsanne, roussanne, viognier, cabernet sauvignon, taminga, muscadelle***	merlot, cabernet franc, shiraz, cinsaut, barbera, sangiovese, touriga
1300	colombard, palomino, grenache	cabernet sauvignon, mondeuse, ruby cabernet, valdiguie
1350	muscat gordo blanco, trebbiano	mataro, petit verdot, carignan, graciano, grenache
1400	clairette, grenache blanc, doradillo, biancone	tarrango

*   Few areas in Australia have a degree-day maximum that does not exceed 1050. Viticulture in such areas, besides being restricted to a choice of the earliest ripening grape varieties, would probably be precluded for climatic reasons, that is, spring frosts, cold winds, altitude and so on.

**   Most of the early ripening German varieties, such as siegerrebe, and lesser known Italian and Portuguese varieties, such as malvasia bianca (malmsey), have been omitted, as they are not yet grown in Australia on a commercial scale.

***   Gladstones (*Viticulture and Environment*, p. 67) places both semillon and muscadelle in the 1200 degree-day group. He reports that muscadelle is the latest ripening of Bordeaux white varieties, David Morris of Morris Wines, who grows both varieties at Rutherglen, believes that semillon is the earlier ripener. Even though David was ripening muscadelle for fortified wine purposes, it was still at least two weeks behind semillon.

expected maturity. On the other hand, a narrow diurnal range might give rise to earlier than expected maturity. Therefore in sites with a very wide or narrow diurnal range, Gladstones makes an adjustment to raw temperature data in months where the range exceeds 13°C by reducing it by 0.25°C for every 1°C of range over 13°C and increasing it by the same ratio in months where the range is less than 10°C.

The resulting degree-day count, subject to all three adjustments, is in Gladstones' view 'biologically effective'.

Having ascertained the method of calculating biologically effective degree days for prospective grape-growing regions, Gladstones seeks to correlate those particular regions with suitable grape varieties, that is, varieties that will come to full maturity within that region. He does this by formulating a table of degree days commencing at 1050 and dividing this table into eight groups at 50 degree days apart until he reaches 1400 degree days. Red, white and rosé wine styles and the grape varieties from which they are made are set beside the appropriate degree-day group, based on the number of degree days that each variety needs to come to ripeness. The table on p. 19 sets out wine grape varieties in general commercial use in Australia and the number of degree days required for maturity where dry table wines are to be made.

Of grape varieties mentioned in the notes on wine regions, I have included varieties actually grown in any particular region and also mentioned, where possible, varieties suitable for that region that accord with the practical experience of winegrowers within that region.

In general in my description of regions and sub-regions, I have used the following adjectives in relation to various degree-day groups: very cool HDD 1050–1200; cool 1201–1500; warm 1501–1800; hot 1801–2100; very hot above 2101.

During the 1990s the world became alarmed about the increasing degradation of the environment by the use of chemical fertilisers and sprays in agriculture and concerned that such practices would irreparably damage our future way of life and were simply not sustainable. So how are these principles of sustainability applied to viticulture?

For many years it has been realised that the vine uses sunlight as a source of energy to convert carbon in the atmosphere and water in the earth to carbohydrates (i.e. sugars) in its grapes, which with relatively minor human interference and the assistance of yeasts in the atmosphere begin the process of fermentation to give us wine. During its growth cycle, the vine needs assistance from trace elements (see pp. 15–16). What sustainable viticulture is about is presenting these essential nutrients to the vine naturally. To do this, it is necessary to adopt the cultivation methods used by our forefathers. That is, natural compost and green cover crops grown between rows, which can provide nutrients for soil microbes. Thus the health of the soil is directly proportional to the quantity and diversity of these microbes. In a vineyard environment, compost may be made from marc (i.e. fermented skins, seeds and stalks) and other organic items such as chicken or other animal manure and sawdust. Such compost should be laid out in heaps and regularly aerated, providing oxygen for the microbe population, which over a period of weeks will convert the basic ingredients into a black 'earth', rich in nutrients. This black 'earth' may then be mulched back under the vines and allowed to meld back into the vineyard soils. Thus, the microbes released into the vineyard provide a new source of vine health, converting mineralised forms of the elements mentioned above into organic forms, a diet easier for the plant to use.

Healthy soils help to combat parasitic insects and harmful fungi. Vines will also need help to keep harmful insects at bay. Here too biological controls can be effective. Employ ducks to dine on the snails, chickens to devour any weevils and guinea fowl to lunch on the grasshoppers. As for fungal spores, which can also cause problems for vines, weather conditions need to be carefully watched and preventative measures like the application of retardants such as sulphur (a chemical, but used on vines for perhaps as long as 5000 years) or natural oils. All of this was common viticultural practice to our forefathers.

So perhaps we should be considering those viticultors who will succed us and leave them soils which are worth cultivating.

Rating system

NR (not rated)   Vineyards or wineries marked NR are either too new to have been rated or their wines have not been tasted within the last two years by the author.

60 or less   bad wines with major faults.

61–70   poor wines with some winemaking faults.

71–75   Average. Occasionally wines with faults may be found.

76–80   Overall a consistently good standard.

81–85   There are some excellent wines here among others of a high standard. Worth a detour.

86–90   Extraordinarily good. Certainly worth a special trip, but make sure there is wine available for sale.

91–100   The highest standards and the very best wines that Australia can offer. Make an appointment to visit.

Part I

VICTORIA

❦ WESTERN VICTORIA ZONE

This is a substantial tract of Victoria, stretching from Ballarat in the east to the South Australian border and the western Victorian coast. It comprises three actual and proposed wine regions at the present—The Grampians, Henty and the Pyrenees.

THE GRAMPIANS REGION

Centred around the village of Great Western and the towns of Stawell to the north-west and Ararat to the south-east, the Grampians wine region is a child of the great Victorian goldrush of the 1850s and 1860s. Its first vineyards were planted by those ever-present miners' suppliers, who usually made much more money providing the miners with the picks and shovels and other necessities of mining than most of their clients ever made by using them. Jean Pierre Trouette and Anne Marie Blampied were two such *providores* who moved to the Great Western region in 1858 after a profitable stay at the north-east Victorian mining town of Beechworth. In the next few years they planted their St Peter's vineyard. The brothers Joseph and Henry Best were two other *providores* who established a profitable butchery in Ararat. They too purchased land at Great Western, Joseph founding his Great Western estate, some say in 1862 or 1865, while Henry planted Concongella virtually across the road in 1866.

The early wines from this region were table wines, matured at Great Western in 'drives' which were tunnels beneath the winery excavated by former miners. Later that century and in the twentieth, they were extended and put to even better use as the wine fame of the region came to be based firmly on *methode champenoise* sparkling wines, made there by a Frenchman, Charles Pierlot. He had been brought to Great Western by Hans Irvine, the purchaser of Great Western after Joseph's death in 1887. Its reputation as a sparkling wine producer soared during the first half of the twentieth century, especially after Seppelt purchased Great Western from Hans Irvine in 1918 and popularised sparkling wine nationally. The production of table wines, however, though much smaller, never ceased. Colin Preece, Seppelt Great Western winemaker from 1932 to 1963, made some superb reds during that time.

Great Western today, and the Grampians region generally, specialise once more in table wines, though its local sparkling wines—now chiefly made of the classic Champagne grape varieties, pinot noir, meunier and chardonnay—remain of high quality.

Location: latitude 37°09'S, longitude 142°50'E, about 220 km west-north-west of Melbourne
Altitude: 330 m
Topography and soils: Moderately undulating with vineyards planted both on slopes and flats. Hard, mottled yellow duplex soils with yellow, clayey subsoils (flats) (Dy 3.41, Dy 3.42) and hard red duplex soils with red-brown, clayey subsoils (slopes) (Dr 2.21,

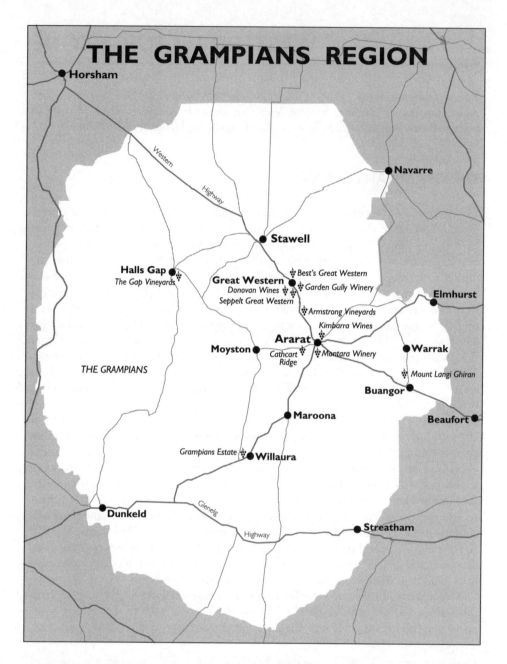

Dr 2.22). Subsoils drain only moderately well. Soil types are only moderately fertile. pH: acid to neutral.

Climate: MJT 20.2°C, MAR 12.2°C, HDD (raw) 1464, AR 591 mm (Oct–Mar 238 mm), RH 59% (9am), AI 362 mm, SH 8.3. Warm and dry with risk of spring frosts on flatter areas. Moderate evaporation, radiation and relative humidity.

A 'continental' climate—cool nights, warm days. Annual rainfall is slightly winter-dominant. Other water resources: drip irrigation from surface storage dams only, as creeks and bores are sometimes saline.

Harvest time: Mid-March to mid-May

Principal grape varieties: Red—shiraz, cabernet sauvignon, pinot noir*, meunier*; White—riesling, chardonnay*, ondenc* (*also used for sparkling wine base)

Major wine styles: Shiraz (the Grampians Region forms the western extremity of the Central Victorian Shiraz crescent, which produces wines of intense berry and black pepper characters occasionally accompanied by a tang of eucalyptus. Other constituent parts of the crescent, proceeding from west to east, are the Pyrenees Region, Bendigo Region and the proposed Heathcote regions); Sparkling; Riesling

Leading wineries and vineyards: Seppelts Great Western, Mount Langhi Ghiran, Best's Concongella.

Armstrong Vineyards NR

Lot 1 Military Road, Armstrong, Vic 3381
Ph 03 8277 6073, Fax 03 8277 6035,
Email armstrong@picknowl.com.au

Owner/chief winemaker: Tony Royal
Year of foundation: 1989
Tonnes produced on average each year: 33 of which about 12 are presently used for the maker's own label
Location: Armstrong near Great Western
Area: 6.5 ha
Soils: typical powdery sandy loams over a clay sub-soil. Low fertility
Varieties planted: White—none; Red—shiraz
Leading wine: Armstrong Vineyards Shiraz
Notes: This is the vineyard of former Seppelt Great Western winemaker Tony Royal. There are no cellar door sales. Sales are made through retail outlets in Adelaide and Melbourne.

Best's Great Western R88

Concongella, Great Western, Vic 3377
Ph 03 5356 2250, Fax 03 5356 2430

Owner: Best's Wines Pty Ltd (the Thomson family)
Chief winemaker: Viv Thomson
Year of foundation: Concongella 1866 (winery and vineyard); Rhymney Reef 1996 (vineyard)
Tonnes crushed on average each year: Concongella 157; Rhymney Reef first commercial crop due 2001
Location: Great Western and Rhymney
Area: Great Western (Concongella) 21 ha, Rhymney Reef 60 ha (40 of which are planted)
Soils: Great Western, powdery sandy loams overlying a deep clay subsoil. Rhymney Reef, deep quartz loam over deep red clay
Varieties planted: (Concongella) White—chardonnay, gewurztraminer, ondenc, riesling; Red—cabernet sauvignon, cabernet franc, dolcetto, merlot, meunier, pinot noir, shiraz; (Rhymney Reef): White—riesling; Red—merlot, pinot noir, shiraz
Leading wines: Thomson Family Shiraz, Bin 0 Shiraz, Cabernet Sauvignon, Chardonnay, Riesling
Notes: This is the original vineyard site of Henry Best and there are still four hectares of vines existing from his first plantings over 130 years ago. The Thomson family itself can look back on a century of involvement with Great Western viticulture and three-quarters of a century of involvement with Concongella. Its wines, especially Shiraz, consistently rank among the best of the region. The Rhymney Reef vineyard will considerably increase production in the years to come. Cellar door

sales: Mon–Sat 10am–5pm, Sun of Victorian holiday periods noon–4pm. Closed other Sundays and Christmas Day.

Cathcart Ridge NR

Moyston Road, Cathcart via Ararat, Vic 3377
Ph 03 5352 1997, Fax 03 5352 1558,
Email finewines@netconnect.com.au

Owner: Farnhill family
Chief winemaker: David Farnhill
Year of foundation: 1975
Tonnes crushed on average each year: 100, rising in 2003 to 250 when a new vineyard at Rhymney Reef comes into production. All is and will be used for Cathcart Ridge and Mount Ararat Estate labels
Location: Ararat
Area: (Cathcart Ridge) 10 ha plus 160 ha at Great Western which commenced in 1998; (Rhymney Reef) 30 ha
Soils: (Cathcart Ridge) shale underlying gravelly loam, not overly fertile; (Rhymney Reef) red loam over shale
Varieties planted: (Carthcart Ridge) White—chardonnay, riesling; Red—cabernet sauvignon, merlot, shiraz; (Rhymney Reef) White—pinot gris; Red—sangiovese, dolcetto
Leading wines: Cathcart Ridge Cabernet Sauvignon, Merlot, Shiraz
Notes: David Farnhill has established a new vineyard at Rhymney Reef, which is planted to the increasingly popular Italian varieties sangiovese and dolcetto, as well as the Franco-Italian pinot gris (grigio). Cellar door sales: 7 days 10am–5pm, barbecue area.

Donovan Wines NR

Main Street, Great Western, Vic 3377 (cellar door)
Ph 03 5358 2727, Fax 03 5358 3931

Owner: Donovan family
Chief winemaker: Simon Clayfield

Year of foundation: 1978
Tonnes crushed on average each year: 10
Location: winery and vineyard, Pomonal Road, Stawell
Area: 5 ha
Soils: sandy loam over clay
Varieties planted: White—chardonnay; Red—cabernet sauvignon, shiraz
Leading wines: Donovan Wines Shiraz
Notes: Like most of the makers in the Grampians region, Peter Donovan makes sturdy Shiraz reds of great character. Cellar door sales: Mon–Sat 10am–5pm, Sun noon–5pm.

FAA (a provisional name) NR

c/- Mount Langhi Ghiran (see p. 30)

Owners: a joint venture between Mount Langhi Ghiran, M. Chapoutier and US interests
Chief winemaker: Trevor Mast
Year of foundation: 1999
Tonnes produced on average each year: vineyard is not yet in bearing
Location: Malakoff (vineyard)
Area: 80 ha proposed over 3 years. 32 ha have already been planted
Soils: brown-yellow clay and gravels
Varieties planted: White—none; Red—shiraz
Leading wines: none yet made but certain to be Shiraz
Notes: Early days yet for this joint venture but there may be some outstanding red. No cellar door sales.

The Gap Vineyard (formerly Boroka Vineyards) NR

Pomonal Road, Halls Gap, Vic 3380
Ph 03 5356 4252, Fax 03 5356 4645,
Email langhi@netconnect.com.au

Owners: Mount Langhi Ghiran Vineyards
Chief winemaker: Trevor Mast
Year of foundation: 1970
Tonnes crushed on average each year: 15

Location: Hall's Gap
Area: 11 ha
Soils: sandy loams overlying medium clays ranging from orange to red, typical of the upper and intermediate slopes of Hall's Gap and the outwash slopes of the Grampians
Varieties: White—riesling; Red—cabernet sauvignon, merlot, shiraz
Leading wines: The Gap Vineyard Shiraz, Cabernet, Shiraz-Cabernet
Notes: Mount Langhi Ghiran purchased this vineyard in 1998 and a high standard of reds can now be expected. Cellar door sales: Wed–Sun 10–5. Every day in school holidays.

Garden Gully Winery R84

Western Highway, Great Western, Vic 3377
(east of the village)
Ph/Fax 03 5356 2400

Owners: Brian Fletcher, Warren Randall and a syndicate of business people
Chief winemakers: Brian Fletcher, Warren Randall
Year of foundation: 1987
Tonnes crushed on average each year: 30
Location: Great Western
Area: 6 ha
Soils: brown loam over clay
Varieties planted: White—riesling; Red—shiraz
Leading wines: Garden Gully Shiraz, Sparkling Shiraz
Notes: Garden Gully is the creation of two former winemakers at Seppelt Great Western, Brian Fletcher and Warren Randall, and the leading wines reflect the expertise learnt there. When you add to that expertise a 6 ha vineyard with old shiraz vines, you have a formula for successful Shiraz. Cellar door sales: Mon–Fri 10.30am–5.30pm, Sat–Sun 10am–5.30pm.

Grampians Estate NR

'Thermopylae', Mafeking Road, Willaura, Vic 3379
Ph 03 5354 6245, Fax 03 5354 6251, Email tguthrie@netconnect.com.au

Owner: Grampians Estate Wine Co Pty Ltd
Chief winemaker: Simon Clayfield
Year of foundation: 1989
Tonnes crushed on average each year: 10
Location: Willaura
Area: 3.2 ha
Soils: granite sand
Varieties planted: White—chardonnay; Red—shiraz
Leading wines: Mafeking Gold Chardonnay, Mafeking Shiraz
Notes: Grampians Estate is yet another vineyard established close to the site of an old gold area, in this case the Mafeking mine discovered near Willaura in 1900. Cellar door sales by appointment.

Kimbarra Wines NR

422 Barkly Street, Ararat, Vic 3377
Ph 03 5356 2343, Fax 03 5352 1950, Email kimbarrawines@netconnect.com.au

Owners: The Leeke Brothers (Jim, David and Peter and their respective families)
Chief winemaker: The Leeke Brothers plus contract
Year of foundation: 1978
Tonnes produced on average each year: 100 of which 20 are used for the Kimbarra label
Location: 5 km east of Great Western off the Western Highway
Area: 12 ha
Soils: sandy loams over mottled red clay
Varieties planted: White—riesling; Red—cabernet sauvignon, shiraz
Leading wine: Kimbarra Riesling
Notes: The wines regularly win silver and bronze medals at local shows. Cellar door sales: Barkly Street, Ararat, Mon–Fri 9am–5pm.

Montara Winery R83

Chalambar Road, Ararat, Vic 3377
Ph 03 5352 3868, Fax 03 5352 4968,
Email montara@netconnect.com.au

Owner: McRae family
Chief winemaker: Mike McRae
Year of foundation: 1970
Tonnes crushed on average each year: 120
Location: Ararat
Area: 20 ha
Soils: rich red loam over shale
Varieties planted: White—chardonnay,
chasselas, riesling; Red—cabernet sauvignon,
merlot, pinot noir, shiraz
Leading wines: Montara Pinot Noir,
Chardonnay, Shiraz, Riesling
Notes: A maker of good Shiraz in the manner
of the region and, less frequently, very good
Pinot Noir. Cellar door sales: Mon–Sat
10am–5pm, Sun noon–4pm.

Mount Langhi Ghiran R88

Warrak-Buangor Road, Buangor via
Ararat, Vic 3375
Ph 03 5354 3207, Fax 03 5354 3277,
Email langhi@netconnect.com.au

Owner: Mount Langhi Ghiran Vineyards Pty Ltd
Chief winemaker: Trevor Mast
Year of foundation: 1966
Tonnes crushed on average each year: 520, but
increasing to 1000 as new plantings come into
bearing
Location: Buangor
Area: 80 ha, including 5 ha of non-bearing vines
Soils: deep granite sand over clay and also
sandy loam over red-brown clay loam with
'buckshot' (commonly called red duplex or red
podsol)
Varieties planted: White—chardonnay, pinot
gris, riesling, viognier; Red—cabernet franc,
cabernet sauvignon, merlot, sangiovese, shiraz
Leading wines: Mount Langhi Ghiran Shiraz,
Cabernet-Merlot, Riesling

Notes: Mount Langhi Ghiran is located in the
Central Victorian crescent which produces some
of the most intense Shiraz in Australia. Black
pepper with the occasional whiff of eucalyptus
on nose and deep meaningful berry, pepper and
tannin palates. These wines are the essence of
great Shiraz and establish the Grampians as a
specialist region. Mount Langhi Ghiran Riesling
can also be rather special. Trevor Mast also
owns the 4 ha Mount Chalambar vineyard
which was planted to chardonnay and produced
sparkling wines for several years. It has now
been grafted over to riesling. How the
pendulum of fashion swings! Cellar door sales:
Mon–Fri 9am–5pm, weekends noon–5pm.

Seppelt Great Western R91

Western Highway, Great Western,
Vic 3377
Ph 03 5361 2222, Fax 03 5361 2200,
Email GWCD@cellardoor.com.au

Owner: Southcorp Wines
Chief winemaker: Paul Lapsley
Year of foundation: 1865
Tonnes crushed on average each year: not
disclosed but estimated at 1000
Location: Great Western
Area: 143 ha
Soils: infertile yellow duplex soils on flats, a
better red duplex soil on hillsides; soils incline
to acidity
Varieties planted: White—chardonnay, ondenc,
riesling; Red—cabernet sauvignon, shiraz,
tempranillo
Leading wines: Salinger (superb sparkling
white made from pinot noir and chardonnay
and often including a small proportion of
meunier), Great Western Reserve Shiraz (200
cases), Great Western Shiraz, Chardonnay,
Cabernet Sauvignon, Sparkling Burgundy and
the Victorian Portfolio, Chalambar Shiraz,
Harpers Range Cabernet Sauvignon, Rhymney
Sauvignon Blanc, Corella Ridge Chardonnay,
Sheoak Riesling

Notes: This is the vineyard founded by Joseph Best which was purchased after his death in 1887 by Hans Irvine, a leading figure in the business and political life of Victoria from 1880 onwards. Irvine's passion in wine was champagne, which was one of his chief objectives in making the purchase and for which in 1890 he brought Charles Pierlot to Australia from Champagne to make the wine. Champagne making and the popularisation of this Australian sparkling wine style was his lasting contribution to Australian wine. At Great Western he expanded the cellars substantially and also much enlarged the vineyards by planting a white grape variety, which he understood to be 'white pinot'. Irvine's White, as it came to be called, turned out to be ondenc, a fairly ordinary white variety from the south of France. On Irvine's retirement in 1918, the estate was purchased by Seppelt, which is now part of Southcorp Wines. The cellars are famous for their 'drives', about 1.6 km of tunnels dug by miners in the late nineteenth century for the purpose of maturing sparkling wine. Its most outstanding winemaker during the middle of the twentieth century was Colin Preece (1932–1963), destined to be remembered more for his red wines than his sparklings which, during the last 20 years, because of the introduction of the classic champagne varieties—chardonnay, meunier and pinot noir—have improved tremendously in quality. Today Seppelt Great Western is vast and dedicated to making sparkling wine from sources all over Australia. There are, however, small parcels of Great Western Shiraz still made. Cellar door sales: 7 days 10am–5pm.

THE PYRENEES REGION

It is said that there were vines at Avoca even before the goldrushes of the 1850s, which is not unremarkable considering the usual pattern of south-east Australian rural settlement. First came the explorers, in Avoca's case the ubiquitous Major Thomas Mitchell, Surveyor-General of New South Wales, in 1836. Then the graziers began arriving in the mid-1840s with their cattle and sheep and often with a few vines, looking for permanent water. Then came the prospectors with their picks and gold pans in 1853. Avoca saw them all. As for the vineyards, they expanded. Near Avoca, the Mackereth family worked a vineyard of 40 acres (16 ha) in the early years of the twentieth century. Like those of the Yarra Valley, this vineyard eventually fell to the dairy cow. About the same time Kofoed had a vineyard of 20 acres (8 ha) at Mountain Creek which went out of production soon after the Second World War. But at no time was Avoca's wine industry the *raison d'etre* of the region. By 1950, it had become the land of wool and mutton.

During all this time, table wine was in the doldrums and the only expanding vineyards were those devoted to the production of brandy. So it was that Nathan and Wyeth, important wine and spirit distributors, formed a joint venture in 1960 with their French principal, Remy Martin of Cognac, to produce Australian brandy at a site 7 kilometres west of Avoca, at the foot of the Pyrenees range. On the 80 hectares purchased, they planted ugni blanc and doradillo, two varieties then very much in vogue for distillation and the production of brandy. By 1970, the taxation rates on local brandy and the public taste in wine had changed entirely. Back to the drawing board, Chateau

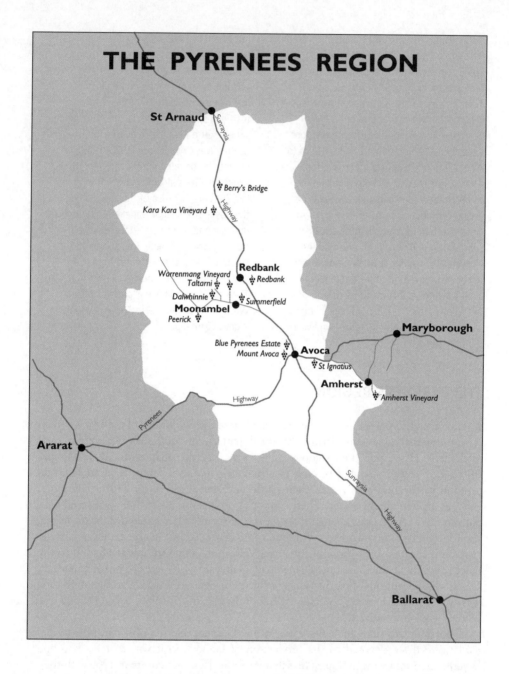

THE PYRENEES REGION

Remy virtually ceased production of brandy and grafted its doradillo vines to cabernet sauvignon, while the ugni blanc vines were used for the production of sparkling wine. By 1982, as Remy searched for better quality sparkling wine, areas of ugni blanc began to be grafted over to chardonnay. Pinot noir and meunier were also planted.

By this time, many other vineyards had been planted in the region. Taltarni (beginning in 1969), Mount Avoca (1970), Redbank (1973) and Dalwhinnie (1976) are some of the wineries in operation. The region is now proud of its wine industry and rightly insists on its title 'the land of wool and wine'.

Location: Avoca latitude 37°05'S, longitude 143°29'E; Moonambel is about 12 km north of Avoca, about 175 km north-west of Melbourne
Altitude: 250–600 m
Topography and soils: Undulating vineyards on the slopes of the Victorian Pyrenees. Soils similar to those of Great Western but often gravelly with a quartz and clay content. pH: tending to be acid.
Climate: MJT 20°C, MAR na, HDD 1532, AR 542 mm (Oct–Apr 258 mm), RH 45%, AI na, SH 8.75. Slightly warmer but similar to Great Western. Annual rainfall is chiefly in winter and spring. Other water resources are limited, drip irrigation being supplied from surface dams or bores.
Harvest time: Mid-March to mid-May
Principal grape varieties: Red—cabernet franc, merlot, pinot meunier; White—semillon, riesling
Major wine styles: Shiraz, Chardonnay, Sauvignon Blanc, Sparkling
Leading wineries: Dalwhinnie, Peerick, Taltarni

Amherst Vineyard R80

Talbot Avoca Road, Amherst, Vic 3467
Ph 03 5463 2105, Fax 03 5463 2091,
Email amherstwinery@origin.net.au

Owners: Norman and Elizabeth Jones
Chief winemaker: Rod Stott (contract)
Year of foundation: 1990
Tonnes crushed on average each year: 12
Location: Amherst
Area: 4 ha
Soils: clayey loam
Varieties planted: White—chardonnay;
Red—cabernet sauvignon, shiraz
Leading wine: Amherst Shiraz
Notes: Norman Jones decided to start slowly and build solidly. That is why Amherst is quite small but it is growing. Like many in the region, Norman is proud of his Shiraz. No cellar door sales.

Berrys Bridge Wines R83

Forsters Road, Carapooee, St Arnaud, Vic 3478
Ph 03 5496 3220, Fax 03 5496 3322,
Email jholt@berrysbridge.com.au

Owners: Roger Milner, Jane Holt and Ian McDonald
Chief winemaker: Jane Holt
Year of foundation: 1990
Tonnes crushed on average each year: 30
Location: Carapooee, St Arnaud
Area: 7 ha
Soils: red duplex clays
Varieties planted: White—none;
Red—cabernet sauvignon, merlot, shiraz
Leading wines: Berrys Bridge Shiraz, Berrys Bridge Cabernet Sauvignon
Notes: Roger Milner is a geologist by profession and should know his dirt. Although the red duplex clays of Berrys Bridge are a fairly common Australian vineyard soil, when they are brought together with the favourable

St Arnaud climate, generous Shiraz reds and Cabernet reds result. Jane Holt who graduated from the Charles Sturt University School of oenology in 2000 is the winemaker. Cellar door sales: weekends and public holidays.

Blue Pyrenees Estate R85

Vinoca Road, Avoca, Vic 3467
Ph 03 5465 3202, Fax 03 5465 3529,
Email ken.field@remy-cointreau.com

Owner: Remy Cointreau SA
Chief winemakers: Kim Hart, Greg Dedman
Year of foundation: 1963
Tonnes crushed on average each year: 1500, of which 1100 are used for the Estate's own wines
Location: Avoca
Area: 225 ha
Soils: this is a vineyard of considerable soil diversity. Its soils have been derived from red sandstone, giving yellow to red soils, older alluviums, yielding gravelly and sandy loams and colluvial material producing almost pure loam without clays
Varieties planted: White—chardonnay, sauvignon blanc, semillon, viognier;
Red—cabernet franc, cabernet sauvignon, merlot, meunier, pinot noir, shiraz
Leading wines: Blue Pyrenees Estate Chardonnay, Red (a blend of cabernets, merlot and shiraz), Estate Reserve and Midnight Cuvee (both made by the classic Champagne method)
Notes: Blue Pyrenees Estate is the former Chateau Remy which, from 1960, specialised in brandy, then in sparkling wine of modest quality (made primarily from ugni blanc until it had finalised the planting of specialised sparkling varieties), then in much improved sparkling wine (but not usually of a quality to rival Australia's best brands). It now specialises in white, red, and sparkling wines, the Estate red being one of the more elegant Pyrenees wines, while the Estate Sparkling can hold its own with most of Australia's best. Cellar door sales: Mon–Fri 10am–4.30pm, weekends 10am–5pm.

Dalwhinnie R90

Taltarni Road, Moonambel, Vic 3478
Ph 03 5467 2388, Fax 03 5467 2237

Owner: Dalwhinnie Wines Pty Ltd
Chief winemaker: David Jones
Year of foundation: 1976
Tonnes crushed on average each year: 100
Location: Moonambel
Area: There are two vineyards, respectively 16 ha and 10.42 ha, 26.42 ha in all
Soils: gravel, quartz, clay
Varieties planted: White—chardonnay;
Red—cabernet franc, cabernet sauvignon, merlot, pinot noir, shiraz
Leading wines: Dalwhinnie Eagle Series Special Shiraz, Chardonnay, Moonambel Shiraz, Moonambel Cabernet Sauvignon
Notes: From year to year Dalwhinnie is brilliantly consistent, its Chardonnay and Shiraz (both Eagle and Reserve) always superb. Cellar door sales: 7 days 10am–5pm.

Glenlofty (vineyard only) NR

Warrenmang Road, Elmhurst, Vic 3469

Owner: Southcorp Wines
Chief winemaker: Paul Lapsley
Year of foundation: 1995
Tonnes crushed on average each year: not disclosed but estimated at 800
Location: Elmhurst
Area: 113 ha
Soils: red to yellow friable clay loams
Varieties planted: White—chardonnay, marsanne, roussanne, sauvignon blanc, semillon; Red—cabernet sauvignon, merlot, nebbiolo, shiraz
Leading wines: this vineyard has not yet established itself as an individual vineyard within any of the Southcorp labels, though it

presently contributes towards the Seppelt Victorian Portfolio range
Notes: This is a vineyard only. There are no local cellar door sales.

Kara Kara Vineyard R84

Sunraysia Highway, St Arnaud, Vic 3478 (10 km south of town)
Ph/Fax 03 5496 3294,
Email kara@ruralnet.net.au

Owner: S. & M. Zsigmond Pty Ltd
Chief winemakers: John Ellis, Steve Zsigmond
Year of foundation: 1977
Tonnes crushed on average each year: 20, of which 15 are used for Kara Kara labels
Location: Kara Kara
Area: 8 ha
Soils: a thin (20cm) layer of a fine grey sandy quartzy loam over red orange and yellow layers of clay
Varieties planted: White—chardonnay, sauvignon blanc, semillon; Red—cabernet sauvignon, shiraz
Leading wines: Kara Kara Chardonnay, Sauvignon Blanc, Shiraz-Cabernet blend
Notes: The most northerly of the Pyrenees wineries, Kara Kara is a true wine estate, utilising only its own grapes for its own wines. The estate concentrates on white wines, unusual for the Pyrenees area which is more renowned for reds. The Chardonnay is very good, the Sauvignon Blanc fresh and zingy. Cellar door sales: daily 9am–6pm.

Mount Avoca R85

Moates Lane, Avoca, Vic 3467
Ph 03 5465 3282, Fax 03 5465 3544,
Email info@mountavoca.com

Owners: John and Arda Barry
Chief winemaker: Matthew Barry
Year of foundation: 1970
Tonnes crushed on average each year: 180
Location: Avoca

Area: 23.72 ha
Soils: clay and gravel
Varieties planted: White—chardonnay, sauvignon blanc, semillon, trebbiano; Red—cabernet franc, cabernet sauvignon, merlot, shiraz
Leading wines: Mount Avoca Reserve (Range) Cabernet Franc, Merlot, Shiraz, Cabernet, Noble Semillon. Traditional (Range): Sauvignon Blanc, Chardonnay, Cabernet, Shiraz
Notes: Like many of the Avoca vineyards, Mount Avoca sits upon old gold diggings, which have proved remarkably suitable for premium wine production. It is a proper wine estate, entirely reliant upon its own fruit resources for all its wines. Its Sauvignon Blanc is zesty and herbaceous and its reds are in the mainstream of Pyrenees regional quality. Cellar door sales: Mon–Fri 9am–5pm, weekends and public holidays 10am–5pm, closed Christmas Day, Boxing Day and New Year's Day.

Peerick Vineyard R87

Wild Dog Track, Moonambel, Vic 3478
Ph 03 5467 2207, Fax 03 9817 1611,
Email mejessup@peerick.com.au

Owners: Chris and Merryl Jessup
Chief winemaker: contract
Year of foundation: 1990
Tonnes produced on average each year: 40, of which 30 are utilised for Peerick's own labels
Location: Moonambel
Area: 6 ha
Soils: Cambrian slate
Varieties planted: White—sauvignon blanc, viognier; Red—cabernet franc, cabernet sauvignon, merlot, shiraz
Leading wines: Peerick Vineyard Shiraz, Sauvignon Blanc, Cabernet Sauvignon
Notes: Peerick Vineyard is an exciting addition to the vineyards of the Pyrenees. Its Sauvignon Blanc is fresh and vigorous, its Viognier soft, complex and nutty in flavour, its Shiraz deep-flavoured and very stylish and its Cabernet

Sauvignon deeply berry-flavoured with the potential to improve for many years. Visit soon. Cellar door sales: weekends 11am–4pm.

Redbank R80

Sunraysia Highway, Redbank, Vic 3467
Ph 03 5467 7255, Fax 03 5467 7248,
Email neillrobb@bigpond.com

Owners: Neill and Sally Robb
Chief winemaker: Neill Robb
Year of foundation: 1973
Tonnes crushed on average each year: 520 from its own vineyard sources and from growers, all used for Redbank's own labels
Location: Redbank
Area: 20 ha
Soils: quartz gravel over red clay, which in Neill Robb's words is 'good enough to eat'
Varieties planted: White—none; Red—cabernet franc, cabernet sauvignon, malbec, merlot, pinot noir, shiraz
Leading wines: Redbank Sally's Paddock (a red blend from a single vineyard), Neill Robb's Private Bin Cabernet
Notes: Now well established (having celebrated its 25th anniversary in 1998), Redbank concentrates on the red wines which are the forte of the region. Its Sally's Paddock blend is usually excellent. Cellar door sales: Mon–Sat 9am–5pm, Sun 10am–5pm.

St Ignatius Vineyard NR

Sunraysia Highway, Avoca, Vic 3467 (5 km south of the town on the eastern side)
Ph/Fax 03 5465 3542

Owners: Enrique and Silvia Diaz
Chief winemaker: Enrique Diaz
Year of foundation: 1992
Tonnes crushed on average each year: 12, but will increase as new plantings come into bearing. All is used for St Ignatius wines
Location: Avoca

Area: 6 ha
Soils: surface gravel over a mixture of quartz aggregate and friable red clay. Naturally slightly acidic and lacking nitrogen and phosphorus
Varieties planted: White—chardonnay, sauvignon blanc; Red—cabernet sauvignon, merlot, sangiovese, shiraz
Leading wines: Hangman's Gully Shiraz
Notes: The winery opened in 1999. The restaurant followed soon after. Cellar door sales: daily 10am–5pm. Restaurant open for lunch and dinner by appointment.

Summerfield Vineyards R76

Main Road, Moonambel, Vic 3478
Ph 03 5467 2264, Fax 03 5467 2380,
Email smrfld@origin.net.au

Owner: Ian Summerfield
Chief winemaker: Ian Summerfield, assisted by Mark Summerfield
Year of foundation: 1970
Tonnes crushed on average each year: 70
Location: Moonambel
Area: 8 ha, including new plantings
Soils: quartz clay
Varieties planted: White—sauvignon blanc, trebbiano; Red—cabernet sauvignon, merlot, shiraz
Leading wines: Summerfield Vineyards Reserve Shiraz, Reserve Cabernet
Notes: Ian Summerfield makes robust reds which always assist in withstanding the chill of a Victorian winter. He has had widespread Show success in Victoria with his full-bodied, earthy Shiraz. Cellar door sales: daily 9am–6pm.

Taltarni R86

Taltarni Road, Moonambel, Vic 3478
Ph 03 5467 2218, Fax 03 5467 2306,
Email taltarni@netconnect.com.au

Owner: Red Earth Nominees Pty Ltd
Chief winemaker: Chris Markell

Year of foundation: 1972
Tonnes crushed on average each year: 950
Location: Moonambel
Area: 320 ha
Soils: well drained schist, red clay over quartz
Varieties planted: White—chardonnay, chenin blanc, riesling, sauvignon blanc; Red—cabernet franc, cabernet sauvignon, malbec, merlot, meunier, pinot noir, sangiovese, shiraz
Leading wines: Taltarni Sauvignon Blanc, Shiraz, Cabernet Sauvignon (still wines); Cuvee Brut, Brut Tache (sparkling)
Notes: One of the pioneers of the Moonambel area of the Pyrenees region, for a long time Taltarni was renowned for the tannic 'size' of its reds, some of which never quite rewarded the patience required for them to soften into balance. Nowadays, more emphasis is laid on fruit and the reds are not so big but still need cellaring and the patience to go with it. Taltarni Sauvignon Blanc is usually suitably herbaceous and refreshingly acid. Taltarni also owns Clover Hill at Lebrina in Tasmania, some of whose sparkling wine is now used to lift the quality of the Pyrenees sparkling material. Cellar door sales: 7 days 10am–5pm.

Warrenmang Vineyard Resort 🍇 R85

Mountain Creek Road, Moonambel, Vic 3478
Ph 03 5467 2233, Fax 03 5467 2309, Email mail@pyreneeswines.com.au

Owners: Luigi and Athalie Bazzani
Chief winemaker: Allen Hart
Year of foundation: 1974
Tonnes crushed on average each year: 100
Location: Moonambel
Area: 22 ha, comprising two vineyards—one at Moonambel (12.5 ha) and the other at Avoca (9.5 ha)
Soils: sandy loam above moisture-retentive red clay subsoil
Varieties planted: (Moonambel) White—chardonnay, sauvignon blanc, traminer; Red—cabernet franc, cabernet sauvignon, dolcetto, merlot, shiraz. (Avoca) White—pinot grigio; Red—barbera, brunello, nebbiolo, shiraz
Leading wines: Warrenmang Estate Shiraz, Grand Pyrenees, Luigi Riserva
Notes: Warrenmang is much more than just a winery. It is a true resort and a very plush one at that with accommodation for up to 84 guests and a highly regarded restaurant. Its reds are very much in the mainstream of the big Pyrenees style. Cellar door sales: 7 days 10am–5pm.

HENTY REGION

Edward Henty had the honour of establishing the first permanent settlement in what was to become known 17 years later as the colony of Victoria. He landed with his three brothers, Stephen, John and Francis at Portland Bay on 19 November 1834, having crossed Bass Strait from Launceston in Tasmania. Also aboard his ship, the *Thistle*, were merino sheep and the first grapevines ever brought into the Colony. Though lacking official permission from the Government of New South Wales to settle anywhere in Victoria (called Southern New South Wales at this time), the Hentys soon established their honourable intentions by erecting several permanent buildings in the town. Their occupation was later recognised by the Government when it appointed Edward a magistrate of the town. In 1837, Stephen Henty explored the hinterland, following the footsteps of Major Mitchell, who had journeyed overland

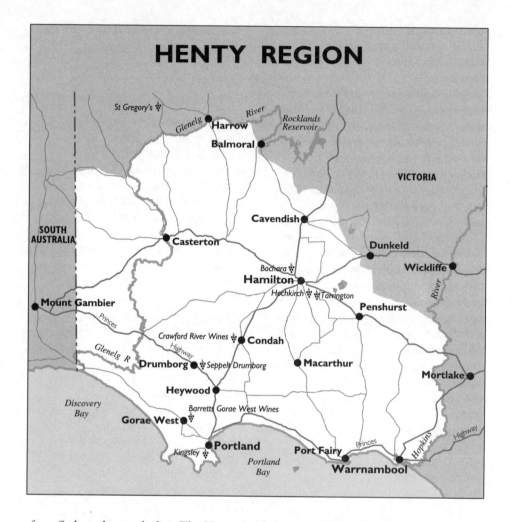

HENTY REGION

from Sydney the year before. The Henty family later established four grazing properties in the district and during the 19th and 20th centuries, south-western Victoria became a centre of the wool industry.

Today, Portland is a thriving seaport and the centre of aluminium and fertiliser producing industries. Warrnambool, the most eastern and largest city of the district, situated at the western end of Victoria's Great Ocean Road, remains a popular tourist destination while Hamilton, the district's major inland city, services the pastoral activities which still surround it. Since the decline of the wool industry, however, other more intensive rural activities including viticulture have emerged.

What happened to Edward Henty's vines remains a mystery. He planted no recorded vineyard, although by repute an ancient muscat hambourg vine descended from his collection still thrives at Ararat, in the Grampians Wine Region; and, having recently discovered another descendant near Portland, the local viticultural society is busy cultivating cuttings for historical and tourist interest.

This Victorian wine region is somewhat of a paradox. Its first settler was a Tasmanian while its modern pioneer of viticulture was a South Australian. Karl Seppelt was at this time very much one of Australia's wine explorers. In the early 1960s he had persuaded the Seppelt board that new grapegrowing territory, suitable for table wines, should be found in the south of South Australia or Victoria, as suitable land in Coonawarra, then starting to be recognised as an area of great quality, was then becoming scarcer and ever more expensive. He located two areas he thought to be of promise: Keppoch to the north of Coonawarra (now the region of Padthaway) and Drumborg in south-west Victoria. The first trial blocks, consisting of riesling and meunier, were planted in 1965, to be vinified at Seppelt's Great Western winery.

Drumborg is now 100 ha in vineyard area and is still vinified at the much larger Great Western. The next plantings (2 hectares of riesling and cabernet sauvignon), intended as a diversification project (then a popular concept amongst graziers) occurred in 1975 at the Crawford River property of John Thomson near Condah. John erected his winery on the site in 1981 and the local production industry was born. The Thomson vineyard now covers 9 hectares. Also at this time other 5- and 6-hectare vineyards were established near Drumborg and neighbouring Heywood. Since then the later years of the 20th century have seen vineyards cultivated throughout the region, though mostly in the vicinity of Portland and Hamilton.

Location: latitude 37°35'S longitude 143°50'E to 142°30', west-south-west of Melbourne about 210–305 km ranging from the Hopkins River in the east to the South Australian border in the west
Elevation: from sea level to about 280 m. The peak of Mount Dundas is 466 m above sea level
Topography and soils: This is a region of coastal plains in the south-west consisting of unconsolidated fine-textured soils, rising to basalt uplands which result from two distinct periods of volcanic activity, the first period occurring about 2 million years ago. In the south-west around Drumborg and in the centre of the region around Hamilton there are extensive areas of fertile well-drained red kraznozem soils, while areas around Branxholme south-west of Hamilton have red volcanic soils over a limestone base. The second phase of vulcanism occurred as recently as 8000 BC and created landmarks such as Mount Napier and Tower Hill in the south east of the region. Here there are fertile and well-drained volcanic tuffs, suitable for intensive horticulture. To the west and north-west of Hamilton are the Merino and Dundas tablelands. The Merino tablelands around Coleraine and Casterton are characterised by deeply dissected landscape with remnants of the still-evident plateau. Fertile soils here result from sedimentary marine deposits. The Dundas tableland features gently rolling hills with distinctive Red Gum trees. Soils here are moderate in their fertility and are derived from weathered granite and rhyolite.
Climate: MJT Portland 17.3°C, Heywood 17.4°C, Hamilton 17.8°C, MAR na, HDD Portland raw 1204, 1263 adjusted for latitude and daily temperature range, 1231 adjusted for vine sites; Heywood raw 1180, 1172 adjusted for latitude and daily temperature range, 1199 adusted for vine sites; Hamilton raw 1197, 1151 adjusted for latitude and daily temperature range, 1189 adjusted for vine sites all according to Gladstones, AR Portland

851 mm (Oct–Apr 351mm), Heywood 861mm (Oct–Apr 373 mm), Hamilton 692 mm (Oct–Apr 327 mm), RH (at 3pm Oct–Apr), Portland 64, Heywood 56, Hamilton 46 AI na, SH Portland 1502, Heywood 1490, Hamilton 1632. The region has a cool to mild climate. Its highest temperatures are recorded in February and lowest in July. Temperature variations are least in the coastal areas, but are much greater in its northern parts. Generally it is a region which is cool and moderately wet and whose southern parts favour viticulture due to its longer growing season and more moderate conditions.

The drainage basins of the region are three in number. The major one is the Glenelg River which rises in the western Grampians and flows west and south to create the northern and part of the western boundary of the region. It debouches into the Great Southern Ocean near Nelson. Major tributaries of the Glenelg are the Wannon and Crawford Rivers, which drain the centre of the region, while its eastern part is drained by the Hopkins River. The third basin is the Portland Coast, whose smaller streams, the Moyne, Shaw, Eumeralla and Fitzroy Rivers also flow into the Southern Ocean. In the coastal regions during the growing season the incidence of frosts due to the moderating influence of the sea is low, but this increases inland as altitude is gained. So care should be taken in the selection of vineyard sites. Overall however, frost risk is not as great as other Victorian inland wine regions.

Harvest Time: Chardonnay (for sparkling wine): Portland 1st week in April, Heywood 1st week in April usually a day or two later than Portland, Hamilton same as Heywood; table wine: Portland second week of April (about 9 days after Sparkling), Heywood 3rd week of April (about 5 days after Portland), Hamilton about the same time as Heywood or marginally (about a day) earlier. *Sauvignon Blanc*: similar to chardonnay table wine. *Riesling*: Portland 4th week of April, Heywood 1st week of May, Hamilton 2nd week of May. *Pinot Noir* (for sparkling wine): as for chardonnay in all centres. For table wine: Portland 2nd week of April, Heywood 3rd week of April slightly later than Portland, Hamilton about the same time or marginally earlier (about a day) than Heywood. *Merlot*: Portland 1st week of May, Heywood 2nd week of May, Hamilton 3rd week of May. *Shiraz*: Portland and Heywood 1st week of May, Hamilton 2nd week of May. *Cabernet Sauvignon*: Portland 3rd week of May, Heywood late in the 3rd week of May, Hamilton 4th week in May. There will be occasional years when cabernet sauvignon fails to reach complete maturity.

Principal grape varieties: Red—pinot noir (40%), meunier (10%), shiraz (10%), cabernet sauvignon (5%); White—chardonnay (15%), riesling (10%), sauvignon blanc (5%), semillon (5%). Others in very small areas: pinot gris.

Major wine styles: Sparkling whites: the classic champagne varieties pinot noir, chardonnay and meunier have now had at least 15 years' experience of Drumborg conditions. In the case of meunier it has been longer. As a result the Drumborg 'base wines' are now of a consistently excellent quality and the sparkling wines to which they contribute or indeed form the whole are magnificent. The wine most often seen is Salinger, which vies with a very few others to be Australia's top sparkling wine. *Riesling*: the Seppelt Drumborg vineyard leads the way with this variety. Though cropping can be irregular in quantity, rieslings invariably show extreme delicacy on nose and palate. Their predominant characters are the much sought-after lime citrus aromas and flavours and they finish with a keen acidity that usually holds them in good

stead for years of beneficial development, if this is desired. The problems with riesling in this region are two-fold. The first is wind which may upset flowering and therefore cause reduced levels of cropping. The second is botrytis to which riesling is susceptible, especially if the season is cool damp and late-ripening. But who really cares! Botrytised Rieslings are often nectar from the gods. *Sauvignon Blanc* and *Semillon-Sauvignon Blanc*: excellent wines of typical capsicum character which are not overly pungent (Crawford River is a fine example). *Chardonnay*: superbly stylish table wines of complexity and balance (Seppelts). *Pinot Noir*: promising full bodied reds of softness and generosity (Seppelts). *Cabernet Sauvignon*: intense reds with aromas and palates of berry and blackcurrant, deftly balanced oak and soft tannin (Seppelts).
Leading wineries: Seppelt Drumborg, Crawford River Wines, Hochkirch

Barretts Gorae West Wines   NR

Nelson Highway, Gorae West, Vic 3305
(about 20 km north-west of Portland)
Ph 03 5526 5251

Owners: Rod and Sandra Barrett
Chief winemaker: Rod Barrett
Year of foundation: 1983
Tonnes crushed on average each year: 15
Location: Gorae West
Area: 4.5 ha
Soils: basaltic red soils of volcanic origin
Varieties planted: White—riesling, traminer;
Red—cabernet sauvignon, pinot noir
Leading wines: Barretts Riesling, Pinot Noir
Notes: In an area very suited to riesling, the Barretts wisely planted this variety and traminer. Cellar door sales: 7 days 11am–5pm.

Bochara Wine Co.   NR

Glenelg Highway, Bochara, Vic 3301
(12 km west of Hamilton)
Ph 03 5570 8274, fax 03 5570 8334

Owners: Martin Slocombe and Kylie McIntyre
Chief winemaker: Martin Slocombe,
Kylie McIntyre (viticulturalist)
Year of foundation: 1998
Tonnes crushed on average each year: 7, but expected to increase as vines mature
Location: Bochara
Area: 2.2 ha

Soils: buckshot gravel over clay planted on a north facing slope at an altitude of 130 m ASL
Varieties planted: White—sauvignon blanc;
Red—meunier, pinot noir
Leading wine: Pinot Noir
Notes: Bochara's first vintage was 2001 and so it is early days for former Coldstream Hills winemaker Martin Slocombe and Yalumba viticulturalist Kylie McIntyre. Cellar door sales to be opened late 2001.

Crawford River Wines   R87

Upper Hotspur Road, Condah, Vic 3305
(about 8 km west of the town)
Ph 03 5578 2267, Fax 03 5578 2240,
Email crawfordriver@140.aone.net.au

Owner: Crawford River Wines
Chief winemaker: John Thomson
Year of foundation: 1975
Tonnes crushed on average each year: 60
Location: Condah
Area: 9 ha
Soils: basaltic loam over clay and limestone
Varieties planted: White—riesling, sauvignon blanc, semillon; Red—cabernet franc, cabernet sauvignon, merlot
Leading wines: Crawford River Riesling, Cabernet Sauvignon
Notes: Crawford River is a working western Victorian grazing property. It happens that, for the last 20 years or so, John Thomson has

been broadening his pastoral experience by viticulture and winemaking and it has worked extremely well. All his wines are estate grown and no fruit is brought in from outside. His Rieslings (usually dry but accompanied by an occasional botrytised) are exceptionally good and his Cabernet Sauvignon is full-flavoured with ripe berry and cassis characters. Cellar door sales: 7 days 9am–5pm.

Hochkirch **R84**

Penshurst Road, Tarrington, Vic 3301
Ph/Fax 03 5573 5200

Owners: John and Jennifer Nagorcka
Chief winemaker: John Nagorcka.
Year of foundation: vineyard 1990, winery 1997
Tonnes crushed on average each year: 35, of which 20 are used for Hochkirch wine labels
Location: Tarrington near Hamilton
Area: 8 ha
Soils: basalt derived brown gravelly loam over gravel over clay
Varieties planted: White—chardonnay, riesling, semillon; Red—cabernet sauvignon, pinot noir
Leading wine: Hochkirch Pinot Noir
Notes: A fairly recent arrival on the Henty scene, making good Pinot and proving the suitability of this region for the pinot noir variety. Cellar door sales: 11am–5pm most days.

Kingsley **NR**

6 Kingsley Court, Portland, Vic 3305
Ph 03 5523 1864, Fax 03 5523 1644

Owner: Tom Beauglehole
Chief winemaker: contract
Year of foundation: 1983
Tonnes produced on average each year: 32, of which 15 are used for Kingsley's own labels
Location: Gorae West (vineyards) and Portland (cellar door sales)
Area: 9 ha

Soils: very fertile deep red gravelly 'buckshot', rich in iron
Varieties planted: White—chardonnay, riesling; Red—cabernet sauvignon
Leading wines: Kingsley Riesling, Cabernet Sauvignon
Notes: Another area vineyard which has produced very good Riesling. Cellar door sales: 7 days 1pm–4pm.

Seppelt Drumborg (vineyard only) **R91**

Princes Highway, Drumborg, Vic 3305

Owner: Southcorp Wines
Chief winemaker: Paul Lapsley
Year of foundation: 1964
Tonnes crushed on average each year: not disclosed but estimated at 550
Location: Drumborg
Area: 100 ha, including 40 ha of new plantings
Soils: red-brown earths to black loams overlying grey clay; grey loam overlying red clay
Varieties planted: White—chardonnay, pinot gris, riesling, sauvignon blanc; Red—cabernet sauvignon, meunier, pinot noir
Leading wine: Seppelt Drumborg Riesling
Notes: An important, if somewhat intermittent, jewel in the Seppelt crown, Drumborg has been renowned for producing a distinctly Germanic style of riesling, supremely elegant and very stylish. In some years in the past it produced none at all, but these days the riesling is still superb and production is in reasonable but not exciting quantity. The vineyard also contributes much to the quality of Seppelt sparkling wines, Salinger and Fleur de Lys, and to other Victorian table wines in its range. There are no cellar door sales here.

Tarrington Vineyards   **NR**

Hamilton Highway, Tarrington, Vic 3301
(south-east of Hamilton)
Ph/Fax 03 5572 4509, Email
tarringtonwines@bigpond.com

Owner: Tarrington Vineyards
Chief winemaker: Tamara Irish
Year of foundation: 1993
Tonnes crushed on average each year: 5
Location: Tarrington
Area: 2.4 ha
Soils: free-draining 'buckshot' gravel, with
clay/loam over marl

Varieties planted: White—chardonnay;
Red—pinot noir
Leading wines: Tarrington Vineyards Pinot Noir,
Chardonnay
Notes: A small vineyard with a small
production devoted entirely to Pinot Noir, but
five different clones and Chardonnay, four
different clones. Two very complex wines,
neither of which I have tasted, should be the
result. Cellar door sales: Summer weekends
and public holidays 10am–6pm; other
weekends and public holidays 11am–5pm.
All other times by appointment.

OTHER WINERIES OF WESTERN VICTORIA

The chief urban centre of the Western Victoria Wine Zone is Ballarat, which like
Bendigo to the north, was founded on the gold diggings of the 1850s. The Eureka
Stockade, a revolt of volatile miners against an equally hot-tempered government, is
legendary and very much an integral part of Ballarat's and Australia's history. Here
once more, the vine followed the mine.

Australia's first roving wine reporter, Ebenezer Ward, records a vineyard at Dead
Horse Gully in 1864, planted some five years previously by a Frenchman. Hopefully it
was not his wine that killed the horse. Undoubtedly there were other local vineyards—
miners are ever a thirsty lot—but recorded history is absent.

Ballarat's modern wine era commenced in 1971 with the planting, by Melbourne
businessman Ian Home, of the Yellowglen Vineyard near Smythesdale initially to
cabernet sauvignon and shiraz. Other plantings (chardonnay and pinot noir) took
place in 1979. Home was convinced that his vineyard was suitable for the production of sparkling wines and in 1982 Dominique Landragin, then employed by
Seppelt at Great Western, joined Home at Yellowglen. What followed was the
meteoric rise of Yellowglen 'Champagne' and the merger with Mildara Wines in
1984. Since then, the vineyards and wineries of Ballarat have grown steadily but not
spectacularly, which may be illustrative of the difficulties of viticulture in this very
cool part of Australia.

Location: latitude 37°35'S, longitude 143°50'E, about 110 km west-north-west of
Melbourne
Altitude: 437 m
Topography and soils: One of the lower parts of the western section of the Great
Dividing Range, it is undulating country with a northerly aspect, one of the few factors
favouring viticulture here. For soil information, see individual vineyard entries.

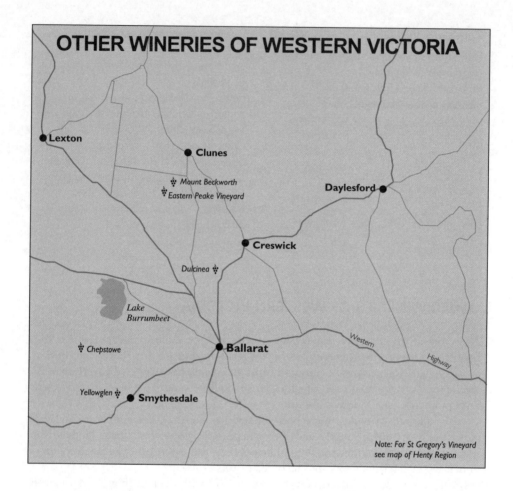

Climate: MJT 17.3°C, MAR na, HDD (raw) 1072, 1154 adjusted for vine sites, AR 719 mm (Oct–Apr 367 mm), RH 37% (G), AI na, SH 7.6. Ballarat is extremely cool with a high degree of frost risk. Careful site selection is imperative and then only early ripening varieties such as chardonnay and pinot noir should be planted.

Harvest time: Chardonnay early to mid-April, pinot noir late April to early May.

Principal grape varieties: White—chardonnay; Red—pinot noir

Total area: na

Major wine styles: Sparkling, Chardonnay, Pinot Noir

Leading wineries: Dulcinea, Chepstowe

Chepstowe Vineyard R88

Fitzpatrick's Lane, Carngham, Vic 3351
Ph 03 5344 9412, Fax 03 5344 9403,
Email chepvyd@tpgi.com.au

Owner: William Wallace
Chief winemaker: John Ellis (contract)
Year of foundation: 1994
Tonnes crushed on average each year: 10, but
will increase as vines come into full bearing
Location: Carngham near Ballarat
Area: 3 ha
Soils: sandy clay loam 60 cm deep over quartzy
broken rock subsoil, the vineyard being on a
steep slope with a north-easterly aspect
Varieties planted: White—chardonnay;
Red—pinot noir
Leading wines: Chepstowe Chardonnay and
Pinot Noir, wines of great style
Notes: Chepstowe is an exciting new addition
to the Ballarat district, already recognised as a
very cool area well-suited to those classic
Burgundian varieties, pinot noir and
chardonnay. Its vines are still very young but
Chepstowe seems destined to become an
obligatory destination for the Pinot Noir and
Chardonnay enthusiast. Cellar door sales:
10am–5pm weekdays, weekends and public
holidays except Christmas Day, Good Friday
and Anzac day. Phone ahead to avoid
disappointment on the very few days when the
cellar door is closed for any other reason.

Dulcinea R83

Jubilee Road, Sulky, Ballarat, Vic 3352
Ph 03 5334 6440, Ph/Fax 03 5334 6828,
Email dulcinea@cbl.com.au

Owners: Rod and Veronica Stott
Chief winemaker: Rod Stott
Year of foundation: 1983
Tonnes crushed on average each year: 50
Location: Sulky near Ballarat
Area: 5 ha
Soils: Ordovician soils, shallow clayey needing

mulching and feeding, vines high-trellised to
avoid frosts
Varieties planted: White—chardonnay,
sauvignon blanc; Red—cabernet sauvignon,
pinot noir, shiraz
Leading wines: Dulcinea Chardonnay, Pinot Noir
Notes: Dulcinea's best wines are from those
varieties best-suited to the district, Pinot Noir
and Chardonnay. Dulcinea's wine show record
is good, though smaller-scale production
means that it is restricted to smaller regional
wine shows. Cellar door sales: 7 days
10am–6pm.

Eastern Peake NR

Clunes Road, Coghills Creek, Vic 3364
Ph 03 5343 4245, Fax 03 5343 4365

Owners: Norman Latta and Di Pym
Chief winemaker: Norman Latta
Year of foundation: 1983
Tonnes crushed on average each year: 20
Location: Coghills Creek
Area: 5 ha
Soils: grey basalt over 'buckshot' clay
Varieties planted: White—chardonnay (1.5 ha);
Red—pinot noir (3.5 ha)
Leading wines: Eastern Peake Pinot Noir,
Chardonnay
Notes: Establishing Eastern Peake was a
12-year labour of love for Norman Latta and
Di Pym. Their first vintage was 1995 and their
Pinot Noir was rewarded with bronze medals
at Rutherglen and Ballarat in 1997. So the
varietal selection certainly corresponded with
the requirements of the area. Cellar door sales:
weekends and public holidays 10am–5pm.

Mount Beckworth Wines NR

Learmonth Road, Tourello via Creswick,
Vic 3363
Ph/Fax 03 5343 4207

Owners: Paul and Jane Lesock
Chief winemaker: Paul Lesock

Year of foundation: 1984
Tonnes crushed on average each year: 15 all of
which are used for Mount Beckworth's own
labels
Location: Tourello, near Creswick
Area: 5 ha
Soils: a slight north-facing slope of red loamy
clay running down to heavier black clay
Varieties planted: White—chardonnay;
Red—cabernet sauvignon, pinot noir, merlot
shiraz
Leading wines: Mount Beckworth Unwooded
Chardonnay, Pinot Noir, Cabernet Merlot,
Shiraz
Notes: Paul Lesock believes that Ballarat is a
chardonnay and pinot noir area, his own wines
being consistent award winners at the Ballarat,
Hobart and Victorian wine shows. Cellar door
sales: weekends 10am–6pm and by
appointment.

St Gregory's **R82**

Bringalbert South Road, Bringalbert
South via Apsley, Vic 3319
Ph 03 5586 5225, 03 9772 2196 (H)

Owner/chief winemaker: Gregory Flynn
Year of foundation: 1983
Tonnes crushed on average each year: not
disclosed but estimated at 10
Location: Bringalbert South
Area: 2.4 ha

Soils: not known
Varieties planted: White—none;
Red—cabernet sauvignon, shiraz, touriga
Leading wine: St Gregory's Port
Notes: A very small vineyard, devoted entirely
to a drier port-style than is commonly
encountered in Australia. Cellar door sales by
appointment.

Yellowglen **R83**

Whytes Road, Smythesdale, Vic 3351
Ph 03 5342 8617, Fax 03 5333 7102

Owner: Mildara Blass Ltd
Chief winemaker: Charles Hargraves
Year of foundation: 1971
Tonnes produced on average each year:
all fruit save an extremely small amount
of vineyard-produced pinot noir (about
20 tonnes) is brought in from outside
Location: Smythesdale
Area: 5 ha
Soils: quartz, gravelly duplex soils on a clay
base
Varieties planted: White—none; Red—pinot
noir
Leading wine: Cuvee Victoria
Notes: Yellowglen these days is a sparkling
wine production plant. The fruit grown on its
vineyard forms a minute part of vastly bigger
quantities from elsewhere. Cellar door sales:
weekdays 9am–5pm; weekends 10am–5pm.

❧ CENTRAL VICTORIA ZONE

Like most of Victoria, this is a broad area nurtured first by grazing and later exalted by gold. It is surprisingly diverse with terrain varying from the cooler uplands of midland Victoria northwards to the warmer dunes of the central Murray Valley.

After a slow start to its regional registration process, Central Victorian zone now encompasses the wine regions of Goulburn Valley and Bendigo, the proposed Heathcote region (when its rival proposers finally settle upon its boundaries), the proposed Central Victorian High Country region and the proposed Strathbogie Ranges region.

BENDIGO REGION

Bendigo followed a fairly typical pattern of New South Wales colonial settlement. It was settled by graziers in the 1840s and, after the creation of Victoria in 1851, became the focus of a huge goldrush and the 'golden' years that followed. At its greatest extent, its gold-bearing area encompassed about 370 square kilometres.

Typically once again, vines are said to have followed the miners, arriving in the area about 1855. However, Ebenezer Ward, the peripatetic wine correspondent, noted vines in the area that appeared to be 15 years old when he passed through in 1864. He also noted several younger vineyards so it would seem that most if not all of the first flush of viticulture in Bendigo was gold-inspired. Even so, by 1859, Bendigo's vineyard area was scarcely greater than 16 hectares and most of this would have been sold as fresh fruit. But only two years later, by 1861, this had grown to 38 hectares. Although no-one is quite certain when the first Bendigo wines were made, certainly by 1862 Bendigo wines were in existence (for the early vintner George Bruhn was awarded 1st prize at the White Hills Exhibition for a white and a red). By 1869 its vineyard area had expanded to nearly 200 hectares and though vineyard growth slowed during the 1870s, by 1880, its area comprised 214 hectares.

It is said that there were more than 100 wineries in production. Its wines were quite famous. One in particular, when shown at the Vienna Exhibition in 1873, caused a walkout by the French judges who alleged that it was so good, it just had to be French. The range of wines produced was also quite broad, ranging from light dry red and white types, through bigger shiraz to quite sweet dessert wines. As a wine region, Bendigo began to decline in 1893 when phylloxera was discovered and thereafter its fall was swift, the Victorian government ordering the wholesale uprooting of vineyards as it had done in Geelong's case some years earlier. Thus Bendigo was to be lost to other forms of agriculture for three quarters of a century.

The modern era of Bendigo wine began in 1969 when Bendigo pharmacist Stuart Anderson planted Balgownie. Though other vineyards were planted in the early to mid-1970s, the eclat created by his dense-coloured reds made Victoria very aware of the area's potential. Today the region is well-established and equally well-respected as one of Victoria's premium areas.

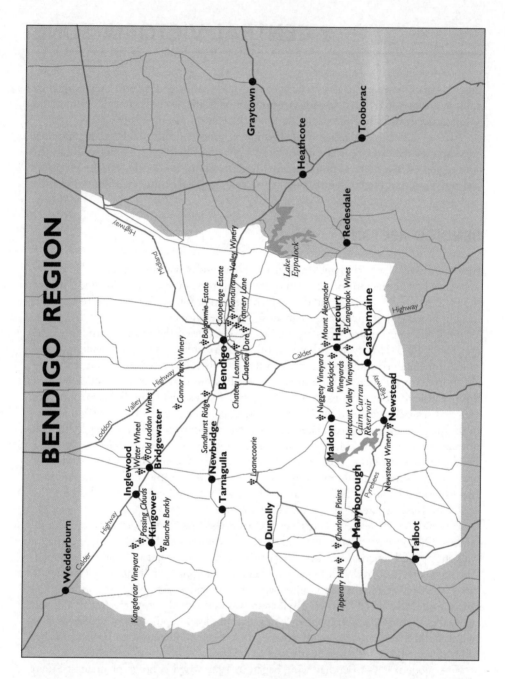

Location: Bendigo (city) latitude 36°46'S, longitude 144°17'E, about 130 km north-west of Melbourne. The region begins just south of Wedderburn and proceeds easterly in a straight line to a point just east of the Campaspe River. The boundary then turns south running parallel with the eastern bank of the Campaspe until it reaches

Knowsley, where it turns west and runs along the northern shores of Lake Eppalock, again turning south as it leaves the Lake. It turns west at a point on the Campaspe north of Metcalfe East and then proceeds west through Metcalfe, Fryerstown and Guildford until it turns south once more (south of Newstead), veering to the west again 7 km west of Mount Franklin. It turns north near Evansford, proceeds north-east virtually to Talbot and then north-west to Natte Yallock, then along the Avoca River until Logan and north-east back to its starting point. Its principal cities and towns are Bendigo, Castlemaine, Maryborough, Dunolly and Bridgewater.

Altitude: 230–744 m (the peak of Mount Alexander). Briefly, it can be said to extend from the northern slopes of the Great Divide to the plains of the flat riverine country, which runs on outside the northern boundary of the region to the Murray River.

Topography and soils: Its land forms include slightly undulating alluvial plains in the north and north-west, the volcanic plains of the catchments of the Campaspe and Loddon Rivers (which together form the major drainage basins of the region), undulating granite hills and sedimentary rises. There are also isolated mountains (Mount Alexander and Mount Tarrengower) in the south near Harcourt and Maldon.

In the Campaspe Valley soils vary from brown loams on the flood plains, red gradational and duplex soils on the volcanic plains, coarse uniform sandy soils on rocky crests in the granitic areas, and yellow duplex soils on the slopes. In the Loddon catchment, on the volcanic plains there are similar red-brown gradational and duplex soils while on the flood plains, red duplex soils with sandy loam top-soils above non-mottled clay subsoils are found. In the granitic areas the more gentle slopes are composed of yellow and yellow grey duplex and red duplex, the sedimentary rises being formed of red and yellow duplex soils with shallow stony soils on isolated rocky ridges. Drainage in the region is generally good.

Climate: Bendigo MJT 21°C, MAR na, HDD 1579 (raw), 1571 (adj for lat and daily temp. range), AR 546 mm (Oct–Apr 267 mm), RH 36%, AI na, SH 1894 (Oct–Apr). In its northern and western parts it has a typically warm but not extreme inland Australian climate. In its southern higher areas it is slightly cooler and damper. The climate as a whole favours robust red table wines. Its rainfall is generally low but evenly spread from month to month between November and March, though supplementary irrigation is sometimes necessary on shallower soils. Its low relative humidity assists in the prevention of mildews and rots. Weather is even during ripening with clear sunny days.

Harvest time: As befits a large region with varying mesoclimates, shiraz ripening is quite diverse. Some typical times in various areas of the region are as follows. *Chardonnay*: immediate north-west of Bendigo city (Maiden Gully) first week of March, further north-west of Bendigo city (Bridgewater) first to second week of March, immediate south of Bendigo city second week of April, further south from Bendigo city (Harcourt) first week of March. *Shiraz*: in most areas two to three weeks after chardonnay and at Castlemaine-Harcourt fractionally later.

Principal grape varieties: White—chardonnay, sauvignon blanc; Red—shiraz, cabernet sauvignon

Total area: not known but certainly not less than 250 ha and increasing

Major wine styles: *Shiraz*: deeply coloured wines showing distinct black pepper characters on nose and palate. Sometimes a eucalyptus nuance can be discerned. Such wines are rich and long-lasting (8+ years in good years). *Cabernet Sauvignon*: as with Shiraz, these are wines of deep red-purple hues, built usually for long-term 8–10 years maturation. Complex and richly structured wines with an emphasis on ripe berry fruit. *Leading wineries*: Passing Clouds, Water Wheel

Balgownie Estate R81

Hermitage Road, Maiden Gully, Vic 3551 (8 km west of Bendigo off the Marong road)
Ph 03 5449 6222, Fax 03 5449 6506, Email vineyard@balgownie.com

Owners: Des and Rod Forrester
Chief winemaker: Tobias Ansted
Year of foundation: 1969
Tonnes crushed on average each year: 100 (a further 100 tonnes is purchased from contracted growers in the region)
Location: Maiden Gully
Area: 32 ha
Soils: alluvial clay loam over silty clays
Varieties planted: White—chardonnay, viognier; Red—cabernet franc, cabernet sauvignon, merlot, pinot noir, shiraz
Leading wines: Balgownie Estate Cabernet Sauvignon, Shiraz, Pinot Noir. (The old Balgownie Cuvee second label has been dropped and a new second label, Maiden Gully, introduced.)
Notes: Founded by master-winemaker Stuart Anderson in 1969, Balgownie was purchased by Mildara Blass in 1985. Its lights were dimmed for a while but these days are tending to glow a little brighter, as the vineyard's inherent quality shines through. Balgownie's show results are consistently good, with silver and bronze medals in capital city wine shows for the Estate Cabernet Sauvignon and Estate Shiraz. The Estate changed hands in 1999 when it was purchased from Mildara Blass by Des and Rod Forrester. Cellar door sales: Mon–Sat 10am–5pm, Sun by appointment.

Blackjack Vineyards R81

Just off Blackjack Road on Calder Highway, Harcourt, Vic 3453
Ph/Fax 03 5474 2355

Owners: McKenzie and Pollock families
Chief winemakers: Ken Pollock and Ian McKenzie
Year of foundation: 1988
Tonnes crushed on average each year: 45
Location: Harcourt
Area: 6 ha
Soils: granitic sand with quartz and granite 'floaters'
Varieties planted: White—none; Red—cabernet sauvignon, merlot, pinot noir, shiraz
Leading wines: Blackjack Vineyards Shiraz
Notes: Like many Australian vineyards, Blackjack is located on the site of an old orchard. It has a rising reputation, not diminished by the trophy won for best 1994 Shiraz at the Royal Melbourne wine show. Its owner, Ian McKenzie, is not to be confused with Ian McKenzie formerly of Seppelt. Cellar door sales: weekends and public holidays 11am–5pm.

Blanche Barkly Wines NR

Rheola Road, Kingower, Vic 3517
Ph 03 5438 8223

Owners: David and Arleen Reimers
Chief winemaker: David Reimers
Year of foundation: 1972
Tonnes crushed on average each year: 25
Location: Kingower
Area: 3.6 ha
Soils: ironstone, quartz, black loamy clay, auriferous country

Varieties planted: White—none; Red—cabernet franc, cabernet sauvignon, mondeuse, shiraz
Leading wine: Blanche Barkly Alexander Cabernet Sauvignon, George Henry Cabernet Sauvignon, Johann Cabernet Sauvignon, Mary Eileen Shiraz
Notes: This is an old established Bendigo winery, well respected for its reds. Cellar door sales: weekends and public holidays 10am–5pm, at other times by appointment.

Charlotte Plains **NR**

Dooleys Road, Maryborough, Vic 3465
Ph 03 5461 3137

Owners: Ian and Vera Kemp
Chief winemaker: Roland Kaval (contract)
Year of foundation: 1990
Tonnes crushed on average each year: 3
Location: Simpson, 5 km north of Maryborough
Area: 1.6 ha
Soils: thin alluvial soils and sandy clay loam, which hold moisture quite well during dry summers
Varieties planted: White—sauvignon blanc; Red—shiraz
Leading wine: Charlotte Plains Shiraz
Notes: A small vineyard (close planted, 25 rows each 100 m long, 1.5 m apart). Charlotte Plains has not entered wine shows because of its tiny production, but a Winestate tasting in 1997 produced an encouraging 4-star rating for its 1996 Shiraz. Sales by mailing list only. Tastings by appointment.

Chateau Dore Winery and Receptions **NR**

303 Mandurang Road, Mandurang, Vic 3551
Ph 03 5439 5278

Owners: Ivan and Jan Gross
Chief winemaker: Ivan Gross
Year of foundation: 1860 (ceased original operation about 1900, re-established 1969)
Tonnes crushed on average each year: 10
Location: Mandurang
Area: 3 ha
Soils: slate country, sandy loams and ironstone over red clay, loam with gravel beds
Varieties planted: White—chardonnay, riesling; Red—cabernet sauvignon, shiraz
Leading wine: Chateau Dore Shiraz
Notes: The ancestral winery was built by Ivan's great-grandfather in the 1860s and was put to work again when winemaking recommenced. Cellar door sales: daily 10.30am–5pm.

Chateau Leamon **R80**

5528 Calder Highway, Bendigo, Vic 3550
Ph 03 5447 7995, Fax 03 5447 0855

Owner: Alma Leamon
Chief winemaker: Ian Leamon
Year of foundation: 1973
Tonnes crushed on average each year: 60
Location: Bendigo
Area: 5.6 ha
Soils: clayey loams
Varieties planted: White—semillon; Red—cabernet sauvignon, merlot, shiraz
Leading wines: Chateau Leamon Shiraz
Notes: Bendigo is of course a very good Shiraz area, Chateau Leamon's Shiraz being typical of the region. Cellar door sales: 6 days (closed Tues).

Connor Park **R81**

69 Connor Road, Leichardt, Vic 3516
about 25 km north west of Bendigo
Ph 03 5437 5234, Fax 03 5437 5204,
Email conner@netcom.au

Owners: Ross and Robyn Lougoon
Chief winemaker: Ross Lougoon
Year of foundation: (vineyard) late 1960s; (winery) 1994
Tonnes crushed on average each year: 60
Location: Leichardt

Area: 10 ha
Soils: sandy loamy creek flats over clay
Varieties planted: White—riesling, semillon;
Red—cabernet sauvignon, merlot, shiraz
Leading wines: Connor Park Shiraz, Sparkling
Shiraz
Notes: Connor Park is small but fortunate to
have a vineyard which is now over 30 years
old. Its speciality is Shiraz, both still and
sparkling. Cellar door sales: daily
10am–6pm.

Cooperage Estate R82

15 Markovitch Lane, Junortoun, Bendigo
Vic 3551
Ph 03 5449 3581, Fax 03 5449 3681,
Email bendigocoopers@bigpond.com

Owner/chief winemaker: Graham Gregurek
Year of foundation: 1991
Tonnes crushed on average each year: 10
Location: Junortoun near Bendigo
Area: 2.5 ha
Soils: quartz clays typical gold bearing country
Varieties planted: Red—cabernet sauvignon,
shiraz
Leading wine: Cooperage Estate Shiraz
Notes: Cooperage Estate is a logical
diversification of Graham Gregurek's Bendigo
cooperage business. As one might expect the
Estate's reds receive excellent oak. A promising
new name in the Bendigo region. No cellar
door sales. Sales by mail order.

Harcourt Valley Vineyards NR

Calder Highway, Harcourt, Vic 3453
Ph 03 5474 2223, Fax 03 5474 2293

Owners: John and Barbara Livingstone
Chief winemaker: John Livingstone
Year of foundation: 1982
Tonnes crushed on average each year: 20
Location: Harcourt
Area: 4 ha
Soils: granitic

Varieties planted: White—chardonnay, riesling;
Red—cabernet sauvignon, malbec, shiraz
Leading wines: Barbara's Shiraz
Notes: Robust reds typical of the region.
Cellar door sales: 11am–6pm daily.

Kangderaar Vineyard NR

Wehla-Kingower Road, Rheola, Vic 3517
Ph/Fax 03 5438 8292

Owners: James and Christine Nealy
Chief winemaker: James Nealy
Year of foundation: 1980
Tonnes crushed on average each year: 10
Location: Rheola
Area: 4.5 ha
Soils: granitic sand, very dry and 'thirsty' in
Christine Nealy's own words
Varieties planted: White—chardonnay,
gewurztraminer, riesling; Red—cabernet
sauvignon, merlot, touriga
Leading wines: Kangderaar Chardonnay,
Cabernet-Merlot, Sauvignon Blanc
Notes: Another small regional vineyard with
consistent standards. Its 1996 Cabernet
Sauvignon won bronzes at Ballarat and the
Victorian wine show. A Sauvignon Blanc is also
made from grapes purchased from a nearby
vineyard. Cellar door sales: Mon–Sat
9am–5pm, Sun 10am–5pm.

Laanecoorie NR

Bendigo Road, Betley, Vic 3472
Ph 03 5468 7260, Fax 03 5468 7388

Owners: John and Rosa McQuilten
Chief winemaker: John Ellis (contract)
Year of foundation: 1982
Tonnes produced on average each year: 20
Location: Betley
Area: 6 ha
Soils: alluvial with sandy clay loam
Varieties planted: White—none; Red—cabernet
franc, cabernet sauvignon, merlot, shiraz
Leading wines: Laanecoorie (a blend of the

three varieties mentioned), Shiraz
Notes: Cellar door sales by appointment.

Langanook Wines NR

91 McKitterick's Road, Sutton Grange
(near Harcourt) Vic 3448
Ph/Fax 03 5474 8250
Email mhunter@netcon.net.au

Owner/chief winemaker: Matt Hunter
Year of foundation: 1985
Tonnes crushed on average each year: 15
Location: Sutton Grange
Area: 1.5 ha
Soils: deep friable granite soils
Varieties planted: White—chardonnay,
viognier; Red—cabernet franc, cabernet
sauvignon, merlot, shiraz
Leading wines: Langanook Cabernet
Sauvignon Merlot and Cabernet Franc,
Langanook Chardonnay
Notes: Located on the slopes of Mt Alexander,
the Langanook vineyard should be suited to
cabernet and its Bordeaux cousins. Cellar door
sales by appointment only.

Mandurang Valley Winery R81

77 Faderson's Lane, Mandurang, Vic 3551
Ph 03 5439 5367, Fax 03 5439 3850

Owners: Wes and Pamela Vine
Chief winemaker: Wes Vine
Year of foundation: 1994
Tonnes crushed on average each year: 6, but
will increase to 12 by 2002. About 20 tonnes
of fruit are used in the production of
Mandurang Valley's own wines, the difference
is purchased from local growers
Location: Mandurang, south east of Bendigo
Area: 2 ha
Soils: deep alluvial loams on lower areas and
tight shales on the rises
Varieties planted: White—chardonnay, riesling;
Red—cabernet sauvignon, pinot noir, shiraz
Leading wines: Mandurang Valley Shiraz,

Cabernet Sauvignon, Pinot Noir, Riesling
Notes: A small vineyard typical of Bendigo's
granite slopes. Cellar door sales: weekends
11am–5pm. At other times by appointment.

Mount Alexander NR

Calder Highway, North Harcourt,
Vic 3453
Ph 03 5474 2262, Fax 03 5474 2553

Owner/chief winemaker: Keith Walkden
Year of foundation: 1983
Tonnes crushed on average each year: 65
Location: North Harcourt
Area: 16 ha
Soils: granitic loam
Varieties planted: White—chardonnay, muller-
thurgau, muscadelle, riesling, sauvignon blanc,
semillon; Red—cabernet franc, cabernet
sauvignon, meunier, muscat a petits grains
rouge, pinot noir, shiraz touriga tinta cao
Leading wines: Mount Alexander Vintage Port,
Cabernet Sauvignon, Chardonnay, Pinot Noir,
Semillon, Shiraz
Notes: For the Bendigo region, Mount
Alexander is quite a large maker with a diverse
range of wines and fruit brandies. There is
also a cider. Cellar door sales: Mon–Sat
9.30am–5.30pm. Picnic and barbecue
facilities.

Newstead Winery R81

Old Newstead Butter Co-op, Tivey St,
Newstead, Vic 3462 (to be replaced in
late 2001 by a new winery at the
Welshman's Reef Vineyard which is
4 km north of Newstead)
Ph/Fax 03 5476 2733, Fax 03 5476 2536

Owners: A partnership of Ronald Snep, Julia
Elkins, Cliff Stubbs and Maureen O'Connor
Chief winemaker: Ronald Snep
Year of foundation: 1992
Tonnes crushed on average each year: 60, of
which 50 are used for Newstead's own labels

Location: Newstead on the Pyrenees Highway south-west of Castlemaine.
Area: there are two vineyards, Welshman's Reef 8 ha and Burnt Acre 1.5 ha
Soils: hard soils of low fertility consisting of quartz, iron and shale
Varieties planted: White—chardonnay, semillon; Red—cabernet sauvignon, merlot, shiraz
Leading wines: Welshman's Reef Semillon, Shiraz
Notes: A popular winery, whose wines are typical of the area and whose labels represent the work of local artists. Cellar door sales: weekends and public holidays 10am–5pm, other times by appointment.

Nuggetty Vineyard   **NR**

Maldon-Shelborne Road, Maldon, Vic 3463 (about 4 km north-west of Maldon and about 20 km south west of Bendigo)
Ph 03 5475 1347, Fax 03 5475 1647, Email nuggettyvineyard@hitech.net.au

Owners: Greg and Jackie Dedman
Chief winemaker: Greg Dedman
Year of foundation: 1994
Tonnes crushed on average each year: presently 8, anticipated to grow to 50 when the vineyard is fully established and bearing
Location: Maldon
Area: 6 ha increasing to 10
Soils: podsolic duplex over red and yellow clay, granitic sand over granite
Varieties planted: White—pinot gris, sauvignon blanc, semillon; Red—cabernet sauvignon, merlot, shiraz
Leading wine: Nuggetty Ranges Shiraz
Notes: A small winery with hand-made wines whose Shiraz reds already have won gold and silver medals at the Ballarat and Stanthorpe Small Winemakers shows. Cellar door sales: weekends and public holidays 10am–4pm, other times by appointment.

Old Loddon Wines   **R80**

5 Serpentine Road, Bridgewater, Vic 3516
Ph 03 5437 3197, Fax 03 5437 3201, Email loddon@netcon.net.au

Owners: Russell and Jill Burdett
Chief winemaker: Russell Burdett
Year of foundation: 1986 (vineyard), 1997 (winery)
Tonnes crushed on average each year: 10
Location: Bridgewater
Area: 2.8 ha
Soils: loamy river flats
Varieties planted: Red—cabernet franc, cabernet sauvignon, merlot, shiraz
Leading wine: Old Loddon Cabernet Sauvignon
Notes: Russell Burdett is a Cabernet enthusiast and his Old Loddon Vineyard is devoted chiefly to cabernet sauvignon and its cousins. Cellar door sales: weekend 10am–5pm, other times by appointment.

Passing Clouds   **R85**

RMB 440 Kurting Road, Kingower, Vic 3517
Ph 03 5438 8257, Fax 03 5438 8246

Owners: Graeme Leith and Sue Mackinnon
Chief winemakers: Graeme Leith, Greg Bennett
Year of foundation: 1974
Tonnes crushed on average each year: 60, including fruit grown on neighbouring vineyards
Location: Kingower
Area: 6 ha
Soils: Passing Clouds is on old creek flats and its vines are well established on non-irrigated deep sandy loam
Varieties planted: Red—cabernet franc, cabernet sauvignon, pinot noir, shiraz
Leading wines: Passing Clouds Graeme's Blend Shiraz-Cabernet, Angel Cabernets
Notes: After a quarter of a century, Graeme Leith and Sue Mackinnon have a wealth of experience of the Kingower area. This is a

vineyard renowned for its smooth Shiraz dominant Graeme's Blend and the classy Angel Cabernets. Cellar door sales: daily 12pm–5pm but as the wines are often in short supply it is best to ring first.

Sandhurst Ridge R79

156 Forest Drive, Marong, Vic 3515
(about 17 km north-west of Bendigo)
Ph/Fax 03 5435 2534

Owners/chief winemakers: Paul and George Greblo
Year of foundation: 1990
Tonnes crushed on average each year: 40
Location: Marong
Area: 5.8 ha
Soils: a thin loamy layer above a heavy red clay rich in gravelly quartz and ironstone
Varieties planted: White—chardonnay, sauvignon blanc; Red—cabernet sauvignon, merlot, shiraz
Leading wines: Sandhurst Ridge Sauvignon Blanc-Cabernet Sauvignon, Shiraz
Notes: Sandhurst Ridge is a new small to medium sized winery specialising in hand-crafted reds. Cellar door sales: Sat noon–5pm, Sun 1pm–5pm, other times by appointment.

Tannery Lane Vineyard NR

174 Tannery Lane, Mandurang, Vic 3551
12 km south east of Bendigo
Ph 03 5439 5011, Fax 03 5444 1400

Owners: Hugh and Adele Williams
Chief winemaker: (contract)
Year of foundation: 1990
Tonnes crushed on average each year: 8.75, about half of which are used for Tannery Lane's own labels
Location: Mandurang
Area: 2 ha
Soils: a thin layer of loamy clayey soil over a shale and rock subsoil
Varieties planted: Red—cabernet franc,

cabernet sauvignon, merlot sangiovese, shiraz
Leading wine: Tannery Lane Shiraz
Notes: A very small boutique winery whose ownership has recently changed hands. Cellar door sales by appointment.

Tipperary Hill Estate NR

Alma-Bowenvale Road, Alma,
Maryborough, Vic 3465
about 7 km north west of Maryborough
Ph/Fax 03 5461 3312

Owners: Paul and Margaret Flowers
Chief winemaker: Paul Flowers
Year of foundation: 1986
Tonnes crushed on average each year: 7
Location: Alma
Area: 2.5 ha
Soils: alluvial soils on a sandstone, quartz and ironstone reef
Varieties planted: White—none; Red—cabernet franc, cabernet sauvignon, merlot, pinot noir, shiraz
Leading wines: Tulkara Shiraz, Cabernets, Pinot-Shiraz
Notes: A pretty spot close to a state forest near an old gold-mining area. There is a restaurant and a picnic ground. Cellar door sales: weekends 10am–5pm or by appointment.

Water Wheel Vineyards R85

Bridgewater on Loddon, Bridgewater,
Vic 3516
Ph 03 5437 3060, Fax 03 5437 3082

Owner: Cumming Murphy Nominees Pty Ltd
Chief winemakers: Bill Trevaskis and Peter Cumming
Year of foundation: 1972
Tonnes crushed on average each year: 450 and increasing
Location: Bridgewater on Loddon, 38 km north west of Bendigo
Area: 96 ha
Soils: white light loam for the whites; red

sticky clay with small pieces of limestone for the reds
Varieties planted: White—chardonnay, sauvignon blanc; Red—cabernet sauvignon, shiraz
Leading wines: Water Wheel Sauvignon Blanc, Shiraz

Notes: Water Wheel is currently in expansive mode. Its vineyard area now nearly doubled in size is limstone-based and all planted to shiraz.
Cellar door sales: daily 11am–5pm except May to September when hours are Mon–Fri 11am–5pm, weekends and public holidays 1pm–4pm.

CENTRAL VICTORIAN HIGH COUNTRY (INTERIM DETERMINATION)

This region consists of what might be called the upper catchment area of the Goulburn River (not the valley itself which has its own separate region). An alternate name might be the Upper Goulburn Valley. High and cool, its southern boundary stretches westerly and south-westerly from Mount Buller in the east through the forests of the Great Divide and then generally north-westerly as far as Broadford on the Hume Highway and briefly north along the highway to Tallarook. It then extends easterly and north-easterly on the southern side of the Strathbogie Ranges to Mansfield and Mount Buller beyond.

Like much of Central Victoria, the region was first settled by squatters in the late 1830s. In its central and eastern parts, these enterprising gentlemen grazed their sheep on large pastoral 'runs' with ill-defined boundaries which were often the subject of dispute. Indeed during the 1840s *caveat emptor* became a common phrase in relation to land purchases in the region, so common in fact that there is to this day a locality called 'Caveat' within the region. From the 1850s to the end of the 19th century, gold fossicking was an occupation for many and gold mining continues to this day. Grazing remained dominant, however, and the droving of cattle and sheep from their pastures in the valleys to their summer grazing above the treeline in October and November and their return journey in May became a common sight. Timber getting was also a large part of the local economy and this too continues as softwood forests reach maturity. Though farming continues on a smaller scale, it has been joined by viticulture and tourism as a source of income for the region. The principal centres of the region are Alexandra, Eildon, Mansfield and Yea.

As a wine region, its history is quite recent. Delatite was founded in 1968. Alan Cuthbertson established Murrundindi in 1977. Other later participants have been the Steen family at Strath Creek and Luis Riebl at Tallarook.There are now over 350 ha of vineyards in the region with six wineries.

Location: Mansfield, latitude 37°3'S, longitude 146°7'E. About 138 km directly north-east of Melbourne.
Altitude: predominantly above 300 m with peaks to 1800 m. Most vineyards are planted between 200 m and 800 m in altitude.
Topography and soils: The region is hilly and comprises the physiographic area of the east Victorian Uplands of dissected high plateaux on various resistant rocks bordered

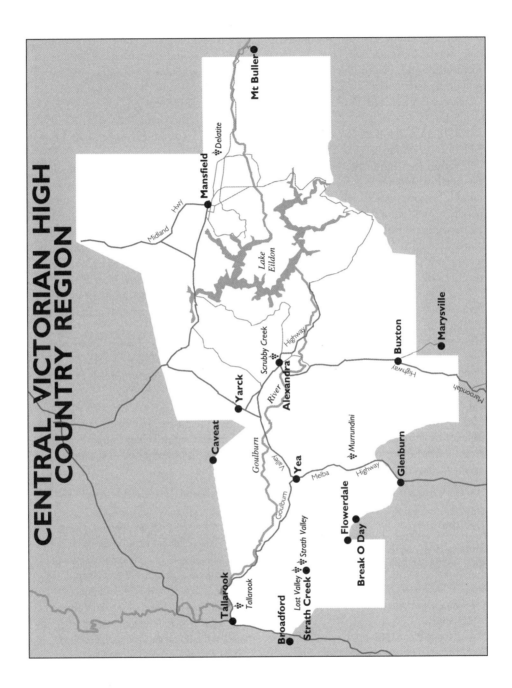

CENTRAL VICTORIAN HIGH COUNTRY REGION

by the Victorian Alps, the Riverine alluvial plain and the moderately high plateaux and strike ridges of the west Victorian Uplands. It is notable for Upper Devonian volcanic and granitic complexes and in the east for the occurrence of Upper Devonian volcanics and thick Upper Devonian and Lower Carboniferous non-marine sediments.

Soil types found on the vineyards in the region include loam, granite, sand/orange clay, clay loam/sandstone, grey clay/loam, gravelly clay and mudstone, shale, granite loams and sand, brown clay loam, red granitic loam, granular porous clay and raised sedimentay metamorphosed rock. Clay and loam soil types are the most common.

Climate: Mansfield, MJT 19.9°C, MAR 14.1°C, HDD 1438 raw cut off at 19°C, AR 718.8 mm (Oct–Apr 383.8 mm) RH na, AI na, SH na; Alexandra, MJT 20.25°C, MAR 13.15°C, HDD, 1407 raw cut off at 19°C, AR 710.5 mm (Oct–Apr 356.3 mm) RH 55%, (9am Jan) AI na, SH 94.4 pa.

Within the region the mean annual rainfall rises from 640 mm to 1000 mm along the north-west flank to more than 1400 mm in the east and south-east. Annual average rainfall for vineyards is within the range of 640 mm to 796 mm. Some vineyards experience snow showers during winter. The climate within the region is generally drier and warmer than that of surrounding regions, with a higher number of clear days. The climate could be termed 'alpine Mediterranean', that is, there is a predominance of winter rain and a relative summer drought. The alpine surrounds exert a definite cooling influence. Both frost and fungus diseases have a relatively low incidence.

Almost all vineyards are irrigated by drip-irrigation systems, supplied by surface dams, which are in turn filled by run-off or natural springs. Bore water is generally not available in sufficient quantity.

Harvest time: later than adjoining areas of lower elevation and with lower yields. Generally in March for early maturing varieties to mid-May for those later.

Principal grape varieties: White—chardonnay; Red—cabernet sauvignon, shiraz, pinot noir, merlot

Total area: 368 ha (2000)

Major wine styles: It is rather early to make definitive judgments, but based on the wine styles of Delatite and Murrundindi, Riesling, Gewurztraminer and Chardonnay hold high promise in whites, while blends of Cabernet Sauvignon and Merlot make elegant reds.

Leading wineries: Lost Valley, Murrundindi, Delatite.

Delatite   **R85**

Stoneys Road, Mansfield, Vic 3722
Ph 03 5775 2922, Fax 03 5775 2911

Owners: Ritchie family
Chief winemaker: Ros Ritchie, David Ritchie (viticulturalist)
Year of foundation: 1968
Tonnes crushed on average each year: 210
Location: Mansfield
Area: 25 ha
Soils: striated ironstone rock; the vineyard has minimum drip irrigation
Varieties planted: White—chardonnay, gewurztraminer, pinot gris, riesling, sauvignon blanc; Red—cabernet franc, cabernet sauvignon, malbec, merlot, pinot noir, shiraz
Leading wines: Demelza NV (sparkling), Riesling, Dead Man's Hill Gewurztraminer, Devil's River (a red blend of the 'Bordeaux' varities planted), RJ (a super-premium red blend of the Bordeaux varieties mentioned above), Chardonnay, Sauvignon Blanc
Notes: A vineyard with an excellent view of the Mount Buller massif, it has a fine reputation for its delicate varietals Riesling and Gewurztraminer and also its fruit-driven reds.
Cellar door sales: daily 10am–4pm.

Henke **NR**

175 Henke Lane, Yarck, Vic 3719
Ph/Fax 03 5797 6277

Owners/chief winemaker: Tim and Caroline
Miller
Year of foundation: 1970
Tonnes crushed on average each year: 5
Location: Yarck
Area: 2.4 ha
Soils: porous clayey soil, not high in fertility,
which has been much improved by mulching
Varieties planted: White—none; Red—cabernet
sauvignon, shiraz
Leading wines: Henke Shiraz, Shiraz Cabernet
Notes: Good blends of Shiraz and Cabernet.
Cellar door sales by appointment and mail
order.

Lost Valley Winery **R86**

36 Yamby Road, Strath Creek, Vic 3658
Ph 03 5797 0212, Fax 03 9821 5278

Owners: Dr Robert Ippaso and Shane Jackman
Chief winemaker: Alex White (contract)
Year of foundation: 1995
Tonnes produced on average each year: 20, all
of which are used for Lost Valley's own labels
Location: Strath Creek
Are: 3.2 ha
Soils: granitic clay
Varieties planted: White—cortese, verdelho;
Red—merlot, shiraz
Leading wines: Lost Valley Shiraz, Cortese,
Merlot, Verdelho
Notes: Lost Valley has one of the very few
Australian plantings of the Italian white varietal
cortese (used exclusively to make the stylish
whites of Gavi, about the only memorable
native white variety of Piedmont). Cellar door
sales by mail order. Tasting by appointment.

Murrundindi **R7**

RMB 6070 Cummins Lane, Murrundindi,
Vic 3717
Ph 03 5797 8217, Fax 03 5797 8422

Owners: Alan and Janet Cuthbertson
Chief winemakers: Hugh and Alan
Cuthbertson
Year of foundation: 1977
Tonnes crushed on average each year: 45, of
which about 30 are used for the Murrundindi
labels
Location: Murrundindi
Area: 15 ha
Soils: gravel, mudstone, quartz
Varieties planted: White—chardonnay;
Red—cabernet sauvignon, merlot, shiraz
Leading wines: Murrundindi Chardonnay,
Cabernets
Notes: Located near Yea in an undoubtedly
cool area, Murrundindi makes unmistakeably
cool-area wines. It produces very good
Chardonnay and an excellent Cabernets. These
are not 'big' wines in any warm area sense of
the word, but fruit-driven and elegant in the
best high country style. Cellar door sales by
appointment or mail order.

Scrubby Creek Wines **NR**

566 Crystal Creek Road, Alexandra,
Vic 3714
Ph 03 5772 2191, Fax 03 5772 1048,
Email cottages@crystalck.com

Owners: Stastra and Napier families
Chief winemaker: Martin Williams (contract)
Year of foundation: 1995
Tonnes crushed on average each year: 25, of
which 10 are used for Scrubby Creek Wines'
own labels
Location: Alexandra
Area: 3.5 ha
Soils: clayey sandy loam
Varieties planted: White—chardonnay;
Red—none

Leading wines: Scrubby Creek Chardonnay
Notes: This is a partnership between the Stastra and Napier families who own neighbouring vineyards. Cellar door sales: daily 9am–5pm

Strath Valley Vineyard NR

Strath Valley Road, Strath Creek, Vic 3658
Ph 03 5784 9229, Fax 03 5784 9381

Owners: Chris and Robyn Steen
Chief winemaker: (contract)
Year of foundation: 1994
Tonnes produced on average each year: 140, of which about 20 are used for Boundary Range labels
Location: Strath Creek
Area: 12.5 ha
Soils: clay over mudstone/gravel
Varieties planted: White—chardonnay, sauvignon blanc; Red—cabernet sauvignon, shiraz
Leading wines: Boundary Range Shiraz, Sauvignon Blanc
Notes: This is a vineyard specialising in Shiraz and Sauvignon Blanc. Cellar door sales: weekends and by appointment.

Tallarook R84

Dabyminga, Ennis Road, Tallarook, Vic 3659
Ph/Fax 03 5793 8399,
Email tallarook@msn.com.au

Owners: Tallarook Wines Pty Ltd
Chief winemaker: Martin Williams (contract)
Year of foundation: 1992
Location: Tallarook
Area: 12.4 ha
Soils: variable soils, chiefly red duplex and deep loams
Varieties planted: White—chardonnay, marsanne, roussanne, viognier; Red—pinot noir, shiraz
Leading wines: Tallarook Chardonnay, Pinot Noir
Notes: Tallarook has both vines and wines of great promise. It is a vineyard of variable microclimates. Part is cool and accordingly its Chardonnays are generous yet have finesse. Part is warm and will suit the northern Rhone white varieties now planted and, of course, shiraz. No cellar door sales. Sales by mail order.

GOULBURN VALLEY REGION

The Goulburn Valley owes its existence as a vineyard area to the massive contribution of Chateau Tahbilk, without which it may long ago have been returned to pastoral pursuits. Founded in 1860 by a group of investors led by a poet (R. H. Horne), Tabilk Vineyard Proprietary with its capital of $50 000 purchased 259 hectares of land adjoining the right bank of the Goulburn River, north of Seymour, and by the end of 1861 had 87 hectares under vine. Substantial cellars were constructed and by 1877 Tabilk's production reached 17 500 cases a year. By this time, Chateau Tahbilk (the name was first used in 1879) was owned and capably managed by John Pinney Bear in whose family it remained until 1926. It was then purchased by the Purbrick family and shortly afterwards was occupied by Eric Purbrick. The Purbrick family has owned Chateau Tahbilk ever since.

Mitchelton, the vision of the late Ross Shelmerdine and the region's other major winery, is of much more recent origin. Lying about 5 km from Chateau Tahbilk and abutting the left bank of the Goulburn River, it became part of Victoria's wine resurgence in the late 1960s. Its vines were established in sandy country on their own

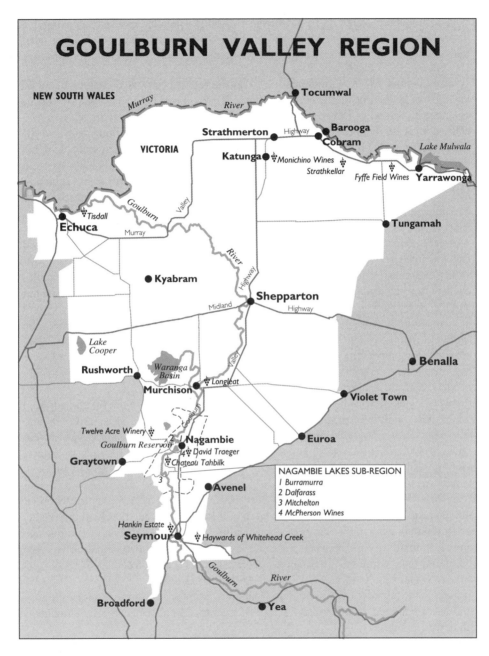

GOULBURN VALLEY REGION

NEW SOUTH WALES

Murray   River

● **Tocumwal**

VICTORIA

Strathmerton ●   Highway   ● **Barooga**
● **Cobram**

Katunga ● ⚘ *Monichino Wines* ⚘   *Lake Mulwala*
Strathkellar   *Fyffe Field Wines* ⚘   **Yarrawonga**

Goulburn   *Valley*
⚘ *Tisdall*
Echuca ●   *Murray*   ● **Tungamah**

River

● **Kyabram**   *Highway*

Shepparton ●
Midland   *Highway*

Lake
Cooper   ● **Benalla**
Waranga
Rushworth   *Basin*   ⚘ *Longleat*
Murchison ●   *Valley*   ● **Violet Town**

Twelve Acre Winery ⚘   2
Goulburn Reservoir   1 ● **Nagambie**   ● **Euroa**
4 ⚘ *David Traeger*
Graytown ●   ⚘ *Chateau Tahbilk*

3   **NAGAMBIE LAKES SUB-REGION**
● **Avenel**   1 Burramurra
2 Dalfarass
3 Mitchelton
4 McPherson Wines

Hankin Estate ⚘
Seymour ●   ⚘ *Haywards of Whitehead Creek*

Goulburn   *River*

Broadford ●   ● **Yea**

rootstocks in the belief that phylloxera had ceased to be a hazard and anyhow would not present a danger in such soil. They were first planted in 1969. Its modern winery with its distinctive 'witch's hat' tower was completed in 1974. Mitchelton was purchased by Petaluma Limited in 1994. Sadly, phylloxera has now appeared in the Mitchelton vineyard and replacement vines are now planted on resistant rootstocks.

The Goulburn Valley is by no means Australia's premier vineyard area but has deservedly built a reputation for sturdy, reliable Cabernet and Shiraz reds and, considering its generally warm climate, distinctive Marsannes and surprisingly delicate Rieslings.

Location: latitude 37°25'S, longitude 145°20'E, the region begins at Broadford, about 62 km north of Melbourne on the Hume Highway. It then proceeds north as a narrow tongue of land until it reaches Tallarook and thereafter on its eastern boundary travels in a generally north-easterly direction near Avenel, Euroa, Violet Town and Tungamah and the Murray River west of Rutherglen. It then travels westward along the southern bank of that river, past the junction with its namesake river to a point just west of Echuca, where it turns generally south-east, its western boundary passing through such towns as Rushworth and Graytown back to its point of commencement. Its principal towns are Seymour, Nagambie, Euroa, Shepparton, Yarrawonga, Cobram, Strathmerton and Echuca.

Altitude: 140 m

Topography and soils: The region generally follows the northerly course of the Goulburn River, which rises near Mount Buller in the Victorian Alps. From there, the river flows swiftly westwards through Lake Eildon and the surrounding steeply mountainous country to reach its wine region south-east of Tallarook. From there, the country is flat and the river's flow is slower, though it is subject to flooding in many places in times of heavy rain. Its sandy, gravelly soils, mainly alluvial in origin, accordingly reflect the history of their river. Further away from the river beds, both current and ancient, there are the typical moderately fertile, hard, red duplex soils, found in many vineyard areas of south-eastern Australia. Water resources of the Goulburn Valley are regarded as very good as there are aquifers at 30 metres.

Climate: Seymour, MJT 20.9°C, MAR na, HDD (raw) 1694, 1485 cut off and adjusted for latitude, daily temperature range but not adjusted for vine sites, AR 596 mm (Oct–Apr 293 mm), RH 41%, AI na, SH 8.7. Euroa, MJT 21.8°C, MAR na, HDD (raw) 1898, 1460 cut off and adjusted for latitude, daily temperature range and vine sites Gladstones, AR 649 mm (Oct–Apr 308 mm), RH 46% (both Gladstones). Goulburn Valley, MJT 21.2°C, MAR 13.7°C, HDD (raw) 1681, AR 597 mm (Oct–Mar 248 mm), RH 52% (9am), AI 309 mm, SH 9 (D&S). Quite warm in summer, though not as warm as Rutherglen and the north-east, the Goulburn Valley has a reputation for table wines of good quality. Slightly less than half the average annual rainfall occurs between October and March and drip-irrigation is now becoming more common. The region also experiences spring frosts and is phylloxerated, new plantings requiring phylloxera-resistant rootstocks.

Harvest time: chardonnay, sauvignon blanc in March; marsanne and riesling in mid-March to mid-April; shiraz in late March to late April; cabernet sauvignon mid-April to mid-May.

Principal grape varieties: Red—shiraz, cabernet sauvignon, merlot, cabernet franc; White—chardonnay, marsanne, riesling, sauvignon blanc, semillon, viognier, verdelho.

Major wine styles: White—Marsanne, Chardonnay, Riesling; Red—Shiraz, Cabernet Sauvignon

Leading wineries: David Traeger, Mitchelon, Tahbilk

Burramurra NR

Banwood Park, Nagambie, Vic 3608
Ph/Fax 03 5794 2755,
Email burramurra@hotmail.com

Owners: Patrick and Merryl McNamara
Chief winemaker: Don Lewis of Mitchelton
(contract)
Year of foundation: 1989
Tonnes produced on average each year: 60,
of which 15 are used for Burramurra's own
labels
Location: Nagambie Lakes
Area: 6 ha
Soils: fronting a large lake on its western
boundary, the vineyard is composed of red
Goulburn Valley loam. Its proximity to the lake
ensures that the vineyard remains frost-free
during spring and relatively cool during the
searing north-westerly winds of summer
Varieties planted: White—none; Red—cabernet
sauvignon, merlot
Leading wine: Burramurra (a blend of the
above varieties)
Notes: This is a new name in the Goulburn
Valley, making only one wine, a Cabernet
Merlot blend. There are no cellar door sales.
Sales by mail order.

Dalfarras R85

Goulburn Valley Highway, Nagambie,
Vic 3608 (2 km south of Nagambie)
Ph 03 5794 2637, Fax 03 5794 2360

Owners: Rosa and Alister Purbrick
Chief winemaker: Alister Purbrick
Year of foundation: 1998
Tonnes crushed on average each year: 2500 (in
2nd year of winery operation) to be increased
to 4000. About 320 tonnes is used for
Dalfarras labels
Location: Nagambie
Area: no vineyard owned
Soils: na
Leading wines: Dalfarras Marsanne,

Chardonnay, Sauvignon Blanc, Cabernet
Sauvignon, Shiraz
Notes: Dalfarras has a new home and a new
winery, which will specialise in Nagambie Lakes
fruit for marsanne and chardonnay. Other red
and white varieties from other regions renowned
for their quality will also be used from time to
time. Cellar door sales: available late 2002.

David Traeger Wines R86

139 High Street, Nagambie, Vic 3608
Ph 03 5794 2514, Fax 03 5794 1776,
Email traeger@eck.net.au

Owners/chief winemaker: David and
Honey-Anne Traeger
Year of foundation: 1986
Tonnes crushed on average each year: 300
Locations: Nagambie (winery), Avenel (21 ha),
Graytown (12 ha)
Area: 33 ha
Soils: Avenel, red clay loam with good fertility
and water-holding capacity; Graytown, river
loam over gravel
Varieties planted: White—verdelho;
Red—cabernet sauvignon, grenache, merlot,
petit verdot, shiraz, tempranillo
Leading wines: David Traeger Verdelho, Shiraz,
Cabernet Blend
Notes: David Traeger is an old Goulburn Valley
hand who happens also to be a Verdelho
enthusiast. Indeed he proudly states that his
was the only Verdelho to have won gold at the
Royal Melbourne Wine Show *last* century. He
must have carried out some painstaking
research. His Shiraz also is usually very good.
Cellar door sales: daily 10am–5pm.

Fyffe Field Wines R80

Murray Valley Highway, Yarrawonga,
Vic 3730 (midway between Yarrawonga
and Cobram)
Ph 03 5748 4282, Fax 03 5748 4284,
Email fyfewine@mcmedia.com.au

Owners: Graeme and Liz Diamond
Chief winemaker: David Traeger (contract)
Year of foundation: 1993
Tonnes produced on average each year: 50, of which 15 are used for Fyffe Field's own labels.
Area: 6.4 ha
Soils: clayey loam
Varieties planted: White—semillon, verdelho; Red—cabernet sauvignon, merlot, petit verdot, shiraz, touriga
Leading wines: Fyffe Field Diamond White (Semillon), Cabernet Sauvignon, Shiraz-Petit Verdot
Notes: Winners of numerous bronze medals at local and small-winemaker shows and also a gold at the prestigious Victorian Wine Show, Fyffe Field features some very drinkable reds and a collection of over 1800 ornamental pigs.
Cellar door sales: daily 10am–5pm.

Hankin Estate R85

Johnsons Lane, Northwood via Seymour, Vic 3660
Ph/Fax 03 5792 2396,
Email Enidhankin@bigpond.com

Owner: Dr Max Hankin
Chief winemaker: Dr Max Hankin
Year of foundation: 1975
Tonnes produced on average each year: 25, of which all are used for Hankin Estate wines
Location: Northwood near Seymour
Area: 15 ha
Soils: alluvial loam on gravel or sand
Varieties planted: White—sauvignon blanc, semillon, verdelho; Red—cabernet franc, cabernet sauvignon, grenache, malbec, merlot, shiraz
Leading wines: Hankin Estate Merlot Shiraz Cabernets
Notes: Max Hankin regularly exhibits at the excellent Victorian Wine Show. A few years ago he discovered that his vineyard had succumbed to phylloxera and this obliged him to replant both existing and new varieties on phylloxera-resistant rootstocks. One of the new varieties planted was merlot, exhibited in 2000 and striking gold, which proves I suppose that it's an illwind that blows nobody any good.
Cellar door sales: weekends 10am–5pm.
Sales by mail order also.

Haywards of Whitehead Creek NR

Hall Lane, Seymour, Vic 3660
Ph 03 5792 3050

Owners: Mr and Mrs B. Hayward
Chief winemakers: Sid and David Hayward
Year of foundation: 1975
Tonnes crushed on average each year: 10
Location: Whitehead Creek
Area: 5 ha
Soils: clay loam over mottled clay
Varieties planted: White—riesling; Red—cabernet sauvignon, malbec, pinot noir, shiraz
Leading wines: Haywards of Whitehead Creek Shiraz, Cabernet Sauvignon
Notes: Cellar door sales: Mon–Sat 9am–6pm, Sun 10am–6pm, closed Good Friday and Christmas Day.

Longleat NR

Old Weir Road, Murchison, Vic 3610
Ph 03 5826 2294, Fax 03 5826 2510,
Email james@longleatwines.com

Owner: Longleat Estate Pty Ltd
Chief winemaker: David Traeger (contract)
Year of foundation: 1975
Tonnes crushed on average each year: 59, of which about 18 tonnes are used for the Longleat labels
Location: Murchison
Area: 9 ha
Soils: sandy loam on a clay base
Varieties planted: White—riesling, semillon; Red—cabernet sauvignon, shiraz
Leading wines: Longleat Shiraz, Cabernet Sauvignon, Riesling

Notes: Under new ownership since 1998, Longleat is currently expanding its plantings. Cellar door sales: Thurs–Mon 10am–5pm.

McPherson Wines NR

Goulburn Valley Highway, Nagambie, Vic 3608
Ph 03 5794 2890, Fax 03 5794 2805,
Ph 02 9436 1644 (H), Fax 02 9436 3144,
Email sschwarz@mcphersonwines.com.au

Owner: McPherson Wines Pty Ltd
Chief winemaker: Andrew Dean
Year of foundation: 1993
Tonnes crushed on average each year: 11 000, including 350 presently from the Goulburn Valley; other fruit is sourced from Mildura. About 6350 tonnes are used for McPherson's own labels, including all the Goulburn Valley fruit. (The gross tonnes crushed include fruit purchased from contract growers.)
Locations: Nagambie (Goulburn Valley) and Mildura (Murray Darling)
Area: 40 ha (Nagambie), 60 ha (Mildura)
Soils: Nagambie, red loam over a gravelly base; Mildura, sandy loam
Varieties planted: (Nagambie) White— chardonnay, marsanne, sauvignon blanc, verdelho; Red—cabernet sauvignon, merlot, shiraz. (Mildura) White—chardonnay, colombard, sauvignon blanc, verdelho; Red—cabernet sauvignon, grenache, merlot, ruby cabernet, sangiovese, shiraz
Leading wines: McPherson Chardonnay, Semillon, Shiraz, Cabernet Sauvignon
Notes: This is a relatively new and potentially very large enterprise, which will come into greater prominence in the later years of the first decade of the new millennium, when more fruit from its Nagambie vineyard becomes available. Cellar door sales: facilities available from late 2000.

Mitchelton R88

Mitchellstown, Nagambie, Vic 3608
Ph 03 5794 2710, Fax 03 5794 2615,
Email mitchelton@mitchelton.com.au

Owner: Petaluma Ltd
Chief winemaker: Don Lewis
Year of foundation: 1969
Tonnes crushed on average each year: 3000, about half of which is produced by Mitchelton's own vineyards, other fruit being sourced from various growers throughout the Goulburn Valley and other parts of Victoria
Location: Mitchellstown
Area: 154.2 ha
Soils: typically alluvial, with soils varying from sandy loams to fine clay loams; red-brown earths predominantly overlying lighter clay dominant soils; pH 5.5–6.5 (very slightly acidic)
Varieties planted: White—chardonnay, marsanne, riesling, roussanne, semillon, viognier; Red—cabernet franc, cabernet sauvignon, merlot, shiraz
Leading wines: Mitchelton Print Shiraz, Blackwood Park Riesling and Botrytis Riesling Mitchelton regional wines, Marsanne, Shiraz, Viognier, the Preece range and the Thomas Mitchell range
Notes: Like its near neighbour Chateau Tahbilk, 5 km away, Mitchelton is typically riverine, light sandy loam soils from ancient Goulburn River beds and a warm but not scorching climate with cooling river breezes. All of this produces stable fruit, from which Don Lewis makes superb award-winning Rieslings, Marsannes and Shiraz. Cellar door sales: daily 10am–5pm. There is also an award-winning restaurant open daily for lunch.

Monichino Wines R80

Berry's Road, Katunga, Vic 3644
Ph 03 5864 6452, Fax 03 5864 6538,
Email monichino@cnl.com.au

Owners: Carlo and Terry Monichino and Ann Sergi (nee Monichino)
Chief winemakers: (table wines) Terry Monichino and (fortified) Carlo Monichino
Year of foundation: 1962
Tonnes crushed on average each year: 200, of which 180 are used for Monichino's own labels
Location: Katunga
Area: 20 ha
Soils: heavy clay loam to llighter red clay sand
Varieties planted: White—chardonnay, orange muscat, riesling, sauvignon blanc, semillon, white frontignac; Red—brown frontignac, cabernet franc, cabernet sauvignon, merlot, shiraz
Leading wines: Monichino Chardonnay, Botrytis Semillon, Shiraz, Merlot, Cabernet Sauvignon and a range of Ports and Muscats
Notes: A winery and vineyard little known north of the Murray but with a consistent record of silver and bronze awards at Victorian and other wine shows. Cellar door sales: Mon–Sat 9am–5pm, Sun 10am–5pm.

Strathkellar R79

Murray Valley Highway, Cobram, Vic 3644
Ph 03 5873 5274, Fax 03 5873 5270

Owners: Dick and Margaret Parkes
Chief winemaker: (Chateau Tahbilk) contract
Year of foundation: 1990
Tonnes produced on average each year: 50, of which 16 are used for Strathkellar's own labels
Location: Cobram
Area: 5.5 ha
Soils: typical red Murray River sand
Varieties planted: White—chardonnay, chenin blanc; Red—shiraz
Leading wine: Strathkellar Chenin Blanc
Notes: A small producer of a good Chardonnay, remarkably delicate for the area. Cellar door sales: daily 10am–6pm or by appointment.

Tahbilk
(formerly Chateau Tahbilk) R85

Tabilk, Vic 3608 (8 km south-west of Nagambie)
Ph 03 5794 2555, Fax 03 5794 2360

Owners: Purbrick family
Chief winemaker: Alister Purbrick
Year of foundation: 1860
Tonnes crushed on average each year: 3100
Location: Tabilk
Area: 155 ha; there are also two other vineyards, AHN of 81 ha and Pogue of 55 ha
Soils: Chateau Tahbilk, fine sand, sandy loam and red loam; AHN, red loam; Pogue, fine sand
Varieties planted: (Chateau Tahbilk Vineyard) White—chardonnay, chenin blanc, marsanne, riesling, roussanne, sauvignon blanc, semillon, viognier; Red—cabernet franc, cabernet sauvignon, malbec, merlot, shiraz. (AHN) White—chardonnay; Red—shiraz. (Pogue) White—chardonnay, sauvignon blanc, verdelho; Red—cabernet sauvignon, merlot, shiraz
Leading wines: Chateau Tahbilk 1860 Vines Shiraz, Reserve Cabernet Sauvignon
Notes: Chateau Tahbilk is one of the historical showplaces of Australian wine. Though it deserves reverence, it is a veteran that is still very much alive. Soon, however (though it is the one Australian wine estate entirely worthy of the name), it plans to drop the name 'Chateau' and become simply 'Tahbilk', a brave step but one in keeping with the beginning of a new century, and paradoxically a return to its original 1860 name. With one exception, reds are Tahbilk's forte—the 1962 Reserve Cabernet Sauvignon was a show wine that was still remarkably resilient 25 years later. Of course there are the few rows of the original plantings of shiraz which somehow escaped the march of phylloxera a century ago. These too now receive the respect and identity due to worthy veterans. The exception to the reds

is the Marsanne which, in good years and given due cellaring, develops a marvellous honeysuckle character on nose and palate. Cellar door sales: Mon–Sat 9am–5pm. Sun and public holidays 11am–5pm. Closed Christmas Day.

Tisdall **NR**

19–29 Cornelia Creek Road, Echuca, Vic 3564
Winery Ph 03 5482 1911,
Fax 03 5482 2516
(home) Ph 02 9966 4804,
Fax 02 9966 4805

Owner: The Ballande Group
Chief winemaker: John Ellis (contract)
Year of foundation: 1979
Tonnes crushed on average each year: 800, all of which are used for Tisdall labels
Location: Echuca
Area: 87 ha
Soils: red clay loam at eastern end passing into typical deep Murray River sand at western end
Varieties planted: White—chardonnay, chenin blanc, colombard, riesling; Red—cabernet sauvignon, gamay, malbec, merlot, ruby cabernet, shiraz
Leading wines: Tisdall Merlot, Cabernet

Sauvignon, Shiraz, Cabernet-Merlot, Unoaked Chardonnay, Chenin Blanc-Semillon
Notes: Dr Peter Tisdall established this winery and vineyard in the late 1970s and during the 1980s it was one of Victoria's leading brands. It then fell on hard times, but has recently been resuscitated by the Ballande Group, as a result of which Tisdall wines are once more seen in Australia's wine shops.

Twelve Acre Winery **NR**

RMB 1628 Nagambie-Rushworth Road, Bailieston, Vic 3608
Ph/Fax 03 5794 2020,
Email 12acres@mcmedia.net.au

Owners/chief winemakers: Peter and Jana Prygodicz
Year of foundation: 1990
Tonnes crushed on average each year: 13
Location: Bailieston
Area: no vineyard—all fruit presently purchased from growers
Leading wines: Twelve Acres Shiraz, Merlot, Cabernet Sauvignon
Notes: A promising winery whose Shiraz has won a trophy at the excellent Victorian wine show. Cellar door sales: weekends and public holidays 10am–6pm.

Nagambie Lakes Sub-region

About a ninety minute drive north of Melbourne on the Goulburn Valley Highway, this sub-region is situated around the town of Nagambie across the Great Divide on the warm Goulburn River plains. Politicians of the late 19th century were noted for their enthusiasm for irrigation schemes and for transforming 'deserts' into 'promised lands'. (One needs only to look at the history of Mildura and Renmark for contemporary examples.) The Nagambie area, whilst scarcely a desert, had been severely affected by a four-year drought (1877–81). The 'Lakes', therefore, are in a sense man-made, as it is the Goulburn River Weir constructed in 1888 that created them. The river water so restrained, inundated the lowlands upstream around Nagambie. So highly regarded was this scheme that it was featured on coins and banknotes issued by the Federal Government from 1913 until 1933. Today the lakes are a picturesque area of tall stands of river red gums, quiet billabongs and occasional river breezes.

As a wine area, the sub-region can boast of some of the oldest shiraz vines in the world. Wine grapes have been grown here for over 140 years. Tahbilk, which recently reverted to its original name after many years of 'Chateauhood', was commenced in 1860 and remains to this day one of the most tranquil wine estates of Australia, a showpiece of living Australian wine history with its gabled wooden tower, original cellars and gravel courtyard, set among the red gums and billabongs. With the resurgence of interest in table wine in the 1960s, Tahbilk was joined by Mitchelton as one of the feature wineries of the sub-region. Mitchelton has another ambience. A tall tower topped by a witch's hat has soared above its surrounding buildings and vineyards for over 30 years since its foundation in 1969. More recently the sub-region has seen David Traeger (once winemaker at Mitchelton) establish his own winery and cellar at Nagambie while in 1999 Alister and Rosa Purbrick also erected the new Dalfarras winery, named after their popular wine brand which began in 1991.

Location: latitude 36°50'S, longitude, 145°20'E, about 115 km north of Melbourne
Altitude: about 140 m
Topography and soils: the generally flat sub-region is of course dominated by its 'Lakes', a large body of water which moderates what would otherwise be a warm vineyard environment. The lakes reduce the area's susceptibilty to frost and maintain a cooling influence in times of intense heat. The soils are deep red duplex (Dr2) well-drained and granular, but not uncommon in south-eastern Australian viticultural areas. They are naturally low in phosphorus and nitrogen, moderate in potassium and high in iron oxide. The top soil varies in depth from 10–50 cm and lies above river gravel and sand, ancient remnants of many older Goulburn Rivers, some of which still flow underground today and are still tapped into for supplementary water. This is one of those Australian sub-regions which are quite rare in that about 16 per cent of its surface area is covered by water.
Climate: Mangalore Airport, MJT 21.45°C, MAR 14.15°C, HDD 1561 raw but cut off at 19°C, otherwise not adjusted, AR 590 mm (Oct–Apr 311 mm), RH 58% (9am Jan), 34% (3pm Jan), AI na, SH na. A moderately warm sub-region whose boundaries are never more than 3 km from the tempering influence of the water mass (i.e. the Lakes themselves, the Goulburn River and its associated lagoons), which also provide a longer growing season due to less fluctuation in the temperature range and some protection against frosts.
Total area: 526.5 ha (1999)
Principal grape varieties: White—chardonnay, marsanne, riesling, rousanne, sauvignon blanc, verdelho, viognier; Red—shiraz, cabernet sauvignon, merlot
Principal wines: Chardonnay, Marsanne, Verdelho, Shiraz, Cabernet Sauvignon, Cabernet-Merlot
Wineries within the sub-region: Burramurra, Dalfarras, McPherson Wines, Mitchelton, Tahbilk, David Traeger Wines (see above for notes).

HEATHCOTE REGION (PROPOSED)

At the time of writing there were two groups of Heathcote vignerons, one favouring a larger area to be called Heathcote (stretching as far north as Rochester, Graytown to the east, as far south as Toobarac and as far west as Lake Eppalock) and the other, a much smaller area surrounding the town and its immediate vicinity. An obvious solution might have been to call the larger area Heathcote or Greater Heathcote and the smaller, 'Heathcote Town' or 'Heathcote Village'. As there is no objection from wine authorities to the name 'Heathcote' being used in conjunction with some other qualifying adjective, each group would thereby have access to a name that has become synonymous with quality in Australian Shiraz. A region of Greater Heathcote and a sub-region Heathcote Town might then both be registered. Names such as these are intended to be noticed by the wine-conscious consumer. There is, of course, a French parallel in the Beaujolais appellations Brouilly and Cotes de Brouilly, the former four times as big as the latter.

From pre-history two tribal groups, the Nerboolok and the Pipandoor people ranged over the whole area until Major Thomas Mitchell and his bullock wagons literally carved a path through the region from present-day Redesdale to Graytown in 1836. He was followed almost immediately by land-hungry squatters, droving large mobs of sheep in search of new pastures and by the early 1840s the whole area was settled. The region's population was swollen enormously by the gold rushes of the 1850s and Heathcote became an urban hub of 20 000, most of whom as usual moved off when the gold ran out. Since that time this area of Victoria has become largely agricultural.

Wine followed the mine as it has in many other areas of rural Victoria. There was a vigneron named Freeman in Toobarac in the early 1860s, whose wine was said to have been of good quality and later a Mr George Robinson established a vineyard of 13 hectares at the northern end of Heathcote, called Mayfield. This was devastated by phylloxera in the late 1890s. However, one vineyard escaped that plague and provides a continuity from the 19th century to the 21st. This was the Graytown vineyard established by an Italian, Signor Goberna, in 1891. From him it passed to Gildo Segafredo, who owned it for 30 years. It is now owned by David Traeger, the well-known winemaker of Nagambie.

The modern development of viticulture in the region can be said to have commenced in 1955, when Paul Osicka Snr planted his Major's Creek vineyard with cuttings from Graytown Vineyard. Its first wines were sold in Melbourne in the early 1960s. In the 1970s interest in viticulture grew apace and further vineyards were planted: one such was Red Hill (in 1971), now named Red Edge, by present owner Peter Dredge. Another was McIvor Creek (1973). Other now famous vineyards followed, Mount Ida and Jasper Hill each being founded in 1975, while another vineyard whose fame has recently soared into the wine stratosphere is Wild Duck Creek, whose skilful winemaker David Anderson has created the new red sensation 'Duck Muck'. There are now many others.

Location: Heathcote (town) latitude 36°54'S, longitude 144°46'E, about 120 km north-north-west of Melbourne. As proposed, the region is bordered on the west mostly by the

Bendigo Region and on the east in part by the Goulburn Valley Region. It stretches north almost as far as Rochester and south to a point on the Northern Highway slightly south of Tooborac, then runs basically west to Barfold before turning north once more.
Elevation: Situated on the northern slopes of the Great Divide, the region is generally elevated at altitudes of between 160 m and 320 m, though there are peaks of over 500 m.
Topography and soils: The region is drained on its western side by the Campaspe and Coliban Rivers, while in the east and north some areas drain into the Goulburn River and Cornella Creek which flows into Lake Cooper. Its distinguishing feature is its Heathcote 'red' soil, which occurs because of the decomposition of Heathcote 'Green-stone', which is a metamorphosed Cambrian era igneous intrusion rock. During the course of about 500 million years, this disconnected series of ridges has weathered and flowed down over sedimentary layers previously formed alongside it. These sedimentary layers now vary from folded shales to clay pans with corresponding variations in drainage. The Heathcote 'red' country commences about 20 km east of Heathcote town, runs south of the town, turning north at the town's western edge and then proceeds north along the Mount Ida Range, past Mount Camel and along the Mount Camel Range about 60 km to the north.
Climate: MJT 21°C, MAR 13.1°C, HDD 1476 raw, taken from 6 years' temperature readings at a meteorological station in Heathcote town and thought to be marginally low, AR 578 mm (Oct–Apr 279 mm) (May–Sept 299 mm), RH 43.5% taken at 3pm (Oct–Mar), SH 8.5 per day (Oct–Mar). Though situated on the northern slopes of the Great Divide, this region is generally slightly cooler than the regions to its west and east though warmer than the proposed Macedon Ranges region to its south. Within the region, as is to be expected, the climate warms as one moves north, but on the whole the temperature differences are relatively slight. This is due to the tempering influence of the Mount Camel range, which runs south-north from Tooborac to Corop. The hills running west from Tooborac also shelter the south of the region from the much cooler Macedon Ranges region. During the growing season the prevailing winds from the south and south east are cool and temper what might be, without them, a much warmer region.

A number of the vineyards in the central and eastern parts of the region are 'dryland', that is, use no irrigation at all, relying on natural rainfall and on the moisture-holding propensities of their soils and subsoils, for example, Jasper Hill. Others such as Osicka's, are aided by natural aquifers quite close to the surface. The majority however, in accordance with the usual Australian practice, have minimal drip irrigation from surface catchment dams or bores. Some in the north of the region have in effect irrigation licences to draw water from the Waranga Western Channel.
Harvest time: Chardonnay—2nd week in March to early April; Shiraz—2nd–3rd weeks in April; Cabernet Sauvignon—late April to early May. Harvest dates in the north of the region are generally two weeks earlier for any particular variety.
Principal grape varieties: Shiraz—easily the most widely planted grape variety of the region; Cabernet Sauvignon—very much a junior partner in this region; Merlot—a promising newcomer starting to be quite widely planted but never likely to be dominant; Chardonnay—really in quite small proportions as befits a region famous for its reds. Other plantings are minor.

Major wine styles: Shiraz. Typically, shiraz makes a full-bodied, ripe yet supple wine tasting of chocolate, berries with occasional traces of eucalypt. Tannins are soft and when well-made, are well-integrated into the palate without any jarring notes. Heathcote's claim to fame rests virtually entirely on this variety.

Barnadown Run NR

390 Cornella Road, Toolleen, Vic 3551
Ph 03 5433 6376, Fax 03 5433 6386,
Email sales@barnadown.com.au

Owner/chief winemaker: Andrew Mills
Year of foundation: 1995
Tonnes crushed on average each year:17, all of which is used for Barnadown Run's own labels
Location: Toolleen
Area: 5 ha
Soils: red Cambrian clay loam
Varieties planted: White—chardonnay; Red—cabernet franc, cabernet sauvignon, malbec, merlot, shiraz
Leading wines: Barnadown Run Cabernet, Shiraz
Notes: Barnadown Run is a young vineyard of promise. Bronze medals at the 1998 and 1999 Victorian Wine Shows confirm a solid standard. Cellar door sales: daily 10am–5pm.

Brown Brothers Patricia Vineyard (vineyard only)

Year of foundation: 1999
Tonnes produced on average each year: not yet bearing
Location: Mount Camel Range (between Corop and Colbinabbin)
Area: 196 ha (175 ha in course of establishment)
Soils: well-drained red Cambrian
Varieties planted: White—roussanne; Red—dolcetto, durif, graciano, malbec, merlot, petit verdot, sangiovese, shiraz, tempranillo
Leading wines: probably Shiraz but no wine has yet been made from this vineyard
Notes: By any standards, this is a big vineyard. Due to its warmer location and vineyard

composition, it will produce virtually all red but whether it will produce Heathcote Shiraz as classic as the region's cooler, more southerly parts remains debatable. However, Brown Brothers will not die wondering. No cellar door facilities.

Cambrien NR

C/-Jasper Hill (*qv*)

Owners: Jasper Hill and M. Chapoutier
Chief winemaker: Ron Laughton
Year of foundation: 1998
Tonnes produced on average each year: vineyards are not yet in full bearing. First vintage anticipated in 2003
Locations: Mount Camel Range (Ladys Path); Heathcote 10 km further south
Area: Ladys Path (Mount Camel Range) 4 ha; Heathcote 4 ha
Soils: red Cambrian, very deep
Varieties planted: White—none; Red—shiraz
Leading wines: nothing yet made, but certain to be Shiraz
Notes: This is a joint venture between the renowned owner of Jasper Hill, Ron Laughton, and the equally famous Rhone maker Chapoutier. Seemingly a union of all the talents. However no wine has yet been tasted.

Eppalock Ridge R87

833 North Redesdale Road, Redesdale, Vic 3444
Ph 03 5425 3135, Fax 03 5425 3233,
Email eppalockridge@netgazer.net.au

Owners: Rod and Sue Hourigan
Chief winemaker: Rod Hourigan
Year of foundation: 1979

Tonnes crushed on average each year: 33, all of which is used for the Eppalock Ridge labels
Location: Redesdale
Area: 1.6 ha (production also includes fruit from 13 ha neighbouring vineyards)
Soils: heavy black through to red basalts through to lighter clay loams
Varieties planted: White—none;
Red—cabernet franc, cabernet sauvignon, malbec, merlot, shiraz
Leading wines: Eppalock Ridge Shiraz, Eppalock Ridge Cabernet Merlot
Notes: A red only winery with Shiraz wines of exciting quality and a Cabernet blend almost neck and neck. Cellar door sales: weekends 10am–6pm; weekdays usually open but ring ahead.

Heathcote Winery R86

185 High Street, Heathcote, Vic 3523
Ph 03 5433 2595, Fax 03 5433 3081
Email ausvine@netspace.net.au

Owner: Heathcote Winery and Vineyard Pty Ltd
Chief winemaker: Mark Kelly
Year of foundation: 1978
Tonnes crushed on average each year: 175, of which 80 are used for Heathcote Winery labels
Location: Heathcote
Area: 30 ha consisting of three vineyards—Newton's Lane (12 ha), Kemp (14 ha) and Slaughterhouse (4 ha)
Soils: Newton's Lane and Kemp consist of Heathcote 'red' soil, a Cambrian red soil which results from the decomposition of Heathcote Greenstone, a igneous intrusion rock flowing over previously adjoining sedimentary layers. Slaughterhouse is composed of the recent alluvial soil created by McIvor Creek
Varieties planted: White—chardonnay, chenin blanc, roussanne, verdelho, viognier;
Red—aglianico, mammolo, shiraz, tinto cao, touriga
Leading wines: Heathcote Winery Cambrian Viognier, Mail Coach Shiraz, Chardonnay

Notes: Comparisons with the northern Rhone area of France may be odious but as Heathcote Winery has developed an excellent reputation for Shiraz, so it may be about to do the same with Viognier and if so Heathcote Winery is the place to visit. Cellar door sales: during summer daily 10am–6pm; during winter, Thurs–Sun 11am–5pm.

Huntleigh R80

Tunnicliffe's Lane, Heathcote, Vic 3523
Ph/Fax 03 5433 2795
Email sequoia@netlink.com.au

Owners: the Hunt family
Chief winemaker: Leigh Hunt
Year of foundation: 1975
Tonnes crushed on average each year: 7, all of which are used for Huntleigh's own labels
Location: Heathcote
Area: 5.5 ha
Soils: variable soils ranging from fertile red clay to sandy loam, mostly planted with an easterly aspect. A small proportion of the vines are drip-irrigated
Varieties planted: White—gewurztraminer, riesling; Red—cabernet franc, cabernet sauvignon, merlot, shiraz
Leading wines: Huntleigh Cabernet Sauvignon
Notes: In an area where shiraz is king, Leigh Hunt prefers his Cabernet Sauvignon because of its complexity. Cellar door sales: mid-week, weekends and most public holidays 10am–5.30pm.

Jasper Hill R92

Drummonds Lane, Heathcote, Vic 3523
Ph 03 5433 2528, Fax 03 5433 3143

Owners: Ron and Elva Laughton
Chief winemaker: Mario Marson with Ron Laughton
Year of foundation: 1975
Tonnes crushed on average each year: 50
Location: Heathcote

Area: 24 ha (some not bearing)
Soils: red Cambrian soil about 4 m deep; this dryland vineyard's soils have good moisture retention
Varieties planted: White—riesling, semillon; Red—cabernet franc, nebbiolo, shiraz
Leading wines: Jasper Hill Georgia's Paddock Shiraz, Riesling, Emily's Paddock Shiraz (which usually has a 5% addition of cabernet franc)
Notes: The overwhelming influence of soil is shown by this vineyard and the adjoining Mount Ida (both on red Cambrian soils). Both produce magnificent Shiraz. Apart from invitations to the occasional international exhibition, Jasper Hill does not enter its wines in wine shows. It does not need to. It has such renown that its wines sell out automatically to a hungry mailing list in a very short time after release, which usually takes place on 1 September each year. Accordingly Jasper Hill is rarely open for cellar door sales.

McIvor Creek **NR**

Costerfield Road, Heathcote, Vic 3523
Ph 03 5433 3000, Fax 03 5433 3456

Owners: Peter and Robyn Turley
Chief winemaker: Peter Turley
Year of foundation: 1973
Tonnes crushed on average each year: 10
Location: Heathcote
Area: 2.8 ha
Soils: Robyn Turley describes the soil as 'clay and rocks'
Varieties planted: Whites—none; Red—cabernet franc, cabernet sauvignon
Leading wine: McIvor Creek Cabernet-Shiraz
Notes: A Heathcote winery with a reduced acreage and good Cabernet-Shiraz reds. There are barbecue facilities and also arts and crafts. Cellar door sales: 7 days 10am–5.30pm.

Mount Ida (vineyard only) **R92**

Northern Highway, Heathcote, Vic 3523

Owner: Mildara Blass Ltd
Chief winemaker: Nick Walker
Year of foundation: 1978
Tonnes crushed on average each year: 30
Location: Heathcote
Area: 6 ha
Soils: red Cambrian loam
Varieties planted: White—none; Red—cabernet sauvignon, shiraz
Leading wines: Mount Ida Shiraz
Notes: Mount Ida produces a renowned Shiraz, which usually contains about 10% cabernet. The brilliant 1998 follows in the footsteps of the illustrious 1996. It is all due to the famous Heathcote 'red' soils of the vineyard. There are no cellar door sales.

Munari **R83**

cnr Northern Highway and Schoolhouse Lane, Heathcote, Vic 3523 (about 13 km north of Heathcote)
Ph 03 5433 3366, Fax 03 5433 3905, Email munari@netcon.net.au

Owners: Adrian and Deborah Munari
Chief winemaker: Adrian Munari
Year of foundation: 1992
Tonnes crushed on average each year: 13, and increasing, all of which is used for Munari labels
Location: Ladys Creek, Heathcote
Area: 7 ha
Varieties planted: White—chardonnay; Red—cabernet franc, cabernet sauvignon, malbec, merlot, shiraz
Leading wines: Munari Ladys Creek Shiraz, Schoolhouse Red Cabernet
Notes: Adrian Munari is an enthusiastic and skilful winemaker and his reds will almost certainly improve as his vines come to maturity. Munari wines have already won medals of all colours, chiefly silver and bronze, its top

performance being a gold at the excellent Victorian Wines Show. Well worth a visit.

Paul Osicka **R87**

Graytown, Vic 3608
Ph 03 5794 9235, Fax 03 5794 9288,
Email osvin@mcmedia.com.au

Owner: Paul Osicka Wines Pty Ltd
Chief winemaker: Paul Osicka
Year of foundation: 1955
Tonnes crushed on average each year: 100
Location: Graytown (in the east of the region)
Area: 13 ha
Soils: Red sandy loam above a mixture of quartzy gravel and ironstone buckshot
Varieties planted: White—riesling, roussanne; Red—cabernet franc, cabernet sauvignon, merlot, shiraz
Leading wines: Paul Osicka Shiraz, Cabernet Sauvignon, Merlot
Notes: This consistent winery, now established over 45 years—long before table wine became fashionable—deserves to be better known because of its very good reds. Cellar door sales: Mon–Sat 10am–5pm, Sun noon–5pm.

Red Edge **R82**

Golden Gully Road, Heathcote, Vic 3523
Ph 03 9337 5695, Fax 03 9337 7550

Owners: Peter and Judy Dredge
Chief winemaker: Peter Dredge
Year of foundation: 1971, purchased by present owners in 1994
Tonnes crushed on average each year: 6, but will increase. All will be used for Red Edge wines.
Location: Heathcote (500 m from the heart of town)
Area: 15 ha, of which 13 are presently not bearing

Soils: Heathcote 'red'
Varieties planted: White—none; Red—cabernet sauvignon, graciano, mourvedre, shiraz, tempranillo
Leading wines: Red Edge Shiraz, Cabernet
Notes: Red Edge is an unirrigated vineyard and organic growing techniques are basically followed. Cellar door sales by appointment. Production is presently very small and all sold to Melbourne restaurants and a few retailers.

Wild Duck Creek **R88**

Spring Flat Road, Heathcote, Vic 3523
(5 km west of Heathcote near Wild Duck Creek)
Ph/Fax 03 5433 3133

Owners: David and Diana Anderson
Chief winemaker: David Anderson
Year of foundation: 1980
Tonnes crushed on average each year: 60, all of which is used for Wild Duck Creek labels
Location: Heathcote
Area: 10 ha
Soils: a mixture of shales and mudstone with quartzy gravel and 'buckshot', some Heathcote 'red', and also alluvial soils
Varieties planted: White—none; Red—cabernet franc, cabernet sauvignon, malbec, merlot, petit verdot, shiraz
Leading wines: Wild Duck Creek Spring Flat Shiraz, Alans Cabernet (a blend of the 'Bordeaux' varieties)
Notes: David Anderson is a committed red winemaker, devoted to quality and complexity in his wines. He became quite famous recently when noted US critic Robert Parker commended his Duck Muck (a super ripe Shiraz blended with Cabernet to make a huge red). Cellar door sales by appointment (a must for the true devotee of fine wine).

Heathcote Sub-Region (proposed)

The sub-region, if registered, will include all but two (Barnadown Run and Eppalock Ridge) of the wineries mentioned above. The proponents of the sub-region argue that it is discrete, and geologically and climatically different from the greater Heathcote Region.

Their argument runs as follows:

1 The sub-region is described as and confined to the valley and foothills engulfed by the McIvor/Mount Ida fault and the Heathcote/Knowsley East fault.
2 Its boundary north-south (through its centre) includes the central segment of the Heathcote Greenstone belt lying between the Cobaw Batholith to the south and Mount Camel to the north. This central segment has been described as having a greater geological complexity than the segments to its north and south. The geology of the sub-region is generally more uniform and less disparate than that of the greater region.
3 Apart from a few bores, the sub-region is generally non-irrigated, none of the vineyards within it sourcing water from a perennial watercourse or man-made channel.
4 The sub-region is more elevated than the northern parts of the region, generally having altitudes between 180 m and 320 m as opposed to altitudes around 100 m in the north.
5 The mean average annual rainfall of Heathcote is 579 mm as opposed to that of Rochester (which is just outside the northern boundary of the greater region) at 447 mm and further that there is up to 1.5° difference in mean temperature between the Heathcote sub-region and the northern parts of the greater region, leading to a much earlier ripening season and to potentially different fruit characters.

STRATHBOGIE RANGES REGION (PROPOSED)

The first white contact with the region was in 1824 when Hume and Hovell traversed it on their southward and return journeys of exploration. Twenty-two years later came the advent of white settlement in 1846. Archaeological evidence (a gravesite and stone tools) has shown, however, that the area was inhabited by aborigines long before this. The region's major road (the Hume Freeway) runs close to Hume's track and is, of course, named after him. Later in the 19th century during the clearing of the land for grazing purposes, the collection of wattle bark for use in tanning became a useful focus of employment. Further areas of forest were felled and the timber utilised when the rail line from Melbourne to Sydney was being constructed. Later still, after sustainable grazing was established around Strathbogie and Terip Terip, dairying became a popular agricultural diversification.

The region's first vineyard was supposedly established by the Tubbs family near Longwood about 1900. It produced both table and fortified under the label St Helena but later died out, probably because of phylloxera. The region's modern wine history began when Dr Peter Tisdall established the Mount Helen vineyard in 1975 and the first wine was made by John Ellis at Echuca in 1979. Mount Helen was followed by

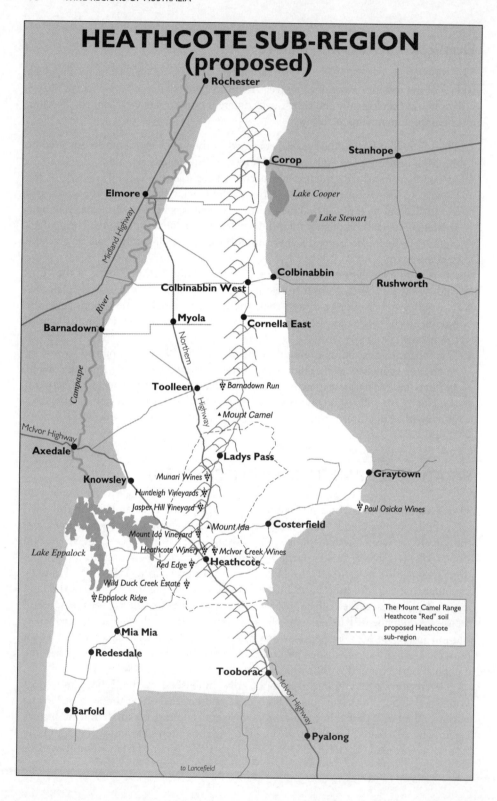

HEATHCOTE SUB-REGION
(proposed)

Rochester

Corop

Stanhope

Elmore

Lake Cooper

Lake Stewart

Midland Highway

River

Colbinabbin

Colbinabbin West

Rushworth

Barnadown

Myola

Cornella East

Campaspe

Northern

Toolleen

Barnadown Run

Highway

Mount Camel

McIvor Highway

Axedale

Ladys Pass

Knowsley

Munari Wines

Graytown

Huntleigh Vineyards

Jasper Hill Vineyard

Paul Osicka Wines

Mount Ida

Mount Ida Vineyard

Costerfield

Lake Eppalock

Heathcote Winery

McIvor Creek Wines

Red Edge

Heathcote

Wild Duck Creek Estate

Eppalock Ridge

Mia Mia

Redesdale

Tooborac

McIvor Highway

Barfold

Pyalong

to Lancefield

The Mount Camel Range
Heathcote "Red" soil

proposed Heathcote
sub-region

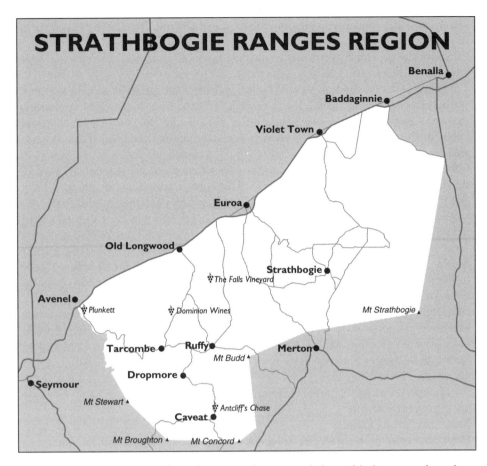

STRATHBOGIE RANGES REGION

Benalla

Baddaginnie

Violet Town

Euroa

Old Longwood

Strathbogie

🍇 The Falls Vineyard

Avenel

🍇 Plunkett

🍇 Dominion Wines

Mt Strathbogie ▲

Tarcombe

Ruffy

Merton

Mt Budd ▲

Dropmore

Seymour

Mt Stewart ▲

🍇 Antcliff's Chase

Caveat

Mt Broughton ▲   Mt Concord ▲

Plunkett's in 1979. Since then the region has expanded steadily because of its slow ripening summer and autumn and the relatively high acids retained by the fruit, which make it very popular for sparkling and delicate table wines, as witness the establishment of a Domaine Chandon vineyard in 1994. Its red grapes also have exceptional colour and flavour. The region now has 880 hectares under vine.

Location: Avenel, latitude 36°55'S, longitude 145°21'E, about 100 km north-north-east of Melbourne; Euroa, latitude 36°46'S, longitude 145°41'E about 130 km north-east of Melbourne. The Strathbogie Ranges region is a substantial portion of higher Victoria. Commencing near Avenel, its north-western boundary runs along the Hume Freeway as far as Baddiginnie near Benalla, where the boundary turns south-east and south to reach its south-eastern point at Mount Strathbogie, from where it turns west and south-west to reach Mount Budd and then south and south-west to ascend Mount Concord, then traversing west to Mount Broughton. It finally returns to its starting point at Avenel via Mount Stewart and Hughes Creek. It encompasses no major cities or towns, its centres of population being Avenel and Euroa (each just outside the region), Violet Town and Strathbogie. Its regional wine neighbours are

Goulburn Valley to its north-west and the proposed Central Victoria High Country to its south and south-east.

Elevation: the general region varies in altitude from 140 m to 1007 m. Vineyard sites range from 160 m to 600 m.

Topography and soils: the Ranges are granitic and the soils, generally acidic (4–5 pH), are deep to moderately deep alluvial or colluvial sand and sandy loams containing ironstone gravel or quartz over Callabonna clay, usually the first clay B horizon, although there is a second clay horizon (Coonunga) and a third formed from weathered granite rock.

Climate: Euroa, outside but adjacent to the lower western and north-western parts of the region, MJT 22.1°C, MAR 13.9°C, HDD 1610 (raw but cut off at 19°C), AR 655 mm (Oct–Apr 310 mm) RH 33% (3pm Jan); Strathbogie, MJT 19.1°C, MAR 13.5°C, HDD 1162 raw but cut off at 19°C, AR 985 mm (Oct–Apr 425 mm) RH 37% (3pm Jan). In its warmer parts adjacent to the Goulburn Valley region the Strathbogie Ranges region is distinctly warm, but as the country rises to the east, it becomes much cooler and more suitable for finer table wines. Rainfall occurs chiefly in the period winter to early spring and varies from 650 mm to 1000 mm annually. Spring frosts are an occasional hazard

Harvest times: As in all wine regions, these are dependent on cropping levels, seasonal weather conditions and disease pressure. During vintage 2000 in this region, the following harvest dates generally occurred: chardonnay and riesling—3rd week in March; merlot and cabernet franc—2nd week in April; shiraz—4th week in April; cabernet sauvignon—1st week in May

Principal grape varieties: White—chardonnay, riesling; Red—cabernet franc, cabernet sauvignon, merlot, shiraz

Total Area: 880 ha (2000)

Major wine styles: at this stage, the author is peering into his crystal ball, but Chardonnay, Riesling, Sauvignon Blanc and Shiraz must be mentioned.

Leading wineries: Dominion Wines, The Falls Vineyard, Plunkett

Antcliff's Chase NR

Caveat, via Seymour, Vic 3660
Ph/Fax 03 5790 4333

Owners: Chris Antcliff Bennett and Nonie Bennett
Chief winemaker: Chris Antcliff Bennett
Year of foundation: 1982
Tonnes crushed on average each year: 30
Location: Caveat, Strathbogie Ranges
Area: 4.4 ha
Soils: a well-drained slope with volcanic loam
Varieties planted: White—chardonnay, riesling; Red—cabernet franc, cabernet sauvignon, merlot, pinot noir

Leading wines: Antcliffs Chase Riesling, Pinot Noir
Notes: At 600 m in altitude, Antcliffs Chase is high and cool in the Strathbogie Ranges—a location that seems suitable for riesling and perhaps pinot noir. Cellar door sales: weekends 10am–5pm. Ring ahead.

Dominion Wines R86

Upton Road, Strathbogie, via Avenel, Vic 3664
Ph 03 5796 2718, Fax 03 5796 2705,
Email chuter@netspace.net.au

Owner: Dominion Wines Ltd
Chief winemaker: Rob Dolan (consultant),
Travis Bush (winemaker)
Year of foundation: 1996, first vintage 1999
Tonnes crushed on average each year: 3500,
which includes contract crushing, 150 for
Dominion's own labels
Location: Strathbogie, via Avenel
Area: 90 ha
Soils: sedimentary sandy clay loams overlaying
orange clays of varying depths to 1.5 m and of
granite derivation
Varieties planted: White—chardonnay, riesling,
sauvignon blanc, verdelho; Red—cabernet
sauvignon, merlot, pinot noir, shiraz
Leading wines: its brands will be Dominion
Estate, Alexander Park, Vinus and Saddle
Mountain
Notes: Dominion Wines is a brave new 'big'
player in Australian and overseas wine
markets. Its first wines promise well for its
future. Cellar door sales: daily 10am–5pm.

The Falls Vineyard R85

Longwood-Gobur Road (adjacent to the
Ruffy Road), Euroa, Vic 3666
(on the slopes of the Strathbogie Ranges
about 5 km from the Hume Freeway)
Ph 03 5798 5291, Fax 03 5798 5437

Owners: Andrew and Elly Cameron
Chief winemaker: Andrew Cameron
Year of foundation: 1969
Tonnes crushed on average each year: 12, all
of which is used for Falls Vineyard wines
Location: Euroa
Area: 1.6 ha
Soils: granitic loam typical of the Strathbogie
Ranges
Varieties planted: White—none; Red—shiraz
Leading wines: Longwood Shiraz, The Falls
Shiraz
Notes: Andrew Cameron is primarily a grazier
who originally planted a vineyard to win a bet
after he had toured Bordeaux and Burgundy

with a friend in the late 1960s. He began
practical winemaking as most farmers do with
simple equipment such as second-hand
stainless milk vats, which are often an ideal size
for small crops of grapes. This former hobby
has turned into something more, a small
specialist winery. Cellar door sales. Ring ahead.

Normans Strathbogie Ranges (formerly Mount Helen) (vineyard only) NR

Upton Road, Avenel, Vic 3664

Owner: Normans Wines Ltd (in receivership)
Chief winemaker: Peter Fraser
Year of foundation: 1975
Tonnes produced on average each year: 700
Location: Strathbogie Ranges
Area: 84 ha
Soils: granitic topsoil over granite and
granodiorite, granitic loams
Varieties planted: White—chardonnay, riesling,
sauvignon blanc; Red—cabernet franc,
cabernet sauvignon, merlot, pinot noir, shiraz
End use of grapes: The Strathbogie Ranges
vineyard contributes to the many Normans
table wines, but has not yet been accorded the
distinction of being part of its regional range.
Notes: Located high in the Strathbogies
between 420–480 m in altitude, the former
Mount Helen Vineyard commands majestic
views over the Goulburn Valley far below. Its
wines however have not over the years proved
equally majestic. Perhaps a continuity of
proprietorship over a considerable period
might make the wines of this vineyard as
spectacular as its views.

Plunkett R82

Lambing Gully Road, Avenel, Vic 3147
Cellar door sales: Hume Highway, Avenel
Ph 03 5796 2150, Fax 03 5796 2147

Owners: Plunkett family
Chief winemaker: Sam Plunkett

Year of foundation: 1968
Tonnes crushed on average each year: 750, of which 150 are used for Plunkett labels
Locations: Avenel (winery); 'Whitegate Farm', Strathbogie Ranges (100 ha), Avenel (2.8 ha) and Mulwala (20 ha) (vineyards)
Area: 122.8 ha in three vineyards
Soils: Strathbogie Ranges, granite top soil over granite and granodiorite; Avenel, ironstone with an abundance of surface rock; Mulwala, red clay loam with some sand ridges

Varieties planted: White—chardonnay, gewurztraminer, riesling, sauvignon blanc, semillon; Red—cabernet franc, cabernet sauvignon, merlot, pinot noir, shiraz
Leading wines: Blackwood Ridge Chardonnay, Shiraz, Reserve Shiraz
Notes: This winery is strong in its complex Chardonnay and well-flavoured Shiraz styles. Cellar door sales (Avenel only): daily 11am–5pm.

❦ Pinot Noir

Great Pinot Noir has been said to be the result not only of great winemaking but also of the art of barrel selection. This may be true as far as treatment goes, but it omits one crucial factor. Premium grape varieties are like thoroughbred horses. They are highly sensitive not only to their treatment but also to their environment. This applies particularly to pinot noir, which is the most pernickety of all noble red cultivars.

It is generally agreed that the style of pinot that most fulfils the red wine lover's expectations of the variety is Burgundy, that is, reds of medium to full colour, of fragrant but complex 'berry', violet and gamey-earthy aromas and soft yet full savoury-sweet berry flavours without any jarring or astringent tannins on finish. If our putative Pinot, when made, results in any other style of red, it seems plain and unworthy of recognition as a good Pinot. It must also be capable of developing well in bottle. This would seem to suggest that climatic and soil (terroir) characteristics similar to those of Burgundy are required. Given that we will never be able or indeed want to duplicate exactly the Burgundian climate and terroir, the search must focus on an Australian terroir that approximates the conditions in which pinot noir is recognised to produce a noble wine. If, therefore, it is to succeed in Australia, it positively demands a long, cool growing season which points to southern Victoria, Tasmania, the Adelaide Hills of South Australia and the southern regions of Western Australia.

Within southern Victoria, several areas have already proved themselves suitable for pinot noir: the Yarra Valley, south-western Gippsland, the Mornington Peninsula and Geelong. Within Tasmania, there are three sites which produce excellent pinot noir: Bicheno on the east coast, Pipers Brook and Hobart. South Australia's Adelaide Hills is also gaining a reputation for pinot quality and areas in the south of Western Australia, such as Albany, Denmark and Pemberton, are showing much promise. These are of course generalisations—not every part of the Yarra Valley or any of the others is totally suitable and there are probably others quite suitable that have yet to see even one pinot vine.

Pinot noir is not only very site- and climate-specific but also maker-specific—it requires the experience of the makers of great pinot. What are the parameters of site, climate and viticultural and winemaking techniques for these sites? To help answer this, the advice was sought of eight makers of Australian pinot noir who most certainly have achieved eminence in this field.

At Freycinet near Bicheno on Tasmania's east coast, Geoff Bull, his daughter Lindy and winemaker Claudio Radenti make a phenomenal Pinot Noir that absolutely radiates fruit aromas and flavours, being at the same time robust, complex and subtle and capable of ageing well. Freycinet is set in an amphitheatre facing north-east. It is a natural suntrap and rain shadow in an otherwise extremely cool area. It has good cold-air drainage so it suffers little frost damage and is protected from the worst of Tasmania's often howling winds. Its soil is podsolic over red clay and well-drained. Its rainfall is about 750 mm annually and it has supplementary irrigation to relieve extreme drought stress. As for technique in viticulture, Freycinet's chief purpose is to expose the ripening fruit to sunlight and to achieve ripeness between 13° and 14°

Baume. In winemaking, the grapes are fermented up to 32°C in a roto-fermenter and the wine allowed to reach dryness. It is then transferred to barrel to undergo malolactic fermentation. Only about one-quarter new oak is used each year in barrel maturation. The rest of the barrels are from one to four years old. After 10 months it is bottled. Claudio states his purpose, quite simply as 'to let the fruit express itself'.

In north-east Tasmania at Pipers Brook, pinot noir has become Andrew Pirie's favoured red variety as in most years it suits local conditions much more than cabernet sauvignon. His premium pinots are grown on red basalt soil, high in iron. It is well-drained but has a sufficient clay content to ensure retention of some moisture. Its climate is very cool and has appropriate humidity that Pirie believes gives pinot the fleshiness it requires to become a top wine. Rainfall is about 750 mm annually, falling mainly in winter, though the growing season does account for slightly less than half.

As for viticulture, Pirie uses vertical shoot positioning (VSP), Lyre and Scott Henry trellissing. Hedging and leaf-plucking are carried out when necessary. Andrew believes that pinot crops optimally at about 5 tonnes per hectare. In the winery, he uses open fermentation and ferments on wild yeasts to about 32°C, using 'pigeage' to cool 'hotspots' in the ferment, which takes on average 11 days to carry through to dryness. The wine is then transferred to casks to undergo its malolactic fermentation. He has no particular French oak preferences, but relies on Burgundian coopers to provide an oak that he has tasted and liked in red Burgundies.

Across Bass Strait, south of Leongatha in Gippsland lies the Bass Phillip vineyard, home of what is arguably Australia's finest pinot noir. There are other varieties of course, a fraction of chardonnay and a skerrick of gamay. Both are fascinating in their own ways, especially the gamay, but pinot noir is Phillip Jones' all-conquering passion. To Jones, the soil of a vineyard is the soul of pinot noir excellence, affecting not only the basic structure of the wine but also its aromatic characters, though these complexities are not noticed until some years after bottling. His soils at Bass Phillip are very old and he has identified five different types in that 4-hectare vineyard. Although there is little limestone (a favourite moisture-holding soil constituent of the Burgundians), the vineyard does have adequate clay content for water retention and sufficient numbers of small stones which trap capillary water. He knows that in every vintage his Premium wine (and that is its name) will come from exactly the same patch of soil, as it develops more layers of flavour than other wines that may be made from soils a mere 50 metres away. To Phillip, soils suitable for the best pinot must have a constant water regime in the root zones of the vine, that is, a clayey, rubbly, pebbly texture to hold water, but not excessive water. Within those soil parameters, the climate requirements of pinot noir are fairly simple, though critical—a long, slow, cool summer and autumn and an ambient humidity at those times to preserve root moisture and canopy humidity. Pinot noir must never be allowed to 'dry out'.

In Gippsland's extremely cool climate, proper canopy management is essential. The canopy must allow bunches to be exposed to sunlight for development and ripening and, importantly, to avoid vegetal flavour. Phillip Jones believes that pinot noir is more representative of its site of origin than any other variety, because it is less primary-fruit dominated. It is also important to have 'balanced' fruit on the vine (i.e. fruit that does not produce excessive malic acid, which will in turn, after malolactic fermentation, produce excessive lactic characters). Above all, for premium pinot, overcropping must be avoided at all costs. Jones suggests no more than five tonnes to the hectare.

As for winemaking, Phillip Jones favours warm to hot ferments (30–32°C) on wild yeasts, using only a small percentage of stalks. For oak, he uses light toast Allier and, depending on vintage, 30–50% of new wood. As Phillip says, 'oak should be a balancing medium in pinot noir, never a flavour component'.

Due to winemaker Gary Farr's experience at Domaine Dujac over the years, Bannockburn has built a reputation for the excellence of its Pinot. Farr believes that we in Australia are beginning to learn about suitable soils for pinot noir, having discovered that the right climate is also crucially important. He too believes that soil drainage is a vital factor in succeeding with pinot noir which, he says, prefers a cool and damp climate. Gary has both close-planted and standard-row vineyards and hedges—the close-planted vines for exposure to sunlight and for spray access. The standard row vines are not vigorous and usually do not need hedging.

In winemaking, he ferments his pinot fruit on natural (wild) yeasts to about 32°C and it rarely needs cooling. The classic Burgundian 'pigeage' technique is used when necessary to control 'hotspots' in the ferment and the whole process, to the total dryness of the wine, usually lasts from 14 to 20 days. The wine is then transferred to barrel and proceeds naturally to malolactic fermentation. As for oak, Gary prefers Allier or Vosges, but normally the percentage of new oak used does not exceed one-third.

The Yarra Valley is perhaps the northernmost latitude for successful pinot making, that is, at normal altitudes. As one goes north, so the Australian climate warms and it is necessary to seek a suitable pinot site at higher altitudes to obtain the necessary coolness of climate for the variety. In the Yarra, one of its most successful pinot makers has been David Lance at Diamond Valley Vineyards. His pinot vineyard is located on a hillside with soils of clay over mudstone. Because of the hillside, they are well-drained and they are low enough in fertility to discourage excessive vigour in the pinot vines. Diamond Valley usually has a long, slow, ripening season and David Lance prefers autumns to be dry and cool to stop vegetative growth and to cause his pinot vines to drop their basal leaves. He feels that the vines should be subjected to a 'drought' stress at this time, so that the fruit is ripened.

As for viticultural techniques, his trellising is designed to expose his pinot fruit to light. Leaf-plucking is also carried out when necessary. In the winery, he ferments his pinot between 30°C and 32°C on cultured yeasts for five to six days and does not favour stem return to the must. For maturation, he uses new Nevers oak, but never more than 20% in any one vintage.

During the past decade, a friendly rivalry has arisen between Diamond Valley and that other producer of premium Yarra Valley Pinot Noir, Coldstream Hills. Coldstream, on the southern side of the valley, produces its Reserve Pinot Noir from estate-grown fruit sourced primarily from the mature, 12-year-old pinot vines on its steep, north-facing Amphitheatre vineyard. Winemaker James Halliday* believes that the Amphitheatre soils, which consist of a sandy, clay loam over broken sandstone, are well-drained and sufficiently moisture-retentive to favour the production of high-quality pinot fruit. He accepts that for premium pinot, the soil must never be allowed to dry out. As in Diamond Valley, the growth and ripening season is long and slow and spring rainfall is usually reliable. Irrigation to preserve optimal humidity is necessary in some years.

In its viticulture, Coldstream cultivates about 3200 vines to the hectare. Its rows are 2.1 m apart and the separation between vines is 1.5 m. It employs vertical shoot positioning with movable foliage wires. Spring growth is usually very vigorous and trimming is usually carried out two to three times during the growing season. Leaf-plucking is also used. As for winemaking, Halliday cold-soaks (i.e. macerates) part of the crushed pinot must prior to fermentation and follows basic Burgundian practice, though normally cultured yeasts are used to begin fermentation. (Since 1993, however, Coldstream has experimented with wild yeasts for this purpose.) Whole bunches are added to the ferment, which runs hot (up to 32°C). The must is foot-stamped (pigeage) to remove hotspots. About halfway through fermentation, the must is inoculated for malolactic fermentation and when it has reached 2° Baume, both free-run juice and pressings are combined and run off into barrel to complete primary ferment and the subsequent malo. For maturation, he believes that a tight-grained French oak is most suitable for premium pinot and uses new Dargaud and Jaegli barrels of Troncais and 'Bourgogne' oak up to a level of 60% in Coldstream Hills Reserve Pinot.

In the Adelaide Hills, a region where it might be contended that pinot noir has not yet proved itself, Lenswood seems to hold out most promise for the variety. Tim Knappstein at Lenswood Vineyard grows his pinot noir on a shallow, red-grey loam over a subsoil of crumbly clay and gravelly ironstone. It is well-drained and its climate is cool and slow-ripening. In his pinot viticulture, Tim believes that it is important to allow sunlight into the canopy to encourage ripening. As a consequence, he practises shoot-thinning and leaf-plucking. In his winemaking, after a pre-ferment maceration (chilled for up to four days), he ferments his must of wholly destemmed berries (sometimes with up to 20% whole bunches) at temperatures up to 32°C with a post-fermentation maceration, with the result that the total 'fermentation' time (including pre- and post-) is 13 to 15 days. Tim matures his pinot in new and one-year-old oak, using up to 50% new oak. His oak preferences are Allier, Troncais and Vosges and he is increasingly favouring the 'pinot' barrel made by the Seguin Moreau cooperage at Chagny in Burgundy. This is a mixed stave barrel of high toast, utilising wood from the forests of central France.

As a wine-growing area, Pemberton is a cool, slow-ripening region, less than 20 years old. Picardy, the estate of Bill Pannell, founder of Moss Wood in Margaret River (which is now owned by Keith and Claire Mugford) is younger still, completing only its third vintage in 1998. Bill has always been a Burgundy enthusiast, so it was only natural that pinot noir would be planted on the loamy, gravelly, clay 'karri' soils of Picardy. Pinot must be in the Pannell genes, as winemaker son Dan shares his father's enthusiasm. Pemberton's 'karri' soils can be a little heavy in places, but not at Picardy. There, Dan feels they are ideal for pinot, draining freely enough yet holding sufficient moisture to prevent excessive drought stress, which is extremely important at Picardy as it is not irrigated.

In his viticultural techniques, Dan uses vertical shoot positioning, leaf-plucks and hedges the rows when necessary. In the winery, Dan utilises the whole range of Burgundian winemaking practice: pre-fermentation maceration, fermentation up to

32°C, pigeage, addition of whole bunches and post-fermentation maceration. His fermentation process takes up to two weeks to complete. In maturation, Dan favours tight-grained French oak, preferably Allier and Troncais, and only 25% new, the balance being similar oak up to three years old. Dan shares the author's opinion that Pemberton pinot often has a naturally smoky nose and flavour (which is certainly not mercaptan nor the result of excessive maturation in high-toast new oak). This appears to be a genuine *goût de terroir*.

Pinot noir growing and making practice in the cooler areas of Australia seems to be becoming standardised, which is no bad thing. What is needed is a cool, slow-ripening climate and suitable gravelly soils with a degree of clay—a growth regime which permits retention of some humidity both above and below ground (never letting the vine 'dry out'), but permitting good drainage and ripening of fruit slowly but surely. Certainly hedging and leaf-plucking may at times be necessary to assist ripening. Its wines should be fermented quickly up to 32°C. 'Pigeage' may be employed to remove hotspots in the fermenting must; some whole bunch fermentation may be employed and both pre- and post-fermentation maceration can be very effective, provided that care is taken at all times to avoid oxidation. As for oak maturation, there are, as we have seen, differing approaches. The result of such site selection, growth regime and winemaking technique should at least be a recognisable Pinot Noir of decent quality.

* Halliday retired from Southcorp's employment in 2000. Coldstream Hills' winemaker was at the time of writing Andrew Fleming.

❦ PORT PHILLIP ZONE

This is the heartland of Victorian table wine and all that cool area Victorian viti-culture is about. The Port Phillip Zone is dominated by and within easy reach of metropolitan Melbourne to the north east of the Bay and encompasses the wine regions of Mornington Peninsula, Yarra Valley, Geelong and Sunbury and the proposed region of Macedon Ranges.

WINERIES WITHIN PORT PHILLIP ZONE BUT OUTSIDE ANY REGION

Carlei Estate Wines and The Green Vineyards **R86**

Lot 2 Albers Road, Upper Beaconsfield, Vic 3808
Ph /Fax 5944 4599

Owners: Serge and Mariangela Carlei
Chief winemaker: Serge Carlei
Year of foundation: 1994
Tonnes crushed on average each year: 70, all of which are used for Carlei Estate or Green Vineyards wines
Location: Upper Beaconsfield
Area: 4 ha
Soils: friable grey loam over clay
Varieties planted: White—chardonnay; Red—pinot noir
Leading wines: Carlei Estate Pinot Noir, Chardonnay; the Green Vineyards range—Chardonnay, Sauvignon Blanc, Pinot Noir, Riesling, Shiraz, Cabernet Sauvignon
Notes: Serge Carlei is a man of deep and sincerely held beliefs and those beliefs concern the viability of 'green' viticulture in cool climates. 'Conventional' wisdom holds that anti-fungal sprays are obligatory in areas which are cool and damp. Carlei disagrees, arguing that fruit grown biodynamically has a greater resistance to mildews and moulds than conventionally grown grapes. They have stronger cell walls, penetrated only with difficulty by mildews and a lesser nitrate content, which is crucial, because higher nitrate content feeds not only the plant but also the attacking moulds. As regards fertilisers, he contends that they upset the salt balance of the plant with the result that the plant overfeeds and this leads to excessive vigour, fruit shading from that excessive foliage, lack of air movement, which encourages moulds and mildews, reduced light penetration which hinders fruit ripening and also excessive cropping levels, all of which encourage disease. He is a man with a mission and that is to persuade the winegrowing world that biodynamic viticulture is the best possible viticultural course. Carlei's practice is not only to use his own certified organic fruit but also to purchase fruit from vineyards which are cultivated as closely as possible to his own beliefs and so he ranges wide with his contracts and his choices, purchasing from his own local area, which he believes one day might become a wine region in its own right: the Kardinia Hills, as well as the Yarra Valley, Sunbury and Heathcote. So after all that, what are his wines like? In a word, excellent! Cellar door sales: weekends and public holidays 11am–6pm or by appointment.

Chestnut Hill Vineyard **R82**

1280 Pakenham Road, Mount Burnett,
Vic 3781
Ph/Fax 03 5942 7314

Owner/chief winemaker: Charlie Javor
Year of foundation: (vineyard) 1985, (winery)
1991
Tonnes produced on average each year: 17, all
of which is used for Chestnut Hill wines
Location: Mount Burnett
Area: 3.2 ha
Soils: clay loam
Varieties planted: White—chardonnay,
sauvignon blanc; Red—pinot noir, shiraz
Leading wines: Chestnut Hill Chardonnay,
Shiraz, Pinot Noir
Notes: Just outside the Yarra Valley, literally on
the wrong side of the hill, but very promising
nevertheless is Chestnut Hill Vineyard. Planted
with varieties quite suitable for the area,
Chestnut Hill produces crisp fresh whites and
good reds. Cellar door sales: weekends and
public holidays 10.30am–5.30pm.

Paternoster **R75**

Paternoster Road, Emerald, Vic 3782
Ph 03 5968 3197

Owner/chief winemaker: Philip Hession
Year of foundation: 1985
Tonnes crushed on average each year: 10, all
of which is used for Paternoster wines
Location: Emerald
Area: 1.6 ha
Soils: reddish mountain loam
Varieties planted: White—chardonnay;
Red—cabernet sauvignon, pinot noir. There is
also a premium wine; Jack of Hearts, which
consists of the best single barrel of red or white
Leading wines: Paternoster Chardonnay, Pinot
Noir. There is also a premium wine, Jack of
Hearts, which consists of the best single barrel
of red or white
Notes: A small vineyard just beyond the
southern boundary of the Yarra Valley and
sharing many of its characteristics, Paternoster
is 330 m in altitude, close planted and
organically grown. Its wines are unfiltered
and treated with minimal amounts of sulfur.
Cellar door sales: weekends 11am–6pm.

YARRA VALLEY REGION

The Yarra Valley is Victoria's oldest vineyard area, dating from 1837 when William Ryrie travelled overland with his cattle from the Monaro region of southern New South Wales to squat at Yering in what is now the Yarra Valley. By 1840, he had planted an acre (0.4 ha) of vines. From its first settlement in 1835, Victoria grew rapidly, being particularly fortunate in that many of its immigrants, chiefly those from Switzerland and Germany, were wine-conscious if not actually skilled in viticulture and wine production.

Commencing in 1849 with the arrival of Paul de Castella, Swiss settlers were particularly active in the development of the Yarra vine. Paul purchased part of Ryrie's run at Yering including the vineyard and expanded it rapidly until, by 1857, it comprised nearly 100 acres (40 ha). It included 20 000 cabernet sauvignon cuttings imported from Chateau Lafite in Pauillac. Also during the 1850s, the Deschamps brothers planted vineyards near Lilydale. In 1862, Hubert de Castella began to plant St Hubert's, a few kilometres to the south-east of Yering, and other Swiss settlers such as Guillaume de Pury of Yeringberg also planted vineyards about this time.

Yarra wine, especially from Yering and St Hubert's, was to win many international prizes over the next 30 years and became much sought-after in Melbourne, Australia's

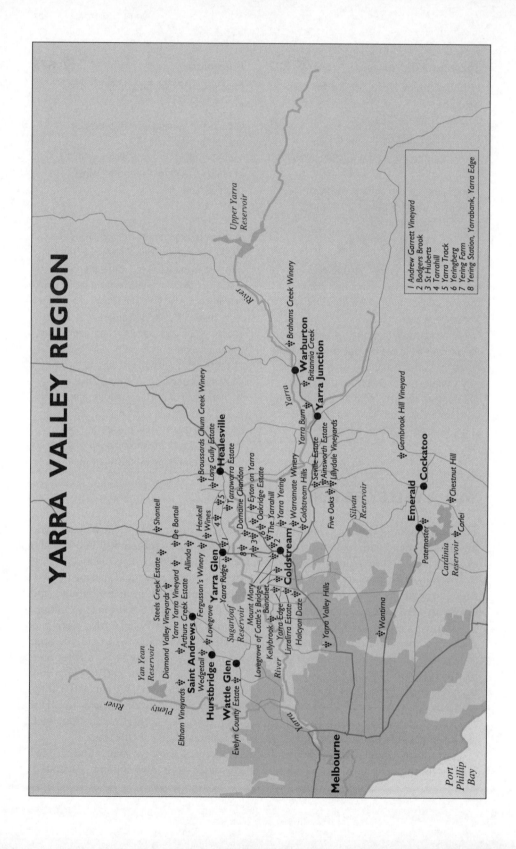

YARRA VALLEY REGION

1 Andrew Garrett Vineyard
2 Badgers Brook
3 St Huberts
4 Tarrahill
5 Yarra Track
6 Yeringberg
7 Yering Farm
8 Yering Station, Yarrabank, Yarra Edge

Melbourne

Port Phillip Bay

Saint Andrews
Hurstbridge
Wattle Glen
Yarra Glen
Healesville
Coldstream
Yarra Junction
Warburton
Emerald
Cockatoo

Yan Yean Reservoir
Sugarloaf Reservoir
Silvan Reservoir
Cardinia Reservoir
Upper Yarra Reservoir

Eltham Vineyards
Diamond Valley Vineyards
Steels Creek Estate
Yarra Yarra Vineyard
Arthurs Creek Estate
Allinda
Fergusson's Winery
Wedgetail
Lovegrove
Yarra Ridge
Shantell
De Bortoli
Henkell Wines
Broussards Chum Creek Winery
Long Gully Estate
Tarrawarra Estate
Domaine Chandon
Eyton on Yarra
Oakridge Estate
The Yarrahill
Yarra Yering
Warramate Winery
Coldstream Hills
Seville Estate
Ainsworth Estate
Lillydale Vineyards
Five Oaks
Gembrook Hill Vineyard
Chestnut Hill
Carlei
Paternoster
Yarra Valley Hills
Wantirna
Halcyon Daze
Lirralirra Estate
Yarra Edge
Kellybrook
Blanchet
Lovegrove of Cattle's Bridge
Mount Mary
Evelyn County Estate
Britannia Creek
Brahams Creek Winery

Plenty River
Yarra River
Yarra River

Yarra Burn

largest and most prosperous city at that time. Indeed, by 1890, the Yarra was at the height of its reputation. Its decline and fall over the next 30 years was due to two quite diverse causes: a general lack of interest in table wines and the preference of wine drinkers for stronger fortified wines, for which Yarra wine was not suited; and the election of a Victorian government that wished to encourage teetotalism and the consumption of more milk. By the 1920s, viticulture in the Yarra Valley had succumbed, not to phylloxera as in other places but to the dairy cow.

The Yarra Valley's rebirth coincided with the general rise of interest in Australian wine in the 1960s. Quite close to its original site, St Hubert's was re-established on a former chicken farm in 1968. In the following year, a minute portion of the original Yeringberg was replanted by the founder's grandson, also Guillaume de Pury, there being no need for a winery as the 'new' winery of 1885 did quite nicely. The medical profession lent a hand as usual—Mount Mary near Lilydale was planted in 1971 by Dr John Middleton and Seville Estate near Seville was established the following year by Middleton's medical partner, Peter McMahon. During the 1980s, retired lawyers such as James Halliday and Louis Bialkower also contributed to its phoenix-like revival. Coldstream Hills and Yarra Ridge bear witness to their efforts.

The Yarra has grown apace and over 30 wineries are now scattered about the Valley, including the important Domaine Chandon, offshoot of Moet & Chandon of Epernay. More importantly—or perhaps alarmingly for some—the 'big battalions' of the Australian wine industry now have a Yarra address, either by way of vineyard ownership or by having purchased an existing winery and continuing to trade under the original name. For example, Mildara Wines purchased the remaining 50% of Yarra Ridge in 1995, having owned half for several years; McWilliam's wines bought Lillydale Vineyards in 1994; BRL Hardy purchased Yarra Burn in 1996; and Southcorp Wines acquired Coldstream Hills in the same year. Certainly their presence has ensured a consistency of quality and national distribution for many more Yarra wines but, it is hoped, at no cost to their regional origin. It seems unlikely that the dairy cow will cause upheaval ever again in the Yarra vignoble. A more pressing and present danger is the ever-expanding eastern suburbia of Melbourne.

Location: latitude 37°45'S, longitude 145°21'E. Situated about 35 km north-east of Melbourne, around and to the north, east and south of Lilydale, and around Coldstream, Yarra Glen, Dixons Creek, Healesville, St Andrews and Seville.
Elevation: 50–400 m
Topography and soils: vineyards are planted on both flat and undulating country which is quite steep in parts. Soils are of two principal types. One is the hard red duplex soils (Dr 2.21, Dr 2.22) which appear grey-brown in colour with a subsoil of red-brown clay. The other major soil type is a very vigorous, deep red loam (Dr 2.42), common around the Seville area and other areas in the southern part of the Valley. This deep red loam country can cause excessive vigour in vines, over-luxuriant growth of foliage and consequent problems in fruit ripening. Good but not excessive drainage is important and this depends on the clay content of the subsoils, which varies from place to place within the Valley. Both major soil types are acidic.
Climate: (local) MJT 18.8°C, MAR na, HDD 1250, AR 1008 mm, RH 57%, AI na,

SH na; (Healesville) MJT 17.9°C, MAR na, HDD (raw) 1251, 1352 adjusted for vine sites, AR 1008 mm (Oct–Apr 597 mm), RH na, AI na, SH 7.5; (Gladstones) MJT 19.4°C, MAR 11°C, HDD 1489, AR 911 mm (Oct–Mar 404 mm), RH 63% (9am), AI 52 mm, SH 7.4 (Dry and Smart). Generally cool, even in its 'warmest' areas, with higher and more exposed areas downright cold. Northerly aspects are most favoured because of their warmth, but these are most exposed to wind and rain which, if combined at critical flowering times (December), can be devastating, as they also may be during ripening (March–April). For this reason too, fungal diseases can present difficulties. In addition, spring frosts can be a problem in low-lying vineyards. During ripening, birds are another hazard. Annual rainfall (750 mm in the northern Yarra Valley (Yarra Glen) and 1150 mm on the southern side of the Valley) does not preclude water stress in the January–March period and the consequent need for drip irrigation from surface dams.

Harvest time: late March (for sparkling wine base) to late May

Principal grape varieties: Red—pinot noir*, cabernet sauvignon, shiraz, merlot, cabernet franc, malbec; White—chardonnay*, sauvignon blanc, semillon, riesling (*indicates use for sparkling wine base)

Major wine styles: *Chardonnay* The Yarra Valley shares with the Adelaide Hills the distinction of being Australia's leading Chardonnay region. These are wines of excellent fruit-acid balance showing typical cool area aromatics and flavours of lime, peach, melon and fig with the ability to age well over 5–10 years. *Pinot Noir* As with its Chardonnays, the Valley produces premium wine from its higher and southerly areas. Elegant reds of good palate structure and lovely soft characters which recall violets, cherries, strawberries and plums. These are wines which usually age well over a moderate term (i.e. 3–5 years) and sometimes longer. *Cabernet Sauvignon* Often on a par with the famous reds of Coonawarra and Margaret River, these are Cabernets of great distinction and depth of mint and berry fruit. They lack the weight of Coonawarra, but compensate in that respect by marvellous elegance and style. They too age well over 8–10 years. *Shiraz* Distinctive on nose because of a pepperiness of the white not black variety, these too have lovely medium weight palates. Complex flavours often include raspberries and plum. Here again are reds which will improve over 8–10 years.

Leading wineries and vineyards: Diamond Valley, Yeringberg, Domaine Chandon, Yarra Yering, Coldstream Hills, Wantirna Estate, Mount Mary, De Bortoli, Yering Farm, Arthurs Creek, Yarra Edge, Yarrabank Vineyards, Seville Estate, Gembrooke Hill. (No other wine region in Australia has such sustained quality in all areas of table and sparkling wine.)

Ainsworth Estate   **R82**

110 Ducks Lane, Seville, Vic 3139
Ph 03 5964 4711, Fax 03 5964 4311,
Email sales@ainsworth-estate.com.au

Owners: Kerri and Denis Craig
Chief winemaker: Dennis Craig and Al

Fencaros (contract)
Year of foundation: 1994
Tonnes produced on average each year: 72, of which about half are used for Ainsworth Estate labels
Location: Seville
Area: 8 ha

Soils: red kraznozems and some grey loam
Varieties planted: White—chardonnay;
Red—pinot noir, shiraz
Leading wines: Ainsworth Estate Unwooded
Chardonnay, Chardonnay, Pinot Noir
Notes: Ainsworth Estate is a promising new
player in the southern Yarra Valley. With its
first wine release, an Unwooded Chardonnay,
it received a bronze medal. Cellar door sales:
daily 10.30am–5pm.

Allinda **R82**

119 Lorimers Lane, Dixons Creek,
Vic 3775
Ph 03 5965 2450, Fax 03 5965 2467

Owner/chief winemaker: Al Fencaros
Year of foundation: 1991
Tonnes crushed on average each year: 150, of
which 35 are used for Allinda's own labels
Location: Dixons Creek
Area: 3 ha
Soils: shallow grey loam over mudstone clay
subsoil
Varieties planted: White—chardonnay, riesling;
Red—cabernet franc, cabernet sauvignon,
merlot, pinot noir
Leading wines: Allinda Cabernets, Chardonnay
Notes: Allinda is primarily a contract crushing
and winemaking establishment, but its
Chardonnay standards are good. Cellar door
sales: 11am–5pm weekends and public
holidays.

Andrew Garrett Vineyard
(vineyard only) **R84**

134A The Parade, Norwood, SA 5067
Ph 08 8379 0119, Fax 08 8379 7228,
Email agarrett@andrewgarrettgroup.com.au

Owner: International Vineyards
Chief winemaker: Andrew Garrett
Year of foundation: 1996
Tonnes crushed on average each year: na
Location: Yarra Glen

Area: 117 ha
Soils: clay loam and sandy loam
Varieties planted: White—chardonnay;
Red—cabernet sauvignon
Leading wines: Yarra Glen Grand Chardonnay,
Cabernet Sauvignon
Notes: A Yarra re-incarnation for this enthusiastic
South Australian winemaker. Chardonnay and
Cabernet Sauvignon are the highlights. Cellar
door sales: at the Grand Hotel Yarra Glen.
Otherwise, sales by retail or mail order.

Arthurs Creek Estate
(vineyard only) **R91**

'Kurnalpi', Strathewen Road,
Arthurs Creek, Vic 3099
Ph/Fax 03 9714 8202

Owner: The Arthurs Creek Estate Pty Ltd
Chief winemaker: contract, Gary Baldwin
(consultant)
Year of foundation: 1975
Tonnes produced on average each year: 20,
but should increase when new plantings of
merlot come into bearing
Location: Arthurs Creek
Area: 7.6 ha
Soils: grey loam
Varieties planted: White—chardonnay;
Red—cabernet sauvignon, merlot
Leading wines: Arthurs Creek Cabernet
Sauvignon, Chardonnay
Notes: Arthurs Creek lies on the western edge
of the Yarra and seems ideally suited for
cabernet sauvignon. Its owner, S. E. K. Hulme,
is a leading Melbourne QC with not only a
passion for great Cabernet but also a great
deal of patience. Why? He first began trial
plantings at Arthurs Creek in 1975. In 1976 he
planted cabernet sauvignon and the first wine
from this vineyard was made in 1979. From
then on, vintages came and went but no wine
was released until 1992. By that time the
Arthurs Creek cellars must have resembled
Aladdin's cave, as Melbourne wine consultant

Joe Sullivan went about the arduous but immensely pleasurable task of assessing the quality of 13 vintages of Cabernet Sauvignon. Since 1992 the wines have been exhibited regularly. The 1992, 1994 and 1995 have won gold medals and trophies at various Victorian wine shows. The Cabernets are usually concentrated and very powerful (the 1995 which I tasted early in 2000 is particularly so) and often need 10 years maturation, but that is the way of great Cabernet. The Chardonnay too has proved worthy of gold. The Cabernet Sauvignon is released at four and a half years of age; the Chardonnay at one and a half. Sales are by retail. Inquire at Sullivan Wine Agencies, 12 Balwyn Road, Balwyn North, Vic 3104, Ph 03 9857 9298, Fax 03 9816 3307.

Badgers Brook Vineyard   **R80**

874 Maroondah Highway, Coldstream
Ph 03 5962 4130, Fax 03 5962 4238

Owners: Mary and Michael Warren
Chief winemaker: Michael Warren
Year of foundation: 1993, vineyard planted 1989
Tonnes produced on average each year: 15, about 9 of which is used for Badgers Brook labels. (A further 50 tonnes of fruit is purchased)
Location: Coldstream on the Melbourne side of Eyton on Yarra
Area: 6.3 ha
Soils: shallow grey loam with gravel leading into clay
Varieties planted: White—chardonnay, sauvignon blanc; Red—cabernet sauvignon, pinot noir, shiraz
Leading wines: Badgers Brook Pinot Noir. A second label Storm Ridge featuring blends of Yarra Valley and Mornington Peninsula fruit is also produced
Notes: Badgers Brook is a small Yarra cellar door outlet whose emphasis is on Pinot Noir.
Cellar door sales: weekends and public holidays 10am–5pm.

Bianchet Vineyard and Winery   **NR**

Lot 3 Victoria Road, Lilydale, Vic 3140
Ph 03 9739 1779, Fax 03 9739 1277

Owners: privately owned
Chief winemaker: Keith Salter
Year of foundation: 1976
Tonnes crushed on average each year: 30
Location: Lilydale
Area: 6 ha
Soils: grey loam with gravelly shale subsoil over yellow clay
Varieties planted: White—chardonnay, riesling, semillon, traminer, verduzzo; Red—cabernet franc, cabernet sauvignon, merlot, pinot noir, shiraz
Leading wines: Bianchet Chardonnay, Pinot Noir, Verduzzo
Notes: For many years owned by the late Lou Bianchet and now under new ownership. A point of interest here is the unusual Verduzzo.
Cellar door sales: daily 10am–6pm.

Brahams Creek Winery   **R73**

Woods Point Road, East Warburton, Vic 3799
Ph/Fax 03 5966 2802

Owners: Gordon Valentine, Geoffrey Richardson and Don Valentine
Chief winemaker: Geoffrey Richardson, B. Wilson (consultant)
Year of foundation: 1990
Tonnes crushed on average each year: 11, but should increase from 2001
Location: East Warburton
Area: 4.6 ha
Soils: a north facing vineyard with grey loam on a clay base
Varieties planted: White—chardonnay, sauvignon blanc; Red—cabernet sauvignon, merlot, pinot noir
Leading wines: Brahams Creek Chardonnay, Pinot Noir
Notes: Cellar door sales: 11am–5pm weekends and public holidays.

Britannia Creek Wines **NR**

75 Britannia Creek Road, Wesburn,
Vic 3799 (about 1 km from Yarra Junction)
Ph 03 5967 1006, Fax 03 5780 1426

Owners: Charlie Brydon and Remy van de Wiel
Chief winemaker: Charlie Brydon
Tonnes produced on average each year: 25, all
of which are used for Britannia Falls labels
Location: Wesburn
Area: 5 ha
Soils: a shallow light brown sandy loam over a
grey clay subsoil. A non-irrigated vineyard of
low fertility
Varieties planted: White—chenin blanc,
sauvignon blanc, semillon; Red—cabernet
franc, cabernet sauvignon, malbec, merlot,
petit verdot
Leading wines: Britannia Falls Sauvignon Blanc,
Semillon, Cabernets
Notes: By varietal inclination, Charlie Brydon is
obviously a Bordeaux enthusiast. I have not
tasted his wines. Cellar door sales: weekends
11am–6pm.

Broussards Chum Creek Winery **NR**

28 Cunningham Road, Healesville,
Vic 3777
Ph 03 5962 5551

Owner: James Broussard
Chief winemaker: (contract)
Year of foundation: 1977
Tonnes produced each year on average: 20
Location: Healesville
Area: 3 ha
Soils: grey loam
Varieties planted: White—chardonnay;
Red—cabernet sauvignon, pinot noir
Leading wines: Chum Creek, Chardonnay,
Cabernet Sauvignon, Pinot Noir
Notes: This small Yarra winery sells most of its
fruit, retaining only 3 tonnes for its own
winemaking purposes. Cellar door sales:
weekends and public holidays 10am–6pm.

Coldstream Hills **R93**

31 Maddens Lane, Coldstream, Vic 3770
Ph 03 5964 9388, Fax 03 5964 9389

Owner: Southcorp Wines
Chief winemaker: Andrew Fleming
Year of foundation: 1985
Tonnes crushed on average each year: 1000,
all of which are used for Coldstream Hills
labels
Location: Coldstream. There are five vineyards
owned or managed by Coldstream Hills: in the
Lower Yarra Valley there are Coldstream Hills,
Briarston and Fernhill; in the Upper Yarra Valley
are Deer Farm and Peggies
Area: 90 ha
Soils: the first four vineyard sites are basically
Yarra Valley grey loam, the last (Peggies)
consists basically of the more vigorous red
loam
Varieties planted: White—chardonnay, pinot
gris, sauvignon blanc; Red—cabernet franc,
cabernet sauvignon, malbec, merlot, meunier,
petit verdot, pinot noir, shiraz
Leading wines: Coldstream Hills Reserve Pinot
Noir, Reserve Chardonnay, Reserve Cabernet
Sauvignon (which in appropriate years usually
form between 15 and 20% of the crop)
Notes: Acquired by Southcorp Wines in 1996,
the premium Yarra Valley winery, Coldstream
Hills, was formerly the property of a publicly
listed company, founded by eminent wine
writer, judge and maker, James Halliday.
Halliday retired from Coldstream Hills in 2000.
Since his retirement there has been absolutely
no dimunition in the quality of its leading
wines, which proceed from strength to
strength. Southcorp Wines recognise the
extreme importance of this jewel in its Yarra
crown and indeed would be foollish not to.
Cellar door sales: 7 days 10am–5pm.

De Bortoli Wines Yarra Valley R92

Pinnacle Lane, Dixons Creek, Vic 3775
Ph 03 5965 2271, Fax 03 5965 2464,
Email dbw@debortoli.com.au

Owner: De Bortoli family
Chief winemaker: Stephen Webber
(Winemakers: David Slingsby Smith, David
Bicknell)
Year of foundation: 1971 (as Chateau Yarrinya)
Tonnes crushed on average each year: 1951
(from the Yarra Valley), 1246 (from the King
Valley) and 515 (from other Victorian sources)
Location: Dixons Creek
Area: 138 ha (Yarra Valley), increasing to
180 ha within a few years
Soils: the Dixons Creek vineyard is undulating
with a wide variety of aspects. Its soils are
shallow sandy clays over yellow mottled
mudstone. They are quite fertile, but do not
drain well, necessitating the provision of
surface drainage to avoid waterlogging
Varieties planted: White—chardonnay,
gewurztraminer, riesling, sauvignon blanc,
semillon; Red—cabernet sauvignon, merlot,
petit verdot, pinot noir, shiraz, zinfandel
Leading wines: De Bortoli Yarra Valley market
three wine ranges above which are two
'flagship' reds, 'Melba' and 'Reserve Shiraz'.
Melba, named after Dame Nellie Melba, is
blended from the best wines made in any
given vintage from the 'Bordeaux' varieties
grown at the Dixons Creek vineyard. It is made
only when vintage conditions are favourable.
The Reserve Shiraz is a small batch red virtually
hand-made, receiving up to 5 days 'cold soak'
before a warm ferment involving 6 hand-
plunges per day during fermentation.
Fermentation is completed in small oak. This is
followed by maturation in a selection of top
quality barrels, which are then blended and
receive further maturation in French and
American barriques for up to 20 months. The
super premium range is Yarra Valley, produced
from the best parcels of Yarra Valley fruit of
the vintage. Below this is Gulf Station a range
of earlier-drinking Yarra Valley table wines of
good quality. The third level is Windy Peak,
Victorian table wines predominantly from the
Yarra, King and Murray Valleys
Notes: The De Bortoli purchase of Graeme
Miller's Chateau Yarrinya in 1987 has been a
great success and the De Bortoli family, in the
years since, have proved to some sceptical
wine critics that its Yarra wines are as good as
any in the Valley and a lot better than most.
Many trophies have been won in the past
decade, especially by the Chardonnay and
Cabernet Sauvignon (more recently a Jimmy
Watson Trophy in 1997 for a 1996 Reserve
Shiraz). De Bortoli also conducts a fine
restaurant specialising in northern Italian
cucina, open every day for lunch and on
Saturday night only for dinner. Cellar door
sales: 7 days 10am–5pm.

Diamond Valley Vineyards R96

Kinglake Road, St Andrews, Vic 3761
Ph 03 9710 1484, Fax 03 9710 1369

Owners: David and Katherine Lance
Chief winemakers: David and James Lance
Year of foundation: 1976
Tonnes crushed on average each year: 145, of
which 80 are used for Diamond Valley labels
Location: St Andrews
Area: 3.5 ha
Soils: thin Silurian layer over a mudstone base,
'mean and lean', as Kathy Lance says
Varieties planted: White—chardonnay;
Red—cabernet franc, cabernet sauvignon,
malbec, merlot, pinot noir
Leading wines: Diamond Valley Close Planted
Pinot Noir, Estate Pinot Noir, Estate
Chardonnay, Estate Cabernet
Notes: With numerous trophies (34 at last
count) and a multitude of gold medals to their
credit, master winemaker Dr David Lance and
his wife Kathy have created a monumental
reputation for excellence for Diamond Valley

Vineyards, especially in Pinot Noir, both the Close Planted and the Estate. Its Estate Chardonnay can also be relied upon to give a great deal of pleasure. The 'Blue Label' has now been replaced but not in colour (it is still a bright blue) by 'Yarra Valley', as the defining name for the non-estate range. There are no cellar door sales. Tasting and sales are strictly by appointment or by mailing list. The Lances also own the Phillip Island vineyard and winery in the Gippsland wine zone.

Domaine Chandon R94

'Green Point', Maroondah Highway, Coldstream, Vic 3770
Ph 03 9739 1110, Fax 03 9739 1095

Owner: Moet & Chandon (Epernay, France)
Chief winemaker: Dr Tony Jordan, Neville Rowe, James Gosper
Year of foundation: 1985
Tonnes crushed on average each year: 880, all of which are used in Domaine Chandon own wines, the total crushed being 3000
Location: Coldstream
Area: 80 ha
Soils: fine sandy clay loam, grey in colour over silty clay subsoil
Varieties planted: White—chardonnay, sauvignon blanc; Red—meunier, pinot noir, shiraz
Leading wines: Chandon Vintage Brut
Notes: Domaine Chandon's name is synonymous with sparkling excellence. Each year its wines improve from best to even better. The sparkling wines are blended from superb fruit purchased from virtually all the cooler regions of Australia. The Green Point Chardonnay is 100 per cent estate grown, made and bottled and of superb quality. Sales are made in the Green Point Room by the glass or bottle, open daily 10.30am–4.30pm. Food and guided tours available.

Eltham Vineyards NR

225 Shaws Road, Arthurs Creek, Vic 3099
Ph 03 9439 4144, Fax 03 9439 5121

Owner/chief winemaker: George Apted and John Graves
Year of foundation: 1986
Tonnes crushed on average each year: 10, all of which is used for Eltham Vineyards own labels
Location: Arthurs Creek
Area: 2.5 ha
Soils: clay, 'hilly and hungry', in George Apted's words
Varieties planted: White—chardonnay; Red—cabernet franc, cabernet sauvignon, merlot, pinot noir
Leading wines: Eltham Vineyards Pinot Noir, Chardonnay, Cabernet-Merlot
Notes: A very small vineyard with local distribution but no cellar door sales.

Evelyn County Estate R85

35 New Road, Kangaroo Ground, Vic 3097 (on the western boundary of the region near Diamond Creek, a tributary of the Yarra River)
Ph 03 9437 1668, Fax 03 9437 1232, Email rmale@netspace.net.au

Owners: Robyn and Roger Male
Chief winemaker: David Lance (contract)
Year of foundation: 1995, 1st Vintage: 1998
Tonnes crushed on average each year: 62 and increasing, 24 of which are presently used for Evelyn County's own labels
Location: Kangaroo Ground
Area: 7 ha of vines all on Scott-Henry trellising and 2x1 metre close planting
Soils: the vineyard has been established on a narrow strip of rich black (slightly acidic) volcanic soil atypical in the region
Varieties planted: White—chardonnay, sauvignon blanc; Red—cabernet sauvignon,

merlot, pinot noir, tempranillo
Leading wines: Evelyn County Chardonnay,
Merlot, Sauvignon Blanc
Notes: Evelyn County has begun extremely
well. Its whites are fresh and vigorous and its
reds promise mightily. Show results show a
pleasing silver and bronze consistency. Golds
will surely follow as its vines mature. Cellar
door sales: daily but ring ahead.

Eyton on Yarra R86

Cnr Maroondah Highway and Hill Road,
Coldstream, Vic 3770
Ph 03 5962 2119, Fax 03 5962 5319

Owner: Deidre Cowan
Chief winemaker: Matt Aldridge
Year of foundation: 1989 (as Yarra Vale)
Tonnes crushed on average each year: 350, of
which 230 are used for Eyton on Yarra's wines
Location: Coldstream
Area: 50 ha consisting of two vineyards, Eyton
10 ha and Dalry Road 40 ha
Soils: Eyton, yellow grey podsolic clay; Dalry
Road, brown black loamy clay (river flat)
Varieties planted: White—chardonnay, riesling,
sauvignon blanc, traminer; Red—cabernet
franc, cabernet sauvignon, merlot, pinot noir,
shiraz
Leading wines: Eyton on Yarra NDC Reserve
range, Eyton on Yarra Chardonnay, Cabernet-
Merlot
Notes: Purchased by the late Newell Cowan in
1994 and extensively refurbished in the years
since, Eyton on Yarra is one of the showplaces
of the Valley, boasting a modern winery, cellar
door and restaurant complex. Under
winemaker Matt Aldridge, its white and reds
have attained an enviable standard. Cellar door
sales: 7 days 10am–5pm, restaurant
noon–3pm.

Fergusson's Winery R85

Wills Road, Yarra Glen, Vic 3793
Ph 03 5965 2237, Fax 03 5965 2405,
Email fergussons@paradigm4.com.au

Owners: Peter and Louise Fergusson
Chief winemaker: Christopher Keyes
Year of foundation: 1968
Tonnes crushed on average each year: 150
Location: Yarra Glen
Area: 16 ha
Soils: grey brown sandy clay loam over a heavy
orange clay subsoil interspersed with schist
Varieties planted: White—chardonnay,
sauvignon blanc; Red—cabernet franc,
cabernet sauvignon, pinot noir, shiraz
Leading Wines: Fergusson's, Victoria
Chardonnay, Jeremy Shiraz, Benjamin Cabernet
Notes: A typically good Yarra winery with
excellent Chardonnay and Cabernet and—still
quite rare in the Yarra—a very good white
peppery Shiraz. All the wines are estate grown
and made and named after the Fergusson
children. There is a restaurant and cellar door
sales: 11am–5pm each day.

Five Oaks R78

60 Aitken Road, Seville, Vic 3139
Ph 03 5964 3704, Fax 03 5964 3064,
Email FiveOaks@bigpond.com

Owners: Judy and Wally Zuk
Chief winemaker: Wally Zuk
Year of foundation: 1978 as Oakridge Estate
which has now relocated to Maroondah
Highway Coldstream (*qv*). As Five Oaks 1998
Tonnes produced on average each year: 25,
all used for Five Oaks' own labels. A further
5 tonnes is purchased
Location: Seville
Area: 3 ha
Soils: a rich red volcanic loam over 20 m deep
above a brown coal seam 1–2 m thick
Varieties planted: White—riesling;
Red—cabernet sauvignon, merlot

Leading wines: Five Oaks Cabernet Sauvignon, Cabernet Sauvignon-Merlot

Notes: Five Oaks continues on the site where Oakridge Estate existed for 20 years. Wine show entries have gained a respectable number of bronze medals. Cabernet Sauvignon is the pick here. Cellar door sales: weekends and public holidays 10am–5pm. At other times by appointment.

Gembrook Hill Vineyard **R90**

Launching Place Road, Gembrook, Vic 3783
Ph 03 5968 1622, Fax 03 5968 1699

Owners: June and Ian Marks
Chief winemaker: Helen Smyth
Year of foundation: 1983
Tonnes crushed on average each year: 18
Location: Gembrook
Area: 6 ha
Soils: red volcanic loam, well drained, of low fertility and pH
Varieties planted: White—chardonnay, sauvignon blanc, semillon; Red—pinot noir
Leading wines: Gembrook Hill Sauvignon Blanc, Chardonnay, Pinot Noir
Notes: Gembrook Hill opened its new winery in time for vintage 2000. The strengths of Gembrook Hill, and they are formidable, lie in all the varieties grown. For lovers of Sauvignon Blanc there is a wine of very complex tropical aromas and flavours. For the Chardonnay aficionado, a wine of great finesse and style, while the Pinot enthusiast cannot fail to be immensely gratified by an elegant medium-bodied wine, which recalls some of the better *climats* of the Cote d'Or. Standards here are excellent. Tastings and cellar door sales by appointment only.

Halcyon Daze **NR**

19 Uplands Road, Chirnside Park, Vic 3116
Ph/Fax 03 9726 7111

Owners: Richard and Cheryl Rackley
Chief winemaker: Richard Rackley
Year of foundation: 1982
Tonnes crushed on average each year: 40, about 5 of which are used for Halcyon Daze labels
Location: Chirnside Park
Area: 6.25 ha
Soils: grey loam over a clay base
Varieties planted: White—chardonnay, riesling; Red—cabernet franc, cabernet sauvignon, merlot
Leading wines: Halcyon Daze Cabernet Blend, Pinot Noir, 'Halcyon' (a methode champenoise sparkling wine), Riesling
Notes: A smaller winery which utilises about an eighth of its own fruit for winemaking, while the rest is sold to other winemakers. Cellar door sales by appointment only.

Hanson
(see Tarrahill Vineyard entry)

Henkell Wines **NR**

Melba Highway, Yarra Glen, Vic 3755
Ph 03 5965 2016

Owner: Hans A. Henkell
Chief winemaker: Rob Dolan (contract)
Year of foundation: 1988
Tonnes produced on average each year: 200, a minimal amount is used for the Henkell label—most grapes go to Yarra Ridge
Location: Dixons Creek
Area: 17.7 ha
Soils: grey clay loam over a clay base with some stones
Varieties planted: White—chardonnay, sauvignon blanc; Red—cabernet sauvignon, pinot noir

Leading wine: Henkell Chardonnay
Notes: Hans Henkell is a member of the famous Henkell winemaking family in Germany. Although not a professional winemaker himself, his family roots are deep in winemaking—hence, Henkell Yarra Valley. Rob Dolan always does an excellent job. Cellar door sales: weekends and public holidays 11am–5pm.

Hoddles Creek (vineyards only) NR

Prices Road, Gladysdale, Vic 3797 and Beenak Road, Beenak, Vic 3797

Owner: BRL Hardy Ltd
Tonnes produced each year on average: 640
Locations: Gladysdale and Beenak
Area: 87.25 ha consisting of two vineyards, Prices Road 30 ha and Beenak Road 57.25 ha
Soils: (Prices Road) deep rich red loam, (Beenak Road) clay loam red volcanic
Varieties planted: White—chardonnay, sauvignon blanc; Red—meunier, pinot noir
Leading wines: Fruit from these vineyards is utilised in BRL Hardy premium labels for sparkling and table wine use, depending on the ripeness of the year. In years of good ripeness, most may be used in table wine. In less than successful years most finds its way into sparkling wine
Notes: Though Hoddles Creek and Beenak are several kilometres apart, they are here listed under the Hoddles Creek name to avoid duplication because their end use, varieties and soil are essentially the same. Specifically they contribute to Yarra Burn, Eileen Hardy Chardonnay and other premium brands of the company. No cellar door facilities.

Kellybrook R78

Fulford Road, Wonga Park, Vic 3115
Ph 03 9722 1304, Fax 03 9722 2092

Owners: Darren and Farley Kelly
Chief winemaker: Darren Kelly

Year of foundation: 1970
Tonnes crushed on average each year: 40
Location: Wonga Park
Area: 8 ha
Soils: grey topsoil over clay over mudstone
Varieties planted: White—chardonnay, riesling, traminer; Red—cabernet sauvignon, merlot, pinot noir, shiraz
Leading wine: Kellybrook Shiraz
Notes: Kellybrook is one of the older established Yarra wineries with a good reputation for Chardonnay. It also makes a range of ciders including an apple brandy in the Calvados style. Cellar door sales: Mon–Sat 9am–6pm, Sun 11am–6pm.

Lillydale Vineyards R88

10 Davross Court, Seville, Vic 3139
Ph 03 5964 2016, Fax 03 5964 3009

Owner: McWilliam's Wines Pty Limited
Winemakers: Max McWilliam and Jim Brayne
Year of foundation: 1976
Tonnes crushed on average each year: 142, all of which is used for Lillydale Vineyards own labels
Location: Seville
Area: 15 ha
Soils: a fertile grey loam topsoil between 20 and 30 cm deep over a free-draining yellow clay about 60 cm deep over dense clay and mudstone
Varieties planted: White—chardonnay, gewurztraminer, sauvignon blanc; Red—cabernet sauvignon, pinot noir
Leading wines: Lillydale Yarra Sauvignon Blanc, Yarra Chardonnay, Yarra Pinot Noir, Yarra Cabernet Merlot
Notes: Since 1994 when it was acquired by McWilliams Wines, the wines of Lillydale Estate, under Jim Brayne's expert tutelage, go from strength to strength. Especially good have been recent years of Cabernet Merlot and Pinot Noir. Cellar door sales: daily 11am–5pm, except Christmas and Good

Friday. There is also a restaurant open for lunch daily except Christmas and Good Friday. Open for dinner Fri–Sat but reservations are necessary.

Lirralirra Estate NR

15 Paynes Road, Chirnside Park, Vic 3116
Ph/Fax 03 9735 0224

Owners: Alan and Joycelin Smith
Chief winemaker: Alan Smith
Year of foundation: 1981
Tonnes produced on average each year: less than 5
Location: Chirnside Park
Area: 2.1 ha
Soils: grey sandy loam over heavy clay over extremely weathered silt stone
Varieties planted: White—sauvignon blanc, semillon; Red—cabernet franc, cabernet sauvignon merlot, pinot noir
Leading wines: Lirralirra Estate Semillon, Pinot Noir, Cabernets, Sauvignon Blanc
Notes: This is a small family-owned vineyard and winery located in the western end of the Valley in one of its warmer and lower (80 m altitude) parts. The Pinot Noir is considered very good. Cellar door sales: 10am–6pm each day during January. At other times, weekends and public holidays, 10am–6pm.

Long Gully Estate R84

Long Gully Road, Healesville, Vic 3777
Ph/Fax 03 5962 3663,
Email longgully@netspace.net.au

Owners: Irma and Rainer Klapp
Chief winemaker: Peter Florance
Year of foundation: 1982
Tonnes crushed on average each year: 275, about 250 of which are used for Long Gully labels
Location: Healesville
Area: 45 ha
Soils: dark brown–black volcanic clay through to buckshot gravel
Varieties planted: White—chardonnay, riesling, sauvignon blanc, semillon; Red—cabernet sauvignon, merlot, pinot noir, shiraz
Leading wines: Irma's Cabernet Sauvignon, Long Gully Merlot, Sauvignon Blanc
Notes: Long Gully is a well-established Yarra winery producing good Sauvignons Blancs and very good Cabernets. Cellar door sales: daily 11am–5pm.

Lovegrove of Cottle's Bridge NR

1420 Heidelberg-Kinglake Road, Cottle's Bridge, Vic 3099
Ph 03 9718 1569, Fax 03 9718 1928,
Email lovegrovewinery@ozemail.com.au

Owners: Stephen Bennett and Louise Heathcote
Winemakers: Stephen Bennett and Karen Coulston
Year of foundation: 1981
Tonnes produced on average each year: 20, all of which are used for Lovegrove Winery labels
Location: Cottle's Bridge
Area: 4 ha
Soils: topsoil is a 15–30 cm layer of clayey loam intermixed with mudstone and gravel. Beneath is a clay subsoil
Varieties planted: White—chardonnay, sauvignon blanc; Red—cabernet sauvignon, merlot, pinot noir
Leading wines: Lovegrove methode Champenoise, Chardonnay, Pinot Noir, Cabernet-Merlot
Notes: This is a winery under relatively new ownership. Its wines have not been recently tasted. Cellar door sales: weekends and public holidays 11am–6pm. Otherwise by appointment.

Mount Mary Vineyard R93

Coldstream West Road, Lilydale,
Vic 3140
Ph 03 9739 1761, Fax 03 9739 0137

Owners: John and Marli Middleton
Chief winemakers: John Middleton and
McGregor Forbes
Year of foundation: 1971
Tonnes crushed on average each year: 52
Location: Lilydale
Area: 15 ha, including new plantings which
have not yet come into bearing
Soils: grey silurian over mudstone on sandy
clay loam—duplex podsols
Varieties planted: White—chardonnay,
muscadelle, sauvignon blanc, semillon;
Red—cabernet franc, cabernet sauvignon,
malbec, merlot, petit verdot, pinot noir
Leading wines: Mount Mary Quintet (a red
blend of the 'Bordeaux' varieties listed above),
Chardonnay, Pinot Noir, Triolet (a white blend
of sauvignon blanc, semillon and muscadelle
a la Graves).
Notes: Though he was not quite the first to
replant vines commercially in the Yarra Valley,
Dr John Middleton is certainly one of its
veterans, a winemaker with over 40 years'
experience of the Valley and an energetic
proponent of its elegant wines, many of which
are his own. Hectare for hectare, his
production is quite small, but his quality is
extremely high. He always recommends that
his wines be tasted with appropriate food in a
true dining situation, for in that way the true
mettle of a wine can be gauged. Every wine
lover should taste a Quintet or a Pinot Noir at
least once in a lifetime. Regrettably there are
no cellar door sales.

Oakridge Estate R87

864 Maroondah Highway, Coldstream,
Vic 3770
Ph 03 9739 1920, Fax 03 9739 1923,
Email mz@oakridgevyds.com.au

Owner: Evans & Tate Ltd
Chief winemaker: Michael Zitzlaff
Year of foundation: 1978
Tonnes crushed on average each year: 420, all
of which is used for Oakridge wines
Location: Coldstream
Area: 50 ha
Soils: grey loam over yellow clay
Varieties planted: White—chardonnay,
sauvignon blanc, semillon; Red—cabernet
sauvignon, merlot, pinot noir, shiraz
Leading wines: There are two wine ranges,
Oakridge Estate, which features Cabernet-
Merlot, Chardonnay, Pinot Noir, Sauvignon
Blanc and the Reserve, which consists of
Cabernet, Chardonnay, Merlot
Notes: In February 1998, after 20 years at its
Seville site, Oakridge moved its lock, stock and
particularly its barrels to Coldstream, where it
now has a handsome new winery and cellar
door complex and a flourishing new vineyard.
It is important to note that in its 'upsizing', the
quality of Oakridge reds has not suffered one
iota. The whites also are very good. Cellar door
sales: 11am–5pm daily. Light lunches are also
available.

Portet Winemakers R87

11 Constance Street, East Hawthorn,
Vic 3123
Ph 03 9882 3547, Fax 03 9882 0997,
Email portetdo@netconnect.com.au

Owner/chief winemaker: Dominique Portet
Year of foundation: 2000
Tonnes crushed on average each year: 100
Locations: Yarra Valley and Heathcote
Area and soils: no vineyards are yet owned or
planted. All fruit is presently contract grown
Varieties planted: none yet, but they will be,
White—sauvignon blanc; Red—cabernet
sauvignon, shiraz
Leading wine: Portet Winemakers Sauvignon
Blanc
Notes: The name Portet can be traced back at

least ten generations and its involvement with wine lasts as long. Dominique Portet retired from Taltarni in 1998, spent half a year in Provence but did not write a word and returned to Australia late in 1999, his enthusiasm for winemaking undiminished despite a quarter of a century at Taltarni. He is now engaged in establishing Portet Winemakers. As befits a true Bordelais, his specialities will be Sauvignon Blanc, Cabernet Sauvignon and also, recognising his Australian adoption, Shiraz. Already he has made an excellent Sauvignon Blanc. He will build his own winery in the Yarra Valley and continue his profession. There are as yet no cellar door sales.

Seville Estate R90

Linwood Road, Seville, Vic 3139
Ph 03 5964 2622, Fax 03 5964 2633

Owner: Brokenwood Wines Pty Ltd and the partners of Brokenwood Wines
Chief winemaker: Iain Riggs (viticulturalist), Alistair Butt (winemaker)
Year of foundation: 1972
Tonnes crushed on average each year: 25
Location: Seville
Area: 8 ha
Soils: red volcanic kraznozem; grey loams also
Varieties planted: White—chardonnay; Red—cabernet franc, cabernet sauvignon, merlot, pinot noir, shiraz
Leading wines: Seville Estate Chardonnay, Cabernet Sauvignon, Shiraz, Pinot Noir
Notes: Established in 1972 on the rich red loams of Seville as one of the first of the reborn Yarra Valley vineyards by former proprietors Peter and Margaret McMahon, Seville Estate has always been one of the region's leading vineyards. It was purchased from Peter and Margaret in 1997 by Brokenwood Wines and has since developed a fine 'white pepper' Shiraz and also excellent Chardonnay, while continuing to produce very good Cabernet Sauvignon and Pinot Noir. In rating Seville, the author must here declare his interest as a member of Brokenwood and its tasting panel, but there is no doubt because of trophies won during the entirety of its existence that it is a top class vineyard and very much among the Yarra Valley's elite. Cellar door sales: weekends and public holidays 10am–4pm.

Shantell R85

1974 Melba Highway, Dixons Creek, Vic 3775
Ph 03 5965 2155, Fax 03 5965 2331, Email shantell@dragon.net.au

Owners: Shan and Turid Shanmugam
Chief winemakers: Shan and Turid Shanmugam
Year of foundation: 1980
Tonnes crushed on average each year: 50, of which 45 are used for Shantell's own wines
Location: Dixons Creek
Area: 10 ha
Soils: light grey clay loam over yellow clay subsoil
Varieties planted: White—chardonnay, semillon; Red—cabernet sauvignon, pinot noir, shiraz
Leading wines: Shantell Chardonnay, Cabernet Sauvignon
Notes: The wine styles of Shantell are fluent and stylish, typical of the higher levels of Yarra winemaking, and its Cabernet Sauvignon is always worth cellaring. Its Chardonnays also display the typical elegance of the vineyard and are always worthy of attention. Cellar door sales: Thurs–Mon 10am–5pm.

St Huberts R88

St Huberts Road, Coldstream, Vic 3770
Ph 03 9739 1118, Fax 03 9739 1015

Owner: Mildara Blass
Chief winemaker: Matt Steele
Year of foundation: 1966 (originally in a slightly different spot, 1862)

Tonnes crushed on average each year: 300
Location: Coldstream
Area: 21 ha
Soils: grey loams over clay
Varieties planted: White—chardonnay,
roussanne; Red—cabernet sauvignon, merlot,
pinot noir
Leading wines: St Huberts Chardonnay, Pinot
Noir, Reserve Cabernet Sauvignon
Notes: For St Huberts, ownership has been a
roller-coaster ride during the past 35 years. In
the modern era, that is since 1966, it has been
through five sets of proprietors, the longest
ownership being that of the Cester family to
whom it owes its renaissance. Cellar door
sales: weekdays 9am–5pm, weekends and
public holidays 10.30am–5.30pm.

Steels Creek Estate NR

Sewell Road, Steels Creek, Vic 3775
Ph/Fax 03 5965 2448,
Email scemail@steelsckestate.com.au

Owners: Simon and Kerri Peirce
Chief winemaker: Simon Peirce
Year of foundation: 1981
Tonnes produced on average each year: 7
Location: Steels Creek
Area: 1.7 ha
Soils: light grey sandy loam over shallow clay
containing mudstone
Varieties planted: White—colombard,
chardonnay; Red—cabernet franc, cabernet
sauvignon, shiraz
Leading wines: Steels Creek Chardonnay,
Cabernet Sauvignon
Notes: Solid wine show results from the local
show but I have not tasted its wines. Cellar
door sales: weekends and public holidays
10am–6pm.

Tarrahill Vineyard R85

340 Old Healesville Road, Yarra Glen,
Vic 3775
Sales office: 49 Cleveland Ave, Lower
Plenty, Vic 3093
Ph 03 9439 7425, Fax 03 9439 4217

Owner/chief winemaker: Dr Ian Hanson
Year of foundation: 1983
Tonnes crushed on average each year: 12
Location: Two vineyards, Yarra Glen and Lower
Plenty
Area: 4 ha
Soils: brown clay loam over mostly a sandy clay
base; elsewhere the base is gravel
Varieties planted: White—sauvignon blanc;
Red—cabernet franc, cabernet sauvignon,
pinot noir
Leading wines: Hanson Cabernets, Tarra's
Block, Cabernet Sauvignon
Notes: Ian Hanson is a Cabernet enthusiast
and dentist and somehow finds the time to
combine both professions successfully. His
'dusty' Tarra's Block Cabernet Franc is always
carefully made and recent Pinots have been
very good. No cellar door sales. Sales by
mailing list to the above address.

TarraWarra Estate R87

Healesville Road, Yarra Glen, Vic 3775
Ph 03 5962 3311, Fax 03 5962 3887,
Email mmatthews@tarrawarra.com.au

Owner: Tarrawarra Estate Pty Ltd
Chief winemaker: Clare Halloron
Year of foundation: 1983
Tonnes crushed on average each year: 337
(vintage 2000) all used for TarraWarra, Tunnel
Hill and Kidron labels. This should increase as
younger vines mature
Locations: TarraWarra (just over halfway
between Yarra Glen and Healesville), and
Coldstream (vineyard only)
Area: 69.58 ha, TarraWarra Estate (23.88 ha),

Watts Point Vineyards (5 ha), Tarrawarra Grange (40.7 ha)
Soils: light well-drained grey soils over clay; Watts Point, dark clay loam over shale
Varieties planted: White—chardonnay at TarraWarra Estate and Grange, sauvignon blanc at Tarrawarra Grange; Red—cabernet sauvignon, merlot and shiraz at Tarrawarra Grange Vineyard, pinot noir at each vineyard
Leading wines: TarraWarra Pinot Noir, TarraWarra Chardonnay; second label—Tunnel Hill Pinot Noir, Tunnel Hill Chardonnay. Look out also for the Tin Cows Shiraz and Merlot reds from Tarrawarra Grange Vineyard. There is also a kosher wine of good quality, Kidron Chardonnay
Notes: Since its first wines in the mid-1980s, TarraWarra Estate has become one of the established estates of the Yarra Valley and has created an enviable reputation for Chardonnays and Pinots of the highest quality. Its Pinot Noir 1995, for example, won the Pinot Noir/Burgundy Trophy (equivalent to the world's best Pinot) at the International Wine Challenge in London in 1997. Since 1996 it has been in expansive mode, establishing the Tarrawarra Grange Vineyard at Coldstream, as a result of which it now has available under its Tunnel Hill label a Merlot and a Shiraz. This is a maker of excellent Pinot Noir in a region renowned for this variety. Cellar door sales: 7 days 10.30am–4.30pm.

Wantirna Estate R93

Bushy Park Lane, Wantirna South, Vic 3152
Ph 03 9801 2367, Fax 03 9887 0225

Owners: Reg, Bertina and Maryann Egan
Chief winemakers: Reg and Maryann Egan
Year of foundation: 1963
Tonnes crushed on average each year: 17
Location: Wantirna South
Area: 4 ha

Soils: light grey clay topsoil over a 'porridgey' marl subsoil
Varieties planted: White—chardonnay; Red—cabernet franc, cabernet sauvignon, merlot, petit verdot, pinot noir
Leading wines: Wantirna Estate Cabernet Merlot (a blend of the Bordeaux red varieties mentioned above), Pinot Noir, Chardonnay
Notes: Reg Egan is one of the pioneers of modern Yarra Valley viticulture and Wantirna Estate is the expression of Reg's determination to succeed and succeed he certainly has! It is a vineyard of great quality, which produces elite Pinot Noir and Chardonnay amongst the very best of their kinds in the Valley. Unfortunately there are no cellar door sales. Mailing list only.

Warramate Winery R83

27 Maddens Lane, Gruyere, Vic 3770
Ph/Fax 03 5964 9219

Owners: Jack and June Church
Chief winemakers: Jack and David Church
Year of foundation: 1969
Tonnes crushed on average each year: 12, all of which are used for Warramate labels
Location: Gruyere
Area: 2 ha
Soils: grey loam soils over clay and rocks, similar to its neighbours, Coldstream Hills and Yarra Yering
Varieties planted: White—riesling; Red—cabernet franc, cabernet sauvignon, merlot, shiraz
Leading wines: Warramate Cabernet, Shiraz, Riesling
Notes: A family-run estate utilising only its own fruit, Jack Church planted the Warramate vineyard in 1969. It is unirrigated and low-yielding at 6 tonnes to the hectare. Jack is now one of the veterans of the reborn Yarra Valley, planting his vineyard in the pre-chardonnay era. Instead, a typically elegant Yarra Riesling is made and these days his son David, yet another medical man but also a qualified winemaker, is

in the thick of things at vintage. Warramate Shiraz is also excellent. Cellar door sales: weekends and public holidays 10am–6pm, at other times by appointment only.

Wedgetail Estate R84

40 Hildebrand Road, Cottle's Bridge, Vic 3099
Ph/Fax 03 9714 8661,
Email wedge@netspace.net.au

Owners: Dena Ashbolt and Guy Lamothe
Chief winemaker: Guy Lamothe
Year of foundation: 1994
Tonnes produced on average each year: 20, all of which are used for Wedgetail labels
Location: Cottle's Bridge, about a 25 minute drive north west of Yarra Glen
Area: 6 ha
Soils: this is an undulating vineyard of quite steep slopes (up to 30°) with loamy and gravelly loamy topsoil ranging in depth from 15 to 30 cm. The subsoil is yellow clay about 80 cm deep above sandstone. Its pinot grows on a north to east facing slope, its chardonnay on a slope facing south
Varieties planted: White—chardonnay; Red—cabernet sauvignon, merlot, pinot noir, shiraz
Leading wines: Wedgetail Estate Pinot Noir, Chardonnay
Notes: A quite exciting newcomer to the wineries of the Yarra, whose Pinot Noir and Chardonnay are especially worth tasting. No cellar door sales. Tasting by appointment. Sales by mail order.

Yarrabank Vineyards, R90
(see also entry for Yering Station)

42 Melba Highway, Yarra Glen, Vic 3775
Ph 03 9730 2188, Fax 03 9730 2189

Owners: Yering Station and Champagne Devaux
Chief winemakers: Tom Carson, Claude

Thibaut and others from Champagne Devaux (consultants)
Year of foundation: 1993
Tonnes crushed on average each year: na, but production is increasing. 5000 cases will be released from vintage 2000
Locations: Yarra Valley, Upper Yarra Valley, Mornington and Macedon
Soils: see note on Yering Station
Varieties planted: White—chardonnay; Red—pinot noir
Leading wines: Yarrabank Vintage Cuvee, Crème de Cuvee (a demi sec)
Notes: Yarrabank Vineyards is a joint venture between Yering Station and Champagne Devaux, specialising in premium sparkling wines.

Yarra Burn R89

Settlement Road, Yarra Junction, Vic 3797
Ph 03 5967 1428, Fax 03 5967 1146

Owner: BRL Hardy Ltd
Chief winemakers: Steve Pannell (red), Ed Carr (sparkling), Tom Newton (white)
Year of foundation: 1975
Tonnes crushed on average each year: 75
Location: Yarra Junction
Area: 9.5 ha
Soils: grey-brown sandy loam, and grey clay
Varieties planted: White—chardonnay, semillon; Red—cabernet franc, cabernet sauvignon, merlot, pinot noir
Leading wines: Yarra Burn Bastard Hill Pinot Noir (appears in good years), Yarra Burn Cabernet Sauvignon, Yarra Burn Chardonnay
Notes: Yarra Burn was purchased by BRL Hardy in 1995. Prior to that it had been owned by its founders, David and Christine Fyffe. Winemaking standards at all BRL Hardy wineries are high and Yarra Burn is no exception. There are excellent Cabernet Sauvignons here, not to mention Pinots Noirs and Chardonnays. In exceptional years, Bastard

Hill Pinot Noir (from Hoddles Creek) is also released. For the time being until and if BRL Hardy decide on a winery development elsehwere in the Valley, all Hoddles Creek fruit is crushed here. Cellar door sales: 7 days 10am–5pm.

Yarra Edge (vineyard only) **R90**

Edward Road, Lilydale, Vic 3140
Ph/Fax see Yering Station

Owners: Doug and Graham Rathbone
Chief winemaker: Tom Carson
Year of foundation: 1984
Tonnes crushed on average each year: 40
Location: Lilydale
Area: 12.6 ha, 5 ha of which have only recently come into bearing
Soils: grey loam clay over shale base
Varieties planted: White—chardonnay; Red—cabernet franc, cabernet sauvignon, malbec, merlot, pinot noir
Leading wines: Yarra Edge Chardonnay, Cabernet
Notes: Yarra Edge has been recently purchased by the proprietors of Yering Station, where the wines are now made. Yarra Edge has been in the past a consistent medal winner at various Victorian wine shows in particular for its Chardonnay. Cellar door sales are at Yering Station.

The Yarrahill **R86**

886 Maroondah Highway, Coldstream, Vic 3775
Ph 03 5962 2983, Fax 03 5964 9314,
Email mf@yarrahill.com.au

Owners: Rob Dolan and a group of three Yarra Valley growers
Chief winemaker: Rob Dolan
Year of foundation: 1998
Tonnes produced on average each year: 750, of which 300 are used at this stage for Yarrahill's own labels

Location: Coldstream (three vineyards)
Area: 82.5 ha
Soils: grey/red clay loam topsoils to a depth of 30–40 cm above a yellow clay subsoil
Varieties planted: White—chardonnay, sauvignon blanc, semillon; Red—cabernet sauvignon, merlot, pinot noir, shiraz
Leading wines: The Yarrahill Sauvignon Blanc, Chardonnay, Pinot Noir, Shiraz, Merlot, Cabernet Sauvignon
Notes: Rob Dolan formerly of Yarra Ridge and now winemaker at Dominion Wines in the Strathbogie Ranges, has made two vintages and is proud of his specialities, Pinot Noir and Chardonnay. A winery and cellar door facilities were erected earlier this year. Cellar door sales: Maroondah Highway, next to Eyton on Yarra, and also at the winery daily.

Yarra Ridge Vineyard **R84**

Glenview Road, Yarra Glen, Vic 3755
Ph 03 9730 1022, Fax 03 9730 1131

Owner: Mildara-Blass
Chief winemaker: Matt Steele
Tonnes crushed on average each year: 2500, 2300 of which are used for Yarra Ridge labels
Location: Yarra Glen
Area: 102 ha, vineyards owned or leased are, Homestead Block 24 ha, Racecourse 27 ha, Dairy Vineyard 34 ha, Henkell 17 ha
Soils: grey loam over grey clay base, some river flat silt
Varieties planted: White—chardonnay, sauvignon blanc; Red—cabernet sauvignon, merlot, petit verdot, pinot noir, shiraz
Leading wines: Yarra Ridge Chardonnay, Sauvignon Blanc, Pinot Noir, Cabernet Sauvignon, Merlot, Shiraz, Yarra Ridge Reserve Chardonnay, Pinot Noir
Notes: Yarra Ridge is the centre of Mildara Blass' Yarra Valley winemaking and crushes fruit from all over the Yarra Valley. Hence the large tonnage crushed. Cellar door sales: 7 days 10am–5pm.

Yarra Track Wines R85

518 Old Healesville Road, Yarra Glen,
Vic 3775
Ph/Fax 03 9730 1349,
Email yarratrack@telstraeasymail.com.au

Owners: Yarra Track Winery Pty Ltd (Jim and
Diana Viggers)
Chief winemaker: Martin Williams (contract)
Year of foundation: 1989
Tonnes produced on average each year: 60, of
which 10 are used for Yarra Track's own labels
Location: Yarra Glen
Area: 6.5 ha
Soils: loose to medium density slightly clayey
silty sand over stiffer grey and brown silty clay
over extremely weathered mudstone. Slightly
acid
Varieties planted: White—chardonnay;
Red—pinot noir
Leading wines: Yarra Track Chardonnay,
Pinot Noir
Notes: A vineyard of much promise specialising
in two of the Yarra's major varieties, which are
made extremely well. Cellar door sales:
weekends and public holidays 10am–5pm or
by mail order. Gourmet platters are available.

Yarra Vale R84

Paynes Road, Seville, Vic 3139
Ph/Fax 03 9735 1819

Owner: Morwood Grange Pty Ltd
Chief winemaker: Domenic Bucci
Year of foundation: 1991
Tonnes crushed on average each year: 25
Location: Seville
Area: 6 ha
Soils: red loam
Varieties planted: White—none; Red—cabernet
sauvignon, merlot
Leading wines: Yarra Vale Cabernet Sauvignon,
Merlot
Notes: No cellar door sales. The wines are mostly
sold through restaurants and wine retailers.

Yarra Valley Hills R81

Lot 1 Delaneys Road, Warranwood,
Vic 3134
Ph 03 5962 4173, Fax 03 5962 4059

Owners: Dromana Estate and Wine Investment
Fund Ltd
Chief winemaker: Garry Crittenden
Year of foundation: 1989
Tonnes crushed on average each year: 150, all
of which, together with a further 50 tonnes
purchased, are used for Yarra Valley Hills labels
Locations: Warranwood, Gruyere and
Healesville (vineyard)
Area: 18 ha
Soils: grey loams over clay
Varieties planted: White—chardonnay, riesling,
sauvignon blanc; Red—cabernet franc,
cabernet sauvignon, malbec, merlot, pinot noir
Leading wines: Yarra Valley Hills Pinot Noir,
Cabernet Sauvignon, Chardonnay, Sauvignon
Blanc
Notes: Ownership has changed hands recently
and winemaking has moved to Dromana
Estate. Knowing the purchasers as I do, there
will certainly be no diminution of quality and
Yarra Valley wines of the highest standard will
continue to be made. No cellar door sales.

Yarra Yarra Vineyard R88

239 Hunts Lane, Steels Creek, Vic 3775
Ph/Fax 03 5965 2380, 5965 2086

Owners: Ian and Anne Maclean
Chief winemaker: Ian Maclean
Year of foundation: 1979
Tonnes crushed on average each year: 25, all
used for Yarra Yarra's own labels
Location: Steels Creek
Area: 7 ha
Soils: grey loam over shaley clayey subsoil
Varieties planted: White—sauvignon blanc,
semillon viognier; Red—cabernet franc,
cabernet sauvignon, merlot, shiraz
Leading wines: Yarra Yarra Vineyard Cabernets,

Reserve Cabernet Sauvignon, Sauvignon Semillon
Notes: There is a long continuity of winemaking at Yarra Yarra Vineyard and, except for shiraz and viognier, a total devotion to Bordeaux varieties for Ian Maclean, who is a Bordeaux enthusiast and has spent two vintages at Domaine de Chevalier in Graves. Tasting by appointment only, weekends and public holidays. Sales by mail order.

Yarra Yering R93

Briarty Road, Gruyere, Vic 3770
Ph 03 5964 9267, Fax 03 5964 9239

Owner/chief winemaker: Dr Bailey Carrodus
Year of foundation: 1969
Tonnes crushed on average each year: 90, rising to 130 as newly planted vines come into bearing
Location: Gruyere
Area: 32.03 ha
Soils: grey silty clay loams over deep clay
Varieties planted: White—chardonnay, marsanne, viognier; Red—alvarelhao, bastardo, cabernet sauvignon, malbec, merlot, nebbiolo, pinot noir, roriz, sangiovese, shiraz, souzao, tinta amarello, tinta cao, touriga
Leading wines: Yarra Yering No 1 Dry Red (Cabernet Malbec Merlot), No 2 Dry Red (Shiraz Marsanne Viognier), Pinot Noir, Merlot, Chardonnay, Underhill Shiraz, Portsorts (a blend of the port varieties mentioned above)
Notes: What can one say about Dr Bailey Carrodus? He has certainly been a pioneer of modern Yarra winemaking and viticulture and often controversial in his winemaking methods. And Yarra Yering? A whole catalogue of grape varieties is grown but it has never been a mish-mash, only order and superb quality. The No 1 Dry Red (the Bordeaux blend) is never less than excellent, nor is the Pinot Noir. And the Underhill Shiraz is a benchmark for cool-area winemakers everywhere. Cellar door sales:

first weekend in May only, Sat 10am–5pm, Sun noon–5pm.

Yeringberg R96

Maroondah Highway, Coldstream, Vic 3770
Ph 03 9739 1453, Fax 03 9739 0048

Owner: Yeringberg Pty Ltd
Chief winemaker: Guill de Pury
Year of foundation: 1863 to 1921, ceasing at that time for economic reasons, and 1969
Tonnes crushed on average each year: 16
Location: Coldstream
Area: 2 ha
Soils: grey loams on heavy grey clay subsoil with interspersed 'buckshot' gravel
Varieties planted: White—chardonnay, marsanne, roussanne; Red—cabernet franc, cabernet sauvignon, malbec, merlot, pinot noir
Leading wines: Yeringberg Chardonnay, Yeringberg (a white blend of marsanne and roussanne), Yeringberg Pinot Noir, Yeringberg (a red blend of the 'Bordeaux' varieties, cabernet sauvignon, cabernet franc, malbec and merlot)
Notes: Yeringberg has belonged to the de Pury family for over 130 years and, as a vineyard, is tiny. Yet Guill de Pury's leading wines lead in every sense of the word—elegance, balance, style, length of palate, regional typicity and ageing potential. Only one word can aptly describe Yeringberg and that is 'Superb!'. Cellar door sales: usually only one weekend in May (which should be ascertained by telephone inquiry). Otherwise strictly by appointment.

Yering Farm R91

St Huberts Road, Yering, Vic 3770
Ph 03 9735 4161, Fax 03 9735 4012, Email yeringfarm@xcel.net.au

Owners: Alan and Louise Johns
Chief winemaker: Alan Johns

Year of foundation: 1989
Tonnes produced on average each year: 100,
about 55 tonnes of which are used for Yering
Farm wines
Location: Yering on St Huberts Road near the
Melba Highway
Area: 12 ha
Soils: grey loam over a clay base
Varieties planted: White—chardonnay,
sauvignon blanc; Red—cabernet sauvignon,
merlot, pinot noir, shiraz
Leading wines: Yering Farm Cabernet,
Chardonnay
Notes: Yering Farm made its first wines in
1992 and ever since has had a consistently
successful wine show record in Victorian and
other wine shows. It is quite a new name to
me, but even on slight acquaintance, it is one
of excellence. An exciting winery not to be
missed. Cellar door sales and tasting:
weekends and public holidays 10am–4pm,
weekdays by appointment only.

Yering Station   **R90**

38 Melba Highway, Yerring, Vic 3770
Ph 03 9730 1107, Fax 03 9739 0135,
Email yarrabank@bigpond.com

Owners: Rathbone family
Chief winemaker: Tom Carson
Year of foundation: originally established 1838
by William Ryrie as the first Yarra vineyard,
then owned from 1849 onwards by Paul de
Castella, under whom it reached the zenith of
its nineteenth-century fame. After ceasing to
be a vineyard in the early years of the

twentieth century, it was re-established in
1988 by the Dominguez family, who
subsequently resold in 1996 to the present
proprietors.
Tonnes crushed on average each year: 600, all
of which is used for Yering Station labels
Location: Yering towards Yarra Glen on the
Melba Highway
Area: 55 ha
Soils: grey loams over aging mudstones
Varieties planted: White—chardonnay, furmint,
sauvignon blanc, marsanne, viognier;
Red—cabernet franc, cabernet sauvignon,
malbec, merlot, nebbiolo, petit verdot,
pinot noir, sangiovese, shiraz
Leading wines: There are two wine ranges,
Yering Station and Barak's Bridge. The Yering
Station range is varietal. The Barak's Bridge
range is also varietal but may include wine
from regions other than the Yarra Valley as
well as a Yarra Valley component
Notes: No expense has been spared since the
present proprietors assumed ownership in
1996. Fifty hectares of vineyard have been
planted and a brand new winery erected for
1997 vintage. The vines planted in 1996–97,
have mostly come into bearing and with the
older planting of 8 hectares are already making
exciting wines. The Chardonnay and Pinot Noir
are exemplary here. Cellar door sales:
weekdays 10am–5pm, weekends and public
holidays 10am–6pm. There is also a
restaurant/wine bar at which the Yering
Station table wines and the Yarrabank
Sparklings may be matched with food.

MORNINGTON PENINSULA REGION

It could be argued that the Mornington Peninsula is yet another born-again Victorian
viticultural area. In 1891, about 8 hectares of vineyard were listed in a Victorian government report on fruit and vegetables as existing in the region around Somerville, but
they were not noteworthy and, as in the Yarra Valley, died out for economic reasons in
the 1920s. Its next flirtation with the vine occurred in the early 1950s, when the late

MORNINGTON PENINSULA REGION

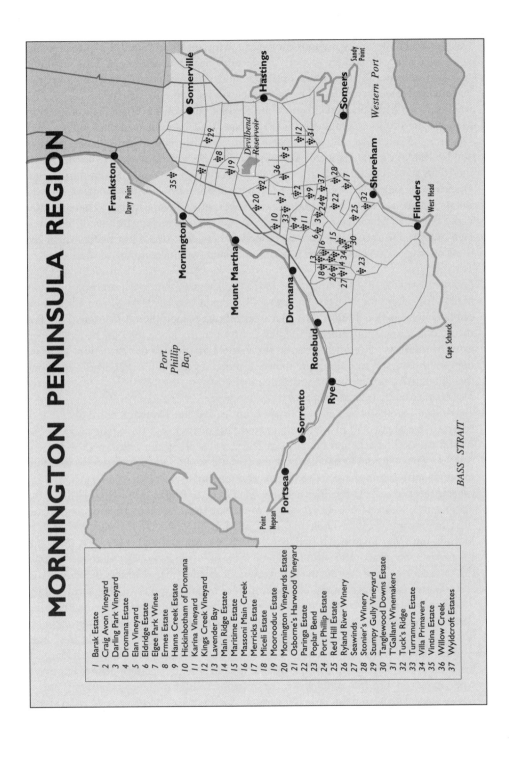

1. Barak Estate
2. Craig Avon Vineyard
3. Darling Park Vineyard
4. Dromana Estate
5. Elan Vineyard
6. Eldridge Estate
7. Elgee Park Wines
8. Ermes Estate
9. Hanns Creek Estate
10. Hickinbotham of Dromana
11. Karina Vineyard
12. Kings Creek Vineyard
13. Lavender Bay
14. Main Ridge Estate
15. Maritime Estate
16. Massoni Main Creek
17. Merricks Estate
18. Miceli Estate
19. Moorooduc Estate
20. Mornington Vineyards Estate
21. Osborne's Harwood Vineyard
22. Paringa Estate
23. Poplar Bend
24. Port Phillip Estate
25. Red Hill Estate
26. Ryland River Winery
27. Seawinds
28. Stonier's Winery
29. Stumpy Gully Vineyard
30. Tanglewood Downs Estate
31. T'Gallant Winemakers
32. Tuck's Ridge
33. Turramurra Estate
34. Villa Primavera
35. Vintina Estate
36. Willow Creek
37. Wyldcroft Estates

Douglas Seabrook (of the famous Melbourne wine merchant family) planted riesling vines on a relative's holiday property at Arthur's Seat near Dromana. This small and very private vineyard flourished until the mid-1960s when it was burnt out in a bushfire and never replanted. The Mornington vine came to stay in the early 1970s when Baillieu Myer planted cabernet and riesling vines on his Elgee Park property at Merricks North. Shortly afterwards (1975), Nat White commenced planting his small property at Main Ridge, the Keffords began to establish their Merricks Estate in 1976 and by 1980 the permanence of Mornington Peninsula wine seemed assured. During the 1980s and 1990s, an explosion of viticultural enthusiasm on the peninsula saw new vineyards springing up everywhere. Though varietal and stylistic comparisons with Burgundy are inevitable, Mornington Peninsula is now growing rapidly. There are now many bigger vineyards and, as elsewhere in Australia, conglomerations of 'businessmen' involved in broad-acre vineyard establishment. But this is not necessarily a bad thing as long as our wine quality is maintained and exports continue to increase.

Location: latitude 38°20'S, longitude 144°58'E, about 60 km south and south-east of Melbourne, along the Nepean Highway. The region extends from Mount Eliza south of Frankston on Port Phillip Bay, south-easterly to Somerville on Western Port Bay then along the western shore of the bay south until the bay joins Bass Strait. It then extends south-westerly and westerly along the Bass Strait coast to Point Nepean, then south-east and east along the southern shore of Port Phillip and north-east along that shore to Mount Eliza (the starting point).

Elevation: virtually from sea-level to 250 m

Topography and soils: The peninsula rises from sea-level at Dromana quite steeply to a central ridge about 250 m high in the Red Hill district and then falls away to the coastal strip at Merricks and Balnarring. The most usual soil is a yellow podsol, but soil types do vary—around Dromana there are skeletal acidic soils, while around Red Hill in the region's centre there are red loams (kraznozems).

Climate: MJT 18.8°C (Mornington) (averaged over 20 years), 20°C (Red Hill South) (1995 only), MAR 11.4°C (1995 only), HDD vary from 1050 to 1600 depending on site (for example, 1240 at Dromana, 1431 at Mornington), AR 736 mm, RH 55% at Mornington. Mornington MJT 18.8°C, MAR na, HDD (raw) 1427, AR 736 mm (Oct–Apr 386 mm), RH 48%, AI na, SH 6.7 (Gladstones). Moderately cool (Moorooduc) to cool (Dromana) to very cool (Red Hill), ripening depending on altitude and exposure to wind chill. Similar in certain aspects to the Yarra Valley, though of course the Mornington Peninsula is more maritime, with the neighbouring Bass Strait providing bleak, wet and windy weather. This may seriously interfere with flowering and also with ripening, but has the advantage of being virtually frost-free. Annual rainfall varies from 730–950 mm, increasing with altitude. Supplementary irrigation is often necessary during the summer and autumn ripening period. Excessive vine vigour can also be a problem on the volcanic soil (kraznozem) country.

Harvest time: late March for early red varieties such as pinot noir to late May for shiraz and cabernet sauvignon

Principal varieties: Red—pinot noir, cabernet sauvignon, merlot, cabernet franc, shiraz, meunier; White—chardonnay, sauvignon blanc, pinot gris, riesling, gewurztraminer.

Major wine styles: Undoubtedly Pinot Noir and Chardonnay are the major successes of the Mornington Peninsula, both as table wines and as sparkling wine when made by the classic method. Shiraz too is proving its worth in selected warmer sites. Cabernet Sauvignon, however, seems to be limited to the lower and warmer north-eastern areas of the peninsula and sometimes when grown on more vigorous soils shows distinctly 'green' methoxypyrazine characters. Gamay Noir a jus blanc is also making a welcome appearance and fresh fruity Beaujolais-like reds may be a pleasing result in a few years. Among other wines, Pinot Gris shows great promise as an unwooded fresh fruit-driven style.
Leading wineries: Main Ridge Estate, Stoniers Winery, T'Gallant Winemakers, Dromana Estate, Paringa Estate, Miceli, Port Phillip Estate, Lavender Bay, Willow Creek Vineyard, Elgee Park, Merricks Estate, Moorooduc Estate.

Barak Estate NR

Barak Road, Moorooduc, Vic 3933
Ph/Fax 03 5978 8439

Owner/chief winemaker: James Williamson
Year of foundation: 1989
Tonnes crushed on average each year: 8, all of which are used in Barak Estate wines
Location: Moorooduc
Area: 2.5 ha
Soils: grey loam over shale over clay
Varieties planted: White—chardonnay; Red—cabernet sauvignon, shiraz
Leading wines: Barak Estate Chardonnay, Cabernet, Shiraz
Notes: A small family vineyard with a rustic winery, hand-built by owner/maker James Williamson. Accommodation is also available. Cellar door sales: weekends and public holidays or by appointment.

Craig Avon Vineyard R85

Craig Avon Lane, Merricks North, Vic 3926
Ph 03 5989 7465, Fax 03 5989 7615

Owner/chief winemaker: Ken Lang
Year of foundation: 1986
Tonnes crushed on average each year: 18, all of which are used for Craig Avon wines
Location: Merricks North
Area: 3 ha

Soils: quite deep red clay/loam, tertiary basalt
Varieties planted: White—chardonnay; Red—cabernet franc, cabernet sauvignon, merlot, pinot noir
Leading wines: Chardonnay, Cabernet
Notes: This is one of the best sites on the peninsula, protected from the south and the west. It is obviously a good site for the Bordeaux varieties, which result in a very supple red. Chardonnay is also very good. Cellar door sales: noon–5pm weekends and public holidays.

Darling Park Vineyard NR

Red Hill Road, Red Hill, Vic 3937
Ph (winery) 03 5989 2324,
(H) 03 5989 2732, Fax 03 5989 2254

Owners: John and Delys Sargeant
Chief winemakers: John Sargeant (reds), consultant (whites)
Year of foundation: 1986
Tonnes crushed on average each year: 20, all used for Darling Park wines
Location: Red Hill
Area: 3 ha
Soils: there are two vineyards, the cellar door block of red volcanic loam (1.6 ha) and the Home block of grey dusty loam over broken mudstone (1.4 ha). The latter is described more colourfully by Delys Sergeant as 'pulverised dinosaur bones over split rock'

Varieties planted: White—chardonnay, pinot gris; Red—pinot noir, cabernet franc, cabernet sauvignon, merlot, tempranillo
Leading wines: Darling Park Querida (a rosé style made from the Bordeaux varietals mentioned above), Pinot Gris, Pinot Noir, Cabernet Merlot, Chardonnay
Notes: At Darling Park, there is an unusual rosé style Querida. There is also a popular restaurant open for lunch. Cellar door sales and restaurant open weekends and public holidays.

Dromana Estate **R90**

Harrisons Road, Dromana, Vic 3936
Ph 03 5987 3800, Fax 03 5981 0714,
Email devyd@onaustralia.com.au

Owner: Dromana Estate Ltd
Chief winemakers: Garry Crittenden and Judy Gifford-Watson
Year of foundation: 1982
Tonnes crushed on average each year: 360, all of which are used for Dromana Estate labels
Location: Dromana
Area: 85 ha, consisting of two vineyards, the Dromana home block (5 ha) and Tuerong Park (80 ha)
Soils: Dromana, sandy loam over a clay base. Tuerong Park, sandy loam over well-drained clay
Varieties planted: (Dromana) White—arneis, chardonnay, sauvignon blanc; Red—cabernet sauvignon, merlot, pinot noir, shiraz. (King Valley) White—none; Red—barbera, dolcetto, marzemino, nebbiolo, sangiovese. (Tuerong Park) White—arneis, chardonnay, pinot gris, sauvignon blanc, viognier; Red—cabernet sauvignon, merlot, pinot noir, shiraz
Leading wines: Dromana Estate Reserve Chardonnay, Pinot Noir
Notes: In the first edition I forecast, quite accurately as it has turned out, that Garry Crittenden was 'a tremendously energetic force'. In the very short time since, much more

has happened. Not only does he continue to make three ranges of very good wine, Dromana Estate, Schinus and the Italian varietal range 'I', but he has arranged a merger with Mornington Vineyards Estate, has entered a 30-year lease of property at Tuerong Park to create a 80 ha vineyard and a new 1000 tonne winery, has purchased Yarra Valley Hills and has organised a successful listing on the Australian Stock Exchange. The result of all this will be that Dromana Estate will become a 'Group' and easily the largest vigneron on the Mornington Peninsula. And the wines emerging? Excellent, of course. Cellar door sales: daily 11am–4pm.

Elan Vineyard & Winery **R75**

17 Turners Road, Bittern, Vic 3918
Ph 03 5983 1858, Fax 03 5983 2321,
Email elanvin@mpgdp.org.au

Owners: Selma and Jonathan Lowther
Chief winemaker: Selma Lowther
Year of foundation: 1990
Tonnes crushed on average each year: 8, all of which are used for Elan Estate wines
Location: Bittern
Area: 2.4 ha
Soils: grey sandy loam over clay subsoil
Varieties planted: White—chardonnay, riesling; Red—cabernet sauvignon, gamay, merlot, shiraz
Leading wine: Elan Cabernet Merlot
Notes: This is a typically small Mornington Peninsula vineyard with a selection of estate-made wines. Cellar door sales: first weekend of the month, public holidays or by appointment.

Eldridge Estate *(formerly Peninsula Estate)* **R85**

120 Arthurs Seat Road, Red Hill, Vic 3937
Ph 03 5989 2644, Fax 03 5989 2089,
Email david@eldridgeestate.com.au

Owners: Wendy and David Lloyd
Chief winemaker: David Lloyd
Year of foundation: 1995
Tonnes crushed on average each year: 10
Location: Red Hill
Area: 2.8 ha
Soils: old red volcanic clay
Varieties planted: White—chardonnay,
sauvignon blanc, semillon; Red—gamay noir a
jus blanc, merlot, pinot noir
Leading wines: Eldridge Estate Chardonnay,
Pinot Noir, Gamay
Notes: Eldridge Estate is one of the few
Australian vineyards to plant gamay in what
appears to be climatically suitable country
and the results for Eldridge have been most
gratifying. A true lighter red style should find
an enthusiastic market in Australia provided
it is not a Rosé, not priced for a millionaire's
pocket only (as are some Pinots) and is not
extractive on the one hand, or sweet and
insipid on the other (as are most 'lighter'
Australian reds). Gamay as made in Beaujolais
is a glorious, easy-drinking, fruit-driven red
with good structure and Australian climates
in cooler areas with suitable soils should be
ideal, good enough in fact to send shivers
up the spines of the southern Burgundians.
Those other Burgundians, Pinot Noir and
Chardonnay, are also equally at home at
Eldridge, regularly winning gold and silver
medals at local shows. All of which proves
that many self-taught winemakers of
experience, and David Lloyd is one, do not
need honours degrees in winemaking to
produce delightful reds and whites, as
Eldridge does. Cellar door sales: weekends
and school holidays 11am–5pm. Open every
day from Jan 2002.

Elgee Park Wines **R86**

Junction Road, Merricks North, Vic 3926
Ph/Fax 03 5989 7338,
Email elgee@pac.com.au

Owner: Baillieu Myer family
Chief winemakers: Tod Dexter (contract)
Chardonnay, Cabernet-Merlot, Pinot Noir,
Riesling; Kevin McCarthy (contract) Pinot Gris,
Viognier
Year of foundation: 1972
Tonnes crushed on average each year: 30, all
of which are used for Elgee Park wines
Location: Merricks North
Area: 4.5 ha
Soils: grey loam clay subsoil
Varieties planted: White—chardonnay, pinot
gris, riesling, viognier; Red—cabernet franc,
cabernet sauvignon, merlot, pinot noir
Leading wines: Elgee Park Chardonnay, Pinot
Noir, Viognier, Cuvee Brut
Notes: This was arguably the first vineyard and
winery on the Mornington Peninsula in its
twentieth-century renaissance. The winery no
longer operates, most wines being made under
contract by Tod Dexter who, as one would
expect, makes excellent Elgee Park Chardonnay.
Cellar door sales: once-a-year event, the Sunday
of the Queen's Birthday weekend. At any other
times tasting is strictly by appointment.

Ermes Estate **NR**

2 Godings Road, Moorooduc, Vic 3933
Ph 03 5978 8376, Fax 03 5978 8396

Owners: Ermes and Denise Zucchet
Chief winemaker: Ermes Zucchet
Year of foundation: 1989
Tonnes crushed on average each year: 15, all
of which are used in Ermes Estate wines
Location: Moorooduc
Area: 2.5 ha
Soils: light sandy clay loam
Varieties planted: White—chardonnay,
malvasia, pinot gris, riesling; Red—cabernet
sauvignon, merlot
Leading wine: Ermes Estate Cabernet
Sauvignon
Notes: A consistent bronze medallist at local
wine shows, Ermes Estate is run

enthusiastically as a family vineyard by Ermes and Denise Zucchet. With its northerly aspect and its location in one of the warmer parts of the peninsula, it ripens cabernet sauvignon quite satisfactorily. A light Italian lunch is served on the third Sunday of each month. Cellar door sales: weekends and public holidays, 11am–5pm.

Hanns Creek Estate NR

Kentucky Road, Merricks North, Vic 3926
Ph 03 5989 7266, Fax 03 5989 7500

Owner/chief winemaker: Tony
Aubrey-Slocock
Year of foundation: 1987
Tonnes crushed on average each year: 30, all of which are used for Hanns Creek wines
Location: Merricks North
Area: 5.3 ha
Soils: red clay
Varieties planted: White—chardonnay; Red—cabernet sauvignon, pinot noir, shiraz
Leading wines: Hanns Creek Estate Chardonnay, Cabernet Sauvignon, 'Chanticleer', a still base wine made from pinot noir and chardonnay grapes
Notes: Hanns Creek Estate is a small Mornington Peninsula winery. There is also a bookings only restaurant open for lunch each weekend whose French style cuisine is much appreciated. Cellar door sales: 11am–5pm each day.

Harwood Vineyard
(see Osborn's Vineyard entry)

Hickinbotham of Dromana R72

Nepean Highway near Wallaces Road, Dromana, Vic 3936
Ph/Fax 03 5981 0355

Owners: Terryn and Andrew Hickinbotham
Chief winemaker: Andrew Hickinbotham
Year of foundation: 1988

Tonnes crushed on average each year: 85, about half of which are used for Hickinbotham labels
Location: Dromana
Area: 6 ha
Soils: a range of soils from sandy loam to heavier red loams
Varieties planted: White—aligote, chardonnay, taminga; Red—cabernet franc, cabernet sauvignon, merlot, pinot noir, shiraz
Leading wines: Hickinbotham of Dromana Chardonnay, Pinot, Merlot, Shiraz
Notes: Andrew Hickinbotham is the third generation of the wine-involved Hickinbotham family. His grandfather, Alan, was the mainspring in the introduction of the oenology course at Roseworthy in the 1930s. His father, Ian, is still very much engaged in wine-writing and education after many years of winemaking in Coonawarra, the Barossa Valley and Geelong. In the past decade at Dromana, the Hickinbothams have built up a strong reputation for pinot noir. Cellar door sales: 11am–6pm weekends, public holidays 11am–5pm, daily during January 11am–5pm.

Karina Vineyard NR

Harrison's Road, Dromana, Vic 3936
Ph/Fax 03 5981 0137

Owners: Gerard and Joy Terpstra
Chief winemaker: Gerard Terpstra
Year of foundation: 1984
Tonnes crushed on average each year: 25, all of which are used for Karina Vineyard labels
Location: Dromana
Area: 3.5 ha
Soils: grey sandy loam over a clay subsoil
Varieties planted: White—chardonnay, riesling, sauvignon blanc; Red—cabernet sauvignon, merlot, pinot noir
Leading wines: Karina Vineyard Chardonnay, Cabernet-Merlot
Notes: A vineyard with mature vines whose recent wine showings have produced bronze

awards at local shows. Cellar door sales: weekends and public holidays 11am–5pm; daily during January, same hours.

Kings Creek Winery   R85

237 Myers Road, Bittern, Vic 3918
Ph 03 5983 2102, Fax 03 5983 5153

Owner: Kings Creek Winery Pty Ltd
Chief winemakers: Brien Cole and Ian Wood
Year of foundation: 1981
Tonnes crushed on average each year: 80 and increasing, all of which are used for Kings Creek labels
Location: Bittern
Area: 96 ha (four vineyards, all locally situated)
Soils: sandy topsoil over a clay base
Varieties planted: White—chardonnay, pinot gris, sauvignon blanc; Red—cabernet franc, cabernet sauvignon, merlot, pinot noir, sangiovese, shiraz
Leading wines: Kings Creek Reserve Chardonnay, Pinot Noir
Notes: Kings Creek Winery is expanding and seems destined to become much more widely known. With a production potential of 1000 tonnes, this seems inevitable. The hope is, of course, that it will remain at its present high standard and there is no reason whatever to suppose that it will not, as long as it produces Chardonnay and Pinot Noir of its present excellent quality. Cellar door sales: daily 11am–5pm.

Kooyong Vineyard and Winery   R88

110 Hunts Road, Tuerong, Vic 3918
Ph 03 5989 7355, Fax 03 5989 7677

Owners: Chris and Gail Aylward
Chief winemaker: Sandro Mosele
Year of foundation: 1996 (vineyard), 2001 (winery)
Tonnes crushed on average each year: 180, of which 100 are currently used for Kooyong wines

Location: Tuerong
Area: 33 ha
Soils: sandy clay loam over yellow clay
Varieties planted: White—chardonnay; Red—pinot noir
Leading wines: Kooyong Chardonnay, Pinot Noir
Notes: It is accepted practice now that in order to achieve greater intensity of flavour, yields of pinot noir must not exceed 5 tonnes to the hectare. Kooyong strictly adheres to this practice and to many others including 'pigeage' to ensure that traditional Pinot of excellent quality is produced. The Mornington Peninsula region overall produces excellent Pinot Noir and Kooyong, an exciting newcomer, is among the best. There is also a top-class Chardonnay. Unfortunately, there are no cellar door sales and visits are strictly by appointment only.

Lavender Bay Vineyard   R87

39 Paringa Road, Red Hill South, Vic 3937
Ph 03 9553 8816, Fax 03 9553 8817

Owners: Kevin and Barbara Luscombe
Chief winemaker: Gary Crittenden (contract)
Year of foundation: 1988
Tonnes crushed on average each year: 7, all of which are used for Lavender Bay wines
Location: Red Hill South
Area: 2 ha
Soils: deep red volcanic loam
Varieties planted: White—chardonnay; Red—pinot noir
Leading wines: Lavender Bay Chardonnay, Pinot Noir
Notes: There are unfortunately no cellar door sales, as all wine is sold through distributors and local restaurants. If ever you have an opportunity to taste Lavender Bay Chardonnay or Pinot Noir, do not pass it up as wine quality is superb.

Main Ridge Estate R93

William Road, Red Hill, Vic 3937
Ph 03 5989 2686, Fax 03 5931 0000,
Email mainridge@satlink.com.au

Owners: Nat and Rosalie White
Chief winemaker: Nat White
Year of foundation: 1975
Tonnes crushed on average each year: 12,
all of which are used for Main Ridge wines
Location: Red Hill
Area: 3 ha
Soils: deep red volcanic loam
Varieties planted: White—chardonnay;
Red—meunier, pinot noir
Leading wines: Main Ridge Chardonnay,
Half Acre Pinot Noir
Notes: In cricket parlance, Nat White is the
perfect all-rounder, equally skilful in vineyard
and winery. If he were Burgundian, he would
surely be one of the senior proprietaire-
recoltants of his village, revered by his juniors
and much sought-after as a guru of the vine.
But he is Australian, has had more than
25 years experience in viticulture and winemaking in what was, prior to his arrival,
seriously unknown country, has resisted the
temptation of economies of scale and remains
lord of a small domain. In so doing he has
mastered the arts of Chardonnay and Pinot Noir
and created an unmatched degree of elegance
and style. At least that is what his wines tell
me! Cellar door sales: weekdays noon–4pm,
weekends noon–5pm. Lunch served on
Sundays.

Maritime Estate   R85

Tuck's Road, Red Hill, Vic 3937
Ph 03 5989 2735, Fax 03 9882 8325

Owners: John and Kevin Ruljancich
Chief winemaker: (contract)
Year of foundation: 1988
Tonnes crushed on average each year: 15, all
of which is used for Maritime Estate labels

Location: Red Hill
Area: 4.7 ha
Soils: red volcanic loam on basalt
Varieties planted: White—chardonnay (1.6 ha),
pinot gris (0.8 ha); Red—pinot noir (2.2 ha).
Leading wines: Maritime Estate Chardonnay,
Pinot Noir
Notes: In the first edition I reported briefly on
the excellence of the Maritime Estate
Chardonnays and Pinots, two varieties totally
suited to vineyard and region. That standard
continues. Cellar door sales: daily 11am–5pm
from 27 December to 26 January. At other
times 11am–5pm every weekend and public
holiday.

Massoni Main Creek   R82

Main Creek Vineyard, 1058 Mornington-
Flinders Road, Red Hill, Vic 3937
Winery (not open to the public) Brasser,
Ave, Dromana, 3936
Ph 03 5989 2352, Fax 03 5989 2014

Owner: Ian Home
Chief winemakers: Ian Home and Samuel
Tyrrell
Year of foundation: 1984
Tonnes crushed on average each year: 8, from
Red Hill vineyard. About 125 tonnes from
sources are required for labels other than
Massoni Main Creek Chardonnay
Location: Red Hill
Area: 2 ha (Main Creek Vineyard)
Soils: brown clay loam
Varieties planted: White—chardonnay;
Red—none
Leading wines: Massoni Main Creek
Chardonnay, Pinot Noir
Notes: Ian and Sue Home are expanding their
wine production, but lovers of the bigger style
Chardonnay and Pinot Noir of Massoni Main
Creek need not be too concerned. Those robust
wines will continue. Added to the range which
was confined previously to Massoni Main Creek
Chardonnay, Massoni Main Creek Pinot Noir

and Lectus (a sparkler) are the Homes wines, Chardonnay, Pinot Noir (each from purchased Mornington Peninsula fruit) and a Cabernet Merlot (presently from Langhorne Creek). Cellar door sales: Queen's Birthday weekend (three days), at other times by appointment.

Merricks Estate R86

Thompsons Lane, Merricks, Vic 3916
Ph 03 5989 8416, 03 9612 7285,
Fax 03 9629 4035

Owners: George and Jacqui Kefford
Chief winemakers: Mike Zitzlaff and Paul Evans (contract)
Year of foundation: 1977
Tonnes crushed on average each year: 25, all of which are used for Merricks Estate wines
Location: Merricks
Area: 3 ha
Soils: brown clay loam over red clay with some 'buckshot'
Varieties planted: White—chardonnay; Red—cabernet sauvignon, pinot noir, shiraz
Leading wines: Merricks Estate Shiraz, Pinot Noir and Chardonnay
Notes: Merricks Estate is now one of the senior Mornington vineyards, producing a well respected and award winning Shiraz. It has won recent trophies for Chardonnay and Pinot Noir also. Cellar door sales: first weekend of each month noon–5pm, public holiday weekends, 26–31 December and every weekend in January.

Miceli Winery R88

Main Creek Road, Main Ridge, Vic 3928
Ph 03 5979 2930, Fax 03 5989 2755,
Email miceli@alphalink.com.au

Owners: Anthony and Pauline Miceli
Chief winemaker: Anthony Miceli
Year of foundation: 1991
Tonnes crushed on average each year: 24, all of which are used for Miceli wines
Location: Main Ridge
Area: 3 ha
Soils: deep red basalt soil
Varieties planted: White—chardonnay, pinot gris; Red—pinot noir
Leading wines: Miceli Chardonnay, Pinot Noir, Pinot Grigio
Notes: I wrote in the first edition that Miceli is a small family winery in the heart of the Mornington Peninsula. So it is, and also very upbeat, having had considerable show success with all three of its very stylish wines. This is a winery not to be missed. Cellar door sales: noon–5pm first weekend of each month, all weekends in January and all public holiday weekends.

Moorooduc Estate R86

501 Derril Road, Moorooduc, Vic 3933
Ph 03 5971 8506, Ph/Fax 03 5971 8550,
Email moorooduc@ozemail.com.au

Owners: Richard and Jill McIntyre
Chief winemaker: Richard McIntyre
Year of foundation: 1983
Tonnes crushed on average each year: 48, all of which are used for Moorooduc Estate wines
Location: Moorooduc
Area: 5 ha
Soils: duplex light sandy loam on a yellow clay subsoil
Varieties planted: White—chardonnay, sauvignon blanc, semillon; Red—cabernet franc, cabernet sauvignon, merlot, pinot noir, shiraz
Leading wines: Moorooduc Estate Wild Yeast Chardonnay and Wild Yeast Pinot Noir, Shiraz, Pinot Noir, Chardonnay, Cabernet, Semillon-Sauvignon Blanc (all conventionally fermented)
Notes: Richard McIntyre is one of the legion of Australian medical men to whom wine is a passionate pursuit. Wine developments here include fermentation on wild yeasts for Chardonnay and Pinot Noir in the Burgundian manner and also a fruit-driven Shiraz (so different from the extractive styles of warmer

climes). The other wines, Chardonnay, Pinot Noir and Cabernet are as usual of the fuller bodied style as befits the slightly warmer microclimate of Moorooduc. There are changes also at cellar door, which is now open every weekend throughout the year 11am–5pm. In addition there is a restaurant open for Friday dinner, Saturday lunch and dinner, and Sunday lunch. Accommodation is also available.

Mornington Vineyards Estate R85

Moorooduc Road, Moorooduc South, Vic 3933
Ph/Fax 03 5974 2097,
Email devyd@onaustralia.com.au

Owners: Hugh and Isabelle Robinson
Chief winemaker: Garry Crittenden
Year of foundation: 1988
Tonnes crushed on average each year: 150, of which 50 are presently used for Mornington Estate wines
Location: Moorooduc South
Area: 20 ha
Soils: sandy loam over red clay
Varieties planted: White—chardonnay, pinot gris, sauvignon blanc; Red—merlot, pinot noir, shiraz
Leading wines: Mornington Estate Pinot Noir, Chardonnay, Sauvignon Blanc
Notes: In June 2000 Mornington Estate merged with Dromana Estate and national distribution is now under way. All Estate fruit is now used for the label. The Estate's particular strengths are those of its region, Pinot Noir and Chardonnay, though there is also a good fruit-driven Shiraz. Cellar door sales: weekends and public holidays 11am–5pm excluding Christmas Day and Good Friday.

Osborn's Harwood Vineyard R84

166 Foxey's Road, Tuerong (formerly Ellerina Road, Merricks North), Vic 3926
Ph 03 5989 7417, Fax 03 5989 7510

Owners: Frank and Pam Osborn
Chief winemaker: Richard McIntyre (contract)
Year of foundation: 1988
Tonnes crushed on average each year: 50, about 20 of which are used for the owners' own labels
Location: Tuerong
Area: 6 ha
Soils: clay loam on clay
Varieties planted: White—chardonnay; Red—cabernet sauvignon, merlot, pinot noir, shiraz
Leading wines: Osborn's Chardonnay, Pinot Noir
Notes: With its vines established on grey clay-loam soils, the Osborn's Harwood Vineyard is sited on a north-facing slope, which is doubly virtuous because it not only protects from any adverse Bass Strait winds, but also adds extra touches of warmth to its microclimate. Its mainstay wines are Chardonnay and Pinot Noir. Cellar door sales: open Festival and holiday weekends or by appointment.

Paringa Estate R90

44 Paringa Road, Red Hill South, Vic 3937
Ph 03 5989 2669, Fax 03 5931 0135

Owners: Lindsay and Margaret McCall
Chief winemaker: Lindsay McCall
Year of foundation: 1985
Tonnes crushed on average each year: 30, all of which are used for Paringa Estate wines
Location: Red Hill South
Area: 4 ha
Soils: deep red volcanic clay
Varieties planted: White—chardonnay, pinot gris; Red—pinot noir, shiraz
Leading wines: Paringa Estate, Pinot Noir, Shiraz, Sparkling Shiraz
Notes: Paringa Estate is by any measure an outstanding winery. It was a pioneer of Shiraz on the Peninsula and that pioneering spirit has led to many well-justified trophies for the variety. But Pinot Noir is also strong at Paringa.

As forecast in the first edition, cabernet sauvignon has now disappeared and been replaced by pinot gris. This is another 'must' vineyard on any Mornington Peninsula visit. Cellar door sales: daily 11am–5pm. In addition there is a restaurant.

Poplar Bend NR

Main Creek Road, Main Ridge, Vic 3928
Ph 03 5989 6046, Fax 03 5989 6460

Owners: Wallace family
Chief winemaker: (contract)
Year of foundation: 1988
Tonnes crushed on average each year: 3
Location: Main Ridge
Area: 0.3 ha
Soils: rich red clay volcanic loams
Varieties planted: White—none; Red—pinot noir (Mariafeld clone)
Leading wine: Poplar Bend Shiraz
Notes: A very small family-run winery which purchases local shiraz fruit. Cellar door sales: weekends and public holidays 11am–5pm or by appointment.

Port Phillip Estate R88

261 Red Hill Road, Red Hill, Vic 3937
Ph/Fax 03 5989 2708,
Email sales@portphillip.net

Owners: Giogio and Dianne Gjergja
Chief winemaker: Lindsay McCall (contract)
Year of foundation: 1987
Tonnes crushed on average each year: 60
Location: Red Hill
Area: 6 ha
Soils: red and grey basalt loam
Varieties planted: White—chardonnay, sauvignon blanc; Red—pinot noir, shiraz
Leading wines: Port Phillip Estate Reserve Pinot Noir, Shiraz
Notes: Ownership changed hands in 2000, but winemaking continues in the skilful hands of Lindsay McCall and remains extremely strong.

Shiraz of course has come into the foreground at Port Phillip, but wines such as Port Phillip Estate Reserve Pinot Noir are benchmarks of the Mornington Peninsula. Do not fail to visit at least once in your lifetime. Cellar door sales: weekends and public holidays daily noon–5pm and 27 December until mid-January.

Red Hill Estate R85

53 Red Hill Shoreham Road, Red Hill South, Vic 3937
Ph 03 5989 2838, Fax 03 5989 2855,
Email winemaker@redhillestate.com.au

Owners: Sir Peter and Lady Derham
Chief winemaker: Michael Kyberd
Year of foundation: 1989
Tonnes crushed on average each year: 80, all of which were used for Red Hill Estate wines until 2000. The amount crushed at vintage 2000 was considerably more (600 tonnes) as stage II of an expansion plan began with that vintage. The plan is to increase crush to 2000 tonnes by 2005
Location: Red Hill South
Area: Red Hill Estate 9.6 ha, plus a number of other vineyards of varying meso-climates in the peninsula, including the Yabby Lake vineyard at Moorooduc
Soils: Red Hill Estate, deep fertile red volcanic loam; Yabby Lake, sandy loam with a bleached A horizon
Varieties planted: White—chardonnay, pinot gris; Red—pinot noir
Leading wines: Red Hill Estate Blanc de Blanc (sparkling), Blanc de Noirs (sparkling), Chardonnay, Pinot Noir, Pinot Gris
Notes: Red Hill Estate has been a very successful small winery in a premium wine region in Australia. All that is in the process of changing as the expansion mentioned above will see a vastly increased amount of Red Hill Estate wine on both Australian and international markets and most likely an Australian Stock Exchange listing in the next

few years. There will also be a new winery away from the Estate. It is an ambitious plan deserving of success because of the quality of the Estate wines and the region generally. Cellar door sales at the Estate will continue, 11am–5pm each day. There is also a restaurant.

Ryland River Winery NR

Main Creek Road, Main Ridge, Vic 3928
Ph 03 5989 6098,
Ph/Fax 03 9899 0184 (H)

Owners: John and Valerie Bray
Chief winemaker: John Bray
Year of foundation: 1986
Tonnes crushed on average each year: 40
Location: Main Ridge
Area: 3.5 ha
Soils: red volcanic loam
Varieties planted: White—chardonnay, sauvignon blanc, semillon; Red—cabernet sauvignon, merlot, shiraz
Leading wines: Ryland River Cabernet Sauvignon, Merlot, Shiraz, Semillon, Sauvignon Blanc
Notes: By Mornington Peninsula standards, Ryland River is a small- to medium-sized winery. There is also a herb garden and trout fishing. Cellar door sales: 10am–6pm weekends and public holidays, other times by appointment.

Seawinds NR

Main Creek Road, Main Ridge, Vic 3928
Ph 03 5989 6204,
Email muffie@netlink.com.au

Owner: Dr Douglas Schwebel
Chief winemaker: T'Gallant (contract)
Year of foundation: 1989
Tonnes crushed on average each year: 14, of which about half are used for Seawinds wines
Location: Main Ridge
Area: 2.6 ha
Soils: red volcanic loam

Varieties planted: White—chardonnay, sauvignon blanc; Red—pinot noir
Leading wine: Seawinds Sauvignon Blanc, Pinot Noir, Chardonnay
Notes: Seawinds is now an established vineyard on a west-facing slope about 200 metres above sea level. No cellar door sales.

Stonier's Winery R93

362 Frankston-Flinders Road, Merricks, Vic 3916
Ph 03 5989 8300, Fax 03 5989 8709,
Email stoniers@stoniers.com.au

Owner: Petaluma Ltd
Chief winemaker: Tod Dexter
Year of foundation: 1978
Tonnes crushed on average each year: 250 (all used for Stonier wines)
Location: Merricks
Area: 40 ha, including four different vineyards at Merricks, Merricks North, Cape Schanck and Shoreham
Soils: Merricks, chocolate brown deep clay loam over red clay
Varieties planted: White—chardonnay, sauvignon blanc; Red—cabernet franc, cabernet sauvignon, merlot, pinot noir
Leading wines: Stonier's Reserve Chardonnay, Reserve Pinot Noir
Notes: A few years ago I wrote that Stoniers was the outstanding winery of the region. In the past three years, many challengers have come forward—and doubtless there will be many more, as standards throughout the region improve—but perfection can still be found in Stonier Reserve Pinot Noir. This is another winery which deserves to be on any winelover's short list. Cellar door sales: daily noon–5pm.

Stumpy Gully Vineyard NR

1247 Stumpy Gully Road, Moorooduc,
Vic 3933
Ph 03 5978 8429, Fax 03 5978 8419,
Email sgvzant@dragon.net.au

Owners: Frank and Wendy Zantwoort
Chief winemakers: Wendy Zantwoort, Maitena
Zantwoort, Ewan Campbell
Year of foundation: 1989
Tonnes crushed on average each year: 100,
about 60 of which are used for Stumpy Gully
wines
Location: Moorooduc
Area: 30.8 ha, consisting of two vineyards at
Moorooduc—the winery block (10.8 ha) and a
nearby vineyard of 20 ha planted in 1998
Soils: rich black topsoil up to 60 cm in depth
over red gritty clay
Varieties planted: White—chardonnay,
marsanne, pinot gris, riesling, sauvignon blanc;
Red—cabernet sauvignon, merlot, pinot noir,
sangiovese, shiraz
Leading wines: Stumpy Gully Sauvignon Blanc,
Marsanne, Cabernet Sauvignon
Notes: Like many other wineries on the
Peninsula, Stumpy Gully is growing. Vintage
2001 saw the new vineyard come into bearing
and a slight increase in production. Cellar door
sales: weekends 11am–5pm.

Tanglewood Downs Estate NR

Bulldog Creek Road, Merricks North,
Vic 3926
Ph 03 5974 3325, Fax 03 5974 4170

Owners: Ken and Wendy Bilham
Chief winemaker: Ken Bilham
Year of foundation: 1984
Tonnes crushed on average each year: 16
Location: Merricks North
Area: 3 ha
Soils: grey clay loam with patches of quartz
Varieties planted: White—chardonnay,
gewurztraminer, riesling; Red—pinot noir

(4 clones—mv6, d5v12, mariafeld and a newer
burgundy clone), cabernet franc, cabernet
sauvignon, merlot
Leading wines: Tanglewood Downs Pinot Noir
Notes: Tanglewood Downs is a well sheltered
vineyard with extensive views over Port Phillip
Bay. Its soil is not fertile, but its structure and
water-holding capacity have been much
improved by extensive mulching and
Scott-Henry trellising has maximised sunlight
exposure. As can easily be seen from the list of
varieties, Ken Bilham tends to specialise in
Pinot and is justifiably pleased with this red
which is usually worth an award at the
Victorian Wines Show (he won a Gold in
1991). He also makes a little Shiraz, a variety
which is still quite rare on the peninsula. Cellar
door sales: daily noon–5pm. Winery lunch
each Sun noon–4pm.

T'Gallant Winemakers R92

Mornington-Flinders Road, Main Ridge,
Vic 3928
Ph 03 5989 6565, Fax 03 5989 6577

Owners/chief winemakers: Kathleen Quealy
and Kevin McCarthy
Year of foundation: 1990
Tonnes crushed on average each year: 300
Location: Main Ridge
Area: 50 ha
Soils: deep red volcanic loam
Varieties planted: White—chardonnay, pinot
gris; Red—muscat, pinot noir
Leading wines: T'Gallant Holystone,
Chardonnay, Pinot Grigio, Imogen Pinot Gris,
Tribute Pinot Gris, Pinot Noir
Notes: It is usual to think of pioneers as
grizzled veterans of many hardships. So it is
quite unusual that Kathleen Quealy and Kevin
McCarthy should ever be thought to fit the
mould, but they do. I cannot tell you about the
hardships. I suppose there have been some.
Most winemakers have them. But in the
decade or so that T'Gallant has operated, the

Quealy–McCarthy team has popularised
Holystone, a blended Pinot Noir Chardonnay
Rosé. Then it introduced Pinot Gris in two
styles: Alsatian (a dry fuller-bodied style) and
Italian (lighter but still dry and fruity and called,
swapping French for Italian, Grigio). Now it has
subdivided the French quotient into three
Pinots Gris, Tribute (the dry bottling), Imogen
(a 'vendange tardive' style) and Triumph (a rich
and sweet version, selection de grains nobles
or beerenauslese if you prefer German). When
these have been digested, there is always
Lyncroft Pinot Noir, no subdivisions here, just a
delicious violet-scented very stylishly
'Burgundian' Pinot. T'Gallant is one more
Mornington imperative! Cellar door sales: daily
11am–5pm.

Tuck's Ridge at Red Hill R83

37 Red Hill Shoreham Road, Red Hill
South, Vic 3937
Ph 03 5989 8660, Fax 03 5989 8579

Owner: Peter Hollick
Chief winemaker: Daniel Greene
Year of foundation: 1986
Tonnes crushed on average each year: 250, all
of which are used for Tuck's Ridge labels
Location: Red Hill South
Area: 26.5 ha consisting of two vineyards, the
winery block (13 ha) and Callanan's Road
(13.5 ha), but fruit is sourced from 26 other
Mornington Peninsula vineyards
Soils: rich red volcanic loam
Varieties planted: White—chardonnay, riesling,
semillon; Red—merlot, meunier, pinot noir
Leading wines: Tuck's Ridge Pinot Noir, Merlot.
A second label Callanan's Road, has replaced
the Altera label
Notes: One of the bigger estates of the region,
Tuck's Ridge is another exciting young winery
whose wines were first enthusiastically received
in 1993. Since then, if anything, its standards
have improved and will continue to do so as its
vines come to maturity. Look out for the Pinot

Noir. Cellar door sales: weekends and public
holidays noon–5pm.

Turramurra Estate Vineyard NR

295 Wallaces Road, Dromana, Vic 3936
Phone 03 5987 1146, Fax 03 5987 1286

Owners: David and Paula Leslie
Chief winemaker: David Leslie
Year of foundation: 1989
Tonnes produced on average each year: 75, all
of which are used for Turramurra Estate's own
wines
Location: Dromana
Area: 9 ha
Soils: the vineyard is 85 metres above sea level
with a north-west aspect overlooking Port
Phillip. Its soils are thin (5–10 cm deep) and
sandy lying over fractured sedimentary rock
and clay (yellow podsol)
Varieties planted: White—chardonnay,
sauvignon blanc; Red—cabernet franc,
cabernet sauvignon, merlot, pinot noir, shiraz
Leading wines: Turramurra Estate Chardonnay,
Sauvignon Blanc (a fume style), Pinot Noir,
Cabernet, Shiraz
Notes: Turramurra Estate is a relatively new
vineyard with its first vintage made in 1996. As
David Leslie says, his vineyard soils present 'no
vigour problems'. The vines are now mature
and should produce good wines in the future.
Cellar door sales: first weekend of each month
noon–5pm.

Villa Primavera (formerly Tuerong Estate Vineyard) NR

Mornington-Flinders Road, Red Hill,
Vic 3937
Ph/Fax 03 5989 2129

Owners: Gennaro and Jenny Mazzella
Chief winemaker: (contract)
Year of foundation: 1984
Tonnes crushed on average each year: 5, all of
which are used for Villa Primavera wines

Location: Red Hill
Area: 4 ha
Soils: deep red volcanic loam
Varieties planted: White—chardonnay, pinot grigio; Red—pinot noir
Leading wine: Villa Primavera Sparkling (Methode Champenoise)
Notes: This is a small family-owned vineyard with a restaurant, 'Gennaro's Table', which is open for dinner on Saturday, lunch on Sundays and most public holidays, and daily from 26 December to 26 January. Tasting hours 10am–5pm.

Vintina Estate NR

1282 Nepean Highway, Mount Eliza, Vic 3930
Ph 03 9787 8166, Fax 03 9775 2935

Owners: Jim and Tina Filippone
Chief winemaker: Jim Filippone
Year of foundation: 1985
Tonnes crushed on average each year: 4
Location: Mount Eliza
Area: 1.6 ha
Soils: grey sandy loam over a clay subsoil
Varieties planted: White—chardonnay, pinot gris; Red—cabernet sauvignon, pinot noir
Leading wines: Vintina Estate Louisa Chardonnay, Mitchel James Cabernet Sauvignon
Notes: Vintina Estate Chardonnays have won some critical support from time to time. Cellar door sales: 7 days 11am–5pm.

Willow Creek Vinyard R87

166 Balnarring Road, Merricks North, Vic 3926
Ph 03 5989 7448, Fax 03 5989 7584,
Email adin@willow-creek.com.au

Owners: Harris, Ball and Knowles families
Chief winemaker: Simon Black
Year of foundation: 1989
Tonnes crushed on average each year: 150, but increasing to 500 in the next few vintages
Location: Merricks North
Area: 12.8 ha
Soils: red chocolate grey and black loam with limestone deposits
Varieties planted: White—chardonnay; Red—cabernet sauvignon, pinot noir
Leading wines: Willow Creek Vineyard Pinot Noir, Tulum Chardonnay
Notes: Willow Creek Vineyard is growing, if not in area, certainly in tonnes crushed. It has an excellent record since its first vintages for Pinot Noir and Chardonnay, two varieties for which the region is eminently suited. Yet another Mornington Peninsula winery whose wines must be tasted. Cellar door sales: 10am–5pm daily. There is also a restaurant open daily for lunch and Fri–Sat for dinner.

Wyldcroft Estates NR

Stanleys Road, Red Hill South, Vic 3937
Ph/Fax 03 5989 2646, Fax 03 9783 9469

Owners: Devendra and Shashi Singh
Chief winemaker: contract
Year of foundation: 1987
Tonnes crushed on average each year: 12, all of which are used for Wyldcroft Estate wines
Location: Red Hill South
Area: 3.5 ha
Soils: deep red volcanic loam
Varieties planted: White—chardonnay; Red—cabernet sauvignon, pinot noir, shiraz
Leading wines: Wyldcroft Estate Pinot Noir, Shiraz
Notes: Cellar door sales: daily 11am–5pm.

GEELONG REGION

Geelong is at once one of the oldest and youngest Australian wine regions. Its vineyards were founded 150 years ago by Swiss and German immigrants, encouraged by Sophie de Montmollin, wife of the Superintendent of Melbourne Charles La Trobe. They soon prospered and by 1860 there were over 200 hectares under vine. But it was a fleeting prosperity. Fifteen years later, phylloxera chose Geelong as its point of entry and began its devastation of Australia. The Victorian government, anxious to localise the outbreak, offered a bounty for the uprooting of its vineyards. Despite this, the progress of the louse was inexorable. By the turn of the century there were few, if any, vineyards remaining in Geelong and phylloxera was well established in Victoria.

Nearly 70 years later, in 1966, came the renaissance of Geelong wine when Daryl and Nini Sefton planted their Idyll vineyard. Two years later, Tom Maltby established the Anakie vineyard (now called Zambelli) and the Geelong region was set for steady growth in the 1970s (Mount Duneed 1970, Tarcoola 1971, The Minya 1974, Bannockburn 1974, Asher 1975, Prince Albert 1975) and further growth still in the 1980s (Innisfail 1980, Waybourne 1980, the Hickinbotham family lease of Anakie in 1981, Scotchman's Hill 1982, Staughton Vale 1986). Though pinot noir has certainly been extremely successful in the region (witness Bannockburn, Scotchman's Hill and, in some years, Prince Albert) and Geelong is growing rapidly, it is not yet a name that hangs from every winelover's lips. Despite this lack of recognition, vineyard area in the Geelong region increased by 66 per cent in the three years from 1996–99. But it is still a small vineyard area (in the year 2000, almost but not quite as big as it was 130 years ago) and there is a lack of a definite profile. It is just such a lack of profile that worries Geelong at the present time, as it watches the rapid growth of other wine regions such as the Yarra Valley and the Mornington Peninsula. Although Scotchman's Hill and Bannockburn are the largest and best wineries in the region, Geelong seems to require the presence of one of the 'big battalions', a major wine company to stabilise the wine identity of the region and to make it nationally recognisable.

Location: latitude 38°7'S, longitude 144°22'E, about 70 km south-west of Melbourne along the Princes Highway. Though reasonably small in its area of vines under cultivation, Geelong is quite widespread with vineyards to the east, north, north-west and south-west of the centre of the city up to 30 km away.

Elevation: 20–300 m

Topography and soils: quite steep and undulating country especially to the north and north-west of Geelong (around Anakie, to about 350 m). Lower hills to the east and south. There are two basic soils: (i) heavy grey soils on basalt, found north of the Barwon River, these are brownish-grey in colour and overlie grey and yellow-grey clay subsoils, being slightly acid in nature; (ii) red duplex soils (podsolic, sandy loams overlying yellow-grey heavy clay subsoils), quite acid in nature. Other soils in the region are limestone-based rendzinas and terra rossas.

Climate: MJT 18.8°C, MAR na, HDD (raw) 1457 (cut off and as adjusted for latitude daily temperature range and vine sites 1354), AR 541 mm (Oct–Apr 301 mm), RH 52% (Gladstones). MJT 19°C, MAR 9.4°C, HDD (raw) 1471, AR 538 mm

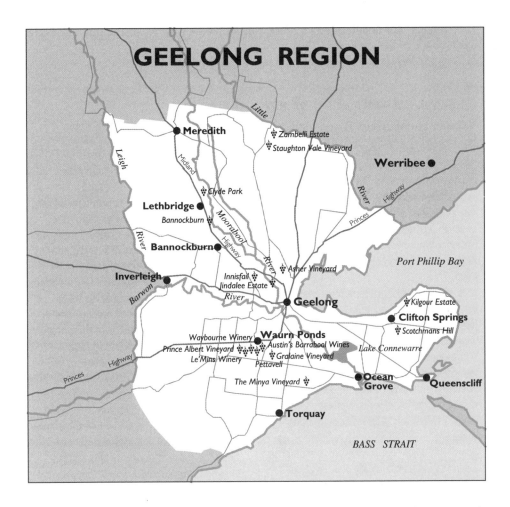

GEELONG REGION

Meredith
Zambelli Estate
Staughton Vale Vineyard
Werribee
Little
Leigh
Midland
Clyde Park
Lethbridge
Bannockburn
Moorabool
Highway
River
River
Highway
Princes
Bannockburn
Asher Vineyard
Port Phillip Bay
River
Inverleigh
Innisfail
Jindalee Estate
Barwon
River
Geelong
Kilgour Estate
Clifton Springs
Scotchmans Hill
Waybourne Winery
Waurn Ponds
Austin's Barrabool Wines
Prince Albert Vineyard
Gralaine Vineyard
Lake Connewarre
Le'Mins Winery
Pettavell
Princes
Highway
The Minya Vineyard
Ocean
Grove
Queenscliff
Torquay
BASS STRAIT

(Oct–Mar 311 mm), RH 62% (9am), AI 266 mm, SH 7.8. (Dry & Smart). Quite cool and dry with low radiation. Wind chill and frosts sometimes a problem at flowering. Maritime influences (Bass Strait) in its eastern and southern parts. Annual rainfall figures are very low at 538 mm and 541 mm and certainly indicate a need for supplementation by drip irrigation from surface dams during ripening.

Harvest time: mid-March (pinot noir) to late April (riesling, shiraz and cabernet sauvignon)

Principal varieties: White—chardonnay, riesling, sauvignon blanc, semillon, pinot gris; Red—pinot noir, shiraz, cabernet sauvignon, merlot

Total area: 363 ha (1999)

Major wine styles: The Chardonnays of Geelong are usually excellent cool-area examples of the variety. Well-structured yet delicate, capable of aging, and perhaps as close to 'Burgundian' as Australia comes. In Geelong, Pinot Noir is typified by Bannockburn and Scotchman's Hill. On the one hand there is Bannockburn, wines of finesse which are at once subtle and stylish yet well able to take five years' bottle age.

Scotchman's Hill usually shows a fuller, fruitier palate with good structure and body, again able to take bottle age.
Leading wineries: Bannockburn, Scotchman's Hill, Jindalee

Austin's Barrabool Wines R82

50 Lemins Road, Waurn Ponds, Vic 3221
Ph 03 5241 8114, Fax 03 5241 8122

Owners: Richard and Pamela Austin
Chief winemaker: John Ellis (contract)
Year of foundation: 1982
Tonnes crushed on average each year: 30, all of which are used for Austin's Barrabool Wines
Location: Waurn Ponds and Sutherland's Creek
Area: 1.5 ha Waurn Ponds, 19 ha Sutherland's Creek
Soils: Waurn Ponds, rich terra rossa over a limestone base; Sutherland's Creek, a north facing slope with very similar soils
Varieties planted: (Waurn Ponds)
White—riesling, chardonnay; Red—cabernet sauvignon. (Sutherlands Creek)
White—chardonnay, riesling; Red—cabernet sauvignon, merlot, pinot noir, shiraz
Leading wines: Austin's Barrabool Chardonnay, Shiraz
Notes: The Waurn Ponds vineyard is another of Geelong's old sites originally planted about 150 years ago by the Swiss family Triboulet. Very good Chardonnay and Shiraz is produced. Tasting by appointment only.

Bannockburn Vineyards R90

Midland Highway, Bannockburn,
Vic 3331
Ph 03 5281 1363, Fax 03 5281 1349

Owner: Bannockburn Vineyard Pty Ltd
Chief winemaker: Gary Farr
Year of foundation: 1974
Tonnes crushed on average each year: 100
Location: Bannockburn
Area: 17.5 ha
Soils: heavy clay loam over limestone and over

'buckshot' clay
Varieties planted: White—chardonnay, sauvignon blanc; Red—cabernet sauvignon, malbec, merlot, pinot noir, shiraz
Leading wines: Bannockburn Pinot Noir, Chardonnay, Shiraz
Notes: Not only is Bannockburn within a very cool area, it is also very low yielding. But when outrageous fortune flings its arrows (in this case 10 minutes of hail) as it did prior to 1998 vintage, then even the most experienced of winemakers realises that there is something more to winemaking than simply skill. The unlucky '98 vintage was all but wiped out, only 10 per cent of normal crop being picked. And so, south-east Australian blends were substituted for its estate favourites, Chardonnay, Pinot Noir and Shiraz—and excellent wines they proved to be, showing Gary Farr is indeed a skilful, if not a lucky winemaker. Since then there have been two excellent vintages of differing styles, the forward but fruity '99s and the ripe and balanced 2000. I wish Gary Farr much better luck in the future. No cellar door sales.

Clyde Park NR

Midland Highway, Bannockburn, Vic 3331
Ph/Fax 03 5281 7274, (H) 03 9827 2311,
Fax 03 9827 5045,
Email info@clydepark.com

Owners: Terry Jongebloed and Sue Dixon
Chief winemaker: Roland Kaval
Year of foundation: 1980
Tonnes crushed on average each year: 50, but increasing to 100 by 2005, all of which are or will be used for Clyde Park labels
Location: Bannockburn

Area: 14 ha
Soils: black volcanic loam over a limestone base
Varieties planted: White—chardonnay, pinot
gris, sauvignon blanc; Red—pinot noir, shiraz
Leading wines: Clyde Park Chardonnay, Pinot
Gris, Pinot Noir
Notes: Owned by Bannockburn winemaker
Gary Farr until 1994, and now by Terry
Jongebloed and Sue Dixon, Clyde Park is
steadily expanding and may expand further in
the first few years of the new millennium.
Cellar door sales: weekends.

Gralaine Vineyard NR

65 Feehan's Road, Mount Duneed,
Vic 3216
Ph 0429 009 973, Fax 03 9886 7377

Owners: Graeme and Elaine Carroll
Chief winemaker: John Ellis (contract)
Year of foundation: 1983
Tonnes crushed on average each year: 7, all
used for Gralaine Merlot
Location: Mount Duneed
Area: 4 ha
Soils: light sandy loam over reactive clay over
yellow clay
Varieties planted: White—none; Red—cabernet
sauvignon, merlot
Leading wine: Gralaine Merlot
Notes: Gralaine is almost a merlot monoculture
and has moved deeper into merlot with recent
vineyard expansion. However, there are a few
cabernet vines. The Merlot is made by John
Ellis, who is an excellent winemaker. There are
no cellar door sales. The wines, however, may
be tasted at Hanging Rock Winery, Newham
Victoria.

Innisfail Vineyards and Winery NR

Cross Street, Batesford, Vic 3221
Ph 03 5276 1258, Fax 03 5221 8442

Owner: Shaaron Griffiths
Chief winemaker: Ron Griffiths

Year of foundation: 1980
Tonnes crushed on average each year: 35
Location: Batesford
Area: 6 ha
Soils: heavy volcanic loam over a limestone
base
Varieties planted: White—chardonnay, riesling;
Red—cabernet sauvignon, merlot, pinot noir
Leading wine: Innisfail Chardonnay
Notes: The Griffiths have a small but mature
vineyard, make their own wine and have a
good reputation for their Chardonnay.
No cellar door sales.

Jindalee Estate Geelong (formerly Idyll Vineyard) R86

265 Ballan Road, Moorabool, Vic 3221
Ph 03 5277 2836, Fax 03 5277 2840,
Email jindwine@mail.austasia.net

Owners: Vince and David Littore, Bill Mithen
Chief winemaker: Scott Ireland
Year of foundation: 1999 (purchase of Idyll
Vineyard), 1966 (foundation of Idyll Vineyard)
Tonnes produced on average each year: 100
Location: Moorabool
Area: 14 ha
Soils: dark brown soil over clay and limestone
Varieties planted: White—chardonnay,
gewurztraminer; Red—cabernet sauvignon,
shiraz
Leading wine: Fettlers Rest Shiraz
Notes: Jindalee has created a good reputation
for easy drinking wines from its
Murray–Darling vineyards. There is no reason
why its Geelong wines should not be even
better. Cellar door sales: 7 days 10am–5pm.

Kilgour Estate NR

85 McAdams Lane, Bellarine, Vic 3223
Ph/Fax 03 5251 2223

Owner: Anne Timms
Chief winemaker: Karen Coulston (consultant)
Year of foundation: 1989

Tonnes crushed on average each year: 60, all of which are used for Kilgour Estate labels
Location: Bellarine
Area: 10 ha
Soils: heavy sandy loam leading to sand over a limestone base
Varieties planted: White—chardonnay, pinot gris; Red—cabernet franc, cabernet sauvignon, merlot, pinot noir
Leading wines: Kilgour Estate Pinot Noir, Chardonnay, Pinot Gris, Cabernet Sauvignon, Pinot Noir, 97 Methode Traditionale (a sparkling pale pink wine)
Notes: Kilgour Estate is beautifully situated with panoramic views over Port Phillip, Corio Bay and Bass Strait. There is a restaurant and outdoor barbecue facilities. Cellar door sales: Wed–Sun 10.30am–5pm, daily during January. The restaurant, specialising in local seafood, serves dinner Fri–Sat and lunch Sat–Sun. Reservations are advisable.

Le'Mins Winery R75

40 Lemins Road, Waurn Ponds, Vic 3216
Ph 03 5241 8168

Owner/chief winemaker: Steve Jones
Year of foundation: 1994
Tonnes produced on average each year: 2, all of which are used for Lemins Winery Pinot Noir
Location: Waurn Ponds
Area: 0.7 ha
Soils: the vineyard faces north and has rich brown terra rossa soils over limestone
Varieties planted: White—chardonnay (3 rows); Red—pinot noir
Leading wines: Lemins Winery Pinot Noir
Notes: This is almost a pinot noir monoculture. Steve Jones converted part of this former kiwifruit plantation to pinot noir in 1994 and is slowly increasing the area of vines. No cellar door sales.

Melbourne Wine Co R83

C/- Jindalee Estate, 265 Ballan Road, Moorabool, Vic 3221
Ph 03 5281 7477, Fax 03 5281 7377,
Email mwc@pipeline.com.au

Owners: Scott Ireland and Jennifer Lilburn
Chief winemaker: Scott Ireland
Year of foundation: 1995
Tonnes crushed on average each year: 30
Location: Geelong
Area: no vineyards are owned
Soils: no vineyards are owned
Varieties utilised: White—chardonnay, pinot gris; Red—pinot noir, shiraz
Leading wines: Provenance Chardonnay, Pinot Noir
Notes: Scott Ireland makes his wines at the old Idyll Winery. Buying excellent parcels of fruit from local growers, he has created a Geelong brand, Provenance, and very good it is with smooth fruit-driven pinots and shiraz. There are no cellar door sales, but the wines may be found at retailers.

The Minya Vineyard and Winery NR

Minya Lane, Connewarre, Vic 3227
Ph 03 5264 1397

Owners: Jeff and Sue Dans
Chief winemaker: Sue Dans
Year of foundation: 1974
Tonnes crushed on average each year: 20
Location: Connewarre
Area: 4 ha
Soils: light sandy loam
Varieties planted: White—chardonnay; Red—cabernet sauvignon, grenache, merlot, shiraz
Leading wines: The Minya Grenache, Cabernet Sauvignon-Shiraz-Merlot
Notes: This small vineyard is within sea-spray of Bass Strait and requires wind breaks and also netting protection from the many birds in

the area. Unusually for the region, The Minya cultivates grenache. Cabin accommodation is available. Cellar door sales: weekends after Christmas until Easter, most public holidays and by appointment.

Pettavel Geelong Wines **NR**

545 Princes Highway, Waurn Ponds, Vic 3216 (corner of Pettavel Road)
Ph 03 5266 1120, Fax 03 5266 1140

Owners: Michael and Sandi Fitzpatrick
Chief winemaker: Peter Flewellyn
Year of foundation: 2001 (cellar door); 1989 Sutherlands Creek, 1999 Waurn Ponds
Tonnes on average each year: 500, of which 50 are presently used for Pettavel labels
Locations: Waurn Ponds (cellar door) and Sutherlands Creek
Area: 72 ha
Soils: rich grey-brown volcanic self-mulching soils over limestone
Varieties planted: (Sutherlands Creek) White—chardonnay, sauvignon blanc, semillon; Red—cabernet franc, cabernet sauvignon, merlot, petit verdot, pinot noir, shiraz. (Waurn Ponds) Red—shiraz
Leading wines: Pettavel Chardonnay
Notes: A new millennium and a new middling-large winery for the Geelong Region. Certainly the Waurn Ponds winery and vineyard are very recent but Mike Fitzpatrick is a veteran of the region, having established his Sutherlands Creek vineyard in 1989. Its first vintage under the new Pettavel Geelong label (named after David Louis Pettavel, the Swiss pioneer of Geelong viticulture in the 1840s) was Chardonnay 2000. Its cellar door has been recently opened, daily 10am–6pm. There is also a restaurant.

Prince Albert Vineyard **R77**

100 Lemins Road, Waurn Ponds, Vic 3216
Ph/Fax 03 5241 8091

Owners: Susan and Bruce Hyett
Chief winemaker: Bruce Hyett
Year of foundation: 1975
Tonnes crushed on average each year: 8, all of which are used for Prince Albert Pinot Noir
Location: Waurn Ponds
Area: 1.75 ha
Soils: red clay 25 cm deep over marl 10 cm deep
Varieties planted: White—none; Red—pinot noir
Leading wine: Prince Albert Pinot Noir
Notes: Prince Albert is a monoculture, and like all monoculture suffers rather more from variable vintages than vineyards with several varieties. In top years for Pinot Noir, Prince Albert can be very good, but wine faults do show occasionally. Prince Albert is also a certified organic winery. Cellar door sales by appointment.

Scotchman's Hill **R90**

190 Scotchman's Road, Drysdale, Vic 3222
Ph 03 5251 3176, Fax 03 5253 1743,
Email info@scotchmans.com.au

Owners: Browne family
Chief winemaker: Robin Brockett
Year of foundation: 1982
Tonnes crushed on average each year: 600, all of which are used for Scotchman's Hill and Spray Farm labels
Location: Drysdale
Area: 60 ha
Soils: black, heavy volcanic clay over broken basalt
Varieties planted: White—chardonnay, riesling, sauvignon blanc; Red—cabernet franc, cabernet sauvignon, merlot, pinot noir
Leading wines: Scotchman's Hill Chardonnay, Pinot Noir

Notes: Located east of Geelong on the Bellarine Peninsula and with a cool, maritime climate, Scotchman's Hill has rapidly built up an excellent reputation for its Pinot Noir and Chardonnay which should not be missed. It is now well-established and the biggest vineyard and winery of the region. Spray Farm is the Scotchman's Hill Group's second wine. The Spray Farm wines receive a shorter maturation period and are intended for earlier drinking. Spray Farm is located at 2275 Portarlington Road Bellarine. Its phone and fax numbers are the same as Scotchman's Hill. Cellar door sales are available at both addresses from 10.30am–5.30pm daily at Scotchman's Hill and between the same hours at weekends at Spray Farm, which also has a café open for lunch and afternoon tea.

Staughton Vale Vineyard NR

20 Staughton Vale Road (cnr Ballan Road), Anakie, Vic 3221
Ph 03 5284 1477, Fax 03 5284 1229

Owners: Paul and Lyn Chambers
Chief winemaker: Paul Chambers
Year of foundation: 1986
Tonnes crushed on average each year: 40, all of which are used for Staughton Vale wines
Location: Anakie
Area: 7 ha
Soils: part of an old volcanic cone—black basalt soils over 'scoria'
Varieties planted: White—chardonnay, riesling, semillon; Red—cabernet franc, cabernet sauvignon, malbec, merlot, petit verdot, pinot noir
Leading wines: Staughton (a blend of the Bordeaux red varieties listed above), Staughton Riesling
Notes: Staughton Vale is a close-planted vineyard with a vine density of 3200 vines to the hectare. Cellar door sales: Fri–Mon and public holidays 10am–5pm, other times by appointment. A restaurant, open for lunch and

morning and afternoon tea, is located in the vineyard.

Waybourne Winery NR

60 Lemins Road, Waurn Ponds, Vic 3221
Ph/Fax 03 5241 8477

Owners: Tony and Kaye Volpato
Chief winemaker: Tony Volpato
Year of foundation: 1978
Tonnes crushed on average each year: 10
Location: Waurn Ponds
Area: 1.6 ha
Soils: red terra rossa over limestone base
Varieties planted: White—chardonnay, frontignac, pinot gris, riesling; Red—cabernet sauvignon
Leading wines: Waybourne Cabernet Sauvignon, Riesling
Notes: Adjoining Prince Albert Vineyard and sharing a rich basaltic soil over a limestone base, Waybourne is another vineyard planted in the centre of the historic Geelong wine-growing district. Perhaps the soil here is too rich as it promotes vigorous vine growth at the expense of fruit, making cultivation and sulfur spraying extremely difficult and yielding only a small crop. Tasting and cellar door sales by appointment only. The tasting room includes a small gallery.

Zambelli Estate Wines (formerly Mount Anakie Wines) NR

Staughton Vale Road, Anakie, Vic 3221
Ph 03 5284 1452, Fax 03 5284 1405

Owner: O Zambelli
Chief winemaker: O Zambelli
Year of foundation: 1969
Tonnes crushed on average each year: 60, all of which are used for Zambelli labels
Location: Anakie
Area: 18 ha
Soils: black volcanic soils over 'scoria'—broken lava rock, part of an old volcanic cone

Varieties planted: White—biancone, chardonnay, riesling, semillon; Red—cabernet franc, cabernet sauvignon, shiraz
Leading wines: Mount Anakie Shiraz, Chardonnay

Notes: Founded by Tom Maltby in 1969 and for several years leased to Hickinbotham Winemakers, this is another longstanding Geelong vineyard. Cellar door sales: 7 days 11am–5pm.

SUNBURY REGION

The region was first crossed by Hume and Hovell in 1824 on their mistaken way to Western Port Bay, a journey which ended at Corio Bay off Port Phillip. But it was not a journey in vain, though it may have seemed so at the time. They found valuable pastoral land, needing little clearance, natural grassland virtually devoid of eucalypts. This was later to encourage John Batman, a free settler in Van Diemens Land, in 1835 to make the initial barterings with Aboriginal tribes that led to the settlement of what was ultimately to be called Melbourne. Batman did not plan a future metropolis—what initially interested him and his immediate circle, the Port Phillip Association, were its grazing prospects. Shortly after, these were exploited by members of that Association, who moved their flocks to what is today the Sunbury area, so named by Jackson Brothers after Sunbury on Thames in England. Discoveries of gold at Bendigo in the 1850s also created a demand for overnight accommodation in the area and in 1859 the area received its first railway service.

The first vineyards appeared there during the late 1850s. James Goodall Francis, later to be a premier of Victoria, erected his Goona Warra homestead and winery in 1858, at the same time employing European vignerons to plant a terraced vineyard. In 1865 James Johnston, a man of varying business interests—hotel-keeper, grazier, newspaper proprietor and politician—erected Craiglee, having the year before planted 16 acres of vines, including riesling and hermitage. Those two varieties later proved the most successful on the site. His 1872 Craiglee Hermitage, an award-winner at the Vienna Exposition in 1875, is the oldest Australian wine I have ever tasted and quite remarkable for its 102 years of age at the time of tasting. By 1870, there were over 300 acres of vines in and around Sunbury. Later the region miraculously avoided phylloxera, which devastated both Geelong and later Bendigo. Although the region continued to produce wine until the late 1920s, the nineteenth century was its golden age. By the time of the Great Depression, sheer economics forced the grubbing out of the vines and, as in most former vineyards, the substitution of more viable sheep and wool.

The Carmody family came to Craiglee in 1961 and, in 1976, Patrick Carmody planted the first vines it had seen in virtually 50 years. In 1979 came the first vintage of reborn Craiglee. Since then the Sunbury region has grown steadily. Goona Warra was re-established in 1983 and several more old Sunbury names, such as Old Winilba, are with us once more. In 1997, the region produced 150 tonnes of fruit from 82.5 ha of mostly young vines. Plantings in 1998 were anticipated to be a further 150 hectares with the 500-tonne criterion being reached by 2000. Growth in this region in the future may be threatened by the onset of Melbourne's western and north-western suburbs.

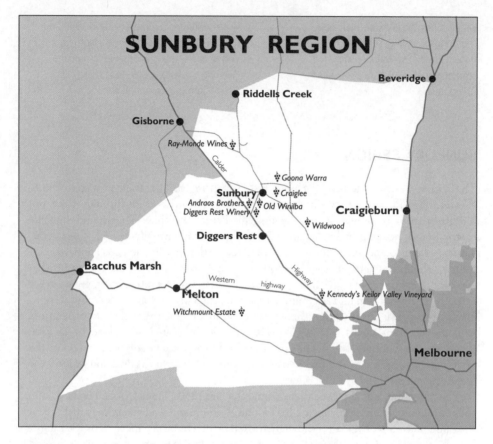

Location: latitude 37°35'S, longitude 144°44'E about 30 km north-west of Melbourne
Elevation: 50–400 m (contour boundary)
Topography and soils: The region is flat to undulating, rising to the north and north-west to a 400-metre contour line, forming the boundary between it and the Macedon Ranges region. It is a mixture of igneous and sedimentary rocks, the igneous rocks being chiefly new basalt formed during the Pleistocene period with small areas of older basalt from the Lower Tertiary period. There are also areas of Upper Palaeozoic granite and granodiorite. The sedimentary rocks are formed from small areas of Tertiary sand, clay and lignite and shale, sandstone, mudstone and limestone, Silurian, slate and sandstone from the Ordovician age.

Its major soil is hard alkaline red duplex (Dr 2.23 Northcote), quite common in vineyard areas of south-eastern Australia with some areas of cracking clays and others of hard acidic duplex soils. There are also free-draining sandy loams (alluvial) along creek valleys, which are acidic (pH 5.5).

Climate: (local) Sunbury (Weather Station Melbourne Airport) MJT 19.6°C, MAR 10.5°C, HDD (raw) 1400, AR 562 mm (Oct–Apr 292.3 mm), RH 73% (av % Oct–March) (3pm). AI na, SH na. Cf Melbourne: MJT 19.6°C, MAR na, HDD (raw) 1554, 1501 (cut off and adjusted for altitude daily temperature range and vine sites),

AR 658 (Oct–Apr 394 mm), RH 48% (Jan 3pm), AI na, SH 6.7 (Gladstones). Additional local data: Sunbury AR 592 mm (Oct–Apr 301.2 mm).

Sunbury is undoubtedly much warmer and drier than Macedon Ranges to its north and north-west, but can share heavy damaging winds. By comparison, Melbourne to the south-east is warmer, possibly due to an urban warming factor, and wetter (possibly due to closer proximity to Port Phillip and its maritime effect). Practical experience (Pat Carmody carried out his twentieth vintage at Craiglee in 1998) has shown that the region is climatically suited to all but the latest ripening grape-types, that is, only late Southern French varieties such as grenache and mourvedre and Italians such as sangiovese may fail to ripen. As in most parts of vinous Australia, irrigation is necessary and is effected through surface catchment in private dams, through town water supplies and by pumping from some creeks. Bore water is likely to be salty. Frost is a slight risk. At Craiglee, situated on fairly flat ground, it has affected the vineyard only twice in 20 years (1982 and 1997). Birds account for about 1% crop loss at Craiglee which is not netted. This is due to a natural absence of trees in the region and such a loss is much lower than in other regions, such as the Yarra Valley and Mornington Peninsula.

Harvest time: chardonnay early to mid-April, shiraz mid-April to early May

Principal varieties: White—chardonnay, sauvignon blanc; Red—cabernet sauvignon, shiraz, pinot noir

Major wine styles: *Chardonnay* Young Chardonnay from this region generally shows melony aromas, which are made more complex by barrel and malolactic fermentation. In good years the wine is well balanced with good acidity, causing it to age well over 5 years. If a French comparison is needed, Sunbury Chardonnays tend to 'Chablis' style in youth, filling out on palate with 3+ years bottle age. *Shiraz* In good years, the Shiraz of the region is medium-bodied and fruit-driven, accepting subtle French oak extremely well. On nose it is typically but not heavily peppery, inclining more to white than black pepper, and this coupled with cherry fruit aromas causes great aromatic complexity. Its palate is medium bodied, of berry and spice flavours with well integrated, lightly peppery tannins. In all, these are wines of excellent vinosity and quite long in the mouth. In poor years, the wines can be thin, ungenerous and a trifle green. *Pinot Noir* This is a bigger, darker more solid style of Pinot than in other regions of the Port Phillip Zone, lacking elegance by comparison, but certainly not in ripeness or extract.

Leading wineries: Andraos Brothers, Wildwood Vineyards, Witchmount Estate

Andraos Brothers at Old Winilba **R85**

150 Vineyard Road, Sunbury, Vic 3429
Ph 03 9740 9703, Fax 03 9740 1357,
Email andraos@melb.alexia.net.au

Owners: Fred and Sam Andraos
Chief winemakers: Fred Andraos, Mario Marson (consultant)
Year of foundation: originally 1864, closed 1912, re-established 1989
Tonnes crushed on average each year: 20
Location: Sunbury
Area: 6 ha
Soils: volcanic ash of a light to dark brown colour; between 220 and 250 m in altitude, the vineyard is sited on an east-facing slope
Varieties planted: White—chardonnay, riesling, sauvignon blanc, semillon; Red—cabernet sauvignon, pinot noir, shiraz

Leading wines: Andraos Brothers Cabernet, Shiraz, Semillon

Notes: Andraos Brothers have a most consistent show record especially for their reds, winning silvers and bronzes and the occasional gold at local wine shows. A restaurant, Estelle's, is open for lunch and dinner Fri–Sun. Cellar door sales: weekends and publc holidays 11am–5pm.

Craiglee NR

Sunbury Road, Sunbury, Vic 3429
Ph 03 9744 4489, Fax 03 9744 4489

Owners: Carmody family
Chief winemaker: Pat Carmody
Year of foundation: 1976
Tonnes crushed on average each year: 40
Location: Sunbury
Area: 10 ha
Soils: sandy loams, clay loams
Varieties planted: White—chardonnay, sauvignon blanc; Red—cabernet sauvignon, pinot noir, shiraz
Leading wines: Craiglee Shiraz, Chardonnay
Notes: Modern Craiglee is a vineyard of nostalgia for me as its nineteenth-century incarnation produced the oldest Australian wine I have ever tasted—1872 Craiglee Hermitage. Regrettably, Craiglees of more current vintages have not recently come my way. Cellar door sales: Sundays and public holidays 10am–5pm, other times by appointment.

Diggers Rest Winery NR

205 Old Vineyard Road, Sunbury, Vic 3429
Ph/Fax 03 9740 1660

Owners: Joseph and Elie Obeid
Chief winemaker: Peter Dredge
Year of foundation: 1987
Tonnes crushed on average each year: 18, of which 16 are used for Diggers Rest wines
Location: Sunbury

Area: 5.5 ha
Soils: black basaltic and quartzite clay gravel
Varieties planted: White—chardonnay; Red—cabernet sauvignon, pinot noir, shiraz
Leading wines: Diggers Rest Shiraz, Cabernet Sauvignon, Chardonnay
Notes: Diggers Rest consistently wins silver and bronze awards for its Shiraz and Cabernet Sauvignon at the Victorian Wines Show. Cellar door sales: by appointment.

Goona Warra R83

Sunbury Road, Sunbury, Vic 3429
Ph 03 9740 7766, Fax 03 9744 7648

Owners: Goona Warra Vineyard Ltd
Chief winemaker: John Barnier
Year of foundation: 1863, re-established 1983
Tonnes crushed on average each year: 35, but this should increase slightly as new plantings of merlot come into bearing
Location: Sunbury
Area: 6 ha
Soils: black basaltic clays on hills varying to sandy loams on river flats
Varieties planted: White—chardonnay, roussanne, semillon; Red—cabernet franc, cabernet sauvignon, merlot, pinot noir
Leading wines: Goona Warra Cabernet Franc, Chardonnay, Semillon
Notes: Goona Warra, like Craiglee, is a reincarnation of another nineteenth-century Victorian vineyard. Cabernet Franc is its forte and is very good. Sunday lunch is available in the historic bluestone winery building erected in 1863. Cellar door sales: daily 10am–5pm except Good Friday and Boxing Day.

Kennedy's Keilor Valley Vineyard NR

Overnewton Road, Keilor, Vic 3036
Ph/Fax 03 9331 6246

Owners: Colin and Denise Kennedy
Chief winemaker: Peter Dredge (contract)

Year of foundation: 1989
Tonnes crushed on average each year: 8, of which half are used for Keilor Valley Vineyard wines
Location: Keilor
Area: 2 ha
Soils: rich red soil, clay subsoil
Varieties planted: White—chardonnay; Red—cabernet sauvignon
Leading wines: Kennedy's Keilor Valley Chardonnay (lightly wooded)
Notes: There are no cellar door sales. Sales by personal contact and through a local distributor.

Ray-Monde Wines R78

250 Dalrymple Road, Sunbury, Vic 3429
Ph 03 5427 2777, Fax 03 5428 3390,
Email jtlakey@iaa.com.au

Owners: Lakey family
Chief winemakers: John and Vincent Lakey
Year of foundation: 1988
Tonnes crushed on average each year: 15, all of which are used for Ray-Monde Pinot Noir
Location: Sunbury
Area: 5 ha
Soils: heavy basalt clay, which can cause drainage problems in wet years and red weathered basaltic soils containing 'buckshot' which have better structure and noticeably better drainage
Varieties planted: White—none; Red—pinot noir
Leading wine: Ray-Monde Pinot Noir
Notes: As is increasingly the case with Pinot Noir in Australia, Ray-Monde is experimenting with wild yeast fermentation. The results are sometimes unusual. Cellar door sales by appointment made on Sunday between 11am–5pm.

Wildwood Vineyards R85

St Johns Lane, Wildwood, Bulla, Vic 3428
Ph 03 9307 1118, Fax 03 9331 1590,
Email wildwoodvine@bigpond.com

Owner: Dr Wayne G. Stott
Chief winemakers: Wayne Stott and Peter Dredge
Year of foundation: 1983
Tonnes crushed on average each year: 25, but this will increase as the newly planted vineyard area comes into bearing
Location: Bulla
Area: 16 ha
Soils: heavy black basalt on the tops of the slopes, where the 'Bordeaux' varieties are planted and lighter terra rossa over limestone for the others
Varieties planted: White—chardonnay, viognier; Red—cabernet franc, cabernet sauvignon, merlot, petit verdot, pinot noir, shiraz
Leading wines: Wildwood Chardonnay, Cabernets, Shiraz
Notes: The Wildwood vineyard area has recently been doubled, so production will certainly increase in the next few vintages. Wayne Stott will also be hoping for a break to the three-year drought which has reduced production from his established vineyard. But a gold medal for Wildwood Shiraz 99 at the Ballarat Show has certainly increased his enthusiasm. Cellar door sales: 7 days 10am–6pm.

Witchmount Estate R83

557 Leakes Road, Rockbank, Vic 3335
Ph 03 9747 1155, Fax 03 9747 1744

Owners: M. and G. Ramunno
Chief winemaker: Peter Dredge (contract)
Year of foundation: 1991
Tonnes crushed on average each year: 30, but this will increase as new plantings come into production

Location: Rockbank
Area: 15 ha
Soils: red loam
Varieties planted: White—chardonnay,
sauvignon blanc; Red—cabernet franc,
cabernet sauvignon, nebbiolo, shiraz
Leading wines: Witchmount Cabernet
Sauvignon, Shiraz, Chardonnay, Nebbiolo

Notes: Witchmount has been a consistent
medal winner at local wine shows almost since
its inception. Cabernet Sauvignon and
Chardonnay are the strong varieties here.
Cellar door sales: Wed–Sun noon–10pm. An
Italian restaurant and function rooms open for
lunch and dinner.

MACEDON RANGES REGION (PROPOSED)

First traversed in 1824 by Hume and Hovell during their mistaken journey to Port Phillip (they were heading for Westernport), the Macedon Ranges were crossed and reported on by the energetic Surveyor General of New South Wales, Major Thomas Mitchell in 1836. There were earlier attempts at settlement in Southern Victoria soon after Hume and Hovell, for example, the failed attempt from Tasmania in 1827 by Hume's old school friend, John Batman, who finally succeeded by surreptitiously settling in Melbourne in May 1835. He was followed in August of the same year by John Pascoe Fawkner, who took up land at Monegeeta west of Romsey but did not settle there. In 1837, the New South Wales government recognised Batman's *fait accompli* and the area was officially opened for settlement, but by then there were over 200 squatters in the area stretching from Melbourne to Mount Macedon. Like much of rural Australia at that time, grazing was the chief pursuit, the towns in the general area beginning to develop in the 1840s. In the 1850s, the goldrushes to the north-west (Castlemaine and Bendigo) furthered their development. By the time Burke and Wills pushed north through the region in 1860 on their ill-fated north–south traverse of the continent, the Macedon Ranges were well settled, both legally by the station owners and rather more irregularly by bushrangers. From this time also and well into the twentieth century, the cool heights of the area became known as a refuge from the heat of the Australian summer and so became a holiday and health resort.

The viticultural history of the region began as usual with early graziers and farmers planting small vineyards in the 1840s and 1850s (see David Dunstan's *Better than Pommard*, 1994). These were at Carlsruhe, Darraweit Guim and Riddells Creek. Other vineyards were also planted in the general area at this time and later in the nineteenth century. None have survived, being victims of the 1890s eastern Australian recession, the adjoining warmer Sunbury vineyard area (also thriving in the later years of the nineteenth century) and the loss of English markets.

The Macedon region resumed its viticultural associations in 1968 when a Melbourne restaurateur, Tom Lazar, began to plant his Virgin Hills vineyard at Lauriston. He was soon followed by Gordon Knight at Granite Hills (1970). Later in the 1970s came Gordon Cope-Williams at Romsey (1977) and in the early 1980s John Ellis began Hanging Rock (1982). Since then many vineyards and wineries have been established in this rapidly expanding area, but there has been some dispute as to the name and extent of the region. In an area, part of which is very suited to the production of

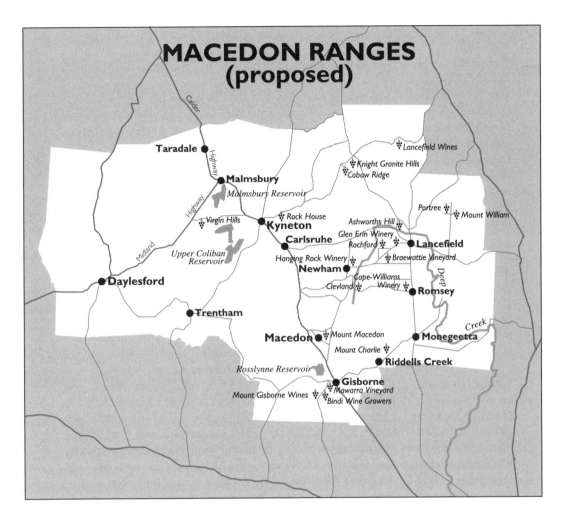

MACEDON RANGES (proposed)

sparkling wines, some makers have registered the name 'Macedon' to use for sparkling wines, provided they are made from the classic Champagne varieties grown within the region and by the classic champagne method. While this is understandable, there are other warmer parts of Macedon where red table wine grapes happily grow and ripen (e.g. Knight Granite Hills) and there are other areas (e.g. around Daylesford) which are simply not geographically part of the Macedon Ranges. So the solution proposed was a change of name to 'Greater Macedon', with a slight extension to the western boundary, and the eastern portion of the region becoming a sub-region 'Macedon Ranges'. Unfortunately this was not acceptable to the Geographical Indications board as it included a predominantly 'red' vineyard in the west of the sub-region and so was deemed not 'homogeneous' enough. So the region remains in unregistered limbo.

Location: Kyneton, latitude 37°16'S, longitude 144°25'E; Gisborne, latitude 33°30'S, longitude 144°37'E; Woodend, latitude 37°22'S, longitude 144°33'E; Lancefield, latitude 37°22'S, longitude 144°48'E. The region is about 65 km north-north-west of Melbourne.

Elevation: from about 400 m (Gisborne) to about 600 m (Woodend) with a mean altitude of 492 m.

Topography and soils: Geologically the Macedon Ranges region lies within an area of Ordovician and Silurian sedimentary rocks extending from east of Ballarat to east of Mount Macedon. These are bounded on the east by the Cambrian greenstones forming part of the Heathcote greenstone belt. In their turn these rocks have been intruded by Devonian granitic rocks forming the Cobaw Ranges in the north of the region. These also have been intruded by tertiary basalts and trachytes due to volcanic activity. The results of this are gently rounded hills punctuated by the granitic Cobaw Ranges to the north and the extinct volcanoes Mount Macedon, Mount Gisborne and Bullengarook in the south.

The soils resulting from the Ordovician and Silurian sandstones and shales are acidic duplex shallow brown-yellow clay loams of low fertility occurring in the west and south-west of the region, but also extending to the base of Mount Macedon, Macedon and Bullengarook and also to the Cobaw Ranges in parts. The soils derived from the granites of the Cobaw Ranges and parts of Mount Macedon on the steeper slopes are mostly free-draining uniform or gradational sandy to stony shallow loams. The soils around Romsey, to the south and east of Gisborne and around Woodend are rich gradational sometimes red friable clayey soils. They are volcanic in origin and are frequently found in contact with the Ordovician and Silurian duplex soils along old stream valleys.

Climate: Kyneton, MJT 18.4, MAR 12.6°C, HDD 1041, AR 828 mm, RH 61.9% (3pm); Macedon, MJT 17.4, MAR 12.2°C, HDD 1005, AR 853 mm, RH 59.8% (3pm) (both local); Cf Macedon MJT 17.7°C, MAR 12.8°C, HDD (raw) 1035, AR 753 mm (Oct–Mar 294 mm), RH 64% (9am), AI 168 mm, SH 8 (Dry & Smart). The Macedon Ranges region is undoubtedly cold. By way of comparison, the statistics for Reims in Champagne are MJT 18.3, MAR 16.3, HDD 1031, AR 700 mm, RH 58% (1pm July), SH 6.2 (Gladstones). The heat summations are some of the lowest in Australia and are very similar to those in Reims. No wonder then that the region has shown itself to be very suitable for sparkling wine style and early ripening still whites. The heat summations are also much lower than the neighbouring region to the north, Bendigo, where medium- to full-bodied red wines of good to excellent quality are made from cabernet sauvignon and shiraz grapes. This suggests that such varieties are generally unsuitable for the Macedon Ranges region, except in extremely favourable locations. Virgin Hills, which makes a classic Australian cool-area red, is such an exception. It is predominantly cabernet sauvignon, which as a general rule in this region ripens late in May and on some occasions early in June. The cause of this apparent anomaly is its sheltered north-facing microclimate and the very small crops that the Virgin Hills vines carry. Even earlier ripening red cultivars, such as pinot noir, must be regarded as marginal for table wines in this region. As a comparison, the HDD of Dijon in the north of the Cote d'Or is 1223, much warmer than Kyneton. Leongatha in Gippsland at about 1300 is similarly better placed. It would seem that there needs to be quite favourable lengthy ripening conditions or a warm and sheltered location for a Macedon Ranges site to obtain medium- to full-body in Pinot Noir in most years. In Macedon Ranges, therefore, microclimate is all-important in the production of even medium-bodied reds.

Strong, cold winds at flowering may also present serious problems unless vineyards are naturally sheltered or have wind breaks and sometimes even these are not enough to prevent loss. Frosts too can present problems, so sites with good air drainage should be chosen. Other problems may include birds, both native and imported, but these may be alleviated if there are alternative food supplies or if vineyards are netted.

The district is a substantial catchment area. Irrigation water is of good quality and, if used, is supplied to vineyards from surface dams and bores.

Harvest time: for chardonnay and pinot noir, late April to May, for other varieties, ripening may extend as late as mid-June, subject to favourable conditions at this difficult time of the year

Principal varieties: White—chardonnay; Red—pinot noir; other varieties often found in the region include sauvignon blanc, semillon, riesling and traminer, as well as cabernet sauvignon, merlot, cabernet franc and shiraz

Total area: 200 ha approx.

Major wine styles: *Sparkling Macedon* Champagne method sparkling wines of great finesse and style made from the classic varieties chardonnay and pinot noir (occasionally with a touch of meunier). Some of the best sparkling wines in Australia. Epitomised by Hanging Rock Macedon, but there are several other very good styles. *Chardonnay* A firmer 'Chablis' style of Chardonnay with good structure and malolactic firmly under control, often with minerally flavours (probably a terroir characteristic), quite distinctive. Ages well. Bindi Winegrowers Quartz Chardonnay is especially good. *Pinot Noir* Different and more 'Australian' than the more ethereal Pinots of Mornington Peninsula or the 'Burgundian' styles of the Yarra Valley, these are reds of good depth of colour, plummy in aroma and generous yet tight on palate. 'Chunky' seems an appropriate adjective for them in good years. *Shiraz* Generous reds of medium bodied 'berry' flavours with integrated tannins (e.g. Knight Granite Hills) that age well.

Ashworths Hill NR

104 Ashworths Road, Lancefield, Vic 3435
Ph/Fax 03 5429 1689

Owners: Peg and Ken Reaburn
Chief winemakers: (contract) John Ellis (whites), Ann Manning (reds)
Year of foundation: 1984 (vineyard), 1995 (winery)
Tonnes crushed on average each year: 3 (in 1998)
Location: Lancefield
Area: 4 ha
Soils: a range of soils varying from red loam through shot clay to grey loam

Varieties planted: White—chardonnay, riesling, and small amounts of flora, orang muscat and tullilah; Red—cabernet sauvignon, meunier, pinot noir
Leading wines: Ashworths Hill Cabernet, Pinot Noir
Notes: This is a small vineyard indicative of the widespread interest shown in vines by farmers throughout Australia. At an altitude of 500–527 m, Ashworths Hill is on marginal wine-growing country. As Peg Reaburn says, 'we have the best views, but are windswept'. In the high places such as this, spring can be both kind and cruel. High winds after budburst and late frosts can destroy or seriously retard

a promising crop in a few hours. Cellar door sales: Wed–Mon 10am–6pm.

Bindi Wine Growers R90

343 Melton Road, Gisborne, Vic 3437
Ph/Fax 03 5428 2564

Owner: Dhillon family
Chief winemaker: Michael Dhillon
Year of foundation: 1988
Tonnes crushed on average each year: 20
Location: Gisborne
Area: 6.5 ha
Soils: shattered quartz over alluvial clay
Varieties planted: White—chardonnay;
Red—pinot noir
Leading wines: Bindi Chardonnay, Chardonnay Quartz, Macedon Methode Champenoise, Pinot Noir Block Five, Pinot Noir Original Vineyard
Notes: Bindi is a classic Macedon Ranges vineyard well-suited to its varieties. Its Quartz Chardonnay is hard-edged and flinty, very 'Chablis'-like while its Original Vineyard Pinot Noir is also full-flavoured and plummy with a firmer palate structure than Pinots from other Port Phillip regions. They are fascinating wines which age particularly well in good years. Its Macedon Sparkling styles are also never less than excellent. Mail orders. No cellar door sales.

Braewattie Vineyard R86

351 Rochford Road, Rochford, Vic 3442
Ph 03 5429 1266, Fax 03 5429 1015

Owners: Des and Maggi Ryan
Chief winemakers: John Ellis, John Flynn (contract)
Year of foundation: 1993
Tonnes produced on average each year: 45, of which 6 are presently used for Braewattie wines
Location: Rochford
Area: 5.5 ha

Soils: free-draining red volcanic loam over basalt. The vineyard is situated at 560–600 m in altitude on the middle reaches of a north-easterly slope giving maximum sunlight exposure and has good air drainage, which minimises frost risks
Varieties planted: White—chardonnay; Red—pinot noir
Leading wines: Braewattie Chardonnay, Pinot Noir
Notes: Braewattie is planted to the Macedon Ranges sub-region's most suitable varieties and its first wines are extremely promising. Cellar door sales by appointment only.

Cleveland R83

Shannons Road, Lancefield, Vic 3435
Ph 03 5429 1449, Fax 03 5429 2017

Owners: Keith and Lynette Brien
Chief winemaker: Keith Brien
Year of foundation: 1984
Tonnes crushed on average each year: 40, of which 30 are grown at Cleveland, the balance purchased from local growers or from Heathcote for making Cleveland Shiraz
Location: Lancefield
Area: 4 ha
Soils: podsolic with varying depths of grey sandy loam over ironstone gravel and well-drained
Varieties planted: White—chardonnay, pinot gris; Red—pinot noir
Leading wines: Cleveland Brut Macedon, Pinot Noir, Chardonnay, Shiraz (made from shiraz from the neighbouring Heathcote region)
Notes: Cleveland is a consistent medallist for its sparkling wines at smaller regional wine shows. At Cleveland there is also an historic homestead built in 1890 as well as two bed and breakfast rooms and a restaurant. Cellar door sales: daily 9am–5pm.

Cobaw Ridge R86

31 Perc Boyers Lane, East Pastoria,
via Kyneton, Vic 3444
Ph/Fax 03 5423 5227

Owners: Nelly and Alan Cooper
Chief winemaker: Alan Cooper
Year of foundation: 1985
Tonnes crushed on average each year: 20, all
of which used for Cobaw Ridge wines
Location: East Pastoria
Area: 4 ha
Soils: free-draining granitic sand
Varieties planted: White—chardonnay;
Red—lagrein dunkel, pinot noir, shiraz
Leading wines: Cobaw Ridge Chardonnay,
Shiraz, Lagrein Dunkel
Notes: Tucked away 618 m up in the Cobaw
Ranges in the north-east of the Greater
Macedon Region, Cobaw Ridge is remarkably
cool. It is remarkable also for its Lagrein
Dunkel, a rare red from the Alto Adige area of
Northern Italy, what used to be in the early
20th century the Sud Tirol province of the
Austro-Hungarian Empire. World War I
changed all that but like Alsace in France, it
did not change the bi-lingualism of many of
the inhabitants or the grape varieties they
grew. Alan Cooper is a Lagrein enthusiast and
you may or may not be convinced by the
variety, which is certainly different. What is not
different is the great quality of his Shiraz and
Chardonnay. Certainly a place to visit, but
don't get lost in the nearby Cobaw National
Park. It gets quite cold at night. Cellar door
sales: weekends 10am–5pm, at other times
telephone first.

Cope-Williams Winery R83

Glenfern Road, Romsey, Vic 3434
Ph 03 5429 5428, Fax 03 5429 5655,
Email winesales@cope-williams.com.au

Owner: Cope-Williams family
Chief winemaker: Gordon Cope-Williams
Year of foundation: 1977
Tonnes crushed on average each year: 75
Location: Romsey
Area: 10 ha
Soils: Romsey red loam, decomposed basalt
Varieties planted: White—chardonnay;
Red—cabernet franc, cabernet sauvignon,
merlot, pinot noir
Leading wines: Romsey Brut, Cope-Williams
Chardonnay, Pinot Noir, Cabernet-Merlot,
Willow Liqueur
Notes: Cricket is a popular game in Australia,
but Gordon Cope-Williams has enshrined it at
Romsey, where sparkling wine and cricket are
integral parts of the local ethos. Here the only
'fine legs' you will encounter are on the field
or in the wine glasses. The sparkling wines are
well flavoured but with a delicacy imposed by
the region and 'Willow' will certainly cause no
tears. The Chardonnay, Pinot Noir and
Cabernet-Merlot are also very well made.
There are also a Royal Tennis Court and full
conference facilities with 21 rooms. Cellar door
sales: daily 10am–5.30pm.

Glen Erin Vin Retreat (formerly Glen Erin Grange) NR

Rochford Road, Lancefield, Vic 3435
(4 km west of the town)
Ph 03 5429 1041, Fax 03 5429 2053

Owners: Brian and Kim Scales
Chief winemaker: John Ellis (contract)
Year of foundation: 1993
Tonnes crushed on average each year: 6
Location: Lancefield
Area: 4.8 ha
Soils: volcanic loam on a clay base
Varieties planted: White—chardonnay,
gewurztraminer; Red—merlot, pinot noir
Leading wines: Glen Erin Macedon (Sparkling)
Chardonnay, Pinot Noir
Notes: Cellar door sales: weekends and public
holidays 10am–5pm, weekdays by
appointment. There is also a restaurant open

Friday night for dinner, Saturday lunch and dinner and Sunday lunch.

Hanging Rock Winery R87

The Jim Jim, 88 Jim Road, Newham, Vic 3442
Ph 03 5427 0542, Fax 03 5427 0310, Email hrw@hangingrock.com.au

Owner: The Hanging Rock Winery Pty Ltd
Chief winemaker: John Ellis
Year of foundation: 1982
Tonnes crushed on average each year: 1500, of which 500 are used for Hanging Rock wines
Location: Newham
Area: 6.5 ha
Soils: volcanic decomposing basalt
Varieties planted: White—chardonnay, gewurtztraminer, pinot gris, sauvignon blanc, semillon; Red—pinot noir
Leading wines: Hanging Rock 'Macedon' (a champagne method sparkling wine), The Jim Jim Sauvignon Blanc, Hanging Rock Heathcote Shiraz
Notes: Hanging Rock is planted on one of the old lava flows of the 'Jim Jim', an extinct volcano. At 650 m in altitude, it is a very cool if not cold site and as such has proved itself ideal for early ripening and sparkling wine varieties. Hanging Rock 'Macedon', of rich autolysed nose and palate characters, is a very fine sparkling wine. The Jim Jim Sauvignon Blanc is also excellent, as is the Heathcote Shiraz. John Ellis is also kept extremely busy as a very popular contract winemaker. Cellar door sales: 7 days 10am–5pm.

Knight's Granite Hills Wines R85

1481 Burke and Wills Track, Bayneton, via Lancefield, Vic 3444
Ph 03 5423 7264, Fax 03 5423 7288, Email ghknight@access.com.au

Owner: Knight family
Chief winemaker: Llew Knight
Year of foundation: 1970
Tonnes crushed on average each year: 90
Location: Bayneton
Area: 11 ha
Soils: coarse sandy decomposed granite loam over clay or granite boulders
Varieties planted: White—chardonnay, riesling; Red—cabernet franc, cabernet sauvignon, merlot, pinot noir, shiraz
Leading wines: Granite Hills Chardonnay, Riesling, Sparkling, Shiraz, Cabernet Sauvignon
Notes: Located on the northern side of the Great Dividing Range, where the climate is generous enough to ripen shiraz and the 'Bordeaux' varieties, this winery is certainly one of the veterans of the region and yet its wine styles have not become weary. It maintains an excellent record at various Victorian wine shows with many gold and silver awards. Its highlights are a seriously good Shiraz and a fresh stylish Riesling. Cellar door sales: Mon–Sat 9am–6pm, Sun 10am–6pm.

Lancefield Winery NR

Scrubby Camp Road, Emu Flat, Lancefield, Vic 3435
Ph 03 5433 5292, Fax 03 5433 5114

Owner/chief winemaker: Andrew Pattison
Year of foundation: 1985 (original location), 1995 (new location)
Tonnes crushed on average each year: 12
Location: Lancefield and Pipers Creek (near Kyneton)
Area: Lancefield 2.5 ha, Pipers Creek 3 ha
Soils: Lancefield granitic sand, Pipers Creek red volcanic loam
Varieties planted: (Pipers Creek) White—none; Red—cabernet franc, cabernet sauvignon, merlot. (Lancefield) White—chardonnay, gewurtztraminer; Red—pinot noir, shiraz
Leading wines: Pattison Cabernet-Merlot, Lancefield Winery Chardonnay
Notes: Andrew Pattison is primarily a

grape-grower, but crushes 50 tonnes of fruit for his own winery purposes. Cellar door sales: Wed–Sun. There is also a café.

Mawarra Vineyard R80

69 Short Road, Gisborne, Vic 3437
Ph 03 5428 2228, Fax 03 5428 4816,
Email bob@winetours.com.au

Owner: Bob Nixon and Associates Pty Ltd
Chief winemaker: John Ellis (contract)
Year of foundation: 1978
Tonnes crushed on average each year: 15
Location: Gisborne
Area: 4 ha
Soils: volcanic grey loam over a clay base
Varieties planted: White—chardonnay, semillon; Red—pinot noir
Leading wines: Mawarra Chardonnay-Semillon, Pinot Noir
Notes: Highlights here are crisp whites and Pinot Noir. Cellar door sales: 7 days 10am–5pm.

Mount Charlie Winery R79

228 Mount Charlie Road, Riddells Creek, Vic 3431
Ph/Fax 03 5428 6946

Owners: Trefor and Olive Morgan
Chief winemaker: Professor Trefor Morgan
Year of foundation: 1988
Tonnes crushed on average each year: 6
Location: Riddells Creek
Area: 2 ha
Soils: granitic
Varieties planted: White—chardonnay, sauvignon blanc; Red—cabernet sauvignon, merlot, shiraz
Leading wines: Mount Charlie Chardonnay, Sauvignon Blanc, Red (a blend of the red varieties mentioned)
Notes: Trefor Morgan is a graduate in Wine Science from Charles Sturt University. His vineyard is on the southern side of the

Macedon spur and the most southerly in the region. Despite this general aspect, the vineyard is situated on a north-facing knoll which provides protection from cold southerly winds, giving the vines a favourable microclimate in which to ripen red varieties, which can be difficult in less favourable parts of the Macedon Ranges. Cellar door sales: most Sundays by appointment. Sales also by mail order.

Mount Gisborne Wines R89

83 Waterson Road, Gisborne, Vic 3437
Ph/Fax 03 5428 2834,
Email m.g.w@bigpond.com

Owner: David and Mary Ell
Chief winemakers: Stuart Anderson, David Ell
Year of foundation: 1986
Tonnes crushed on average each year: 14
Location: Gisborne
Area: 3.2 ha
Soils: volcanic decomposing basalt
Varieties planted: White—chardonnay; Red—pinot noir
Leading wines: Mount Gisborne Chardonnay, Pinot Noir
Notes: A specialist vineyard under consultancy from Stuart Anderson, a specialist winemaker. The Pinots are outstanding in the bigger chunky Macedon style. Generally open on weekends or by appointment.

Mount Macedon R82

off Bawden Road, midway between Mount Macedon and Woodend, Vic 3441
Ph 03 5427 2735, Fax 03 5427 1071,
Email wine@mtmacedonwinery.com.au

Owners: Brian and June Neylon
Chief winemaker: Ian Deacon (consultant)
Year of foundation: 1989
Tonnes crushed on average each year: 25, but will increase as new plantings come into bearing

Locations: Mount Macedon and Pipers Creek
Area: Mount Macedon 9.8 ha, Pipers Creek 4 ha
Soils: Mount Macedon, volcanic with brown
clay loams and friable red clay loams, Pipers
Creek, granitic sand
Varieties planted: White—chardonnay,
gewurztraminer; Red—cabernet sauvignon,
merlot, meunier, pinot noir, shiraz
Leading wines: Mount Macedon Chardonnay,
Pinot Noir, Shiraz, Cabernet Sauvignon,
Sparkling Wines
Notes: At 680 m above sea level in such an
area, Mount Macedon is obviously a very cool,
even cold site. The new owners have brought
a vineyard at Pipers Creek near Kyneton into
the fold. So some different styles of whites and
reds may result. Cellar door sales: 7 days
10am–5pm.

Mount William Winery R80

Mount William Road, Tantaraboo,
via Kilmore, Vic 3764
Ph 03 5429 1595, Fax 03 5429 1998,
Email mtwilliam@connect.net.au

Owners: Murray and Adrienne Cousins
Chief winemaker: Murray Cousins
Year of foundation: 1987
Tonnes crushed on average each year:
20, which, together with a further 8 tonnes
purchased from local growers, fill the needs of
the winery
Location: Tantaraboo
Area: 7 ha
Soils: grey loam 60 cm deep over mudstone
over a clay base, red volcanic loam 30 cm
deep over a clay base
Varieties planted: White—chardonnay,
semillon; Red—cabernet franc, merlot, pinot
noir
Leading wines: Louise Clare Sparkling Red,
Chardonnay, Pinot Noir, Riesling
Notes: At 600 m in altitude and with snow
quite often in winter, Mount William has a
climate that can only be described as cold.

No wonder then that there is low
flavour-developing ripening and that vintage
extends from mid-April (chardonnay) to early
June (semillon). Cellar door sales: weekends
11am–5pm, at other times by appointment.

Portree R80

72 Powell's Track via Mount William
Road, Lancefield, Vic 3455
Ph 03 5429 1422, Fax 03 5429 2205

Owners: Ken and Lyn Murchison
Chief winemaker: Ken Murchison
Year of foundation: 1983
Tonnes crushed on average each year: 40, of
which 10 are used for Portree wines
Location: Lancefield
Area: 5 ha
Soils: red basalt (chardonnay), grey loam
(cabernet franc)
Varieties planted: White—chardonnay;
Red—cabernet franc, pinot noir
Leading wines: Portree Chardonnay
Notes: Ken Murchison ages his Chardonnays
for three years before release, a process which
certainly adds to complexity. His Cabernet
Franc Quarry Red is a full round early drinking
style not unlike the wines of Chinon on the
Loire. Cellar door sales: weekends and public
holidays 11am–5pm.

Rochford R86

146 Otts Road, Rochford, Vic 3442
Ph 03 5429 1428, Fax 03 5429 1066,
Email admin@rochfordwines.com.au

Owners: Helmut and Yvonne Konecsny
Chief winemaker: David Creed
Year of foundation: 1983
Tonnes crushed on average each year: 60,
increasing to 150 by 2005, all of which is or
will be used for Rochford wines
Location: Rochford
Area: 21 ha, not all of this is yet in bearing
Soils: red volcanic loam of good drainage

Varieties planted: White—chardonnay, pinot gris, riesling; Red—cabernet sauvignon, merlot, pinot noir
Leading wines: Rochford Pinot Noir, Chardonnay, Pinot Gris
Notes: Rochford has found that cabernet sauvignon does not suit its terroir in all vintages and so it has been removed and replaced by pinot noir, a much more suitable variety in the area and a trophy winner for Rochford at the local wine show. Cellar door sales: 7 days 10am–4pm.

Rock House **NR**

St Agnes Hill, Calder Highway, Kyneton, Vic 3444
Ph 03 5422 2205, Fax 03 9388 9355, Email rlacey@lincolne.com.au

Owners: Maxwell Finlason and Ray Lacey
Chief winemaker: Malcolm Stewart
Tonnes produced on average each year: 35, of which 5 are used for Rock House wines
Location: Kyneton
Area: 6 ha
Soils: no information
Varieties planted: White—riesling; Red—cabernet sauvignon, merlot
Leading wines: Kyneton Assemblage (a red blend), Riesling

Notes: No cellar door sales. Sales only through local licensed outlets.

Virgin Hills **R85**

17 Piper Street, Kyneton, Vic 3444
Ph 03 5422 3032, Fax 03 5422 3045

Owner: Michael Hope
Chief winemaker: Chris Smales
Year of foundation: 1968 (first vintage 1973)
Tonnes crushed on average each year: 60, of which about 35 are used for Virgin Hills wines
Location: Lauriston (vineyard), Kyneton (winery/cellar door)
Area: 14 ha
Soils: sandy loam of weathered granite over clay, well drained
Varieties planted: White—chardonnay; Red—cabernet sauvignon, malbec, merlot
Leading wine: Virgin Hills (a blend of the red varieties mentioned above)
Notes: In an isolated, very high and cool area, not always ideal for the varieties grown, Virgin Hills makes one of Australia's most notable and long-living reds. During the late 1990s Virgin Hills entered a troubled period of ownership from which hopefully it has now emerged, once more to re-establish a premium reputation. Cellar door sales: at Kyneton only, weekdays 10am–4pm, weekends 10am–5pm.

Like most Victorian agricultural regions, Gippsland had its viticultural origins in the nineteenth century and met a similar economic fate in the early years of the twentieth. Its rebirth also began about 1970, but it has had a slow growth since then. Apart from Chardonnay in the hands of makers like Ken Eckersley at Nicholson River, and Pinot Noir made by that master of Pinot, Phillip Jones at Bass Phillip, Gippsland wines await a final verdict. Certainly in ripe warm years such as 1983 and 1991, the Chardonnays and Pinots of Gippsland can be magnificently full-flavoured and even Cabernet Sauvignon ripens well, but Gippsland's problem is that such years are atypical. In cooler years, later ripening reds and whites, though delightful in their fruit character, seem to gain insufficient weight to interest the normal consumer of Australian wines. Cool areas, however, do not need such wines and Gippsland, which is most definitely cool, needs only to point to its Chardonnays and Pinots as wines deserving of the greatest respect.

Location: that part of Victoria approximately between latitude 145°30'E and 150°E and longitude 37°30'S and 39°S, a vast area stretching virtually from the south-eastern suburbs of Melbourne, south to the south-east coast of Victoria then east to the New South Wales border at Cape Howe. It stretches north-west from there into the Snowy Mountains, returning westerly mainly through the alpine country to its starting point. There are no official wine regions or sub-regions at the present time as the area, in terms of wine production, is too small. It would seem logical for the future, however, in view of the present viticultural sites, to divide Gippsland into three regions, West, South and East, which is the way I have classified the wineries.

Topography and soils: as must be expected in an area so large, these are very variable, from the lush green hills of western Gippsland, via the flood plains, lakes and coastal sands of central and eastern Gippsland to the temperate rainforests, alpine country and snowfields of the north and east.

Climate: Bairnsdale (East Gippsland), MJT 18°C, MAR na, HDD 1331, AR 696 mm (Oct–Apr 428 mm), RH 53%, AI na, SH 8; Leongatha (South-West Gippsland), MJT 18.1°C, MAR na, HDD 1301, AR 998 mm (Oct–Apr 530 mm), RH na, AI na, SH 6.5 (Gladstones). Windy and often wet along the Bass Strait coast in spring and early summer. In some years also, except for grape varieties such as pinot noir and chardonnay, autumn rain and cold bring the ripening season to an end too soon for the full maturation of most popular Australian wine grape varieties, a problem that Gippsland shares with northern Tasmania. In higher areas, it is sometimes frosty with snow in winter at altitudes above 1000 m.

Harvest time: late March to May

Principal varieties: Red—pinot noir, cabernet sauvignon, merlot; White—chardonnay, riesling, sauvignon blanc

Total area: na

Major wine styles: Chardonnay, Pinot Noir

Leading wineries: Bass Phillip, Phillip Island Vineyard, Narkoojee, Lyre Bird Hill Winery, Nicholson River Winery

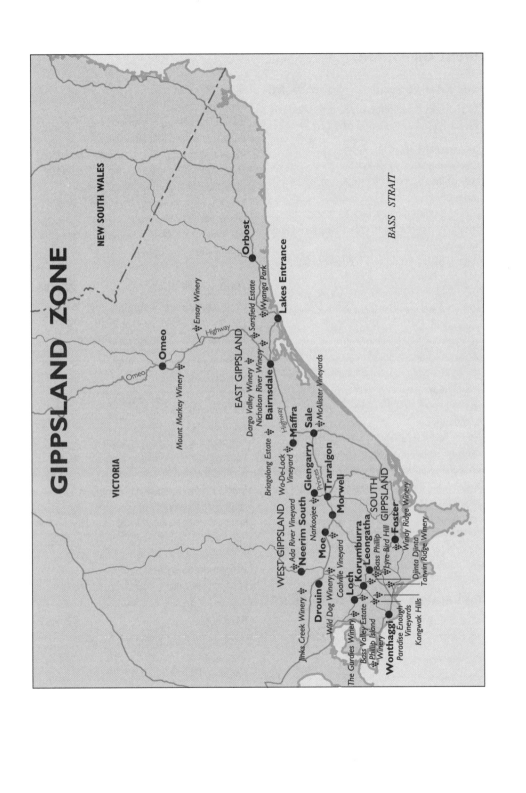

WEST GIPPSLAND

Ada River Vineyard NR

2330 Main Road, Neerim South, Vic 3831
Ph 03 5628 1221, Fax 03 5623 6723

Owners: Peter and Chris Kelliher
Chief winemaker: Peter Kelliher
Year of foundation: 1983 (vineyard), 1995
(wine sales)
Tonnes produced on average each year: 20
Locations: Neerim South (West Gippsland) and
Yarra Valley
Area: 9 ha consisting of 6 ha (Neerim South)
and 3 ha (Yarra Valley)
Soils: Neerim South, rich red volcanic soil; Yarra
Valley, typical grey clay loam (neither vineyard
is irrigated)
Varieties planted: (Neerim South)
White—chardonnay; Red—cabernet
sauvignon, pinot noir. (Yarra Valley) White—
chardonnay, gewurztraminer; Red—pinot noir
Leading wines: Gippsland Pinot Noir,
Chardonnay
Notes: Ada River vineyard is situated in the
heart of Gippsland's cheese country (the
homes of Gippsland Blue and Jindi Brie are
within 5 km of the vineyard. The Ada River
reds, especially the Cabernet (very good in
warmer years) make very interesting
companions to these premium cheeses.
Cellar door sales: at Neerim South, weekends
and public holidays 10am–6pm.

Coalville Vineyard NR

Moe South Road, Moe, Vic 3825
Ph 03 5127 4229, Fax 03 5127 2148

Owners: Peter and Libby Beasley
Chief winemaker: Peter Beasley
Year of foundation: 1972
Tonnes crushed on average each year: 20
Location: Moe
Area: 5 ha
Soils: sandy loam over red clay not far above

seams of brown coal
Varieties planted: White—chardonnay;
Red—cabernet franc, cabernet sauvignon,
malbec, merlot, pinot noir, shiraz
Leading wines: Coalville Cabernet Sauvignon
Notes: Coalville Vineyard is the workaday life
of vintage car enthusiast, Peter Beasley.
In warm years, it ripens cabernet very well.
I remember its 1991 well. Coalville has a
restaurant overlooking its vineyard. Cellar door
sales: 7 days 10am–5pm.

Jinks Creek Winery R85

Tonimbuk Road, Tonimbuk, Vic 3815
Ph 03 5629 8502, Fax 03 5629 2342,
Email JINKSCK@wgcomp.com.au

Owner/chief winemaker: Andrew Clarke
Year of foundation: 1981
Tonnes crushed on average each year: 7.5
Location: Jinks Creek
Area: 2.4 ha
Soils: granitic free-draining loam
Varieties planted: White—sauvignon blanc;
Red—pinot noir
Leading wines: Jinks Creek Sauvignon Blanc,
Pinot Noir, Chardonnay
Notes: A small estate in West Gippsland on the
road from Bunyip to Gembrook in the Yarra
Valley. It has a very small but much sought-
after production. Cellar door sales by
appointment only.

Narkoojee R87

RMB 1110 Francis Road, Glengarry,
Vic 3854
Ph/Fax 03 5192 4257

Owners: Harry and Val Friend
Chief winemakers: Harry and Axel Friend
Year of foundation: 1980
Tonnes crushed on average each year: 30
Location: Glengarry

Area: 4 ha
Soils: deep fertile alluvial soils comprising various mixtures of clay, silt, sand and ironstone gravels. A lyre trellis is used to minimise mildews and maximise fruit exposure
Varieties planted: White—chardonnay; Red—cabernet franc, cabernet sauvignon, merlot, pinot noir
Leading wines: Narkoojee Chardonnay, Cabernets, Cabernet-Merlot, The Athelstan Merlot
Notes: Narkoojee is renowned for its big flavoursome Chardonnays which should not be missed. Its reds are also a treasure. Cellar door sales: weekends, but telephone first.

Wild Dog Winery NR

South Road, Warragul, Vic 3820
Ph 03 5623 1117, Fax 03 5623 6402,
Email farfarm@nex.net.au

Owner: John and Helen Farrington
Chief winemaker: John Farrington
Year of foundation: 1981 (wine made from 1988)
Tonnes crushed on average each year: 60
Location: Warragul
Area: 12.5 ha
Soils: deep red Gippsland loam (kraznozem) about 3 m deep with poor moisture retention; drip irrigation available but rarely used
Varieties planted: White—chardonnay, riesling, semillon; Red—cabernet franc, cabernet sauvignon, pinot noir, shiraz
Leading wines: Wild Dog Shiraz, Pinot Noir-Rosé,
Notes: Wild by name but the wines are not wild by nature. In fact, there is quite good Shiraz here. Cellar door sales: every day 9am–5pm, except Christmas and Good Friday.

SOUTH GIPPSLAND

Bass Phillip R97

cnr Hunt and Tosch's Road, Leongatha South, Vic 3953
Ph 03 5664 3341, Fax 03 5664 3209

Owners: Phillip and Sairung Jones
Chief winemaker: Phillip Jones
Year of foundation: 1979
Tonnes crushed on average each year: 20, rising to 50 by 2002 as new vineyards come into bearing
Location: Leongatha South and Leongatha
Area: 18 ha Leongatha South (the Estate vineyard 4 ha), Leongatha (the Village vineyard 10 ha). Belrose (Leongatha South 4 ha)
Soils: the Estate, deep silty loams, rich in minerals of ancient volcanic origin, with some areas of raised sea-bed; Village, deep clay loams, ancient volcanic loams with 'buckshot' (high ironstone content); Belrose, rich loamy mudstone soils

Varieties planted: White—a little chardonnay; Red—a little gamay, pinot noir very much in the majority
Leading wines: (Estate) Bass Phillip Reserve Pinot Noir, Premium Pinot Noir, Pinot Noir; (Village) Village Pinot Noir, Crown Pinot Noir
Notes: Bass Phillip is very much the holy water of Australian Pinot Noir and, like holy water, it is dispensed unfortunately in tiny quantities. Carrying the ecclesiastical analogy further, its proprietor-winemaker, Phillip Jones, who controls one of the very few Australian vineyards that can aptly be called a 'domaine', is most certainly the Apostle of Pinot, totally devoted to pinot noir and its propagation. This religious fervour is tempered by Phillip's vast knowledge of his vineyard's climate and soil parameters. Pinot must certainly not be grown everywhere. It is, as Phillip says, very fussy about its microclimates, but he has found his own little spot in Leongatha South to be, if not

infallible, as close as it is possible to be to that sublime state. The Bass Phillip Chardonnay is also excellent. The vines on the new Village vineyard, which are cropped at very low levels, are still quite young but show much promise and so Pinotphiles can expect great wines in the future. Visits by appointment only.

Bass Valley Estate NR

St Helier Road, Loch, Vic 3945
Ph 03 5659 6321, Fax 03 5659 0256,
Email rogercutler@net-tech.com.au

Owner: Robert Cutler
Chief winemaker: Roger Cutler
Year of foundation: 1989
Tonnes crushed on average each year: 14
Location: Loch
Area: 2.8 ha
Soils: grey loam with slight clay content, sandstone subsoil
Varieties planted: White—riesling; Red—cabernet sauvignon, pinot noir, shiraz
Leading wines: Bass Valley Estate Cabernet Sauvignon
Notes: Like many Gippsland vineyards, Bass Valley Estate is a small family-operated winery with a very cool climate, its cabernet sauvignon not ripening until late in May. Its local wine show results are consistently good. Cellar door sales: 7 days 10am–6pm.

Djinta Djinta NR

cnr South Gippsland Highway and Stevens Road, Kardella South, Vic 3950 (between Korimburra and Leongatha)
Ph 03 5658 1163, Fax 03 5658 1863,
Email djintadjinta@dcsi.net.au

Owners: Peter and Helen Harley
Chief winemaker: Peter Harley
Year of foundation: 1988 (first wine 1995)
Tonnes produced on average each year: 11
Area: 2.2 ha
Soils: Strzelecki Grey i.e. silty clay loams about

1 metre deep over decomposing slate and mudstone. The vineyard is planted on north/south-facing slopes to facilitate drainage and to maximise exposure to the sun
Varieties planted: White—marsanne, roussanne, sauvignon blanc, semillon, viognier; Red—cabernet franc, cabernet sauvignon, merlot
Leading wines: Djinta Djinta Sauvignon Blanc Semillon, Marsanne Roussanne Viognier, Merlot Cabernet, Sauvignon, Cabernet Franc
Notes: Peter is both a chef and a qualified winemaker and by inclination prefers the Bordeaux white and red varieties and the Rhone whites to the more usual pinot noir and chardonnay of South Gippsland. His Sauvignon Blanc has received a trophy at a local show and has been well reviewed. Cellar door sales: weekends and public holidays 9am–6pm, other times by appointment. There is also a restaurant featuring local produce and local wines.

Kongwak Hills NR

1030 Korumburra–Wonthaggi Road, Kongwak, Vic 3951
Ph 03 5657 3267

Owner/chief winemaker: Peter Kimmer
Year of foundation: 1989
Tonnes produced on average each year: 7
Location: Kongwak
Area: 2 ha
Soils: grey-brown loam on a sandstone base
Varieties planted: White—chardonnay; Red—cabernet sauvignon, malbec, merlot, pinot noir, shiraz
Leading wines: Kongwak Hills Cabernet-Malbec-Merlot blend, Pinot Noir
Notes: Cellar door sales: weekends and public holidays 10am–5pm.

Lyre Bird Hill Winery and Guesthouse

 R86

Inverloch Road, Koonwarra, Vic 3954
Ph 03 5664 3204, Fax 03 5664 3206,
Email rowen@lyrebirdhill.com.au

Owners: Owen and Robyn Schmidt
Chief winemaker: Owen Schmidt
Year of foundation: 1987
Tonnes crushed on average each year: 12, with a further 12 purchased
Location: Koonwarra
Area: 2.4 ha
Soils: high acid duplex with black sandy loam topsoil, an intervening layer of gravel and a red gravelly subsoil
Varieties planted: White—chardonnay, riesling, traminer; Red—cabernet sauvignon, pinot noir, shiraz
Leading wines: Lyre Bird Hill Pinot Noir, Shiraz
Notes: Lyre Bird Hill is a restful place and well worth a special trip. Owen Schmidt has done well with his Pinot Noir in recent years, although he is 'particularly pleased' with his Shiraz. Robyn Schmidt provides excellent bed and breakfast accommodation and there are dinners by arrangement. Cellar door sales: weekends and public holidays 10am–5pm.

Paradise Enough Vineyards

 NR

Stewarts Road, Kongwak, Vic 3951
Ph 03 5657 4241, Fax 03 5657 4229

Owners: John Bell and Sue Armstrong
Chief winemaker: John Bell
Year of foundation: 1987
Tonnes crushed on average each year: 10
Location: Kongwak
Area: 6 ha
Soils: fine sandy loam over fine sandy clay, average drainage, over sandstone rock; a sheltered microclimate
Varieties planted: White—chardonnay; Red—cabernet franc, cabernet sauvignon, merlot, pinot noir, shiraz

Leading wine: Paradise Enough Reserve Chardonnay
Notes: John Bell is very Burgundian in his viticultural and winemaking approach, regarding his dry-land chardonnay and pinot noir as his two premium varieties. His wines are also non-interventionist, low sulfur and unfiltered. He is very much a disciple of Phillip Jones and it seems that is the way things in South Gippsland should be. Cellar door sales: weekends and public holidays noon–5pm, other times by appointment.

Phillip Island Vineyard and Winery

 R92

Berry's Beach Road, Phillip Island, Vic 3922
Ph/Fax 03 5956 8465

Owners: David and Catherine Lance
Chief winemaker: Dr David Lance
Year of foundation: 1994
Tonnes produced on average each year: 15, and a further 25 are purchased from local growers
Location: Phillip Island
Area: 2 ha
Soils: rich volcanically derived soil with some pebbles and small stones over a well drained clay subsoil
Varieties planted: White—chardonnay, sauvignon blanc; Red—cabernet sauvignon, merlot, pinot noir
Leading wines: Phillip Island Sauvignon Blanc, Nobbies Pinot Noir, Chardonnay
Notes: Phillip Island Vineyard and Winery has gone from success to success since its foundation in 1995. Seven trophies in its first five years are eloquent testimony to the skill and care that goes into its winemaking. The backbone of this good fortune has been not only winemaking expertise (that goes without saying when the names David Lance and Diamond Valley are mentioned) but also the grape varieties most suited to the local terroir,

sauvignon blanc, chardonnay, and pinot noir. Phillip Island Winery is another must on any winelover's short list of places to go! Cellar door sales: daily November–March 11am–7pm, April–October 11am–5pm.

Tarwin Ridge Wines NR

Wintles Road, Leongatha South, Vic 3953
Ph 03 5664 3211, Fax 03 8660 2114,
Email anstee@dcsi.net.au

Owners: Brian Anstee and Rhonda Givoni
Chief winemaker: Brian Anstee
Year of foundation: 1983
Tonnes crushed on average each year: 11
Location: Leongatha South
Area: 2.8 ha
Soils: light grey sandy loam over clay
Varieties planted: White—sauvignon blanc, semillon; Red—cabernet sauvignon, merlot, pinot noir
Leading wines: Tarwin Ridge Sauvignon Blanc, Pinot Noir, Cabernet-Merlot, Sparkling Red and White
Notes: Cellar door sales: May–October only, some Sundays but ring ahead. Other times by appointment.

The Gurdies Winery NR

215 Gurdies St Helier Road, The Gurdies, Vic 3984
Ph 03 5997 6208, Fax 03 5997 6511

Owners: Peter Svans, Peter Kozik and Yolanda Kozik
Chief winemaker: Peter Kozik
Year of foundation: 1982

Tonnes crushed on average each year: 12
Location: The Gurdies
Area: 4 ha
Soils: sandy loam with excellent drainage
Varieties planted: White—chardonnay, riesling; Red—cabernet sauvignon, merlot, pinot noir, shiraz
Leading wines: The Gurdies Cabernet Sauvignon, Cabernet-Merlot, Merlot, Reserve Pinot Noir
Notes: Rehabilitation at The Gurdies is now complete and the vineyard is growing with plans to double the existing area within the next few years. Cellar door sales: 7 days 10am–5pm.

Windy Ridge Winery NR

527 Fish Creek Foster Road, Foster, Vic 3960
Ph 03 5682 2035,
Email windyrdg@tpgi.com.au

Owners: Graeme and Georgia Wilson
Chief winemaker: Graeme Wilson
Year of foundation: 1978
Tonnes crushed on average each year: 5
Location: Foster
Area: 3 ha
Soils: duplex black loams, 20–30 cm deep, over clay subsoil
Varieties planted: White—traminer; Red—cabernet sauvignon, malbec, pinot noir
Leading wines: Windy Ridge Cabernet Sauvignon and Malbec, Pinot Noir
Notes: Cellar door sales: public holiday weekends only 10am–5pm.

EAST GIPPSLAND

Briagolong Estate   NR

Valencia–Briagolong Road, Briagolong,
Vic 3860
Ph 03 5147 2322, Fax 03 5147 2400,
Email briagest@netspace.net.au

Owners: Gordon and Christine McIntosh
Chief winemaker: Gordon McIntosh
Year of foundation: 1975
Tonnes crushed on average each year: 5
Location: Briagolong, north of Maffra
Area: 3 ha
Soils: highly leached Tanjil series, a thin layer of
sandy loam over very sticky clay
Varieties planted: White—chardonnay,
sauvignon blanc; Red—pinot noir
Leading wines: Briagolong Estate Pinot Noir,
Chardonnay
Notes: A small wine estate with a very low
rainfall and without irrigation, only making
wine from its own fruit, which accounts for a
very small production. Cellar door sales: by
appointment.

Dargo Valley Winery   NR

Lower Dargo Road, Dargo, Vic 3862
Ph 03 5140 1228, Fax 03 5140 1388

Owners: Hermann and Pam Bila
Chief winemaker: Hermann Bila
Year of foundation: 1985
Tonnes produced on average each year: 4
Location: Dargo
Area: 2.6 ha
Soils: rich alluvial river flats
Varieties planted: White—chardonnay,
gewurztraminer, riesling, sauvignon blanc;
Red—cabernet sauvignon, pinot noir
Leading wines: Dargo Valley Chardonnay,
Cabernet Sauvignon
Notes: Dargo Valley Winery is a family run
business with bed and breakfast and
bunkroom accommodation. There is a fully

licensed restaurant serving all meals daily
except Thursday when it is closed. Reservations
are required. Cellar door hours: noon–5pm,
weekends 10am–8pm.

Ensay Winery   NR

Great Alpine Road (formerly Omeo
Highway), Ensay, Vic 3895
Ph 03 5157 3203, Fax 03 5157 3372,
Email ensaywine@tpg.com.au

Owners: David and Jenny Coy
Chief winemaker: David Coy
Year of foundation: 1992
Tonnes crushed on average each year: 2
Location: Ensay
Area: 3 ha
Soils: granitic clay loam, free-draining
Varieties planted: White—chardonnay;
Red—cabernet sauvignon, merlot, pinot noir,
shiraz
Leading wines: Ensay Winery Chardonnay,
Shiraz
Notes: Situated about 220 m in altitude in an
isolated area and in a rain shadow, the Ensay
Winery is about an hour's drive from Mount
Hotham on Lakes Entrance watershed. The
vineyard is drip irrigated. Vertical shoot
positioning is employed. Cellar door sales:
weekends 11am–5pm, other times by
appointment.

McAlister Vineyards   NR

Golden Beach Road, Longford, Vic 3851
Ph/Fax 03 5149 7229

Owners: Maureen and Peter Edwards
Chief winemaker: Peter Edwards
Year of foundation: 1975
Tonnes crushed on average each year: 11
Location: Longford
Area: 2 ha

Soils: silicate in nature with clay and ironstone protrusion on a limestone base
Varieties planted: White—none; Red—cabernet franc, cabernet sauvignon, merlot, petit verdot
Leading wine: The McAlister (a blend of the 'Bordeaux' varieties listed above)
Notes: Though McAlister Vineyards may not be called a monoculture, it is certainly a 'Bordeaux' culture, one wine only being produced. Cellar door sales by appointment only.

Mount Markey Winery NR

Swifts Creek-Omeo Road, Cassilis, Vic 3896
Ph 03 5159 4328, Fax 03 5159 4599, Email mtmarkey@tpg.com.au

Owners: Howard and Christine Reddish
Chief winemaker: Howard Reddish
Year of foundation: 1991
Tonnes crushed on average each year: 14
Location: Mount Markey (winery), Cassilis (vineyard)
Area: 5 ha (Mount Markey 3 ha and Cassilis 2 ha)
Soils: Mount Markey, gold mining schist, quite free-draining; Cassilis, granitic soil on top of granite
Varieties planted: White—chardonnay, kerner, pinot gris, sauvignon blanc, traminer; Red—cabernet sauvignon, meunier, pinot noir, shiraz
Leading wines: Mount Markey Chardonnay, Lone Hand Cabernet, Rose of Australia Honey Mead. There are also elderberry wine and herb and fruit vinegars
Notes: At nearly 500 m in altitude, Mount Markey is on the Lakes Entrance catchment of the Great Dividing Range and during summer is about 20 per cent warmer than Melbourne. It is a dry area, which means that drip irrigation is needed in times of moisture stress. Cellar door sales: 6 days 10am–5pm except Tuesday unless it is a public holiday. There is also a potters' gallery.

Nicholson River Winery R85

Liddell's Road, Nicholson, Vic 3882 (about 3 km north of Princes Highway, between Bairnsdale and Lakes Entrance)
Ph 03 5156 8241, Fax 03 5156 8433, Email nichowine@net-tech.com

Owners: K. and J. Eckersley
Chief winemaker: Ken Eckersley
Year of foundation: 1978
Tonnes crushed on average each year: 20, but will increase as young, recently planted vines come into bearing
Location: Nicholson
Area: 8 ha
Soils: gravelly to sandy loams
Varieties planted: White—chardonnay, riesling, sauvignon blanc, semillon; Red—merlot, pinot noir
Leading wines: Nicholson River Chardonnay, Pinot Noir, Botrytised Semillon, Sparkling Wines
Notes: Ken Eckersley is one of the pioneers of modern Gippsland viticulture. He is quite famous for his full-bodied Chardonnays, usually wines of immense depth of flavour and complexity. His Chardonnay-style has evolved through the last 20 years from the big rich wooded styles of the 1980s to the finer-boned less-wooded wines of the present time, but his devotion to quality remains. Like many smaller makers, Nicholson River is also exploring its export opportunities. Cellar door sales: December to Easter 10am–4pm. At other times ring ahead to make an appointment.

Sarsfield Estate NR

345 Duncan Road, Sarsfield, Vic 3875
Ph 03 5156 8962, Fax 03 5156 8970

Owners: Peter Albrecht and Suzanne Rutschmann
Chief winemaker: Suzanne Rutschmann
Year of foundation: 1992
Tonnes produced on average each year: 15, all

of which are or will be used for Sarsfield Estate wines
Location: Sarsfield
Area: 2 ha
Soils: dark sandy loam over light clay. The vineyard is planted on a north-facing slope sheltered from strong winds
Varieties planted: White—none; Red—cabernet franc, cabernet sauvignon, merlot, pinot noir, shiraz
Leading wines: Sarsfield Estate Cabernets-Shiraz, Pinot Noir
Notes: A new small vineyard off the Omeo Highway at Sarsfield between Bairnsdale and Bruthen, specialising in reds. No cellar door sales. Its wines are available through mailing list and at selected restaurants and bottle shops.

Wa-de-Lock Vineyard NR

Stratford–Maffra Road, Vic 3860
(Vineyards and Winery)
76 Tyers Street (i.e. Princes Highway)
Stratford, Vic 3862 (Cellar Door)
Ph 03 5147 7050, Fax 03 5147 7030,
Email wadelock@i-o.net.au

Owners: Graeme and Astrid Little
Chief winemaker: Graeme Little
Year of foundation: 1987
Tonnes crushed on average each year: 17, but will increase as new plantings come into bearing
Location: Stratford (cellar door); Maffra (vineyard)
Area: 5.64 ha not all yet bearing
Soils: the vineyard is established on an elevated north-east-facing slope with good air drainage. Soils are sandy loam with porous clay and broken sedimentary sandstone throughout. Good drainage
Varieties planted: White—chardonnay (clone I10V5), sauvignon blanc (H5V10); Red—cabernet sauvignon (G9V3), nebbiolo (vars), pinor noir (MV6), shiraz (PT23)

Leading wines: Wa-de-Lock Pinot Noir, Sauvignon Blanc, Chardonnay
Notes: As well as being a consistent winner of silver and bronze awards at Victorian regional wine shows, Wa-de-Lock has expanded. Its cellar door sales has moved to Stratford and now stocks wines from sixteen Gippsland wineries, cheeses from six different cheesemakers and smoked goods from two Gippsland smoke houses. It is an obvious place to stop for the food and wines for a picnic lunch. There is also a café and wine-bar. Open 7 days 10am–6pm.

Wyanga Park NR

Baades Road, Lakes Entrance, Vic 3909
Ph 03 5155 1508, Fax 03 5155 1443

Owners: Geoff and Lindel Mahlook
Chief winemaker: (contract)
Year of foundation: 1970 (vineyard), 1980 (winery)
Tonnes crushed on average each year: 70
Location: Lakes Entrance
Area: 6.4 ha, some fruit is bought in from local growers
Soils: gravel through to sandy loam, well drained, 60 m in altitude abutting north arm of lake
Varieties planted: White—chardonnay, riesling, sauvignon, traminer; Red—cabernet sauvignon, pinor noir
Leading wines: Wyanga Park Sauvignon Blanc, Cabernet Sauvignon
Notes: Wyanga Park is an unusual Australian vineyard site for two reasons: it sometimes experiences a California-like sea mist coming off Bass Strait and it also offers a lake cruise as a means of access to its restaurant and cellar-door facility. It serves morning tea and lunch daily and dinner on Thurs to Sat nights. Cellar door sales: 7 days Mon–Sat 9am–5pm, Sun 10am–5pm.

❦ NORTH EAST VICTORIA ZONE

This is yet another Victorian zone whose future was firmly founded upon the gold discoveries of the Beechworth and Rutherglen fields in the second half of the 19th century. It is a zone of extremes, both in climate and terrain, varying from the snowy alpine peaks of Mount Hotham to the hot plains of the eastern Murray Valley. There are currently three registered wine regions, Rutherglen, Alpine Valleys and Beechworth. One other, King Valley, seems permanently affixed to interim registration status. The remaining grape-growing area, Glenrowan, famous for its fortified wines, has not yet requested regionalisation.

RUTHERGLEN REGION

By the 1820s, the exploration and settlement of New South Wales was expanding not only to the north and the west but rather more accessibly to the south and south-west. In 1824 the explorers Hume and Hovell crossed what they called the Hume River near present-day Albury. The river was renamed the Murray five years later by Charles Sturt, who discovered it much further west, at its junction with the Murrumbidgee. Hume and Hovell went on to discover Corio Bay (part of Port Phillip) which they mistakenly thought was Westernport, the objective of their expedition. The peripatetic Sir Thomas Mitchell also passed close to the area in 1836 on his return journey from Portland.

The Rutherglen story really begins in 1837 when E. P. S. Sturt, a Commissioner for Crown Lands, toured the area to extract fees from squatters. Official records of the area began in 1841 when the New South Wales Lands Department noted a cattle run at Wahgunyah being held by two licensees. By 1845, there were many squatters' runs and over 800 settlers were recorded as living between the Murray and Goulburn Rivers. Within a decade, Victoria had achieved its independence from New South Wales and the river-boat trade on the Murray originating in South Australia, and inspired by the gold rush to Beechworth in 1852, had also begun to develop. By 1860 further gold discoveries in the region had consolidated Wahgunyah's status as a thriving river-port and when in 1860 a further gold discovery was made only 10 km away, it seemed that the prosperity of the area was established. Within a few months a town sprang up, and was soon named Rutherglen by one John Wallace, a Scot and a successful former 'digger', who called it after his birthplace. Gold, however, was a fickle ally and soon, due to difficult 'leads', production began to fall and the population of the town dwindled. By 1870, the area's economy was agricultural, but the romance of gold was not forgotten. It was a love affair to be renewed in the 1890s.

It has often been said that the vine marched arm in arm with the gold seekers, but perhaps in Rutherglen's case it preceded the discoveries that were to be so important to the development of Australia in the 1850s. The story has it that in 1851 three German settlers, Frauenfelder, Schumbach and Rau (who were perhaps former indentured agricultural labourers from New South Wales, brought to that Colony in the

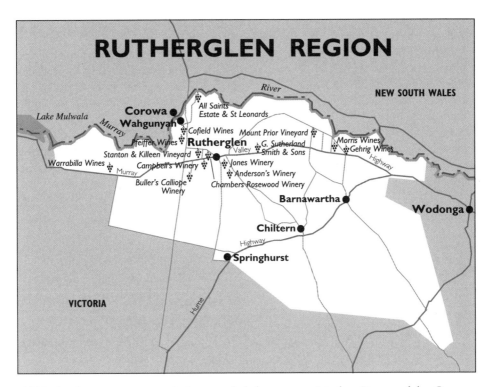

1840s for their vinous expertise) persuaded the squatter Lindsay Brown of the Goora-madda run to be allowed to plant some vines there. The vines flourished and were quickly followed by more plantings. Former gold miners such as George Morris and John Campbell also took up the vine. By 1865, Morris, Campbell, Sutherland Smith and Gehrig were all vignerons of the Rutherglen district. By 1881, there were over 800 hectares of vines in the area.

The coming of the railway in 1879 also spurred on vinous expansion. Winemakers could now ship their produce to Melbourne and, indeed, overseas to London, where tastes were growing for the sturdy reds and fortifieds that the Rutherglen district, with its abundance of sun, made so well. And when, with the fall of wool and wheat prices in the late 1880s, the Victorian Government stepped in with cash bounties for vine-growing, six-and-a-half million litres of wine poured from the local wine presses. Within a few years, Rutherglen was the showplace of the north-east.

By 1900, the Rutherglen wine boom had abated. There were three causes: the election of a teetotal Government that abolished the vine bounty; the financial malaise that afflicted all of eastern Australia in the mid-1890s; and, much more serious, the onset of phylloxera. Phylloxera had wiped out the Geelong vineyards over 20 years earlier and had seriously set back Bendigo and the Goulburn Valley in the 1890s. Now it was Rutherglen's turn. Even though its march was inexorable, the industry was not wiped out. In 1908, in a sensible effort to combat phylloxera, Francois de Castella, son of Hubert of Yarra Valley fame, was sent to Europe to investigate new grape varieties as well as new techniques that allowed new vines to be grafted onto phylloxera-resistant root stock. His collection of new varieties was established in the Rutherglen Viticultural College, which later became the Rutherglen Research Institute.

While Rutherglen recovered from phylloxera, it never regained its former glory. Although wine tastes, such as they were in the early 20th century, favoured its products (many millions of litres of strong reds and fortifieds were exported from Australia), it was South Australia that benefited most and, of course, suffered most when the crash finally came in late 1929. Rutherglen struggled on, its luscious tokays and muscats fortifying it against any further decline in its fortunes, until the 1960s, when the wine volcano began to erupt once more. But as the boom has progressed from red table wines to white, Rutherglen has not been well equipped to receive the benefits. Current fashion does not favour its best products, Tokay and Muscat, which have often been called Australia's most distinctive wines. This is a great pity. It is just as well that 'big' reds have always had their followers, as Rutherglen's reds are no laggards in this respect.

Location: latitude 36°30'S, longitude 146°32'E, about 240 km north-east of Melbourne.
Elevation: The vineyards of the region are between 160 and 250 metres in altitude.
Topography and soils: The region is mainly flat, although there are slight undulations. Part of the Shepparton formation, its soils consist mainly of alluvial clay, silt, sand and gravel deposits spread over older marine sediments. They are accompanied in some places by lacustrine (lake) and aeolian (wind) deposits and are extremely deep, at places more than 50 metres. They have been mostly deposited by older river systems flowing west and north-west from the Victorian Alps. The two major soil types were classified in 1961 by Poutsma and Skene as Rutherglen Loam and (less prosaically) as Black Dog Fine Sandy Loam, the latter soil occurring in the southern part of the region. These soils are distinctive to the region and differ markedly from those in the Corowa area, across the River Murray, and soils to the south in the Glenrowan area of the Warby Ranges.
Climate: MJT 22.3°C, MAR 15.4, HDD 1775, AR 590 mm (Oct–Mar 258 mm), RH 50%, AI 375 mm, SH 9.3 (Dry & Smart), MJT 22.4°C, MAR na, HDD 1580 (adjusted for vine sites), AR 608 mm (Oct–Apr 311 mm), RH 26%, AI na, SH 9.6 (Gladstones), MJT 22.35°C (local), MAR 14.45°C (local), HDD 1817 (raw from Gladstones' data), AR 597.2 mm (local), RH 48% (local). Rutherglen undoubtedly has a very warm growing season with a substantial amount of its annual rainfall falling during that season. It has also been stressed that the region enjoys ripening temperatures comparable with other great fortified wine producing areas of the world, for example, Frontignan in Southern France and Setubal in Portugal. What is perhaps more important is that in Rutherglen's case, its low relative humidity leads to a partial shrivelling (without botrytis) of the berries during and after ripening. Such shrivelling results in an intense, very sweet style, but without the complexity of botrytis cinerea. A low natural humidity is also important in the control of downy mildew and less noble types of botrytis. Another factor differentiating its climate from areas nearer the coast is an absence of cooling afternoon breezes, cut off as it is from any maritime influences, though Wahgunyah, sitting on a bend in the Murray River, does sometimes experience a cooling river breeze in the evenings called the 'Wahgunyah Doctor'.

Irrigation is not essential for winegrowing in this region, but as in most other Australian sites, it is recommended certainly for the establishment of young vineyards and for times of moisture stress thereafter. Drip irrigation is found in many vineyards, water being supplied either from the Murray River or from private surface dams. The usual spray programs are adopted to counteract mildews. As for other problems, the Rutherglen region is frost-prone so vines tend to be trained high and clean cultivation techniques adopted. Colin Campbell allows about a 5 per cent crop loss every year for frosts and birds.

Harvest time: typical ripening dates are: chardonnay—in the east of region, second week of March, in the west of region, mid-March. Shiraz—in the east of region, end of March, in the west of region, end of March/early April. Cabernet sauvignon—in the east of region, mid-April, in the west of region, third week of April.

Principal varieties: White—chardonnay, muscadelle, riesling, semillon, trebbiano; Red—cabernet sauvignon, durif, grenache, muscat à petits grains rouge, shiraz, touriga

Major wine styles: Historically, Rutherglen had two major wine styles: the first and most important being the marvellously rich fortified Muscats, Tokays (from the muscadelle variety) and port style; the second, the huge tannic dry reds, which were formidably big wines, and required equally heroic palates to consume them. Such wines often needed many years' cellaring to come into balance, if, indeed, they ever did. It is regrettable that during the past 25 years, popular taste has moved away from fortified wines, however good they may be and also, with some exceptions, from Australian reds that need long cellaring. But such is fashion. It is hoped that Rutherglen makers persist in their traditional styles, especially in making those luscious fortifieds!

The Muscats, made from the Rutherglen brown muscat (muscat a petits grains rouges) usually present a tawny brown hue and show that indescribable mix of muscat and rancio characters on nose and palate. These wines are the icons of Rutherglen orthodoxy. The Tokays made from the muscadelle grape are usually an aged golden brown in shade with distinctive aromas of cold tea and, again, that marvellous integration of old wood, old spirit and old wine called 'rancio'. Such fascinating characters are replicated on palate. The port styles, whether tawny or vintage, can only be compared to those of McLaren Vale, but the vintage style is usually more earthy and less driven by blackberry fruit.

Though today those superb fortified styles are still produced, they need time, skill and the economic motive to continue in such production. Unless the pendulum of fashion swings away from table wines and in their favour, Rutherglen winemakers will not waste their time producing fortified wines they cannot sell. That is why eight makers of Rutherglen Muscat (All Saints Estate, R.L. Buller & Son, Campbells, Chambers Rosewood Vineyards, Morris Wines, Pfeiffer Wines, Seppelt [formerly of Rutherglen but now of the Barossa Valley] and Stanton & Killeen) have introduced a classification system, dividing Rutherglen Muscat into four categories that mark a progression in richness, complexity and intensity of flavour. They are as follows: *Rutherglen Muscat* this should show fresh raisin aromas, rich fruit, clean spirit and good length of flavour on palate; *Classic Rutherglen Muscat* this should offer a greater level of richness and complexity, arising through the blending of selected parcels of wine, often matured in various sizes of oak casks to impart dry 'rancio' characters, produced from maturation in seasoned wood; *Grand Rutherglen Muscat* this style goes a step further in the procession to perfection, displaying even greater levels of intensity, depth and concentrated flavour, mature rancio characters and complexity; *Rare Rutherglen Muscat* this is the *ne plus ultra*, the peak, pinnacle and paragon of all Rutherglen muscat, fully developed and displaying the richest and most complete Muscat characters that are possible in the region. The Muscats of Rutherglen have their own identifying mark of regional authenticity, a stylised R above a bunch of grapes surrounded by the words Muscat of Rutherglen within an oval logotype.

Apart from the fortifieds and the big reds, the region also produces honestly made white wines, Chardonnays and Semillons typical of warmer areas, which are good present drinking, but hardly ever memorable.

Leading wineries: (fortified) Morris Wines, Chambers Rosewood Vineyards, Campbell's Winery, R.L. Buller & Son; (table wines) Campbell, All Saints, Morris.

Note: In the following winery notes, because of the unique nature of Rutherglen and in connection with the seven Rutherglen domiciled wineries mentioned above—five of which are rated below—fortified wine classifications have been given separately from table wine classifications. FR = Fortified rating, WR = Table wine rating.

All Saints Estates  FR88 WR84

All Saints Road, Wahgunyah, Vic 3687
Ph 03 6033 1922, Fax 03 6033 3515,
Email wine@allsaintswine.com.au

Owner/chief winemaker: Peter Brown
Year of foundation: 1864
Tonnes crushed on average each year: 350
Location: Wahgunyah
Area: 50 ha
Soils: sandy loam over clay
Varieties planted: White—chardonnay, marsanne, muscadelle, riesling, sauvignon blanc, semillon;
Red—cabernet sauvignon, merlot, muscat a petits grains rouges, pinot noir, shiraz
Leading wines: All Saints Estate Chardonnay, Shiraz, Cabernet Sauvignon, Muscat, Tokay.
Notes: Under the ownership and wine supervision of Peter Brown, the historic All Saints Estate grows in strength. Its red brick castellated winery, built in 1880, looks back to the solidity of the Victorian era. Its benchmark wines are its rich and luscious fortifieds, but its Carlyle Chardonnay and Shiraz are often very good. Cellar door sales: Mon–Sat 9am–5.30pm, Sun 10am–5.30pm. Closed Christmas Day. There is also a restaurant, The Terrace, open Mon–Fri 10am–5pm and for dinner Sat from 7pm. Closed Christmas Day and Good Friday.

Anderson's Winery NR

Chiltern Road, Rutherglen, Vic 3685
(2 km from Rutherglen Post Office)
Ph 03 6032 8111

Owner: Anderson family
Chief winemaker: Howard Anderson
Year of foundation: 1992 (vineyard), 1993 (winery)
Tonnes crushed on average each year: 22
Location: Rutherglen
Area: 5 ha
Soils: clay loam with 'buckshot' over clay base
Varieties planted: White—none; Red—durif, shiraz
Leading wines: Anderson Shiraz, Sparkling Shiraz, Sparkling Merlot
Notes: Howard Anderson spent 14 years at Seppelt Great Western and still puts his sparkling expertise to good use in Rutherglen by making three sparkling wines at his winery. Sparkling whites are not often made in this region so it is not surprising that some of the

fruit used for this purpose comes from the King Valley. There are of course other sparkling reds in the region, usually made from shiraz and/or durif. Apart from the sparkling wines, there is usually a good Shiraz. Cellar door sales: 7 days 10am–5pm.

R.L. Buller & Son Rutherglen **FR88 WR82**

Three Chain Road, Rutherglen, Vic 3685 (about 5 km west of the town)
Ph 03 6032 9660, Fax 03 6032 8005, Email bullers@albury.net.au

Owner: Val Buller
Chief winemaker: Andrew Buller
Year of foundation: 1921
Tonnes crushed on average each year: 80
Locations: Rutherglen and Indigo Valley within the Rutherglen region
Area: 22.81 ha at Rutherglen and 10 ha planted at Indigo Valley with 40 ha more available there
Soils: Rutherglen, light red loam over clay; Indigo Valley, granitic sand over red loamy subsoil
Varieties planted: (Rutherglen) White—chasselas, muscadelle, white frontignac; Red—cinsaut, grenache, mondeuse, muscat a petits grains rouge, shiraz. (Indigo Valley) White—chardonnay, marsanne, sauvignon blanc; Red—cabernet franc, cabernet sauvignon, durif, merlot, pinot noir
Leading wines: Calliope Shiraz, Rare Rutherglen Muscat
Notes: Buller is an old and respected name in Rutherglen, not quite as old perhaps as the originals, Morris, Chambers and Campbell, but its non-irrigated Rutherglen vineyard makes great fortified wines in the same style. The Indigo Valley vineyard, which produces more delicate table wine fruit, presently sells its fruit but when market opportunities arise, will be utilised for wines under the Buller label.
Cellar door sales: Mon–Sat 9am–5pm,

Sun 10am–5pm. Closed Christmas Day and Good Friday.

Campbell's Winery **FR91 WR85**

Murray Valley Highway, Rutherglen, Vic 3685
Ph 03 6032 9458, Fax 03 6032 9870

Owners: Campbell family
Chief winemaker: Colin Campbell
Year of foundation: 1870
Tonnes crushed on average each year: 900, of which 650 are used for Campbell's wines
Location: Rutherglen
Area: 70 ha
Soils: red clay loam
Varieties planted: White—chardonnay, muscadelle, riesling, semillon, sylvaner, trebbiano; Red—cabernet sauvignon, durif, muscat a petits grains rouge, ruby cabernet, shiraz
Leading wines: Campbell's Bobbie Burns Shiraz, Chardonnay, Rutherglen Muscat
Notes: The Campbell winery was founded by John Campbell, a Scottish goldminer who came to the region in 1858. Like all good Scots, he had a great respect for Bobbie Burns and named his winery after him. Colin Campbell, the present chief winemaker, has been the driving force behind the move to classify Rutherglen Muscat, wines which he totally understands and makes expertly. His Bobbie Burns reds are also typical of the region, 'big' in the Rutherglen style but never jarringly astringent. His whites too have a delicacy that is hard to match in the region.
Cellar door sales: Mon–Sat 9am–5pm, Sun 10am–5pm.

Chambers Rosewood Vineyards **FR95 WR74**

Barkly Street, Rutherglen, Vic 3685
Ph 03 6032 8641, Fax 03 6032 8101

Owners: Chambers Rosewood Pty Ltd
Chief winemaker: Bill Chambers
Year of foundation: 1858
Tonnes crushed on average each year: 125, with a further 5 tonnes purchased
Location: Rutherglen
Area: 5 ha
Soils: red duplex
Varieties planted: White—gouais, muscadelle, palomino, riesling; Red—cabernet sauvignon, cinsaut, grenache, muscat a petits grains rouge, shiraz, touriga
Leading wines: Chambers Rosewood Muscat, Tokay, other Fortifieds
Notes: Chambers Rosewood is one of the magic names of north-east Victorian fortified wines, always vying with Morris as the quintessence of Rutherglen Muscat style. If anything, the Chambers style is lighter and a touch more elegant, but both wines are fantastically good and Bill Chambers, winemaker and senior wine judge, is one of the stalwarts of the industry. Cellar door sales: Mon–Sat 9am–5pm, Sun 11am–5pm. Closed Christmas Day and Good Friday.

Cofield Wines NR

Distillery Road, Wahgunyah, Vic 3687
Ph 03 6033 3798, Fax 03 6033 0798

Owners: Karen and Max Cofield
Chief winemaker: Damien Cofield
Year of foundation: 1990
Tonnes crushed on average each year: 10
Location: Wahgunyah (2 vineyards)
Area: 8 ha
Soils: light free-draining sandy soil in one vineyard, and heavier clay loam in the other
Varieties planted: White—chardonnay, muscadelle, semillon; Red—cabernet sauvignon, durif, merlot, sangiovese, shiraz
Leading wines: Cofield Sparkling Shiraz
Notes: Cellar door sales: Mon–Sat 8am–5pm, Sun 10am–5pm. The 'Pickled Sisters' Café is open Wed–Mon 10am–4pm.

Gehrig Wines NR

Cnr Murray Valley Highway and
Howlong Road, Barnawartha, Vic 3688
Ph 03 6026 7296, Fax 03 6026 7424,
Email gehrig@hotkey.net.au

Owner: Gehrig family
Chief winemaker: Brian Gehrig
Year of foundation: 1858
Tonnes crushed on average each year: 120
Location: Barnawartha
Area: 20 ha
Soils: loam over clay base, water retentive
Varieties planted: White—chardonnay, chenin blanc, muscadelle, riesling, trebbiano; Red—cabernet sauvignon, cinsaut, durif, merlot, muscat a petits grains rouge, pinot noir, shiraz
Leading wines: Gehrig Estate Chardonnay, Cabernet-Shiraz, Vintage Port
Notes: Cellar door sales: Mon–Sat 9am–5pm, Sun 10am–5pm. There is also the Café Courtyard.

Jones Winery R80

Chiltern Road, Rutherglen, Vic 3685
Ph 03 6032 8496, Fax 03 6032 8495,
Email jones@joneswinery.com

Owners: Arthur and Mandy Jones and Leanne Schloen
Chief winemaker: Mandy Jones
Year of foundation: founded in 1860 and purchased by the Jones family in 1927
Tonnes crushed on average each year: 15, the vineyard is currently being expanded
Location: Rutherglen
Area: 12 ha
Soils: red clay
Varieties planted: White—pedro ximenes; Red—muscat a petits grains rouge, shiraz
Leading wines: L J Shiraz, Classique Dry Red
Notes: The Jones Vineyard changed hands in 1998 and has been brought into the 21st century by the skilled winemaking of Mandy

Jones, who was making wine in Bordeaux for a decade until the recent purchase. Cellar door sales: Fri–Sat 10am–5pm, Sun and public holidays 10am–4pm.

Morris Wines **FR95 WR84**

Mia Mia Road, Rutherglen, Vic 3685
Ph 03 6026 7303, Fax 03 6026 7445

Owner: Orlando Wyndham
Chief winemaker: David Morris
Year of foundation: 1859
Tonnes crushed on average each year: 1600
Location: Rutherglen
Area: 100 ha, consisting of 2 vineyards; Mia Mia 55 ha and Knights 45 ha
Soils: red loam over red-yellow podsolic subsoil
Varieties planted: White—chardonnay, muscadelle, palomino, semillon; Red—cabernet sauvignon, cinsaut, durif, muscat a petits grain rouge, shiraz, touriga
Leading wines: Morris Old Premium Muscat, Tokay, Morris Durif
Notes: I said in the 1st edition that a Morris Liqueur Muscat is the taste experience of a lifetime. I see no reason to change that opinion. Cellar door sales: Mon–Sat 9am–5pm, Sun 10am–5pm.

Mount Prior Vineyard **NR**

Cnr River Road and Popes Lane, Rutherglen, Vic 3685
Ph 03 6026 5591, Fax 03 6026 5590,
Email mtprior@bigpond.com

Owner: Jim Sawyer
Chief winemaker: Tony Lacy assisted by James Asch
Year of foundation: 1860
Tonnes crushed on average each year: 200, increasing to 250 as the vines mature
Location: Rutherglen
Area: 47 ha
Soils: red loam over shale rock and red loam over clay

Varieties planted: White—chardonnay, chenin blanc, semillon; Red—cabernet sauvignon, durif, grenache, malbec, merlot, shiraz
Leading wines: Mount Prior Chardonnay, Shiraz, Cabernet-Merlot, Durif
Notes: Mount Prior has a gracious old Rutherglen house built in the booming 1880s and now run as a guest house with five rooms and an award-winning restaurant using top local produce, all set in two hectares of garden—an excellent place to taste its wines. The restaurant is open to the public each day. Cellar door sales: 7 days 9am–5pm.

Pfeiffer Wines **NR**

Distillery Road, Wahgunyah, Vic 3687
Ph 03 6033 2805, Fax 03 6033 3158

Owners: Chris and Robyn Pfeiffer
Chief winemaker: Chris Pfeiffer
Year of foundation: 1984
Tonnes crushed on average each year: 300, all used for Pfeiffer and Carlyle labels
Location: Wahgunyah
Area: 32 ha in two blocks
Soils: alluvial sandy loam over gravel and heavy loam over clay and gravel
Varieties planted: White—chardonnay, frontignac, muscadelle, riesling; Red—cabernet franc, cabernet sanzey, cabernet sauvignon, gamay, merlot, muscat a petits grains rouge, pinot noir, shiraz, touriga and small areas of 26 other Portuguese varieties
Leading Wines: Pfeiffer Riesling, Marsanne, Chardonnay, Frontignac, Ensemble (a rosé style), Gamay, Pinot Noir, Shiraz, Cabernet Sauvignon, Auslese Tokay, Christophers Vintage Port, Old Distillery Port (a tawny), Old Distillery Muscat, Old Distillery Tokay, Fino Sherry. There is also the lesser priced Carlyle range made from fruit purchased in the district
Notes: With his wife Robyn, Chris Pfeiffer purchased the old Seppelt Distillery at Wahgunyah in 1984. Chris, a winemaker of great experience in fortified and also table

wines, worked as group fortified winemaker until that time and since then has acquired a vast amount of show judging experience. The result is a full range of both fortified and table wines at his winery. Cellar door sales: Mon–Sat 9am–5pm, Sun 11am–4pm, closed Christmas and Boxing Days, Good Friday and Anzac Day morning.

St Leonards R84

St Leonards Road, Wahgunyah, Vic 3687
Ph 03 6033 1004, Fax 03 6033 3636,
Email wine@stleonardswine.com.au

Owner/chief winemaker: Peter Brown
Year of foundation: 1860
Tonnes crushed on average each year: 160
Location: Wahgunyah
Area: 22 ha
Soils: sandy loam and clay
Varieties planted: White—chardonnay, chenin blanc, orange muscat, sauvignon blanc, semillon; Red—cabernet franc, cabernet sauvignon, malbec, shiraz
Leading wines: St Leonards Chardonnay, Shiraz
Notes: St Leonards is a tranquil place, gracefully sheltered on the banks of a lagoon of the nearby Murray River. Its table wines are always consistently good. Cellar door sales: 11am–5pm daily. There is also the Lazy Grape Café open during the same hours each day. Closed Good Friday and Christmas Day.

Stanton and Killeen Vineyard NR

Jacks Road off Murray Valley Highway, Rutherglen, Vic 3685
Ph 03 6032 9457, Fax 03 6032 8018,
Email skwines@neto.net.au

Owner: Killeen family
Chief winemaker: Chris Killeen
Year of foundation: 1875
Tonnes crushed on average each year: 200
Location: Rutherglen
Area: 40 ha

Soils: red loams a metre deep over clay
Varieties planted: White—muscadelle; Red—cabernet franc, cabernet sauvignon, durif, merlot, muscat a petits grains rouge, shiraz, tinta baroca, tinta cao, touriga nacional
Leading wines: Stanton & Killeen Durif, Jacks Block Shiraz, Vintage Port, Muscat
Notes: A very good maker of reds and fortifieds which are firmly in the mainstream of regional style. Cellar door sales: Mon–Sat 9am–5pm, Sun 10am–5pm.

G Sutherland Smith & Sons Pty Ltd NR

Cnr Murray Valley Highway and Falkiners Road, Rutherglen, Vic 3685 (7 km east of the town)
Ph/Fax 03 6032 8177

Owner: George Sutherland Smith and Sons Pty Ltd
Chief winemaker: George Sutherland Smith
Year of foundation: 1993
Tonnes crushed on average each year: 20
Location: Rutherglen
Area: 5 ha consisting of three vineyards, at Glenrowan, Wooragee near Beechworth and Rutherglen
Soils: Rutherglen vineyard, red loam over red-yellow podsol
Varieties planted: White—riesling, traminer; Red—cabernet sauvignon, merlot, shiraz
Leading wines: Sutherland Smith Riesling, Chardonnay, Josephine Riesling-Traminer, Cabernet-Shiraz, Cabernet-Shiraz-Merlot, Tawny Port
Notes: Cellar door sales: weekends, Victorian school holidays and public holidays.

Warrabilla Wines NR

Murray Valley Highway, Rutherglen, Vic 3685 (18 km west of the town)
Ph/Fax 03 6035 7242

Owners: Andrew and Carol Smith
Chief winemaker: Andrew Smith
Year of foundation: 1991
Tonnes crushed on average each year: 85
Location: Rutherglen
Area: 14.8 ha
Soils: deep rich red loam to sandy loam with 'buckshot'

Varieties planted: White—chardonnay, riesling; Red—cabernet sauvignon, durif, merlot, muscat a petits grains rouge, shiraz
Leading wines: Warrabilla Shiraz, Durif, Cabenet
Notes: Warrabilla's principal wines are reds, very much in the mainstream of regional style.
Cellar door sales: 7 days 10am–5pm.

ALPINE VALLEYS

Like most of the North East Victorian wine zone, the Ovens Valley was an area settled by graziers in the 1840s. In the ensuing decade it was transformed by the lure of gold with the result that most of its present-day towns and villages mark their origin from this time. Mining fever continued in the Ovens Valley and surrounds for all the rest of the 19th century, made more permanent by the invention in the early 1850s of 'reef mining', a quartz crushing process that made gold-panning seem rather casual. In the Flagstaff Range area alone 44 gold bearing reefs were identified.

The name 'Alpine Valleys' was something of a compromise between those who wished to call the region 'Ovens Valley' and others who preferred Mount Buffalo Ranges and other names. As a wine-producing region, 'Ovens Valley' may have been more evocative, recalling as it does, the Shiraz, made by Wynns in the 1960s and 1970s and the range of Brown Brothers wines from the Everton Hills (also in the Ovens Valley) made at the same time. But Alpine Valleys is a region of several valleys, encompassing not only the valley of the Ovens River but the Buckland Valley and that of the Kiewa.

Location: Myrtleford, latitude 36°31'S longitude 146°44'E, about 250 km north-east of Melbourne; Bright, latitude 36°40'S longitude 146°53'E, about 256 km north-east of Melbourne
Elevation: Bright 300 m
Topography and soils: In the Ovens River catchment area, four distinct river terraces and a recent flood plain have been identified. There are two more elevated terraces associated with Mount Buffalo. The soils on the present flood plain commence at 300 m elevation upstream of Eurobin in the Ovens and Buckland Valleys and upstream from Nug Nug in the Buffalo River Valley to a 180 m elevation downstream from Rocky Point Bridge. Such soils have no profile development and are the most fertile soils. They can be described as recent alluvial soils consisting mostly of sandy loams and fine sandy clay loams. Such soils produce high yields of grapes of lesser value to winemakers than fruit produced on higher terrace soils.

The soils on the lowest river terrace are greyish-brown gradational soils, still very young and highly fertile with little soil profile development. Soil types are similar to those on the flood plain. The elevation of these soils is 180–200 m.

On the second lowest terrace, soils are again greyish-brown to brown gradational. Soils here show more profile surface features ranging from fine sandy loam to fine sandy clay loam with a slight increase in texture at a quarter of a metre depth but not

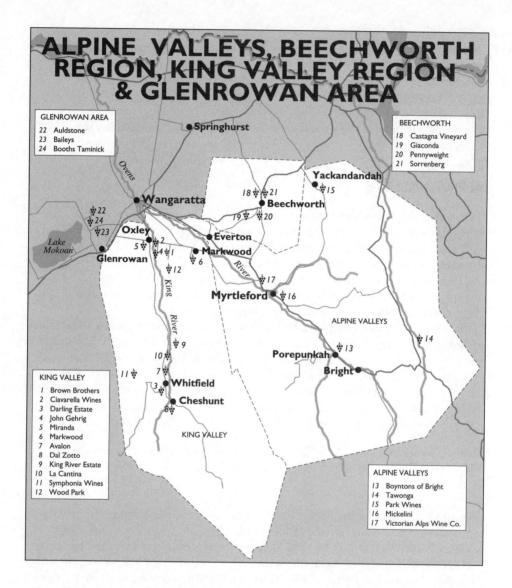

ALPINE VALLEYS, BEECHWORTH REGION, KING VALLEY REGION & GLENROWAN AREA

GLENROWAN AREA

22 Auldstone
23 Baileys
24 Booths Taminick

BEECHWORTH

18 Castagna Vineyard
19 Giaconda
20 Pennyweight
21 Sorrenberg

KING VALLEY

1   Brown Brothers
2   Ciavarella Wines
3   Darling Estate
4   John Gehrig
5   Miranda
6   Markwood
7   Avalon
8   Dal Zotto
9   King River Estate
10 La Cantina
11 Symphonia Wines
12 Wood Park

ALPINE VALLEYS

13 Boyntons of Bright
14 Tawonga
15 Park Wines
16 Mickelini
17 Victorian Alps Wine Co.

exceeding a clay loam. In soils on the lowest and second lowest river terrace, vigour control is necessary to produce fruit of very good quality. Sites where soil textures become lighter than fine sandy loam at a depth of three-quarters of a metre or more will aid vigour control, as some moisture stress can be imposed during January and February. The elevation of this terrace is about 220 m.

The second highest terrace has duplex soils on older sediments. Its soils vary greatly between upstream and downstream locations. Upstream from Rocky Point Bridge there are lighter soils of a yellowish-brown to reddish-brown colour, with textures not exceeding clay loams in the B horizon, whereas downstream from that bridge there are much heavier soil features with medium clay B horizons common. In elevation these soils vary from 240 m down to 180 m. Vigour control is less necessary because of the clay layers in the profile and the vines can be stressed. The fruit produced is usually excellent.

The highest terrace has duplex reddish-brown to red-brown soils. These soils are at an elevation of 240–250 m and soil features change abruptly from fine sandy clay loams to reddish or red-brown medium clays with stable structure. As the soils are fairly fertile, some vigour control may still be necessary, but the fruit produced is of very high quality.

Forming a ring around Mount Buffalo, there are very old dark-red duplex soils. These soils are on ancient river terraces at an elevation of 300 m and in some slightly higher areas (320 m) are overlain with colluvial material. Though vigour control has to be practised, these too produce excellent fruit.

On the hills, soils vary from gradational to duplex and in colour from yellowish-brown to reddish-brown. They occur at an elevation of 300–340 m upstream of Rocky Point Bridge and at an elevation of 240–280 m downstream of this bridge. They have less depth in profile and gravel with medium clay is often found at depths of less than one metre. Here vine vigour is more easily managed because of lower fertility and moisture stress during January and February. Gently sloping hills with an easterly to north easterly aspect are favoured because there is often a deeper layer of surface soil.
Climate: Bright (300 m altitude) MJT 20.4°C, MAR 13.6°C, HDD (raw) 1608, 1246 adjusted, AR 1218 mm (Oct–Apr 617 mm), RH na (Ovens Research Station). Myrtleford MJT 21.3°C, MAR 13.9°C, HDD 1482, cut off at 19°C, AR 902 mm (Oct–Apr 425 mm), RH 56% (Jan 3pm), AI na, SH na.

The southern end of the Valley (Bright and Porepunkah) is very suitable for the production of excellent 'cool area' table wines, particularly Chardonnays.

In these alpine valleys, which basically run from the Victorian Alps (altitude about 2000 m) in the south-east to the north-west, vineyard site selection should be made with extreme care as there is a considerable risk of frost. Sites with free air drainage should be chosen to avoid streams of cold air which flow in springtime along the valleys to the flatter lands around Wangaratta. Throughout North Eastern Victoria, phylloxera is an ever-present risk and all vineyards should be established on phylloxera-resistant rootstocks.
Harvest time: (Bright) chardonnay late March to early April, shiraz late April to early May, late May.
Principal varieties: White—chardonnay, sauvignon blanc; Red—cabernet sauvignon, merlot, shiraz, pinot noir
Area: 480 ha (2000) (80 ha planned for 2001 and beyond)
Major wine styles: The area is undoubtedly cool and shares with the neighbouring King Valley many farmers of Italian origin who for many years relied on tobacco as their major cash crop. With the decline of tobacco about 20 years ago many diversified into wine grapes such as sauvignon blanc and merlot as well as the more usual varieties such as shiraz and cabernet sauvignon, together with pinot noir and chardonnay, which were popular as sparkling base wine. Now the pendulum is swinging to Italian varietals, such as sangiovese, barbera and nebbiolo. The area has yet to establish a wine identity, other than as a source of grapes for large wine companies.
Leading wineries: Victorian Alps Winery, Boynton

Boynton's Wines R83

Great Alpine Road, Porepunkah, Vic 3740
Ph 03 5756 2356, Fax 03 5756 2610,
Email boyntons@bright.albury.net.au

Owner/chief winemaker: Kel Boynton
Year of foundation: winery and cellar door,
1989; vineyard, 1997
Tonnes crushed on average each year: 175
Location: Porepunkah (about 10 km from
Bright)
Area: 16 ha
Soils: deep alluvial red soils washed down from
the adjacent hills, forming terraces on which
the vineyard is planted
Varieties planted: White—chardonnay, pinot
gris, riesling, sauvignon blanc; Red—cabernet
sauvignon, durif, merlot, meunier, petit verdot,
pinot noir, shiraz
Leading wines: Boyntons Cabernet Sauvignon,
Merlot, Shiraz, Chardonnay
Notes: Boyntons was my introduction to the
wines of this region long before it became
one. The depth of fruit and lack of extraction
and hot tannins surprised me, accustomed as I
was to the wines of Rutherglen further north.
Since then the wines have retained their
quality. Cellar door sales: daily 10am–5pm.

Michelini Wines NR

Great Alpine Road, Myrtleford, Vic 3737
Ph 03 5751 1990, Fax 03 5751 1410,
Email MicheliniWines@bigpond.com

Owner: Vallunga Pty Ltd
Chief winemaker: Josephine Horn
Year of foundation: 1966
Tonnes crushed on average each year: 800, of
which 50 are used for Michelini wines
Location: Myrtleford (winery), Buckland Valley,
Porepunkah (vineyards)
Area: 36 ha
Soils: red loam
Varieties planted: White—chardonnay;
Red—marzemino, merlot, pinot noir

Leading wines: Michelini Riesling, Cabernet
Sauvignon, Shiraz, Merlot, Marzemino,
Chardonnay, Fragolino
Notes: The winery is recent, the vineyards
established and the show record good, and,
as befits the Michelini family of winegrowers,
there is an emphasis on Italian varieties such
as marzemino, but there are also more usual
varieties like merlot. Cellar door sales: daily
10am–5pm.

Park Wines NR

Sanatorium Road, Allans Flat,
Yackandandah, Vic 3691
Ph 03 6027 1564, Fax 03 6027 1561,
Email parkwine@hotkey.net.au

Owners: Rod and Julia Park
Chief winemaker: Rod Park
Year of foundation: 1982
Tonnes produced on average each year: 9
Location: Allans Flat
Area: 6.25 ha
Soils: rich clay/loams
Varieties planted: White—chardonnay, riesling;
Red—cabernet franc, cabernet sauvignon,
merlot
Leading wines: Park Wines Chardonnay,
Cabernet Sauvignon
Notes: Rod Park's practice is to mature his
Cabernet 'in the highest quality French oak'
for 2 years and his Chardonnay for 12 months.
I am partial to high quality French oak but
unfortunately have not been able to taste the
wines. Cellar door sales: most weekends,
public and school holidays 10am–5pm.
At other times ring ahead to make an
appointment.

Tawonga Vineyards NR

2 Drummond Street, Tawonga, Vic 3697
Ph /Fax 03 5754 4945

Owner/chief winemaker: John Adams
Year of foundation: 1994

Tonnes produced on average each year: 10, increasing as newly grafted wines come into bearing
Location: Tawonga, Kiewa Valley
Area: 3.6 ha
Soils: deep red loamy clay and shallow red loam over ancient river stone soils
Varieties planted: White—verdelho, viognier; Red—merlot, shiraz, chambourcin
Leading wines: Tawonga Chardonnay, Shiraz
Notes: Cellar door sales by appointment.

Victorian Alps Winery   **R86**

Cnr Great Alpine and Snow Roads, Gapsted, Vic 3737
Ph 03 5751 1992, Fax 03 5751 1368,
Email vicalps@netc.net.au

Owners: Victorian Alps Wine Co (a venture of Kingston Estate, Shayne Cunningham, four King Valley growers and one Buffalo Valley grower)
Chief winemaker: Shayne Cunningham, Michael Cope-Williams (winemaker)

Year of foundation: 1997
Tonnes crushed on average each year: 5000
Location: Gapsted (winery and 10 ha vineyard)
Area: 10 ha but the winery is also a contract crushing facility for local growers and also many other wineries buying fruit from the region and adjoining regions
Soils: a south-west facing slope with reddish-brown fine loam to sandy clay loam over shale and quartz
Varieties planted: White—none; Red—cabernet sauvignon, merlot, petit verdot, shiraz
Leading wines: Gapsted Durif, Merlot, Cabernet Sauvignon
Notes: This new corporate entity involves principals who bring together their own individual skills in an arrangement for the common good. The new winery will crush and vinify some of the considerable quantities of fruit now emanating from the Alpine Valleys.
Cellar door sales: Fri–Sun and holidays 10am–5pm.

BEECHWORTH REGION

The Beechworth region must be one of the rare areas of inland Victoria not traversed by the peripatetic Major Mitchell, if only because Messrs Hume and Hovell had beaten him to it, passing that way 12 years earlier. In 1838, William and George Faithful, overlanding from Sydney with sheep, reached the Ovens district. George founded the Oxley Plains run and William headed south towards present-day Benalla, but was waylaid by Aborigines who killed 17 of his party of 19. Due to these events, Dr G. E. McKay halted at Myrrhee, where he briefly settled before being driven away by Aborigines. He later settled at Warrowly where he again offended the local tribe who, attacking with spears and guns, killed all but 7 of 3000 head of cattle. Dr McKay was not present at the time of the attack, but while hunting for his missing cattle was the first to see the present site of Beechworth. Dr McKay was to prosper, seizing the opportunities presented by the Beechworth Gold Rush in the 1850s to open stores selling goods to local miners in Beechworth, Stanley, Quartz Reef (Gapsted) and Myrtleford. Gold fever raged throughout the Ovens Valley during that decade and was heightened by the new technique of reef mining (as opposed to gold panning). After the fever had abated, most of those infected moved on to other Eldorados, however, gold mining remained an important local industry for another century, waxing and waning as the world required or relaxed its reliance upon gold. Beechworth too was notorious for its bushrangers, the most infamous of whom were the Kelly Gang and it was from Beechworth gaol that Ned Kelly made his final trip to Melbourne in 1880.

Sales of agricultural land also began in the mid-1850s, many of the purchasers being successful local miners. With the growth of agricultural settlement came a corresponding diversity of production. Wheat, oats, potatoes, tobacco, hops, all were tried and most succeeded. The first reference to viticulture occurs about the same time (1856), when a Mr Rochlitz is recorded by the local press (*The Ovens and Murray Advertiser*) as having introduced '95 different descriptions of grapes from Adelaide at very great expense and trouble'. By 1863 Mr Rochlitz was fulfilling the role of nurseryman and supplying the district with propagation material. Winemaking by French and German miners started about the same time: Bertrand, Grandjoux, Chevalier, Zimmermann, Neuber—such are the names. Their vineyards were small. In fact, by 1865 there were only 36 hectares of vineyard in the region. Vineyard growth was steady but slow for the rest of the century, 49 ha of vineyard being recorded by 1892. By Federation, however, viticulture was declining with vineyard area being only 40 ha. Probably due to the arrival of phylloxera, which had decimated nearby Rutherglen, by 1910 there were only 13 ha and by 1916 only 2 ha. A revival, of sorts, began in 1945 when 2 ha were established at Everton Hills, a property purchased in 1950 by Brown Brothers and subsequently enlarged. Brown Brothers made their sought-after Everton Hills wines until 1978 when the vineyard was sold and not re-established due to low production.

The modern era of Beechworth viticulture can be said to have begun in 1980 when Rick Kinzbrunner established his Giaconda Vineyard between Everton Hills and Beechworth. By vintage 1998, viticulture in the region had virtually reached its 1865 level and by 2000 about 74 ha of vineyard existed once more in Beechworth.

Location: Beechworth latitude 36°21'S, longitutde 146°19'E about 250 km north-east of Melbourne.
Elevation: Beechworth 552 m; Mount Stanley (peak) 1050 m; Stanley township 700–800 m
Topography and soils: The region is distinguished from neighbouring regions by the fact that it encompasses a single distinct massif (Mount Stanley) of considerable elevation (1050 m) and does not include any significant streams. It has two major soil types: Ordovician greywacke, sandstone, mudstone and shales, and Devonian granites and grandiorite. Close to Beechworth most of the arable land is between 500–650 m in altitude and is derived primarily of mudstones. To the south-east of Beechworth, there are large tracts of rich agricultural and horticultural land surrounding Stanley (at 700–800 m altitude) which consist of mudstone and granite soils. These change primarily to granite between Stanley and Mount Stanley further to the south-east. To the west, the country declines in altitude to 280 m and here there are three different granites unique to the area: Golden Ball Silicified Quartz, Golden Ball Adamelite and Everton Grandiorite Porphyrite. In the north-east of the region around Wooragee at an altitude of between 320 and 400 metres, there is a tract of rich Permian soils associated with colluvial outwashes (the result of ancient glacial activity). These are

basically surrounded by granite. The region's vineyards are found primarily above 350 metres in altitude as opposed to those of nearby regions which are located below that height.

Climate: Beechworth MJT 20.4°C, MAR 14.1°C, HDD 1420 adjusted for altitude, AR 921 mm (Oct–Apr 470 mm) RH 44% (9am Jan), AI na (local), SH 9.3 (Gladstones). Stanley HDD 1240 adjusted for altitude, AR 1234 mm (Oct–Apr 556 mm). Wooragee HDD 1687 adjusted for altitude, AR 785 mm (Oct–Apr 372 mm). Golden Ball area HDD 1725 adjusted for altitude.

Being north of the Great Divide, the region is primarily influenced by weather patterns that affect the east coast of Australia rather than its southern coasts. Thus the region's rainfall results from low pressure troughs forming over the east coast and being drawn inland, or tropical wet weather patterns weakening and being pushed south-east across the continent by cold fronts coming from the south-west. Frost is a risk, but generally the region is at a high altitude and so much less at risk than if it were lower, since cold air sinks from the high hilltops into the river valleys of surrounding regions.

The region has no major rivers or irrigation schemes and relies on natural rainfall, springs and bores for water and surface dams for collection, though the soils in the region because of their porous nature do not lend themselves to dam construction. Water quality is good but potential yields of water at 18 000 litres per hour are low.

Harvest times: Chardonnay from 2nd week of March to 1st week of April, cabernet sauvignon from 3rd to 4th week of April, but occasionally earlier

Principal varieties: chardonnay, shiraz, cabernet sauvignon, pinot noir

Area: (2000) 97.9 ha

Major wine styles: Chardonnay, Shiraz, Pinot Noir

Leading wineries: Giaconda, Castagna

Castagna **R85**

Ressom Lane, Beechworth, Vic 3747
Ph 03 5728 2888, Fax 03 5728 2898,
Email castagna@enigma.com.au

Owner: Julian and Carolann Castagna
Chief winemaker: Julian Castagna
Year of foundation: 1997
Tonnes produced on average each year: 12
Location: Beechworth
Area: 2 ha
Soils: granitic soils on clay
Varieties planted: White—viognier;
Red—cabernet sauvignon, nebbiolo, sangiovese, shiraz
Leading wines: Castagna Allegro Rose, Genesis Shiraz
Notes: Some very interesting red styles will

emanate from Castagna. Planned are a Shiraz-Viognier, as Julian Castagna hopes, in the style of Côte Rotie, a Sangiovese Cabernet to rival some of the better wines of the Chianti region and a Nebbiolo, all savoury reds which Julian prefers. He may also make a Viognier from time to time. There are no cellar door sales, but appointments may be made, if you are in the region.

Giaconda **R10**

McClay Road, Beechworth, Vic 3747
Ph/Fax 03 5727 0246

Owner/chief winemaker: Rick Kinzbrunner
Year of foundation: 1981
Tonnes crushed on average each year: 15, this will increase as a new adjoining vineyard

comes into bearing
Location: Beechworth (2 vineyards)
Area: 6.4 ha (original 1981 planting 2.8 ha,
new 1996 planting 3.6 ha)
Soils: mixture of gravel and clay
Varieties planted: White—chardonnay,
roussanne; Red—cabernet sauvignon, pinot
noir, shiraz
Leading wines: Giaconda Chardonnay, Pinot
Noir, Cabernet Sauvignon
Notes: Giaconda is expanding, more than
doubling its vineyard size. But, that said, its
increased production will hardly flood the
market. However, being aware of Giaconda's
peerless standards of quality, the new vineyard
will provide wines of exceptional interest, a
Shiraz and a Roussanne to add to the great
distinction of the Chardonnay and Pinot Noir.
Cellar door sales by appointment only.

Pennyweight NR

Pennyweight Lane, Beechworth, Vic 3747
Ph 03 5728 1747, Fax 03 5728 1704,
Email pennywgt@netc.net.au

Owners: Stephen and Elizabeth Morris
Chief winemaker: Stephen N. Morris
Year of foundation: 1982
Tonnes crushed on average each year: 25
Location: Beechworth
Area: 3 ha
Soils: red duplex
Varieties planted: White—palomino, riesling,
semillon; Red—cabernet sauvignon, gamay,

pinot noir, shiraz
Leading wines: Pennyweight Pinot Noir, Shiraz,
Cabernet Blend, Riesling, Fortifieds
Notes: Pennyweight follows organic principles
and is non-irrigated. Cellar door sales:
Thurs–Tues 10am–5pm, Sun 11am–5pm,
closed Wednesdays, Good Friday and
Christmas Day.

Sorrenberg NR

Alma Road, Beechworth, Vic 3747
Ph/Fax 03 5728 2278

Owners: Barry and Jan Morey
Chief winemaker: Barry Morey
Year of foundation: 1984
Tonnes crushed on average each year: 23
Location: Beechworth
Area: 3 ha
Soils: granitic
Varieties planted: White—chardonnay,
sauvignon blanc, semillon; Red—cabernet
franc, cabernet sauvignon, gamay, merlot,
pinot noir
Leading wines: Sorrenberg Sauvignon Blanc,
Semillon, Chardonnay, Gamay, Cabernet
Sauvignon, Cabernet Franc, Merlot
Notes: Sorrenberg is one of the few Australian
vineyards to grow gamay and match it up with
granitic soil. So for Beaujolais lovers there is
often a bigger style of Gamay reminiscent of
some of the firmer appellations of Beaujolais.
Cellar door: ring ahead to see if an
appointment is possible.

KING VALLEY REGION (INTERIM REGISTRATION)

The King Valley was developed in the 1970s as a winegrowing area chiefly by Italian
farmers who wished for an alternative to an ever-shrinking tobacco market and by
graziers who wished to diversify from beef production. Its most famous early wines were
the Koombahla Rieslings and Cabernets made by Brown Brothers in the 1970s and
1980s. That company later went on to develop the high altitude Whitlands vineyard
while continuing to purchase substantial amounts of fruit from local growers.

Location: Wangaratta, latitude 36°23'S, longitude 146°23'E, about 200 km north-east of Melbourne; Whitfield, latitude 36°47'S, longitude 146°20'E, about 47 km south-east of Wangaratta

Elevation: Wangaratta 150 m; Whitfield, valley floor 200 m, steeply sloping to Whitlands 800 m

Topography and soils: The King River flows north-north-west to meet the Ovens near Wangaratta. At its source, in the Alpine National Park, the country is mountainous, but the vineyards commence some 40 km to the north around Cheshunt and Whitfield. Around Whitfield there is extremely steep and undulating country which remains hilly and undulating until the river reaches flood plains near Milawa. Around Whitlands the soils are volcanic brown loams over clay. At lower altitudes to the north the soils have formed on river deposits derived from Ordovician sedimentary rock and from rock formed from acid lava flows during the Devonian period. When the river leaves its valley and debouches on to the plain, there are deep red alluvial loams (Milawa).

Climate: Wangaratta MJT 22.6°C, MAR, na HDD (raw) 1874, (adjusted for vine sites) 1580, AR 640mm (Oct–Apr 325mm), RH 26% (3pm Jan), AI na, SH 9.5 (Gladstones). Milawa (south-east of Wangaratta) (alt 155 m) MWTM 22.8°C, HDD na, AR 660mm, RH na. Banksdale (central King Valley) (alt 450 m) MWTM 20.6°C, HDD na, AR 900 mm, RH na. Whitfield AR 1097 (Oct–Apr 463mm). Whitlands (alt 800m) MTWM 19°C, HDD na, AR 1410mm, RH na.

The King River Valley therefore seems suitable for all styles of Australian wine from the richest fortifieds (on its warm northern plains near Wangaratta) to fine sparkling and table wines at Whitlands. The region becomes increasingly cooler as the river is followed upstream to its Alpine source and the country gains in altitude. Whitlands has in fact proved to be an excellent area for the production of sparkling base wine and for delicate white table wines.

Phylloxera remains a grave risk here and vines must be planted on an appropriately resistant rootstock. Frosts too are a serious risk.

Harvest time: This will vary with altitude. Chardonnay: at 150 m late February, at 200 m early March, at 600 m 3rd week of March, at 800 m end of first week of April. Cabernet sauvignon: 150 m mid-March, at 200 m 3rd week of March, at 600 m 3rd week of April. At 800 m, cabernet sauvignon will not ripen fully and probably should not be planted at altitudes in excess of 600 m.

Principal varieties: White—chardonnay, sauvignon blanc; Red—cabernet sauvignon, shiraz

Area: na

Major wine styles: except for some Brown Brothers and Miranda wines, very little table wine appears nationally under the King River Valley GI. Much more is purchased by outside wine companies and disappears into bigger blends of South East Australian origin, which is a pity for the proposed region produces excellent Chardonnay, Sauvignon Blanc, Cabernet Sauvignon and Shiraz—far too good to be consigned to the anonymity of a brand.

Leading wineries: Brown Brothers, Symphonia Wines

Avalon Vineyard NR

RMB 9586 Wangaratta, Vic 3678
Ph 03 5729 3629, Fax 03 5729 3635

Owner: Groom family
Chief winemaker: Doug Groom
Year of foundation: 1981
Tonnes produced on average each year: 100, 45 of which are used for Avalon Vineyard wines
Location: Whitfield, 4km north of the town on the Whitfield–Wangaratta road
Area: 10 ha
Soils: red clay loams of volcanic origin, generally quite acidic requiring annual applications of lime
Varieties planted: White—chardonnay, sauvignon blanc, semillon; Red—cabernet franc, cabernet sauvignon, malbec, merlot, pinot noir, shiraz, tempranillo
Leading wines: Avalon Shiraz
Notes: A little known vineyard with a good reputation for Shiraz. Cellar door sales: daily 10am–5pm.

Brown Brothers R90

Snow Road, Milawa, Vic 3678
Ph 03 5720 5500, Fax 03 5720 5511,
Email bbmv@brown-brothers.com.au

Owners: Brown family
Chief winemaker: Terry Barnett
Year of foundation: 1889
Tonnes crushed on average each year: 12 500
Locations: cellar door and winery—Milawa. Vineyards—Milawa, Banksdale, Whitlands, Mystic Park (Swan Hill region), Patricia Vineyard (Heathcote Region)
Area: Milawa 83 ha, King Park 4.85 ha, Hurdle Creek 11.3 ha, Banksdale 95 ha, Whitlands 44 ha, Mystic Park (see Swan Hill region), Patricia (see Heathcote region)
Soils: Milawa, 3 vineyards alluvial red sandy loam to a depth of 1.2 metres. Moderate pH. Typical King and Ovens Valley flood-plain soils;

Banksdale, tertiary eocene basalt slightly acidic; Whitlands, volcanic, brown loam/clay about 2 metres deep on a kaolin clay base, low to moderate pH; Mystic Park, see Swan Hill region; Patricia Vineyard, see Heathcote region.
Varieties planted: (Milawa) White—chenin blanc, gewurztraminer, riesling, sauvignon blanc, white frontignac; Red—barbera, cabernet franc, cabernet sauvignon, dolcetto, fer, graciano, merlot, mondeuse, muscat a petits grains rouge, pinot noir, shiraz. However, within the three Milawa vineyards there are different emphases depending on the success of particular varieties. Thus Milawa itself is regarded as most successful for:
White—riesling (for botrytised Noble Riesling); Red—dolcetto, graciano, mondeuse (for the Shiraz Mondeuse Cabernet dry red blend), muscat a petits grains rouge (for Muscat).
King Park: White—none; Red—dolcetto.
Hurdle Creek: White—riesling; Red—none.
Banksdale: White—chardonnay, pinot grigio; Red—barbera, cabernet sauvignon, merlot, shiraz. Here the site, being midway between Milawa and Whitlands, has been carefully chosen for these varieties.
Whitlands: White—chardonnay, gewurztraminer, meunier, pinot gris, riesling, sauvignon blanc; Red—cabernet franc, cabernet sauvignon, malbec, merlot, pinot noir. Outstanding here have been the 'champagne' varieties, pinot noir, meunier and chardonnay, made as base wine with, in some years, some chardonnay and pinot noir left to ripen fully for table wine. Sauvignon blanc also develops complex aromas and flavours, as does gewurztraminer. For Mystic Park, see Swan Hill region. For Patricia Vineyard, see Heathcote region
Leading wines: (Milawa vineyard) Brown Brothers Shiraz-Mondeuse-Cabernet, Noble Riesling, Dolcetto, Muscat; (Banksdale) Brown Brothers Shiraz, Pinot Grigio, Barbera; (Whitlands) Brown Brothers Sparkling Wines, Sauvignon Blanc, Gewurztraminer. For Mystic Park and Patricia Vineyard, see respective regions

Notes: One of the great wineries of Australia, Brown Brothers has now become a giant, still expanding. For almost 40 years I have watched it grow from a small but innovative winery, operated by John Brown Senior with the assistance of his sons, to the Victorian behemoth it is today. Remarkably, it is still strongly family-owned, though Peter Brown now owns and operates All Saints and St Leonards on his own account in the Rutherglen region. The story of Brown Brothers is really the story of the Australian wine industry over the last 40 years, but in microcosm. There is a strong interest in high-quality table wine and sparkling wines, though a few good quality fortified wines remain, and an equally strong desire to provide patrons with a wide variety of varietal wines, while always exploring new and perhaps better regions for the production of such wines as well as export markets. May Brown Brothers long flourish! Cellar door sales: daily 9am–5pm. There is also the Epicurean Centre, open daily from 11am–3pm for lunch. Closed Good Friday and Christmas Day.

Ciavarella **NR**

Evans Lane, Oxley, Vic 3678
Ph/Fax 03 5727 3384

Owners: Cyril and Jan Ciavarella
Chief winemaker: Cyril Ciavarella
Year of foundation: 1978
Tonnes crushed on average each year: 30
Locations: Oxley and North Wangaratta
Area: 6 ha
Soils: sandy loams
Varieties planted: White—chardonnay, chenin blanc, semillon verdelho; Red—cabernet sauvignon, durif, merlot, shiraz
Leading wines: Ciavarella Chardonnay (lightly wooded), Chenin Blanc, Shiraz, Cabernet Sauvignon, Dolcino (a sweet red), Late Harvest Chenin Blanc
Notes: A small winery and vineyard making a

very pleasant lightly wooded Chardonnay. Cellar door sales: Mon–Sat 9am–6pm, Sun 10am–6pm.

Dal Zotto Wines **NR**

Edi Road, Cheshunt, Vic 3678
Ph 03 5729 8321, Fax 03 5729 8490

Owners: Dal Zotto family
Chief winemakers: Ottorino Dal Zotto and Warren Proft
Year of foundation: 1987
Tonnes produced on average each year: 70
Location: Cheshunt and Whitfield in the south of the King Valley
Area: 39.5 ha, two vineyards, 17.5 ha at Cheshunt, and 22 ha at Whitfield
Soils: Cheshunt, reddish clay soil interspersed with gravel dark loams; Whitfield, sandy red soil with some clay, well-drained
Varieties planted: White—chardonnay, riesling; Red—barbera, cabernet sauvignon, marzemino, merlot, sangiovese, shiraz
Leading wines: Dal Zotto Chardonnay, Shiraz, Merlot, Cabernet-Merlot
Notes: As in other King Valley wineries, there is an emphasis here on merlot and also Italian varieties such as barbera and sangiovese, but the whites also are prize winners at local and small-maker shows. Cellar door sales at Cheshunt Thurs–Mon 11am–5pm.

Darling Estate **NR**

Koombahla Vineyard, Whitfield, Vic 3678
Ph/Fax 03 5729 8396

Owner: Koombahla Vineyard Pty Ltd
Chief winemaker: Guy. Darling
Year of foundation: 1970 (vineyard); 1990 (winery)
Tonnes crushed on average each year: 350, about 5 of which are used for Darling Estate wines
Locations: Koombahla Vineyard, Whitfield and Nambucca Vineyard, Cheshunt

Area: 23.5 ha consisting of two vineyards, Koombahla (22 ha) and Nambucca (1.5 ha)
Soils: clay loam of volcanic origin
Varieties planted: (Nambucca) White—chenin blanc; Red—gamay, pinot noir. (Koombahla) White—chardonnay, riesling, sauvignon blanc; Red—cabernet franc, cabernet sauvignon, merlot, pinot noir, shiraz
Leading wines: Darling Estate Cabernet Sauvignon, Shiraz, Cabernets
Notes: Guy Darling is the pioneer of winegrowing in the King Valley, starting at a time when tobacco was king of the Valley. His Koombahla Vineyard supplied Brown Brothers for many years, making the name Koombahla quite famous among lovers of Brown Brothers wines. These days the fruit sales are more widely spread. Cellar door sales by appointment.

John Gehrig NR

Off the Snow Road, Oxley, Vic 3678
Ph 03 5727 3395, Fax 03 5727 3699

Owners: John and Elizabeth Gehrig
Chief winemaker: John Gehrig
Year of foundation: 1976
Tonnes crushed on average each year: 90
Location: Oxley
Area: 6 ha
Soils: alluvial sandy loam on a clay subsoil
Varieties planted: White—chardonnay, chenin blanc, riesling; Red—cabernet franc, cabernet sauvignon, durif, malbec, merlot, muscat a petits grains rouge, pinot noir, petit verdot
Leading wines: John Gehrig Pinot Noir, Merlot
Notes: A consistent bronze medallist at the Rutherglen Show. Cellar door sales: daily 9am–5pm.

King River Estate R80

Edi, King Valley, Vic 3678
Ph 03 5729 3689, Fax 03 5729 3688

Owner/chief winemaker: Trevor Knaggs
Year of foundation: vineyard 1990, winery 1996
Tonnes produced on average each year: 150, of which 30 are used for King River Estate Wines
Location: Edi, between Whitfield and Moyhu, 35 km south of Wangaratta
Area: 20 ha
Soils: sandy, gravelly loam soils
Varieties planted: White—chardonnay, verdelho, viognier; Red—barbera, cabernet sauvignon, merlot, sangiovese, shiraz
Leading wine: King River Estate Merlot
Notes: Merlot is the pick here. Cellar door sales by appointment.

La Cantina King Valley NR

Honey's Lane, King Valley, Vic 3678
Ph 03 5729 3615, Fax 03 5729 3613

Owner/chief winemaker: Gino Corsini
Year of foundation: 1997
Tonnes produced on average each year: 16, increasing as new vines come into bearing
Location: King Valley
Area: 20 ha
Soils: red clay loam with flaky shale
Varieties planted: White—chardonnay, riesling; Red—cabernet sauvignon, dolcetto, merlot, shiraz
Leading wines: La Cantina Cabernet Sauvignon, Shiraz
Notes: This winery produces 'No-Preservatives Added' wines, which I have not tasted. Cellar door sales: weekends and public holidays 10am–5pm. At other times by appointment.

Markwood NR

Morris Lane, Markwood, Vic 3678
Ph/Fax 03 5727 0361,
Email rick@netc.net.au

Owner/chief winemaker: Rick Morris
Year of foundation: 1971

Tonnes crushed on average each year: 10
Location: Markwood
Area: 2.5 ha
Soils: alluvial grey loam
Varieties planted: White—chardonnay,
palomino; Red—cabernet sauvignon, shiraz
Leading wines: Markwood Cabernet
Sauvignon
Notes: Cellar door sales, 7 days 9am–5pm.

Miranda High Country Wines  **R80**

Cnr Snow Road and Whitfield Road,
Oxley, Vic 3678
Ph/Fax 03 5727 3399,
Cellar door ph 03 5727 3888,
Email info@mirandawines.com.au

Owner: Miranda Wines Pty Ltd
Chief winemaker: Garry Wall
Year of foundation: 1997 (vineyards), 1998
(winery)
Tonnes crushed on average each year: 1500
Location: Oxley
Area: 36 ha
Soils: sandy loam
Varieties planted: White—chardonnay;
Red—cabernet sauvignon, merlot, petit
verdot, shiraz
Leading wines: Miranda Show Reserve
Merlot, Miranda High Country Range
Notes: Miranda purchase quite an amount of
fruit from both the King and Alpine Valleys
regions for the making of its High Country
wines which have won many awards at various
Australian and overseas wineshows. Cellar
door sales: daily 10am–6pm.

Symphonia Wines **R83**

Boggy Creek Road, Myrrhee, Vic 3732
Ph/Fax 03 5729 7519,
Email readsymphonia@bigpond.com

Owner/chief winemaker: Peter Read
Year of foundation: 1981 (vineyard), 1998
(winery)

Tonnes produced on average each year: 300, of
which 6 are presently used for Symphonia wines
Location: Myrrhee
Area: 25 ha
Soils: red duplex soils of volcanic derivation
Varieties planted: White—arneis, chardonnay,
petit manseng, viognier; Red—cabernet
sauvignon, dolcetto, merlot, meunier, pinot
noir, saperavi, tannat, tempranillo
Leading wines: Symphonia Merlot, Quintus
(a blend of merlot, cabernet sauvignon,
tannat, sapewravi and tempranillo), Saperavi,
Cabernet plus Tannat and Merlot, Pinot
Chardonnay Methode Champenoise
Notes: This is a fascinating winery for students
of varieties, for there is a wide range of
French, Spanish, Italian and even a Russian,
saperavi. Wine quality is also very good as
witness the numerous awards won at small
winemakers shows. Peter Read's production
under his Symphonia label is small, but his
wines are well worth tasting. Cellar door sales:
by appointment.

Wood Park Wines ᵥ**NR**

Kneebone Gap Road, Bobinawarrah,
Vic 3678
Ph 03 5727 3367, Fax 03 5727 3682

Owner: the Stokes family and John Leviny
Chief winemaker: John Stokes
Year of foundation: 1989
Tonnes produced on average each year: 180,
of which 50 are used for Wood Park wines
Location: winery and vineyard Bobinawarrah,
vineyard Meadow Creek
Area: 16 ha
Soils: sedimentary derived shale mudstone,
gravelly clay based shallow profile
Varieties planted: White—chardonnay,
roussanne, viognier; Red—cabernet sauvignon,
petit verdot
Leading wines: Wood Park Cabernet
Sauvignon-Shiraz, Chardonnay (barrel
fermented)

Notes: Wood Park vineyard has supplied fruit to Brown Brothers since 1990 and Meadow Creek Chardonnay is always a joy to taste. These days John Stokes barrel-ferments the Chardonnay and uses wild yeasts for fermentation. The winery is a little off the beaten track, so make an appointment. It is accessible via the Snow Road. (Turn south off the Snow Road just east of Markwood on to the Carboor Road. Travel for 6 km then turn left to the east on to Kneebones Gap and travel a further 3 km to find Wood Park.)

OTHER WINERIES WITHIN THE NORTH EAST VICTORIA ZONE

Auldstone Cellars NR

Booths Road, Taminick, Vic 3675
Ph 03 5766 2237

Owners: Michael Reid and Nancy Reid
Chief winemaker: Michael Reid
Year of foundation: 1891 as Herceynia; 1987 as Auldstone
Tonnes crushed on average each year: 100, about half of which are used for Auldstone's own labels
Location: Taminick
Area: 20 ha
Soils: deep red granite sandy loams
Varieties planted: White—chardonnay, riesling, traminer; Red—cabernet sauvignon, merlot, muscat a petits grains rouge, shiraz
Leading wines: Auldstone Cabernet, Sparkling Shiraz, Shiraz, Muscat
Notes: The Reids are great enthusiasts for the Taminick area and demonstrated this by spending several years restoring the old Herceynia Winery and its surrounding vineyard. Cellar door sales: Thurs–Sat 9am–5pm, Sun 10am–5pm. Lunch is also available at weekends.

Baileys of Glenrowan   R86

Cnr Taminick Gap Road and Upper Taminick Road, Glenrowan, Vic 3675
Ph 03 5766 2392, Fax 03 5766 2596

Owner: Mildara Blass Ltd
Chief winemaker: Daiel Bettio
Year of foundation: 1870

Tonnes crushed on average each year: 1500
Location: Taminick
Area: 149 ha
Soils: deep red fertile granite soils providing both good water retention and drainage
Varieties planted: White—muscadelle; Red—cabernet sauvignon, merlot, muscat a petits grains rouge, shiraz, touriga
Leading wines: Baileys of Glenrowan 1920s Block Shiraz, 1904 Block Shiraz, Founders Liqueur Muscat
Notes: This vineyard and winery has a grand old reputation for its Muscat and its 'Hermitage'—a name no longer permissible but certainly unforgettable in the minds of older red wine drinkers. It was a red that needed many years to mature and was occasionally described as 'food, wine and a good cigar'. The 'Hermitage' style as expressed by the 1920s Block Shiraz is lighter and more elegant these days but never puny and the Muscats are unmatched save for a select few from Rutherglen to the north-east. Cellar door sales: Mon–Fri 9am–5pm, weekends and public holidays 10am–5pm.

Booths Taminick Cellars NR

Booths Road, Taminick, Vic 3675
Ph 03 5766 2282, Fax 03 5766 2151

Owners: Booth family
Chief winemaker: Peter Booth
Year of foundation: 1904
Tonnes crushed on average each year: 90
Location: Taminick

Area: 20 ha
Soils: granite soils
Varieties planted: White—chardonnay,
trebbiano; Red—cabernet sauvignon, merlot,
muscat a petits grains rouge, shiraz

Leading wines: Booths Cabernet-Merlot,
Muscat, Shiraz
Notes: A producer of the traditional 'big' red
style of the North East. Cellar door sales:
Mon–Sat 9am–5pm, Sun 10am–5pm.

✤ From gold to gold

As has been often stated in Australian wine history, the wine followed the mine and, though in Rutherglen's case this situation might just have been the reverse, miners were generally a thirsty lot and usually a purveyor of victuals found his gold much more easily than any digger. It is true that gold was found in the main street of Rutherglen but before, not after, the settlement of the town. Afterwards, the only ones to find it in the streets of Rutherglen were the merchants. The streets were never quite paved with gold and when miners did ultimately tire of mining in one place, the unlucky moved on to the next whispered Eldorado while the more successful settled where they were. Very few places had more than one goldrush though Rutherglen was an exception. After the gold craze of the late 1850s and early 1860s, the region settled down to an agricultural stability, during which successful vineyards were developed.

The wine styles which suited the region were obviously the heavy alcoholic reds and fortifieds that were also in favour in London in the last thirty years of the century. They travelled well—the existing level of alcohol and a little more added for the journey saw to that. So by the late 1880s an export trade was developing, aided by the opening of the railway to Melbourne. Though the local gentry favoured 'Champagne' such as that made by Mr Hans Irvine of Great Western, the less discerning local palates (much to the disgust of Mr Hubert de Castella of the Yarra Valley), later favoured richer, more alcoholic wines, just the kind that Rutherglen was making its speciality. It was about this time that Rutherglen's second goldrush began and also that the region's Muscats and Tokays began to make their mark. In a minute way they still do, for the best of the region's Muscats may contain a fraction of the dark green muscaty essence of wine that first made its appearance a century ago. Such wines are unique and if there are degrees of uniqueness—which pedagogues say there most certainly are not—then the Tokays of the region are even more unique, for nowhere else in the world are there similar wines made from muscadelle, a minor Bordeaux white variety. The wines of the same name made in Hungary are superficially similar, but these are not made from muscadelle.

So how are Muscats and Tokays made? The method of making is quite similar, though of course the grape varieties are different. Tokay, as we have seen, is made from muscadelle, a bit-player in the making of Sauternes in the Bordeaux region of France. Muscat is made from muscat a petits grains rouges (the muscat with little red berries). The grapes are picked at their ripest, depending on season. This may be as low as 15° Baume or as high as 20° Baume. By that time they are shrivelled but should not be botrytised. Noble rot is no part of this style. They are fermented for 1–2 days on skins in the normal manner of red wine, but such a fermentation usually reduces the Baume by only 1–2 degrees. The juice, still very sweet, is then run off and the must is pressed. Both free-run and pressings are added together. The wines, very high in natural sugar, are then fortified with a neutral high strength grape spirit to about 18.5% alcohol. The purpose of this is to stabilise what would otherwise be a very unstable liquid and to preserve the sweetness. Having been placed in large old oak vats for about 12 months to clarify, they are then graded and placed in small old oak barrels where they age and evaporate for many years. It is during this period that they gain their complexity, intensity of flavour and lusciousness. They are then examined once more and, for the very best wines, refreshed with younger material before bottling.

Both Muscats and Tokays range in quality and price. The cheapest wines are usually of the youngest average age (about 4–5 years). The most expensive may be a blend of very old wines (average 60+ years) and much younger wines (3–4 years) and therefore average about 30 years. They do not improve in bottle and may, due to relatively high alcohol content, cause their cork to disintegrate if kept too long. They are usually served at room temperature, though younger wines served slightly chilled do have their admirers. After opening they retain their character for several weeks before losing freshness. Companion foods are usually dried fruits and nuts and, in the case of Muscats, rich desserts such as Christmas puddings. Nor should we forget creamy blue cheeses, such as Gippsland Blue, for which an old Muscat can make a perfect partner. As for Tokay, it goes well with such confections as creme caramel.

What are the typical characters of such wines? In colour, Muscats of young average age are pinky red to amber in hue. Older wines are more tawny and verge into olive green on the edges of the glass. In Tokay, its colour varies from gold-amber in young wines to deep brown in aged wines, also with tinges of green on the edges.

Aromatically, young Muscats smell of raisins or muscatels with occasional orange peel overtones, though this must not be confused with the typical botrytis nose. With age their nose becomes very complex with intense muscatel characters and also 'rancio' (a mixture of old wine, spirit, volatility due to years of evaporation, and old oak). Young Tokays, on the other hand, show confectionery aromas, caramel, toffee and the merest hint of muscat (after all, muscadelle is a card-carrying family member). With age these change to 'cold tea' and later to more complex butterscotch and rancio characters.

On palate, a young Muscat is distinctly grapey and fresh with intense flavours that suggest nothing else but muscat. Though a sweet wine, it should finish relatively dry and clean and should not cloy. Its senior colleague, like the mousse of a good old Champagne, hits the tongue with an explosion of flavour. Old raisins, fruit peel, rancio and old spirit all clamour for attention in a luscious liquid that lasts and lasts. In its youth, Tokay has sweet toffee characters. With age, it gains complexity and must, like Muscat, be blended with younger wine to retain its freshness. Unlike Muscat, it is never quite as complex and, though those butterscotch, cold tea and rancio characters are present, it does not quite have that Muscat intensity, lingering rather than exploding on the palate.

There is another point. Both Muscats and Tokays have excellent 'legs'. Swirl the glass around and watch those viscous streams of old wine trickle treacle-like into the bottom of the glass. And a word of warning—old fortified wines can be very hard on the teeth, pricking into every cavity and playing the very devil with the gums. But don't let this worry you; old Muscats and Tokays are a never-to-be-forgotten experience and these days they are the only gold that you will find on the streets of Rutherglen.

❧ NORTH WEST VICTORIA ZONE

This is an improbable wine zone which, without irrigation, can only be described as arid. It is due to the devotion of the 19th century Chaffey Brothers to irrigation engineering on the Murray River that it exists at all. This zone is centred upon the city of Mildura in the extreme north west of Victoria and further to the south east, Swan Hill. It encompasses the wine regions of Murray–Darling and Swan Hill, each of which cross the Murray into New South Wales. Apart from its irrigation country, this area is a desert, with some wheat grown in the southern parts. It is largely an area producing good to average quality white wine, especially Chardonnay and Semillon.

MURRAY–DARLING REGION

Perhaps that brilliant young nineteenth-century lawyer/journalist/politician Alfred Deakin should be credited with the idea of first using irrigation in Australia on a large commercial scale. He had visited California in the 1880s and had viewed for himself the work of two irrigation engineers, George and William Chaffey. He invited them to visit Victoria. On their arrival in Mildura they immediately recognised the suitability of the red plains for irrigation. But the Chaffeys required land and water rights and the Victorian bureaucracy retarded the process of acquiring those rights so much that in frustration they turned to Renmark in neighbouring South Australia and began an irrigation scheme there. Their departure to South Australia proved to be just the spur that the Victorian government required. Within two months the red tape had been cut away and an offer was made to the Chaffeys. After its commencement in 1887, the Mildura scheme rapidly expanded and within a few months about 200 hectares had been cleared for occupation, about 27 kilometres of main irrigation channel established and temporary pumping stations erected. The population had also increased to 270. However, many problems confronted the settlers in getting their produce to the Melbourne market. Carriage of goods by road was slow and perishable produce often suffered in the process. River transport to areas where the produce could be transshipped by rail was often spasmodic due to low or non-existent river heights. It was not until the arrival of the railway in 1903 (when transport times to Melbourne could be reduced from over a week to one day) that the problems were permanently solved.

From the start, horticulture was highly important in the region. Though some wines (chiefly fortified) were made very early in the region's history (from 1891), the emphasis was on dried fruits. Later in the twentieth century, though dried fruits have remained important, this has switched to citrus and multi-purpose grapes. These days wine grapes have become even more important as imported citrus concentrate drives citrus growers away from that industry and there is greater demand for specialised wine grapes.

The first winery in the region, the Mildura Wine Co at Merbein, was established by W. B. Chaffey in 1888, its name being changed to Mildara in 1938. McWilliam's followed suit in 1952 at Robinvale, Hungerford Hill Wines began its winery (now

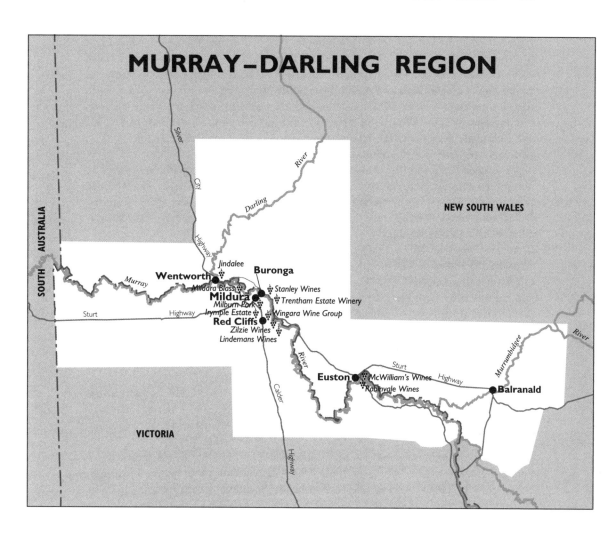

MURRAY–DARLING REGION

NEW SOUTH WALES

SOUTH AUSTRALIA

Silver

City

Darling

River

Highway

Murray

Jindalee

Wentworth

Buronga

Mildara Blass

Stanley Wines

Mildura

Trentham Estate Winery

Milburn Park

Irymple Estate

Vingara Wine Group

Sturt   *Highway*

Red Cliffs

Zilzie Wines

Lindemans Wines

River

Calder

Sturt   *Highway*

Murrumbidgee

River

Euston

McWilliam's Wines

Robinvale Wines

Balranald

VICTORIA

Highway

owned by BRL Hardy) in 1963 and later Lindemans (now part of Southcorp Wines) erected Karadoc in 1974. Since then six other wineries have come into production in the region. Nine wineries within a region as large as this may not sound too many, but their production is enormous. It can be said that Murray–Darling is the industrial heartland of Australian wine production.

In wine terms, the region is known as a producer of good average quality Chardonnays, mostly marketed at keen prices, a reputation now supplanting that of producer of softpack white wine. The region is in the process of transformation from an area of multi-purpose grapes for common white wine to one of good to very good (but not outstanding quality) varietal white wine grapes.

Location: Mildura latitude 34°7'S, longitude 142°7'E, about 450 km north-west of Melbourne, is the commercial centre of this large region. The region runs in a south easterly direction about 350 km from the South Australian border along the Murray to its junction with the Wakool River in New South Wales, encompassing lands on both the Victorian and New South Wales sides of the River Murray. Other viticultural areas forming part of it are Wentworth, Dareton, Buronga, Balranald and Euston (NSW) and Robinvale, Nangiloc, Red Cliffs, Merbein and Lake Cullulleraine (Vic).

Elevation: (general) 30–100 m above sea-level, (vineyards) 50–85 m.

Topography and soils: On first acquaintance, the region is generally flat and featureless, but subtle differences in height are important in affecting drainage. Occasionally breaking the flatness of the terrain are gentle dune-swale formations. Its soils are the typical pink-brown 'Mallee' type quite common in north-west Victoria. These sit over a limestone and clay subsoil.

Climate: Sunraysia MJT 23.6°C, MAR 13.7, HDD 2244 (raw), AR 283 mm (Oct–March 134 mm), RH 49% (9am), AI 637 mm, SH 9.7 (Dry & Smart). Contrast Gladstones Merbein MJT 23.3°C, MAR na, HDD 2191 (raw), 1719 (cut-off at 19°C and adjusted for latitude and daily temperature range but not for vine sites), AR 275 mm (Oct–Apr 147 mm), RH 30% (3pm), AI na, SH 9.8. Throughout its area, the Murray–Darling region is very hot with low humidity and negligible growing season rainfall. Continentality is high with wide shifts in diurnal temperature ranges, but not enough to make spring frosts a problem. Due to its dry climate and low rainfall, the region has lower incidence of disease than cooler, wetter areas.

Irrigation is a necessity and there are a large number of such schemes within the region. Because of this and the warmth of the climate, fairly heavy crops of some varieties are able to be ripened. Such fruit is sought primarily by wineries for bottled wines of lesser price brackets and for current-drinking soft-pack wines.

Harvest time: chardonnay, mid-February, other varieties correspondingly later

Principal grape varieties: White—sultana (5029 ha bearing, 145 ha, non-bearing), chardonnay (4260 ha bearing, 78 ha non-bearing), muscat gordo blanco (1775 ha bearing, 98 ha non-bearing), semillon (1021 ha bearing, 657 ha non-bearing), colombard (836 ha bearing, 177 ha non-bearing); Red—shiraz (2820 ha bearing, 964 ha non-bearing), cabernet sauvignon (3053 ha bearing, 719 ha non-bearing), merlot (1534 ha bearing, 467 ha non-bearing), ruby cabernet (722 ha bearing, 234 ha non-bearing), carina (405 ha bearing, 69 ha non-bearing)

Total area: (2000) 27 592 ha

Major wine styles: Although Semillon of good quality has been reported from Lake Culluleraine, from the region itself, only Chardonnay can be said to be of interest. Its style is ripe and usually fairly forward and should be drunk within two years of vintage.

Leading wineries: Jindalee Murray–Darling, Milburn Park, Trentham Estate, Wingara

Irymple Estate Winery NR

2086 Karadoc Avenue, Irymple, Vic 3498
Ph/Fax 03 5024 5759,
Email mfiliz@vic.ozland.net.au

Owner: Filiz family
Chief winemaker: Brian Wilson (contract)
Year of foundation: 1988
Tonnes produced on average each year: 110,
of which about 70 are used for Irymple Estate
wines
Location: Irymple
Area: 4 ha
Soils: light clay to loam
Varieties planted: White—chardonnay, chenin
blanc, frontignac, sauvignon blanc, semillon,
sultana, verdelho, waltham cross;
Red—cabernet sauvignon, merlot, ruby
cabernet, shiraz
Leading wines: Irymple Estate Shiraz,
Chardonnay
Notes: I have not tasted the wines, and there
are no cellar door sales. Sales are made by
direct mail order.

Jindalee Murray Darling (vineyards only) R83

265 Ballan Road, Moorabool, Vic 3221
Phone 03 5277 2836, Fax 03 5277 2840,
Email jindwine@mail.austasia.net

Owners: Vince and David Littore, Bill Mithen
Chief winemaker: Scott Ireland
Year of foundation: 1997
Tonnes produced on average each year: 5000,
of which 1500 are used for Jindalee
Murray–Darling wines
Location: (vineyards) Coomealla, Gol Gol,
Wentworth
Area: 400 ha
Soils: sandy loams over a calcareous base
Varieties planted: White—chardonnay,
colombard; Red—cabernet sauvignon, merlot,
shiraz
Leading wines: Jindalee Chardonnay

Notes: Jindalee Chardonnays are generously
flavoured soft wines, always worth drinking.
Cellar door sales from Jindalee Estate, Geelong
daily 10am–5pm.

Lindemans Karadoc Winery R80

Eddy Road, Karadoc, Vic 3496
Ph 03 5051 3333, Fax 03 5051 3390

Owner: Southcorp Wines
Chief winemaker: Peter Taylor
Year of foundation: 1974
Tonnes crushed on average each year: not
disclosed but Karadoc has a make/store
capacity of 100 million litres, 30% of which is
for the Southcorp Wine group Chardonnay
requirements almost two-thirds of which is for
production of Bin 65 Chardonnay, which now
exceeds 2 million cases in production annually
Location: Karadoc (vineyard and winery), Lake
Culluleraine (vineyard)
Area: Karadoc 108.1 ha, Lake Culluleraine
200.8 ha
Soils: Karadoc, red-brown earths over grey
loamy clay. Lake Culluleraine, sand loam over
clay base with limestone marl
Varieties planted: (Karadoc) White—most will
be planted to Chardonnay by 2002; Red—
shiraz. (Lake Culluleraine) White—chardonnay,
semillon; Red—merlot
Leading wines: Bin 65 Chardonnay and other
white wines of the Southcorp group (all are
usually South East Australian blends)
Notes: Karadoc is a catchment for Southcorp
white wines from many sources. Even the use of
the word 'wine' is inappropriate, for not only do
wine and grapes come to Karadoc, but also
musts and juices. Its importance is as a
production and storage centre for chardonnay—
grapes, musts and wines. Other white varieties
such as Lake Culluleraine semillon are also
processed there. What is being phased out is
the very purpose of the winery's original
construction—wine cask production. These days
the emphasis is on Chardonnay, especially for

the production of that world leader—Bin 65. Apart from this, little more can be said about Karadoc, except that it is vast.

McWilliam's Wines NR

22 Moore Street, Robinvale, Vic 3549
Ph 03 5026 4004, Fax 03 5026 4479

Owner: McWilliam's Wines Pty Ltd
Chief winemaker: Matthew McWilliam
Year of foundation: 1963
Tonnes crushed on average each year: 8000
Location: Robinvale
Area: no local vineyards owned, all fruit is purchased from local growers
Leading wines: various McWilliam's fortified wines
Notes: This is a production facility only with a winemaking emphasis on fortified wine. Cellar door sales: Mon–Fri 9am–noon, 1pm–4.30pm.

Milburn Park Winery (formerly Alambie Wines) R82

Campbell Ave, Irymple, Vic 3498
Ph 03 5024 6800, Fax 03 5024 6605,
Email mpark@cranswick.com.au

Owner: Cranswick Premium Wines Ltd
Chief winemaker: Gary Magilton
Year of foundation: 1977
Tonnes crushed on average each year: 4500 for Milburn Park's own brands
Location: Irymple
Soils: terra rossa over limestone and red loam over yellow clay
Varieties planted: no vineyards owned. All fruit is purchased from contract growers
Leading wines: Milburn Park Chardonnay, Shiraz
Notes: In recent years, Milburn Park Chardonnay has won two Melbourne Show trophies and it proves the suitability of local chardonnay when blended with smaller quantities of cool area fruit for show purposes. Cellar door sales: Mon–Sat 10am–4.30pm

Mildara Blass R78

Wentworth Road, Merbein, Vic 3505
Ph 03 5025 2303, Fax 03 5025 2566

Owner: Mildara Blass Ltd
Chief winemaker: David Tierney
Year of foundation: 1888
Tonnes crushed on average each year: 14 000
Location: Merbein
Area: 580 ha (Parkers Field)
Soils: sandy loam over calcareous clay
Varieties planted: White—chardonnay; Red—cabernet sauvignon, merlot, petit verdot, shiraz
Leading wines: Church Hill range, Black Marlin range, Mildara Fortifieds
Notes: Merbein winery is part of the Mildara Blass 'engine room', where its lower-priced brands are produced. Cellar door sales: 7 days 10am–5pm except Christmas Day and Good Friday.

Robinvale Wines NR

Lot 43b Sealake Road, Robinvale, Vic 3549
Ph 03 5026 3955, Fax 03 5026 1123

Owner: Caracatsonoudis family
Chief winemaker: William Caracatsonoudis
Year of foundation: 1976
Tonnes crushed on average each year: 200, all of which is used for Robinvale and Demeter wines
Location: Robinvale (winery and vineyard)
Area: 44.3 ha (Robinvale) 33.5 ha, (Swan Hill) 10.8 ha
Soils: organic and biodynamic soils
Varieties planted: White—chardonnay, chenin blanc, kerner, sauvignon blanc; Red—cabernet franc, cabernet sauvignon, merlot, shiraz, touriga, zinfandel
Leading wines: Robinvale Wines Zinfandel-Merlot, Oak Chardonnay, Demeter Chardonnay, Classic Dry White, Preservative-Free Wines

Notes: Robinvale Wines is a member of the Organic Vignerons Association of Australia and specialises in bio-dynamically grown grapes. It makes both alcoholic wines and non-alcoholic beverages and has won many minor awards at the Swan Hill Show. Cellar door sales: 7 days 10am–6pm

Stanley Wines **NR**

Silver City Highway, Buronga, NSW 2648
Ph 03 5023 4341, Fax 03 5023 4344

Owner: BRL Hardy Ltd
Chief winemaker: Lincoln Sauer
Year of foundation: 1963 (Hungerford Hill),
1984 (Thomas Hardy & Sons)
Tonnes crushed on average each year: 70 000
Location: Buronga Hill (winery only)
Area: 180 ha
Soils: sandy loams over limestone
Varieties planted: no vineyard owned
Leading wines: Stanley, Buronga Ridge and other BRL Hardy products
Notes: Chiefly engaged in soft pack production but crushes other quantities of grapes for bottled wines in the BRL Hardy ranges.
Cellar door sales: 10am–4pm weekdays, Sat 10.30am–4pm, Sun noon–4pm.

Trentham Estate **R80**

Sturt Highway, Trentham Cliffs, NSW 2738
Ph 03 5024 8888, Fax 03 5024 8800

Owner: Murphy family
Chief winemaker: Anthony Murphy
Year of foundation: 1909 (vineyard), 1988 (winery)
Tonnes crushed on average each year: 1000, of which 800 are used for Trentham Estate wines
Location: Trentham Cliffs
Area: 50 ha
Soils: loamy sand to sandy clay over various limestone layers
Varieties planted: White—chardonnay, colombard, riesling, sauvignon blanc, taminga, viognier; Red—cabernet sauvignon, grenache, merlot, nebbiolo, ruby cabernet, shiraz, tannat
Leading wines: Trentham Estate Chardonnay, Sauvignon Blanc, Merlot, Cabernet-Merlot, Shiraz
Notes: Certainly one of the leading wineries in this region, producing both reds and whites of consistently good quality. Cellar door sales: weekdays 8.30am–5pm, weekends 9.30am–5pm. Restaurant and barbecue Tues–Sun 11am–3pm.

Wingara Wine Group **R80**

Kulkyne Way, Red Cliffs, Vic 3496
Ph 03 5029 1666, Fax 03 5024 3316

Owner: Wingara Wine Group Pty Ltd
Chief winemaker: Linda Jakubans
Year of foundation: 1980
Tonnes crushed on average each year: 18 800, of which 5000 are used for Wingara Wine Group labels
Location: Red Cliffs
Area: 350 ha
Soils: typical sandy loams often over limestone
Varieties planted: White—chardonnay, colombard, sauvignon blanc, semillon; Red—cabernet sauvignon, merlot, ruby cabernet, shiraz
Leading wines: the Deakin Estate range, Deakin Select
Notes: A large winery by most standards with a high quality and two brands, Deakin Estate and Deakin Select. Since 1987, Deakin Estate has won 10 gold medals and many more minor medals for its wines. There are no cellar door sales, but there is a lake for picnicking.

Zilzie Wines **NR**

Kulkyne Way, Karadoc, Vic 3496
Ph 03 5025 8100, Fax 03 5025 8116,
Email zilziewines@a1.com.au

Owner: Forbes family
Chief winemaker: Bob Shields
Year of foundation: 1979 (vineyards), 1999 (winery)
Tonnes produced on average each year: 10 000, of which about 650 are used for Zilzie wines
Location: Karadoc
Area: 500 ha
Soils: sandy clay loam over limestone

Varieties planted: White—chardonnay, sauvignon blanc, semillon; Red—cabernet sauvignon, merlot, petit verdot, shiraz
Leading wines: Zilzie Chardonnay, Cabernet Sauvignon, Merlot, Shiraz
Notes: Zilzie is a new winery with established vineyards. It presently makes a comparatively small quantity of wine for its own purposes, but also sells fruit, makes bulk wine and contract crushes. No cellar door sales.

SWAN HILL REGION

Like much of the rest of Victoria, Swan Hill was first explored by that indefatigable Surveyor General of New South Wales, Major Thomas Mitchell, in 1836. Describing its soil as 'of the richest description . . . and capable of being converted into good wheat land and easily irrigated at any time by the river (Murray)', Mitchell named it Swan Hill after a 'point of ground between the two rivers (Murray and Little Murray)' where there was a 'shallow lagoon' with 'swans and waterfowl so abundant that . . . their noise disturbed us throughout the night'. As predicted by Mitchell, landowners in the Swan Hill area were irrigating their lands as early as the 1880s and the planting of muscats and sultanas for dried fruit production in the Nyah district commenced in 1900. However, early irrigation schemes were often insufficient and unreliable, resulting in the salinity of certain areas and the financial failure of some irrigation trusts and private companies formed to subdivide agricultural land and supply water. The region's first winery, St Andrews, was built in 1930 at Tresco by the Thomson family. After World War II, many Sicilian immigrants planted wine grapes and stone fruits in the district. In 1951, when many wine areas in Australia were suffering acute economic stress, R L Buller & Son showed its faith in the future of wine and in the region by erecting Swan Hill's second winery at Beverford. There are now three wineries operating in the region and, in addition, Brown Brothers of Milawa with its Mystic Park Estate. Carpinteri Vineyards has also established a substantial presence in the region.
Location: latitude 35°20'S, longitude 143°15'E, about 370–400 km north-west of Melbourne and 180 km south-east of Mildura, being partly in Victoria and partly in New South Wales, straddling the Murray River. Its northern boundary is the junction of the Murray and Wakool Rivers.
Elevation: 60–85 m above sea-level
Topography and soils: The region is generally flat. Calcareous earths are quite common throughout. These consist of red-brown loamy sand, sandy loam (Tachera) or loam surface soils above subsoils of sandy clayey loams, associated with the ancient miocene sea-bed and overlying lake, river and wind-borne deposits. These are over 80 m deep. Surface soils are neutral to alkaline; subsoils strongly alkaline. Surface soils are usually permeable, but permeability is restricted in all but the most sandy of subsoils. Rarer soils in the region are sandy earths, hard red duplex and brownish sands.

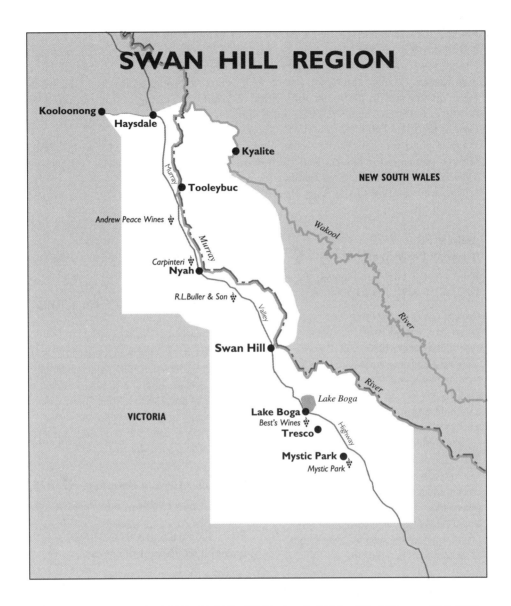

SWAN HILL REGION

Kooloonong

Haysdale

Kyalite

NEW SOUTH WALES

Murray

Tooleybuc

Andrew Peace Wines

Murray

Carpinteri
Nyah

R.L.Buller & Son

Wakool

Valley

River

Swan Hill

River

Lake Boga

VICTORIA

Lake Boga
Best's Wines
Tresco

Highway

Mystic Park
Mystic Park

Climate: MJT 23.6°C, MAR 14.3°C, HDD (raw) 2138, AR 345 mm, RH 52%, AI 497 mm, SH 9.3 (Dry & Smart). Compare Gladstones' MJT 23.4°C, MAR na, HDD (raw) 2181, 1718 (cut off and adjusted for latitude and daily temperature range), AR 345 mm (Oct–Apr 178 mm), RH 29%, AI na, SH 9.7. Mystic Park MTWM 23.5°C (Brown Bros). Though undeniably a hot region, Swan Hill is slightly cooler than Murray–Darling and has a higher natural rainfall (345 mm p.a.). Its higher Mean Annual Range (MAR) temperature indicates a longer and slower ripening period. Irrigation is provided by three schemes within the region. Nyah is fed directly from the Murray River through pumps in the Nyah township. Tresco and Woorinen are supplied through the Torumbarry Scheme, which diverts water from the Murray near Echuca and channels it 160 km via a series of canals, creeks, weirs and lakes to its points of use. Other growers within the region obtain water either direct from the Murray River or from Kangaroo Lake. The region has no major climatic problems. Its chief concern is water quality and in particular the degree of salinity occurring during run-off after flooding of upstream rivers or heavy local rain.

Harvest time: late February to mid-March for most wine varieties

Principal grape varieties: White—chardonnay, colombard, riesling and chenin blanc, sultana, muscat gordo blanco; Red—shiraz, cabernet sauvignon, grenache and mataro

Major wine styles: Shiraz, Chardonnay

Leading wineries: Best's Lake Boga, Brown Brothers

Andrew Peace Wines (formerly Peace Wines)   NR

Murray Valley Highway, Piangal, Vic 3597
Ph 03 5030 5291, Fax 03 5030 5605

Owners: A & C & J & P Peace
Winemaker: Andrew Peace
Year of foundation: 1980
Tonnes crushed on average each year: 800
Location of vineyard: Piangal
Area: 100 ha
Soils: red loams and rich black alluvial soils
Varieties planted: White—chardonnay, crouchen, muscat gordo blanco, riesling; Red—cabernet sauvignon, grenache, mourvedre, ruby cabernet, shiraz
Leading wines: Andrew Peace range, Ashwood Grove range
Notes: Initially highly regarded for a 1995 Chardonnay, but not seen for some time. Cellar door sales by appointment.

Best's Wines Lake Boga   R79

St Andrews, Lake Boga, Vic 3584
Ph 03 5037 2154, Fax 03 5037 2678

Owner: Best's Wines Pty Ltd
Chief winemaker: Viv Thomson
Year of foundation: 1930
Tonnes crushed on average each year: 400
Location: Lake Boga
Area: 29 ha

Soils: light sandy loam over limestone
Varieties planted: White—chardonnay, chenin blanc, colombard, muscadelle, muscat gordo blanco, riesling; Red—cabernet sauvignon, muscat a petits grains rouge, grenache, merlot, shiraz
Leading wines: Best's Victoria range
Notes: This was the first winery established in the Swan Hill region in 1930. Wines under the Victoria label are either 100% from Swan Hill or blends of Best's Swan Hill and Concongella vineyards (see Grampians). Cellar door sales: Mon–Sat 10am–5pm; Sun, long weekends and school holidays noon–4pm.

R L Buller Pty Ltd Beverford   R78

Murray Valley Highway, Beverford,
Vic 3590
Ph 03 5037 6305, Fax 03 5037 6803,
Email bullers@swanhill.com.au

Owner: R L Buller & Son Pty Ltd
Chief winemaker: Richard Buller
Year of foundation: 1952
Tonnes crushed on average each year: 5000, of which 1200 are used for R L Buller wines
Location: Beverford
Area: 27.5 ha (fruit is also purchased from local growers)
Soils: soils range from sandy loam over limestone to grey alluvial loams
Varieties planted: White—colombard,

frontignac, muscat gordo blanco, pedro
ximenes, semillon; Red—cabernet sauvignon,
grenache, muscat a petits grains rouge, shiraz,
touriga
Leading wines: Magee Cabernet-Shiraz,
Semillon-Chardonnay, Victoria Classic Shiraz-
Grenache-Mataro, Beverford Chenin Blanc,
Chardonnay, Fortifieds
Notes: The second oldest winery in the region,
specialising in reds. Wines made at Beverford
are kept separate from the company's other
wines made at Rutherglen. Cellar door sales:
Mon–Sat 9am–5pm

Brown Brothers Mystic Park (vineyard only) **R80**
Gorton Drive, Mystic Park, Vic 3581

Owner: Brown Brothers
Year of foundation: 1968
Tonnes produced on average each year: 1000
Location: Mystic Park
Area: 128 ha and growing (at 2001, this
vineyard contains many young non-bearing
vines)
Soils: tachera sandy loam to a depth of 1 metre
Varieties planted: White—chenin blanc,
colombard, crouchen, flora, muscadelle,

orange muscat, semillon, sylvaner;
Red—cabernet sauvignon, grenache,
muscat a petits grain rouge, shiraz, tarrango
Leading wines: Brown Brothers Orange
Muscat, Tarrango
Notes: This large vineyard helps to satisfy the
fruit needs of Brown Brothers. No local cellar
door sales.

Carpinteri Vineyards **NR**
Murray Valley Highway, Nyah, Vic 3594
Ph 03 5030 2569, Fax 03 5030 2680,
Email carp@ruralnet.net.au

Owners:V & K, C & T Carpinteri
Chief winemaker: Michael Kyberd (contract)
Year of foundation: 1999
Tonnes produced on average each year: 520,
of which 30 are used for Carpinteri wines
Location: Nyah
Area: 32 ha
Soils: sandy loam over limestone
Varieties planted: White—calmeria,
chardonnay, muscat gordo blanco, sultana;
Red—grenache, malbec, mataro, black muscat
Leading wines: little wine yet produced
Notes: No cellar door sales. Sales by mail order.

PART II

TASMANIA

❦ Wine in Tasmania

Wine was produced in Tasmania as long ago as 1826, but the vine suffered obvious disadvantages in the island colony. Its extremely cool climate, the lack of skilled labour and viticultural knowledge, and a very small market were factors that greatly discouraged the development of a viable industry. By 1850, viticulture in Tasmania was extinct, and the only subsequent flicker of interest occurred later in the 19th century when an Italian entrepreneur planned to plant grapes on Maria Island, a venture that was ultimately abandoned.

The industry's rebirth occurred during the 1950s and 1960s as a result of persistence by two migrants, the French engineer, Jean Miguet, who planted vines near Launceston and Claudio Alcorso, an Italian, who started plantings further south on the Derwent River just west of Hobart. In 1967, vines appeared once more in the Tamar Valley, when Graham Wiltshire established a vineyard near Legana. By 1974 Dr Andrew Pirie was pioneering the Pipers Brook area.

Since then, bearing in mind its climatic limitations and the consequent restrictions on grape varieties that will ripen fully in that climate, Tasmanian viticulture has expanded quite rapidly. Pinot Noir, Chardonnay and, to a lesser extent, Riesling are some of the varieties that have been particularly successful, but as a rule only locations with a favourably warm and long season (parts of the Tamar Valley and the East Coast) will ripen Cabernet Sauvignon. The result is that Tasmanian Cabernet rarely, if ever, rivals the mainstream styles of Australian Cabernet. (There is no doubt that Cabernet wines of great quality can be made, the Tamar Ridge Cabernet Sauvignon 1998 being a case in point.)

By year's end 1999, the Tasmanian wine industry was in expansive mode. The 1998 statistics are bracketed beside the 1999 figures. There were 94 (87) licensed wine producers, 119 (112) individual vineyards, 26 (23) wineries, 595 (522) planted and 73 (60) newly planted hectares of vineyard of which 463 (445) hectares were in bearing. Yields were 3199 (3113) tonnes. By mainland standards these statistics are minute, but for lovers of elegant whites, enticing reds and stylish sparklings, they are very encouraging. Though their vineyards are small, having an average area of not quite 4 hectares, Tasmanian vignerons on the whole are enthusiastic with their sights set firmly on quality.

Some years ago, I suspect in the absence of sufficient marketing wherewithal, the Tasmanian government's Tasmanian Appellation scheme quietly folded. As a geographical indication, Tasmania is simply a wine zone without any more specific designation at the present time, but moves are afoot in the Tamar Valley to regionalise, as the qualifying conditions for this purpose already exist. However, regionalisation needs to be effective in the marketplace and without accompanying marketing nous and a viable budget would lead to very little. So it remains to be seen whether the vignerons of the Tamar Valley are brave enough to take this step.

The Tasmanian government, through its Commissioner for Licensing, divides Tasmanian viticulture into seven wine-producing areas which I have consolidated for the purposes of this book into four as regards grouping of wineries and vineyards.

Location: The North East latitude 41°07'S, longitude 147°05'E (Pipers River); latitude 42°059'S, longitude 148°05'E (Swansea–Bicheno). The Tamar Valley and the North West, latitude 41°25'S, longitude 147°10'E (Launceston). The South latitude 42°65'S, longitude 147°30'E (Derwent Valley); latitude 42°60'S, longitude 147°40'E (Coal River); latitude 43°02'S, longitude 147°E (Huon Valley).

Elevation: Pipers Brook, 120 m; Swansea–Bicheno, 25 m; The Tamar Valley, 80 m; Derwent Valley, 60 m; Coal River Valley, 65 m; Huon Valley, 50 m

Topography and soils: Tasmania is, of course, an extension of the Australian mainland, separated only recently in geological time by Bass Strait. Its topography is very similar to south-eastern New South Wales and southern Victoria with quite mountainous terrain in the western and central parts of the island and warmer coastal aspects on its eastern side. Its southerly situation also means that it is constantly exposed to the predominantly southerly and westerly winds of the Roaring Forties. Tasmania also shares many of the soil types of the mainland. Generally, in the north there are deep sandy earths of a reddish colour, while in the south, soils are thinner and sandstone-based.

Climate: *North and east*. Launceston MJT 17.7°C, MAR na, HDD (raw) 1155 and 1281 (cut off and as adjusted for latitude, daily temperature range and vine sites), AR 725 mm (Oct–Apr 348 mm), RH 46% (3pm Jan), AI na, SH 7.6 (Gladstones), Cf MJT 17.2°C, MAR 10.3°C, HDD (raw) 1020, AR 788 mm (Oct–Mar 311 mm), RH 65% (9am Jan), AI 224 mm, SH 7.3 (Dry & Smart). St Helens MJT 16.7°C, MAR na, HDD (raw) 1017 and 1264 (cut off and as adjusted for latitude, daily temperature range and vine sites), AR 782 mm (Oct–Apr 431 mm), RH 59% (3pm Jan), AI na, SH 7.6. *South*. Risdon MJT 16.8°C, MAR na, HDD (raw) 1039 and 1182 (cut off and as adjusted for latitude, daily temperature range and vine sites), AR 596 mm (Oct–Apr 356 mm), RH 51% (3pm Jan), AI na, SH 6.8. Hobart MJT 16.7°C, MAR na, HDD (raw) 1019 and 1158 (cut off and as adjusted for latitude, daily temperature range and vine sites), AR 622 mm (Oct–Apr 359 mm), RH 52% (3pm Jan), AI na, SH 6.7. I have mentioned that generally Tasmania is an extremely cool zone. It is interesting to note, however, that most of Tasmania's modern viticultural development took place during the 1980s and that in *Viticulture and Environment* Dr Gladstones quite reasonably postulates Tasmania is becoming warmer.

The question should therefore be asked, is Tasmania's viticulture being reborn during a false dawn? Will the trend continue or be reversed? Whatever the answers may be, Tasmania's future vine sites will continue to need the most careful planning and the present ones all the protection that they can obtain from late spring frosts and high winds.

Harvest time: *North and east*. Pinot noir and chardonnay early to mid-April, cabernet sauvignon late May, riesling slightly earlier. *South*. Pinot noir and chardonnay early April, riesling early May

Principal varieties: White—chardonnay, riesling, sauvignon blanc; Red—pinot noir, cabernet sauvignon

Other varieties: White—gewurztraminer, muller thurgau, pinot gris, semillon; Red—cabernet franc, gamay, meunier, petit verdot, shiraz

Total area as at 1999: *North and East Tasmania* (incorporating the North East Tamar Valley, the North West and Eastern Tasmania) 451 ha, tonnes produced 2445;

South Tasmania (incorporating Coal Valley, Derwent Valley and Huon/Channel) 144 ha, tonnes produced 754.
Major wine styles: Pinot Noir, Chardonnay, Riesling, Sparkling White (Champagne style)
Leading wineries and vineyards of Northern Tasmania: Clover Hill, Tamar Ridge, Pipers Brook, Silk Hill, East Arm, Golders Vineyard, Rosevears Estate, Delamere, Lalla Gully.
Leading wineries and vineyards of Eastern Tasmania: Freycinet Vineyards, Spring Vale Vineyard, Craigie Knowe, Apsley Gorge.
Leading wineries and vineyards in Southern Tasmania: Derwent Estate, Meadowbank, Moorilla Estate, Elsewhere Vineyard, Treehouse Vineyard.

WINERIES WITHOUT VINEYARDS SPECIALISING IN MAKING WINE FROM TASMANIA-WIDE SOURCES

Hood Wines   **R85**

Denholms Road, Cambridge, Tas 7170
Ph 03 6248 5844, 03 6243 7320,
Fax 03 6243 0226

Owners: Andrew and Jennifer Hood
Chief winemaker: Andrew Hood
Year of foundation: 1990
Tonnes crushed on average each year: 300, of which 50 are used for Andrew Hood's own label, Wellington Wines, the rest as contract winemaker for many vineyards throughout Tasmania

Location: Cambridge (winery)
Area: na
Soils: na
Varieties planted: na
Leading wines: Wellington Riesling, Chardonnay, Pinot Noir, Iced Riesling
Notes: Andrew Hood is primarily a contract winemaker for many small vineyards throughout Tasmania. In his own right, he concentrates on fine-fruit styles of Riesling, Chardonnay and Pinot Noir, which are of excellent quality. He also makes a freeze-dried sweeter style of Riesling. Cellar door sales by appointment.

NORTHERN TASMANIA (TAMAR VALLEY, PIPERS BROOK AND THE NORTH WEST)

Brook Eden Vineyard   **NR**

167 Adams Road, Lebrina, Tas 7254
Ph 03 6395 6211

Owners: John and Sheila Bezemer
Chief winemaker: John Bezemer
Year of foundation: 1987 (vineyard), 1993 (winery)
Tonnes crushed on average each year: 10
Location: Lebrina

Area: 2 ha
Soils: Red basalt (kraznozems) drains well but also holds moisture
Varieties planted: White—chardonnay, riesling; Red—cabernet sauvignon, pinot noir
Leading wines: Brook Eden Pinot Noir, Chardonnay
Notes: A small vineyard and winery that is part of a larger pastoral property. Cellar door sales: 10am–5pm daily.

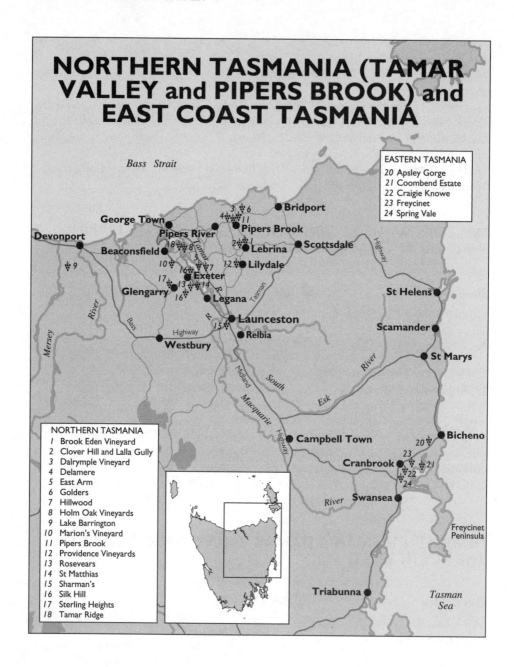

NORTHERN TASMANIA (TAMAR VALLEY and PIPERS BROOK) and EAST COAST TASMANIA

Bass   Strait

EASTERN TASMANIA
20 Apsley Gorge
21 Coombend Estate
22 Craigie Knowe
23 Freycinet
24 Spring Vale

Devonport

George Town

Pipers River

Beaconsfield

Pipers Brook

3   6
4   11
2   1   Lebrina
Bridport

Scottsdale

9

10

18   8
5
16   7
17   13   14
16   Legana
Exeter

12   Lilydale

Glengarry

St Helens

15
Launceston
Relbia

Scamander

Westbury
Highway

St Marys

Mersey River

Bass

Midland

Macquarie

South

Esk River

Campbell Town

20
23
Cranbrook   22   21
24

Bicheno

River   Swansea

Freycinet
Peninsula

Triabunna

Tasman
Sea

NORTHERN TASMANIA
1   Brook Eden Vineyard
2   Clover Hill and Lalla Gully
3   Dalrymple Vineyard
4   Delamere
5   East Arm
6   Golders
7   Hillwood
8   Holm Oak Vineyards
9   Lake Barrington
10   Marion's Vineyard
11   Pipers Brook
12   Providence Vineyards
13   Rosevears
14   St Matthias
15   Sharman's
16   Silk Hill
17   Sterling Heights
18   Tamar Ridge

Clover Hill **R93**

Clover Hill Road, Lebrina, Tas 7254
Ph 03 6395 6114, Fax 03 6395 6257

Owner: Tasmania Vineyards Pty Ltd
Chief winemaker: Chris Markell
Year of foundation: 1986
Tonnes produced on average each year: 160, of which 150 are used for Clover Hill wines
Location: Lebrina, about 10 minutes drive south-west of Pipers Brook and about 20 minutes north-east of Launceston
Area: 21 ha
Soils: well drained, deep volcanic soils, dark red in colour
Varieties planted: White—chardonnay; Red—meunier, pinot noir
Leading wines: Clover Hill Vintage Sparkling Wines (made by the classic champagne method)
Notes: Only one wine is produced and it is a classic, showing the ideal nature of this area for sparkling wine. You will note that 10 tonnes of fruit appears to remain after Clover Hill needs have been satisfied. This is used for Taltarni non-Tasmanian sparkling wine to give further freshness and elegance. Base wines are made at Clover Hill and then transported to Taltarni for champenisation and a minimum 30 months maturation on lees. Clover Hill is the archetypal Tasmanian sparkling white, extremely elegant and often tending to acidity when young. With some bottle age it becomes quite creamy and makes a marvellous aperitif style. Cellar door sales daily September to June 10am–5pm.

Dalrymple Vineyard **NR**

1337 Pipers Brook Road, Pipers Brook, Tas 7254
Ph/Fax 03 6382 7222,
Email dalrymple.wine@microtech.com.au

Owners: Dr Bertel and Anne Sundstrup
Chief winemaker: Dr Bertel Sundstrup

Year of foundation: 1987
Tonnes crushed on average each year: 70, of which 58 are used for Dalrymple wines
Location: Pipers Brook
Area: 11 ha
Soils: Situated upon rich red basaltic soil on the edge of an extinct volcano crater with a clay subsoil over a high underground water table, the vineyard enjoys a favourable north-east aspect and so maximum sunshine hours are obtained
Varieties planted: White—chardonnay, pinot gris, sauvignon blanc; Red—pinot noir
Leading wines: Dalrymple Vineyard Pinot Noir, Chardonnay, Sparkling
Notes: Dr Bertel Sundstrup retired recently, but not from winemaking. He has completed his studies in oenology at Charles Sturt University and continues to win trophies at wine shows especially for his Pinot Noir. Cellar door sales: daily 10am–5pm except Christmas Day.

Delamere **R84**

4238 Bridport Road, Pipers Brook, Tas 7254
Ph 03 6382 7190, Fax 03 6382 7250,
Email delamere@telstra.easymail.com.au

Owners: Richard and Dallas Richardson
Chief winemaker: Richard Richardson
Year of foundation: 1983
Tonnes crushed on average each year: 29
Location: Pipers Brook
Area: 3.5 ha
Soils: kraznozem, a deep well-structured, well-drained soil, having good moisture retention and a pH that is neutral to slightly acid
Varieties planted: White—chardonnay; Red—pinot noir
Leading wines: Delamere Vineyard Reserve Pinot Noir, Reserve Chardonnay, Sparkling Cuvée
Notes: Like all the wisest red producers of Pipers Brook, Richard Richardson specialises in Pinot Noir, producing a fine-boned, fruit driven

red. He also makes tiny amounts of Chardonnay. Cellar door sales: daily 10am–5pm.

East Arm Vineyard R86

111 Archers Road, East Arm,
via Hillwood, Tas 7250
Ph 03 6334 0266, Fax 03 6334 1405,
Email jwetten@medeserve.com.au

Owners: Dr John Wettenhall and Anita James
Chief winemaker: contract
Year of foundation: 1993
Tonnes produced on average each year: 12
Location: East Arm near Hillwood
Area: 2.5 ha
Soils: the vineyard is situated on an east-north-east facing slope quite steep in parts. Its soils are sandy loams overlying gravelly clay. Drainage is good and rocks within the vineyard allow for heat-retention during the day. The vineyard is trellised entirely by the Scott-Henry system
Varieties planted: White—chardonnay, pinot gris, riesling; Red—pinot noir
Leading wines: East Arm Vineyard Riesling, Pinot Noir, Chardonnay
Notes: John Wettenhall, who recently graduated from Charles Sturt University in oenology, is one more of the legion of medical men in the grip of the grape. Three golds (two for Riesling and one for Pinot Noir) at the Tasmanian Wine Show highlight the promise of this vineyard. It is early days for cellar door sales. Arrangements to taste East Arm wines may be made by contacting Dr Wettenhall.

Golders Vineyard R85

Bridport Road, Pipers Brook, Tas 7254
Ph/Fax 03 6395 4142

Owner/ chief winemaker: Richard Crabtree
Year of foundation: 1993
Tonnes produced on average each year: 8
Location: Pipers Brook

Area: 2.5 ha (only part of which is bearing)
Soils: red kraznozems (red volcanic loam over basalt)
Varieties planted: White—chardonnay; Red—pinot noir
Leading wines: Golders Vineyard Chardonnay, Pinot Noir
Notes: Situated on a north-east facing slope 5km from Bass Strait, Golders Vineyard specialises in the two varieties most suited to Pipers Brook, Pinot Noir and Chardonnay, both of which are very good. Cellar door sales by appointment.

Hillwood NR

Leam Road, Hillwood, Tas 7252
Ph 03 6334 4595 or 0418 500 672,
Fax 03 6334 3050

Owners: Geoff Carr and Barbara Ruttelle
Chief winemaker: Geoff Carr
Year of foundation: 1991
Tonnes produced on average each year: 5
Location: Hillwood
Area: 1 ha
Soils: ironstone gravel
Varieties planted: White—sauvignon blanc; Red—cabernet sauvignon, merlot, pinot noir
Leading wines: Hillwood Cabernet Sauvignon, Hillwood Sauvignon Blanc
Notes: A very small vineyard whose wines are unknown to me. No cellar door sales.

Holm Oak Winery NR

11 West Bay Road, Rowella, Tas 7270
Ph 03 6394 7577, Fax 03 6394 7350

Owners: Nicholas and Cynthia Butler
Chief winemaker: Nicholas Butler
Year of foundation: 1983
Tonnes crushed on average each year: 42
Location: Rowella (Tamar Valley)
Area: 6.2 ha
Soils: alluvial soils over gravelly, ironstone clays
Varieties planted: White—riesling;

Red—cabernet franc, cabernet sauvignon, merlot, pinot noir
Leading wines: Holm Oak Pinot Noir, Cabernet Sauvignon (a blend of the 'Bordeaux' varieties), Pinot Noir-Chardonnay (a still pink wine), Riesling, Merlot
Notes: Now one of the Tamar Valley's older vineyards, Holm Oak is located in a very favourable position for ripening cabernet sauvignon. Its fuller-style Cabernet is of very good quality and helps keep the 'Bordeaux' flag flying in this very cool state. Cellar door sales: daily 10am–5pm.

Ironpot Bay NR

Rowella Vineyard
West Bay Road, Rowella, Tas 7250
Ph 03 6394 7320, Fax 03 6394 7346

Owner: Rod Cuthbert
Chief winemaker: Andrew Hood (contract)
Year of foundation: 1988
Tonnes crushed on average each year: 50, about 30 of which are used for Ironpot Bay wines
Location: Deviot (Tamar Valley)
Area: 4.1 ha
Soils: loam over clay
Varieties planted: White—chardonnay, gewurztraminer, pinot gris, sauvignon blanc, semillon; Red—none
Leading wines: Ironpot Bay Chardonnay, Semillon-Sauvignon Blanc, Pinot Grigio
Notes: Ironpot Bay specialises in unwooded whites and has won many awards for such wines. Cellar door sales by appointment.

Lake Barrington Vineyard NR

1133–1136 West Kentish Road, Sheffield, Tas 7306
Ph 03 6491 1249, Fax 03 6334 2892, Email nutvine@netspace.net.au

Owner: Maree Taylor
Chief winemakers: Andrew Hood (still wines),

Steve Lubiana (sparkling) (contract)
Year of foundation: 1986
Tonnes crushed on average each year: 7
Location: Sheffield
Area: 3.2 ha (2 ha of which are non-bearing)
Soils: red clay
Varieties planted: White—chardonnay, riesling; Red—pinot noir
Leading wines: Lake Barrington Chardonnay, Pinot Noir, Alexandra (sparkling)
Notes: Lake Barrington Vineyard is a consistent winner of bronze and silver awards for its Chardonnay and Pinot Noir and has won a trophy for Alexandra at local wine shows. Cellar door sales: Wed–Sun 10am–5.30pm November–April. Closed at other times.

Lalla Gully Vineyard R84

Brooks Road, Lalla, Tas 7267
Ph/Fax see Clover Hill

Owners: Tasmania Vineyards Pty Ltd
Chief winemaker: Chris Markell
Year of foundation: 1989
Tonnes crushed on average each year: 30
Location: Lalla Gully
Area: 6 ha
Soils: grey loam with limestone deposits in subsoil
Varieties planted: White—chardonnay, sauvignon blanc; Red—pinot noir
Leading wines: Lalla Gully Chardonnay, Sauvignon Blanc
Notes: A recent change of ownership has introduced Taltarni and Chris Markell to another nearby vineyard in north-east Tasmania. The varieties planted are ideal for the area and some excellent table wines should result. No cellar door sales. Wines are distributed by Taltarni.

Marion's Vineyard NR

Foreshore Drive, Deviot, Tas 7275
Ph/Fax 03 6394 7434

Owners: Mark and Marion Semmens
Chief winemaker: Marion Semmens
Year of foundation: 1980
Tonnes crushed on average each year: 58
Location: Deviot (Tamar Valley)
Area: 11 ha
Soils: doleritic and ironstone gravel. As Mark
Semmens says, 'a lot of rock!'.
Varieties planted: White—chardonnay,
gewurztraminer, muller-thurgau, pinot gris,
viognier; Red—cabernet franc, cabernet
sauvignon, cascade (a labrusca cross), merlot,
pinot noir, rkatsitelli
Leading wines: Marion's Vineyard Cabernet
Sauvignon
Notes: Arriving in Tasmania initially as tourists
from California, Mark and Marion Semmens
liked the look of what they saw. Twenty years
later they still do, although instead of a 12 ha
rocky bush block above the Tamar River, they
now gaze upon 11 ha of mature vineyard and
a winery as their own contribution to this part
of the Tamar Valley, which is one of the few
areas in Tasmania capable of ripening
cabernet sauvignon. Cellar door sales: daily
10am–5pm.

Notley Gorge NR

Loop Road, Glengarry, Tas 7275
Ph 03 6396 1166, Fax 03 6396 1200

Owner: Dr M Beamish
Chief winemaker: Andrew Hood (contract)
Year of foundation: 1982
Tonnes crushed on average each year: 50, of
which about 35 are used for Notley Gorge's
own labels
Location: Glengarry, about 6 km west of Exeter
Area: 8 ha
Soils: duplex soils over a clay base
Varieties planted: White—chardonnay,
sauvignon blanc; Red—cabernet sauvignon,
merlot, pinot noir
Leading wines: Notley Gorge Pinot Noir
Notes: The present Notley Gorge estate is an
amalgamation of the former Notley Gorge and
Glengarry vineyards. It sprang to prominence
with a top gold for Pinot Noir at the Royal
Melbourne Wine Show, an award that can but
underscore Tasmania's reputation as a producer
of fine Pinot Noir and Andrew Hood as one of
its leading makers. Cellar door sales: by
appointment.

Pipers Brook Vineyard R87

1216 Pipers Brook Road, Pipers Brook,
Tas 7254
Ph 03 6322 4444, Fax 03 6382 7226,
Email cwansink@pbv.com.au

Owner: Pipers Brook Vineyard Ltd
Chief winemaker: Dr Andrew Pirie
Year of foundation: 1974
Tonnes crushed on average each year: 1000,
all of which are used for Pipers Brook and
Ninth Island wines
Location: Pipers Brook winery, Pipers Brook;
Ninth Island Winery, Pipers River. Vineyards at
Pipers Brook, Timperon Hills, Strathlynn, Pier,
Bird, Buchanan, Leura, Rochaix, HeemsKerk
Area: 245.73 ha (all vineyards)
Soils: Pipers Brook, Timperon and Hills—
kraznozems/ferrosols (deep friable tertiary
basaltic soils); Strathlynn and Pier—red basalt
and biscay (cracking black clay), Bird—
kraznozems/ferrosol; Buchanan—podsolic,
sandy silt on a heavy clay base;
Heemskerk—kraznozems/ferrosols;
Leura—ferrosols/kraznozems; Rochaix—
ferrosols running into ironstone silt, red
kraznozems
Varieties planted: Pipers Brook Vineyard:
White—chardonnay (4.1ha), gewurztraminer
(1.5 ha) riesling, (5.3ha); Red—cabernet franc
(0.8 ha), pinot noir (4.1 ha). Timperon:
White—chardonnay (6.42 ha), pinot gris

(0.35 ha); Red—pinot noir (6.3 ha). Hills: White—chardonnay (3.4 ha), pinot gris (0.88 ha), riesling (0.57 ha), sauvignon blanc (2.1 ha), semillon (0.8 ha); Red—pinot noir (3.74 ha). Strathlynn: White—chardonnay (9.18 ha), gewurztraminer (0.72 ha), pinot gris (1.47 ha), riesling (0.41 ha), sauvignon blanc (10.09 ha); Red—cabernet franc (2.29 ha), cabernet sauvignon (3.04 ha), pinot noir (8.08 ha). Bird: White—riesling (3.75 ha); Red—pinot noir (8.99 ha). Buchanan: White—chardonnay (1.32 ha), frontignac (0.84 ha), riesling (1.08 ha), sauvignon blanc (0.99 ha), semillon (0.39 ha); Red—cabernet sauvignon (1.46 ha), merlot (1.03 ha), pinot noir (2.14 ha). Rochaix: White—chardonnay (8.89 ha), pinot gris (0.24 ha), riesling (1.59 ha), sauvignon blanc (3.18 ha); Red—merlot (0.55 ha), pinot noir (7.54 ha), mixed (0.1 ha). Heemskerk Vineyard: White—chardonnay (23.31 ha), pinot gris (1.97 ha), riesling (2.11 ha); Red—meunier (2.76 ha), pinot noir (10.58 ha), mixed (0.09 ha). Leura: White—chardonnay (11.52 ha), pinot gris (4 ha); Red—meunier (5.14 ha), pinot noir (36.03 ha), mixed (0.21 ha). Pier: White—chardonnay (1.75 ha), riesling (1.16 ha), sauvignon blanc (0.82 ha), semillon (1.02 ha); Red—merlot (0.92 ha), pinot noir (0.37 ha)

Leading wines: Pipers Brook Vineyard Summit Chardonnay, Vineyard Reserve Chardonnay, 'The Blackwood' Pinot Noir, Vineyard Reserve Pinot Noir, Pirie Vintage (Sparkling), Pipers Brook Vineyard Estate Wines Chardonnay, Pinot Noir (formerly Pellion), Riesling, Gewurztraminer, Pinot Gris, Cabernet (formerly Opimian).

Notes: Since its public listing, great changes have taken place at Pipers Brook. From the middle of 2000, the wines were regraded into three levels of ascending quality (and price) in the Pipers Brook Vineyard range. These are Estate, Reserve and Single Site. Pipers Brook emphasises that the differences are as follows: *Estate*: (this is an upgrade from the previous standard Pipers Brook Vineyard label) i) they are estate grown and made from mature, low-yielding vines; ii) there is a sharper quality focus and less volume; and iii) the varietals in this range are Riesling, Gewurztraminer, Pinot Gris, Sauvignon Blanc, Chardonnay, Pinot Noir and Cabernet: *Reserve*: (these are wines from sites that have been the subject of long term evaluation) i) they have been selected according to a benchmark by a tasting panel; ii) they have cellaring potential; iii) they are released in limited quantities; and iv) the varietals selected are Pinot Noir and Chardonnay. *Single Site*: (these are the best wines from single sites—there are no blends) i) these are from the most proven terroir from well-established low-yielding vineyards; ii) they are wines linked to special terroir; iii) they have excellent cellaring potential; iv) before selection, such wines have to meet extremely high selection criteria; v) they are released in extremely limited quantities; and vi) they are restricted at the present time to Summit Chardonnay, Blackwood Vineyard Pinot Noir and Upper Slopes Riesling. Other varieties may be included as quality is proven. Cellar door sales: at Pipers Brook open daily 10am–5pm; Strathlynn vineyard, 95 Rosevears Drive, Rosevears daily 10am–5pm.

Ninth Island **R81**

40 Baxters Road, Pipers River, Tas 7252
Ph 03 6332 4444, Fax 03 6382 7226

Owner: Pipers Brook Vineyard Ltd
Chief winemaker: Dr Andrew Pirie
Tonnes crushed on average each year: see Pipers Brook
Location: (winery) Pipers River
Area : na (part of Pipers Brook)
Soils: na (part of Pipers Brook)
Varieties planted: (part of Pipers Brook)
Leading wines: Ninth Island Tamar Cabernets, Pinot Noir, Chardonnay, Riesling, Sauvignon Blanc, Pinot Grigio

Notes: Ninth Island, the second label of Pipers Brook Vineyard, is well known in mainland Australia. It is restricted to wine originating in Tasmania. Cellar door sales: daily 10am–5pm (closed during the winter months).

Providence Vineyards NR

236 Lalla Road, Lalla, Tas 7267
Ph 03 6395 1290, Fax 03 6395 2088,
Email providence.vineyards@bigpond.com

Owner: Stuart and Brenda Bryce
Chief winemaker: Andrew Hood (contract)
Year of foundation: 1956
Tonnes produced on average each year: 16, about 8 of which are used for Providence Vineyard wines
Location: Lalla
Area: 2.17 ha
Soils: heavy clay dolerite loam with high water capacity and poor drainage. The vineyard is situated on a north-east facing slope, is drip irrigated and completely bird-netted during the growing season
Varieties planted: White—chardonnay, riesling, semillon; Red—pinot noir
Leading wines: Providence Chardonnay (lightly wooded), Pinot Noir
Notes: Providence Vineyard is an historic site in Tasmanian viticultural terms, for part of it was originally planted in 1956 by Tasmanian wine pioneer, Jean Miguet. It was originally called La Provence, but to avoid further litigation (an action in passing off instituted by the French government had been successfully defended by Stuart Bryce in 1994), Stuart changed his vineyard's name to Providence Vineyards in 1996. His wines regularly win gold, silver and bronze awards at local and mainland wine shows. Cellar door sales: 10am–5pm daily.

Rosevears Estate R85

1A Waldhorn Drive, Rosevears, Tas 7277
Ph 03 6330 1800, Fax 03 6330 1810,
Email rosevearsestates@bigpond.com

Owners: M. Beamish, R. Cuthbert and R. Martin
Chief winemaker: Shane McKerrow (winemaker), Jim Chatto (consultant)
Year of foundation: 1999
Tonnes produced on average each year: 140, of which 100 are used for Rosevears Estate wines
Location: Rosevears
Area: 26 ha consisting of four vineyards, Notley Gorge (8 ha), Glengarry (5.5 ha), Batman Bridge (5.5 ha) and Rosevears (7 ha)
Soils: Notley Gorge and Glengarry, duplex soils over a clay base; Batman Bridge, loam, clay subsoils; Rosevears, red basalt
Varieties planted: White—chardonnay, pinot gris, riesling, sauvignon blanc, traminer; Red—cabernet sauvignon, merlot, pinot noir
Leading wines: Rosevears Estate Pinot Noir, Cabernet Sauvignon, Riesling, Chardonnay, Sparkling, Pinot Noir Rose, Notley Gorge range
Notes: Rosevears Estate is a partnership between Dr Michael Beamish of Notley Gorge, Rod Cuthbert of Ironpot Bay and R. Martin of Batman Bridge Vineyard. Cellar door sales: daily 10am–5pm. There is also a restaurant.

St Matthias NR

Rosevears Drive, West Tamar, Tas 7277
Ph 03 6330 1700, Fax 03 6330 1975

Owner: a syndicate of Hobart businessmen with Tim Goddard as Chief Executive
Chief winemaker: Michael Glover
Year of foundation: 1982
Tonnes produced on average each year: 70
Location: Rosevears
Area: 15 ha
Soils: reddish-brown clayey loams intermixed with ironstone
Varieties planted: White—chardonnay, riesling;

Red—cabernet sauvignon, merlot, pinot noir, shiraz

Leading wines: Moorilla range, St Matthias range

Notes: St Matthias shares common ownership with the more famous Moorilla Estate at Berriedale near Hobart. Its vineyard has a warm north-easterly aspect over the Tamar River. Cellar door sales: daily 10am–5pm.

Sharmans (formerly Glenbothy Vineyard) NR

RSD 175 Glenwood Road, Relbia, Tas 7258
Ph/Fax 03 6343 0773,
Email msharman@qotas.net

Owners: Mike and Philippa Sharman
Chief winemaker: (contract)
Year of foundation: 1987
Tonnes produced on average each year: 28, about half of which is used for Sharman wines
Location: Relbia (just south of Launceston)
Area: 3.2 ha
Soils: shallow sandy clay loam over clay with patches of river-washed stone scattered through it
Varieties planted: White—chardonnay, riesling, sauvignon blanc, schonburger; Red—cabernet sauvignon, pinot noir
Leading wines: Glenbothy Vineyard Chardonnay, Pinot Noir, Riesling
Notes: A vineyard with a comparatively low profile, winning bronze awards at local wine shows. Cellar door sales: weekends 10am–4pm, other times by appointment.

Silk Hill Vineyard R86

324 Motor Road, Deviot, Tas 7275
Ph 03 6394 7385, Fax 03 6394 7392,
Email silkhill@primus.com.au

Owners: Gavin and Ann Scott
Chief winemaker: Gavin Scott
Year of foundation: 1982

Tonnes produced on average each year: 8
Location: Deviot (vineyard and winery), Robigana (vineyard)
Area: 1.5 ha (includes both vineyards)
Soils: Deviot: ironstone loam over clay. Robigana: grey sandy loam over gravel over clay.
Varieties planted: White—none; Red—pinot noir
Leading wine: Silk Hill Pinot Noir
Notes: Silk Hill reveals just how important it is to match 'climat' with variety. Here pinot noir thrives. Certainly Gavin Scott's show results stress this. His Pinots are built to last a while also. Trophies for the best Tasmanian wine in older classes were awarded at the Royal Hobart Show 1996 and the Qantas Trophy for the best Pinot Noir of Show at Hobart in 1997 prove that his Pinots are not pleasant drinking forward styles meant like some to be consumed within 12–18 months. Cellar door sales: tastings by appointment.

Sterling Heights R83

77 Faulkners Road, Winkleigh, Tas 7275
Ph/Fax 03 6396 3214, Mob 0419 594 115

Owners: Geoff and Jenny Wells
Chief winemaker: Alain Rousseau (contract)
Year of foundation: 1988
Tonnes produced on average each year: 15
Location: Winkleigh
Area: 1.9 ha
Soils: grey sandy loam over varying subsoils with an east-north-east aspect
Varieties planted: White—chardonnay, gewurztraminer, riesling; Red—cabernet franc, meunier, pinot noir
Leading wines: Sterling Heights Pinot Noir
Notes: For Geoff Wells, Sterling Heights Pinot Noir has been a consistent performer at local wine shows and its quality is undoubted. What is stifling Sterling Heights and many other small vineyards throughout Australia is the Wine Equalisation Tax. Previous exemptions

from sales tax for very small makers have now been abolished, ensuring that winemaking in small quantity is no longer viable: small makers are using less and less of their own fruit and simply becoming growers for larger wineries. The inevitable result will be a loss of diversity and the growth of uniformity, a great pity for the lover of rare wines from small vineyards. Cellar door sales (while they last) by appointment and at Esk market on Sundays.

Tamar Ridge **R90**

Auburn Road, Kayena, Tas 7250
Ph 03 6394 7002, Fax 03 6394 7003,
Email tamridge@southcon.com.au

Owner: Josef Chromy
Chief winemaker: Julian Alcorso
Year of foundation: 1994 (vineyard), 1999 (winery)
Tonnes produced on average each year: 200 but increasing to 500 by 2005

Location: Kayena, West Tamar
Area: 55 ha
Soils: grey sandy clay loam to sandy loam
Varieties planted: White—chardonnay, gewurztraminer, pinot gris, riesling, sauvignon blanc; Red—cabernet sauvignon, merlot, pinot noir
Leading wines: Tamar Ridge Riesling, Pinot Noir, Cabernet Sauvignon
Notes: Under the experienced winemaking hand of Julian Alcorso, Tamar Ridge has got off to a flying start. This remarkable new winery is well worth a special trip, if only for its Cabernet Sauvignon, a variety generally difficult to ripen in Tasmania but which ripens extremely well in this part of the Tamar. Its Riesling and Pinot Noir are also very good. Don't miss it. Cellar door sales: daily 10am–5pm.

EAST COAST TASMANIA

Apsley Gorge   **R81**

'The Gulch', Bicheno, Tas 7215
Ph 03 6375 1221, Fax 03 6375 1589

Owner/chief winemaker: Brian Franklin
Year of foundation: 1990
Tonnes crushed on average each year: 30
Location: Bicheno
Area: 4 ha
Soils: heavy clay over broken sandstone
Varieties planted: White—chardonnay;
Red—pinot noir
Leading wines: Apsley Gorge Chardonnay,
Pinot Noir
Notes: It is climate that is the secret here. The
vineyard has been established in a north-east
facing valley almost at the entrance to the
Apsley Gorge National Park. As evidenced by
its show results, Apsley Gorge is a vineyard
and winery capable of very high standards,
especially in Pinot Noir, but I found a 1998
Chardonnay slightly disappointing because of a
vegetative character and some off-flavours.
Cellar door sales: by appointment.

Coombend Estate   **NR**

'Coombend', Swansea, Tas 7190
Ph (cellar door) 03 6257 8881,
Fax 03 6257 8484,
Email coombendest@telstra.net.au

Owners: John and Josephine Fenn-Smith
Chief winemaker: Andrew Hood (contract)
Year of foundation: 1986
Tonnes produced on average each year: 23
Location: Swansea (cellar door and vineyard),
halfway between Swansea and Bicheno
Area: 4 ha
Soils: This vineyard is adjacent to Freycinet, but
its soils are slightly different—brownish on a
clay base with a good northerly aspect and
excellent drainage
Varieties planted: White—riesling, sauvignon
blanc; Red—cabernet sauvignon, shiraz
Leading wines: Coombend Estate Sauvignon
Blanc, Cabernet Sauvignon
Notes: Coombend Estate vineyard is part of a
much larger pastoral property. It has gained a
good reputation for its Cabernet Sauvignon,
being located in one of the few Tasmanian
areas that do in fact suit that late-ripening
variety. Farm cottage accommodation is
available on the property. Cellar door sales:
daily from 9am–5pm and by mail order.

Craigie Knowe Vineyard   **R84**

80 Glen Gala Road, Cranbrook,
Tas 7190
Ph 03 6223 5620, Fax 03 6223 5009

Owners: John Austwick and Ray Jensen
Chief winemaker: John Austwick
Year of foundation: 1979
Tonnes crushed on average each year: 10, but
will increase to about 20 when new plantings
come into bearing
Location: Cranbrook
Area: 4.8 ha
Soils: friable red loams over dolerite
(kraznozems), as John Austwick says 'great for
vegetables and grapes'
Varieties planted: White—none; Red—cabernet
franc, cabernet sauvignon, merlot, petit verdot,
pinot noir
Leading wine: Craigie Knowe Cabernet
Sauvignon
Notes: The east coast of Tasmania is the only
spot other than the Tamar Valley where
cabernet sauvignon ripens with any
consistency. John Austwick has a good site and
makes a complex Cabernet from the Bordeaux
brotherhood of varieties, although the French,
as John acknowledges, would be most
surprised to see pinot noir growing alongside
them. Cellar door sales: weekends.

Freycinet R86

15919 Tasman Highway, Bicheno,
Tas 7215
Ph 03 6257 8574, 03 6257 8384,
Fax 03 6257 8454

Owners: Geoff and Susan Bull
Chief winemakers: Claudio Radenti
Year of foundation: 1980
Tonnes crushed on average each year: 90
Location: Bicheno (18 km south)
Area: 9 ha
Soils: rocky podsolic loam over a well-drained
clay subsoil
Varieties planted: White—chardonnay, riesling;
Red—cabernet sauvignon, merlot, pinot noir
Leading wines: Freycinet Pinot Noir, Chardonnay
Notes: Freycinet is one of the great success
stories of Tasmanian viticulture, proving in that
zone that climate and exposure are critical in
the ripening of quality grapes. Freycinet is
situated in a natural amphitheatre, which faces
north, being open to the mildest of Tasmanian
east coast weather. It is sheltered from cold
southerly and westerly winds, and is also in a
rain shadow, which means that supplementary
irrigation is often necessary during the growing
season. Its Pinot Noir is powerful and
concentrated, and its Cabernet Sauvignon is
arguably the 'biggest' in Tasmania, with little
of the leafy, capsicum-like 'green' attributes of
leaner Cabernets. Its Chardonnay also is
excellent. Cellar door sales: Mon–Fri
9am–5pm, weekends 10am–4pm.

Spring Vale Vineyards   85

130 Spring Vale Road, Cranbrook,
Tas 7190
Ph 03 6257 8208, Fax 03 6257 8598

Owners: Rodney and Lyn Lyne
Chief winemaker: Rodney Lyne and contract
Year of foundation: 1986
Tonnes crushed on average each year: 35
Location: Cranbrook
Area: 4 ha
Soils: a rich, red-brown loam over porous clay
with a tendency to promote excessive vigour in
the vines. Its fertility is controlled by trellising
and strict attention to bud numbers.
Varieties planted: White—chardonnay,
gewurztraminer, pinot gris; Red—pinot noir
Leading wine: Spring Vale Pinot Noir
Notes: Spring Vale, part of a much larger
pastoral property owned by the Lyne family
since 1875, is another of those fortunate
vineyards that share the marvellous viticultural
climate of Tasmania's east coast. Like its
neighbours Apsley Gorge and Freycinet, Spring
Vale has built an excellent reputation for rich
and full-flavoured Pinot Noir. Cellar door sales:
daily 10am–5pm.

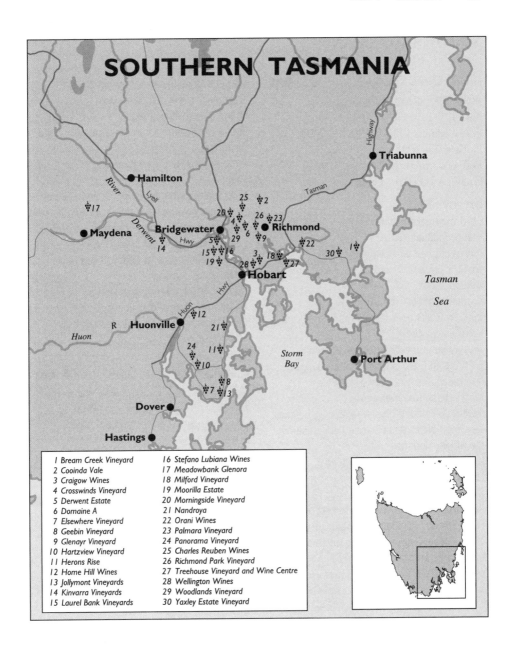

SOUTHERN TASMANIA

1 Bream Creek Vineyard	16 Stefano Lubiana Wines
2 Cooinda Vale	17 Meadowbank Glenora
3 Craigow Wines	18 Milford Vineyard
4 Crosswinds Vineyard	19 Moorilla Estate
5 Derwent Estate	20 Morningside Vineyard
6 Domaine A	21 Nandroya
7 Elsewhere Vineyard	22 Orani Wines
8 Geebin Vineyard	23 Palmara Vineyard
9 Glenayr Vineyard	24 Panorama Vineyard
10 Hartzview Vineyard	25 Charles Reuben Wines
11 Herons Rise	26 Richmond Park Vineyard
12 Home Hill Wines	27 Treehouse Vineyard and Wine Centre
13 Jollymont Vineyards	28 Wellington Wines
14 Kinvarra Vineyards	29 Woodlands Vineyard
15 Laurel Bank Vineyards	30 Yaxley Estate Vineyard

SOUTHERN TASMANIA

Bream Creek Vineyard   **R81**

Marion Bay Road, Bream Creek,
Tas 7175
Postal address (sales) GPO box 2020
Hobart, Tas 7001
Ph/Fax 03 6231 4646,
Email peacock@mpx.com.au

Owner: Fred Peacock
Chief winemaker: Steve Lubiana (contract)
Year of foundation: 1973
Tonnes crushed on average each year: 115,
about 55 of which are used for Bream Creek
wines
Location: Potters Croft, Arthur Highway,
Dunalley (cellar door sales); Bream Creek and
Rowella (vineyards)
Area: Bream Creek 7.5 ha, Rowella 4 ha
Soils: Bream Creek brown basaltic clay loam
over basalt, Rowella, grey silt clay loam,
mudstone derived over gravel
Varieties planted: White—chardonnay, riesling,
savuignon blanc, schonburger; Red—cabernet
sauvignon, pinot noir
Leading wine: Bream Creek Riesling
Notes: The Bream Creek vineyard enjoys
picturesque ocean views overlooking Marion
Bay and Maria Island, itself the subject of Signor
Diego Bernacchi's putative vineyard in the
1880s. Bream Creek is a mature vineyard and
quite old by Tasmanian standards, having been
planted in 1973. Riesling seems to be well-
suited here, though it sometimes does not ripen
until June. Cellar door sales: (as above) or by
mail order to GPO Box 2020, Hobart, Tas 7001.

Charles Reuben Wines   **R78**

777 Middle Tea Tree Road, Tea Tree,
Tas 7017
Ph/Fax 03 6268 1702,
Email chasreuben@eisa.net.au

Owners: Tim and Leonie Krushka
Chief winemaker: Tim Krushka
Year of foundation: 1989
Tonnes produced on average each year: 7 and
increasing
Location: Tea Tree, Coal River Valley
Area: 4 ha
Soils: a black silty clay, locally called marl, but
in reality a form of limestone
Varieties planted: White—chardonnay, riesling.
Red—pinot noir
Leading wines: Charles Reuben Pinot Noir,
Chardonnay, Riesling
Notes: Lighter styles of Pinot and a
Chardonnay with some vegetative characters.
Cellar door sales: September to May, daily
10am–5pm.

Cooinda Vale   **R81**

Barton Vale Road, Campania, Tas 7028
Ph 03 6260 4227, Fax 03 6224 3591, Email
johnpooley@performanceautomobiles.com.au

Owner: Pooley family
Chief winemaker: Andrew Hood (contract)
Year of foundation: 1985
Tonnes produced on average each year: 7 (and
increasing)
Location: Campania
Area: 5 ha
Soils: sandy loam over clay and sandstone
Varieties planted: White—chardonnay, riesling;
Red—cabernet sauvignon, merlot, pinot noir,
shiraz
Leading wines: Cooinda Vale Riesling,
Chardonnay
Notes: This is a small family-owned vineyard
whose whites seem to be in the ascendant at
the present time. Cellar door sales: weekends
11am–4pm.

Craigow Wines **NR**

528 Richmond Road, Cambridge,
Tas 7170
Ph 03 6248 5379, Fax 03 6248 5482,
Email craigow@trump.net.au

Owner: Dr Barry Edwards
Chief winemaker: Julian Alcorso (contract)
Year of foundation: 1989
Tonnes produced on average each year: 80,
most of which are sold to wineries, about
8 tonnes being retained for Craigow wines
Location: Cambridge
Area: 10 ha
Soils: black cracking clay over dolomite rock
Varieties planted: White—chardonnay,
gewurztraminer, riesling, sauvignon blanc;
Red—cabernet sauvignon, merlot, pinot noir
Leading wines: Craigow Chardonnay, Riesling
Notes: No wines have been tasted, but Julian
Alcorso is a very good winemaker. Cellar door
sales: by appointment.

Crosswinds Vineyard **NR**

10 Vineyard Drive, Tea Tree, Tas 7017
Ph/Fax 03 6265 1091,
Email crosswnd@netspace.net.au

Owner: Crosswinds Pty Ltd
Chief winemaker: Andrew Vasiljuk
Year of foundation: 1990
Tonnes crushed on average each year: 20
Locations: Tea Tree (25 km north of Hobart)
and Margate (Brookfield Vineyard, 25 km
south of Hobart)
Area: 3 ha Tea Tree (1 ha of close planted
vineyard, about 4500 vines) and 2 ha at
Brookfield
Soils: Tea Tree, clay loam over dolerite;
Brookfield, deep red loam on a river flat
Varieties planted: Each vineyard has
chardonnay and pinot noir
Leading wine: Crosswinds Pinot Noir
Notes: Yet again pinot noir has proved its
suitability for Tasmanian vineyards. Crosswinds

1998 Pinot Noir is also very consistent, winning
8 bronze awards at wineshows throughout
Australia. Cellar door sales: October–May daily
10am–5pm. At other times weekends only
10am–5pm.

Derwent Estate **R85**

329 Lyell Highway, Granton, Tas 7030
Ph/Fax 03 6263 5802

Owner: Hanigan family.
Chief winemaker: Steve Lubiana (contract)
Year of foundation: 1993
Tonnes produced on average each year: 38,
about 35 of which are sold (the remainder
being used for Derwent Estate wines)
Location: Granton
Area: 4.5 ha
Soils: north-facing vineyard on a moderate
slope with rows running north–south to
maximise sunlight, good chocolate loam-clay
over a limestone base
Varieties planted: White—chardonnay, riesling;
Red—cabernet sauvignon, pinot noir
Leading Wines: Derwent Estate Riesling
Notes: Derwent Estate is obviously a very good
riesling site, its 1998 being judged one of the
best in Tasmania at the 1999 Tasmanian Wine
Show, an award richly deserved. Sales by mail
order only.

Domaine A **R82**

105 Tea Tree Road, Campania, Tas 7026
Ph 03 6260 4174, Fax 03 6260 4390,
Email althaus@domaine-a.com.au

Owners: Ruth and H. Peter Althaus
Chief winemaker: H. Peter Althaus
Year of foundation: 1973
Tonnes crushed on average each year: 75, all
of which are used for Domain A and Stoney
Vineyard wines
Location: Campania (Coal River Valley)
Area: 11 ha
Soils: still often called Stoney Vineyard (the

name is used as a label for its more current drinking wines), the soils are, as the former vineyard name suggests, quite stony with a thin layer of black clay over strongly weathered dolerite and sandstone. They are also quite well-drained
Varieties planted: White—sauvignon blanc; Red—cabernet franc, cabernet sauvignon, merlot, petit verdot, pinot noir
Leading wines: Domaine A Cabernet Sauvignon, Pinot Noir. There is also the second range of reds and whites, Stoney Vineyard, designed for more immediate drinking
Notes: Close-planted on a north-north-east slope, Domaine A now has a well-established, meticulously attended vineyard. As Peter Althaus says, it is an estate 'inspired by the best traditions of the Old World' with a winery influenced by the best technology of the New. Together with the east coast and the Tamar Valley, the Coal River Valley is another Tasmanian site that in good years can ripen cabernet sauvignon satisfactorily. Indeed Domaine A makes award winning Cabernet Sauvignons, sometimes with the addition of a little cabernet franc, merlot and petit verdot. Cellar door sales: Mon–Fri 10am–5pm, weekends by appointment only.

Elsewhere Vineyard R83

42 Dillons Hill Road, Glaziers Bay, Tas 7109
Ph/Fax 03 6295 1228,
Email andrew@elsewherevineyard.com

Owners: Kylie and Andrew Cameron
Chief winemakers: Andrew Hood (still wines, contract) and Steve Lubiana (sparkling wines, contract)
Year of foundation: 1984
Tonnes crushed on average each year: 35, of which 30 are used for Elsewhere Vineyard wines
Location: Glaziers Bay
Area: 11.75 ha (2.5 ha of which are not bearing)

Soils: light sandy loam, a clay subsoil over limestone and granite
Varieties planted: White—chardonnay, with small plantings of riesling, sauvignon blanc, sylvaner and traminer; Red—pinot noir
Leading wines: Elsewhere Vineyard Pinot Noir, Sparkling
Notes: Located in a very cool area, the amusingly named Elsewhere Vineyard is yet another Tasmanian estate with a great reputation for its Pinot Noir, the 1998 vintage of which struck gold and bagged the Trophy for the Chairman's Selection at the 1999 Tasmanian Wine Show. No cellar door sales. sales by mail order.

Geebin Vineyard NR

3729 Channel Highway, Birches Bay, Tas 7162
Ph 03 6267 4750, Fax 03 6267 5090

Owners: Ken and Barbara Jones
Chief winemaker: Andrew Hood (contract)
Year of foundation: 1983
Tonnes crushed on average each year: 0.6
Location: D'Entrecasteaux Channel, 3 km south of Woodbridge
Area: 0.5 ha
Soils: clayey loam
Varieties planted: White—riesling; Red—cabernet sauvignon
Leading wine: Geebin Riesling
Notes: Ken Jones claims that Geebin is the smallest commercial vineyard in Australia. I have not tasted its hard-to-find wines and they will always remain so unless you live virtually next door, but it is remarkable to see cabernet sauvignon so far south. Bed and breakfast accommodation is available, but no cellar door sales. Sales by mail order.

Glenayr Vineyard NR

Back Tea Tree Road, Richmond,
Tas 7025
Ph 03 6260 2388, Fax 03 6260 2691

Owners: Bill Casimaty
Chief winemaker: Andrew Hood (contract)
Year of foundation: 1975
Tonnes crushed on average each year: 2, one
of which (together with 5 tonnes of
chardonnay and pinot noir purchased from the
adjoining Tolpuddle vineyard) is used for
Glenayr wines
Location: Richmond (Coal Valley)
Area: 2 ha
Soils: duplex soils ranging from a heavy black
cracking clay to sandy loam
Varieties planted: White—riesling;
Red—cabernet franc, cabernet sauvignon,
merlot, shiraz
Leading wines: Glenayr Chardonnay, Pinot
Noir, Riesling, Cabernet-Shiraz-Merlot
Notes: Adjacent to the much larger
Tolpuddle vineyard, which is owned partly
by Bill Casimaty and from which some
chardonnay and pinot noir fruit is purchased,
Glenayr wines are made nearby by Andrew
Hood. Quantities are small but the wines
may be purchased at cellar door Mon–Fri
8am–5pm.

Hartzview Vineyard NR

70 Dillons Road, Gardners Bay, Tas 7112
Ph 03 6295 1623, Fax 03 6295 1723

Owners: Robert and Anthea Patterson
Chief winemaker: Robert Patterson
Year of foundation: 1988
Tonnes crushed each year on average: 10
Location: Gardners Bay, Huon Valley
Area: 3 ha
Soils: yellow podsols gradational verging on
duplex
Varieties planted: White—none; Red—pinot
noir

Leading wines: Hartzview Pinot Noir
Notes: Hartzview is a wine centre selling not
only its own wine, but also the wines of other
local winemakers. The range of wines is
extensive. Spacious accommodation is available
for up to six people in a colonial-style
homestead. Cellar door sales: 9am–5pm daily
except Christmas Day; closed in June except
for weekends.

Herons Rise NR

Saddle Road, Kettering, Tas 7155
Ph 03 6267 4339, Fax 03 6267 4245

Owners: Gerry and Sue White
Chief winemaker: Andrew Hood (contract)
Year of foundation: 1984
Tonnes produced on average each year: 3.5
Location: Kettering, D'Entrecasteaux Channel
Area: 1 ha
Soils: heavy clay soils over dolerite
Varieties planted: White—muller-thurdau,
riesling; Red—pinot noir.
Leading wines: Herons Rise Pinot Noir,
Muller-Thurgau
Notes: A small vineyard with two holiday
cottages for visitor accommodation and
sweeping rural and ocean views. Gourmet
dinners served to resident guests. Cellar door
sales: by appointment.

Home Hill Wines R81

73 Nairn Street, Ranelagh, Tas 7109
Ph 03 6264 1028, Fax 03 6264 1069,
Email homehill@bigpond.com

Owners: Terry and Rosemary Bennett
Chief winemaker: Michael Vishacki (contract)
Year of foundation: 1993
Tonnes produced on average each year: 30
Location: Ranelagh, Huon Valley
Area: 4 ha
Soils: grey loam over clay
Varieties planted: White—chardonnay,
sylvaner; Red—pinot noir

Leading wines: Home Hill Wines Pinot Noir, Chardonnay

Notes: By Tasmanian standards, Home Hill is a vineyard slightly larger than average. Its chief wines are made from varieties that are obviously well suited to the area. Its Chardonnay is crisp, flinty and Chablis-like, while its Pinots have won silver and bronze awards at both Tasmanian and mainland wine shows. Cellar door sales: 7 days 10am–5pm Sales by mail order. A restaurant is open Wed–Sun 10am–5pm, featuring the best of Huon Valley produce, oysters, salmon, quail, mushrooms, berries and apples. The restaurant and cellar door are closed Christmas Day, Good Friday and for the month of July.

Jollymont Vineyard NR

Pullens Road, Woodbridge, Tas 7162
Ph 03 6267 4594,
Email pkreet@tasmail.com

Owners: Peter Kreet and Heather Kreet
Chief winemaker: Andrew Hood (contract)
Year of foundation: 1989
Tonnes crushed on average each year: 1
Location: Woodbridge
Area: 0.8 ha
Soils: red-brown dolerite and grey soil mudstone on a north-facing slope
Varieties planted: White—none; Red—pinot noir
Leading wine: Jollymont Vineyard Pinot Noir
Notes: Jollymont is a very small vineyard which has had difficulties in establishment from time to time. Irrigation is not practised. Quality, however, seems to have made up for lack of quantity, for Peter Kreet describes his Pinot as having a flavour intensity engendered by small bunches and small berries. Sales by mail order. Restaurant cellar door and winery opened in 2001.

Kinvarra Vineyard NR

1211 Glenora Road, Plenty, Tas 7140
Ph 03 6286 1333, Fax 03 6286 2026,
Email kinvarra@tasmail.com

Owners: Sue and David Bevan
Chief winemaker: Andrew Hood (contract)
Year of foundation: 1990
Tonnes crushed on average each year: 7, of which 2 are used for Kinvarra Estate wines
Location: Plenty, Derwent Valley
Area: 1 ha
Soils: dolerite loams on a north-facing slope
Varieties planted: White—riesling; Red—pinot noir
Leading wines: Kinvarra Estate Riesling, Pinot Noir
Notes: A small vineyard with a very small production for its own use. However, Tasmanian Wine Show results have been consistently good with silver and bronze awards going equally to Riesling and to Pinot. Cellar door sales: by appointment.

Laurel Bank Vineyard NR

130 Black Snake Lane, Granton, Tas 7030
Ph 03 6263 5977, Fax 03 6263 3117

Owner: Kerry Carland
Chief winemaker: Andrew Hood (contract)
Year of foundation: 1986
Tonnes crushed on average each year: 15, of which 9 are used for Laurel Bank wines
Location: Granton, Derwent Valley
Area: 3 ha
Soils: Quite complex soils ranging from deep black cracking clays with limestone particles which are alkaline through shallower loamy soils (of more normal pH) to shallow dry sandy loam with sub-surface sandstone 'floating' rock (slightly acidic in pH)
Varieties planted: White—riesling, sauvignon blanc; Red—cabernet franc, cabernet sauvignon, merlot, pinot noir

Leading wines: Laurel Bank Pinot Noir, Cabernet-Merlot

Notes: Kerry Carland attempts to match variety to soil type. So he has planted sauvignon blanc on the least fertile sandy loam, riesling in the exposed steeper upper slopes and the reds in sheltered deeper loams. He describes his show entry record as 'erratic', but this refers to frequency rather than quality of exhibit, both his reds, Pinot Noir and the Cabernet Merlot, having won gold (the Cabernet Merlot a Trophy also). Cellar door sales: by appointment.

Meadowbank Glenora R85

Meadowbank, Glenora, Tas 7140
Ph 03 6286 1234, Fax 03 6286 1133,
Email mbw@biz.net.au
Meadowbank, Cambridge,
Cambridge, Tas 7025

Owners: Cartell Pty Ltd
Chief winemaker: Andrew Hood (contract)
Year of foundation: (Glenora) 1974, (Cambridge) 1999
Tonnes crushed on average each year: 80 at Glenora, of which 60 are used for Meadowbank wines; Cambridge not yet bearing
Locations: Glenora, Derwent Valley, Cambridge, Coal River Valley
Area: 11 ha (Glenora), 8.4 ha (Cambridge)
Soils: Glenora, sandy loam. Cambridge, duplex loam over clay
Varieties planted: White—chardonnay, pinot gris, riesling, sauvignon blanc; Red—cabernet sauvignon, pinot noir
Leading wines: Meadowbank Pinot Noir, Henry James Pinot Noir, Chardonnay
Notes: Meadowbank at Glenora is now an old established vineyard with a great reputation for Pinot Noir and also Chardonnay. The vineyard at Cambridge is newly planted and may be used for sparkling wine when it comes into full bearing. Cellar door sales: Glenora weekdays

only 11am–5pm; Cambridge: daily 10am–5pm. There is also a restaurant at Cambridge.

Milford Vineyard NR

1431 Tasman Highway, Cambridge, Tas 7025 (opposite the Tasmanian Golf Club)
Ph 03 6248 3029, Fax 03 6224 2331

Owners: Charles Lewis, Jonathon Dakin, Clive Ockenden and Peter Last
Chief winemaker: Andrew Hood (contract)
Year of foundation: 1984
Tonnes crushed on average each year: 4, (of which 2 are used for Milford Vineyard wines
Location: Cambridge
Area: 1 ha
Soils: well-drained sandy calcareous soil containing sea shells over a clay base
Varieties planted: White—none; Red—pinot noir
Leading wine: Milford Vineyard Pinot Noir
Notes: Milford Pinot Noir has been a consistent show award winner over the years and its 1996 Pinot Noir was the only Tasmanian red to receive a gold award at the 1997 Royal Hobart Wine Show. No cellar door sales. Sales by mail order.

Moorilla Estate (see also St Matthias, Tamar Valley) R84

655 Main Road, Berriedale, Tas 7011
Ph 03 6249 2949, Fax 03 6249 4093

Owners: a syndicate of Hobart businessmen with Tim Goddard as Chief Executive
Chief winemaker: Michael Glover
Year of foundation: 1958
Tonnes crushed on average each year: 200, including fruit from St Matthias and other purchased fruit, about 90 tonnes of which are used for Moorilla wines. The Berriedale vineyard produces about 30 tonnes. Moorilla Cabernet-Merlot and Chardonnay are usually made from fruit from St Matthias
Location: Berriedale, Derwent Valley

Area: 4 ha
Soils: clayey loam, with an excellent aspect
Varieties planted: White—gewurztraminer,
riesling; Red—pinot noir
Leading wines: Moorilla Estate Riesling,
Chardonnay, Reserve Pinot Noir
Notes: Moorilla Estate has a fine reputation for
its Riesling, a style usually drier and more
floral-spicy than the lime–citrus wines of Eden
Valley and Clare. Its Chardonnay and Pinot
Noir are usually excellent also. Its Cabernet
also is very much better since Moorilla has had
its Tamar Valley connection. Cellar door sales:
daily 10am–5pm. There is also a restaurant
open Tues–Sun for lunch.

Morningside Vineyard R83

711 Middle Tea Tree Road, Tea Tree,
Tas 7017
Ph/Fax 03 6268 1748,
Email morningside@trump.net.au

Owners: Peter and Brenda Bosworth
Chief winemaker: Peter Bosworth
Year of foundation: 1980
Tonnes crushed on average each year: 7 and
increasing
Location: Tea Tree, Coal River Valley
Area: 2 ha
Soils: doleritic soils over calcareous clay
Varieties planted: White—chardonnay, riesling;
Red—cabernet franc, cabernet sauvignon, petit
verdot, pinot noir
Leading wines: Morningside Vineyard Pinot
Noir, Chardonnay, Riesling
Notes: So named because of the aspect of the
morning sun, Morningside is a maker of good
plummy berry Pinot Noir. I do not know the
whites. Cellar door sales by appointment.

Nandroya NR

262 Sandfly Road, Margate, Tas 7054
Ph 03 6267 2377, Fax 03 6223 8237,
Email djrees@optomeyes.com.au

Owners: John and Joy Rees
Chief winemaker: Andrew Hood (contract)
Year of foundation: 1989
Tonnes produced on average each year: 2.5
Area: 1 ha
Soils: basalt over clay
Varieties planted: White—sauvignon blanc;
Red—pinot noir
Leading wines: Nandroya Sauvignon Blanc,
Pinot Noir.
Notes: A very small vineyard planted with
varieties appropriate for its climate. Cellar door
sales: daily 10am–5pm.

Orani Vineyard NR

394 Arthur Highway, Sorell, Tas 7172
Ph/Fax 03 6265 1849

Owners: Tony and Angela McDermott
Chief winemaker: Andrew Vasiljuk (contract)
Year of foundation: 1985
Tonnes produced on average each year: 25
Location: Sorell
Area: 5 ha
Soils: loamy soils about 1–2 m deep.
Varieties planted: White—chardonnay, riesling;
Red—cabernet sauvignon, pinot noir
Leading wines: Orani Riesling, Pinot Noir
Notes: Cellar door sales: weekends and public
holidays 9.30am–5.30pm.

Palmara Vineyard NR

1314 Richmond Road, Richmond,
Tas 7025
Ph 03 6260 2462

Owner: Bird family
Chief winemaker: Allan Bird
Year of foundation: 1984
Tonnes crushed on average each year: 5
Location: Richmond, Coal River Valley
Area: 1 ha
Soils: variable soils of great age with some
volcanic ash content overlying an ancient
sandstone and dolerite sea bed and pHs

varying from 5.2 to over 8; quite fertile in the main with vine vigour controlled by a naturally low rainfall (less than 500 mm per annum)
Varieties planted: White—chardonnay, ehrenfelse, semillon, siegerrebe; Red—cabernet sauvignon, pinot noir
Leading wine: Palmara Pinot Noir
Notes: Palmara has been a consistent award winner at local and mainland wine shows for its Pinot Noir. Cellar door sales: weekends and holidays 10am–6pm, closed June–August.

Panorama Vineyard R85

1848 Cygnet Coast Road, Cradoc, Tas 7109
Ph 03 6266 3409, Fax 03 6266 3486, Email panoramavineyard@hotmail.com

Owners: Sharon and Michael Vishacki
Chief winemaker: Michael Vishacki
Year of foundation: 1976
Tonnes produced on average each year: 40
Location: Cradoc, a 45-minute drive south of Hobart
Area: 9 ha
Soils: silty clay loam
Varieties planted: White—chardonnay, sauvignon blanc; Red—cabernet sauvignon, pinot noir
Leading wine: Panorama Vineyard Pinot Noir
Notes: This is a vineyard well worth a special trip along the scenic Cygnet Coast Road. Pinot Noir and Chardonnay are each fine examples of cool area viticulture and the Sauvignon Blanc recalls the grassy asparagus style of Marlborough. Cellar door sales: daily (closed Tues) 10am–5pm; closed Tues, Wed. in June and July.

Richmond Park Vineyard NR

Logie Road, Richmond, Tas 7172
Ph 03 6265 2949, Fax 03 6265 3166, Email tonypark@cosycabins.com

Owners: Tony and Julie Park
Chief winemaker: Andrew Hood (contract)

Year of foundation: 1988
Tonnes produced on average each year: 6
Location: Richmond, Coal River Valley
Area: 3 ha
Soils: heavy top soil 30 cm deep over heavy black clay
Varieties planted: White—chardonnay; Red—pinot noir
Leading wine: Richmond Park Pinot Noir
Notes: No cellar door facilities. Sales by mail order.

Stefano Lubiana Wines NR

Rowbottoms Road, Granton, Tas 7030
Ph 03 6263 7457, Fax 03 6263 7430

Owners: Steve and Monique Lubiana
Chief winemaker: Steve Lubiana
Year of foundation: 1990
Tonnes crushed on average each year: 110
Location: Granton, Derwent Valley
Area: 15 ha
Soils: poor, grey, gravelly soils
Varieties planted: White—chardonnay, pinot grigio, riesling, sauvignon blanc, semillon; Red—cabernet sauvignon, merlot, nebbiolo, pinot noir
Leading wines: Stefano Lubiana Pinot Noir, Sauvignon Blanc, Sparkling Pinot
Notes: Stefano Lubiana has expanded his production in recent vintages, as befits a busy and skilled winemaker. Some popular Italian varieties have been planted and will come on to the market in the next few years. It is to be hoped that the Tasmanian climate will be warm enough to ripen them. Cellar door sales: daily 10am–5pm.

Treehouse Vineyard and Wine Centre R84

257 Richmond Road, Cambridge, Tas 7170
Ph 03 6248 5367, Fax 03 6248 4175, Email treehousevineyard@bigpond.com

Owners: Todd Goebel and Gillian Christian
Chief winemaker: Andrew Hood (contract)
Year of foundation: 1990
Tonnes produced on average each year: 6
Location: Cambridge, Coal River Valley
Area: 2 ha (only one of which is bearing)
Soils: black sandy soils
Varieties planted: White—chardonnay, riesling; Red—cabernet sauvignon, merlot, pinot noir
Leading wines: Treehouse Vineyard Riesling, Chardonny, Pinot Noir, Cabernet-Merlot
Notes: Recent success at the Tasmanian Wine Show with its Riesling and Chardonnay augurs well for Treehouse. Excellent Riesling and very good Chardonnay are available. Cellar door sales: September–April, Wed–Sun 10am–5pm. Light lunches are also available.

Woodlands Vineyard NR

839 Main Road, Tea Tree, Tas 7017
Ph 03 6268 1331, Fax 03 6268 1379

Owner: Woodlands Vineyard Pty Ltd
Chief winemaker: Moorilla (contract)
Year of foundation: 1987
Tonnes produced on average each year: 11, half of which is used for Touchwood Wines
Location: Tea Tree, Coal River Valley
Area: 3 ha
Soils: chocolate loam of volcanic origin over limestone
Varieties planted: White—chardonnay, riesling; Red—cabernet sauvignon, merlot, pinot noir

Leading wines: Touchwood Chardonnay, Pinot Noir
Notes: I have not tasted any wine from Woodlands. No cellar door sales. Sales by mail order.

Yaxley Estate Vineyard NR

31 Dransfield Road, Copping, Tas 7174
Ph/Fax 6253 5222

Owners: Yaxley family
Chief winemaker: Andrew Hood (contract)
Year of foundation: 1992
Tonnes produced on average each year: 5
Location: Copping, off the Arthur Highway
Area: 2 ha
Soils: sandy loam and sand over sandstone and clay of variable depth with some areas of dolerite rock and gravel
Varieties planted: White—chardonnay, pinot gris, sauvignon blanc; Red—pinot noir
Leading wines: Yaxley Estate Pinot Gris, Pinot Noir, Chardonnay
Notes: Yaxley Estate participates in the Tasmanian Wine Show each year with moderate success, its Pinot Gris winning silver and bronze awards at the 1998 and 1999 Shows. Low production prevents entry to many shows. Cellar door sales: winter daily 10am–5pm, summer 9am–6pm.

PART III

SOUTH AUSTRALIA

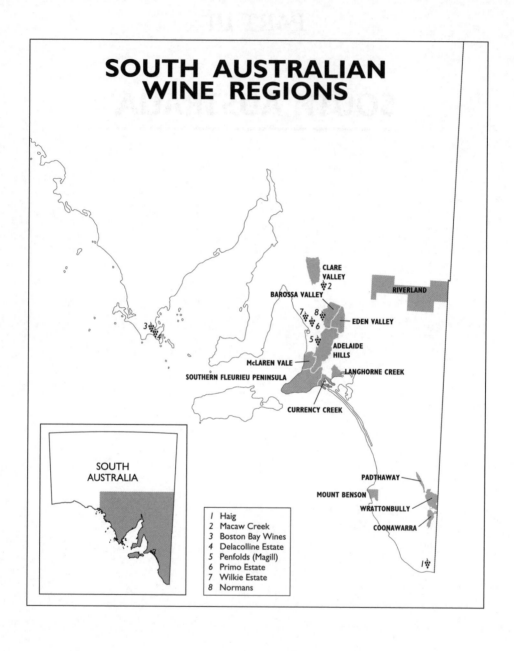

SOUTH AUSTRALIAN WINE REGIONS

CLARE VALLEY

RIVERLAND

BAROSSA VALLEY

EDEN VALLEY

ADELAIDE HILLS

McLAREN VALE

LANGHORNE CREEK

SOUTHERN FLEURIEU PENINSULA

CURRENCY CREEK

SOUTH AUSTRALIA

PADTHAWAY

MOUNT BENSON

WRATTONBULLY

COONAWARRA

1 Haig
2 Macaw Creek
3 Boston Bay Wines
4 Delacolline Estate
5 Penfolds (Magill)
6 Primo Estate
7 Wilkie Estate
8 Normans

☘ THE ADELAIDE SUPERZONE

'Adelaide' is an umbrella zone including 'Barossa', 'Fleurieu' and 'Mount Lofty Ranges' and allows winemakers within those zones to use the name 'Adelaide' instead of their zonal description. In some senses, this seems anomalous, but it does accommodate wine-producing areas such as Adelaide Plains and the very few remaining suburban vineyards of Adelaide, such as Magill, which were once such a force in the growth of South Australian winemaking. It also includes the very new vineyard areas of Kangaroo Island. All wineries in the superzone are marked on the state map.

Leading wineries: Penfolds Magill, Primo Estate

Normans (vineyard only) NR
Evanston Vineyard, Gawler, SA 5118

Owner: Normans Wines Limited (in receivership)
Chief winemaker: Peter Fraser
Year of foundation: 1952
Tonnes produced on average each year: 800
Location: Evanston, near Gawler
Area: 57.9 ha
Soils: heavy brown loam over gravel (floodplain of Gawler River)
Varieties planted: White—chardonnay, chenin blanc, riesling, sauvignon blanc; Red—cabernet sauvignon, pinot noir, shiraz, merlot
Leading wines: the Evanston Vineyard contributes to Norman's various lower and mid-market varietal and regional blends
Notes: No cellar door sales facilities here.

Penfolds Magill R88
78 Penfold Road, Magill, SA 5072
Ph 08 8301 5400, Fax 08 8301 5562

Owner: Southcorp Wines
Chief winemaker: John Duval
Year of foundation: 1844
Tonnes crushed on average each year: 30
Location: Magill
Area: 5.92 ha
Soils: red loam over slate with limestone reefs running through the vineyard

Varieties planted: White—none; Red—shiraz
Leading wine: Penfolds Magill Estate Shiraz
Notes: Magill Estate is where Penfolds began. Dr Christopher Penfolds' original Grange cottage, recently restored, stands as a South Australian viticultural landmark and the dry-grown shiraz vineyard, whose vine-age averages 50 years, is the last of Adelaide's truly suburban vineyards. Its vines sometimes contribute to Grange Hermitage, but its more usual product is the excellent Magill Estate Shiraz, made in the historic adjoining cellars. Cellar door sales: 7 days 8am–5pm. There is also a restaurant.

Primo Estate R88
Old Port Wakefield Road, Virginia, SA 5120
Ph 08 8380 9442, Fax 08 8380 9696, Email primo@senet.com.au

Owners: Joe and Dina Grilli
Chief winemakers: Joe Grilli and Grant Harrison
Year of foundation: 1979
Tonnes crushed on average each year: 400
Location: winery—Virginia; vineyards—Virginia, Angel Gully (Clarendon) and McMurtrie Road (McLaren Vale)
Area: 36.2 ha in total (Virginia 15.6 ha, Angel Gully 12.6 ha, McLaren Vale 8 ha—the latter

vineyards being in McLaren Vale Region)
Soils: Virginia, deep red-brown alluvial soils
varying from sandy loam to clay loam, over
limestone nodules, free-draining; Angel Gully,
dark shallow clay over shale and rock; McLaren
Vale variable from dark clay to grey sandy clay
Varieties planted: (Virginia) White—chardonnay
(1.4 ha), colombard (4.4 ha), riesling (3 ha),
semillon (1 ha); Red—barbera (0.4 ha),
cabernet sauvignon (2.4 ha), nebbiolo (0.4 ha),
shiraz (2.6 ha). (Angel Gully) White—pinot
grigio (1 ha); Red—cabernet sauvignon (4.5
ha), merlot (2 ha), nebbiolo (1 ha), shiraz (4.1
ha) (this vineyard is not yet fully bearing).
(McLaren Vale) White—none; Red—cabernet
sauvignon (4 ha), shiraz (4 ha)
Leading wines: Virginia, Primo Estate
Colombard La Biondina, Shiraz-Sangiovese
Il Briccone (sourced from Virginia and McLaren
Vale and also from sangiovese purchased from
a Virginia grower), Sparkling Red; McLaren
Vale, Joseph Cabernet Sauvignon Merlot
'moda amarone'
Notes: Primo Estate is a winery of finesse and
style existing in the baking heat of the
Adelaide Plains. What Joe Grilli achieves with
colombard (a white variety recommended for
holding its acidity in the warmest of areas but
not much else) is nothing short of miraculous.
In its best years, it is as crisp as the best
sauvignon blanc with many of its herbaceous

characters in common and equally good with
seafood. His reds also, especially Il Briccone
and Joseph, are full-flavoured yet softly Italian
in style and his Sparkling Red completes a
brilliant range. This is a winery not to miss on
any wine tour of Adelaide and surrounds.
Cellar door sales: Mon–Fri 10am–4pm.

Wilkie Estate NR

Lot 1 Heaslip Road, Penfield, SA 5121
Ph 08 8284 7655, Fax 08 8284 7618

Owners: W. Spurr and Trevor Spurr
Chief winemaker: Trevor Spurr
Year of foundation: 1974 re-established 1988
Tonnes crushed on average each year: 60
Location: Penfield
Area: 7.2 ha
Soils: red-brown earths with sandy loam about
50 cm deep
Varieties planted: White—verdelho;
Red—cabernet sauvignon, merlot, ruby
cabernet
Leading wines: Wilkie Estate Cabernet Merlot,
Verdelho
Notes: Wilkie Estate is a certified organic
vigneron. The wines are shown and win
medals regularly at Adelaide, Melbourne and
Rutherglen. They are distributed from Adelaide
and there are no cellar door sales. Sales by
mail order only.

Note: A region called Adelaide Plains has recently received interim registration. (This
information was too late for detailed inclusion in this edition.) The region commences
at Gepps Cross in metropolitan Adelaide, extends west along Grand Junction Road to
the coast (St Vincents Gulf), then skirts the coast north to the mouth of the River
Light. From there it travels north-east as far as Templers and returns south along the
Main North Road (excluding Gawler) to Gepps Cross.

✿ BAROSSA ZONE

This zone, together with Adelaide and Reynella, is the birthplace of South Australian wine. It remains even today as one of its major production areas in terms of wineries, if not in grape production. It folds neatly into two wine regions—Barossa Valley and Eden Valley.

BAROSSA VALLEY REGION

Originally called 'Barrossa' by Colonel William Light in 1837 after a Spanish battle in which he had fought during the Peninsular War, the Valley soon lost its first 'r' due to the early colonists both misspelling and mispronouncing it. This situation was regularised by bureaucracy in 1846 when the hundred of 'Barossa' was proclaimed. Prior to this, during early exploratory work, the expatriate German geologist Johann Menge had favourably reported that the area north-east of Adelaide known as the Barrossa Ranges was first-class farming country, enthusiastically describing it as 'the real cream of South Australia'. In 1839, he persuaded his former employer George Fife Angas, founder of the South Australian Company, to allow his secretary Charles Flaxman to accompany him on a further tour of the area. Flaxman confirmed Menge's report and soon after, acting as Angas' agent, purchased 28 000 acres at one pound per acre.

The South Australian Company, wishing to establish a free colony of smallholders and artisans, insisted that every settler paid in full for his land, which was not to exceed 32 ha in extent. Convict labour and free land grants were certainly not welcome in South Australia. George Fife Angas, however, favoured a superstratum of landed gentry (men of property and capital who could afford to take up large tracts of land). The latter class could purchase much larger tracts of land on two conditions, the first being that they were prepared to subdivide and sell land back to smaller settlers when they had the capital to purchase it, and the second that they retained at least 1600 ha of their original purchase (obviously as a source of employment for more of the farm labourers and artisans, the more successful of whom were already settling the Valley floor. Few blocks as large as this existed on the Valley floor. There were many more in the hills to the east. So the net result of the two policies was that the smallholders purchased smaller, more fertile blocks chiefly in the Valley and engaged in intensive crop farming, dairying, horticulture and day labour while the gentry bought broadacres mainly in the Hills for grazing, though a few of the latter class, such as Joseph Gilbert and Henry Evans, later diversified into wine production. The national origin of the settlers was also different. The smallholders and artisans were largely German or Silesian Lutherans who had left Prussia in protest against a new Lutheran service ordained by Kaiser Friedrich Wilhelm III. The graziers were almost entirely Anglo-Celtic and recreated the orderly estates with which they were familiar in Britain. There was therefore a broad social and economic division between the inhabitants of the Valley and those of the Hills (the Barossa Ranges). The factor that would tend to unite them—though this must not be overstated, for few settlers were prepared in the 1840s to risk a whole livelihood upon it—was a common cognisance of wine.

By the 1840s the first vineyards were appearing both in the Valley and to a lesser extent in the Hills. In 1843, a Silesian family, the Aldenhovens, settled in Bethany and are believed to have planted grapes. By 1847, local wines were being exhibited at the Tanunda and Angaston shows. In the same year, Johann Gramp planted near Jacob's Creek and Joseph Gilbert also began his vineyard at Pewsey Vale in the Hills. Samuel Smith followed with the first vines at Yalumba two years later. Both the gentry and the German smallholders were accustomed to wine with their meals. So winegrowing, for which the country and climate were quite favourable, became popular as one of the general disciplines of local farming life, although by no means the most important one. Indeed, winemaking was to become too popular twenty years afterwards, as the later history of South Australia was to prove.

Winegrowing received a tremendous fillip in 1858 with the enactment of the Wark Act by the South Australian legislature which, mistakenly as it turned out, wished to encourage wine production. The Act permitted expansion of distillery licensing (most wines of this period relied on the addition of some spirit at least for their stability). The result was an explosion of vineyards (vineyard area increased from 300 ha in 1858 to 2650 ha in 1866) and subsequently a general lowering of winemaking standards. As the *Adelaide Observer* pointed out, 'there were prospects that failure would teach them [the vintners] to produce an article which would be prized in the markets of the world'. But markets outside South Australia were extremely hard to find and the local market was flooded.

Left to itself the overproduction stimulated by this legislation may soon have petered out were it not for the irrational optimism generated by the Gladstonian budget of 1860, whereby Australian colonial wines were encouraged to enter Britain because of more favourable duties.

Nonetheless it was during this period (1850 to 1870) that many of the patriarchal families that dominated Australian winemaking for the ensuing century became established—families of German origin such as Seppelt, Gramp and Henschke, and those of Anglo-Saxon heritage such as Smith and Salter. There were of course many others, whose descendants are still resident in the Valley and its vicinity. The Wark legislation was repealed in 1877 and this in turn caused an exodus of the lesser-skilled from the South Australian industry and induced others to concentrate on grape-growing.

By this time export markets were beginning to flourish for Barossa wine. The chief wine styles were a heavy dry red, which would withstand the rigours of a 19 000 km voyage and the often neglectful behaviour of the London dockers at the other end, and fortified sweet reds and whites, the 'ports' and 'sherries' which were to become beloved by the British working classes. By 1900, South Australia was producing about ten million litres of wine annually and the Barossa nearly half of this total.

Despite many anti-German outbursts, prohibition campaigns from temperance groups and British Empire jingoism, the First World War proved only the mildest hiccup in Barossa wine production. Exports were of course affected by the lack of shipping, but those companies which could concentrate upon domestic sales, did so. Only those companies reliant entirely on export failed, such as the Riverton winery

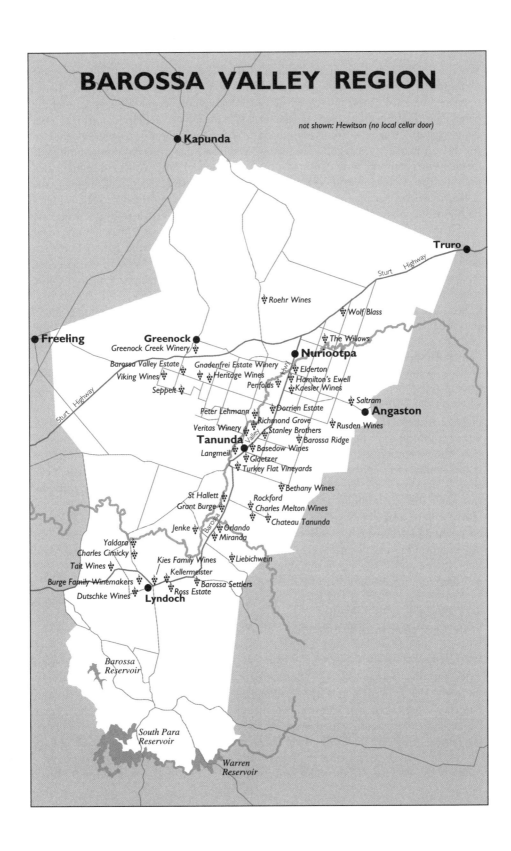

BAROSSA VALLEY REGION

not shown: Hewitson (no local cellar door)

Kapunda

Truro

Sturt Highway

Roehr Wines

Wolf Blass

Freeling

Greenock
Greenock Creek Winery

The Willows

Nuriootpa

Barossa Valley Estate
Viking Wines

Gnadenfrei Estate Winery
Heritage Wines

Elderton
Hamilton's Ewell

Seppelt

Penfolds

Kaesler Wines

Saltram

Peter Lehmann

Dorrien Estate

Angaston

Veritas Winery

Richmond Grove
Stanley Brothers

Rusden Wines

Tanunda

Barossa Ridge

Langmeil

Basedow Wines
Glaetzer
Turkey Flat Vineyards

Bethany Wines

St Hallett
Grant Burge

Rockford
Charles Melton Wines
Chateau Tanunda

Jenke

Orlando
Miranda

Yaldara
Charles Cimicky
Tait Wines

Kies Family Wines
Kellermeister

Liebichwein

Burge Family Winemakers
Dutschke Wines

Ross Estate
Barossa Settlers

Lyndoch

Barossa
Reservoir

South Para
Reservoir

Warren
Reservoir

Wooroora, established to supply London in the boom times of the 1880s, but going under in 1918. The 1920s provided yet another boost to the Barossa economy, thanks to peace, the 1924 export bounty of the Federal government and Winston Churchill's beneficent 'Empire preference' budget of 1925 in favour of Empire fortifieds over Spanish and Portuguese. Yet overproduction and speculation saw a severe decline in the British market from 1928. The whole structure came crashing down during the Great Depression and wine exports (fortified, of course) only recovered immediately prior to the Second World War. Though this war severely curtailed exports, the domestic market became quite buoyant. There was a beer shortage and the soldiers, both Australian and American, substituted fortified wine for their traditional tipple.

This time, the war's end and another victorious peace brought little improvement to a rather flat export market. Indeed, the British seemed to favour lighter European table wines and the traditional fortifieds of Portugal and Spain. At home things began to change, ever so slightly, at first. Lighter style white wines such as Ringold (more refreshing than the heavily alcoholic fortifieds) began to be accepted though in a minor way. There was even talk in the industry of red table wines becoming popular. In 1950, Penfolds dispatched Max Schubert on a study tour to Bordeaux and the lasting result—following much intervening work on the part of its creator—was Grange Hermitage.

During this decade and the 1960s, the Barossa remained the production centre of the Australian wine industry, but there were to be changing emphases especially in white wine handling. Arguably, the greatest of these was a German invention, the pressure fermentation tank, first imported into Australia by Orlando Wines in 1952. Other technical tours de force included inert gas cover of fermenting must, refrigeration, the increasing use of stainless steel and cold stabilisation. One wine result of these technical triumphs was the production of a sparkling white wine of virtually mass appeal—Barossa Pearl. Thousands of young Australians were introduced to wine by this party fizz and millions of bottles were produced. There were also vast social changes taking place in Australia. The post-war immigration scheme was in full swing, encouraging settlement not only by Anglo-Celts but also by Italians, Germans and other central Europeans, most of whom had at least some familiarity with wine. And then, in the mid-1960s, came the long awaited red wine boom. By 1970, table wine consumption surpassed fortified for the first time.

During the 1970s and 1980s, the Barossa maintained its wine production ascendancy, though now in the Valley and amongst its growers there was a sense of neglect by the large companies. During the 1980s many such companies looked beyond the Valley to outside sources, such as the Riverland and the booming Coonawarra and Padthaway regions, for grapes which were lighter and more delicate for the table wine styles that they were producing. The domestic market was now very buoyant and, by the early 1980s, per capita wine consumption exceeded 20 litres annually. In the Barossa a sense of regional identity was stirring, inspired by winemakers such as Peter Lehmann, whose primary winemaking ethics were not only quality but also loyalty to his Barossa growers. By 1990, there were many smaller producers reliant almost entirely on local grapes for wine production and a re-awakening among the larger companies of the awareness of the value of local fruit for robust reds, wood-matured whites and fruity, flavoursome Rieslings. Both large and small wine companies are now proud of proclaiming the Barossa origin of a wine. The future of the Barossa Valley wine region and its growers seems assured.

Location: latitude 34°35'S, longitude 139°00'E, about 80 km north-east of Adelaide
Elevation: varying from south to north from about 300 m at Williamstown to 200 m at Lyndoch, 250 m at Tanunda and 270 m at Nuriootpa; and from east to west 400 m at Mengler's Hill, 250 m at Dorrien, 300 m at Patterson Hill and 380 m at Belvidere. Traditionally, the eastern boundary of the Barossa Valley, separating it from the Eden Valley, has followed the 400-metre contour line, which approximates the ridge of the Barossa Range and differentiates the predominant soils of the Barossa (see below) from the rocky, podsolic soils of the Eden Valley.
Topography and soils: Geologically, the Barossa Valley is an inter-montane basin, having an extensive area of Tertiary deposited sediments. On its eastern side, overlooking the Valley, there is a belt of metamorphosed Cambrian limestone (Angaston marble), adjacent to the northern section of the Kanmantoo trough, where there is also a strong development of high grade metamorphic rock, including gneisses and gneissic granites which form the Barossa Ranges.

In the Valley, there are two dominant soil types: (i) grey and brown clays, red-brown earths, brown earths or black earths over red-brown clay subsoils; and (ii) calcareous solodised solonetz (yellow sands) over red clay subsoils. In the west and north-west of the region (the country around Gomersal), the grey and brown clay soils are less suitable for viticulture due to their cracking characters. The red-brown earths of the hills around Marananga and Greenock and the northern hills in the vicinity of Truro and Stockwell are ideally suited. However, the yellow sands, wherever situated, have a lower water retention capacity and, unless irrigation is available, are not regarded as suitable.
Climate: Nuriootpa MJT 21.2°C, MAR 16.8, HDD raw 1703, AR 504 mm (Oct–Apr 200 mm), RH 49% (9am), 31% (3pm) (Nuriootpa Viticultural Research Centre). Williamstown MJT 19.3°C, MAR 11.6, HDD raw 1336, AR 756 mm (Oct–Apr 266 mm), RH 56% (9am), 33% (3pm) (Mount Crawford Forest); compare with Barossa: MJT 21.4°C, MAR 12.6°C, HDD raw 1715, AR 503 mm (Oct–Mar 161 mm), RH 47% (9am), AI 464 mm, SH 8.8 (Dry & Smart); compare with Nuriootpa: MJT 20.8°C, MAR na, HDD raw 1575, 1443 (as cut-off and adjusted for latitude and daily temperature range), AR 506 mm (Oct–Apr 204 mm), RH 36% (3pm Jan), AI na, SH 8.6 (G).

Undoubtedly Nuriootpa is a warm area, but the Barossa Valley as a whole varies widely in climate. Its north-western areas (adjacent to the northern Adelaide Plains) are as a rule even warmer than Nuriootpa, but the more southerly Williamstown district, being higher, is cooler and wetter.

The Valley is located within the catchment of the North Para River and to a lesser extent that of the Light River, which constitutes part of its northern boundary. Its groundwater is recharged by water from the North Para River and by the higher rainfall and infiltration from the Eden Valley. Because of limited resources, irrigation is tightly controlled in the Barossa Valley. New bores and surface dams are prohibited in order to maintain the sustainability of underground aquifers. All present bores are metered and limited in usage to 100 megalitres per hectare per annum, while present dams are restricted in volume to the ability of the owner to collect natural run-off and to harvest water from transitory stream flows. In the Barossa Valley aquifer, water quality is described as 'good quality at depth, saline at the surface'.

Viticultural problems in the form of heat stress can arise as a result of hot northerly winds during the ripening season, though occasional westerly sea breezes can be an ameliorating factor. Disease risk from downy and powdery mildew and botrytis is low. Starlings, however, are a major problem. Like other older viticultural areas, growers in those areas of the Barossa Valley where there is no risk of soil erosion practise clean cultivation rather than sod culture for moisture retention, but this is gradually changing. As for pruning and harvesting, these are carried out mechanically for all but the youngest and oldest vines. As excessive vine vigour does not present much of a problem, there is little canopy or bunch thinning, though there is some slashing carried out in summer. As a result, canopy and trellis management is carried out on traditional lines to satisfy as much as possible the demands of mechanical harvesting, though some growers are experimenting with more modern Scott-Henry techniques. Many bush-pruned vines still remain and premium wines produced from 'old vines', especially shiraz, have become a speciality of the Valley.

Harvest time: generally in the 7-week period from late February to mid to late April. Typical ripening dates: chardonnay early to mid-March; riesling mid-March; shiraz late March; cabernet sauvignon early to mid-April.

Principal varieties: (1998) White—riesling, semillon; Red—shiraz, cabernet sauvignon, grenache.

Total area: (Barossa GIC Zone) (i.e. includes Eden Valley Region) (1999) 8944 ha.

Major wine styles: (from grapes of Barossa origin) White—Semillon (a fuller style often matured in new American oak), Riesling, Chardonnay (usually oaked), Semillon-Chardonnay (a blend); Red—Shiraz (full-bodied and ripe, often matured in American oak) with Old Vines Shiraz a speciality of many vineyards, Cabernet Sauvignon (full-bodied and rich), Grenache (a full, fruity style usually intended for reasonably early drinking), Shiraz-Grenache-Mataro (a blend) and Cabernet-Merlot (a blend); also, traditionally, fortified reds (of port style), which are at the present time in market disfavour.

Leading wineries and vineyards: Penfolds, Peter Lehmann, Rockford, Seppelt Winery, Saltram Wine Estates, Charles Melton, Wolf Blass, Dorrien Estate, St Hallet, Grant Burge, Glaetzer Wines, Hewitson, Kaesler.

Barossa Ridge Wine Estate   **R78**

Light Pass Road, Vine Vale, Tanunda,
SA 5352
Ph/Fax 08 8563 2811

Owners: Marco and Dianne Litterini
Chief winemaker: Marco Litterini
Year of foundation: 1987

Tonnes produced on average each year: 18
Location: Vine Vale (east of Tanunda)
Area: 3 ha
Soils: alluvial sand, interspersed with water-worn gravel over a base of red clay
Varieties planted: White—none; Red—cabernet franc, cabernet sauvignon, merlot, petit verdot, shiraz

Leading wines: Barossa Ridge Old Creek Shiraz, Rocky Valley Cabernet Sauvignon
Notes: A small family-owned winery in the hamlet of Vine Vale. Cellar door sales by appointment.

Barossa Settlers NR

Trial Hill Road, Lyndoch, SA 5351
Ph 08 8524 4017, Fax 08 8524 4519

Owners: Howard and Joan Haese
Chief winemaker: Howard Haese
Year of foundation: 1983
Tonnes produced on average each year: 350, of which about 20 are used for Barossa Settlers wines
Location: Lyndoch
Area: 35 ha
Soils: fertile loamy top-soil of variable depth over red clay
Varieties planted: White—chardonnay, chenin blanc, muscadelle, pedro, riesling, Red—cabernet sauvignon, grenache, mataro, shiraz
Leading wines: Barossa Settlers Riesling, Shiraz, Cabernet Sauvignon
Notes: The Haese family are primarily growers but do have a vineyard with shiraz vines dating back to 1887, which play a great part in Barossa Settlers Shiraz. Cellar door sales: Mon–Sat 10am–4pm, Sun 11am–4pm.

Barossa Valley Estate NR

Seppeltsfield Road, Marananga, SA 5355
Ph 08 8563 3980,
Email be@chariot.net.au

Owner: Barossa Valley Estate Ltd
Chief winemaker: Natasha Mooney
Year of foundation: 1985
Tonnes crushed on average each year: 2500
Location: (cellar door) Marananga, (winery) Angle Vale
Area: none, see above
Varieties planted: no vineyards are owned

Leading wines: E&E Black Pepper Shiraz, Ebenezer Cabernet-Merlot
Notes: Converted recently from a large grape-growers' co-operative to a public company structure, Barossa Valley Estate is curiously named in that it owns no vineyard of its own, being supplied by many contracted growers throughout the Barossa Valley. However this is not an unusual Australian situation. Its wines are typical of the ultra-rich Barossa styles. Cellar door sales: Mon–Fri 9am–5pm, Sat 10am–5pm, Sun closed.

Basedow Wines NR

161–165 Murray Street, Tanunda, SA 5352
Ph 08 8563 2888, Fax 08 8563 3597

Owners: Hill Wine Group
Chief winemakers: Craig Stansborough, Grant Burge and Brian Light (consultants)
Year of foundation: 1896
Tonnes crushed on average each year: 1750
Location: (cellar door) Tanunda
Area: no vineyards owned, all fruit purchased from Barossa growers
Varieties planted: none
Leading wines: Basedow Barossa Valley Semillon, Shiraz, Riesling, Cabernet, Bush Vine Grenache, Sauvignon Blanc, VO Tawny, Mistella
Notes: This winery was founded in 1896 and remained in Basedow family hands until 1971. John Basedow, the last family owner-winemaker, won a Jimmy Watson trophy in 1970. In the ensuing 31 years, there have been four proprietors, the latest being the Hill family. It owns no vineyards but has a broad range of wines of good quality overall and keenly priced. Perhaps Basedow's most famous table wine of recent years has been its 'Oscar's White Burgundy', now varietally labelled, a lemon and vanilla-scented Semillon matured in American oak with a full-flavoured palate, very typical of the up-front Barossa Semillon style.

Cellar door sales: weekdays 10am–5pm, weekends and public holidays 11am–5pm.

Bethany Wines R83

Bethany Road, Tanunda, SA 5352
Ph 08 8563 2086, Fax 08 8563 0046

Owners: Schrapel families
Chief winemakers: Robert and Geoff Schrapel, Paul Bailey
Year of foundation: 1977
Tonnes crushed on average each year: 350
Location: Bethany (south-east of Tanunda)
Area: 40 ha made up of four vineyards—Homestead, Bethanian, Manse (Barossa) and Trial Hill (Eden Valley)
Soils: Homestead, alluvial soil over red-brown clay and limestone; Bethanian, rich top soil (1 m deep) over clay, some Biscay soil; Manse, flood plain top soil well drained over a clay base; Trial Hill, rich top soil from ½ m to 1 m deep over rocky clay subsoil
Varieties planted: White—chardonnay, frontignac, muscadelle, riesling, semillon; Red—cabernet franc, cabernet sauvignon, grenache, merlot, shiraz
Leading wines: Barossa Valley Semillon, Shiraz, Grenache Shiraz, Old Quarry Tawny
Notes: Bethany is the heartland of the Barossa Valley and the Schrapel family, whose ancestors arrived in 1844, are very much part of its history. After many years as growers, the family constructed its winery in 1977. The strengths here are traditionally Barossan, Shiraz, Shiraz blends with Grenache and well made wood fermented Semillon. Cellar door sales: Mon–Sat 10am–5pm, Sun 1pm–5pm.

Burge Family Winemakers R84

Barossa Valley Way, Lyndoch, SA 5351
Ph 08 8524 4644, Fax 08 8524 4444

Owners: Richard and Bronwyn Burge
Chief winemaker: Rick Burge
Year of foundation: 1928

Tonnes crushed on average each year: 55 rising to 75 by the year 2005, about 50 is presently used for Burge Family wines
Location: Lyndoch
Area: 10 ha
Soils: There are two vineyards flanking the Draycott homestead: Draycott, alluvial loams over red clay; Olive Hill, red-brown clay loams over limestone
Varieties planted: White—muscat blanc, riesling, semillon; Red—cabernet sauvignon, grenache, merlot, mourvedre, nebbiolo, sauzao, shiraz, touriga, zinfandel
Leading wines: Olive Hill Riesling, Semillon, Muscat Blanc Late Harvest, Shiraz-Grenache-Mourvedre, Draycott Shiraz, Cabernet-Merlot, Reserve Shiraz
Notes: The Burge family have been growers in the Barossa since the 19th century and winemakers here since 1928. Rick is a winemaker of great experience who cherishes the traditions of the Valley, the most important of which these days are shiraz and its concomitant Rhone varieties, grenache and mourvedre (mataro, if you prefer Spanish). Now Rick is enjoying a place in the sun, as reviews of his wines have been outstanding—Robert Parker, a recent disciple of Australian Shiraz style, rating a Draycott Shiraz as close to perfection as anyone can get (99/100). Though I am not quite as generous, standards here are very high. Cellar door sales: Mon–Tues, Thurs–Sat 10am–5pm, Sun 11am–5pm. Closed Wed.

Charles Cimicky Wines NR

Gomersal Road, Lyndoch, SA 5351
Ph 08 8524 4025, Fax 08 8524 4772

Owner: Charles Cimicky
Chief winemaker: Charles Cimicky
Year of foundation: 1972
Tonnes crushed on average each year: 500
Location: Lyndoch
Area: 32 ha

Soils: red loam over limestone
Varieties planted: White—none; Red—cabernet sauvignon, merlot, petit verdot, shiraz
Leading wines: Charles Cimicky Shiraz, Grenache
Notes: Charles Cimicky features a Signature Shiraz, which is typical of the generous style of the region. Cellar door sales: Tues–Sat 10am–4pm.

Charles Melton Wines R88

Krondorf Road, Tanunda, SA 5352
Ph 08 8563 3606, Fax 08 8563 3422,
Email cmelton@dove.net.au

Owners: Charlie Melton and Virginia Weckert
Chief winemaker: Charlie Melton
Year of foundation: 1984
Tonnes crushed on average each year: 225
Locations: (winery) Krondorf Road, (vineyards) Krondorf Road, Nitschke Road, Woodlands and Smyth Road
Area: 28.5 ha (Krondorf Road 2.5 ha, Nitschke Road 6 ha, Woodlands 9.2 ha, Smyth Road 10.8 ha)
Soils: Krondorf Road and Nitschke Road, biscay (heavy cracking clays); Woodlands, sandy gravelly loam over clay; Smyth Road, sandy loam over clay and rich red river flat loam
Varieties planted: White—none; Red—(Krondorf Road) (brush-pruned) grenache, shiraz; (Nitschke Road) shiraz; (Woodlands) cabernet sauvignon, grenache, shiraz; (Smyth Road) cabernet sauvignon, (bush-pruned) grenache, shiraz
Leading wines: Charles Melton Nine Popes, Rose of Virginia
Notes: Charlie Melton is one of the mainstays of the Barossa and his wines, along with those of Robert O'Callaghan, are Barossa icons. Indeed, the Barossa Valley when facing a critical loss of identity in the 1980s was fortunate in finding staunch individuals such as Charlie Melton to remind it of its traditions. Otherwise it might today simply be a soulless

production centre processing wines from anywhere. Charlie Melton loves the old bush vines of the valley and uses them to perfection. Expect traditional styles here, of the highest quality! Cellar door sales: 7 days 11am–5pm. Closed Christmas Day and Good Friday.

Chateau Tanunda NR

Basedow Road, Tanunda, SA 5352
Ph/Fax 08 8563 3888

Owner: John Geber
Chief winemaker: Ralph Fowler (contract)
Year of foundation: (originally 1889) re-established 1997
Tonnes produced on average each year: 100
Location: Tanunda
Area: 14 ha
Soils: na
Varieties planted: White—riesling; Red—shiraz
Leading wine: Chateau Tanunda Shiraz
Notes: An impressive building and an old and respected name for Australian brandy for over a century, which is no longer produced here. However, Ralph Fowler is a consultant winemaker of great competence, but I know nothing of the wines. Cellar door sales: daily 10am–5.30pm.

Dorrien Estate R86

Cnr Barossa Valley Way and Siegersdorf Road, Tanunda, SA 5352
Ph 08 8561 2200, Fax 08 8561 2299

Owner: Cellarmasters (Mildara Blass)
Chief winemaker: Simon Adams
Year of foundation: 1982
Tonnes crushed on average each year: 12 000
Location: Tanunda
Area: (Barossa) 5.2 ha, (Eden Valley) 31.9 ha (see also Mt Benson)
Soils: Barossa, loam/clay; Eden Valley, sandy loam over clay
Varieties planted: (Barossa Valley and Eden

Valley) White—chardonnay; Red—cabernet sauvignon, shiraz

Leading wines: Dorrien Estate Bin 6 Chardonnay Semillon, Bin 7 Cabernet Sauvignon-Shiraz, Growers' Shiraz, Rare Print range, New Eden Riesling, Chardonnay, Avon Brae Eden Valley Shiraz

Notes: The successful Cellarmaster operation of direct wine sales was purchased by Mildara in 1997. The Cellarmaster emphasis is these days on regional quality, which it indeed produces at a reasonable price. There are, of course, no cellar door sales.

Dutschke Wines (formerly Willow Bend Wines) NR

Lyndoch Valley Road, Lyndoch, SA 5351
Ph/Fax 08 8524 4169

Owner: (vineyard) Ken Semmler
Chief winemaker: Wayne Dutschke
Year of foundation: 1990
Tonnes produced on average each year: 190 of which 40 are used for Dutschke wines
Location: Lyndoch
Area: 24 ha
Soils: grey sandy loam over clay
Varieties planted: White—chardonnay, frontignac, riesling; Red—cabernet sauvignon, merlot, pinot noir, shiraz
Leading wines: Dutschke Oscar Semmler Shiraz, St Jakobi Shiraz, Willow Bend Merlot, Shiraz, Cabernet Sauvignon
Notes: The wines have not been tasted. No cellar door sales. Mail order only.

Elderton R80

3 Tanunda Road, Nuriootpa, SA 5355
Ph 08 8562 1058, Fax 08 8562 2844,
Email elderton@chariot.net.au
Toll free sales line 1800 888 500

Owner: The Ashmead family
Chief winemakers: Allister Ashmead, Richard Sheedy, James Irvine (contract)

Year of foundation: 1985
Tonnes crushed on average each year: 450 (Elderton also purchases fruit from local growers)
Location: Nuriootpa
Area: 28 ha
Soils: deep river silt over limestone varying to red-brown earth away from the river
Varieties planted: White—riesling, semillon; Red—cabernet sauvignon, merlot, shiraz
Leading wine: Elderton Command Shiraz
Notes: The quality of Elderton Command Shiraz is sensational, typical of the Barossa's best. The many awards, both local and international, say so. The Cabernet Sauvignon, the winner of the Jimmy Watson Trophy in 1993 is also at times very good. Perhaps the problem I found with Elderton is that its other wines are less even in quality. However, I may be a lone voice crying in a distant vineyard. Cellar door sales: Mon–Fri 8.30am–5pm, weekends and public holidays 11am–4pm.

Glaetzer Wines R85

34 Barossa Valley Way, Tanunda, SA 5352
Ph 08 8563 0288, Fax 08 8563 0218,
Email glaetzer@glaetzer.com

Owner: Glaetzer family
Chief winemakers: Colin and Ben Glaetzer
Year of foundation: 1996
Tonnes crushed on average each year: 50
Location: (winery and cellar door sales) Tanunda
Area: no vineyard is owned or leased
Varieties planted: none, all fruit is purchased from growers
Leading wines: Glaetzer Bush Vine Semillon, Bush Vine Grenache-Mourvedre, The Bishop Shiraz
Notes: This winery was established only in 1996, but, as you would expect from a skilled Barossa maker, the wines are full, flavoursome and all-Barossa, being sourced from arguably the best dry-grown area in the valley, Ebenezer,

off very low yielding sandy clay loams over limestone. Cellar door sales: Mon–Sat 10.30am–4.30pm, Sundays and public holidays 1pm–4.30pm.

Gnadenfrei Estate Winery NR

Seppeltsfield Road, Marananga
SA 5355
Ph 08 8562 2522, Fax 08 8562 3470

Owners: Malcolm and Joylene Seppelt
Chief winemaker: Malcolm Seppelt
Year of foundation: 1979
Tonnes crushed on average each year: 28
Location: Marananga
Area: 10 ha
Soils/Varieties planted: riesling, pinot noir, malbec, cabernet sauvignon on clay loam, grenache on gravelly loam, shiraz on black clay
Leading wines: Gnadenfrei Estate Shiraz, Shiraz-Grenache
Notes: This small family cellar specialises in the reds grown on its own vineyard. In addition there are whites and other reds made from grapes purchased locally and from the Eden Valley. There is a restaurant open for lunch from 12.30pm to 3pm every day except Monday unless it is a public holiday. Cellar door sales: Tues–Sun and public holidays 10am–5pm.

Grant Burge R86

Barossa Valley Way, Jacobs Creek,
SA 5352
Ph 08 8563 7400, Fax 08 8563 2800,
Email admin@gbwines.com.au

Owners: Grant and Helen Burge
Chief winemaker: Grant Burge
Year of foundation: 1988
Tonnes crushed on average each year: 3500, of which 2000 are used for Grant Burge wines
Locations: Jacobs Creek and Krondorf (cellar doors), Lyndoch (5 vineyards), Williamstown
Area, soils and varieties planted: 330 ha made

up of 13 vineyards. 1) The Winery Vineyard (Jacobs Creek) deep alluvial soils, planted to chardonnay and shiraz. 2) Corryton Park (Barossa Ranges) sandy loam and loam, planted to cabernet sauvignon, merlot and petit verdot. 3) Summer's (Eden Valley) podzolic soil planted to chardonnay, pinot noir and riesling. 4) Nicolai (Bethany) biscay (black cracking clay) and red-brown earths, planted to shiraz and cabernet sauvignon. 5) Lily Farm (Tanunda) red-brown earths, planted to merlot, riesling, semillon, sauvignon blanc, and muscat a petits grains blanc (white frontignac). 6) The Holy Trinity (Lyndoch) alluvial soils, planted to merlot. 7) Wilsford (Lyndoch) biscay and red-brown earths planted to mourvedre (mataro). 8) Hillcot (Lyndoch) sandy loams and red-brown earths, planted to merlot. 9) Cameron Vale (Lyndoch) red-brown earths and grey loam over red clay, planted to cabernet sauvignon, shiraz and petit verdot. 10) Filsell (Lyndoch) deep alluvial soils planted to shiraz. 11) Miamba (Lyndoch) deep alluvial soils and some red-brown earths, planted to shiraz, cabernet sauvignon, merlot, chardonnay and semillon. 12) Chaff Mill (Lyndoch) gravelly loam over clay, planted to shiraz, grenache, semillon, palomino and pedro. 13) Berghofer (Williamstown) red-brown earths and solodized solonetz, planted to shiraz, cabernet sauvignon, grenache, semillon, riesling, chardonnay and sauvignon blanc.
Leading wines: Grant Burge Meshach Shiraz, Filsell Shiraz, Cameron Vale Cabernet Sauvignon, Hillcot Merlot, Pinot Noir-Chardonnay Brut. Barossa Vines is a second label
Notes: The Grant Burge range of wines is quite varied, but all are characteristically Barossan, from the full-bodied Shiraz styles even to the Sparkling, made from traditional Champagne varieties, all have that added element of ripeness and strength that is Barossa. If you need to appreciate the wine styles of the Barossa, you need go no further than Grant

Burge. Cellar door sales: 7 days 10am–5pm, except Good Friday and Christmas Day.

Greenock Creek Vineyard and Cellars NR

Radford Road, Seppeltsfield, SA 5360
Ph 08 8562 8103, Fax 08 8562 8259,
Email gckwines@dove.net.au

Owners: Michael and Annabelle Waugh
Chief winemaker: Michael Waugh
Year of foundation: 1989
Tonnes crushed on average each year: 55 tonnes but will increase to 120 tonnes as new vines come into bearing
Locations: Seppeltsfield and Marananga
Area: (Seppeltsfield) 16 ha, (Marananga) 6 ha
Soils: deep red earth to sandy loam to bluestone shale
Varieties planted: White—none; Red—cabernet sauvignon, grenache, mataro, shiraz
Leading wines: Greenock Creek Vineyard Cornerstone Grenache, Cabernet Sauvignon, Apricot Block Shiraz, The Roennfeldt Road Shiraz, Cabernet Sauvignon
Notes: Once quite small, this family winery is now growing quickly. Its vineyards are not irrigated. Its wines, made solely from Greenock Creek fruit, are crushed and made off-site and then returned to the cellars for maturing. Its Shiraz, made in the generously flavoured Barossa manner, is most popular. A faithfully restored cottage, Miriam's, is available for bed and breakfast. Cellar door sales: Wed–Mon 11am–5pm unless sold out. Ring ahead. Wines are released in early September.

Hamilton's Ewell Vineyards R82

Siegersdorf Vineyard, Barossa Valley Way,
Nuriootpa, SA 5355
Ph 08 8562 4600, Fax 08 8562 4611,
Email cellardoor@hamiltonewell.com.au

Owners: Mark and Deborah Hamilton
Chief winemaker: (contract)
Year of foundation: originally established near Adelaide by Richard Hamilton in 1837, re-established in 1991 by Mark Hamilton
Tonnes produced on average each year: 1300, 125 of which are used for Hamilton's Ewell wines
Location: Nuriootpa (cellar door)
Area: 251 ha consisting of 131 ha (Barossa Valley floor), encompassing Siegersdorf Vineyard, Railway Vineyard, Fuller's Vineyard, Rohrlach's Block and Tweedie's Gully Vineyard. In addition, there are vineyards owned at Eden Valley (18 ha), Wrattonbully (87 ha) and Southern Riverland (15 ha). The Barossa and Eden Valley vineyards are leased to Southcorp Wines, but some fruit is also used for Hamilton's Ewell wines
Soils: The Barossa and Eden Valley vineyards are leased to Southcorp (see Penfolds entry below). Wrattonbully, terra rossa type soils (i.e. red-brown clay loams over limestone); Southern Riverland, (Nildottie) red sandy loam over a calcareous base
Varieties planted: White—chardonnay, riesling, sauvignon blanc, semillon, traminer; Red—cabernet franc, cabernet sauvignon, grenache, malbec, shiraz
Leading wines: Hamilton's Ewell Vineyard Barossa Valley, Fullers Barn Shiraz
Notes: Hamilton's Ewell is a nostalgic name to many older Australian wine drinkers. The name began to disappear after Mildara Blass acquired it in 1979 and since 1991 Mark Hamilton has been trying to rectify Mildara's omission. At the present time, all the wine offered under Hamilton's Ewell labels originates from the floor of the Barossa Valley, the Shiraz styles being my choice. Cellar door sales: daily, Mon–Fri 9am–5pm, weekends and public holidays 11am–5pm.

Heritage Wines R84

106a Seppeltsfield Road, Marananga,
SA 5355
Ph 08 8562 2880, Fax 08 8562 2692,
Email heritage@dove.net.au

Owners: Stephen and Christine Hoff
Chief winemaker: Stephen Hoff
Year of foundation: 1984
Tonnes crushed on average each year: 65
Location: Marananga
Area: 8 ha
Soils: red-brown earth over clay
Varieties planted: White—none; Red—cabernet
sauvignon, malbec, shiraz
Leading wines: Heritage Barossa Valley Shiraz,
Rossco's Shiraz
Notes: Like many smaller Barossan winemakers,
Stephen Hoff specialises in reds, especially
Shiraz. His speciality is well-worth following.
Cellar door sales: 7 days 11am–5pm.

Hewitson R85

16 McGowan Ave, Unley, SA 5061
Ph 08 8271 5755, Fax 08 8271 5570,
Email dean@hewitson.com.au

Owner/chief winemaker: Dean Hewitson
Year of foundation: 1998
Tonnes crushed on average each year: 90
Location: no cellar door
Area: no vineyards are owned or leased
Leading wines: Hewitson Barossa Shiraz,
Grenache, Old Garden Mourvedre, Eden Valley
Riesling
Notes: Dean Hewitson might by a stretch of
imagination be termed a winemaker of no fixed
abode, except of course that his wines are of
eminently respectable origins, the Barossa Valley,
Eden Valley and McLaren Vale. His Barossa reds
are typical of the full ripe fruit character of the
Valley and his Eden Valley Riesling is extremely
stylish. His McLaren Vale L'Oiseau Shiraz is also
extremely good. He is certainly a winemaker to
follow. Sales by mail order.

Jenke NR

Jenke Road, Rowland Flat, SA 5352
Ph 08 8524 4154, Fax 08 8524 5044,
Email kym@jenke.com.au

Owner/chief winemaker: Kym Jenke
Year of foundation: vineyard 1926, winery 1989
Tonnes crushed on average each year: 550, of
which 130 are used for Jenke wines
Location: Rowland Flat
Area: 45 ha
Soils: alluvial river silt, very deep
Varieties planted: White—chardonnay, riesling,
semillon; Red—cabernet franc, cabernet
sauvignon, grenache, merlot, shiraz
Leading wine: Jenke Semillon
Notes: Kym Jenke is descended from an old
Barossa grapegrowing family who arrived in
1854. His vineyard, dating only from 1926, is
therefore a comparative youngster but its
quality is outstanding, especially its semillon.
Jenke Semillon is an excellent white, ripe in the
best Barossa tradition but never fat or over-
blown. Cellar door sales: 7 days 10am–4.30pm.

Kaesler Wines R85

Barossa Valley Way, Nuriootpa, SA 5355
Ph 08 8562 2711, Fax 08 8562 2788,
Email reid@mail.pealva.net

Owners: Dural Wines Australia Pty Ltd
Chief winemaker: Reid Bosward
Year of foundation: vineyard 1893,
winery 1989
Tonnes crushed on average each year: 180
Location: Nuriootpa
Area: 22 ha
Soils: in large part, the vineyard is established
on red-brown clay loams over a limestone
shale. But there are two other distinct soil
types, a deep brown sandy loam and a red clay
with very little topsoil over limestone shale
Varieties planted: White—palomino, riesling,
semillon, viognier; Red—cabernet sauvignon,
grenache, mataro, shiraz

Leading wines: Kaesler Shiraz-Cabernet-Merlot, Old Vines Shiraz

Notes: A recent change of ownership but no change to the rich stylish reds. Cellar door sales: 7 days 10am–5pm. There is also a restaurant.

Kellermeister R81

Barossa Valley Way, Lyndoch, SA 5351 (about 1.5 km east of the town)
Ph 08 8524 4303, Fax 08 8524 4880, Email kmeister@mail.mdt.net.au

Owners: Ralph and Val Jones
Chief winemaker: Trevor Jones
Year of foundation: 1979
Tonnes crushed on average each year: 300, of which 200 are used for Kellermeister wines
Location: Lyndoch
Area: 5 ha
Soils: red loam clay and limestone over black loam over soft schist rock
Varieties planted: White—none; Red—shiraz
Leading wines: Kellermeister Grenache-Merlot-Cabernet Franc, Dry Grown Shiraz, Old Barossa Tokay, Barossa Liqueur Shiraz Tawny
Notes: Kellermeister purchase a large quantity of their fruit from local growers and its wine range, made by the widely experienced Trevor Jones, is typical of the Barossa. Recent reviews have included a perfect century by wine advocate Robert Parker for the two fortifieds mentioned above. Cellar door sales: 9am–6pm each day.

Kies Family Wines R83

Barossa Valley Way, Lyndoch, SA 5351
Ph/Fax 08 8524 4110

Owners: Michael and Tina Kies
Chief winemaker: James Irvine (contract)
Year of foundation: vineyard 1857, winery 1984
Tonnes crushed on average each year: 220, of which 45 are used for Kies Family Wines

Location: Lyndoch and Hoffnungstahl
Area: 84 ha, (Lyndoch) 17 ha, (Hoffnungstahl) 67 ha
Soils: Hoffnungstahl, dark brown soil; Lyndoch, heavy to sandy loams
Varieties planted: (Lyndoch) White—riesling, semillon; Red—shiraz cabernet sauvignon, merlot, cabernet gros. (Hoffnungstahl) White—chardonnay, riesling, semillon; Red—cabernet franc, shiraz
Leading wine: Kies Family Dedication Shiraz, Riesling
Notes: The Kies Family are chiefly grapegrowers, their ancestors first planting their vineyards in 1880. Today these vineyards are a treasured legacy. Obviously, therefore, Shiraz is the bag here. Cellar door sales: Mon–Fri 10am–4.30pm, weekends and public holidays 10am–5pm. There are also barbecue facilities and a gazebo.

Langmeil Winery R82

Cnr Langmeil and Para Road, Tanunda, SA 5352
Ph 08 8563 2595, Fax 08 8563 3622, Email langmeilwinery@dove.net.au

Owner: Langmeil Pty Ltd
Chief winemaker: Paul Lindner
Year of foundation: 1932
Tonnes produced on average each year: 60, an additional 80 are purchased to satisfy Langmeil Winery needs
Locations: Tanunda (winery, cellar door and Tanunda vineyard); Lyndoch (vineyard)
Area: 14 ha, (Tanunda) 5 ha, (Lyndoch) 9 ha
Soils: Tanunda, old river loam over limestone; Lyndoch, sandy loam over ironstone
Varieties planted: White—none; Red (Tanunda) shiraz; (Lyndoch) cabernet sauvignon, grenache, shiraz
Leading wines: Langmeil Barossa Shiraz, Cabernet Sauvignon
Notes: The Lindner family has been long established in the Barossa and today maintain

those long-established Barossa traditional wines. The reds are the strength here. Cellar door sales: 7 days 11am–4.30pm.

Peter Lehmann Wines   **R91**

Para Road, Tanunda, SA 5352
Ph 08 8563 2500, Fax 08 8563 3402

Owner: Peter Lehmann Wines Ltd (a public company listed since 1993)
Chief winemaker: Andrew Wigan
Year of foundation: 1978 (as Masterson, renamed Masterson Barossa Vignerons in 1979, then named Peter Lehmann Wines Ltd in 1982)
Tonnes crushed on average each year: 7500, of which about 210 are supplied by Peter Lehmann owned vineyards
Locations: (winery and cellar door) Tanunda; (vineyards) Stonewell, The Crossing
Area: Barossa Valley 40 ha (Stonewell 20 ha, The Crossing 20 ha); Clare 20 ha
Soils: Stonewell, variable Biscay soil over shale and red-brown loam over limestone; The Crossing, red duplex over clay; Clare, Trillions Hill, grey brown shallow soil over shale
Varieties planted: (Stonewell) White—none; Red—cabernet sauvignon, malbec, merlot, shiraz; (The Crossing) White—none; Red—cabernet franc, cabernet sauvignon, shiraz; (Clare) White—none; Red—cabernet sauvignon, malbec, merlot, shiraz
Leading wines: Peter Lehmann Stonewell Shiraz, Eight Songs Shiraz, Mentor, Eden Valley Riesling, Clancy's White and Red
Notes: Peter Lehmann, publicly corporatised or not, is a Barossa Valley patriot, a single-minded independent in a multinational world. Though most of his fruit is purchased from growers (over 175 from all over the Valley), the only 'outside' fruit that comes into the winery is from the adjacent Eden Valley region and the company's own vineyard at Clare, which provides some of the red source for its other premium brand, Clancy's. Corporate existence has often been difficult since the company's inception in 1978, but the philosophy has not wavered. His leading wines are red, Stonewell Shiraz, Eight Songs Shiraz, and the very smart Cabernet blend, Mentor, though the Lehmann Eden Valley Rieslings age very gracefully. Cellar door sales: weekdays 9.30am–5pm, weekends and public holidays 10.30am–4.30pm.

Liebichwein   **R80**

Steingarten Road, Rowland Flat, SA 5352
Ph 08 8524 4543, Fax 08 8524 4047

Owners: Liebich family
Chief winemaker: Ron Liebich
Year of foundation: vineyard 1985, winery sales 1992
Tonnes crushed on average each year: 200, of which about 25 are used for Liebichwein labels
Location: Rowland Flat
Area: 24 ha
Soils: The vineyard is divided by a creek. Its northern side is Biscay, south of creek is red-brown earth
Varieties planted: White—chardonnay; Red—cabernet sauvignon, grenache, merlot, pinot noir, shiraz
Leading wine: Darkie Shiraz
Notes: As the extent of the vineyard and the quantity of fruit produced show, Ron and Janet Liebich are primarily growers, but Darkie Shiraz from their Darkie vineyard is a typical generously flavoured Barossa red, well worth a taste. Cellar door sales: daily 11am–5pm, other times by appointment.

Miranda Wines   **R80**

Barossa Valley Way, Rowland Flat, SA 5352
Ph 08 8524 4537, Fax 08 8524 4066, Email info@mirandawines.com.au

Owner: Miranda Wines
Chief winemaker: Gary Wall
Year of foundation: 1919 (as Miranda Wines 1991)

Tonnes crushed on average each year: 6000
Location: Rowland Flat
Area: 25 ha
Soils: sandy loam
Varieties planted: White—chardonnay;
Red—cabernet sauvignon, grenache, merlot,
shiraz
Leading wines: Miranda Show Reserve
Chardonnay, Old Vine Shiraz, Show Reserve
Shiraz-Cabernet
Notes: It must be the Italian influence. Just as
the De Bortoli family added new dimensions of
excellence to Yarra Valley winemaking, so the
Mirandas have put their own quality imprint
on the Barossa. Show success has been
widespread for both whites and reds. Cellar
door sales: weekdays 10am–4.30pm,
weekends 11am–4.30pm.

Orlando R85

Barossa Valley Way, Rowland Flat,
SA 5352
Ph 08 8521 3111, Fax 08 8521 3100

Owner: Orlando Wyndham
Chief winemaker: Philip Laffer
Year of foundation: 1847
Tonnes crushed on average each year: not
disclosed but in excess of 10 000
Location: Rowland Flat (winery)
Area: as well as purchasing local fruit, Orlando
has several vineyards in the Barossa Valley.
These are Jacobs Creek (26 ha), Bungalow
(21 ha), Kluges Estate (34 ha) and Lyndoch
Estate (7 ha), 88 ha in all. (See also Eden Valley)
Soils: Jacobs Creek, red-brown earth with
sandy loam; Bangalow and Kluges, same as
Jacobs Creek; Lyndoch Estate, dark cracking
clays with self-mulching surface soil.
Varieties planted: (Jacobs Creek)
White—riesling; Red—pinot noir, shiraz;
(Bungalow) White—none; Red—cabernet
sauvignon; (Kluges Estate) White—riesling;
Red—cabernet franc, shiraz
Leading wines: Gramps Chardonnay,

Cabernet-Merlot, Jacobs Creek
Shiraz-Cabernet, Chardonnay, Jacobs Creek
Reserve and Limited Release Ranges
Notes: Having celebrated its sesquicentenary in
1997, Orlando is the oldest wine company
resident in the Barossa Valley and one of
Australia's largest. It is now world-famous for
its excellent Jacobs Creek brand, which
absorbs all the fruit from the vineyard of the
same name and a great deal more from other
sources. Cellar door sales: weekdays
10am–5pm, weekends and public holidays
10am–4pm.

Penfolds R95

Tanunda Road, Nuriootpa, SA 5355
Ph 08 8568 9389, Fax 08 8562 1669

Owner: Southcorp Wines
Chief winemaker: John Duval
Year of foundation: 1844
Tonnes crushed on average each year: from
the company's own Barossa vineyards, 1800,
all of which, together with much more fruit
purchased from growers, are used for Penfolds
wines
Locations: Nuriootpa (winery and cellar door);
vineyards see below
Area: 483.71 ha comprising vineyards at
Kalimna (137.2 ha) about 4 km north of
Nuriootpa; Koonunga Hill (30.3 ha) 5 km
north-east of Kalimna; Scholz (28 ha) adjacent
to Koonunga Hill on the south-east; Stonewell
Road (33.21 ha) about 4 km west of
Nuriootpa; Hamilton vineyards, known as
Rohrlachs, Fullers, Siegersdorf, Railway and
Tweedie Gully (leased from Hamilton Ewell
Vineyards until November 2005) and on the
eastern edge of the Barossa Valley between
Nuriootpa and Lyndoch (125 ha); Walton
adjacent to southern boundary of Seppeltsfield
(130 ha), not yet fully planted or bearing.
Soils: Kalimna, varying from deep sandy soil on
sloping areas to sandy loam and heavy red-
brown clays on the flats; Koonunga Hill and

Scholz, red-brown earth over deep red clays; Stonewell Road, mainly deep red clays with some shallow silt-based top soils; Hamilton, mainly deep red and self-mulching grey clay soils; Tweedie Gully, significant areas of rock and shallow topsoils which are prone to drying out rapidly in summer; Walton, predominantly red-brown earths with shallow topsoils on the hilltops, alluvial creek flats and pockets of vertisols
Varieties planted: (Kalimna) White—none; Red—cabernet sauvignon, shiraz. (Koonunga Hill) White—none; Red—cabernet sauvignon, shiraz. (Scholz) White—none; Red—shiraz. (Stonewell Road) White—chardonnay, riesling, semillon; Red—cabernet sauvignon, grenache, shiraz. (Hamilton) White—chardonnay, riesling, sauvignon blanc, semillon; Red—cabernet franc, cabernet sauvignon, grenache, malbec, shiraz. (Walton) White—none; Red—cabernet sauvignon, mourvedre, shiraz
Leading wines: (vineyard of origin) Kalimna—Penfolds Special Bin Block 42 Cabernet Sauvignon, components of Penfolds Grange, Bin 707 Cabernet Sauvignon, Bin 407 Cabernet Sauvignon, Bin 389 Cabernet-Shiraz, Bin 28 Shiraz, St Henri Koonunga Hill Shiraz-Cabernet and RWT Barossa Valley Shiraz. Koonunga Hill—the same as Kalimna with the exception of Special Bin Block 42 Cabernet Sauvignon
Notes: The Barossa Valley vineyards are the heart, soul and backbone of Penfolds premium and super-premium reds. Consonant with the quality to be expected from such wines, the vineyards are farmed conservatively, always with the aim of increasing organic content in soils and with irrigation either absent or kept to a minimum, so that salinity levels are not increased. Accordingly they are very low-yielding. Cellar door sales: Mon–Sat 10am–5pm, Sun 11am–5pm.

Richmond Grove   **R85**

Para Road, Tanunda, SA 5352
Ph 08 8563 2204, Fax 08 8563 2804

Owner: Orlando Wyndham
Chief winemaker: John Vickery
Year of foundation: 1897
Tonnes crushed on average each year: 30 000
Location: Tanunda
Area: 7 ha, also sources fruit from its own Coonawarra vineyard (see entry) and purchases elsewhere (notably from Watervale in the Clare region)
Soils: red duplex, red-brown earth on a clay base
Varieties planted: White—none; Red—cabernet sauvignon
Leading wines: Richmond Grove Barossa Shiraz, Coonawarra Cabernet Sauvignon, Watervale Riesling
Notes: Richmond Grove is a rather peripatetic label. It has moved without difficulty from the Hunter to the Barossa Valley where its latest home is the century-old Orange Grove (Chateau Leonay) winery in Tanunda. It is also the workplace of eminent winemaker John Vickery, who is responsible for among others its excellent Watervale Rieslings. It is now the South Australian 'red' winery for the Orlando-Wyndham group with the Rowland Flat facility as the 'white'. Its Cabernet Sauvignon sourced from Coonawarra is also quite good.
Cellar door sales: weekdays 9am–4.30pm, weekends 11am–4pm.

Rockford   **R90**

Krondorf Road, Tanunda, SA 5352
Ph 08 8563 2729, Fax 08 8563 3787

Owner: Tanunda Vintners Pty Ltd
Chief winemaker: Robert O'Callaghan and Chris Ringland
Year of foundation: 1984
Tonnes crushed on average each year: 450, of which 70 are used for Rockford wines

Location: Tanunda
Area: none, all grapes purchased from private growers
Varieties crushed: White—riesling, frontignac, semillon; Red—alicante bouschet, cabernet sauvignon, grenache, mourvedre, shiraz
Leading wine: Rockford Black Basket Press Shiraz
Notes: Barossa tradition is alive and well at Rockford. If heritage is your thing, there is an 1850s stone settler's cottage and wine making equipment almost as old. If you just love fantastic full-bodied Barossan reds, don't miss Rockford. Cellar door sales: Mon–Sat 11am–5pm (closed Sunday, Good Friday and Christmas Day).

Roehr Wines **NR**

Roehr Road, Ebenezer via Nuriootpa, SA 5355
Ph/Fax 08 8565 6242

Owners: Elmor and Suzanne Roehr
Chief winemaker: (contract)
Year of foundation: vineyard 1851, cellar door 1995
Tonnes produced on average each year: not disclosed but estimated at 75, of which only a very small part is used for Roehr wines
Location: Ebenezer, north-west of Nuriootpa
Area: 20 ha
Soils: iron-laced stony loam of variable depth (15–20 cm) over red clay over limestone
Varieties planted: White—chardonnay; Red—grenache, mataro (mourvedre), shiraz, cabernet sauvignon
Leading wine: Elmer's Ebenezer Old Vine Shiraz
Notes: The Roehr family have been in the Barossa for 150 years. They migrated from Prussia to avoid religious persecution. I have not tasted any wine but Ebenezer, located in the north-west of the Valley, is one of its best locations for shiraz and the vineyard in parts is over 80 years old.

Ross Estate **R84**

Barossa Valley Highway, Lyndoch, SA
Ph 08 8524 4033, Fax 08 8524 4533

Owners: Darius and Pauline Ross
Chief winemaker: Rod Chapman
Year of foundation: 1999
Tonnes produced on average each year: 350 (in 2000) but will increase to 600 tonnes by 2002, most of which will be used for Ross Estate labels
Location: Lyndoch, about 1 km from the town
Area: 43 ha
Soils: variable—generally the topsoils are shallow and grape varieties have been planted to (hopefully) suit soils. Thus shiraz is planted on crests which have ironstone in both top and subsoil. Riesling is planted on shallow light brown earths which are gravelly in the ridges. Cabernet sauvignon and franc are established in loam over clay and chardonnay, semillon and the other varieties are planted in shallow light brown earths
Varieties planted: White—chardonnay, riesling, sauvignon blanc, semillon; Red—cabernet franc, cabernet sauvignon, grenache, merlot, shiraz
Leading wines: Ross Estate Old Vine Grenache, Semillon, Riesling, Shiraz, Cabernet Sauvignon
Notes: Ross Estate is a new but experienced face in the Barossa. Darius Ross is a Polish-born businessman of 30 years' experience in lighting and engineering. His winemaker Rod Chapman formerly of Southcorp has 38 years' experience in winemaking. No wonder then that Ross Estate has been quite successful at recent wine shows. Its best wines are red and amongst those, Shiraz, though there are some good crisp stylish whites. Cellar door sales: Mon–Sat 10am–5pm, Sun 11am–4pm.

Rusden Wines **NR**

Magnolia Road, Tanunda, SA 5352
Ph 08 8563 2976, Fax 08 8563 0885,
Email djandccc@dove.net.au

Owners: Dennis and Chris Canute
Chief winemaker: Christian Canute
Year of foundation: 1998
Tonnes produced on average each year: 135, of which 10 are presently used for Rusden wines (increasing to 60 in the near future)
Location: Tanunda (about 3 km north-east)
Area: 16 ha
Soils: deep sand over clay
Varieties planted: White—chenin blanc, riesling, sauvignon blanc; Red—cabernet sauvignon, grenache, merlot, shiraz, zinfandel
Leading wines: Rusden Wines Grenache, Cabernet Sauvignon, Shiraz, Chenin Blanc
Notes: Rusden Wines is the story of another grower unhappy with big company attitudes. Dennis Canute and a friend started experimental winemaking in 1992, repeated the exercise until 1997, missing only two vintages. 1998 saw 7.5 tonnes crushed and 1999, 10. It is a slow process, establishing a winemaking name but critical mass (about 60 tonnes) should be achieved in a few vintages. I have not tasted the wines. No cellar door sales yet. Sales by mail order.

St Hallett **R86**

St Halletts Road, Tanunda, SA 5352
Ph 08 8563 7000, Fax 08 8563 7001,
Email sthallett@sthalett.com.au

Owner: Banksia Wines (recently purchased by Lion Nathan)
Chief winemaker: Cathy Spratt
Year of foundation: 1944
Tonnes crushed on average each year: 2600
Location: Hallett Valley, Tanunda
Area: 40 ha
Soils: alluvial silty loam, red duplex over clay
Varieties planted: White—chardonnay, riesling, semillon; Red—cabernet sauvignon, mataro (mourvedre), shiraz, touriga
Leading wines: St Hallett Old Block Shiraz, Faith Shiraz, Eden Valley Riesling, Semillon Select

Notes: 'Big Bob' McLean is one of the irrepressible characters of the Australian wine industry. In less than a decade he has taken St Hallett from relative mediocrity to the top of the tree. There have been two compelling reasons for this meteoric rise. The first, as always, is hard work; the second is a realisation of the combined worth of old shiraz vines and Barossa tradition. Old Block Shiraz is a rich style typical of generous Barossa fruit and sourced from several vineyards over 50 years old, that is deceptively drinkable after only a few years yet matures well over a decade. This type of red has certainly struck a responsive chord in red wine consumers with the result that Old Block has many flattering imitations in warmer Australian wine regions. St Hallett has recently merged with Tatachilla of McLaren Vale (Bob McLean insists that St Hallett will remain purely Barossan).
Cellar door sales: Mon–Sat 9am–5pm, Sun 10am–5pm. Closed Christmas Day, New Years Day, Good Friday.

Saltram Wine Estates **R89**

Nuriootpa Road, Angaston, SA 5353
Ph 08 8564 3355, Fax 08 8564 2209

Owner: Mildara Blass
Chief winemaker: Nigel Dolan
Year of foundation: 1859
Tonnes crushed on average each year: 200 (in addition considerable amounts of local fruit are purchased)
Location: Angaston
Area: 20 ha
Soils: sands over medium clay and deep silty loam and red-brown earth over limestone and red clay
Varieties planted: White—chardonnay; Red—cabernet sauvignon, malbec, shiraz
Leading wines: Pepperjack Shiraz, Cabernet Sauvignon, Mamre Brook Shiraz, Cabernet Sauvignon
Notes: Saltram is an old and respected Barossa

name which, during a generation, has passed through several hands—Seagram, Rothbury Estate and now Mildara Blass—with a corresponding effect on quality, that is, until recently. Now with an excellent winemaker, Nigel Dolan, wine quality is again in the ascendant. Cellar door sales: 7 days 9am–5pm.

Seppelt Winery R90

Seppeltsfield Road, Seppeltsfield
via Tanunda, SA 5352
Ph 08 8568 6200, Fax 08 8562 8333

Owner: Southcorp Wines
Chief winemaker: Paul Lapsley (fortified winemaker), James Godfrey
Year of foundation: 1851
Tonnes crushed on average each year: not disclosed but estimated at 1600
Locations: (winery and cellar door) Seppeltsfield, (vineyards) Dorrien, Seppeltsfield, Partalunga (near Mount Pleasant, Adelaide Hills)
Area: 95.15 ha in the Barossa Valley (Dorrien 6.25 ha, Seppeltsfield 88.9 ha), Partalunga (Adelaide Hills) 69.8 ha
Soils: Dorrien, heavy red-brown earth clays; Seppeltsfield, lighter red-brown loams over limestone on higher sections and heavy red-brown earth clays; Partalunga, sand over sandy loam
Varieties planted: (Dorrien) White—none; Red—cabernet sauvignon. (Seppeltsfield) White—palomino; Red—cabernet sauvignon, grenache, shiraz, touriga. (Partalunga) White—chardonnay, riesling, sauvignon blanc; Red—cabernet sauvignon
Leading wines: Seppelt Dorrien Cabernet, Partalunga Chardonnay, Seppeltsfield fortified range in particular Show Sherries (DP 117 Fino, DP 116 Amontillado, DP 38 Oloroso), Show Tawny DP 90, Para Liqueur (100 Year Old, 21 Year Old), Rutherglen DP 63 Muscat, DP 57 Tokay
Notes: Seppeltsfield is famous for its

nineteenth century cellars, full of old fortifieds, which are a joy to the palate and especially to their maker, James Godfrey, a self-confessed Sherry fanatic. His Dorrien Cabernet Sauvignon, a rich, long-living cabernet style, is also especially good. Partalunga Chardonnay has a well-deserved reputation also. Cellar door sales: weekdays including public holidays 10am–5pm, Sat–Sun 11am–5pm.

Stanley Brothers NR

Barossa Valley Way, Tanunda, SA 5352
Ph 08 8563 3375, Fax 08 8563 3758,
Email stanleybros@dove.net.au

Owners: LG & L J Stanley Pty Ltd
Chief winemaker: Lindsay Stanley
Year of foundation: 1994
Tonnes crushed on average each year: 200, of which 100 are used for Stanley Brothers wines
Location: Tanunda
Area: 30 ha
Soils: sand over permeable yellow-clay, water retentive
Varieties planted: White—chardonnay, semillon; Red—cabernet sauvignon, shiraz
Leading wines: Stanley Brothers Thoroughbred Cabernet, John Hancock Shiraz, Full Sister Semillon, Pristine Chardonnay (unwooded)
Notes: I have not seen the wines recently. Cellar door sales: Mon–Fri 10am–5pm, weekends 11am–5pm.

Tait Wines NR

Yaldara Drive, Lyndoch, SA 5351
Ph 08 8524 5000, Fax 08 8524 5220,
Email tait@taitwines.com.au

Owners: Bruno and Michael Tait
Chief winemaker: Bruno Tait
Year of foundation: 1994
Tonnes crushed on average each year: 80, of which about 15 are used for the Tait label
Location: Lyndoch
Area: 4 ha

Soils: shallow clay over limestone
Varieties planted: White—chardonnay,
frontignac; Red—cabernet sauvignon, pinot
noir, shiraz
Leading wines: Tait Wines Shiraz, Cabernet
Sauvignon, Chardonnay
Notes: The Tait family have been connected
with the Barossa Valley for more than
100 years, albeit as coopers, not winemakers.
The small family-owned winery has been in
operation since 1994. Cellar door sales:
weekends and public holidays 11am–5pm.

The Willows Vineyard NR

Light Pass Road, Light Pass, SA 5355
Ph 08 8562 1080, Fax 08 8562 3447

Owners: Scholz family
Chief winemakers: Peter Scholz
Year of foundation: winery and cellar door,
1989
Tonnes crushed on average each year: 300, of
which 85 are used for The Willows Vineyard
wines
Location: Light Pass
Area: 35 ha
Soils: alluvial loams, red-brown earth over clay,
sand over clay
Varieties planted: White—chardonnay, riesling,
semillon, traminer; Red—cabernet sauvignon,
grenache, malbec, pinot noir, shiraz
Leading wines: The Willows Semillon,
Cabernet Sauvignon, Riesling, Shiraz, Sparkling
Red
Notes: The vineyard is extensive and grape
sales still constitute the major part of the
Scholz family's viticultural activities. Indeed the
family have been grapegrowers for over
60 years. However, as a 'value-adding'
concept, the family introduced 'The Willows'
label in the late 1980s and it has been very
successful. Indeed, the Willows Vineyard has
won several major awards for its Semillon.
Cellar door sales: 10.30am–4.30pm most days.

Turkey Flat Vineyards NR

Bethany Road, Tanunda, SA 5352
Ph 08 8563 2851, Fax 08 8563 3610

Owners: Peter and Christie Schulz
Chief winemaker: Peter Schulz
Year of foundation: vineyards 1847, winery
1990
Tonnes crushed on average each year: 200
(a further 50 are purchased from growers to
satisfy the requirements of Turkey Flat
Vineyards)
Location: Tanunda
Area: 30 ha including two new vineyards
recently planted
Soils: red-brown sandy loam over limestone
Varieties planted: White—semillon;
Red—cabernet sauvignon, grenache, mataro
(mourvedre), shiraz
Leading wines: Turkey Flat Semillon, Grenache
Noir, Rose, Butchers Block (a blend of Mataro
Mourvedre, Grenache and Shiraz), Cabernet
Sauvignon, Shiraz
Notes: Named after the bush turkeys that
roamed the Barossa in the nineteenth century,
Turkey Flat opened its cellar door facilities in
1993 but Turkey Flat Vineyard is much more
ancient. The vineyard originated about 1847
and still has some shiraz vines over 150 years
old. It came into the Schulz family about 1870
and has been owned by them ever since. The
red wine styles are typically rich and smooth.
I have not recently tasted its wines. Cellar door
sales: 7 days 11am–5pm.

Veritas Winery NR

Seppeltsfield Road, Dorrien, SA 5355
Ph 08 8562 3300, Fax 08 8562 1177,
Email veritas@terra.net.au

Owners/chief winemakers: Rolf Binder and
Christa Binder Deans
Year of foundation: 1955
Tonnes crushed on average each year: 300
Location: Tanunda

Area: 38 ha in total (Chri-Ro Estate 20 ha, Western Ridge 8 ha, new plantings 10 ha)
Soils: shallow sandy loams over limestone
Varieties planted: White—chardonnay, riesling, sauvignon blanc, semillon; Red—cabernet franc, cabernet sauvignon, grenache, malbec, merlot, mourvedre, shiraz
Leading wines: Hanisch Shiraz, Heysen Shiraz, Shiraz-Mourvedre Pressings, Christa Rolf Shiraz-Grenache, Semillon
Notes: This medium sized winery is now in its second generation of family ownership. The reds have won trophies at the Barossa Show. Cellar door sales: daily 11am–4.30pm.

Viking Wines NR

RSD Seppeltsfield Road, Marananga, SA 5352
Ph 08 8562 3842, Fax 08 8562 4266

Owner: Thord Soderstrom
Chief winemaker: Rolf Binder (contract)
Year of foundation: 1993
Tonnes crushed on average each year: 20
Location: Marananga
Area: 8 ha (dry grown)
Soil: red clay
Varieties planted: White—riesling; Red—cabernet sauvignon, shiraz
Leading wines: Viking Cabernet Sauvignon, Riesling, Shiraz
Notes: The Vikings wandered through the Northern Hemisphere over a thousand years ago. As descendants of those ancient Vikings, Thord and Catherine Soderstrom found their way to Australia and while here were engaged appropriately enough building submarines. So it was entirely logical that, when they decided to come ashore for the last time in 1993, they should buy an old bush-vine vineyard in the Barossa Valley as a weekender. The vineyard has been rehabilitated and Viking's wines are starting to be noticed in the Barossa, as well as in Sweden where they are exported, and they

are no doubt in the mainstream of Valley style. Cellar door sales: Tues–Sun 11am–6pm.

Wolf Blass R87

Bilyara Vineyard, Sturt Highway, Nuriootpa, SA 5355
Ph 08 8562 1955, Fax 08 8562 2156

Owner: Mildara Blass
Chief winemakers: White (Wendy Stuckey), Red (John Glaetzer)
Tonnes crushed on average each year: 30 000 (used for various Wolf Blass and Saltram labels and including fruit purchased from growers)
Locations and area: 408 ha, winery and vineyard—Nuriootpa 7 ha; vineyards—Eden Valley 92 ha, Sevenhill (Clare) 83 ha, Watervale (Clare) 146 ha, Krondorf Vineyards (Barossa) 80 ha
Soils: Nuriootpa, red-brown earth over limestone clay; Eden Valley, loamy sands and sandy loam over red-brown clays; Krondorf, various soils including red-brown earth over limestone, sandy loam over medium clays, Biscay soils; Sevenhill, red podsols; Watervale, red-brown earths over limestone soils
Varieties planted: White—(Eden Valley) riesling; Red—(Nuriootpa and Eden Valley) cabernet sauvignon, shiraz. (Krondorf vineyard, Williamstown) White—chardonnay, semillon; Red—cabernet sauvignon, shiraz. (Sevenhill) White—chardonnay, riesling; Red—cabernet sauvignon, shiraz. (Watervale) White—riesling; Red—cabernet franc, cabernet sauvignon, merlot, shiraz
Leading wines: Wolf Blass range of reds and whites
Notes: A very high standard of both red and white winemaking has been established here, especially in red with Senior Red winemaker John Glaetzer maintaining and even perhaps improving upon the heritage left by Wolf Blass. The regional blends, e.g. Wolf Blass Black Label, are usually sensational as are the reds of Barossa and Clare origin in good years.

Cellar door sales: Mon–Fri 9.15am–4.30pm, weekends 10am–4.30pm.

Yaldara Wines
(formerly Chateau Yaldara)   **NR**

Gomersal Road, Lyndoch, SA 5351
Ph 08 8524 4200, Fax 08 8524 4678
Email yaldara@yaldara.com.au

Owners: Simeon Wines
Chief winemaker: Robert Ruediger
Year of foundation: 1947
Tonnes crushed on average each year: 5000

Location: Lyndoch
Area: 50 ha
Soils: alluvial loam
Varieties planted: White—chardonnay; Red—cabernet sauvignon, shiraz
Leading wines: Yaldara Farms range, Julians range and Lakewood range
Notes: Though it has recently been sold by the Thumm family to publicly listed Simeon Wines, Yaldara remains a showplace, a chateau once called built on the ruins of a Barossa flour mill by its founder Hermann Thumm. Cellar door sales: daily 10am–5pm. There is also a bistro.

EDEN VALLEY REGION

The Eden Valley, which can be broadly described as the upland country above 400 metres in altitude adjacent to the Barossa's eastern boundary, shares its historical roots with the Barossa. In the 1840s, as the Barossa Ranges, it became the broadacre grazing country settled by the new colony's Anglo-Celtic gentry, two of whom—Joseph Gilbert at Pewsey Vale (1847) and Henry Evans at Evandale (1852)—subsequently established vineyards on their properties. At the perimeter of the new region (Angaston), Samuel Smith planted vines in 1849. The nomenclature 'Eden Valley' came into use in the 1860s as a township subdivision, settled by William Lillecrap. The region also became known ultimately as Eden Valley, but not until the 1950s.

In 1862, Johann Christian Henschke settled near present-day Keyneton, then called North Rhine. As part of his general farming activities, he too planted a small vineyard. At this time also, there were both large and small wineries and distilleries in the general area, especially Pewsey Vale which was gaining quite a reputation for its 'Hocks' and 'Rieslings', as well as 'its Shiraz and Carbonet [sic]' reds (Ebenezer Ward). The region expanded substantially during the nineteenth century but never threatened its lowland neighbour in production, nor in popular taste which was then beginning to favour fortified reds rather than table wines. By the 1920s the southern parts of Eden Valley had reverted to grazing; sheer economics had overwhelmed the production of delicate table wine. The Henschke family, however, maintained its link with wine throughout, though it too produced fortified wine in the economically adverse middle years of the twentieth century. The renascence of Eden Valley as a table wine producing area occurred in the 1950s when Cyril Henschke, one of the most skilled and enlightened winemakers of his age, began to market the region's delicate table wines in the eastern states. Soon after this, Eden Valley Rieslings, delicately crafted by the young John Vickery, were also available. Today, the region's forte is still riesling, though in its warmer northern parts, around Keyneton and Moculta, shiraz is extremely successful. Most cool area grape varieties are cultivated and its name is synonymous with style and delicacy.

Location: latitude 34°35'S, longitude 139°E, about 75 km north-east of Adelaide.
Elevation: 380–550 m

Topography and soils: Part of the northern Kanmantoo Trough, the region is hilly and exhibits a strong development of high-grade metamorphic rock amongst which are gneisses and gneissic granites. Its soils are chiefly grey-brown duplex or yellow podsolic skeletal, sharing common characteristics with many other south-eastern and south-western Australian vineyard soils, though in places the soils of the region tend towards infertile leached sands.

Climate: MJT 19.3°C, MAR na, HDD raw 1365, 1251 (cut off and adjusted for latitude and daily temperature range but not for vine sites) (Gladstones), AR (Henschke, Moculta) 534 mm (about 225 mm of which falls Oct–Apr), but further south and at greater altitude higher (Jim Irvine at Eden Valley reporting 680 mm pa), RH 39% (3pm Jan), AI na, SH 8.3. Eden Valley is a cool and dry region, having, in common with other higher altitude areas, great temperature variability, a relatively high number of sunshine hours and low summer rainfall and humidity.

The Valley is a natural drainage basin for two river systems, the North Para, flowing into the Barossa Valley, and the nostalgically named Rhine which flows eastwards into the Murray. Irrigation is a must in the Valley and reliance is placed chiefly on surface dams filled by rainfall rather than on bores, as groundwater flow is often limited, quite poor in quality and often saline. New surface water storage dams in areas which debouch into the Para system have now been limited by legislation to less than 5 million litres in capacity.

In contrast to the more conservative, warm area practices of the Barossa Valley, the winegrowers of Eden Valley have followed the advice of modern viticulturalists and adopted modern, cool area viticultural techniques such as canopy management, vine planting widths and row orientation. Sod culture, which has the benefits of min-imising erosion, water run-off and soil compaction, has also largely replaced clean cultivation. Both under-vine and inter-row mulching are also being utilised to retain moisture and build up nitrogenous material in the soil. In the Eden Valley, as in other cool areas, modern methods of vertical trellising such as Scott Henry and Smart Dyson, which minimise vine vigour and maximise sunlight penetration, are gaining in popularity while leaf plucking also assists in sunlight exposure. In its warmer northern areas, such as Moculta, however, the more traditional techniques of Barossan viticul-ture still exist. Pruning and harvesting are carried out chiefly by machine except on the steepest vineyard blocks.

Viticultural problems encountered in the Valley include botrytis and powdery mildew, which are counteracted by modern spray programs during the growing season. The region's grapes are also the unwelcome target of hungry birds, especially starlings, rosellas and crows, while young vines can be particularly delectable to rabbits and hares which raid from the protection of surrounding bushland. Other afflictions are the Light Brown Apple Moth and eutypa (die-back), a disease caused by a fungus that is often fatal to older vines and results from careless pruning. Spring frosts can also pose problems.

Harvest time: generally for all relevant varieties about 3–4 weeks later than on the floor of the Barossa Valley. Typical are shiraz second week in April, riesling end of April, cabernet sauvignon end of April.

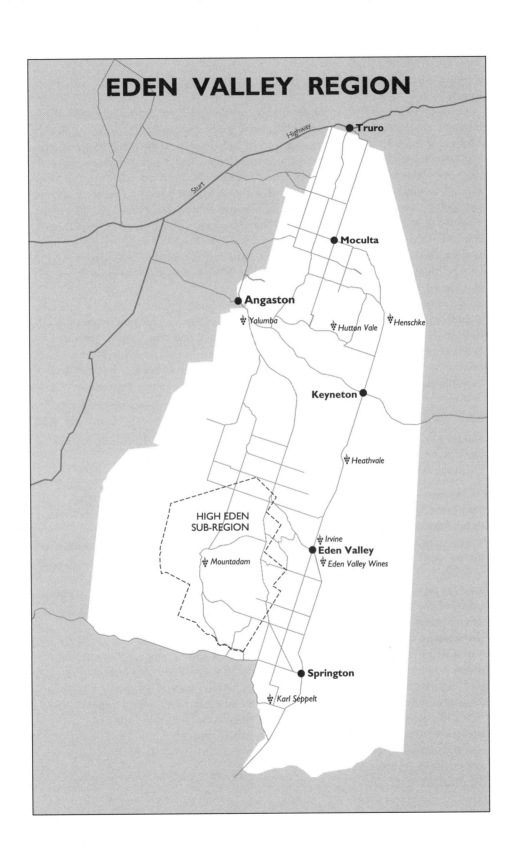

Principal varieties: (1998) White—riesling, chardonnay; Red—cabernet sauvignon, shiraz.

Total area: (1996) 452 ha (may err slightly on the low side due to vine area of the hundred of Moorooroo being included entirely in the Barossa Valley wine region).

Major wine styles: Except in the region's north and along its western and south-western edges, the Eden Valley must be classified generally as a white wine production area. In the north (the Moculta–Keyneton district), greater warmth and old vines produce marvellous fuller-bodied Shiraz reds (Hill of Grace, Mount Edelstone excel). Cabernet sauvignon grows very successfully on the western rim of the Valley (the Woodbury vineyard of Tollana and Mountadam are cases in point) with a fullness of berry flavour, atypical of the region as a whole which generally produces Cabernets of lighter berry and leaf flavours (Pewsey Vale). Pinot noir is the region's third most widely grown red variety. Many smaller producers such as Irvine, Mountadam and Karl Seppelt are also making sparkling wines of good standard.

With a reputation over a century old, the region produces what is generally regarded as Australia's classic riesling style, high flavoured yet elegant wines of floral-lime characters which age over a decade into 'honey and toast' styles, treasured by lovers of older rieslings.

Leading wineries and vineyards: Henschke, Leo Buring, Orlando, Tollana, Irvine, Mountadam, Yalumba.

Eden Valley Wines **R82**

Main Street, Eden Valley, SA 5235
Ph 08 8564 1111, Fax 08 8564 1110,
Email sales@edenvalleywines.com

Owners: Peter and Karolina Thompson
Chief winemaker: Peter Thompson
Year of foundation: 1990
Tonnes crushed on average each year: 150
Location: Eden Valley (winery), Springton (vineyard)
Area: 129 ha
Soils: sand over sandstone and quartz
Varieties planted: White—riesling; Red—cabernet sauvignon, merlot, shiraz
Leading wines: Eden Valley Wines Riesling, Shiraz
Notes: It is anticipated that production from this vineyard will increase to 800 tonnes by 2003. Cellar door sales: 7 days 10am–5pm except Good Friday and Christmas Day, but as most wine is presently sold overseas, cellar door may be closed due to lack of stock, so ring ahead.

Heathvale **R80**

Sawpit Gully Road, Keyneton, SA 5353
Ph/Fax 08 8564 8248

Owners: Trevor and Faye March
Chief winemaker: Paul Bailey (contract)
Year of foundation: vineyard 1987, first wine 1990, first commercial release 1997
Tonnes produced on average each year: 20, of which 7 are currently used for Heathvale wines
Area: 10 ha
Soils: sandy clay loam over sandstone saprolite of low fertility and about 60 cm deep, limited irrigation is used
Leading wines: Heathvale Chardonnay, Shiraz
Notes: A slow but purposeful re-establishment for Heathvale, where wine production ceased in the first decade of last century. It hopes to increase its production to 50 tonnes by 2003. Shiraz is my choice here. Tasting by appointment only.

Heggies

(see Yalumba)

Henschke **R91**

Moculta Road, Keyneton, SA 5353
Ph 08 8564 8223, Fax 08 8564 8294,
Email henschke@dove.net.au

Owner: C A Henschke & Co
Chief winemaker: Stephen Henschke
Year of foundation: 1868
Tonnes crushed on average each year: 550
Location: Keyneton
Area: 54 ha, (Eden Valley Vineyard) 32 ha,
(Mount Edelstone) 16 ha, (Hill of Grace) 6 ha
Soils: Eden Valley, sandy loam over gravel and
bedrock; Mount Edelstone, deep sandy loam,
red podsols over clay loam; Hill of Grace,
alluvial sandy loam over clay
Varieties planted: (Eden Valley Vineyard):
White—chardonnay, gewurztraminer, riesling,
sauvignon blanc, semillon; Red—cabernet
franc, cabernet sauvignon, merlot, shiraz.
(Mount Edelstone) White—none; Red—shiraz.
(Hill of Grace) White—riesling, semillon;
Red—shiraz
Leading wines: Henschke Hill of Grace, Mount
Edelstone, Julius Eden Valley Riesling, Louis
Eden Valley Semillon, Cyril Henschke Cabernet
Sauvignon
Notes: A pioneer maker in the Eden Valley,
Henschke is one of the older family-owned
wine companies in Australia and a famous
name indeed for its Shiraz, the magnificent Hill
of Grace and marvellous Mount Edelstone,
whose greatness was initiated by the late Cyril
Henschke. Since his own accession as
winemaker, Stephen Henschke has
commemorated his father with the Cyril
Henschke Cabernet Sauvignon, a powerful but
very stylish red. Today Stephen is one of
Australia's leading winemakers and his wife,
Pru, is an eminent viticulturist. A must for any
lover of superb reds. Cellar door sales:

weekdays 9am–4.30pm, Sat 9am–12 noon,
public holidays 10am–3pm, closed Sundays,
Good Friday and Christmas Day.

Hill-Smith Estate

(see Yalumba)

Hutton Vale Vineyard **NR**

Stone Jar Road, Angaston, SA 5353
Ph 08 8564 8270, Fax 08 8564 8385,
Email angas@dove.net.au

Owners: Jan and John Angas
Chief winemakers: David Powell and Chris
Ringland (contract)
Year of foundation: vineyard 1910, first
vintage 1987, first release 1994
Tonnes produced on average each year: 90,
of which 4 are used for Hutton Vale wines
Area: 27 ha
Soils: red-brown earths over clay, neutral pH
Varieties planted: White—riesling;
Red—cabernet sauvignon, grenache intermixed
with a few mataro (mourvedre), shiraz
Leading wines: Hutton Vale Shiraz, Riesling,
Grenache-Mataro
Notes: George Fife Angas, ancestor of John
Angas, was the prime mover of the foundation
of South Australia and organiser of much of
the emigration to the colony. Though the
Angas family was interested in wine during the
19th century, its first vineyards were not
planted until the early 20th, when Hutton Vale
and another well-known vineyard, Mount
Edelstone, were established. Mount Edelstone
was later sold to the Henschke family and has
become famous throughout Australia in the
years since. So Hutton Vale has a very solid
historical foundation. Cellar door sales by
appointment only.

Irvine R86

Springhill Vineyard, Basil Roeslers Road,
Eden Valley, SA 5235
Ph/Fax 08 8564 1046

Owner: Marjorie Irvine
Chief winemaker: James Irvine
Year of foundation: 1980
Tonnes crushed on average each year: 95, of
which 65 are used for Irvine labels
Location: Eden Valley
Area: 14 ha
Soils: grey-brown podsols, really a gravel
saddle with quartz reefs and very shallow top
soils, which are ancient and quite poor in
fertility but well-drained and highly acidic
Varieties planted: White—chardonnay, meslier,
pinot gris; Red—merlot, zinfandel
Leading wines: Irvine Grand Merlot, Eden Crest
Merlot
Notes: As well as being an excellent winemaker,
whose consulting skills are widely used
throughout the Barossa and Eden Valleys and
other places, Jim Irvine is nothing if not a merlot
enthusiast, whose passion for the variety began
with a taste of Chateau Petrus years ago. Jim
does not blend his merlot with cabernet
sauvignon as a matter of course, but carefully
scrutinises the quality of each batch, keeping
the best separate. This has resulted in Irvine
Grand Merlots winning several international
prizes. As a style, Irvine Grand Merlot does total
justice to the word 'grand'. It is big in every
sense, from the expressively complex plummy
nose to the big plum-berry and oak flavours and
the noticeable tannins on finish. It is not a wine
to be trifled with. Of course Jim produces a
fascinating red bubbly from merlot but also a
sparkler from the rare variety meslier, a highly
acid white variety from the Aube region of
Champagne. This, too, is wine which must be
experienced. Cellar door sales at Eden Valley
Hotel, Eden Valley where tastings of Irvine wines
are free. Usual hotel hours.

Karl Seppelt (formerly Grand Cru) R82

Dewell's Road, Springton, SA 5235
Ph 08 8568 2378, Fax 08 8568 2799

Owners: Karl and Lotte Seppelt
Chief winemaker: Karl Seppelt and contract
Year of foundation: 1981
Tonnes crushed on average each year: 85,
about 40 of which are used for Karl Seppelt
wines
Location: Springton
Area: 11 ha
Soils: schist–yellow grey loam duplex podsolic
skeletal rocks
Varieties planted: White—chardonnay;
Red—cabernet sauvignon, merlot, meunier,
pinot noir
Leading wines: Karl Seppelt Chardonnay,
Cabernet Sauvignon, Chardonnay Brut
Notes: Australian wine owes a great debt to
Karl Seppelt, who has spent all his working life
in the wine industry. It was he who helped
'discover' the Drumborg and Padthaway wine
regions in the early 1960s. His vineyard, drip
irrigated with salt-free water and on the
southern boundary of the Eden Valley region,
is only a kilometre away from the Adelaide
Hills region. Karl believes it shares more
climatic common ground with the latter than
the former and was intended, he says, as a
retirement hobby. His vineyard has since
become much more and, with 60 tonnes of his
own fruit used for his own wines, is now quite
a large boutique. The Chardonnay is a lightly
wooded style. The Cabernet in warm years can
be quite powerful and concentrated, but
usually softens into an accessible drinking style
after 4–5 years' cellaring. The sparkling wines
are also consistent medal winners. There are
also fortified reds (vintage and tawny 'ports')
and a fino 'sherry'. Cellar door sales: 7 days
10am–5pm.

Leo Buring (vineyard only) R90

Tanunda Road, Nuriootpa, SA 5355

Owner: Southcorp Wines
Chief winemaker: John Duval
Year of establishment: 1931
Tonnes produced on average each year: not
disclosed but estimated at 550
Location: High Eden Vineyard, Eden Valley
Area: 58 ha
Soils: variations of three podsolics: sand over
sandy loam; sandy loam over clay; sandy loam
over mottled clay overlying impermeable
sandstone
Varieties planted: White—chardonnay, riesling,
sauvignon blanc; Red—pinot noir
Leading wines: Leo Buring Leonay, Show
Reserve Rieslings, Eden Valley Riesling
Notes: John Vickery, as acclaimed for his
Rieslings as the late Max Schubert was for his
Grange Hermitage, began his Riesling-
making career with the original Leo Buring.
The name Buring is consonant with Riesling
quality in Australia and much of Australia's
best Riesling originates in the Eden Valley.
Cellar door sales: see Penfolds Nuriootpa
(Barossa Valley).

Mountadam R86

High Eden Ridge, Eden Valley, SA 5235
Ph 08 8564 1101, Fax 08 8564 1064
(Adelaide office Ph 08 8361 3300,
Fax 08 8361 3400)

Owner: Cape Mentelle Vineyards
Chief winemaker: Andrew Ewart
Year of foundation: 1972
Tonnes produced on average each year: 300
(fruit is purchased for other brands made at
the winery)
Location: High Eden, Eden Valley
Area: 50 ha
Soils: coarse podsolic sand over schist and
quartz, quite shallow and free-draining
Varieties planted: White—chardonnay, pinot

gris, viognier; Red—cabernet sauvignon,
merlot, pinot noir
Leading wines: Mountadam Chardonnay,
Cabernet, The Red (a blend of cabernet
sauvignon and merlot). Other brands are David
Wynn and Eden Ridge
Notes: Mountadam, founded in 1972 by the
late David Wynn, long recognised as the
rescuer and resuscitator of present-day
Coonawarra, was, since its first vintage,
carried on by his son Adam, who created a
great reputation for its Chardonnay.
Mountadam was sold recently to Cape
Mentelle Vineyards, itself a subsidiary of the
giant Moet Hennessy Louis Vuitton Group.
Adam Wynn will become Executive Chairman
of Mountadam with special emphasis on the
development of its export markets. Cellar door
sales: 11am–4pm each day, closed Good
Friday and Christmas Day.

Orlando (vineyard only) R90

Karra Yerta Road, Eden Valley, SA 5235

Owner: Orlando Wyndham Pty Ltd
Chief winemaker: (white) Philip Laffer
Year of foundation: 1968
Tonnes crushed on average each year: 215
Locations: Eden Valley (2)
Area: 46.04 ha, Karra Yerta Road, Eden Valley
(44.44 ha) and Steingarten (1.6 ha)
Soils: Karra Yerta, sandy loam over weathered
sandy clay; Steingarten, decomposed schisty
rock
Varieties planted: White—riesling, traminer;
Red—none
Leading wines: St Helga Riesling, Steingarten
Riesling, Jacob's Creek Riesling (part)
Notes: Orlando is blessed by two outstanding
Rieslings from this Region. St Helga is from the
Karra Yerta Road vineyard which is one of the
most reliable Eden Valley sites, always
producing high quality Riesling. Steingarten
Riesling is sourced from its eponymous Eden
Valley vineyard but regrettably is available only

in minute quantities. Cellar door sales: see
Orlando Barossa entry.

Pewsey Vale

(see Yalumba)

Southcorp Wines
(vineyard only) NR

Stonegarden Vineyard, Eden Valley,
SA 5235

Owner: Southcorp Wines (leased for a term of
10 years which commenced in November
1995)
Chief winemaker: John Duval
Year of foundation: (lease) 1995
Tonnes produced on average each year: not
disclosed but estimated at 150
Location: Eden Valley (vineyard)
Area: 21 ha
Soils: thin sandy soils with rocky outcrops
Varieties planted: White—riesling, white
frontignan; Red—cabernet sauvignon,
grenache (100 year old bush vines), shiraz
Leading wines: its production is utilised
generally by the many wines of the group.

Tollana R87

Tanunda Road, Nuriootpa, SA 5355

Owner: Southcorp Wines
Chief winemaker: John Duval
Year of foundation: 1888 (as Tolley, Scott and
Tolley)
Tonnes produced on average each year: 1200
Locations: vineyards at Roeslers Estate Eden
Valley and Woodbury Estate, High Eden
Area: 120 ha, Roeslers (14.4 ha) and
Woodbury (105.6 ha)
Soils: similar to Leo Buring soils
Varieties planted: (Roeslers) White—riesling,
sauvignon blanc, semillon; Red—meunier,
shiraz. (Woodbury) White—chardonnay,
gewurztraminer, riesling; Red—cabernet
sauvignon, pinot noir, shiraz

Leading wines: The Tollana range of Eden
Valley wines
Notes: Tollana is one of the lesser-known
treasures of Southcorp. Its Cabernet Sauvignon
TR222 and its Botrytis Riesling are never less
than very good. Cellar door sales: as for
Penfolds Barossa.

Wolf Blass (vineyards only)

(see Barossa Valley entry)

Yalumba R85

(see also Coonawarra, Koppamurra and
Riverland SA)
Eden Valley Road, Angaston, SA 5353
Ph 08 8561 3200, Fax 08 8561 3393

Owners: Hill Smith family
Chief winemaker: Brian Walsh
Year of foundation: 1849
Tonnes crushed on average each year: 22 500
Locations: Angaston (the winery sits in the
Eden Valley wine region on the boundary of
the Barossa Valley region), Eden Valley,
Coonawarra, Koppamurra, Oxford Landing
(Qualco) est 1958, Barossa Valley—the Nursery
Vineyard (a relocation of the vine nursery and
its associated propagating and grafting
activities formerly at Angaston. This block also
contains old bush trained grenache vines).

i) Angaston vineyards

(Shorts and Old Triangle)

Tonnes crushed on average each year: 55
(aggregated)
Location: Angaston
Area: 7.8 ha (Shorts), 3.25 ha (Old Triangle, all
shiraz)
Soils: red-brown earth over clay limestone base
Varieties planted: (Shorts) White—pinot gris,
viognier; Red—cabernet sauvignon, shiraz.
(Old Triangle) White—none; Red—shiraz
Leading wines: none specified

ii) Heggies (vineyard only) **R84**

off Flaxman's Valley Road, Eden Valley, SA 5253

Chief winemaker: Hugh Reimers
Year of foundation: 1971
Tonnes crushed on average each year: 300
Location: Eden Valley
Area: 48.5 ha
Soils: grey loam over gravel clay base with rocky outcrops
Varieties planted: White—chardonnay, riesling, viognier; Red—merlot, pinot noir
Leading wines: Heggies Vineyard wines

iii) Hill-Smith Estate (vineyard only) **R83**

off Flaxman's Valley Road, Eden Valley, SA 5253

Chief winemaker: Hugh Reimers
Year of foundation: 1971
Tonnes crushed on average each year: 150
Location: Eden Valley
Area: 23.25 ha
Soils: grey loam over gravel
Varieties planted: White—chardonnay, sauvignon blanc; Red—none
Leading wines: Hill-Smith Estate wines

iv) Pewsey Vale (vineyard only) **R87**

Brownes Road, Eden Valley, SA 5235

Chief winemaker: Louisa Rose
Year of foundation: 1847 (the original Pewsey Vale ceased production about 1927); re-established 1963
Tonnes crushed on average each year: 350
Location: Eden Valley
Area: 58.6 ha
Soils: grey loam over gravel and clay
Varieties planted: White—riesling; Red—cabernet sauvignon
Leading wines: the Pewsey Vale Vineyard wines

v) Robert Hill-Smith Vineyard (vineyard only)

Valley and Eden Valley Roads, Angaston

Year of foundation: 1998
Tonnes produced on average each year: not yet bearing
Location: Eden Valley
Area: 6 ha
Soils: red-brown earth over clay
Varieties planted: White—none; Red—shiraz
Leading wines: none specified

Notes: Yalumba is the oldest family owned wine company in Australia. Its founder, Samuel Smith, was a Dorsetshire brewer who settled near Angaston in 1848 and ultimately prospered. His was a typical pioneer's story: very little initial capital but, after working as an orchardist for George Fife Angas, saved enough to buy a smallholding (12 ha) and plant a small vineyard. A trek to the goldfields followed, and modest success after great effort. More land was purchased and some capital improvements made. By the late 1880s, Yalumba had gained quite a reputation for its 'port', which reflected the contemporary change in public taste to stronger reds and fortified wines. So Yalumba continued into the twentieth century, producing strong reds and fortifieds to satisfy its local and overseas markets, though some table wines were made for the then small band of enthusiasts. By 1960 Yalumba, in common with the other established wine companies of that time, was preparing for a table wine revival. As Joseph Gilbert had over a century earlier, it saw its opportunity in Pewsey Vale in the Barossa Ranges, establishing its vineyard there in 1963. Later, in 1971, Yalumba planted its two other 'Hills' vineyards and has subsequently established vineyards at Coonawarra and Koppamurra (see entries). Today it remains one of the larger family-owned Australian wine companies, crushing about 22 500 tonnes of grapes annually. All wines of the company are produced and sold at its Angaston winery. Cellar door sales: weekdays 8.30am–5pm, Saturdays and public holidays 10am–5pm, Sundays 12 noon–5pm.

High Eden Sub-region

Much of the general history of the High Eden Sub-region has been dealt with above. Suffice it to say that one Joseph Gilbert, who arrived in Adelaide in 1839, took advantage of the 'Special Survey' provisions of the South Australian Company to apply, with one Edward Rowland, for the special survey of 15 000 acres (about 6000 ha) in the Barossa Ranges to buy any of the 80 acre (32 ha) blocks within the survey up to 4000 acres (1600 ha) for $2 an acre (i.e. $5 a ha) and to lease the rest for three years at a low rental. Gilbert gave his portion of the survey the name Pewsey Vale after the Vale of Pewsey in Wiltshire where he had lived prior to his arrival in South Australia. 'Pewsey Vale' soon became the centre of various farming activities. Within a decade there were a small vineyard and winery, an orchard and various cash crops such as wheat, barley, maize and potatoes. By the mid-1850s Gilbert's wines began to be noticed. In 1854, he was the most successful exhibitor at the Adelaide Show, his brandy being described as 'a splendid style'. In 1867 Gilbert received a special medal awarded by the Melbourne Intercolonial Wine Exhibition for 'the general excellence of his wines and in recognition of his services and success as a vigneron'. Gilbert's energy was the foundation of the sub-region's wine industry at least until the 1920s when economics and changes of taste forced the discontinuance of the table wines of Pewsey Vale. Pewsey Vale, of course, was to be re-born in the early 1960s when the Angas Parsons and Hill-Smith families took a momentous decision to re-establish vineyards there. The Hill-Smith family also established Hill-Smith Estate some two kilometres to the north-west about the same time. However, it was David Wynn who created the name 'High Eden' when Wynn's planted its High Eden Estate in the early 1970s, and he then established Mountadam in 1972. The Hill-Smith family were again active at this time in planting Heggies, as was Tollana in setting up Woodbury Estate soon after (1973). It was at this time that the future of the Eden Valley and High Eden was assured. Southcorp now own both High Eden and Woodbury and they are the provenance respectively of the best fruit for its Leo Buring and Tollana brands. Mountadam is presently the only winery within the sub-region.

Location: latitude 34°45'S, longitude 139°02'E, about 55–60 km north-east of Adelaide
Elevation: from south (Springton Hill) along High Eden Ridge to north (Heggies) 480–540 metres; from High Eden Ridge (the north–south spine of the sub-region) the altitude slopes down to 450 metres on both the western and eastern sides
Topography and soils: This is an area of hilly country consisting of high ridges and long tapering slopes with many steep slopes. At least 80 per cent of High Eden soil types consist of yellow podsols which are coarse-textured often loose sandy topsoil 25–30 cm thick, over mottled yellow, red and grey, soapy clay 76–152 cm thick passing to pallid

zone and/or decomposed rock materials. Such subsoils often impede water movement and restrict root growth to some extent. Waterlogging can occur in the surface soil 8–30 cm immediately on top of the subsoil. Thus these soils in dry seasons may drought-stress vines because there is little or no moisture reserve in the deeper subsoils. The soils are slightly to moderately acidic with low natural organic matter. There are low or very low levels of phosphate, potassium, calcium, magnesium and molybdenum. Erosion hazard: sheet—moderate; gully—slight; wind—slight.

Of the balance of the subregion's soils, there are three main types:

1 meadow podsols which are typically light brownish-grey sand topsoil 38–46 cm thick over a white sand subsurface soil 46–53 cm thick over yellow-brown stiff clay about 15 cm thick usually over fine sandy clay to a depth over 183 cm. Such soils are typically located on gently sloping coalescing creek flood plains. Such soils have low nutrient element reserves and are acidic. Erosion hazard: wind—moderate to severe.

2 skeletal soils which are found on the tops and upper slopes of steep ridges and have no marked contrast between surface soil and subsoil. They are light grey-brown to grey loose sand over broken rock at about 30–38 cm depth. The very high fine sand and low clay content render this soil very quickly drought-stressed and liable to erosion. They are acidic and low in fertility. Erosion hazard: sheet—moderate; gully—slight; wind—slight.

3 ground-water podsols which are found in creek flood plains, consisting of grey loose sand about 15 cm thick over a bleached horizon passing to light yellow sands with rusty brown streaks and variable coffee rock bands or nodules 53–61 cm deep. There is a high seasonal variation in moisture in such soils ranging from very wet with a high water table to very dry. They are slightly acidic. Seasonal waterlogging is intensified in low-lying areas. The sandy alluvial soils are very liable to drought-stress. Such soils have low nutrient reserves. Erosion hazard: wind—moderate to severe with deposition from adjacent higher areas perhaps proving a difficulty.

In view of the difficult soils mentioned above, vineyard management techniques have been developed to minimise erosion and water run-off. Thus contour planting is widely used in the subregion's vineyards. Indeed some of the largest contour-planted vineyards in the Southern Hemisphere are to be seen in High Eden. Mulching to build organic matter in the soils and to conserve moisture in the predominantly sandy soils is also widely practised. Besides the hazards of erosion already mentioned, birds whether native or imported present a problem immediately before harvest, as do rabbits and hares in newly planted or young vineyards.

Climate: (High Eden) MJT 17.6°C, MAR na, HDD raw 1342, AR 730 mm (Oct–Apr na), RH na, AI na, SH na. High winds during floraison pose a danger during October as these are often accompanied by cold wet weather, resulting in poor fruit set and correspondingly low yields. Thus windbreaks or trellising designed to minimise wind damage for new or even older vineyards may be advisable.

Irrigation requirements within High Eden are high primarily because of the incidence of winter rainfall and the poor water-retention capacity of the subregional soils. These requirements are mostly met by the use of surface water dams (which recharge from run-off) for trickle irrigation, as ground water is limited in quantity and often saline in quality. However, surface water dams have been restricted to domestic and stock dams of less than 5 million litres in capacity without local government approval, so future vineyard development in the subregion is now restricted.

Harvest time: (these dates sometimes vary according to seasonal conditions and vineyard aspect) chardonnay first week of April, riesling third week of April, shiraz fourth week of April, cabernet sauvignon fourth week of April.

Principal varieties: White—riesling, chardonnay; Red—cabernet sauvignon, shiraz

Major wine styles: This sub-region and the surrounding Eden Valley region are famous for Riesling, exemplified by Leo Buring and Tollana. Mountadam has built a good reputation for Chardonnay, while both Tollana and Mountadam have made some excellent Cabernets over recent years.

🍇 Cabernet Sauvignon & Co

Cabernet sauvignon is a grape variety that has received universal recognition. In Bordeaux where it originated, it is blended to a greater or lesser extent with its cohabitant, merlot, but there is often a leavening of its other colleagues, cabernet franc, malbec and petit verdot. It has been present in Australia since 1832, but the migration of its companions, with the exception of malbec, has been much more recent. Merlot and cabernet franc have been present in Australia barely twenty years and petit verdot is even newer. So it is scarcely remarkable that we have not yet seen the best of them in blends. But we are beginning to see them.

At the same time as the acclimatisation of these 'new' varieties, we have witnessed the creation in one case and the rebirth and consolidation in other cases of 'cooler' wine-growing areas. Coonawarra has expanded vastly in the past 30 years. We have seen the growth of Margaret River as one of Australia's premium areas. Mount Barker is also widely respected and the Yarra Valley has been reborn. In all four areas, cabernet sauvignon is a major variety and there is a certain rivalry among the areas for cabernet supremacy. As the prize for such supremacy is increased public recognition and acceptance of that area (and greater sales), it is necessary to examine the cabernet styles of each of the regions to see how they differ. As each has also from time to time made claims to be Australia's 'Medoc', we should examine the significant climate factors of each for any justification of that claim.

The table shows comparisons between the altitudes, the relevant mean daily temperatures, effective degree days, annual mean rainfall, relative humidity and total sunshine hours.

Altitude (m)	47	59	90	130	253
Daily mean temp (°C)	Apr 11.7	Oct 12.6	13.5	13.0	13.1
	May 15.4	Nov 14.8	15.8	15.2	15.6
	Jun 18.3	Dec 17.0	18.0	17.0	17.6
	Jul 20.5	Jan 19.3	20.0	17.9	19.0
	Aug 20.5	Feb 19.6	20.3	18.2	19.0
	Sept 18.3	Mar 17.4	18.8	16.8	17.7
	Oct 13.3	Apr 14.5	16.5	13.3	15.7
Effective degree days adjusted for vine sites	1453	1333	1557	1352	1488

	Medoc	Coonawarra	Margaret River	Yarra Valley (Healesville)	Mt Barker (WA)
Average annual rainfall (mm)					
Apr–Oct	427	Oct–Apr 257	274	597	285
Nov–Mar	406	May–Sept 371	918	411	471
Total	833	628	1192	1008	756
Relative humidity (July)	59% (3pm)	48% (Jan)	56%	57%* (9am Jan)	54%
Sunshine hours	1472	1593	1626	1490	1518

Note: All data according to Gladstones, *Viticulture and Environment*, except for Yarra Valley relative humidity*.

Such comparisons prove little, however, and only tend to emphasise differences rather than similarities. In degree day terms, both Coonawarra and the Yarra Valley are much cooler than the Medoc, while Margaret River is substantially warmer. Mount Barker is closest in degree days, but greater in total sunlight hours. In that respect, the Medoc and the Yarra Valley are least blessed but close, while Coonawarra and Margaret River enjoy a superiority. Both the Medoc and Margaret River have similarities in relative humidity. Margaret River would otherwise be a paradise for botrytis were it not for its dry summer, a condition which does not always come to the rescue of the Yarra Valley. It should also be noted that the Medoc warms much more quickly than any comparable Australian site, for example, 66 degree days in April which virtually triples in May to 181. Coonawarra heat degree days in October (86) are not quite doubled by November and in cooling rates too the Medoc falls more rapidly than Coonawarra (Medoc Sept—253, Oct—133; Coonawarra March—224, Apr—142), though the differences in corresponding latitudes (Coonawarra is more than 5 degrees closer to the equator than the Medoc) would certainly have an influence.

In broad terms there are similarities between the Medoc and Coonawarra. In location, both are reasonably close to the sea, though the Medoc is a peninsula subject to greater air moisture and therefore subject to less frost risk. Altitudes are similar and terrains of both are flat. Coonawarra is on the whole much drier and more liable to frost after budburst; the Medoc warms more quickly; the soils are quite different in nature though similar in drainage (well-drained terra rossa above limestone in the case of Coonawarra's best country and, on the whole, well-drained silty pebbly alluvial soils on a clayey subsoil in the case of Medoc). So perhaps we may simply conclude our climate study with 'Vive la difference!'. If Australia cannot pretend to any 'Medoc' homoclimes, we do at least have magnificent but distinct cabernet styles of our own from the four Australian regions mentioned.

In Margaret River, David Hohnen makes Cape Mentelle Cabernet Sauvignon from the original 1970 five-hectare planting and believes that the best Margaret River Cabernet should be picked ripe but equally should retain its acid balance. Irrigation has helped produce a balanced, stress-free wine, which means good structure, but soft tannins. He leaves his wine in contact with skins for 3–4 weeks. During this time, the tannins have increased but also have softened and become integrated. After primary fermentation, the wine is racked and inoculated to induce malolactic fermentation and then placed in oak, all of which is French and three-quarters of it new. In the following spring after malo is complete, the wine is racked once more and blended into approximately its final form. After this assemblage, it is returned to oak, where it remains for a further fifteen to eighteen months in a temperature-controlled humidified environment, receiving further rackings when necessary. After about eighteen months, it is finally assembled, coarsely filtered and bottled. It is bottle-matured for about two years and released between three and four years of age, designed to be drunk after 10 years and to live for 20. The factor that separates Margaret River from the rest, according to David, is a mulberry, blackberry leafiness that pervades its flavour together with a full, but never harsh tannic finish.

In Coonawarra, Ralph Fowler, formerly of Leconfield, seeks complexity in Cabernet Sauvignon. Simple pleasant fruitiness should be no part of Coonawarra cabernet sauvignon. He makes four or five pickings based on flavour criteria. He seeks and usually finds a mulberry character in the early flavour profile of Coonawarra cabernet. Aromas at this stage are predominantly 'rose-petal' and the baume (although Ralph does not regard this as a criterion) is between 11.5 and 12 degrees. This picking usually accounts for about 20% of the crop. At the next level of flavour ripeness (usually between 12.5 and 13 degrees), he notices berry-cassis flavours with similar aromas and picks about 40% of the fruit. Finally at super-maturity (13 degrees plus), he finds liquorice and leather characters and picks the balance at this point. As for merlot, he uses this variety as an 'alcohol' additive, ripening it as much as possible. It usually forms between 6% and 15% of the final wine. His other chosen variety, petit verdot, with its quite distinct 'green' flavours, ripens very late anyway and forms 4% to 7%. Ralph leaves a part of the wine macerating on skins for 4–5 weeks. This depends on vintage. The oak used is predominantly American (about 55%) and the rest French. The early picked cabernet is put into older oak, which does not dominate its more delicate flavours; the riper material is put into new. Over a period of about 3 months after vintage, the various parcels of wine, including merlot and petit verdot, are put together. The wine then spends at least 15 more months in barrel and is ready to bottle at 20 months of age. A zero sulfur regime is maintained during barrel maturation, but the wine before bottling receives about 20 parts per million. Ralph expects such a wine to come to maturity between 4 and 7 years of age depending on vintage and to live about 15 years. To him, Coonawarra's input into cabernet sauvignon is its 'terroir' and in that terroir there is an intensity of berry and earth flavour which, in Bordeaux terms, I liken to Pauillac.

Another famous Margaret River maker, Vanya Cullen, picks her Cabernet-Merlot on flavour and to a certain extent on baume. The flavours sought are blackcurrant and dark fruit. The baume of such fruit is usually 13 degrees plus. The fruit is crushed conventionally as well as whole berries being added to the must.

Just before completion of fermentation half is run off into barrels at 2 degrees Be to finish its ferment. The other half is fermented out in vat and allowed to macerate for 4–6 weeks in tank. Each portion is inoculated to induce malolactic fermentation. After completion of malo, the wines are blended and put into medium toast Nevers oak, about 40% of which is new and the rest one or two years old. Coopers used are usually Dargaud & Jaegle, Seguin Moreau and Taransaud. The wines spend about 18 months in wood, are racked three times during that period, then egg-white fined and lightly filtered before bottling. The wines receive a further 6 months in bottle before release.

Typically a Cullen Margaret River Cabernet Merlot contains 60% cabernet sauvignon, 25% merlot and 5% cabernet franc, leaving 10% 'swinging' (i.e. varietal proportions may be adjusted according to vintage quality). Petit verdot is also being used in small quantities. Vanya sees a typical Cabernet Merlot as having 'dark fruit flavours, chocolatey oak and good texture'. It also has a life expectancy of 15–20 years.

At Coldstream Hills in the Yarra Valley, very little has changed since the retirement of James Halliday. The Reserve Cabernet is still picked from the north-east-facing G Block of the Amphitheatre Vineyard. The fruit is picked on flavour when intense blackcurrant/herbal characters are detected on nose and palate. The baume of the fruit so picked can vary between 12.5 and 13.5 degrees. About half of the fruit is crushed into open fermenters and fermented down to near dryness (1°–2° Be) and then run off into new oak to finish. The balance is allowed to remain in closed vats fermenting to dryness and remaining in contact with skins for 7–14 days according to vintage. On completion of fermentation each batch is pressed and then inoculated to undergo malolactic fermentation. Rackings take place at least twice before assemblage the following summer, when any merlot that is deemed good enough is added. The assembled wine is then returned to oak until filtration, and bottling when the wine is two years old. The oak used is Seguin Moreau 'Haut Brion' and Dargaux et Jaegli Allier and Nevers. What is sought is a ripe berry and blackcurrant nose with a slight herbal character and a similarly flavoursome palate with length and fine tannins and a dry savoury finish.

✾ LIMESTONE COAST ZONE

The Limestone Coast is aptly named, for it mostly encompasses ancient sea beds of the Southern Ocean. Its registered wine regions are Coonawarra, Mount Benson and Padthaway. Wrattonbully is interim-registered.

ROBE RANGES

An application for a regional geographical indication in this name has been lodged in respect of the area immediately to the south of the present Mount Benson region, where there is a substantial Southcorp vineyard of 240 ha. Its soils are generally sandy loam or loamy sand over limestone. There are also large areas of rendzina (shallow brownish soils over limestone 'calcrete') and small pockets of siliceous sands. The climate is very similar to that of the Mount Benson region. Chief varieties planted here are chardonnay in white and cabernet sauvignon, merlot and shiraz in reds. For Southcorp wines, most of the fruit appears in Lindemans Limestone Coast range.

BORDERTOWN

Bordertown is also part of the Limestone Coast zone. The area is irrigated. There are two major vineyards in the general area. As this area is likely to become a region, some basic climatic detail is given: MJT 22°C, MAR 12.3°C, HDD na, AR 557 mm, AI 358 mm, RH 48%.

Cuppa Cup Vineyard
(vineyard only) **NR**
Bordertown, SA 5268

Owner/manager: Southcorp Wines
Chief winemaker: various winemakers within Southcorp Wines
Year of foundation: 1988
Tonnes crushed on average each year: not disclosed but estimated at 4500, all of which are used in wines of the Southcorp Wines group
Location: Bordertown
Area: 380 ha

Soils: moderately fertile shallow soils over limestone rock or rubble. Soil types differ but include a range of red and brown loams and sandy loams. Well-drained. New plantings have been mounded to maximise the amount of topsoil
Varieties planted: White—chardonnay; Red—cabernet sauvignon, merlot
Leading wines: various Lindeman and Penfolds premium and semi-premium wines
Notes: This is a valued contributor to some of Southcorp's leading wines. There are no local cellar door sales.

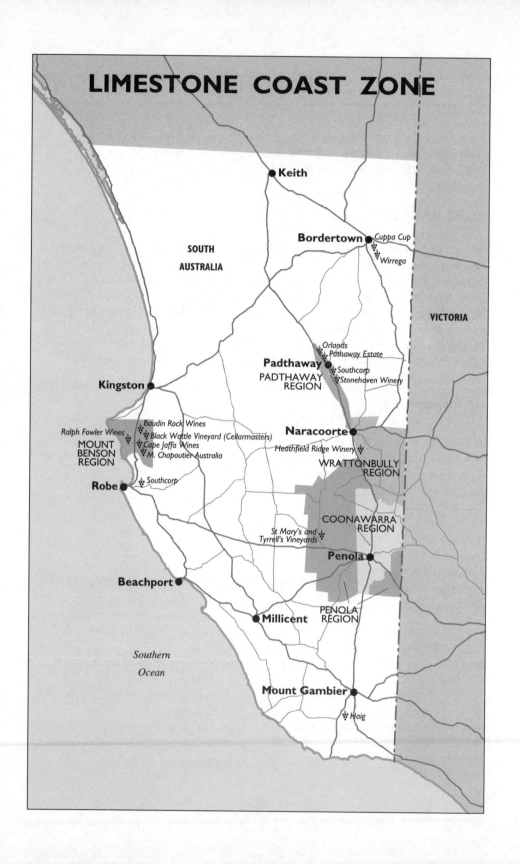

LIMESTONE COAST ZONE

● **Keith**

Bordertown ● 🍇 *Cuppa Cup*
🍇 *Wirrega*

SOUTH

AUSTRALIA

VICTORIA

Orlands
🍇 *Pathaway Estate*
Padthaway 🍇 *Southcorp*
🍇 *Stonehaven Winery*
PADTHAWAY
REGION

Kingston ●

Baudin Rock Wines
Ralph Fowler Wines 🍇 🍇 *Black Wattle Vineyard (Cellarmasters)*
MOUNT 🍇 *Cape Jaffa Wines*
BENSON 🍇 *M. Chapoutier Australia*
REGION

Naracoorte ● 🍇

Heathfield Ridge Winery

WRATTONBULLY
REGION

Robe ● 🍇 *Southcorp*

COONAWARRA
REGION

St Mary's and 🍇
Tyrrell's Vineyards

Penola ●

Beachport ●

PENOLA
REGION

Millicent ●

Southern

Ocean

Mount Gambier ●

🍇 *Haig*

Wirrega Vineyard
(vineyard only)   🍇 **NR**

Mundulla, SA 5270 (about 14 km south-west of Bordertown)

Owners: various syndicates
Manager: Gino Melino
Chief winemaker: Ben Glaetzer (about 1/3 of the fruit grown is made into Wirrega Vineyard wine, which is exported and also marketed in Australia; the majority of fruit is sold to various wineries)
Year of foundation: 1994
Tonnes crushed on average each year: vineyard not yet in full bearing but 2300 tonnes is anticipated

Location: Mundulla
Area: 166 ha
Soils: red duplex over limestone marl, drip irrigated
Varieties planted: White—chardonnay, sauvignon blanc, semillon, verdelho; Red—cabernet sauvignon, merlot, petit verdot, shiraz
Leading wines: fruit sold to various winemakers
Notes: Wirrega Vineyards has been exporting successfully for several years. It is presently seeking to break into the Australian market. No cellar door sales.

COONAWARRA REGION

Coonawarra is certainly the most famous cabernet sauvignon region in Australia and, some would argue, the most renowned wine region in Australia per se. Europeans first touched on the general area about 1800, when Lieutenant James Grant named two inland peaks Mount Schank and Mount Gambier. A closer inspection of the region was made about two years later when Lieutenant Matthew Flinders of HMS *Investigator* and Nicholas Baudin of the *Geographe* mapped the coast from their respective ships. The general area was then forgotten, except by sealing boats and escaped convicts, for over 40 years. After all it was unprepossessing country, predominantly swampy in summer and flooded in winter. Its first squatter at what was to become Penola was Alexander Cameron, who was granted the first occupational licence in south-east South Australia in 1844. He ran considerable numbers of sheep, for wool production was booming and the English midland and northern towns, in the midst of the Industrial Revolution, could scarcely get enough. The first settlers on the Yallum lease to the west of Penola were the Austins, who later sold to the Wells. In October 1861, they resold to John Riddoch, who continued to populate it with sheep.

Like many thousands of others, the Scottish-born Riddoch arrived, aged 25, in the colony of Victoria in 1852, seeking gold. He found it, after initial fossicking success, basically in supplying the needs of miners on the goldfields and was a prosperous merchant in Geelong when he purchased the Yallum run for $60 000. He became the local laird and in 1865 stood successfully for parliament. In 1880, he spent $28 000 in building a grand house at Yallum Park which exists today, and the very next year even entertained royalty, the young Princes George and Albert, who were then midshipmen on HMS *Bacchante*. Yet Riddoch was more than a minor grandee. He was in fact a politician of some skill. He succeeded in having the road from Mount Gambier to Penola constructed and later in 1885 secured a rail link from Mount Gambier to Naracoorte.

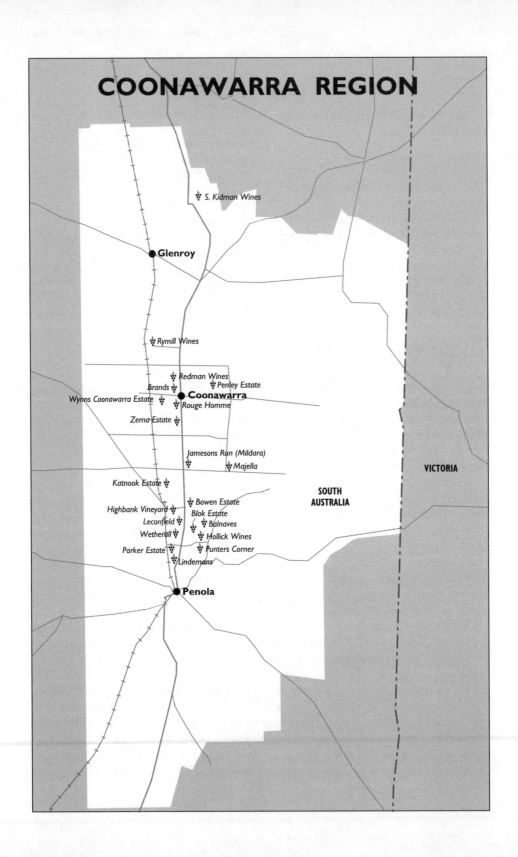

COONAWARRA REGION

S. Kidman Wines

Glenroy

Rymill Wines

Redman Wines
Penley Estate
Brands
Wynns Coonawarra Estate
Coonawarra
Rouge Homme
Zema Estate

Jamesons Run (Mildara)
Majella

Katnook Estate

Bowen Estate
Highbank Vineyard
Blok Estate
Leconfield
Balnaves
Wetherall
Hollick Wines
Parker Estate
Punters Corner
Lindemans

Penola

SOUTH
AUSTRALIA

VICTORIA

Though sheep provided his chief source of income, his interests were not devoted solely to them. By this time, they extended to arboriculture (he acclimatised the radiata pine in the region) and horticulture. In his horticultural endeavours, he was assisted by William Wilson, a Scot, who had also succeeded (rather more modestly than Riddoch) on the goldfields. Wilson had spent some years in vineyards in France and Spain and had later established an excellent Penola garden that, according to a contemporary observer (obviously anticipating the *Guide Michelin*) was 'worth a long journey to see'. The garden was developed on the terra rossa soil existing in the area. There was similar country further north in Riddoch's other domain, Katnook, which was to become known as the Penola Fruit Colony and, later in 1897, Coonawarra.

Exactly why Riddoch subdivided his land is not clear. It may have been, due to Wilson's influence, strictly an interest in horticulture. Perhaps he had overreached himself financially. But he did subdivide in 1890 after a false start in 1889. First, he divided 459 ha into blocks varying from 4 ha to 32 ha on the limestone ridge about 10 kilometres north of Penola. Later a further parcel of 324 ha was subdivided. His sub-division was not spectacularly successful. Initially, only 26 purchasers were found. For the Penola fruit colonists, as the purchasers became known, times rapidly became harder. The Australia-wide bank crashes of 1893 soon affected them and their prices. Droughts later in the 1890s followed by overproduction completed a dismal picture of poor economic returns, but Riddoch in the meantime had fulfilled his undertakings to his purchasers. He had planted a large vineyard on his neighbouring lands, had erected a substantial winery, appointed two winemakers (the first was William Salter, soon followed by Ewen McBain) and continued to purchase their grapes. Viticultural assistance was always available to his Coonawarra 'colonists'. But beyond that he could not go, for he too was dependent on contemporary market forces. Riddoch died in 1901, having realised his own dream of exporting his wine to England.

Without Riddoch's driving force, the Coonawarra viticultural dream began to fade rapidly and his winery was used merely for the making of base wine for brandy distillation. Only a young Bill Redman, who had begun to work for Riddoch a few months before his death, was able later to continue to produce wine by purchasing a 16 ha vineyard block from the estate, though a few other growers struggled on. Their grapes went to the still but Redman was able to prevent the total collapse of table wine making by the sale to Adelaide of table wines for export and later by sales to Woodley Wines of Adelaide. For many years Redman was the only name known outside the district and even then to very few people. His cause was not helped in the 1930s by a state government which instituted a vine-pull scheme designed to convert Coonawarra into a dairying area, but was assisted by one of his reds winning overseas recognition at an Inter-Dominion Exhibition in London.

Yet Coonawarra's turn was to come again after the Second World War. In 1951, the Wynn family purchased the old Riddoch winery and its vineyards and David Wynn publicised the region so successfully that 'Coonawarra' became a buzzword among the few 'claret' drinkers of the time. A minute but growing public curiosity about Coonawarra and red wine generally awakened in turn the interest of Wynns rival producers. Mildara in particular began to purchase land on the terra rossa ridge. Penfolds too purchased vineyard blocks. Later Wynns itself began to increase its holdings substantially and by the mid-1960s Lindemans had also entered Coonawarra, this time by purchasing Rouge Homme, as the Redman family winery and winemaking business had come to be known.

Since then the Coonawarra land boom has continued, not only in the terra rossa country but also in the adjoining intermediate and poorly drained black rendzina soils. What has eventuated, with a logic that is sometimes rare in the wine industry, is that grape varieties for which Coonawarra is traditionally respected—cabernet sauvignon and shiraz—have for the most part been planted on the well-drained terra rossa soils and transitional soils. The white varieties such as chardonnay, sauvignon blanc and semillon and red varieties used for sparkling wine base such as pinot noir have been chiefly planted on the black rendzina.

It was once alleged that soils had little relevance in Australian winemaking. What was important was superior winemaking technique. In Coonawarra's case, that is quite wrong. Coonawarra's winemakers are as technically skilled as any others in Australia but, in red winemaking, their typical terra rossa soils give them a decided edge.

Coonawarra's road to regional status has not been without controversy. Not that it was ever doubted that it should be a region. What was in contention were its boundaries. The first formal declaration of these was at the annual general meeting of the Viticultural Council of the South East of South Australia on 25 October 1984, where it was decided that the Hundreds of Penola and Comaum should be regarded as the boundaries of Coonawarra. At the ensuing annual general meeting (21 October 1985), this decision was reaffirmed. In addition, in the rules of the Coonawarra Vignerons' Association, which was incorporated on 12 November 1985, membership was made available 'to holders of producers' licences, as defined in the Liquor Licensing Act, in the Coonawarra viticultural area, within the Hundreds of Penola and Comaum . . .'. On 18 May 1988, the Viticultural Council repeated its definition in a letter to Karl Seppelt, who was at that time engaged in defining the viticultural regions of South Australia on behalf of the Australian Wine and Brandy Corporation. The Viticultural Council again confirmed the definition of Coonawarra at its meeting on 17 July 1991. It is perhaps unfortunate that nowhere in these resolutions is there any mention of soil type, merely the hundred boundaries of Comaum and Penola and in the 1980s the area had been growing rapidly. However, thought was obviously being given to this problem. The Coonawarra Grapegrowers' Association Inc (CGA) was formed on 11 August 1993. Its qualification for membership rather mysteriously confers eligibility upon growers of wine grapes within the area known as Coonawarra, which is defined as 'that area within the Hundreds of Penola and Comaum and more particularly that wine grape growing area known as Coonawarra . . . which area shall be determined by members at a special general meeting from time to time'. Though, as a definition, it suffers logically in that it is defined in terms of itself (how can Coonawarra be defined by 'members', who may or may not be within its boundaries?) it does allow the CGA to vary its area from time to time. The region was registered by the GIC on 10 May 2000, but its registration provoked a storm of objections subsequently heard by the Administrative Appeals Tribunal, which delivered judgment on 5 October 2001. The Tribunal set aside the boundaries registration by the GIC substituting the boundaries shown in the map on p. 264.

Location: latitude 37°18'S, longitude 140°50'E, about 360 km south-east of Adelaide
Altitude: 59 m
Topography and soils: The general area of which Coonawarra is part is a series of former coastal dunes, rising slightly to the north-east and descending to the south-west, ultimately to the present sea-level, at Beachport, about 90 km away. The region itself is set on a limestone ridge only centimetres above flat country which, prior to various drainage schemes during the early twentieth century, was prone to flooding during winter rainfall, as there were no rivers or creeks in the region to carry the water away naturally. This low plain with its consequent, vigorous growth of grass provided good summer pasture for sheep and cattle. The limestone ridge slightly above was selected for settlement and for the building of roads, because of its superior drainage.

The limestone ridge of Coonawarra is distinct, apparently created about 650 000 years ago in a different geological age to other such ridges in the general area. This distinction lies in the differences in its age, its slightly higher clay content and organic matter. It extends from just to the south of Penola northwards about 16 kilometres. It is nowhere more than 2 kilometres wide and is often much narrower. Its surface is a layer of rich red loam, commonly called terra rossa (classified by KH Northcote as consisting of two soils (Uf 5.31 and Um 6.41)) varying in depth from 5 centimetres to about 60. It is superimposed on pieces of limestone intermixed with clay down to about two to three metres. In turn, this sits above a pure water table, beneath which there is a bed of sandstone. Generally to the west there is a heavier black loam, called black rendzina, which sits above similar substrata. However, both red and black topsoil areas on the eastern boundary are somewhat intermingled. The crucial difference between the soils is their drainage capacity.

The black rendzina soils (often called groundwater or, as classified by KH Northcote, Ug 5.14) are much inferior in this aspect. It has been said that such soils can hold six times as much water as an equivalent depth of sand. Though vines may be grown on the black rendzina (indeed it has been noted that such soils promote excessive growth and sometimes overcropping), its poorer drainage means that the soils warm later than the red soils and therefore that vines grown on it may have a later budburst, a later flowering and even perhaps an imperfect ripening. This would be critical in later-ripening red varieties such as cabernet sauvignon and petit verdot. So the comparatively early ripening white and red varieties such as chardonnay, pinot noir and meunier (all eminently suitable for sparkling wine base) may be grown satisfactorily. Indeed, satisfactory white wine may be made from other early ripening white varieties not customarily used for sparkling wine base (all, it should be noted, with reasonable and not excessive crop levels). Quality red production should not, however, be expected from such soils. There are also brown rendzina soils found in the Coonawarra region. These are similar to terra rossa in all respects except colour and are called in the region 'transitional' soils. They have been planted to grapes quite successfully.
Climate: MJT 19.3°C, HDD raw 1363, 1333 (cut off and as adjusted for latitude, daily temperature range and for vine sites) MAR na, AR 628 mm (Oct–Apr 257 mm), RH 40% (Jan 3pm), AI na, SH 7.5 (G). MJT 19.6°C, MAR 9.8°C, HDD raw 1432, AR 646 mm (Oct–Mar 218 mm), RH na, AI 52 mm, SH 7.8 (D&S). (Local) 18.85°C (average between 3 stations (north, central and south)), MAR 9.75°C (again based on same

average), RH 49% (average Jan). Coonawarra is a cool but sunny area with a low January relative humidity. The climate has been described as Mediterranean and is uniform throughout the region. About 35–40% of its annual rainfall falls in the growing season (Oct–Mar) and can occasionally affect vintage, especially in the south of the region. Irrigation is from bores and is controlled and licensed by statute according to type of crop. Such bores are replenished by groundwater flow and by a shallow water table only 2 metres beneath the surface. A confined aquifer (the Dilwyn Formation) exists about 150 metres beneath the surface, but is not presently used for irrigation. Local lore regards Anzac Day (25 April) as a watershed in ripening, as the weather sometimes changes dramatically after that date. It is said, particularly of cabernet sauvignon, that 'if it is not ripe by Anzac Day, forget it!'. Viticultural problems include spring frosts which can be severe, and powdery and downy mildew, both usually controlled by fungicide sprays. On the bigger properties, pruning and harvesting is usually by machine. For cabernet sauvignon on the classical soils, ripening times are reasonably uniform throughout the centre of the region, though slightly earlier in the north and correspondingly later in the south. Picking for cabernet sauvignon typically commences in the second to third week of April.

Harvest time: generally from late March to early May

Principal grape varieties: White—chardonnay, riesling, sauvignon blanc, semillon; Red—cabernet franc, cabernet sauvignon, merlot, pinot noir, petit verdot, shiraz

Total area: na

Principal wine styles: Cabernet Sauvignon (which may include up to 15% of merlot, cabernet franc and petit verdot in total), Cabernet Merlot (which may include less than 85% cabernet sauvignon, but must include merlot as a predominant secondary variety), Cabernet Verdot (similarly with verdot as predominant secondary variety), Shiraz, Chardonnay.

Leading wineries and vineyards: Lindemans, Rosemount, Wynn's, Parker, Petaluma, Wetherall, Orlando, Penfolds, Jamiesons Run (Mildara), Redman, Yalumba, Brands, Katnook Estate, Penley Estate.

Balnaves R85

Riddoch Highway, Coonawarra, SA 5263
(4 km north of Penola near Bowen Estate)
Ph 08 8737 2946, Fax 08 8737 2945,
Email kirsty.balnaves@balnaves.com.au

Owners: Doug, Annette, Kirsty and Peter Balnaves
Chief winemaker: Peter Bissell
Year of foundation: vineyard 1976, first vintage 1990
Tonnes crushed on average each year: 388, of which 150 are used for Balnaves wines
Location: Coonawarra
Area: 50 ha

Soils: red clay loam over limestone and friable red loam over clay and also sandy soil over clay
Varieties planted: White—chardonnay; Red—cabernet franc, cabernet sauvignon, merlot, shiraz
Leading wine: Balnaves Cabernet Sauvignon
Notes: Doug Balnaves is a Coonawarra winegrower of many years' experience. Wines have been made since 1990 and since 1996 there has been a winery on site, though over half the fruit grown is sold to other wineries. Cabernet Sauvignon is the pick here as it is throughout the region. Cellar door sales: 9am–5pm weekdays, weekends and public holidays 10am–5pm.

The Blok Estate NR

Riddoch Highway, Coonawarra, SA 5263
Ph 08 8737 2734, Fax 08 8737 2994,
Email
theblokestate@telstra.easymail.com.au

Owners: Dianne and John Blok
Chief winemaker: contract
Year of foundation: 1998
Tonnes produced on average each year: 6
Location: Coonawarra
Area: 0.8 ha
Soils: terra rossa
Varieties planted: White—none; Red—cabernet
sauvignon
Leading wines: The Blok Estate Cabernet
Sauvignon, Shiraz
Notes: The Bloks have purchased the former
cellar door site of Nick Haselgrove and produce
a small quantity of Cabernet Sauvignon from
their vineyard. I have not tasted the wine but
wine show entries have produced bronze
awards. Cellar door sales: 7 days 10am–4pm.

Bowen Estate R86

Riddoch Highway, Coonawarra, SA 5263
Ph 08 8737 2229, Fax 08 8737 2173,
Email bowenest@penola.mtx.net.au

Owners: Doug and Joy Bowen
Chief winemaker: Doug Bowen
Year of foundation: 1972, first vintage 1975
Tonnes crushed on average each year: 150
Location: Coonawarra
Area: 34.7 ha
Soils: red clay based loam over limestone
Varieties planted: White—chardonnay;
Red—cabernet franc, cabernet sauvignon,
merlot, petit verdot, shiraz
Leading wines: Bowen Estate Cabernet
Sauvignon, Ampelon, Shiraz
Notes: After Eric Brand and Owen Redman,
Doug Bowen was one of the first 'boutique'
producers of Coonawarra. Restricting cropping
levels to about 6 tonnes per hectare for his
reds, he makes concentrated yet supple reds
and has built a very fine reputation for all his
reds over the years. Cellar door sales: 7 days
10am–5pm except at Christmas and Good
Friday.

Brands of Coonawarra R87

Riddoch Highway, Coonawarra, SA 5263
Ph 08 8736 3260, Fax 08 8736 3208,
Email jbrand@mcwilliams.com.au

Owner: McWilliam's Wines Pty Ltd
Chief winemakers: Jim Brand and Peter
Wienberg
Year of foundation: 1966
Tonnes crushed on average each year: 1500,
increasing to 3500 by 2003 as new vineyards
come into bearing (about 700 tonnes are used
for Brand's wines each vintage)
Location: Coonawarra
Area: 300 ha
Soils: red clay loam over limestone
Varieties planted: White—chardonnay, riesling,
sauvignon blanc; Red—cabernet franc,
cabernet sauvignon, grenache, malbec, merlot,
petit verdot, pinot noir, shiraz
Leading wines: Brand's Stentiford's Reserve Old
Vines Shiraz, Patron's Reserve Cabernet-Shiraz
Merlot, Brand's of Coonawarra Shiraz, Limited
Release Merlot, Cabernet-Merlot, Chardonnay
Notes: Located on some of the most exciting
terra rossa soils of Coonawarra, Brand's have
surged ahead since their purchase by
McWilliams. Their reds and Chardonnay are
prolific medal winners and justifiably so for
their quality is outstanding. All winelovers
deserve a trip to Coonawarra and while there
Brand's must be visited. Cellar door sales:
weekdays 8am–5pm, weekends and public
holidays 10am–4pm.

BRL Hardy (vineyards only)   NR

Riddoch Highway, Coonawarra, SA 5263
Ph 08 8736 5144, Fax 08 8736 5110

Owner: BRL Hardy Ltd
Chief winemaker: Peter Dawson
Year of foundation: 1971
Tonnes crushed on average each year: not
disclosed but estimated at 1450 tonnes
Location: Coonawarra
Area: 143.5 ha, Weatherall Vineyard (24.5 ha),
Father Woods Vineyard (80 ha, planted
1996/97), Kidman Vineyard (27 ha, planted
1995) (leased), Joint Venture Vineyard (BRL
Hardy share) (12 ha)
Soils: Weatherall, transitional soils and black
rendzina; Father Woods Vineyard, small
patches of terra rossa and red gum sand;
Kidman Vineyard, red gum sand; Joint Venture
Vineyard, black rendzina
Varieties planted: White—none;
Red—(Weatherall) cabernet sauvignon, shiraz;
(Father Woods) cabernet sauvignon, merlot;
(Kidman) cabernet sauvignon; (Joint Venture)
cabernet sauvignon
Leading wines: Stonehaven Cabernet
Sauvignon, Thomas Hardy Cabernet Sauvignon
(a small part not wholly Coonawarra)
Notes: BRL Hardy do not market a 100%
Coonawarra Cabernet. It feels that its
vineyards are still young and the fruit produced
is not yet mature enough. Most Coonawarra
fruit finds its way with other fruit from the
Limestone Coast Zone into Stonehaven
Cabernet. No cellar door sales.

Highbank Vineyards   NR

Riddoch Highway, Coonawarra, SA 5263
Ph 08 8736 3311, Fax 08 8736 3122,
Email vice@dove.net.au

Owners: Dennis and Bonnie Vice
Chief winemaker: Trevor Mast (consultant)
Year of foundation: 1986
Tonnes crushed on average each year: 20

Location: Coonawarra
Area: 4 ha
Soils: terra rossa over limestone
Varieties planted: White—none; Red—cabernet
franc, cabernet sauvignon, merlot
Leading wines: Highbank Cabernet Blend,
Merlot
Notes: Highbank's chief wine is a smooth
Cabernet very much in the mid-stream of
Coonawarra style, but when there is sufficient
merlot, a straight Merlot is made. However I
have tasted nothing recently from Highbank.
Set among the Highbank vines, some
accommodation is also available. Cellar door
sales by appointment.

Hollick Wines   R84

Cnr Ravenswood Lane and Riddoch
Highway, Coonawarra, SA 5263
Ph 08 8737 2318, Fax 08 8737 2952,
Email hollick@coonawarra.mtx.net.au

Owners: IB & WC Hollick
Chief winemakers: Ian Hollick, (winemaker)
David Norman
Year of foundation: vineyard 1975, first wine
release 1982
Tonnes crushed on average each year: 550
Location: Coonawarra
Area: 63 ha (20 ha are also owned in
Wrattonbully)
Soils: Coonawarra, classic terra rossa over
limestone; Wrattonbully, terra rossa over
limestone
Varieties planted: White—chardonnay, riesling;
Red—cabernet franc, cabernet sauvignon,
merlot, petit verdot, pinot noir, shiraz,
tempranillo
Leading wines: Hollick Ravenswood Cabernet
Sauvignon, Wilgha Shiraz, Coonawarra
Cabernet Sauvignon-Merlot, Reserve
Chardonnay
Notes: By Coonawarra standards, Hollick is an
estate of modest size but of excellent
reputation. Winning the 1985 Jimmy Watson

trophy in only its third year of operation did not hurt at all. Ian Hollick makes some of Coonawarra's best reds. In particular, the Ravenswood Cabernet Sauvignon, which makes its appearance only in Coonawarra's best years, is outstanding. Cellar door sales: daily 9am–5pm except Good Friday and Christmas Day.

Jamieson's Run/Mildara Winery Coonawarra (formerly Mildara Coonawarra) R88

Riddoch Highway, Coonawarra, SA 5263
Ph 08 8736 3380, Fax 08 8736 3071

Owner: Mildara Blass
Chief winemaker: Andrew Hales
Year of foundation: 1955
Tonnes crushed on average each year: 4900
Location: Coonawarra
Area: 489 ha
Soils: terra rossa with some transitional soils on the western boundaries of the vineyard
Varieties planted: White—chardonnay, sauvignon blanc; Red—cabernet sauvignon, malbec, merlot, meunier, pinot noir, petit verdot, shiraz
Leading wines: Jamiesons Run Reserve, Jamiesons Run range, Robertsons Well range, Mildara Coonawarra range
Notes: Now renamed to recognise the outstanding success of its Jamiesons Run wines, Mildara is, with Wynns and Rouge Homme, one of the veterans of the Coonawarra region. Seniority should engender a certain respect, but the current crop of Jamiesons Run/Mildara reds are deserving of more than respect. They are simply not to be missed. Cellar door sales: daily 10am–4.30pm.

Katnook Estate   R87

Riddoch Highway, Coonawarra, SA 5263
(about halfway between Penola and Coonawarra)
Ph 08 8737 2394, Fax 08 8737 2397,
Email katnook@seol.net.au

Owner: Wingara Wine Group Pty Ltd
Chief winemaker: Wayne Stehbens
Year of foundation: 1979
Tonnes crushed on average each year: 2500, of which 1800 are used for Katnook Estate and Riddoch wines
Location: Coonawarra
Area: 330 ha
Soils: top layer of rich friable red loam varying in depth from a few centimetres to a metre deep, overlying a thin layer of calcareous material, in turn overlying a deep stratum of limestone. A subterranean reservoir of fresh water serves the vines whose root systems are developed enough to reach it
Varieties planted: White—chardonnay, riesling, sauvignon blanc; Red—cabernet sauvignon, merlot, shiraz
Leading wines: Katnook Estate Chardonnay, Cabernet Sauvignon, Merlot, Shiraz
Notes: Katnook is a Coonawarra Estate long married to great quality in Cabernet Sauvignon, Merlot and Shiraz. It also makes a complex Chardonnay and one of the better Sauvignons Blancs of the Region.
Cellar door sales: Mon–Fri 9am–4.30pm, Sat 10am–4.30pm, Sun noon–4.30pm, closed Christmas Day, Boxing Day and Good Friday.

S Kidman Wines   R80

Riddoch Highway, Coonawarra, SA 5263
(about 12 km north of Coonawarra township)
Ph 08 8736 5071, Fax 08 8736 5070,
Email kidman@coonawarra.mtx.net.au

Owners: Sid and Suzie Kidman
Chief winemaker: John Innes
Year of foundation: 1984
Tonnes crushed on average each year: 120
Location: Coonawarra
Area: 15 ha
Soils: terra rossa and sandy loam over red clay
Varieties planted: White—riesling, sauvignon blanc; Red—cabernet sauvignon, shiraz

Leading wines: S Kidman Cabernet Sauvignon, Shiraz, Riesling, Sauvignon Blanc
Notes: The strengths here are its Cabernet Sauvignon and Shiraz. Cellar door sales: 9am–5pm daily.

Leconfield R85

Riddoch Highway, Coonawarra, SA 5263 (about mid-way between Penola and Coonawarra township)
Ph 08 8737 2326, Fax 08 8737 2285, Email leconfield@hamiltonwines.com

Owner: Dr Richard Hamilton
Chief winemaker: Philippa Treadwell
Year of foundation: 1974
Tonnes crushed on average each year: 400
Location: Coonawarra
Area: 28 ha
Soils: terra rossa plus a little black rendzina
Varieties planted: White—chardonnay, riesling; Red—cabernet franc, cabernet sauvignon, merlot, mourvedre, petit verdot, shiraz
Leading wines: Leconfield Cabernet, Merlot, Shiraz, Cabnernets
Notes: Leconfield consistently produces outstanding Cabernets (a blend of Cabernet Sauvignon, Merlot, Petit Verdot and Cabernet Franc), several vintages of which have received world-wide acclaim. This is a Coonawarra red not to be missed. Its other reds are also extremely good, but never outdo the Cabernets. Cellar door sales: Mon–Fri 9am–5pm, weekends 10am–4pm.

Lindemans R93

Riddoch Highway, Coonawarra, SA 5263
Ph 08 8736 3205, Fax 08 8736 3250

Owner: Southcorp Wines
Chief winemaker: Greg Clayfield
Year of foundation: 1971
Tonnes crushed on average each year: not disclosed but estimated at 1700
Location: Coonawarra

Area: 167 ha
Soils: classic central strip terra rossa
Varieties planted: White—none; Red—cabernet sauvignon, merlot, shiraz
Leading wines: Limestone Ridge Shiraz Cabernet, St George Cabernet Sauvignon, Pyrus
Notes: Lindemans have been located in Coonawarra since 1965, when the former Lindemans public company purchased Rouge Homme Wines. It did not really begin to market its own Coonawarra brands till the mid-1970s when Limestone Ridge 1971 was released. After an uncertain start in the early 1970s, the St George Cabernet Sauvignon proved itself in 1976 when a magnificent red was made; Pyrus followed, its 1980 vintage being released in 1983. Of the three, I have a sneaking preference for Limestone Ridge, which for me epitomises classic Coonawarra character, though St George Cabernet Sauvignon and Pyrus (a multi-blend of cabernet sauvignon, cabernet franc, merlot and malbec) have had their moments of triumph. A Jimmy Watson trophy was won in 1981 for the 1980 St George and the same trophy for 1985 Pyrus in 1986. All three are individual vineyard wines. Reds, such as Limestone Ridge, have always been the raison d'être for Lindemans' presence in Coonawarra. May they long continue! Cellar door sales: 7 days 10am–4pm.

Majella R90

Lynn Road, Coonawarra, SA 5263
Ph 08 8736 3055, Fax 08 8736 3057, Email prof@penola.mtx.net.au

Owners: Brian and Anthony Lynn
Chief winemaker: Bruce Gregory
Year of foundation: vineyard 1968, winery 1991
Tonnes crushed on average each year: 120 for Majella wines (balance of fruit is sold)
Location: Coonawarra
Area: 60 ha

Soils: terra rossa running off to sandy loam at the rear of the property
Varieties planted: White—riesling; Red—cabernet sauvignon, merlot, shiraz
Leading wines: Majella Malleea (a Cabernet-Shiraz blend), Shiraz, Cabernet
Notes: Majella has a mature vineyard producing excellent fruit, which goes a long way to explaining the phenomenal success that its reds have enjoyed since its first wines in 1992. In that time over 200 awards have been gained, including 12 trophies and over 50 gold medals, the latest to receive the plaudits of the show judges being Majella Malleea, a traditional Coonawarra blend of Cabernet Sauvignon and Shiraz. This is another Coonawarra winery that must be visited.
Cellar door sales: 7 days 10am–4.30pm.

Orlando (vineyards only) **R89**

Riddoch Highway, Coonawarra, SA 5263

Owners: Orlando Wyndham
Chief winemaker: Phil Laffer
Year of foundation: 1977
Tonnes crushed on average each year: 750
Location: Coonawarra (four separate vineyards)
Area: 130 ha
Soils: terra rossa, plus dark chocolate soil over limestone
Varieties planted: White—none; Red—cabernet sauvignon, shiraz
Leading wines: St Hugo Coonawarra Cabernet Sauvignon, Richmond Grove Coonawarra Cabernet, Russet Ridge, Jacaranda Ridge Cabernet Sauvignon
Notes: Orlando is another large winemaker, which came late to Coonawarra. Its St Hugo Cabernets are of high quality and always reliable, while its super-flagship from Coonawarra, Jacaranda Ridge, makes rather more spasmodic but sensational appearances. Richmond Grove Coonawarra Cabernet is also a recent arrival and usually excellent value. There are no cellar door sales.

Parker Coonawarra Estate **R91**

Riddoch Highway, Coonawarra, SA 5263
Ph 08 8737 3525, Fax 08 8737 3527

Owners: John Parker and family and James Fairfax and interests associated with them
Chief winemaker: Chris Cameron
Year of foundation: vineyard 1985, first wine 1991
Tonnes crushed on average each year: 70, of which about 55 are used for Parker Coonawarra Estate wines
Location: Coonawarra at the southern end of the terra rossa strip
Area: 10 ha
Soils: terra rossa varying in colour from deep red to brown
Varieties planted: White—none; Red—cabernet franc, cabernet sauvignon, merlot, petit verdot
Leading wines: Parker Terra Rossa First Growth (a blend of the four red varieties), Terra Rossa Cabernet Sauvignon, Terra Rossa Merlot
Notes: For the varieties planted in what is their most appropriate Australian home, it is quite justifiable to use terms such as 'First Growth' to describe the superb quality of these wines. They are concentrated powerful reds made with great style and with no expense spared. Like classic Medocs, they should last at least fifteen years. Wines which should not be missed. Cellar door sales: open early 2002 10am–4pm.

Penfolds **R89**

Riddoch Highway, Coonawarra, SA 5263

Owner: Southcorp Wines
Chief winemaker: John Duval
Year of foundation: 1957
Tonnes crushed on average each year: 1000
Location: Coonawarra
Area: 100 ha
Soils: terra rossa
Varieties planted: White—none; Red—cabernet sauvignon, shiraz

Leading wines: Penfolds Bin 128 Coonawarra Shiraz, Bin 707 Cabernet Sauvignon (part) and other special show wines released from time to time

Notes: Penfolds is a veteran of this region, its vineyard dating from the late 1950s. Its Coonawarra Bin 128 Shiraz is always good, sometimes brilliant, but there are occasionally some spectacular show blends of Cabernet. No local cellar door sales.

Penley Estate R87

McLeans Road, Coonawarra, SA 5263
Ph 08 8736 3211, Fax 08 8736 3124,
Email penley@penley.com.au

Owner: Penley Estate Pty Ltd
Chief winemaker: Kym Tolley
Year of foundation: 1988
Tonnes crushed on average each year: 750, half of which are used for Penley Estate wines
Location: Coonawarra
Area: 98 ha of which 10 ha are not yet bearing
Soils: terra rossa and brown sandy loam overlying limestone
Varieties planted: White—chardonnay; Red—cabernet franc, cabernet sauvignon, merlot, pinot noir, shiraz
Leading wines: Penley Estate Cabernet Sauvignon, Merlot, Hyland Shiraz
Notes: Kym Tolley is a winemaker not only by vocation but also by ancestry, being descended from the Penfold and Tolley families. When Coonawarra is added to this winemaking heritage, the results are reds of sumptuous style and whites of elegance. The Penley Estate Coonawarra Cabernet Sauvignon can be simply magnificent. Cellar door sales: 7 days.

Petaluma R90

Riddoch Highway, Coonawarra, SA 5263
Ph 08 8339 4122, Fax 08 8339 5253

Owner: Petaluma Ltd
Chief winemaker: Brian Croser (winemaker) Constantinos Moshos

i) Evans Vineyard

Year of foundation: 1969
Tonnes crushed on average each year: 120
Location: Coonawarra
Area: 15.35 ha
Soils: terra rossa, clay loam well structured over former or highly calcareous material
Varieties planted: White—none; Red—cabernet sauvignon, merlot, petit verdot
Leading wines: Petaluma Coonawarra (a Cabernet-Merlot blend), Petaluma Coonawarra Merlot
Notes: A blend of cabernet sauvignon and merlot, the Petaluma Coonawarra is a superb premium red. It is made in the best traditions of its region without the massive structure of some of its counterparts but with the added style and elegance that one expects from any Petaluma wine. Sales from Bridgewater Mill in the Adelaide Hills. No local cellar door sales.

ii) Sharefarmers Vineyard

Penola Hundred Line Road, Coonawarra, SA 5263

Year of foundation: 1983
Tonnes crushed on average each year: 440
Location: Coonawarra (see Notes)
Area: 48 ha
Soils: terra rossa similar to Evans Vineyard
Varieties planted: White—chardonnay, sauvignon blanc, semillon; Red—cabernet franc, cabernet sauvignon, malbec, merlot, pinot noir
Leading wines: Sharefarmers White, Sharefarmers Red
Notes: As a result of the judgment of the Administrative Appeals Tribunal in October 2001, Sharefarmers Vineyard is now part of the Coonawarra Region. Its wines are of

excellent quality and go under the Sharefarmers label and sometimes into the Petaluma brands. No local cellar door sales.

Punters Corner R82

Riddoch Highway and Racecourse Road, Coonawarra, SA 5263
Ph 08 8737 2007, Fax 08 8737 3138,
Email punters@coonawarra.mtx.net.au

Owners: David Muir and Robert Hance
Chief winemaker: Balnaves (contract)
Year of foundation: vineyards 1975, 1993 as Punters Corner
Tonnes crushed on average each year: 250, of which 120 are used for Punters Corner wines
Location: Coonawarra
Area: three vineyards—12 ha around the cellar door in southern Coonawarra; 16 ha (now 12 years old) on Victoria and Albert Lane in central Coonawarra; and a new vineyard of 60 ha not yet in full bearing 1 km north of V&A Lane
Soils: cellar door block, terra rossa; V&A Lane, terra rossa and sand over clay; new block, terra rossa and transitional brown soils over limestone
Varieties planted: White—chardonnay; Red—cabernet sauvignon, merlot, shiraz
Leading wine: Punters Corner Spartacus Reserve Shiraz
Notes: Located at the southern end of the famous terra rossa bank, its address is the clue to the unusual name of this vineyard—the Penola Racecourse is a few hundred metres away. This amusingly named vineyard is somewhat better than a good eachway bet, having shown great form when its Spartacus Shiraz 1999 dashed off with the Jimmy Watson Trophy in 2000. Other wine show form includes gold awards for Cabernet Sauvignon and Cabernet-Merlots in recent years, otherwise consistent minor placings. Cellar door sales: 10am–5pm each day, except June, July and August when hours are 10am–4pm

weekdays and 10am–5pm weekends and holidays.

Redman Winery R88

Riddoch Highway, Coonawarra, SA 5263
Ph 08 8736 3331, Fax 08 8736 3013

Owners: Redman family
Chief winemakers: Bruce and Malcolm Redman
Year of foundation: 1966
Tonnes crushed on average each year: 250
Location: Coonawarra
Area: 32 ha
Soils: terra rossa virtually 100%
Varieties planted: White—none; Red—cabernet sauvignon, merlot, shiraz
Leading wines: Redman Coonawarra Shiraz, Cabernet Sauvignon, Cabernet Sauvignon-Merlot
Notes: The Redman Winery these days is run by Bruce and Malcolm Redman, grandsons of Bill (who, not without many difficulties, saw Coonawarra safely through the first half of the 20th century) and also sons of the late Owen Redman who founded the winery in 1966. It is very pleasing to report that Redman Winery came back to form after some uncertain times in the 1980s and 1990s with a superb 1998 vintage. Cellar door sales: Mon–Fri 8am–5pm, weekends and public holidays 10am–4pm.

Richmond Grove see Orlando

Rosemount R92

Kirri Billi Vineyard, Riddoch Highway, Coonawarra, SA 5263

Owner: Southcorp Wines
Chief winemaker: Philip Shaw
Year of foundation: 1982
Tonnes crushed on average each year: not disclosed but estimated at 800
Location: Coonawarra (two vineyards, Kirri Billi and Abbey)

Area: 117 ha
Soils: Kirri Billi, classic terra rossa; Abbey, clay loams, outcrops of sandy loam to sand
Varieties planted: White—none; Red—cabernet sauvignon
Leading wine: Reserve Cabernet
Notes: In a little under 30 years, Rosemount has become a national wine company with, I imagine, all the aspirations accompanying such a status. Naturally one of those should be a quality Coonawarra red, appearing annually. One of my Rosemount disappointments has been that great Coonawarra reds have not appeared often enough from Rosemount's older Coonawarra vineyard. With new vineyard plantings in Coonawarra of 80 ha complementing the existing 28 ha and ultimately producing over 1000 tonnes, this should ensure that this comes about more regularly. No cellar door sales.

Rouge Homme **R86**

Riddoch Highway, Coonawarra, SA 5263
Ph 08 8736 3205, Fax 08 8736 3250

Owner: Southcorp Wines
Chief winemaker: Paul Gordon
Year of foundation: 1908 as John Redman & Sons (Bill Redman) and 1954 as Rouge Homme Wines Pty Ltd
Tonnes crushed on average each year: 1250, most of which are used for Rouge Homme wines
Location: Coonawarra
Area: 125 ha
Soils: terra rossa
Varieties planted: White—chardonnay; Red—cabernet franc, cabernet sauvignon, malbec, merlot, petit verdot, pinot noir, shiraz
Leading wines: Rouge Homme Cabernet Sauvignon, Cabernet Merlot
Notes: Rouge Homme is an ancestral name around Coonawarra, second only in age to Wynn's Coonawarra Estate. The winery was purchased by Lindemans Wines (then a public

company) in 1965, which in turn was purchased by Philip Morris and then by Southcorp. So it became a 'brand' but a superior one, retaining its own vineyard and winery and getting first stab at its own vineyard fruit. Both its Cabernet Sauvignon and its Cabernet-Merlot which (when called Richardson's Block) won a Jimmy Watson Trophy, are benchmark Coonawarra styles. Cellar door sales: daily 10am–4pm.

Rymill **R86**

The Riddoch Run Vineyard, Coonawarra, SA 5263
Ph 08 8736 5001, Fax 08 8736 5040,
Email winery@rymill.com.au

Owners: Rymill family
Chief winemaker: John Innes
Year of foundation: 1972
Tonnes crushed on average each year: 1000, of which 800 are used for Rymill wines
Location: Coonawarra
Area: 162 ha, consisting of 100 ha (winery block) and 62 ha (Three Mile Lane)
Soils: Winery, terra rossa of variable depth; Three Mile Lane, part terra rossa and sandy loam over limestone
Varieties planted: White—chardonnay, gewurztraminer, sauvignon blanc; Red—cabernet franc, cabernet sauvignon, merlot, meunier, pinot noir, shiraz
Leading wines: Rymill Cabernet Sauvignon, MC$_2$, Shiraz
Notes: Peter Rymill is a descendant of John Riddoch and used to use the name 'Riddoch Run' as his label in Australian markets. However, confusion with two other 'Riddoch' labels caused some puzzlement in the region and so 'Riddoch Run' was withdrawn and substituted by his own name 'Rymill' on his labels. This is totally justified and indicative these days of the high quality of his wines, especially his reds. Rymill is certainly a winery to visit if in the region. Cellar door sales:

7 days 10am–5pm except Good Friday and Christmas Day.

Southcorp Wines

Remaining vineyards owned by Southcorp in the Coonawarra region include the Terra Rossa Vineyard, located north of Coonawarra, which was established in 1968. It is 45.3 ha in extent, producing about 450 tonnes (not disclosed, but my estimate) of chardonnay, cabernet sauvignon and shiraz. Its production is used variously by Penfolds. There are other vineyards at various places within the region owned by Southcorp Wines. They encompass 198.2 ha, producing on my estimate about 2000 tonnes of chardonnay, riesling, cabernet sauvignon, merlot, petit verdot, pinot noir and shiraz. The production is utilised in Penfolds reds, Seaview sparkling wines and Tollana Botrytis Riesling. Soils are chiefly terra rossa but vary in places to podsolic sands over clay. There are no cellar door outlets in Coonawarra for these vineyards.

Wetherall Wines Coonawarra R90

Riddoch Highway, Coonawarra, SA 5263
Ph 08 8737 2104, Fax 08 8737 2105

Owners: MT and MC Wetherall and BA and MJ Wetherall
Chief winemaker: Michael T Wetherall
Year of foundation: 1965
Tonnes crushed on average each year: 450, of which 25–30 are used for Wetherall wines
Location: Coonawarra
Area: 72 ha
Soils: terra rossa over limestone with some red sandy loams in certain areas
Varieties planted: White—chardonnay; Red—cabernet sauvignon, shiraz
Leading wine: Wetherall Cabernet Sauvignon
Notes: Over 90% of Michael Wetherall's fruit is sold to other wineries, but what he makes is usually of matchless quality. Cabernet Sauvignon in particular is a 'must' here.
Cellar door sales: 7 days 10am–4pm.

Wynn's R92

Memorial Drive, Coonawarra, SA 5263
Ph 08 8736 3266, Fax 08 8736 3202

Owner: Southcorp Wines
Chief Winemaker: Sue Hodder
Year of foundation: 1891, as Wynn's Coonawarra Estate 1951
Tonnes crushed on average each year: 10 000, all of which are used for Wynn's and Southcorp wines
Location: Coonawarra
Area: 900 ha
Soils: terra rossa varying to black rendzina on western edges
Varieties planted: White—chardonnay, riesling; Red—cabernet franc, cabernet sauvignon, merlot, pinot noir, shiraz
Leading wines: Wynn's John Riddoch Cabernet Sauvignon, Michael Shiraz, Coonawarra Estate Black Label Cabernet Sauvignon
Notes: Wynn's is without doubt the largest winegrower and producer in the Coonawarra region and may quite justifiably be called the heart of Coonawarra. The Estate winery is where winemaking in Coonawarra began over a century ago and the larger than life characters associated with it at various times such as John Riddoch, Bill Redman and David Wynn have spelled out Coonawarra's history over the years. The superb John Riddoch Cabernet Sauvignon is arguably Australia's most opulent Cabernet Sauvignon. Cellar door sales: daily 10am–5pm.

Yalumba R88

Riddoch Highway, Penola, SA 5263

Owners: Hill-Smith family
Chief winemaker: Brian Walsh
Year of foundation: 1993
Tonnes crushed on average each year: 300
Location: Penola
Area: 31.35 ha in two vineyards—Menzies 17.71 ha and Hawthorns 13.64 ha

Soils: terra rossa
Varieties planted: (Menzies) White—none;
Red—cabernet sauvignon. (Hawthorns)
White—none; Red—cabernet sauvignon,
merlot, shiraz
Leading wine: Yalumba 'The Menzies'
Coonawarra Cabernet Sauvignon
Notes: The 'Menzies' Cabernet is named after
Sir Robert Menzies, a former Australian prime
minister, who at a dinner once publicly
endorsed the quality of a Yalumba Cabernet.
A cellar door facility was opened late in 2001.

Zema Estate R85

Riddoch Highway, Coonawarra, SA 5263
(just south of Coonawarra township)
Ph 08 8736 3219, Fax 08 8736 3280

Owners: Zema family
Chief winemaker: Tom Simons

Year of foundation: 1982
Tonnes crushed on average each year: 300
Location: Coonawarra
Area 43.85 ha
Soils: terra rossa
Varieties planted: White—sauvignon blanc;
Red—cabernet franc, cabernet sauvignon,
malbec, merlot, petit verdot, shiraz
Leading wines: Zema Family Selection
Cabernet Sauvignon, Cabernet Sauvignon,
Shiraz, Cluny (a blend of the 'Bordeaux'
varieties mentioned above)
Notes: The Zema family is of Italian descent.
This did not stop Demetrio Zema coming to
Penola, planting a vineyard and making
excellent reds in Coonawarra from classic
French varieties. Cabernet Sauvignon,
especially the Family Reserve, is once more to
the fore. Cellar door sales: 7 days 9am–5pm,
except Christmas Day and Good Friday.

PADTHAWAY REGION

The region was first settled by squatters in the 1840s and pastoral leases were issued by the South Australian government in 1851. In that year also, Scottish immigrant Robert Lawson named his grazing run (47 square miles) 'Padthaway', a name derived from the local Aboriginal word *Potaruwt*, meaning 'good water'. Except for sleeper-cutting, grazing continued to be the primary occupation of the district from then until the mid-1930s. This was despite the fact that, in 1926, a Royal Commission report concluded that the area was too valuable to be allowed to remain purely in pastoral occupation. Yet official reports do occasionally emerge from pigeonholes and, from 1936, the area began to be further subdivided and some cereal-growing commenced. The end of the Second World War brought yet more subdivision in the form of soldier-settlement, the establishment of the township of Padthaway in 1952 and, from the mid-1950s, the utilisation of irrigation from the underground aquifers for pasture seed production and stock-fattening.

By the 1960s most wine companies were well aware that their red wine sales were improving. Those established in areas such as Coonawarra knew that they had suitable sites and climate to satisfy this boom. For others not in Coonawarra or other suitable red wine producing areas, and cash-strapped as most family wine companies tended to be, the quandary was whether to buy quite expensive land in such areas or seek new (but basically similar) lands elsewhere at a cheaper price. Seppelt was just such a company. After a close study of the area, inspired by a CSIRO report almost 20 years before and personal inspections by Karl Seppelt, Seppelt purchased land at Keppoch (then a name commonly used for the area) and planted its first experimental vineyard in 1963. Its commercial plantings began the following year. The modern era of Padthaway had begun. Seppelt was followed by Hardy's and Lindemans in 1968.

Early wines began to come from the region in the late 1960s and early in the following decade. Though the country was roughly similar to Coonawarra in soils, its early wines were most definitely not. They were tremendously disappointing—thin red wines coming from over-irrigated callow vines, which proved very difficult to sell. It was with a sense of relief that the companies then established in Padthaway turned with the majority of Australian winedrinkers to white wines later in the 1970s. Following major plantings of riesling, its whites were more successful and Chardonnay too was becoming increasingly desirable in the marketplace. Padthaway's reputation was finally established as a white wine producing area, indeed, later in the mid-1980s as a premium Chardonnay region. In the past decade, however, it has shot forward as a producer of premium Shiraz.

Today, all the major wine companies have substantial vineyards in the region as well as several smaller growers. There are also two wineries, Eliza Padthaway Estate (a small winery specialising in sparkling wines) and BRL Hardy's Stonehaven (a very modern winery with a 10 000-tonne capacity), completed in 1998.

The major disadvantage that Padthaway has suffered over the years is a lack of identity, as large companies tend to use their wines from this region in major blends. Except for very poor reds in its early days and Lindemans' excellent Padthaway Chardonnays in more recent years, Padthaway identity has usually remained a closely kept corporate secret.

Location: latitude 36°37'S, longitude 140°28'E, about 290 km south-east of Adelaide
Elevation: 35–90 m
Topography and soils: Similar to Wrattonbully and Coonawarra to its south, Padthaway was once part of the ancient sea-beds adjoining south-eastern South Australia, after an inundation of the sea 40 million years ago. About 15 million years later, the sea began to recede, leaving the Gambier limestone deposits commonly found in the region. After a further inundation, climatic changes and an uplift of the land surface some 2 million years ago caused the sea to retreat finally, leaving a series of ridges which are the remains of ancient coastal sand dunes parallel to the present coastline. One of these ridges, running from the northern to the southern end of the region, is known as the West Naracoorte Ridge and forms its eastern boundary.

The interdunal plain to its west comprises about 80% of the region. It is quite flat and at an altitude of about 37 metres above sea-level. Its soils are variable. Most common is red duplex (Dr 2.23 Northcote), which is alkaline in nature. The soils of the West Naracoorte Ridge, which rises on average to about 87 metres elevation, are on their slopes red-brown sandy loams (Uc 6 and Um 6 Northcote) of less than half a metre in depth above limestone.
Climate: MJT 20.3°C, MAR 11.25°C, HDD raw 1603, AR 524 mm (Oct–Apr 199 mm), RH 56% (9am Jan) (Bureau of Meteorology), MJT 20.4°C, MAR 11.4°C, HDD raw 1606, AR 526 mm (Oct–Mar 178 mm), RH 65% (9am Jan), AI 475 mm, SH 8.2 (Dry & Smart). MJT 20.2°C, MAR na, HDD raw 1560, 1479 (cut off and as

adjusted for vine sites), AR 509 mm (Oct–Apr 208 mm), RH 35% (3pm Jan), AI na, SH 8.1 (Gladstones). MJT 20.1°C, MAR 10.5°C, HDD na, AR 528 mm (Oct–Apr na), RH 60% (Lindemans local meteorological station).

Variable MJTs between 20.1°C and 20.4°C certainly point to a difference in recording sites, but the raw HDD (1603–1606) makes Padthaway one of the warmer regions of the Limestone Coast zone. Even so, it is scarcely hot and so lends itself well to the production of medium to full-bodied dry white and dry red styles. Frosts are a local hazard as they are virtually throughout the Limestone Coast zone and are generally countered by overhead spray irrigation. Despite this, serious frost damage occurs on a 'one year in ten' basis, with damage occurring more frequently in isolated vineyard depressions. The region is also one of the driest in the zone, irrigation being necessary and practised throughout. In the past, this was carried out by overhead sprinklers, travelling irrigators and flood, but in recent years the region has converted all irrigation systems to drip, except overhead sprinklers used for frost control. The source of irrigation is from bore holes tapping into underground aquifers. Irrigation licences are now required and it has also been suggested that a local winter-flowing creek be diverted to recharge the aquifer throughout the year.

Doubtless the recent vast improvement in Padthaway reds is due to the advent of drip irrigation and the practice of controlled stress applied to the vineyards from budburst to the completion of flowering, which is now reducing yields to about 10 tonnes to the hectare where premium quality is required. With such regimes in place, the future of Padthaway as a quality red area seems assured.

Harvest time: chardonnay early to mid-March, shiraz late March to early April

Principal varieties: White—chardonnay, sauvignon blanc, semillon, riesling; Red—shiraz, cabernet sauvignon, merlot

Total area: 3150 ha

Major wine styles: Chardonnay is definitely the most important wine style of the region. Such wines are usually of the fig-peach spectrum of aromas and flavours, are medium to full-bodied, have excellent length of palate and mature well over 3–5 years. Lindemans has established the region's excellent reputation for this variety.

The Pinot Noirs are light fresh-drinking reds of distinctive pinot character with light strawberry aromas and flavours. They are not to be kept long. Lindemans is the principal exponent of this style.

Shiraz from Orlando Wyndham in particular (Lawson's), are full-bodied reds exhibiting great depth of ripe berry-pepper character both on nose and palate. Also part (50%) of the Eileen Hardy Shiraz 1995, winner of the Jimmy Watson trophy in 1996. Wines such as these are recommended for cellaring for 8–10 years.

Cabernet Sauvignon is rarely seen unblended. It is released either blended with merlot or with cabernet sauvignon from other areas. By itself it has decent berry characters but is rather plain and simple, even disappointing when compared with the wealth of rich berry-blackcurrant character shown by the cabernets of Coonawarra to the south.

Merlot is still to be finally evaluated in the region but is very promising, producing fruity plummy reds of medium to full body when not overcropped.

Leading wineries and vineyards: Orlando, Stonehaven, Lindemans.

BRL Hardy

(see Stonehaven Winery)

Mildara Blass NR

Padthaway SA 5271

Owner: Mildara Blass
Chief winemaker: Andrew Hales
Year of foundation: 1989 (by both Tolley and
Andrew Garrett both subsequently purchased
by Mildara Blass)
Tonnes crushed on average each year: 1700
Location: Padthaway
Area: total 158.7 ha in three vineyards (Tolley
40.4 ha, Garrett 78 ha, Gales 40.3 ha)
Soils: (Garrett) red loam over limestone; (Tolley
and Gales) sand over red clay over limestone
Varieties planted: (Tolley) White—riesling;
Red—cabernet franc, cabernet sauvignon, petit
verdot, shiraz. (Garrett) White—chardonnay,
sauvignon blanc; Red—cabernet franc, pinot
noir, shiraz. (Gales) White—none;
Red—cabernet sauvignon, malbec, merlot,
pinot noir, shiraz
Leading wines: There are no separately
released Mildara Blass Padthaway wines. The
wines are component parts of many of its
premium and semi-premium wine ranges
Notes: No local cellar door sales.

Orlando Wyndham R90

Padthaway, SA 5271

Owner: Simeon Wines Ltd leased and
managed by Orlando Wyndham
Chief winemaker: Philip Laffer
Year of foundation: 1968
Tonnes crushed on average each year: 8000
Location: Padthaway
Area: 490 ha, consisting of two vineyards,
Lawsons and Richmond Grove
Soils: Lawsons, varied, sandy loam over
limestone; Richmond Grove, red duplex over
limestone

Varieties planted: White—chardonnay,
sauvignon blanc; Red—cabernet franc,
cabernet sauvignon, malbec, merlot, shiraz
Leading wines: Lawsons Shiraz, St Hilary
Chardonnay. Orlando Padthaway fruit also
forms part of many premium and semi-
premium blends made by the company,
including Jacob's Creek Reserve wines
Notes: Rated for its magnificently concentrated
Lawsons Shiraz and the often very successful
St Hilary Chardonnay. Orlando's Padthaway
fruit is an essential ingredient in many of their
successful wines. No local cellar door sales.

Padthaway Estate R82

Padthaway Estate, Padthaway, SA 5271
Ph 08 8765 5039, Fax 08 8765 5097,
Email pad_estate@bigpond.com

Owners: Dale Baker and Ian Gray
Chief winemaker: Ulrich Grey-Smith, Nigel Catt
(consultant)
Year of foundation: 1980
Tonnes crushed on average each year: 650, of
which 200 are used for Padthaway Estate
wines
Location: Padthaway
Area: 40 ha
Soils: red duplex above limestone
Varieties planted: White—chardonnay;
Red—cabernet sauvignon, meunier, pinot noir,
shiraz
Leading wines: Padthaway Estate Eliza Pinot
Noir Chardonnay (a sparkling wine),
Unwooded Chardonnay, Chardonnay,
Cabernet Sauvignon
Notes: Padthaway Estate is a charming
homestead dating in part from 1847. Its 40 ha
vineyard is minute by regional comparisons,
but Eliza, its sparkler named after Eliza
Lawson, wife of Robert Lawson, the first settler
of the region, is fresh and cleansing after a
long day's drive. There are other wines also,
Chardonnay in both unwooded and wooded
form and Cabernet Sauvignon, but Eliza is the

pick. Padthaway Estate is open for dinner, bed and breakfast and excellent accommodation is offered. Cellar door sales: in the Old Stables 7 days 10am–4pm.

Southcorp (vineyard only) R87

Padthaway, SA 5271

Owner: Southcorp Wines
Chief winemakers: various within the Southcorp Wines Group
Years of foundation: Seppelt vineyard 1963, Lindeman vineyard 1968, now Penfolds vineyard but formerly Wynns and before Wynns, Glenloth 1968
Tonnes crushed on average each year: not disclosed but estimated at 13 000, all of which are used by the various wineries within the group
Location: Padthaway
Area: 1240 ha
Soils: various; red duplex and red-brown sandy loams
Varieties planted: White—chardonnay; Red—cabernet sauvignon, merlot, pinot noir, shiraz
Leading wines: Lindemans Padthaway Range, Chardonnay, Shiraz, Cabernet Sauvignon, Pinot Noir, Merlot
Notes: The output of this vast vineyard is chiefly divided between Lindemans (see Lindemans, Leading wines) and Penfolds in

many of its premium and semi-premium products. There are no local cellar door sales.

Stonehaven Winery R87

Stonehaven, Keith-Naracoorte Road, Padthaway, SA 5271
Ph 08 8765 6140, Fax 08 8765 6137, Email info@stonehavenvineyards.com.au

Owner: BRL Hardy
Chief winemaker: Tom Newton
Year of foundation: vineyards 1968, winery 1998
Tonnes crushed on average each year: 4500
Location: Padthaway
Area: 450.27 ha, Stonehaven vineyard (411.5 ha), joint venture block (38.77 ha)
Soils: red duplex over limestone varying to sand over limestone on ridges as well as grey loam to clay loam over limestone half metre to a metre and a quarter deep, well-drained
Varieties planted: White—chardonnay, muscadelle, riesling, sauvignon blanc, semillon, traminer, verdelho, viognier; Red—cabernet franc, cabernet sauvignon, malbec, merlot, pinot noir, shiraz
Leading wines: The best fruit produced here is made into Hardy's Stonehaven range by Tom Newton, one of the best winemakers in Australia. The Stonehaven range is currently very good.
Notes: Cellar door sales: daily 10am–4pm.

WRATTONBULLY

Like most of south-eastern South Australia, the early history of the Wrattonbully region was pastoral. The area of what is now the town of Naracoorte was first settled in 1842 by George Ormerod and called the Naracoorte Run. Adjoining this area is Struan, settled at the same time by the Robertson brothers who prospered from grazing and timber-milling, converting local red-gum forests into many thousands of sleepers which were sold to the South Australian Railways. Like John Riddoch at nearby Yallum Park, the Robertsons became the lairds of the district, building a fine mansion and entertaining royalty. Again like Riddoch they subdivided and used part of their land, not for fruit growing and viticulture but for grazing, and smaller grazing properties came into being.

Situated immediately to the north of Coonawarra with its urban centre Naracoorte adjacent to but not forming part of it, Wrattonbully had a history of pastoral and forestry activity until the early 1990s, when the vast growth of its neighbour and the generally like nature of its terrain caused obvious viticultural interest. There had, however, been viticultural development as early as 1968 when the Wrattonbully Vineyard in the southern part of the proposed region was established. Further plantings took place in the early 1970s, but the upsurge did not really begin until 1993. From then until 1997, 950 hectares of vineyard have been established. About 90% of the vines planted have been red. There is currently only one winery within the proposed region, most wine being made outside it. This region, previously to be called Koppamurra, faced legal difficulties concerning the use of its name. 'Koppamurra' is registered as a trademark and cannot be used as a regional description without the consent of the owner of the trademark.

Wrattonbully is an area of modern viticultural techniques yet with an air of caution. Vineyard trellising has been arranged to accommodate vertical shoot positioning: 1.1 metre, single or double wire or Scott Henry. Planting density varies from row widths of 2.2 m to 2.75 m averaging 2000–2700 vines per hectare and Yalumba has taken the precaution of planting 80% of its vines on phylloxera resistant rootstocks.

Location: latitude 36°57'S, longitude 140°46'E, about 310 km south-east of Adelaide
Elevation: 55 to 130 m with most vineyards located between 75 and 100 m above sea-level
Topography and soils: the Naracoorte area is generally recognised to be the most inland of a series of ranges representing the ancient coastal dunes and sea-bed from which the Limestone Coast wine zone derives its name. It is a district of flat lands with undulating rises, having very similar soils to those of Coonawarra to its immediate south. Red sandy clay to clay loams over limestone (terra rossa) are interspersed with red-brown earths and podsols.
Climate: (from Bureau of Meteorology records over a 12-year period) MJT 19.75°C, MAR 10.7°C, HDD raw 1481, AR 565 mm (Oct–Apr 227 mm), RH 49% (Jan 9am), AI na, SH na. Its climate varies only slightly from the premium growth region of Coonawarra to the south, though the important Padthaway region to its north is warmer. Its average summer ripening temperature is one degree warmer than Coonawarra and one degree cooler than Padthaway. Its vineyards are slightly higher in elevation than those of Coonawarra with better air drainage and a consequent lower frost risk, though there is significant frost risk in April–May and mid-August to October. Its climate and lower relative humidity mean a slightly drier vine environment with less risk of botrytis, downy mildew, phomopsis, black spot and other fungal diseases. The chief risk is powdery mildew, which is likely to occur every year.

Irrigation is essential and efficient drip irrigation is employed throughout the region. Though water quality from bores is very good, such usage is restricted by government regulation and irrigation licences are necessary. Such licences have been issued to the maximum permissible amount set by the South Australian government and no additional licences to take water will be granted. Any new winegrower must purchase an existing licence.

Harvest time: Wrattonbully is situated midway between Coonawarra and Padthaway, and harvest dates are similarly placed: chardonnay, sauvignon blanc fourth week of March; merlot, shiraz second week of April; cabernet sauvignon third week of April.
Principal varieties planted: White—chardonnay, sauvignon blanc, semillon and a little riesling; Red—cabernet sauvignon, shiraz, merlot, smaller areas of cabernet franc, pinot noir and meunier
Area: na
Major wine styles: Shiraz, Cabernet Sauvignon
Leading wineries and vineyards: Cranswick, Mildara Blass, Heathfield Ridge.

BRL Hardy Ltd
(vineyard only)   **NR**

Elderslie Road, Naracoorte, SA 5271

Owner: BRL Hardy Ltd
Chief winemaker: Peter Dawson, Tom Newton
(Stonehaven winery)
Years of foundation: 1994
Tonnes crushed on average each year: 1600
Location: Koppamurra
Area: 169 ha consisting of two vineyards—
Elderslie Road 92 ha and Burgess 77 ha
Soils: terra rossa clay over limestone (70%),
red and brown sandy loams over clay (30%)
Varieties planted: (Elderslie Road)
White—chardonnay; Red—cabernet
sauvignon, pinot noir, shiraz. (Burgess)
White—chardonnay; Red—cabernet
sauvignon, meunier, pinot noir, shiraz
Leading wines: no wines are made specifically
from this vineyard, but it does contribute to
the Sir James and Stonehaven ranges
Notes: No cellar door sales.

Cranswick Premium Wines Ltd
(vineyard only)   **R83**

Koppamurra, SA

Chief winemakers: Nick Haselgrove and Paul
Dunnewyk
Year of foundation: 1995
Tonnes crushed on average each year: 500
(other fruit from this area is also purchased
from contract growers)

Location: Koppamurra
Area: 40 ha
Soils: mostly terra rossa dune country
Varieties planted: White—none; Red—cabernet
sauvignon, merlot, shiraz
Leading wines: Haselgrove Bentwing Shiraz,
Cabernet Sauvignon, Chardonnay
Notes: The Bentwing range is entirely regional.
No local cellar door sales.

Heathfield Ridge Winery   **R82**

Cnr Caves Road and Riddoch Highway,
South Naracoorte, SA 5271 (10 km south
of the town within the Koppamurra wine
region)
Ph 08 8762 4133, Fax 08 8762 0141,
Email winery@hthfieldwine.mtx.net

Owners: Tidswell family
Chief winemaker: Pat Tocaciu
Year of foundation: 1998
Tonnes crushed on average each year: 5000, of
which 1000 are used for Heathfield Ridge
wines
Location: Koppamurra
Area: there are two vineyards—Winery
Vineyard 28 ha and Bool Lagoon Vineyard
125 ha
Soils: Winery, shallow sandy loam over
limestone base; Bool Lagoon, terra rossa over
limestone
Varieties planted: White—chardonnay,
sauvignon blanc, semillon; Red—cabernet
sauvignon, merlot, pinot noir, shiraz

Leading wines: Patrick Cabernet Sauvignon, Jennifer Shiraz and the Heathfield range of wines

Notes: Erected in 1998, Heathfield Ridge Winery acts as a contract crusher for many local vineyards. It is also a fully equipped winery which makes excellent wines from its own vineyard at Bool Lagoon and other Limestone Coast vineyards. Cellar door sales: Mon–Sat 10am–5pm, Sun 11am–4pm.

Koppamurra Wines R78

Joanna, 7 km east of Struan, SA 5271
Ph 08 8271 4127, Fax 08 8271 0726,
Email kpmr@koppamurrawines.com.au

Owner: a partnership trading as Koppamurra Wines
Chief winemaker: John Greenshields
Year of foundation: vineyard 1975
Tonnes crushed on average each year: 50 (about 60 tonnes per year are crushed for Koppamurra Wines labels)
Location: Joanna
Area: 11 ha
Soils: terra rossa over limestone
Varieties planted: White— riesling; Red—cabernet franc, cabernet sauvignon, merlot, meunier, shiraz
Leading wines: Koppamurra Wines Cabernet, Merlot and Cabernet Franc, Cabernet Sauvignon
Notes: The wine is made in Adelaide. There are no cellar door sales. Sales by mail order to PO Box 3050, Unley, SA 5061.

Mildara Blass (vineyard only) R83

Langkoop Road, Koppamurra, SA 5271

Owner: Mildara Blass Ltd
Chief winemaker: Andrew Hales
Year of foundation: 1994
Tonnes crushed on average each year: 4000
Location: Wrattonbully
Area: 416 ha
Soils: terra rossa (the old dunes), red-brown loams and duplex soils (lighter sandy soil over clay), these latter soils being interdunal
Varieties planted: White—none; Red—cabernet sauvignon, merlot, petit verdot, shiraz
Leading wine: Schulz's Wrattonbully Shiraz
Notes: This is another large Mildara Blass vineyard, from which only one wine of origin is made at the present time. No local cellar door sales.

Yalumba (vineyard only) NR

Cnr Davies Edwards Road and Old Caves Road, Koppamurra, SA 5271

Owners: Hill-Smith family
Chief winemaker: Brian Walsh
Year of foundation: 1995
Tonnes crushed on average each year: 950
Location: Wrattonbully
Area: 140 ha (not yet fully bearing)
Soils: terra rossa over limestone
Varieties planted: White—chardonnay, sauvignon blanc, viognier; Red—cabernet sauvignon, merlot, shiraz
Leading wines: none yet released
Notes: No local cellar door sales.

MOUNT BENSON REGION

Mount Benson, a name unfamiliar to most wine lovers, is destined to become much more famous. It has the same French connection as the more illustrious Margaret River and arguably even more potential. A compact region situated on the south-east coast of South Australia between Kingston and Robe, it was first explored in April 1802 in a piece of Anglo-French cooperation unusual for its time (the early days of the Napoleonic Wars) by the French navigator, Nicolas Baudin, in *Geographe* and Lieutenant Matthew Flinders in HMS *Investigator*. They had met, not surprisingly, in Encounter Bay when both were mapping the southern coast of Australia. Had they been closer to Europe, they might have tried to blast each other out of the water, but were infinitely more civilised, recalling their presence in the region by naming prominent landmarks along the coast. Thus Lacepede and Guichen Bays and Cape Jaffa were named by Baudin and Baudin Rocks by Flinders, who already had his own name immortalised by the island in Bass Strait.

By 1840, the area had become part of the stock route from Portland to Adelaide. Mount Benson itself was named after a stockman, Harry Benson, and in 1845 the region was settled. The first local industry was grazing and later in the nineteenth century black wattle bark was harvested for the extraction of tannin. Late twentieth-century industries include cray-fishing and afforestation, but that other source of tannin, the grapevine, was not to appear until 1978 when Colin Kidd, viticultural manager of Lindemans, planted a trial vineyard of 80 vines (four rows of 20 vines each of cabernet sauvignon, riesling, traminer and chardonnay) at Cape Jaffa Almond Orchard. All grew well. The first commercial vine planting occurred in 1989 when the first vines of the Mount Benson Vineyard were established.

The Mount Benson region grew rapidly in the late 1990s.

Location: latitude 37°5'S, longitude 139°45'E, about 300 km south-east of Adelaide
Altitude: 10–40 m
Topography and soils: The region is generally undulating with limestone outcrops. Its soils are of 'terra rossa' type similar to the Coonawarra region, which are friable dark brown to dark red subplastic clays above a medium to heavier clay brown-red subsoil and a typical limestone crust. Drainage is generally good.
Climate: (Noolook Forest over 22 years) MJT 18.2°C, MAR na, HDD raw 1226, AR 657 mm (Oct–Apr 222 mm), RH na, AI na, SH na. Mount Benson is a very cool area with obvious maritime influences, southerly sea breezes predominating during summer and autumn. Annual rainfall is 657 mm, falling mainly between April and November. Water of excellent quality for drip irrigation is supplied by two sources, one virtually on top of the other. The first and more shallow is the Gambier Limestone aquifer, in some places as close to the surface as 2 m and in others as deep as 35 m. This aquifer is recharged annually, chiefly by local rainfall occurring between May and November. The second and deeper is the Dilwyn Formation, semi-artesian in nature and believed to be recharged by water from the Gambier Limestone formation and by sources as far away as Western Victoria. Frosts occurring after periods of drought can be a problem in spring, as can strong sea breezes at budburst and flowering. Normal precautions such as wind breaks are taken to obviate wind damage. Compared with Coonawarra, 100 km to the south-east, Mount Benson's growing season starts earlier and finishes later. For example, chardonnay budburst is a week earlier (first week of September), flowering a week later (second week of November), veraison two and a half weeks later (around 7 February) and harvest about 10 days later (around 1 April).
Harvest time: late March to the end of April

Principal grape varieties: (1999) White—chardonnay (bearing) 17.4 ha, (non-bearing) 9.8 ha; sauvignon blanc (bearing) 8 ha, (non-bearing) 6.8 ha. Red—cabernet sauvignon (bearing) 72.3 ha, (non-bearing) 52.1 ha; shiraz (bearing) 45.3 ha, (non-bearing) 34.9 ha
Total area: (1999) (bearing) 160.6 ha, (non-bearing) 135.2 ha–295.8 ha
Major wine styles: Shiraz, Cabernet Sauvignon
Leading wineries and vineyards: Ralph Fowler Vineyards, Black Wattle Vineyards, M Chapoutier.

Baudin Rock Wines NR

Kingston SE, SA 5275
Ph/Fax 08 8768 6217, Email baudinrockwines@bigpond.com

Owner: Robin Ling
Chief winemaker: contract
Year of foundation: 1997
Tonnes produced each year on average: about 20 and growing as the vineyard comes into full production
Location: Mount Benson
Area: 20 ha
Soils: terra rossa
Varieties planted: White—sauvignon blanc; Red—cabernet sauvignon, merlot, shiraz
Leading wines: Baudin Rock Cabernet Sauvignon, Shiraz
Notes: I have not tasted the wines. No cellar door sales.

Black Wattle Vineyards (formerly Cellarmaster Wines) R86

Balmoral Vineyard, Mount Benson via Kingston SE, SA 5275
Ph 08 8768 6264, Fax 08 8778 6114, Email cellar@cellarmasters.com.au

Owner: Cellarmaster Wines Pty Ltd (Mildara Blass)
Chief winemaker: Wayne Dutschke
Year of foundation: 1993
Tonnes produced on average each year: 240
Location: Mt Benson
Area: 42.1 ha
Soils: sand and sandy loam over limestone
Varieties planted: White—chardonnay, sauvignon blanc, verdelho; Red—cabernet franc, cabernet sauvignon, merlot, petit verdot, shiraz
Leading wines: Black Wattle Mt Benson Chardonnay, Cabernet Sauvignon
Notes: Balmoral has all the ingredients of a classic Limestone Coast vineyard, good water, good terra rossa soil and a maritime climate which can turn scorching days into cool nights, though it does create the necessity for wind breaks during the more wind-sensitive times of the grape-growing season. Strangely for a region so close to the sea, spring frosts may be a problem when the earth is cold and the nights are clear. Wine quality is good. No cellar door sales.

Cape Jaffa Wines R81

Limestone Coast Road, Mount Benson, SA 5276
Ph 08 8768 5053, Fax 08 8768 5040

Owner: Cape Jaffa Pty Ltd
Chief winemaker: Derek Hooper
Year of foundation: 1993
Tonnes crushed on average each year: 450, of which 150 are used for Cape Jaffa wines
Location: Mount Benson
Area: 20 ha
Soils: terra rossa
Varieties planted: White—chardonnay, sauvignon blanc, semillon, viognier; Red—cabernet franc, cabernet sauvignon, merlot, petit verdot, shiraz
Leading wines: Cape Jaffa Cabernet

Sauvignon, Chardonnay, Shiraz
Notes: I have tasted nothing recently from
Cape Jaffa. Cellar door sales: daily 10am–5pm.

M Chapoutier Australia R84

Robe Road, Mount Benson via Kingston
SE, SA 5275
Ph 03 9429 8301, Fax 08 8768 5040

Owner: Chapoutier Australia, a company
involving M Chapoutier, Alberic Mazoyer, Cape
Jaffa Wines and one other
Chief winemakers: Jean Philippe Archambaud
and Derek Hooper
Year of foundation: 1998
Tonnes produced on average each year: 55,
but the vineyard is not yet fully in bearing
Location: Mount Benson (see also Heathcote
(Vic) and Pyrenees (Vic))
Area: 35 ha
Soils: terra rossa
Varieties planted: White—marsanne, viognier;
Red—cabernet sauvignon, shiraz
Leading wine: Chapoutier Australia Shiraz
Notes: This is the first of the Chapoutier joint
ventures in Australia. No wines have yet been
released and there are no cellar door sales as
yet.

Ralph Fowler Wines R87

Lot 101 Limestone Coast Road,
Mount Benson, SA 5276
Ph 08 8365 6898, Fax 08 8365 2516,
Email rfwine@senet.com.au

Owners: Ralph and Deborah Fowler
Chief winemaker: Ralph Fowler
Year of foundation: 1998
Tonnes crushed on average each year: 100
Location: Mount Benson
Area: 40 ha, of which 7 ha have been planted
so far
Soils: red sandy loam 20–60 cm deep over
limestone
Varieties planted: White—viognier;
Red—merlot, shiraz
Leading wine: Limestone Coast Shiraz
Notes: Having made the name of Leconfield in
Coonawarra with superb reds for several years,
the very skilled and experienced Ralph Fowler
is now forging his own path. His new vineyard
at Mount Benson is coming to maturity and
already producing good Shiraz. This is a name
to be followed. Sales by mail order to PO Box
631, Magill, SA 5072. No cellar door sales at
present.

PENOLA REGION (INTERIM REGISTRATION)

Penola is a pleasant town in the south-east of South Australia. The history of this
region is shared with that of better-known Coonawarra. Its economy also is dependent
upon the tourism engendered by wine production in the more famous Coonawarra
region. The wine region adjoins Coonawarra on its south-east, south, south-west, west
and north-west.

Location: latitude 37°49'S, longitude 140°83'E, about 365 km south-east of Adelaide
Altitude: 50–60 m
Topography and soils: its better terrain is very similar to Coonawarra. It is generally flat
with limestone outcrops and is what remains of the receded seabed of the Southern
Ocean. Other soils include black rendzina with relatively poor drainage.
Climate: (Penola Forest Reserve Weather Station) MJT 19.2°C, MAR 10.1°C,
HDD 1411 (cut off at 19°C, but not otherwise adjusted), AR 711 mm (Oct–Apr

270 mm), RH 39% (3pm Jan). Generally weather conditions are very similar to Coonawarra but marginally cooler with the same climatic risks and needs for irrigation. The HDD here shows slightly warmer than Coonawarra but this may be because of the location of the weather station.

Harvest time: late March to early May

St Mary's NR

Victoria and Albert Lane, 15 km west of Coonawarra, SA 5263
Ph 08 8736 6070, Fax 08 8736 6045,
Email stmarys@coonawarra.mtx.net.au

Owner: Mulligan family
Chief winemaker: Barry Mulligan
Year of foundation: 1986
Tonnes crushed on average each year: 50
Location: (see above)
Area: 11 ha
Soils: terra rossa soils very similar to the ridge within the defined Coonawarra region
Varieties planted: White—none; Red—cabernet sauvignon, shiraz
Leading wines: St Mary's House Block Cabernet Sauvignon, Shiraz
Notes: The St Mary's vineyard, located west of the defined Coonawarra region but on one of the very similar ridges of terra rossa soils that roll westward towards the coast, is jointly owned by the Mulligan family and Tyrrells Vineyards though the brand St Mary's is owned solely by the Mulligan family. Cellar door sales: 7 days 10am–4pm, closed Christmas Day and Good Friday.

Tyrrells Vineyards NR

St Mary's, Victoria and Albert Lane, 15 km west of Coonawarra, SA 5263

Owner: Tyrrells Vineyards Pty Ltd
Chief winemaker: Andrew Spinaze
Year of foundation: 1995
Tonnes crushed on average each year: 100
Location: west of Coonawarra
Area 14.4 ha
Soils: see St Mary's entry above
Varieties planted: White—none; Red—cabernet franc, cabernet sauvignon, merlot, petit verdot, shiraz
Leading wines: no wines yet released
Notes: This is another instance of Tyrrells expansion to national winemaking status, and some excellent reds are in the pipeline. No cellar door sales.

OTHER LIMESTONE COAST VINEYARDS AND WINERIES (but outside registered or proposed regions)

Haig R80

Square Mile Road, Mount Gambier, SA 5290
Ph 08 8725 5414, Fax 08 8725 0252

Owners: AR and HM Haig
Chief winemaker: Martin Slocombe (contract)
Year of foundation: 1982
Tonnes crushed on average each year: 20, of which about half are used for Haig wines
Location: near the famous Blue Lake, Mount Gambier
Area: 4 ha
Soils: rich, black, volcanic soils over limestone
Varieties planted: White—chardonnay; Red—cabernet sauvignon, gamay, pinot noir
Leading wine: Haig Cabernet Sauvignon
Notes: A vineyard deep in the south-east near the Blue Lake. Good Cabernet styles. Cellar door sales: 7 days 11am–5pm.

❦ Shiraz

The origin of shiraz is to say the least obscure. There is a city in Iran of the same name and a city in Sicily called Syracuse. Did shiraz originate in Persia and proceed via Sicily to Roman Gaul? Who knows and who can ever ascertain its origin except by DNA testing of modern shiraz against current Persian grapevines (if any are left under the Muslim mullahs). When the myths and legends come away, what we are left with is a Northern Rhone grape variety of very respectable reputation, which is solidly ensconsed in many parts of Australia.

Not that its establishment has always been secure. One of the great swings in the popularity pendulum in the past twenty years has been that of shiraz. From the degradation of grubbing-out or grafting in the late 1970s to the exaltation of increasing vineyard area in the late 1990s, such has been its lot. Who now remembers the shiraz muffins of the 1970s? In the late 1970s there was little public excitement in red wines and that was concentrated entirely on cabernet sauvignon. Now there is much more, as Australians recognise just how good our red wines are and how well suited most of our wine regions are to shiraz. Though cabernet sauvignon remains superb in premium regions, such as Coonawarra, Yarra Valley and Margaret River, it performs very ordinarily in warmer regions. Merlot is beginning to make an impact, but again its preferred microclimate seems to be cool to moderately warm (here again Coonawarra, Yarra Valley and Margaret River spring to mind), while pinot noir is restricted to the cooler regions of southern Victoria, Tasmania and perhaps the Lenswood sub-region of the Adelaide Hills.

Where are our best shiraz regions? It all depends on the climates and also the consumers' expectations of the variety. Perhaps the most common hope is for a deeply coloured, aromatically arousing, opulently flavoured wine, richly endowed with berry and pepper fruit, vanillan oak and firm but not hard tannin, a macho red, soft enough to drink comparatively young (2–3 years old), youthfully generous, but not aggressive, on the palate, a wine that will also age gracefully for perhaps another 5–7 years, revealing in due course its complex varietal nuances on nose and palate. For such wines, the shiraz enthusiast should seek out warm to hot climates in areas such as McLaren Vale (incomparable for shiraz in good years), Clare (big shiraz styles with longevity), the Barossa Valley and perhaps the Hunter Valley (although the Hunter style is often more savoury and rarely as rich as the South Australian areas mentioned). In more moderate climates, there are the Bendigo, Heathcote and Great Western regions of central and western Victoria, which make firm shiraz reds of balanced fruit and tannin again long-living and mellow in their more senior years, which some see as having peculiar eucalypt aromas, as well as the more customary black pepper. So too, there are 'cooler' areas such as Sunbury, whose outstanding Shiraz representative is the historic Craiglee, Geelong, where Bannockburn often produces outstandingly 'cool' Shiraz. Also the Yarra Valley, not usually a name dangling from everyone's lips when shiraz is mentioned, is extremely complex in that what are usually seen as 'berry' aromas turn into 'plum' and its 'pepper' transmogrifies from 'black' to 'white'. De Bortoli and Seville Ente are the outstanding names here. But let us not leave Western Australia out of calculations. That state also has an excellent shiraz sub-region, Mount Barker, which shows the typical black pepper, berry and spice characters of Central Victoria, though without that idiosyncratic eucalyptus overlay that is sometimes noticed. Another current and very interesting trend in some regions is the blending of 3–10 per cent of the white grape viognier into shiraz to produce a more supple drinking style. I await developments here with eager anticipation, if only because it may tend to attenuate in some cases the overwhelming influence of American oak.

What are the problems of shiraz today? Very few unless you regard 'too much of a good thing' as a problem. Shiraz seems to flourish virtually everywhere in vinous Australia. Only in our coolest areas does it fail to ripen satisfactorily, producing rather thin 'green' wines. And perhaps in extremely hot areas it occasionally 'bakes' into overripeness, though this is rare. The most common fault is in winemaking—a tendency to use far too much American oak, so that all the nose and palate perceive are lashings of 'coconut', which totally dominate fruit and destroy any claim to finesse that the wine may have. However, our better shiraz makers today seem to be shunning the extremes of American oak and seeking a more subtle path for what might well be called our native variety.

FLEURIEU ZONE

Fleurieu is a considerable area of South Australia, encompassing, as one would expect, the Fleurieu Peninsula and the islands to its south and south west. On the mainland it extends from Glenelg (metropolitan Adelaide) in the north, south along the peninsular coast as far east as the Murray River mouth and pushes back into the hills above McLaren Vale as far as Clarendon. It includes the wine regions of Langhorne Creek, McLaren Vale, Kangaroo Island and the proposed regions of Currency Creek and Southern Fleurieu Peninsula.

LANGHORNE CREEK REGION

The name commemorates Alfred Langhorne, an early overlander, who drove cattle from Sydney in 1841. Having been attacked by Aborigines near the Rufus River, he saw the cattle safely down to what is now the Langhorne Creek area to country he held as a squatter. The spot where he crossed the Bremer River was thereafter known as Langhorne's Crossing and later, after the bridge was built, Langhorne's Bridge or Langhorne's Creek.

In 1850, the South Australian government surveyed and subdivided the area and one of the original purchasers of a selection in that year was Frank Potts, who had arrived in Adelaide aboard the *Buffalo* in 1836. The country selected was part of the flood plain of the Bremer River, which has its sources in the eastern slopes of the Adelaide Hills and flows into Lake Alexandrina, outlet also of the Murray-Darling system. As a flood plain, it not only had the Bremer overflowing its banks nearly every winter but had been the recipient of rich alluvial soil, possibly for many centuries. The first settlers realised this, noting the rich natural grasslands which were ideal for grazing and the soil beneath, excellent for the growth of cereal crops.

Vines were first planted possibly with the encouragement of that ardent South Australian propagator of the vine, Thomas Hardy, who was rising to prominence in the 1860s. Though the exact year is unknown, Frank Potts was one of the first to plant vines (mainly shiraz and verdelho) about that time. Another early grower was Edward Hector of Montura. There is also contemporary diary evidence that Thomas Hardy began to buy wine from Potts in the mid to late 1860s and wine production is confirmed by an 1869 report in a local newspaper that 'a large quantity of wine is being made in the neighbourhood this season. Messrs Hector and Potts, the two largest and most successful growers in the district, are just about to finish their gathering'. In 1883 William Formby bought the land which he later (in 1892) planted with shiraz and cabernet sauvignon and called Metala, some of the original vines of which survive today.

Though the winter flood of the Bremer provided natural irrigation and soaked the deep alluvial soils of the plain, Frank Potts created an innovation and, in so doing, one of Australia's first irrigation schemes. This was the building of an ox-drawn pumping system which harnessed the spring and summer flow of the Bremer by diverting a flow

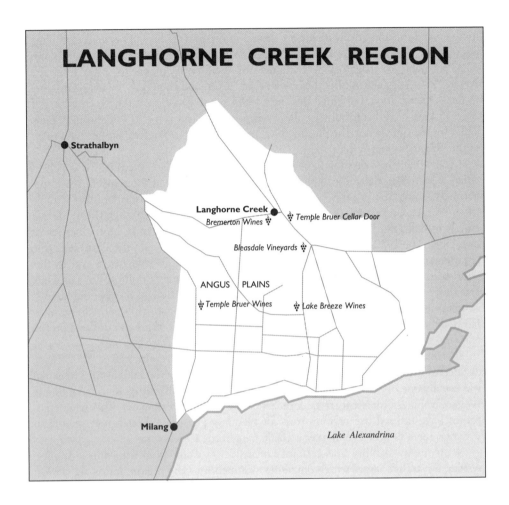

equivalent to 50 cubic metres an hour into a main channel conveying it to the vineyard. In the twentieth century, the development of irrigation in the region continued with the building of levees. They held back the water diverted from the river by way of channels cut into the river banks or the overflow from the river if the winter flood was high enough. In the period from the 1930s to the 1970s, four weirs were built across the river to enable its full flow to be diverted onto the flood plain so that winter and spring irrigation could take place in the vineyards. The region's irrigation capacity was also increased in the late 1950s when wells were bored, though the salinity levels of this supply increased over the next 20 years. In 1980 restrictions were placed on water use and, for a few years after, these restrictions—and encouragement from the South Australian government to recharge the basin with low salinity flood water from its supplying rivers (the Bremer and the Angas)—enabled viticulturalists to use good quality water. But at this time also to ensure the establishment of new young vine varieties and the continuity of economic crop levels, permanent trickle irrigation was introduced. Once more the sub-artesian system began to suffer, water salinity began to increase and the amount available for irrigation began to reduce. This severe problem began to be solved when access to Murray-Darling water from Lake Alexandrina was made available to irrigators in exchange for their entitlements to water from the Angas-Bremer system. At first little water was taken and then only by irrigators close to Lake Alexandrina, but since the early 1990s pipelines of great length (the longest over 35 km) have been built to allow irrigation of land close to Langhorne Creek. Thus, for the time being, the pressure has been taken off the flagging sub-artesian basin of the Angas-Bremer system.

Meanwhile, the Potts family—whose winery and vineyard 'Bleasdale' was named after Dr John Bleasdale, a leading Victorian cleric, who spread the temperance gospel by encouraging the growth of vineyards and the moderate consumption of table wine—was expanding its wine and fortifying spirit production. Though this trade was chiefly in bulk, the Potts family reserved very small quantities of its best wines for its own label. The 1920s and its export demands for fortified reds met the Potts' bulk sale requirements exactly. The 1930s and the Great Depression brought an end to this flourishing trade and later they were compelled to distil over a million litres of wine. Yet they persisted in winemaking and by the 1960s, though the pendulum was swinging back to table wine, the region had been reduced to this one winery only. However, the excellent Metala reds of Saltram also kept this then obscure area on the map and Lindemans produced a soft Shiraz-Ouillade blend from the area.

Its time came in the late 1960s when a young German winemaker, Wolf Blass, decided to 'go solo', making his own red blends in masterly style. Langhorne Creek red was usually one of Wolf's essential building blocks and Wolf's three successive Jimmy Watson trophies brought it to the fore. Since the Blass success, many other wine companies have utilised the region's fruit for blending purposes, though few, save local wineries, seem disposed to market a 100% Langhorne Creek wine.

With the availability and certainty of irrigation water from the Murray-Darling system, Australia's larger wine companies swarmed into the region during the 1990s. Mildara-Blass, Orlando, Rosemount and BRL Hardy have all made significant plantings there. In addition, many smaller local growers have increased plantings and irrigators who once specialised in other crops have made the transition to vines. Today there are four wineries within the region.

Location: latitude 35°13'S, longitude 139°05'E, about 60 km south-east of Adelaide, bounded by the Mount Lofty Ranges to the west and north and Lake Alexandrina to the south
Altitude: from virtually sea-level to 50 m, averaging about 20 m
Topography and soils: Resting on and resulting from the alluvial outwash from the Mount Lofty Ranges, Langhorne Creek is generally flat with very fertile soils. It has a general elevation from about 1 metre (on the shores of Lake Alexandrina, its southern boundary) grading upwards to and bounded by a 50-metre contour line in the north of the region. There are also slight undulations due to sandy loam rises caused by wind action. The light sandy soils of the original outwash are traversed and drained by two rivers, the Bremer and the Angas, which in turn have made their own contributions to the soil complexities of the region, by depositing silts and clays on the plain during

flooding. This in turn has given rise to pockets of silts, loams, clay loams and clay over-lying the original sands and clays.

Climate: (Note: Gladstones and Smart and Dry appear to have used Strathalbyn weather station about 12 km away for their MJTs. The 'local' readings are those of Bill Potts of Early Day Vineyards from his own weather station in the midst of his vineyard. Such data, however, have only been gathered for about 10 years.) MJT 19.2°C, MAR 9°C, HDD raw 1458, AR 388 mm (Oct–Mar 145 mm), RH 60%, AI 383 mm, SH 8.3 (local), MJT 19.9°C, MAR 10.3°C, HDD raw 1521, AR 410 mm (Oct–Apr 135 mm), RH 60% (9am Jan), AI 443 mm, SH 8.3 (Dry & Smart), MJT 19.9°C, MAR na, HDD raw 1655, 1606 (as cut off and adjusted for latitude daily temperature range and for vine sites), AR 495 mm (Oct–Apr 204 mm), RH 43% (3pm Jan). AI na, SH 8.2 (Gladstones). Langhorne Creek has a deceptively mild climate with little variation across its region—deceptive because one would imagine such a region of low rainfall, where vineyard areas are flat and virtually at sea-level, to have little air movement and to be extremely warm. It is certainly not so. It is much cooler than, say, McLaren Vale. There are two reasons for this. The large expanse of water, Lake Alexandrina, is immediately to the south and a prevailing south-west sea breeze blowing across the lake moderates temperatures in Langhorne Creek in summer, a breeze that is apparently much less frequent in Strathalbyn. In winter the lake's influence is also to be felt, again moderating the cold nights that would otherwise make the area more frost-prone. The lake also accounts for the high relative humidity of the region.

The annual rainfall of 388 mm (of which only about 145 mm falls during the growing season (Oct–March)) is low and irrigation is necessary during this season (see above for a brief history of the region's irrigation). There are three sources of irrigation: (A) the area watered by the unique annual flooding of the Bremer and Angas systems; (B) water pumped by pipelines from Lake Alexandrina; and (C) water drawn from the Angas-Bremer sub-artesian basin.

Source A flooding is carried out through a series of floodgates and levee banks which divert water from the rivers and onto surrounding vineyard land, where it remains from 1–2 days until the vineyard soil is saturated. One soaking usually suffices for the ensuing growing season. Water quality, however, varies considerably depending on the salinity of the water in the volume of flow and the time of year in which it occurs. Large flows usually occurring in winter and early spring carry less salinity (about 100 ppm). Smaller earlier flows have much higher salinity (as much as 1800 ppm). Source B has caused many pipelines to be established, including a major pipeline that is utilised by over 40 different landholders. It is available year-round, reliable and its salinity during the last three years has varied from 260 to 340 ppm. This water source alone has caused a major expansion of the Langhorne Creek area, about 80% of the currently planted area being presently irrigated from this source. Source C (the sub-artesian basin of the Angas-Bremer system) is now much diminished as a source of irrigation, though some vineyards do use a mix of this source and lake water for this purpose. Its salinity also can be much higher (250 to 2500 ppms).

Viticultural problems that may occur include excess vine vigour, frost (a slight risk) and mildews, both powdery and downy, but the usual spray program should hold these in check.

Harvest time: Typical phenological dates for Langhorne Creek are cabernet sauvignon, late March to mid to late April, shiraz, similarly
Principal grape varieties: White—chardonnay, verdelho; Red—cabernet sauvignon, shiraz, merlot
Total area: over 5000 ha
Principal wine styles: A difficult question as Langhorne Creek wines are mostly blended with the wines of other regions, the wines of Bleasdale being a notable exception. However, the region's Cabernet Sauvignon and Shiraz reds are distinguished by an accessibility of nose and a suppleness of palate, having good fruit-tannin integration. They not only make excellent blending material but also very good early drinking. The region's two major varieties can be described as follows: Cabernet Sauvignon possessing classical mint, blackcurrant and chocolate characters; Shiraz typically plummy, earthy and chocolatey.
Leading wineries and vineyards: Bleasdale Vineyards, Mildara Blass, Lake Breeze.

Bleasdale Vineyards R90

Wellington Road, Langhorne Creek,
SA 5255 (about 1.5 km east of the town)
Ph 08 8537 3001, Fax 08 8537 3224

Owner: Bleasdale Vineyards Pty Limited
Chief winemakers: Michael Potts and Renae Hirsch
Year of foundation: 1850
Tonnes crushed on average each year: 2400, expected to rise to about 3000 tonnes by 2003 (about three quarters are used for Bleasdale wines)
Location: Langhorne Creek
Area: 62 ha
Soils: red brown alluvial loam
Varieties planted: White—chardonnay, riesling, verdelho; Red—cabernet franc, cabernet sauvignon, grenache, malbec, merlot, petit verdot, shiraz, tinta madeira
Leading wines: Bleasdale Frank Potts (a super-premium 'Bordeaux' blend), Generations (a topflight Shiraz), Mulberry Tree (a premium Cabernet style), Bremerview (a premium Shiraz style)
Notes: Bleasdale reds are an essay in smoothness, lovely supple early maturing wines which are deceptively easy to drink. Cellar door sales: Mon–Sat 9am–5pm, Sun 11am–5pm.

Bremerton Wines R82

Strathalbyn Road, Langhorne Creek,
SA 5255
Ph 08 8537 3093, Fax 08 8537 3109,
Email info@bremerton.com.au

Owners: Craig and Mignonne Willson
Chief winemaker: Rebecca Willson
Year of foundation: 1988
Tonnes crushed on average each year: 300
Location: Langhorne Creek
Area: 40 ha
Soils: part black-grey river loam and part sand over clay
Varieties planted: White—chardonnay, sauvignon blanc, verdelho; Red—cabernet sauvignon, malbec, merlot, petit verdot, shiraz
Leading wines: Bremerton Tamblyn (a red blend of Cabernet Sauvignon, Merlot, Malbec and Shiraz), Verdelho
Notes: The Willsons came to Langhorne Creek from a non-wine media background in a non-wine town, Whyalla. The property purchased was sown to lucerne, a good cash crop. Craig Willson, still with his media involvement but with a growing interest in wine and thoughts of diversifying (what farmer doesn't have them), planted a 3-hectare vineyard in 1991. Bremerton grew from there. Its story is a familiar one in Langhorne Creek—vineyards

gradually taking over the whole region. In the Willsons' case the move to viticulture was spurred on by a flood in 1992 which damaged the lucerne and the buildings. So the decision for wine and vineyard was taken. From a production of 680 cases in 1993 to 20 000 in 2000, Bremerton has seen a swift expansion. The whole family is now involved: Craig as chief executive, his wife Mignonne as weekend chef, daughter Rebecca as winemaker, other daughter Lucy as cellar door manager and her husband Mark as winery manager. Cellar door sales daily. Mignonne's 'mood food' is available on most weekends. Bookings essential.

BRL Hardy (vineyard only) **NR**

Langhorne Creek, SA 5255

Owner: BRL Hardy Limited
Chief winemaker: Peter Dawson
Year of foundation: 1995
Tonnes crushed on average each year: 950
Location: Langhorne Creek
Area: 90.1 ha
Soils: alluvial, red loamy clays, silty sands
Varieties planted: White—none; Red—cabernet franc, cabernet sauvignon, merlot, petit verdot, sangiovese, shiraz
Leading wines: see notes
Notes: Like the rest of the 'big battalions', BRL Hardy gathered its first substantial crop from its recent plantings in 1998 and, until the vineyards reach maturity, the wines made will in all probability be blended into the general run of BRL Hardy reds. No local cellar door sales.

Lake Breeze Wines **R87**

Step Road, Langhorne Creek, SA 5255
(3 km south of the town)
Ph 08 8537 3017, Fax 08 8537 3267,
Email lakebreeze@lm.net.au

Owners: Follett family
Chief winemaker: Greg Follett
Year of foundation: vineyard 1880s, winemaking 1987
Tonnes crushed on average each year: not disclosed but estimated at 800, of which 140 are used for Lake Breeze wines
Location: Langhorne Creek
Area: 80 ha
Soils: alluvial, black-brown soils
Varieties planted: White—chardonnay, white frontignac; Red—cabernet sauvignon, grenache, malbec, merlot, petit verdot, shiraz
Leading wines: Lake Breeze Bernoota Shiraz-Cabernet, Langhorne Creek Reserve Cabernet Sauvignon
Notes: The Follett family began farming in Langhorne Creek in the 1880s, originally growing currants for drying and then replacing them with port and sherry grape varieties in the 1930s, which in turn were replaced by the present table wine varieties 20–30 years ago. Since 1994, Lake Breeze wines have received ten trophies and 38 gold medals. The Lake Breeze Cabernet Sauvignon is especially good. Cellar door sales: 10am–5pm each day.

Mildara Blass **R88**

Lake Plains Road, Langhorne Creek, SA 5255

Owner: Mildara Blass Limited
Chief winemaker: Chris Hatcher
Year of foundation: 1994
Tonnes crushed on average each year: 3600
Location: Langhorne Creek
Area: 245 ha
Soils: rich alluvial loams and sandy clay
Varieties planted: White—none; Red—cabernet sauvignon, merlot, shiraz
Leading wines: Metala Shiraz-Cabernet, Black Label Original Vines Shiraz, Blass Grey Label Cabernet Sauvignon
Notes: The Mildara Blass production from this

region is substantial. But the only wines originating wholly from here are Metala Shiraz Cabernet and Black Label Original Vines Shiraz. No cellar door sales.

Orlando Wyndham (vineyard only)   NR

Clements Road, Langhorne Creek, SA 5255

Owner: Orlando Wyndham
Chief winemaker: Phil Laffer
Year of foundation: 1995
Tonnes crushed on average each year: 5500
Location: Langhorne Creek
Area: 501 ha rising to 640 ha by 2002
Soils: loamy sands to sandy loams of varying depth over sandy clay loam
Varieties planted: White—chardonnay; Red—cabernet franc, merlot, shiraz
Leading wines: Orlando Jacobs Creek Sparkling, Red and Jacobs Creek Reserve Chardonnay
Notes: For Orlando, its Langhorne Creek vineyard represents a very large investment. As well as the vineyard, it has involved the construction of a long water pipeline, but it should return several thousand tonnes of fruit on maturity of the vines. No local cellar door sales.

Rosemount (vineyard only)   NR

Alexandrina, Milang Road, Angas Plains, SA 5255

Owner: Southcorp Wines
Chief winemaker: Philip Shaw
Year of foundation: 1993
Tonnes crushed on average each year: not disclosed but estimated to be about 4500 tonnes

Location: Angas Plains
Area: 300 ha
Soils: red brown sandy loam, clay loams
Varieties planted: White—chardonnay; Red—cabernet sauvignon, grenache, merlot, petit verdot, shiraz
Leading wines: Rosemount produces no wines of origin from its Langhorne Creek vineyard, but it does contribute an important part of the Diamond label range.
Notes: No local cellar door sales.

Temple Bruer Wines   R82

Milang Road, Strathalbyn, SA 5255
Ph 08 8537 0203, Fax 08 8537 0131,
Email templebruer@olis.net.au

Owners: Barbara and David Bruer
Chief winemaker: Nick Bruer
Year of foundation: 1981
Tonnes crushed on average each year: 300 and rising as new plantings come into full bearing (about 150 tonnes are used for Temple Bruer wines)
Location: Langhorne Creek
Area: 27 ha (3 ha not bearing)
Soils: alluvial silt of variable depth over mallee sand over limestone-clay marl
Varieties planted: White—chenin blanc, riesling, verdelho, viognier; Red—cabernet franc, cabernet sauvignon, grenache, malbec, merlot, petit verdot, shiraz
Leading wines: Temple Bruer Cabernet-Merlot, Shiraz-Malbec, Viognier, Chenin Blanc
Notes: The Temple Bruer Vineyards are certified organic. All wines since 1999 have been made organically. Cellar door sales: Wed–Mon 11am–4.30pm, Tues 11am–2pm.

McLAREN VALE REGION

One of the first areas to be settled south of Adelaide (1839), the McLaren Vale region was, prosaically enough, initially named after its first surveyor, John McLaren. It was a name that had some difficulty catching on, the hamlets originally named Gloucester and Bellevue having greater local currency. However, by the 1920s, the name McLaren Vale became commonly accepted.

As was customary in early Australian rural settlements, the pioneers were generally prepared to experiment with any crop that might be of value either domestically or to the local economy. Such was the case with viticulture, where the usual practice was to plant a few vines to see what happened. So it was with the first English settlers who worked their mixed farms south of Adelaide, but none were prepared to risk an entire livelihood on the vine. John Reynell was typical of such settlers. He is reputed to have planted vines on his Reynella farm as early as 1838.

Medicine has often walked arm in arm with the vine. So it was in South Australia, at Magill, east of Adelaide, with Dr Penfold in 1844. Similarly south of Adelaide, where Dr Alexander Kelly planted a vineyard on his Trinity farm near Morphett Vale perhaps even earlier than Dr Penfold. By 1845, there was little doubt that most temperate and explored parts of South Australia appeared eminently suitable for viticulture. By 1850 what is now McLaren Vale witnessed the planting of its first 'commercial' vineyard—12 hectares at Hope Farm (now Seaview) established by George Manning. Five years later, Manning made his first wine, but he still relied on wheat as his principal crop. By 1860 South Australia was about to experience its first wine boom. Dr Kelly saw great export opportunities and, utilising most of his own capital and enlisting the financial support of some of the magnates of Adelaide, such as Sir Thomas Elder, Sir Samuel Davenport and Sir Edward Sterling, he organised the purchase of Crown land near McLaren Vale late in 1862. Tintara, which began to be planted the following year, was to be the region's first truly commercial vineyard and London was to be its market. A decade later, amid recriminations, the company had ground slowly to a halt. In 1873 it closed its doors for the last time. It was 'picked up' quite cheaply in 1876 by an immigrant boy made good, Thomas Hardy, aged 46, then reaching the peak of his commercial activity.

Hardy, a Devonshire lad, had reached Adelaide in 1850 at the age of 20. After time in the goldfields, where he made money, not from gold but from droving cattle to feed the miners, he bought 'Bankside' on the Torrens near Adelaide in 1853. By the late 1850s he was a small but thriving horticulturalist and winemaker and was even exporting small quantities of wine to London. Hardy trod carefully through the depressed 1860s. Tintara was most likely his introduction to McLaren Vale and fortuitously his purchase of Tintara coincided with a general upturn in the South Australian economy as a whole, which had been depressed due to drought, the discovery of gold in Victoria and New South Wales (which caused a drift of South Australian population to those two eastern colonies) and the non-discovery of gold in South Australia (which would have more than reversed the trend). The presence of a successful wine company—for Thomas Hardy & Sons was very successful by 1880—undoubtedly influenced the progress of viticultural development in McLaren Vale and by the 1890s, a new viticultural boom was

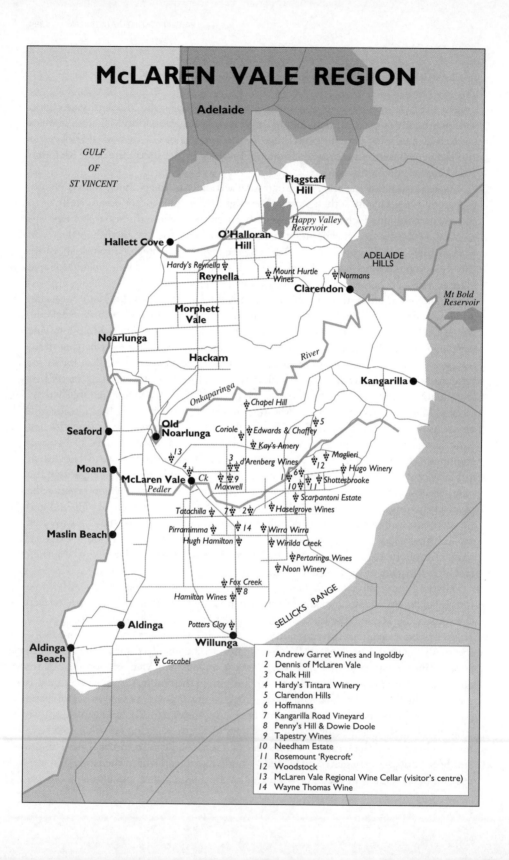

McLAREN VALE REGION

Adelaide

GULF
OF
ST VINCENT

Flagstaff
Hill

*Happy Valley
Reservoir*

O'Halloran
Hill

ADELAIDE
HILLS

Hallett Cove ●

Hardy's Reynella 🍇

Reynella

🍇 *Mount Hurtle
Wines*

🍇 *Normans*

Clarendon ●

*Mt Bold
Reservoir*

Morphett
Vale

Noarlunga

Hackam

River

Kangarilla ●

🍇 *Chapel Hill*

Onkaparinga

Old
Noarlunga

Seaford ●

Coriole 🍇 🍇 *Edwards & Chaffey*

🍇 *5*

🍇 *Kay's Amery*

🍇 *13*

3 🍇 🍇 *d'Arenberg Wines*

🍇 *Maglieri*

🍇 *12*

4 🍇

Moana ●

McLaren Vale ● Ck

🍇 *9*

Maxwell

1 🍇 *6* 🍇

🍇 🍇 *Hugo Winery*

🍇 *Shottesbrooke*

Pedler

10 🍇 🍇 *11*

🍇 *Scarpantoni Estate*

Tatachilla 🍇 *7* 🍇 *2* 🍇 🍇 *Haselgrove Wines*

Maslin Beach ●

Pirramimma 🍇

🍇 *14*

🍇 *Wirra Wirra*

Hugh Hamilton 🍇

🍇 *Wirilda Creek*

🍇 *Pertaringa Wines*

🍇 *Noon Winery*

🍇 *Fox Creek*

🍇 *8*

Hamilton Wines

SELLICKS RANGE

Aldinga ●

Potters Clay 🍇

Willunga ●

Aldinga
Beach ●

🍇 *Cascabel*

1	Andrew Garret Wines and Ingoldby
2	Dennis of McLaren Vale
3	Chalk Hill
4	Hardy's Tintara Winery
5	Clarendon Hills
6	Hoffmanns
7	Kangarilla Road Vineyard
8	Penny's Hill & Dowie Doole
9	Tapestry Wines
10	Needham Estate
11	Rosemount 'Ryecroft'
12	Woodstock
13	McLaren Vale Regional Wine Cellar (visitor's centre)
14	Wayne Thomas Wine

under way, as Australian vignerons began to exploit new opportunities in the British market. In that market, as well as in the various Australian colonial markets, there had been a change in popular taste to heavier and more alcoholic wines. For the British, it was a swing towards cheap fortifieds and medically recommended 'tonic burgundies' (heavy reds), for which the warmer Australian vineyard areas such as the Barossa Valley, Rutherglen and McLaren Vale were particularly suitable. For the Australian wine market, never large, it was probably an aping of British taste. It was at this time (1890–1914) that many of the ancestors of today's McLaren Vale vignerons began to plant their vineyards. Thomas Hardy's involvement in the region from 1876 onwards has been mentioned, but prominent in the 1890s McLaren Vale boom were the Kays and the Johnstons. Later came the Osborns.

For McLaren Vale, these were to become markets set in stone and destined to last— give or take a World War or two and the Great Depression—for seventy years. By the 1960s, McLaren Vale, until then the most stable of Australian wine markets, was once more depressed as the British market fell away and as a consequence local wineries began to close. This time it was the local market to the rescue, as a post-war awareness of wine began to grow, spurred on by post-war migration, a booming economy and a younger generation beginning to be aware of a 'lifestyle' that their parents could never have hoped to enjoy. At first it was a cognisance of charmat-process white wine, the Barossa Pearls and the other sparkling 'jewels' of the day, then 'dry red', then in my case a home-bottling of a hogshead of Seaview Cabernet-Shiraz 1964—that was my first experience of McLaren Vale. By 1967, the local red wine boom had arrived and McLaren Vale was very much part of it. Suddenly, there were many small wineries, unknown names that had previously sold all their wine or their fruit to Emu or Hardy's or Gilbey's of London, names that now needed to sell their product or go under. Go under some of them did, but many survived by turning to winemaking and McLaren Vale began to proliferate with small, interesting names, scarcely heard of before. Some of those families from the red boom of the 1960s are still there, now in the hands of second generation winemakers, and they are still extremely interesting, though they are being eaten up increasingly by the bigger fish of the industry. Further replantings and restructurings were forced on McLaren Vale during the 1970s and 1980s, when first white wine and then chardonnay became extremely popular.

Today McLaren Vale remains predominantly a red wine area. Of course there are many hectares of white grapes planted and how well these varieties prosper in the Vale, especially chardonnay and, though not quite as consistently, sauvignon blanc! But in any good vintage, it is still the reds, especially shiraz and cabernet sauvignon, that create the excitement. There are about 70 wineries in McLaren Vale, not all with cellar door sales, and approximately 270 independent growers, who grow all major and many minor grape varieties, both white and red. Average production has risen to 58 000 tonnes, most of which is crushed, vinified and marketed as McLaren Vale wine.

Location: latitude 35°03', 35°17'S, longitude 138°30' to 138°40', about 40 km south of Adelaide
Altitude: generally from 50 m to 350 m: in the north 100 m around Reynella to 200 m in the Blewitt Springs area with isolated vineyards in the Mount Lofty Ranges to

350 m; in the south, closer to the sea, there are lower vineyards, which commence at 50 m altitude

Topography and soils: Viewed from the town, McLaren Vale has a flat to undulating landscape, rising gently to the north and the east, but rather more steeply to the north-east. Most of its vineyards are planted within a radius of 12 km from the sea in the general area of McLaren Vale–McLaren Flat–Willunga on a wide variety of soils. There are fertile red-brown earths, common podsolic soils of low fertility, terra rossa, rendzinas, solodic and cracking soils. Geologically, the region is divided into two systems: the hard rocks of the Mount Lofty Ranges consisting of shales, siltstone, quartzite, dolomite and tillite and overlying Cambrian carbonate metasediments such as limestone, dolomite and siltstone; and the unconsolidated sediments of the St Vincent Basin, typified by the Willunga and Noarlunga Embayments. Sand deposits are common around the North and South Maslin areas. Tertiary remnants, though extensively eroded over millions of years, still cap the hills and there the old land surface has been ferruginised to form the red-brown ironstone so admired by the original Thomas Hardy, who thought he could taste it in the reds.

Climate: MJT 21°C, MAR 10.8, HDD raw 1913, AR 656 mm (Oct–Mar 182 mm), RH 49% (9am mid Jan), AI 418 mm, SH 8.6 (Dry & Smart). McLaren Vale is a warm to hot region with dry summers, but it is important to stress that it is bounded on its west by the St Vincent Gulf, which exerts a beneficial cooling effect with its on-shore breezes. Its winters are moderate in temperature and wet (474 mm of rain falling between April and September). Relative humidity is low at 49% and supplementary irrigation is necessary. This is usually carried out by drippers, which have as their water source either surface dams or bores from underground aquifers, the chief of which is the Willunga Basin Aquifer, a source of good water quality, which drains into the Gulf via a small number of streams. About 2% of vineyards are irrigated through mains water. It is to be noted that there is a proposal to limit irrigation to 170 mm per year. Regional temperature variability is less than 1.5°C. Air drainage is generally quite good and frost is virtually unknown. Because of the warm, dry climate in spring and summer, mildews are also rarely a problem, though most vineyards are sprayed periodically. There are isolated sandy areas where nematodes exist, but these can be combated by planting on rootstocks. Light brown apple moth is also present from time to time.

Harvest time: chardonnay early to mid-March, sauvignon blanc mid-March, shiraz late March, cabernet sauvignon late March and grenache late April; harvest times can vary by up to two weeks in the various areas within the region

Principal grape varieties: White—chardonnay, semillon; Red—shiraz, cabernet sauvignon

Total area: (2000) 5800 ha

Principal wine styles: The shiraz of McLaren Vale is rich, ripe, generous and soft, yet paradoxically 'long' with acids and tannins firm enough usually to ensure a cellaring life of 5–10 years. Often the wines seem precocious and can be drunk at 1–2 years of age, but they keep excellently. Predominant flavours are blackberry, black pepper and dark chocolate. Traditionally, shiraz was often blended with varieties such as grenache and mourvedre and made into 'Burgundy' or, by itself or blended with grenache, fortified and made into a long-living 'port' style.

The chardonnays have ripe peachy fruit characters both in aroma and flavour that adapt to oak very harmoniously, making the McLaren Vale style one of the best warm area examples of the variety. But McLaren Vale Chardonnay should not usually be kept beyond 3 years.

Again, the cabernet sauvignons are a very ripe style of red with dark berry, black-currant aromatics and flavours and 'dark chocolate'. It is sometimes blended with its 'Bordeaux' brothers, cabernet franc, merlot and petit verdot. Some tasters also find a savoury black olive character on nose and palate. Ageing potential similar to shiraz.

The mystery with sauvignon blanc is why in an area so warm as McLaren Vale, it conforms so well to its grassy, high acid varietal specifications (which after all are based on sauvignon's performance in relatively cool areas) as to make it notable in three years out of five. Why should McLaren Vale sauvignon show its typical herbaceous-tropical characters in such a warm area? The answer is based on two factors. Firstly McLaren Vale predominantly grows the old shy-bearing clone of sauvignon blanc. The small amount of fruit produced therefore is never overcropped· and conforms excellently in most years to sauvignon's typical parameters. Secondly, the foliage produced by such vines is generally luxuriant, giving shaded, methoxypyrazine characters to the small crops of sauvignon blanc, which do not become overripe, though they reach quite high baumes. The best of McLaren Vale Sauvignon Blanc should be drunk young—up to eighteen months of age.

Leading wineries and vineyards: Pirramimma, Rosemount, Kay's Amery, Normans, Cascabel, Chapel Hill, Andrew Garrett and Ingolby Wines, Penny's Hill, D'Arenberg, Edwards and Chaffey, Hamilton, Sylvan Springs, Maglieri, Tyrrells, Mount Hurtle, Pertaringa, Scarpantoni.

Andrew Garrett and Ingoldby Wines R86

Ingoldby Road, McLaren Vale, SA 5171
Ph 08 8383 0005, Fax 08 8323 8550

Owner: Mildara Blass Ltd
Chief winemaker: Charles Hargrave
Year of foundation: Andrew Garrett 1983, Ingoldby 1972 (cellar door sales are now amalgamated)
Tonnes produced on average each year: 900, all used for Mildara Blass wines
Locations: McLaren Flat and McLaren Vale (cellar door at McLaren Vale)
Area: 84.1 ha consisting of Tamar Vineyard (McLaren Flat) 29.7 ha; Ingoldby Road Block (McLaren Vale) 5.7 ha; Logan's Legacy 48.7 ha
Soils: Tamar Vineyard, loamy clay bleached sands; Ingoldby, friable alluvial loam; Logan's

Legacy, sandy loam over limestone
Varieties planted: (Tamar Vineyard) White—chardonnay; Red—cabernet sauvignon, shiraz. (Ingoldby) White—none; Red—cabernet sauvignon, grenache, shiraz. (Logan's Legacy) White—none; Red—barbera, cabernet sauvignon, merlot, petit verdot, sangiovese, shiraz
Leading wines: Ingoldby Chardonnay, Shiraz, Cabernet Sauvignon
Notes: Ingoldby is a respected name for the rich style of McLaren Vale Chardonnay and also for full-bodied McLaren Vale Shiraz. Cellar door sales: daily 9am–5pm.

Cascabel R87

Rogers Road, Willunga, SA 5172
Ph 08 8557 4434, Fax 08 8557 4435,
Email cascabel@intertech.net.au

Owners/chief winemakers: Duncan Ferguson and Susana Fernandez
Year of foundation: 1997
Tonnes crushed on average each year: 45, of which 30 are used for Cascabel wines
Location: Willunga (winery and vineyard)
Area: 7.5 ha
Soils: red stony loam, very deep with good drainage, well-suited to dry-grown vines
Varieties planted: White—roussanne, viognier; Red—graciano, grenache, mataro (mourvedre), shiraz, tempranillo
Leading wines: Cascabel Grenache et al (i.e. Grenache 86%, Shiraz 10%, Mataro 4%), Tempranillo-Graciano, Viognier-Roussanne
Notes: Cascabel is very new. Its vineyard is only just fully planted and of course not yet in full-bearing, but there will be a definite Spanish influence here in the reds and Rhone in the whites. Susana Fernandez is herself Spanish and, as a winemaker, Spanish-trained. Hence the varieties listed above. One suspects the Spanish influence will grow as the vines mature. Grenache may well revert to its Spanish name Garnacha and certainly Mataro will remain Mataro and not become Mourvedre and there may be a Rioja-influenced Tempranilla-Graciano blend. There will be other differences too. Cascabel will follow organic practices, no fertiliser and, as soon as the vines can stand on their own feet, no irrigation with only minimal use of traditional chemicals such as Bordeaux mixture and sulphur. As Susana does not like the 'cooked' characters in McLaren Vale Shiraz and prefers lighter styles with greater maritime influences, one suspects that the reds may have more finesse than most McLaren Vale reds—as indeed proved to be the case after tasting. Cellar door sales by appointment only. Make an appointment!

Chalk Hill Wines R83

Field St, McLaren Vale, SA 5171
Ph 08 8556 2121, Fax 08 8556 2221

Owners: Harvey Family
Chief winemaker: (contract)
Year of foundation: vineyard 1973
Tonnes produced on average each year: not disclosed but 30 tonnes are used each year for Chalk Hill wines
Location: McLaren Vale
Area: not disclosed as Chalk Hill own several vineyards in the region and the 30 tonnes selected for Chalk Hill labels may vary slightly from year to year
Soils: variable from Urrbrae loam (red gravelly loam) to biscay clay (dark brown self-mulching clay loam) to ironstone sandy loam and deep sand in reds and yellows
Varieties planted: White—chardonnay, semillon; Red—cabernet franc, cabernet sauvignon, gamay, grenache, merlot, pinot noir, shiraz
Leading wines: Chalk Hill Chardonnay, Shiraz, Cabernet Sauvignon
Notes: Good mainstream McLaren Vale reds here. Sales by mail order. No cellar door sales.

Chapel Hill Winery R87

Chapel Hill Road, McLaren Vale, SA 5171
Ph 08 8323 8429, Fax 08 8323 9245, Email winery@chapel-hill.com.au

Owner: Chapel Hill Winery Pty Ltd
Chief winemakers: Pam Dunsford, (winemaker) Angela Meaney
Year of foundation: 1979
Tonnes crushed on average each year: 400
Locations: McLaren Vale (cellar door and vineyards), Kangarilla (vineyard), Bakers Gully (vineyard)
Area: 40 ha are owned, a further 31.5 ha at Kangarilla are leased from the previous owner for 5 years
Soils: Chapel Hill, red-brown earths over shale with ironstone; Kangarilla, duplex sand over mottled clays with ironstone; Bakers Gully, red-brown earths over clay with ironstone

Varieties planted: (Chapel Hill)
White—chardonnay; Red—cabernet
sauvignon, merlot, shiraz. (Kangarilla)
White—chardonnay, verdelho; Red—cabernet
sauvignon, malbec, sangiovese, shiraz. (Bakers
Gully)
White—none; Red—cabernet sauvignon, shiraz
Leading wines: Chapel Hill Reserve
Chardonnay, McLaren Vale Shiraz, The Vicar
(a Shiraz-Cabernet blend)
Notes: Chapel Hill changed hands recently and
is now Swiss-owned. As the same winemaking
team remains, this should make no difference
to quality, which is superb. Cellar door sales:
7 days noon–5pm.

Clarendon Hills NR

Brookman Road, Blewitt Springs,
SA 5157
(H) Ph/Fax 08 8364 1484,
(Winery) Ph/Fax 08 8383 0544

Owner/chief winemaker: Roman Bratasiuk
Year of foundation: 1989
Tonnes crushed on average for own label each
year: 325
Area: none (all fruit is purchased from local
growers)
Soils: no vineyard is owned
Varieties planted: none, but varieties purchased
are White—chardonnay; Red—cabernet
sauvignon, grenache, merlot, pinot noir, shiraz
Leading wines: Clarendon Hills Astralis Shiraz,
Romas Grenache (each a single vineyard red)
Notes: Clarendon Hills wines are made from
fruit selected from old dry-grown vineyards in
the Clarendon, Blewitt Springs, and Kangarilla
areas of McLaren Vale. All wines are fermented
on wild yeasts, the whites in French oak, while
the reds are run warm in stainless steel,
receiving an extended maceration. Pressings
are returned to the barrel. All wines are
matured in Burgundian barriques, the whites
for one year, the reds for 18 months. They are
then bottled without fining or filtration. Thus

Roman Bratasiuk is a minimalist winemaker,
preferring to interfere with the winemaking
process as little as possible. I have not tasted
the wines. Cellar door tasting and sales by
appointment only.

Coriole R83

Chaffeys Road, McLaren Vale, SA 5171
Ph 08 8323 8305, Fax 08 8323 9136

Owners: Lloyd family
Chief winemakers: Grant Harrison and Mark
Lloyd
Year of foundation: 1967
Tonnes crushed on average each year: 500
(some fruit is also purchased from local
growers)
Location: McLaren Vale (winery and vineyard)
Area: 30 ha
Soils: red-brown earth over capped limestone;
Lloyd Reserve vineyard, deep red clay; the area
has a high ironstone content
Varieties planted: White—chenin blanc,
semillon; Red—barbera, cabernet sauvignon,
sangiovese, shiraz
Leading wines: Coriole Lloyd Reserve Shiraz,
Mary Kathleen Cabernet Merlot, Redstone,
Sangiovese
Notes: Coriole is located in the 'Seaview' area
of McLaren Vale, distinctive for its red-brown
earths above a limestone substructure. Such
soils produce excellent reds and Coriole is
renowned for its Shiraz both Reserve and
standard. Cellar door sales: Mon–Fri
10am–5pm, weekends and public holidays
11am–5pm.

d'Arenberg Wines R86

Osborn Road, McLaren Vale, SA 5171
Ph 08 8323 8206, Fax 08 8323 8423,
Email winery@darenberg.com.au

Owner: d'Arenberg Pty Ltd
Chief winemaker: Chester Osborn
Year of foundation: 1912

Tonnes crushed on average each year: 825 (a further 1000 tonnes is purchased from local growers)
Location: McLaren Vale
Area: 138 ha, consisting of Osborn Estate (67.2 ha) and Pedler's Divide (70.8 ha)
Soils: variable, but dominated by red-brown loamy sands of the hard red duplex group Dr 2.33 and a sandy version of the structurally similar grey-brown loamy sand classified by Northcote as Dy 3.43—hard mottled yellow duplex soils with yellow clay sub-soils, Dy 5.42 interspersed with limey deposits and impregnated with ironstone patches of black and red friable loams in the groups 6.2 and 6.4 sometimes called terra rossa
Varieties planted: (Osborn Estate) White—chardonnay, marsanne, riesling, sauvignon blanc, viognier; Red—cabernet sauvignon, chambourcin, grenache, mourvedre, shiraz. (Pedler's Divide Vineyard) White—chardonnay, marsanne, roussanne, sauvignon blanc, viognier; Red—cabernet sauvignon, grenache, mourvedre, petit verdot, shiraz
Leading wines: d'Arenberg Dead Arm Shiraz, d'Arry's Original Grenache, Shiraz, Last Ditch Viognier
Notes: With Kay's Amery and Pirramimma, d'Arenberg is an icon of McLaren Vale, a reticule of the Vale tradition of big red and fortified Shiraz styles that made up most of Australia's wine exports in the 70-year period from 1890 to 1960. These days the rough 'tonic Burgundy' and 'working man's Port' edges have been polished away and the red styles are satin-smooth though by no means emasculated. Though such reds are justifiably popular, there is great quality also in Viognier, that most elegant of upper Rhone white varietals. d'Arenberg is an essential McLaren Vale destination. Cellar door sales: daily 10am–5pm.

Dennis of McLaren Vale NR

Kangarilla Road, McLaren Vale, SA 5171
Ph 08 8323 8665, Fax 08 8323 9121

Owners: Dennis family
Chief winemaker: Peter Dennis
Year of foundation: 1969
Tonnes crushed on average each year: 275
Location: McLaren Vale
Area: 25 ha
Soils: deep red loams, sandy loams, some shale
Varieties planted: White—chardonnay, sauvignon blanc, semillon; Red—cabernet sauvignon, grenache, merlot, shiraz
Leading wines: Dennis Shiraz, Chardonnay
Notes: The Dennis family is another of those grapegrowing families that took to winemaking during the red wine boom of the mid to late 1960s. The winery also has an excellent reputation for Chardonnay, rich and ripe in the usual McLaren Vale manner. Cellar door sales: daily 10am–5pm

Dowie Doole R80

182 Main Road, McLaren Vale, SA 5171
Ph 08 8323 7314, Fax 08 8323 7305,
Email leigh.gilligan@vinum.com.au

Owners: Norm Doole, Drew Dowie, Leigh Gilligan
Chief winemaker: Brian Light (contract)
Year of foundation: 1996
Tonnes crushed on average each year: not disclosed but estimated at 400, about 44 of which are used for Dowie Doole wines
Locations: (cellar door) McLaren Vale; (vineyards) Blewitt Springs, McLaren Vale and McLaren Flat
Area: 49.2 ha consisting of McLaren Vale 26 ha, Blewitt Springs 16 ha and two smaller vineyards at McLaren Vale and McLaren Flat totalling 7.2 ha
Soils: Blewitt Springs, sand over reddish semi-porous clay with interspersed ironstone pebbles; McLaren Vale, sandy loam over

limestone. Soil information for smaller vineyards not disclosed.
Varieties planted: (Blewitt Springs) White—chardonnay, chenin blanc; Red—cabernet franc, cabernet sauvignon, merlot, pinot noir. (McLaren Vale) White—chardonnay, sauvignon blanc, semillon; Red—cabernet sauvignon, merlot, pinot noir, shiraz. (Other vineyards) White—none; Reds—grenache, shiraz
Leading wines: Dowie Doole Semillon-Sauvignon Blanc, Merlot
Notes: Dowie Doole is a partnership of three vineyard owners—former Canadian banker Norm Doole, Adelaide architect Drew Dowie and wine marketer Leigh Gilligan. The best of their crop (usually about 10%) is used for their own label. No cellar door sales.

Edwards & Chaffey (formerly Seaview)   **R86**

Chaffey's Road, McLaren Vale, SA 5171
Ph 08 8323 8250, Fac 08 8323 9308

Owner: Southcorp Wines
Chief winemaker: Fiona Donald
Year of foundation: 1850 (as Hope Farm)
Tonnes crushed on average each year: 1500, all of which are used in Edwards and Chaffey and other Southcorp wines
Locations: McLaren Vale (cellar door) and six vineyards (Seaview, CPL, Bethany, Blencowe, Chapel Hill, Park Hill, Aldersey)
Area: 154 ha
Soils: CPL, duplex red-brown earth; Bethany, dark self-mulching clay loam with a tendency to surface cracking, quite fertile; Blencowe, Chapel Hill, Park Hill, Seaview, ranging from duplex red-brown earth on Blencowe and Chapel Hill to more sandy red-brown earth on Seaview; Aldersey, red-brown clay loams over limestone
Varieties planted: White—chardonnay, riesling, sauvignon blanc, semillon; Red—cabernet sauvignon, grenache, shiraz
Leading wines: Edwards & Chaffey Section 353

Chardonnay, Shiraz, Cabernet Sauvignon
Notes: The Edwards & Chaffey regional wines (Section 353) are top class examples of their region, Shiraz and Cabernet styles with power but also a certain finesse, typical of top Southcorp making. Cellar door sales: Mon–Sat and public holidays 10am–5pm, Sun 11am–4pm.

Fox Creek   **R85**

Malpas Road, Willunga, SA 5172
Ph 08 8556 2403, Fax 08 8556 2104,
Email sales@foxcreekwines.com

Owners: Dr James, Helen and Paul Watts and Dr John and Lyn Roberts
Chief winemaker: Daniel Hills
Year of foundation: vineyards 1984, winery 1995
Tonnes crushed on average each year: 1000, of which 350 are used for Fox Creek wines
Location: Willunga
Area: 60 ha
Soils: mostly black clays which crack in summer when dry but respond well to the application of gypsum
Varieties planted: White—chardonnay, sauvignon blanc, semillon, verdelho; Red—cabernet franc, cabernet sauvignon, merlot, shiraz
Leading wines: Fox Creek Reserve Shiraz, Reserve Cabernet Sauvignon, Merlot
Notes: Fox Creek has a fine and totally justified reputation for its rich Shiraz and Cabernet styles. It is also a consistent medal winner at local and capital city wine shows. Cellar door sales: 11am–5pm daily.

Hamilton (formerly Richard Hamilton Wines)   **R86**

Main Road, Willunga, SA 5172
Ph 08 8556 2288, Fax 08 8556 2868,
cellar door Ph 08 8556 222

Owners: Dr Richard Burton Hamilton and family

Chief winemaker: Philiippa Treadwell
Year of foundation: 1972
Tonnes crushed on average each year: 450
Locations: (cellar door) Willunga, (vineyards)
Willunga and McLaren Vale
Area: 57 ha consisting of three vineyards
(Winery block, Hut Block and Gumpr's Block)
Soils: Winery Block, red river clays and loam
based brown soils; Gumpr's Block, red and
brown based loams and biscay soils (black
cracking clay); Hut Block, sandy based grey
loams and red loams over limestone
Varieties planted: White—chardonnay, riesling,
sauvignon blanc, semillon, viognier;
Red—cabernet franc, cabernet sauvignon,
grenache, merlot, mourvedre, petit verdot,
shiraz
Leading wines: Gumpr's Block McLaren Vale
Shiraz, Single Vineyard Centurion 100 year old
Vines Shiraz, Single Vineyard Reserve Burton's
Vineyard Shiraz
Notes: Reversing the more usual south–north
journey, the Hamilton crop travels south to its
Leconfield winery in Coonawarra for making,
but the wines are kept quite distinct. The reds
are mid-stream McLaren Vale style. Cellar door
sales: daily 10am–5pm.

Hardy's Reynella (formerly Reynell)

 R85

Reynella Road, Reynella, SA 5161
Ph 08 8392 2222, Fax 08 8392 2202

Owner: BRL Hardy Ltd
Chief winemakers: Peter Dawson; red
winemaker Stephen Pannell; white winemaker
Tom Newton; sparkling winemaker Ed Carr
Year of foundation: 1853
Tonnes crushed on average each year: 230 from
the company's own vineyards. The company
buys many more tonnes from local growers
Location: (Cellar door, winery and vineyard)
Reynella, (vineyard) Yeenunga, McLaren Vale
Area: Reynella 11.6 ha, Yeenunga, McLaren
Vale 26.4 ha

Soils: Reynella, grey sandy loam over medium
brown clay and red medium clay over
calcareous medium clay; Yeenunga, orange
shaley clay, grey sand containing abundant
ironstone fragments
Varieties planted: (Reynella)
White—chardonnay; Red—cabernet
sauvignon, malbec, merlot, shiraz. (Yeenunga)
White—none; Red—cabernet sauvignon,
grenache, shiraz
Leading wines: Reynella contributes to Tintara,
Thomas Hardy and Chateau Reynella wines.
Yeenunga forms part of Tintara Shiraz and
Grenache Chateau Reynella Cabernet and
Shiraz and Eileen Hardy Shiraz
Notes: Present-day BRL Hardy headquarters
for administration, packaging and sparkling
wines. This is the former Chateau Reynella,
the site of the first vineyard planted in what is
now the McLaren Vale region (in 1838) and
also the oldest wine cellar in the region (the
Old Cave Cellar constructed in 1845). It is
also where Thomas Hardy, then a young
immigrant aged 20, became a farm labourer
for a few months in 1850. Hardy's have been
renowned for years as master blenders and
that tradition continues especially in the
Eileen Hardy Shiraz. Cellar door sales: daily
10am–4.30pm.

Hardy's Tintara (winery only)

 R85

Main Road, McLaren Vale, SA 5171
Ph 08 8323 8676, Fax 08 8323 0151

Owner: BRL Hardy Ltd
Chief winemaker: Peter Dawson
Year of foundation: 1877
Tonnes crushed on average each year: 8000
Location: McLaren Vale
Area/Soils/Varieties planted: see Hardy's
Reynella
Leading wines: Tintara McLaren Vale Shiraz,
Grenache (wines of McLaren Vale origin made
in limited quantity). Tintara Cellars,

Chardonnay, Cabernet Sauvignon, Shiraz
(wines blended from various regions)
Notes: 'Tintara' has been associated with BRL
Hardy since 1877 and today produces the bulk
of BRL Hardy premium wines, including whites
and reds from Adelaide Hills and McLaren Vale
as well as parcels of premium fruit for labels
such as Eileen Hardy Shiraz and Chardonnay
and Thomas Hardy Cabernet. Cellar door sales:
7 days 10am–4.30pm.

Haselgrove Wines R85

Sand Road, McLaren Vale, SA 5171
Ph 08 8323 8706, Fax 08 8323 8049,
Email winery@haselgrove.com.au

Owner: Cranswick Premium Wines Ltd
Chief winemaker: Nick Haselgrove
Year of foundation: 1981
Tonnes crushed on average year: 3000
(700 used for the Haselgrove labels)
Location: McLaren Vale (winery and vineyards)
Area: 14 ha
Soils: sand over clay
Varieties planted: White—viognier;
Red—cabernet sauvignon, merlot, shiraz
Leading wines: H (series), Shiraz, Cabernet,
Viognier, Chardonnay, Sparkling Garnet
Notes: Haselgrove Wines is the South
Australian presence of the Cranswick Premium
Wines group. Its wines are very much in the
milieu of McLaren Vale style. Cellar door sales:
Mon–Fri 9am–5pm, weekends 10am–5pm.

Hoffmanns NR

Ingoldby Road, McLaren Flat, SA 5171
Ph/Fax 08 8383 0232, Email
hoffmanswine@bigpond.com

Owners: Peter and Anthea Hoffmann
Chief winemaker: Nick Holmes (contract)
Year of foundation: vineyard 1978, cellar door
1996
Tonnes crushed on average each year: 28, of
which about 9 are used for Hoffmans label

Location: McLaren Flat
Area: 4 ha
Soils: halocene alluvium, the flood plain of a
major creek, clay base with sandy loam
allowing minimal irrigation
Varieties planted: White—none; Red—cabernet
sauvignon, shiraz
Leading wine: Hoffmanns Cabernet Sauvignon
Notes: A small vineyard for the area. It is
family-owned and the cabernet sauvignon
grown is the old Reynella clone. Cellar door
sales: daily 11am–5pm.

Hugh Hamilton Wines R83

McMurtrie Road, McLaren Vale, SA 5171
Ph 08 8323 8689, Fax 08 8323 9488,
Email hugh@hamiltonwines.com.au

Owner/chief winemaker: Hugh Hamilton
Year of foundation: 1991
Tonnes crushed on average each year: 160, of
which 70 are used for Hugh Hamilton wines
Location: McLaren Vale
Area: 18 ha
Soils: dark loams over clay
Varieties planted: White—chardonnay,
verdelho; Red—cabernet sauvignon, merlot,
sangiovese, shiraz, tempranillo
Leading wines: Hugh Hamilton Chardonnay,
Shiraz
Notes: Hugh Hamilton is a member of the
winemaking Hamilton family of Adelaide.
Hugh's wines are very much in the midstream
of McLaren Vale and I have usually found the
Unwooded Chardonnay and Shiraz to be of
excellent quality. New cellar door facilities are
on a ridge line with outstanding 360° views.
Cellar door sales: weekdays 10am–6pm,
weekends and public holidays 11am–5pm.

Hugo Winery R85

Elliott Road, McLaren Flat, SA 5171
Ph 08 8383 0098, Fax 08 8383 0446,
Email hugowine@iaccess.com.au

Owners: John and Liz Hugo
Chief winemaker: John Hugo
Year of foundation: vineyard 1950, cellar door
1982
Tonnes crushed on average each year: 115
Location: McLaren Flat
Area: 32 ha, part of which is not yet in full
bearing
Soils: red loam over clay
Varieties planted: White—chardonnay,
sauvignon blanc; Red—cabernet franc,
cabernet sauvignon, grenache, shiraz
Leading wines: Hugo Shiraz, Unwooded
Chardonnay, Cabernet Sauvignon
Notes: Hugo is renowned for producing rich
chocolatey Shiraz, of a wealth of flavour,
totally typical of the region. Cellar door sales:
Sun–Fri 10.30am–5pm, Sat noon–5pm.

Kangarilla Road Vineyard and Winery R85

Kangarilla Road, McLaren Flat, SA 5171
Ph 08 8383 0533, Fax 08 8383 0044

Owners: Kevin and Helen O'Brien
Chief winemaker: Kevin O'Brien
Year of foundation: 1975
Tonnes crushed on average each year: 350
Location: McLaren Flat
Area: 13 ha
Soils: predominantly red loam with creek bed
stones
Varieties planted: White—chardonnay,
viognier; Red—carbernet franc, cabernet
sauvignon, shiraz, zinfandel
Leading wines: Kangarilla Road Vineyard
Chardonnay, Shiraz, Cabernet Sauvignon,
Zinfandel, Viognier
Notes: Formerly the Cambrai winery, Kangarilla
Road's claim to fame is that it is one of the
few producers of Zinfandel in the region.
Cellar door sales: weekdays 9am–5pm,
weekends and public holidays 11am–5pm.

Kay's Amery Winery R90

Kays Road, McLaren Vale, SA 5171
Ph 08 8323 8211–01, Fax 08 8323 9199

Owners: Kay family
Chief winemaker: Colin Kay
Year of foundation: 1890
Tonnes crushed on average each year: 80, all
of which (together with about 20 tonnes
purchased) are used for Kay's Amery wines
Location: McLaren Vale
Area: 17 ha
Soils: variable but predominantly ironstone
gravel
Varieties planted: White—muscat blanc,
sauvignon blanc; Red—cabernet sauvignon,
grenache, merlot, mourvedre, pinot noir, shiraz
Leading wines: Kay's Amery Block 6 Shiraz
(from the original plantings in 1892), Cabernet
Sauvignon, Liqueur Muscat, Very Old Tawny
Port
Notes: The winery was completed in 1895 and
a vineyard commenced a few years before and
they are now very much part of McLaren Vale's
and Australia's wine history. Its cellars are built
on the side of a hill according to a model
designed by John Kelly (son of Alexander)
employing the gravity flow principle, very
useful when the only pumps commonly
available were manual. (Steam pumps were
used by some wineries, but they were quite
expensive.) Crushers are on the top level,
fermenters on the second level and, below,
casks and storage tanks. Kay Brothers were for
many years involved in the export to the UK of
heavy reds and fortifieds, which were the forte
of McLaren Vale at that time. In 1926 over
200 000 litres of 'London Blend' (a heavy
fortified red) were exported. All the reds,
including Block 6 Shiraz made from the
original 1892 plantings, are McLaren Vale
classics. This is a winery not to be missed.
Cellar door sales: weekdays 8am–5pm,
weekends and public holidays noon–5pm.

Maglieri R86

Douglas Gully Road, McLaren Flat,
SA 5171
Ph 08 8383 0177, Fax 08 8383 0136

Owner: Mildara Blass
Chief winemaker: Charles Hargrave
Year of foundation: 1972
Tonnes crushed on average each year: 5000,
all going into various Mildara wines
Locations: (winery and vineyard) McLaren Flat,
(vineyards) McLaren Vale, Willunga
Area: 85.4 ha consisting of Strout Vineyard
(7.6 ha), Binney Vineyard (32.8 ha), Willunga
(18.1 ha), Douglas Gully (16.9 ha)
Soils: Douglas Gully, deep sand, Binney and
Strout, good red loam; Willunga, rich dark
slightly alluvial loam, including some biscay
Varieties planted: (Strout) White—chardonnay,
sauvignon blanc; Red—cabernet sauvignon.
(Binney) White—chardonnay; Red—cabernet
sauvignon, merlot, shiraz. (Douglas Gully)
White—none; Red—cabernet sauvignon,
grenache, shiraz. (Willunga) White—none;
Red—cabernet sauvignon, merlot, shiraz
Leading wines: Maglieri Shiraz, Cabernet
Sauvignon, Chardonnay
Notes: Maglieri is a Mildara Blass winery very
much in the main stream of that rich ripe
McLaren Vale style. Cellar door sales: daily
10am–4pm, closed Christmas Day.

Maxwell R83

Cnr Olivers Road and Chalk Hill Road,
McLaren Vale, SA 5171
Ph 08 8323 8200, Fax 08 8323 8900,
Email maxwellwines@senet.com.au

Owner: Mark, Ken and Margaret Maxwell
Chief winemaker: Mark Maxwell
Year of foundation: 1979
Tonnes crushed on average each year: 350, of
which 250 are used for Maxwell wines
Location: McLaren Vale
Area: 16 ha

Soils: brown loam over limestone, well drained
Varieties planted: White— semillon, verdelho;
Red—cabernet sauvignon, grenache, merlot,
shiraz
Leading wines: Maxwell Ellen Street Shiraz,
Lime Cave Cabernet, Maxwell Mead
Notes: The wine highlight here is the
consistently good Ellen Street Shiraz and mead
is another unusual string to the Maxwell bow.
Cellar door sales: daily 10am–5pm, closed
Christmas Day and Good Friday.

Mount Hurtle (formerly Geoff Merrill Wines) R86

291 Pimpala Road, Woodcroft, SA 5161
Ph 08 8381 6877, Fax 08 8322 2244

Owner: Geoff Merrill
Chief winemakers: Geoff Merrill and Goe di
Fabio
Year of foundation: 1980 (Mount Hurtle
Winery, originally built in 1897, was re-opened
in 1986)
Tonnes crushed on average each year: 1500
(including many tonnes of fruit purchased from
local growers)
Location: Woodcroft near Reynella
Area: Reynella 2 ha, Coonawarra 20 ha,
McLaren Vale 51 ha, Goulburn Valley 35 ha
Soils: Reynella, sandy clay loam to red-brown
earths over red clays; Coonawarra,
predominantly terra rossa; McLaren Vale, sandy
loam; Goulburn Valley, sandy, alluvial loam
Varieties planted: (Coonawarra)
White—chardonnay; Red—cabernet
sauvignon. (Other vineyards)
White—chardonnay, sauvignon blanc;
Red—cabernet sauvignon, merlot, sangiovese,
shiraz
Leading wines: Geoff Merrill Reserve Cabernet,
Shiraz, Chardonnay, Premium Chardonnay,
Sauvignon Blanc, Cabernet, Shiraz, Merlot,
Mount Hurtle Sauvignon-Semillon, Grenache
Rose, Grenache Shiraz
Notes: The ebullient Geoff Merrill is one of the

established characters of the Australian wine industry. Paradoxically, his wine styles (in particular his Reserve Chardonnay and Reserve Cabernet Sauvignon) tend to elegance rather than exuberance. The Mount Hurtle label, which was more characteristically McLaren Vale in style than the Reserve, has now been discontinued except for exports and sales to Liquorland stores. Cellar door sales: Mon–Fri 9am–5pm, Sun and public holidays noon–5pm, closed Sat.

Needham Estate NR

Ingoldby Road, McLaren Flat, SA 5171
Ph/Fax 08 8383 0301, Email
cneedham@ctel.com.au

Owners: Clive and Des Needham
Chief winemaker: (contract)
Year of foundation: 1997
Tonnes crushed on average each year: vineyard not yet in full bearing, but a 50 tonne crop is anticipated (no wines yet made)
Location: McLaren Flat
Area: 4.5 ha
Soils: rich loam over a limestone base
Variety planted: White—none; Red—shiraz
Leading wine: no wines yet made
Notes: It is early days yet for Needham Estate. No cellar door sales.

Noon Winery R85

Rifle Range Road, McLaren Vale,
SA 5171
Ph/Fax 08 8323 8290

Owner/chief winemaker: Drew Noon
Year of foundation: 1976
Tonnes crushed on average each year: 50
Location: McLaren Vale
Area: 6 ha (some fruit is also purchased from growers in Langhorne Creek)
Soils: brown loam over red clay, duplex
Varieties planted: White—none;
Red—grenache

Leading wine: Noon Eclipse (a full-bodied Grenache-Shiraz style, typical of McLaren Vale)
Notes: This is a small family-owned winery whose vineyards are mostly unirrigated and vary in age from 25 to 65 years. The reds are the only wines produced and are fermented in small open vats and pressed in basket presses. Cellar door sales: weekends and public holidays only while stocks are available. Ring ahead.

Normans (vineyard only) R88

Chais Clarendon, Grants Gully Road,
Clarendon, SA 5157
Ph 08 8383 6138, Fax 08 8383 6089

Owner: Normans Wines Ltd (in receivership)
Chief winemaker: Peter Fraser
Year of foundation: Normans 1853
Tonnes crushed on average each year: 930 (Clarendon, 30; Eringa Park Vineyard, McLaren Vale, 900)
Locations: Clarendon (winery and cellar door), Eringa Park (vineyard), McLaren Vale
Area: 99.76 ha (Clarendon 3.74 ha, Eringa Park 96.02 ha)
Soils: Clarendon, shallow clay loam over a medium clay sub-soil; Eringa Park, variable according to the topography of the area. Generally on the elevated areas, there are sandy duplex soils of variable depth over poorly to moderately drained clay. Areas near Moritz Road have an extremely shallow layer of sandy soil, which is unsuitable for vineyard development. The flats near Kangarilla Road consist of loamy sand soil over a gravelly clay. This is subject to waterlogging on occasions.
Varieties planted: (Clarendon)
White—chardonnay; Red—cabernet sauvignon, shiraz. (Eringa Park)
White—chardonnay; Red—cabernet sauvignon, grenache, merlot, nebbiolo, shiraz
Leading wines: Chais Clarendon Chardonnay, Shiraz, Cabernet Sauvignon, Regional Series
Notes: Normans is a medium to large company whose winemaking activities are chiefly

concentrated at Monash in the Riverland region. However, it has good vineyards closer to Adelaide at Evanston on the Adelaide Plains and in McLaren Vale. Its Chais Clarendon range is its best, though its reds under this label are often blends of its vineyards in various regions. Cellar door sales: Mon–Fri 9am–5pm, Sat 10am–5pm, Sun and public holidays 11am–5pm.

Pedler Creek Winery (formerly Maxwell Winery)

McLaren Vale
Ph 08 8323 7397

Owners: Scarpantoni family
Winemakers: Michael and Filippo Scarpantoni
Year of foundation: 1998
Tonnes crushed on average each year: 375, none of which are used for Scarpantoni Estate wines at present
Location: McLaren Vale (winery and vineyard)
Area: vineyard 5.2 ha
Soils: red loams and 'biscay'
Variety planted: White—none; Red—shiraz
Leading wines: none at the moment
Notes: This is the old Maxwell winery, which is a contract processing facility without any cellar door sales at the present time.

Penny's Hill

 R86

Willunga Road, McLaren Vale, SA 5171
Ph 08 8323 7535, Fax 08 8323 7536,
Email tparkinson@barrpark.com.au

Owners: Tony and Susie Parkinson
Chief winemaker: Ben Riggs (contract)
Year of foundation: 1988
Tonnes produced on average each year: 500, of which 100 are used for Penny's Hill wines
Location: McLaren Vale
Area: 44 ha
Soils: various loamy soils
Varieties planted: White—chardonnay, semillon; Red—cabernet sauvignon, grenache, merlot, shiraz

Leading wine: Penny's Hill Shiraz
Notes: Located mid-way between McLaren Vale and Willunga, Penny's Hill is an impressive newcomer to the region. Its Chardonnay is crisp and fresh and made in the modern style, while its Shiraz is very impressive, big, chocolatey and welcoming. Cellar door sales: daily 10am–5pm.

Pertaringa Wines

 R86

Hunt and Rifle Range Roads, McLaren Vale, SA 5171
Ph 08 8323 8125, Fax 08 8323 7766

Owners: Geoff Hardy and Ian Leask
Chief winemaker: Geoff Hardy
Year of foundation: 1980
Tonnes crushed on average each year: 350, about 80 of which are used for Pertaringa wines
Location: McLaren Vale
Area: 31 ha
Soils: deep clay loams
Varieties planted: White—chardonnay, riesling, sauvignon blanc, semillon; Red—cabernet sauvignon, pinot noir, shiraz
Leading wines: Pertaringa Shiraz, Cabernet Sauvignon, Sauvignon Blanc
Notes: A very well-regarded vineyard whose fruit has been sought after by major winemakers. These days there is a growing emphasis on winemaking and as one might expect, Shiraz is the star. Cellar door sales: Mon–Fri 10am–5pm, Sat and Sun and long weekends 10am–5pm, closed ordinary weekends.

Pirramimma

 R92

Johnston Road, McLaren Vale, SA 5171
Ph 08 8323 8205, Fax 08 8323 9224

Owners: Johnston family
Chief winemaker: Geoff Johnston
Year of foundation: 1892
Tonnes crushed on average each year: 7500, of which 3000 are used for own label

Location: McLaren Vale
Area: 240 ha
Soils: very variable, heavy black clay loams, red-brown loams, grey loam to light sand over friable clay subsoil
Varieties planted: White—chardonnay, riesling; Red—cabernet sauvignon, grenache, merlot, petit verdot, shiraz
Leading wines: Pirramimma Shiraz, Chardonnay, Petit Verdot
Notes: Pirramimma is part of the soul of McLaren Vale, in the Johnston family's hands since 1892. For the first seventy years of its existence, it made and sold big reds and fortifieds for the London trade, but in the 1960s and 1970s made a successful switch into local markets, at first as a grape grower, then as a maker of excellent reds. Though the winery contract crushes and makes wine for other wineries, it has ceased to sell fruit and has greatly increased production under its own label for export and domestic sales. All the Pirramimma reds are very good, but the star performers here are Shiraz and Petit Verdot, a variety which Pirramimma may justly say it has pioneered in Australia. Cellar door sales: weekdays 9am–5pm, weekends noon–4pm.

Potters Clay R81

Main Road, Willunga, SA 5172
Ph/Fax 08 8556 2922

Owners: John and Donna Bruschi
Chief winemaker: John Bruschi
Year of foundation: vineyards 1994, winery 1998
Tonnes produced on average each year: 225, of which 40 are used for Potters Clay wines
Location: Willunga
Area: 16 ha
Soils: red clay
Varieties planted: White—chardonnay; Red—cabernet franc, cabernet sauvignon, merlot, shiraz
Leading wines: Potters Clay Chardonnay, Shiraz

Notes: Potters Clay is a boutique winery in Willunga specialising in reds, though a Chardonnay is also made. There are no cellar door sales as yet.

Rosemount Estate (McLaren Vale) R91

14 Ingoldby Road, McLaren Flat, SA 5171
Ph 08 8383 0001, Fax 08 8383 0456

Owner: Southcorp Wines
Chief winemaker: Philip Shaw
Year of foundation: 1888 (as Ryecroft)
Tonnes crushed on average each year: 800, from the company's own McLaren Vale vineyards
Area: 80 ha
Soils: varying from Biscay to sand over red clay
Varieties planted: White—chardonnay, riesling, sauvignon blanc, semillon, traminer; Red—cabernet sauvignon, grenache, malbec, merlot, pinot noir, shiraz
Leading wines: Rosemount Grenache-Shiraz-Mourvedre (GSM), Traditional (a blend of the Bordeaux varieties cabernet sauvignon, merlot and petit verdot), Balmoral Shiraz
Notes: Ryecroft is an ancestral name in McLaren Vale, but not seen at the super-premium end of the Rosemount range, which is a pity. Notwithstanding this, the Rosemount reds originating in McLaren Vale are superb and not to be missed, especially the GSM, which is the epitome of McLaren Vale fullness of flavour and style. Balmoral Shiraz is also a benchmark for the region. Cellar door sales: weekdays 10am–4.30pm, weekends 11am–4.30pm.

Scarpantoni Estate Wines R86

Scarpantoni Drive, McLaren Flat, SA 5171
Ph 08 8383 0186, Fax 08 8383 0490, Email scarpantoni.wines@bigpond.com

Owners: Domenico, Paula, Michael and Filippo Scarpantoni
Chief winemakers: Tom Cleland, Michael and Filippo Scarpantoni
Year of foundation: vineyards early 1900s, winery 1979
Tonnes crushed on average each year: 375
Location: McLaren Flat
Area: 32 ha consisting of two vineyards (McLaren Vale 32 ha and Maslin Beach 2 ha)
Soils: McLaren Flat, deep sand and sand over ironstone or clay; Maslin Beach, red-brown soils over limestone
Varieties planted: White—chardonnay, riesling, sauvignon blanc, semillon; Red—cabernet sauvignon, gamay, merlot, petit verdot, shiraz
Leading wines: Scarpantoni Estate Block 3 Shiraz, Unwooded Chardonnay, Cabernet Sauvignon, School Block (a Cabernet-Shiraz-Merlot blend)
Notes: As might be expected, Shiraz is a leading wine here, but there is also a very good red blend and a Sparkling Red 'Black Tempest'. Cellar door sales: weekdays 9am–5pm, weekends 11am–5pm.

Shottesbrooke R84

Bagshaws Road, McLaren Flat, SA 5171
Ph 08 8383 0002, Fax 08 8383 0222

Owners: CJ and NG Holmes
Chief winemaker: Nick Holmes
Year of foundation: 1984
Tonnes crushed on average each year: 350, of which 125 are used for Shottesbrook wines
Location: McLaren Flat
Area: 32 ha consisting of two vineyards (McLaren Flat 20 ha, and Myponga 12 ha)
Soils: McLaren Flat, varying from deep sand over clay to deep sandy loam; Myponga, podsols over clay
Varieties planted: (McLaren Flat)
White—chardonnay; Red—merlot, shiraz.
(Myponga) White—sauvignon blanc;
Red—cabernet sauvignon, malbec, merlot

Leading wines: Shottesbrooke Merlot, Eliza Shiraz, Sauvignon Blanc, Cabernet-Merlot-Malbec
Notes: Shottesbrooke is a consistent award winner for its reds at capital city wine shows. Its Merlot is especially well-known. Cellar door sales: weekdays 10am–4.30pm, weekends and public holidays 11am–5pm.

Sylvan Springs Estates R86

Blythmans Road, McLaren Flat, SA 5171
Ph 08 8383 0500, Fax 08 8323 7726,
Email sallyp@senet.com.au

Owner: David Pridmore
Chief winemaker: Brian Light (contract)
Year of foundation: 1974
Tonnes produced on average each year: 425, of which about 17 are used for Sylvan Springs Estates wines
Locations: (vineyards) McLaren Flat and McLaren Vale
Area: 41.5 ha, McLaren Flat (36.7 ha) and McLaren Vale (4.8 ha)
Soils: McLaren Flat, sand over clay; McLaren Vale, shallow loam over clay subsoil
Varieties planted: White—chardonnay, chenin blanc, riesling, sauvignon blanc, semillon; Red—cabernet sauvignon, grenache, merlot, pinot noir, shiraz, tempranillo
Leading wines: Sylvan Estates Shiraz, Chardonnay, Cabernet Sauvignon
Notes: The Pridmore family's involvement with wine originated in 1892 when ancestor Cyril Pridmore established 'The Wattles' vineyard at McLaren Vale. A winery was later built on the site in 1896, but this property was sold to Penfolds in 1910. So the Pridmore family ultimately became grapegrowers at its Sylvan Park property in McLaren Vale. This in turn was sold in 1978 but not before Digby Pridmore had established 'Sylvan Springs Estates' at Blewitt Springs. David Pridmore purchased this estate in 1990 upon the retirement of Digby. So the Pridmore family are primarily growers,

but do have a wide selection of grape varieties from which to select for their own winemaking. They have certainly chosen quality over quantity, as their Shiraz suggests. Cellar door sales at the McLaren Vale Visitors' Centre (for members of McLaren Vale Winemakers Inc. without 'homes').

Tapestry Wines of McLaren Vale (formerly Merrivale Wines)   R80

Olivers Road, McLaren Vale, SA 5171
Ph 08 8323 9196, Fax 08 8323 9746,
Email tapestry@merrivale.com.au

Owner: Gerard Industries
Chief winemaker: Jon Ketley
Year of foundation: 1973
Tonnes crushed on average each year: 350, of which 130 are used for Merrivale wines
Location: McLaren Vale (winery and vineyard), Bakers Gully (vineyard)
Area: 40 ha in all consisting of two vineyards, McLaren Vale 6.5 ha, Bakers Gully 33.5 ha
Soils: McLaren Vale, red loam over limestone or clay; Bakers Gully, predominantly grey loam over a subsoil of clay with some areas of ironstone over a clay subsoil
Varieties planted: (McLaren Vale) White—chardonnay; Red—cabernet sauvignon, shiraz. (Bakers Gully) White—riesling; Red—cabernet sauvignon, shiraz
Leading wines: Tapestry Bin 388 Cabernet Sauvignon, Bin 338 Shiraz
Notes: Purchased by Gerard Industries in 1997, Tapestry is a medium-sized McLaren Vale winery with a new winemaker, Jon Ketley. Cellar door sales: daily 11am–5pm.

Tatachilla   R86

151 Main Street, McLaren Vale, SA 5171
Ph 08 8323 8656, Fax 08 8323 9096,
Email tatachil@tatachillawinery.com.au

Owner: Banksia Wines Pty Ltd
Chief winemaker: Michael Frangos

Year of foundation: 1994
Tonnes crushed on average each year: 6500, of which 3500 are used for Tatachilla wines
Location: (winery) McLaren Vale, (vineyard) Clarendon
Area: 13 ha
Soils: red clay loam overlying red-brown clays
Varieties planted: White—chardonnay; Red—cabernet sauvignon, merlot
Leading wines: Tatachilla Clarendon Vineyard Merlot, Foundation Shiraz
Notes: Tatachilla amalgamated with St Hallett in 2000 to create a new South Australian wine force, which will be very strong in reds. Tatachilla Merlot is being increasingly recognised as being of top quality and its Foundation Shiraz has been a winner from the outset. Cellar door sales: Mon–Fri 10am–5pm, weekends and public holidays 11am–5pm.

Tyrrells (vineyard only)   R86

Main Road, Willunga, SA 5172

Owner: Tyrrells Vineyards Pty Limited
Chief winemaker: Andrew Spinaze
Year of foundation: 1994
Tonnes crushed on average each year: 350
Location: Willunga
Area: 38.9 ha
Soils: clay loam
Varieties planted: White—chardonnay, sauvignon blanc; Red—cabernet sauvignon, merlot, pinot noir, shiraz
Leading wine: Tyrrells Rufus Stone Shiraz
Notes: This Willunga vineyard is part of Tyrrells 1990s change of identity from Hunter Valley winemaker to Australian winemaker. Not that the Tyrrell family will ever allow the Hunter Valley to become subsidiary to any other Australian region. The Rufus Stone Shiraz is very interesting, commemorating the place in New Forest where in 1100 the dastardly King William Rufus, while out hunting, became fair game himself, receiving an arrow between the eyes (or was it between the shoulders, no-one

quite knows) reputedly from the bow of an ancient Tyrrell. No local cellar door sales.

Wayne Thomas Wines **NR**

26 Kangarilla Road, McLaren Vale,
SA 5171
Ph/Fax 08 8323 9737

Owners: Pat and Wayne Thomas
Chief winemaker: Wayne Thomas
Year of foundation: 1994
Tonnes crushed on average each year: 200, of which 50 are used for Wayne Thomas wines
Area/Soils/Varieties planted: no vineyards are owned
Leading wines: Wayne Thomas Cabernet Sauvignon, Shiraz
Notes: Wayne Thomas is an old McLaren Vale hand having spent some years at Ryecroft and then establishing Fern Hill Estate, which he sold a few years ago. He owns no vineyards but relies for his fruit on contract growers throughout McLaren Vale. Of his two reds Wayne prefers his Cabernet. Cellar door sales: daily noon–5pm.

Wirilda Creek **R85**

McMurtrie Road, McLaren Vale, SA 5171
Ph 08 8323 9688, Fax 08 8323 9260

Owners: Kerry Flanagan and Karen Shertock
Chief winemaker: Kerry Flanagan
Year of foundation: 1992
Tonnes crushed on average each year: 25
Locations: (winery) McLaren Vale, (vineyards) McLaren Vale and Antechamber Bay, Kangaroo Island
Area: (McLaren Vale) 3 ha, (Kangaroo Island) 4 ha
Soils: McLaren Vale, biscay clay soils and alluvial loam; Kangaroo Island, sand with some clay over limestone
Varieties planted: (Wirilda Creek)
White—none; Red—cabernet sauvignon, malbec, merlot, shiraz. (Kangaroo Island)

White—none; Red—cabernet sauvignon, merlot, petit verdot, shiraz
Leading wines: Wirilda Creek Trad Shiraz, St Pats Cabernet-Merlot, Shiraz Rare, Cabernet Rare, Vine Pruners Blend (Shiraz-Cabernet-Merlot)
Notes: This is a vineyard with a good red reputation, which also makes Sauvignon Blanc and Verdelho from purchased grapes. There are also olives, olive and red wine vinegar to be purchased, as well as bed and breakfast accommodation. Cellar door sales: 7 days 11am–5pm.

Wirra Wirra Vineyards **R82**

McMurtrie Road, McLaren Vale, SA 5171
Ph 08 8323 8414, Fax 08 8323 8596,
Email info@wirra.com.au

Owner: RG & RT Trott Pty Limited
Chief winemaker: Ben Riggs
Year of foundation: orginally 1893 then re-established in 1969
Tonnes crushed on average each year: 2500
Location: McLaren Vale
Area: 109 ha consisting of Bethany (McLaren Vale) 22 ha, Scrubby Rise (McLaren Vale) 14 ha, Moray Park (McLaren Flat) 25 ha, Jones Block (McLaren Vale) 16 ha and Finniss (McLaren Vale) 32 ha
Soils: Bethany, sand over clay; Scrubby Rise, black Biscay clay; Moray Park, deep red clay loams; Jones Block, sandy loam over limestone; Finniss, sandy clay over loam
Varieties planted: White—chardonnay, riesling, sauvignon blanc, semillon, viognier;
Red—cabernet sauvignon, grenache, merlot, pinot noir, shiraz
Leading wines: Wirra Wirra RSW Shiraz, Church Block, Riesling, Chardonnay, The Cousins (a sparkling blend of pinot noir and chardonnay)
Notes: At once a blend of the ancient and modern of McLaren Vale, Wirra Wirra was founded in 1893 by RS Wigley, after whom

RSW Shiraz is named, and flourished until 1924 when he died. Winemaking ceased in 1936 and the land was later sold off piecemeal by his family. The winery block (2.8 ha and the derelict winery) was purchased in 1969 by cousins Greg and Roger Trott from the son of Wigley's foreman. Today Wirra Wirra enjoys a very high reputation for quality in both whites and reds. Cellar door sales: Mon–Sat 10am–5pm, Sun and public holidays 11am–5pm.

Woodstock Winery and Coterie

 R85

Douglas Gully Road, McLaren Vale, SA 5171
Ph 08 8383 0156, Fax 08 8383 0437, Email woodstock.winery@mclarenvale.sa.com.au

Owners: Scott and Anne Collett
Chief winemaker: Scott Collett
Year of foundation: 1974

Tonnes crushed on average each year: 300
Location: McLaren Vale
Area: 30 ha
Soils: White sandy soils of varying depth over clay
Varieties planted: White—chardonnay, riesling, semillon; Red—cabernet sauvignon, grenache, shiraz
Leading wines: Woodstock Shiraz, 'The Stocks' Shiraz, Cabernet Sauvignon, Five Feet (a red blend of Cabernet Sauvignon, Petit Verdot and Shiraz), Grenache, Chardonnay, Botrytis Sweet White
Notes: The Woodstock styles are in the main stream of the region. Full yet fruity Grenache, full-bodied Shiraz and big-flavoured Cabernet and a generous Chardonnay complete a typical McLaren Vale portfolio of wines. There is also a luscious Botrytised Riesling. Cellar door sales: weekdays 9am–5pm, weekends and public holidays noon–5pm. The Coterie (restaurant) is open on Sundays and holiday Mondays for lunch.

KANGAROO ISLAND REGION

Like many capes and islands around the southern coasts of the Australian mainland, Kangaroo Island was first sighted by Lieutenant Matthew Flinders RN aboard the *Investigator*. It was so named on 22 March 1802, naturally enough for the large number of kangaroos that Flinders found upon his landing. Many of these were killed to replenish stocks of meat aboard ship.

Flinders was assisted in his endeavour by the French navigator Nicolas Baudin and his surveyor Louis-Claude Freycinet, which explains the large number of French names given to geographical points of interest on the island. Its first semi-permanent inhabitants were whalers and sealers, some of whom were escaped convicts and some Americans, who established a small colony in the area now known as American River. The next stage of habitation was the founding of a small hamlet called Cygnet River, which flourished for some years supplying other small settlements with fruit and vegetables from the fertile lands on the river flats.

Settlement of the Island became official on 27 July 1836, five months before the official proclamation of South Australia as a British colony, but the 'official' settlement near present-day Kingscote proved difficult and by 1840 most of the 'settlers' had moved to the mainland (modern Glenelg) where in modern parlance 'wages and

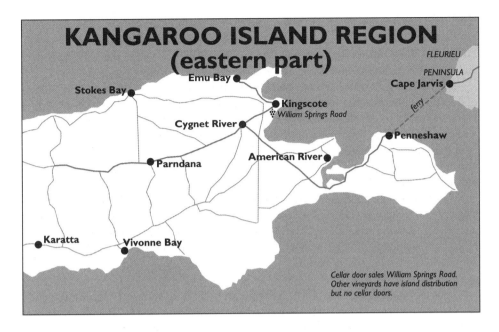

Cellar door sales William Springs Road. Other vineyards have island distribution but no cellar doors.

conditions' were better. The few that did remain were hardy farmers who gradually overcame the hardships of island life and created the modern conception of the dogged perseverance of Kangaroo Island farmers and pastoralists.

During the late 19th century, the Island's predominantly pastoral economy was supplemented by mining (gypsum), quarrying (basalt rock) and distilling (eucalyptus oil). And so the island remained until after World War II, when soldier settlement began around Parndana. The population doubled; agricultural output trebled and until 1990 wool, sheep and fishing remained the chief economic activities on the Island.

Today tourism, exploiting as it does the natural beauty of the Island's spectacular coastline and unspoilt beaches, not to mention its native flora and fauna, dominates the Kangaroo Island economy. There are quality hotels and motels available at the four main Island towns, as well as farmstays and bed and breakfast accommodation. Grain growing and plantation forestry are major agricultural pursuits and other small rural activities include honey and cheese production and viticulture.

Prior to the 1980s, the Island had little history of grape-growing and even that was inauspicious. In the first decade of last century, there was a small planting at American River associated with the Potts family of Langhorne Creek, but the first serious involvement of the Island with viticulture came in 1951 when the Phylloxera Board of South Australia began a rootstock trial at the Parndana Research Station. The collection proved difficult to manage at Parndana and so was moved to Cygnet River in 1955, where the rootstocks developed an unidentified virus, which led to the cessation of the trial and the non-release of any material from it. In the 1970s a small vineyard known as Eastern Cove Wines failed, the vines dying for an unknown reason. However Michael and Rosi Florance succeeded in establishing one hectare of cabernet sauvignon, cabernet franc and merlot vines in 1985, but due to bird damage early yields were very low. At the same time Caj Amadio of Chain of Ponds in the Adelaide Hills also planted a trial plot of pinot noir, shiraz, merlot and riesling. Grapes from these vines were later sent to the Grape and Wine Research Unit at the University of Adelaide where they were assessed and a small quantity of wine made. The results were encouraging.

The first Kangaroo Island wine made from the Florance vineyard was a 1990 blend of the 'Bordeaux' varieties planted there. It was released as a collaborative effort of the Florance family and the Kangaroo Island Trading Co. Though only a few hundred cases were made, the wine was successful. By the mid 1990s five further vineyards had been established. By 1999 there were fourteen. At the present time wine is being marketed under six labels, Kangaroo Island Trading Co, Bay of Shoals, Cape d'Estaing, Dudley Partners, Nepean Ridge and Williams. (Kangaroo Island Trading Co is a company engaged in marketing Kangaroo Island products on the mainland of South Australia. With regard to wine it forms joint ventures with some growers to vinify their fruit and market the ensuing wine. Caj Amadio of Chain of Ponds Vineyards in the Adelaide Hills is its managing director.) Until the year 2000, plantings totalled approximately 70 ha and there were two wineries.

Location: (Kingscote) latitude 35°40'S, longitude 137°38'E, about 112 km south-west of Adelaide. Access by air or passenger ferry to Kingscote or by vehicular ferry to Penneshaw on the eastern end of the Island. (Parndana) latitude 35°48'S, longitude 137°15'E, about 44 km south-west of Kingscote.

Altitude: generally from sea level to about 300 m. The vineyards are located between 10 m and 180 m.

Topography and soils: The Island is a natural extension of the Southern Mount Lofty Ranges, being a thick wedge of sediments created during the Late Precambrian and Cambrian eras in a subsiding marine basin known as the Adelaide Geosyncline. These sediments were faulted and metamorphosed in the ensuing Late Cambrian and Ordovician ages. Since that time the whole island has been intensively weathered to its present reasonably low profile. There are two broad soil–landscape types; the first being soils on the plateau comprising the Seddon and Gosse areas, which are acid duplex soils containing ironstone gravel; the second, on which most of the viticulture is carried out, being calcareous soils comprising both sands and loams and alkaline duplex soils and deep cracking clays (biscay). The soils on the plateau are reasonably uniform, while those in the more weathered coastal areas are much more variable, but predominantly alkaline.

Climate: Kingscote MJT 19.25°C, MAR 7.75°C, HDD 1543 (raw but cut off at 19°C), AR 485 mm (Oct–Apr 164 mm), RH 61% (3pm Jan), AI na, SH na. Parndana MJT 19.75°C, MAR 9.75°C, HDD 1379 (raw but cut off at 19°C), AR 629 mm (Oct–Apr 213.5 mm), RH 65% (Jan 9am), AI na, SH average daily Oct–Apr 6.88. Kangaroo Island has a Mediterranean climate with a very strong maritime influence as nowhere in the Island is further than 22 km from the sea. The Kingscote area is relatively warmer and drier than Parndana. As in most maritime climates (see Margaret River), there are smaller diurnal variations in temperature than in other regions and the vine's growth cycle here is quite long, bud-burst occurring for chardonnay in August and maturity in early to mid-March.

The Island is a windy place, with south-easterlies prevalent in all areas of the Island between December and early February (the Island period between floraison and veraison). These winds may not only cause physical injury to vines but also moisture stress. However, frosts are very rare and are unlikely to occur at any time during the growing season.

Minimal drip irrigation is used on Island vineyards as no significant supplies of groundwater for this purpose have been found, growers being forced to rely on small private surface dams with some supplementary supplies from the South Australian Water reticulation system.

Viticultural problems likely to be encountered include possums, which eat 'anything green', necessitating possum-proof fencing, and birds (bird-netting is essential). Powdery mildew also occurs, but downy mildew has not yet been seen.

Harvest time: Varies slightly according to microclimates, but chardonnay is usually picked early to mid-March with shiraz and cabernet sauvignon being picked from mid-March to mid-April

Principal grape varieties: White—chardonnay; Red—cabernet sauvignon, shiraz

Total area: 70 ha and growing

Principal wine styles: rather early to say, but likely to be red, especially as the region is viewed, in Graham Allison's words as 'Coonawarra without the frost'

Leading vineyard: Florance Vineyard

Bay of Shoals Wines NR

19 Flinders Ave, Kingscote, KI SA 5223
Ph/Fax 08 8553 2229

Owner: Dr John Willoughby
Chief winemakers: Robert Schrapel and Paul Bailey (contract)
Year of foundation: 1993
Tonnes produced on average each year: 7
Location: Bay of Shoals about 1.5 km north of Kingscote
Area: 4 ha
Soils: sand over clay, loam over clay
Varieties planted: White—chardonnay, riesling; Red—cabernet sauvignon, shiraz
Leading wine: Bay of Shoals Cabernet Sauvignon
Notes: No wines tasted. No cellar door sales. Sales by mail order to the above address.

Cape d'Estaing NR

North Coast Road, Wisanger, KI SA 5222
(PO Box 177, Happy Valley, SA 5158)
Ph/Fax 08 8383 6299,
Email annbyers@powercom.com.au

Owner: Cape d'Estaing Pty Ltd (Graham and Jude Allison, Alan and Ann Byers, Marg and Wayne Conaghty and Robin and Heather Moody)
Chief winemakers: Mike Farmilo (contract) and Robin Moody
Year of foundation: 1994
Tonnes produced on average each year: 20 and growing
Location: Wisanger, Kangaroo Island
Area: 10 ha
Soils: dark self-mulching alkaline clays (biscay) and terra rossa
Varieties planted: White—none; Red—cabernet sauvignon, shiraz
Leading wines: Cape d'Estaing Cabernet, Shiraz, Cabernet-Shiraz

Notes: Having overcome the depredations of possums, wallabies and crows, the Cape d'Estaing vineyard is beginning to approach some maturity. Its first wines (1998) were well reviewed by wine advocate Robert Parker and Swiss palate Rene Gabriel and were in fact mostly sold to the US and Europe. No local cellar door sales. Sales by mail order to the above postal address.

Dudley Partners **NR**

Porky Flat Vineyard, Penneshaw,
KI SA 5222
Ph 08 8553 1509, 0408 393 991

Owners: Colin Hopkins, Jeff Howard, Alan Willson and Paul Mansfield
Chief winemaker: contract on site
Year of foundation: 1994, first vintage 1997
Tonnes produced on average each year: 20
Location: Dudley Peninsula, south of Penneshaw
Area: 11 ha consisting of three vineyards (Porky Flat 5 ha, Hog Bay River 2 ha and Sawyers 4 ha)
Soils: sandy loams and clay loams over a limestone base
Varieties planted: (Porky Flat) White—chardonnay, riesling; Red—shiraz. (Hog Bay River) White—none; Red—cabernet sauvignon, merlot. (Sawyers) White—none; Red—cabernet sauvignon, shiraz
Leading wines: Dudley Partners Porky Flat Shiraz, Hog Bay River Cabernet, Shearing Shed Red Shiraz-Cabernet, Peninsula Chardonnay
Notes: No wines have been tasted, but the Dudley Partners are reaching commercial production. There are no cellar door sales, but Kangaroo Island distribution is widespread and some wine is available from a few Adelaide retailers.

Florance Vineyard (vineyard only) **R88**

Gum Creek Road, Cygnet River,
KI SA 5222

Owner: Michael Florance
Chief winemaker: (contract)
Tonnes crushed for Florance wines on average each year: 7 (other fruit produced is sold)
Location: Cygnet River
Area: 4 ha
Soils: sandy loam over clay
Varieties planted: White—none; Red—cabernet franc, cabernet sauvignon, merlot, shiraz
Leading wine: Florance Cabernet Merlot
Notes: The Cabernet Merlot tasted was a fine red by any standards and was the successor to a similar wine of the '96 vintage, which had won a gold medal at the Adelaide Wine Show. Wines such as this augur well for the future of viticulture on the Island. There are no cellar door sales, Florance wines being currently marketed on the mainland by the Kangaroo Island Trading Co.

Nepean Ridge Wines **NR**

Burdon Drive, Kingscote, KI SA 5223
Ph 08 8553 2718, Fax 08 8553 2383

Owners: Rene and Urszula Spruyt
Chief winemaker: Andrew Tolley (contract)
Year of foundation: 1995
Tonnes crushed on average each year: 20
Location: Nepean Ridge, about 4 km south-west of Kingscote
Area: 10.6 ha (3.4 bearing and 7.2 ha due to bear in 2002)
Soils: clay over marl
Varieties planted: White—chardonnay; Red—cabernet sauvignon, merlot, shiraz
Leading wines: Nepean Ridge Chardonnay, Cabernet-Shiraz
Notes: The Nepean Ridge vineyard sits on a south-east facing ridge overlooking Nepean Bay. There Rene Spruyt, former abalone diver

turned vigneron does 'everything from picking to bottling and labelling'. Sales by mail order.

Williams Springs Road **NR**

76 Dauncey Street, Kingscote,
KI SA 5223
Ph 08 8553 2053, Fax 08 8553 3042,
(ah) 08 8553 2206

Owners: Roger and Kate Williams
Chief winemaker: (contract)
Year of foundation: 1995
Tonnes produced on average each year: 3
Location: (vineyard) Williams Springs Road, Kingscote

Area: 10 ha
Soils: sandy loam over clay
Varieties planted: White—chardonnay; Red—cabernet sauvignon, petit verdot, shiraz
Leading wines: Williams Springs Road Chardonnay, Shiraz
Notes: First vintage for Roger and Kate Williams was 1998. The Williams have a joint venture with Kangaroo Island Trading Co to make and market their wine. Cellar door sales and mail orders at 76 Dauncey Street, Kingscote KI 5223.

CURRENCY CREEK REGION (INTERIM)

Goolwa, the region's commercial centre, has since its first settlement been a river town, the first and last port of call on the Murray River and the home of many trading paddle steamers during the 19th century. Indeed the region's raison d'être was the river. Apart from local pastoral activities, there was little else.

The vinous history of the region commenced with the purchase by the Tonkin family of land near Tookayerta Creek in 1969. Four acres (1.6 ha) were initially planted, one each of grenache, cabernet sauvignon, shiraz and riesling. The land was infertile but there were sufficient water and nutrients in the subsoil. So once the vineyard had a start, which it received from fertiliser, it began to thrive. The 1972 vintage saw the first wines of Santa Rosa Winery, as it was then called. That year also witnessed the planting of the first vines at Middleton, then called Marklew, 2.6 ha of riesling and shiraz. This vineyard was purchased in 1988 and renamed Middleton Estate. Other, now substantial, vineyards, Finniss Park Estate and Ballast Stone Estate, also began about this time. These days, there are about 800 ha under vine in the region.

Location: Goolwa latitude 35°30'S, longitude 138°48'E, about 60 km south-east of Adelaide.
Elevation: from sea level to 50 m
Topography and soils: This is low undulating country with two main soil types, sand over clay and a slightly heavier sandy loam. The first type of soil is preferable for vineyards, promoting less vigour in the vines which then concentrate on producing finer fruit flavours. The heavier sandy loam produces more vigour, but less finesse in flavour.
Climate: Goolwa (Hindmarsh Island Marina) MJT 19.45°C, (February is slightly warmer, MFT 19.95°C) MAR 8.3°, HDD 1576 (raw but cut off at 19°C), AR 447 mm (Oct–Apr 178 mm), RH (3pm Jan) 65%, AI na, SH na. Currency Creek has undoubtedly a warm climate but only slightly warmer than neighbouring Langhorne Creek and

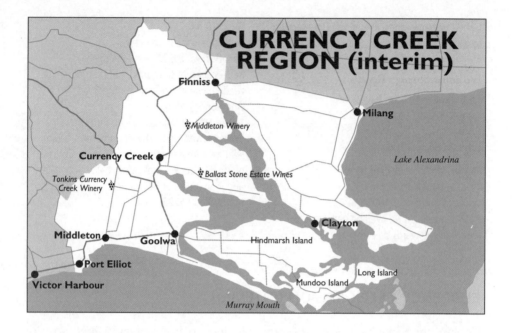

really only lukewarm in comparison to McLaren Vale. Its influences are predominantly maritime, having Encounter Bay to its south and Lake Alexandrina to its east. Prevailing winds during the latter part of the growing season (Jan–Apr) arrive chiefly in the afternoon from the south-east, south and south-west at speeds of between 6 and 30 km per hour. The risk of spring frost is extremely low, only one frost day in September having been recorded in the last 37 years.

Rainfall is comparatively light and supplementary irrigation is necessary. For this purpose, bores are drilled at depths from 20–30 metres. Salinity levels from such bores vary between 300–400 ppm. Private dams also conserve winter run-off. Salinity here averages 100–400 ppm depending upon site. Rivers and creeks such as the Finniss River and Currency Creek are also used for irrigation. Salinity levels here average between 300–400 ppm.

Harvest time: very variable depending on the year. (2000) chardonnay and sauvignon blanc 2nd week of February; shiraz 1st week of April; cabernet sauvignon 2nd week of April. (1999) sauvignon blanc 1st week of March; chardonnay 4th week of March; shiraz and cabernet sauvignon end of 1st week of April. (1998) sauvignon blanc 1st week of March; chardonnay 3rd week of March; shiraz and cabernet sauvignon end of first week of April. (1997) sauvignon blanc and chardonnay 3rd week of March; shiraz and cabernet sauvignon 2nd week of April

Principal grape varieties: White—chardonnay, sauvignon blanc; Red—shiraz, cabernet sauvignon

Total area: (2000) about 800 ha

Major wine styles: Chardonnay, Sauvignon Blanc, Shiraz, Cabernet Sauvignon

Ballast Stone Estate Wines **NR**

Myrtle Grove Road, Currency Creek, SA 5214
Ph 08 8555 4215, Fax 08 8555 4216

Owners: Shaw family
Chief winemaker: John Loxton
Year of foundation: vineyards at McLaren Vale 1972, winery 2000
Tonnes produced on average each year: (2001 vintage) 500, about half of which will be used for Ballast Stone Estate wines. The crush is estimated to rise to 5500 tonnes by 2006
Locations: (vineyards) McLaren Vale and Currency Creek, (winery and cellar door) Currency Creek
Area: 460 ha (McLaren Vale 60 ha, Currency Creek 400 ha)
Soils: McLaren Vale, biscay and red loam; Currency Creek, deep sands over friable clay, biscay and red friable loam
Varieties planted: White—chardonnay, riesling, sauvignon blanc, traminer; Red—cabernet sauvignon, grenache, merlot, petit verdot, shiraz
Leading wines: Ballast Stone Estate Riesling, Sauvignon Blanc, Chardonnay, Grenache, Merlot, Cabernet Sauvignon, Shiraz
Notes: Ballast Stone first wines were released in August 2001. Cellar door sales: daily 10am–4.30pm.

Middleton Winery **NR**

Flagstaff Hill Road, Middleton, SA 5213
Ph 08 8555 4136, Fax 08 8555 4108

Owners: Nigel and Debra Catt
Chief winemaker: Nigel Catt
Year of foundation: vineyard 1972
Tonnes crushed on average each year: 120, of which 50 are used for the Middleton wines

Location: Middleton
Area: 20 ha
Soils: variable ranging from sandy loams over clay to red soils of deep profile
Varieties planted: White—riesling, semillon; Red—cabernet sauvignon, merlot, shiraz
Leading wines: Middleton Riesling, Cabernet, Shiraz
Notes: Middleton Estate is located in a north–south oriented valley just 7 km from the Southern Ocean with vines running east–west and cool maritime breezes to add a necessary touch of humidity. Nigel Catt describes his site as 'perfect'. Cellar door sales: daily 10.30am–5.30pm. There is also a restaurant.

Tonkins Currency Creek Winery (formerly Currency Creek Winery) **NR**

Winery Road, Currency Creek, SA 5214, about 10 km from Goolwa
Ph 08 8555 4069, Fax 08 8555 4100

Owner: Wally Tonkin
Chief winemaker: Warren Randall (contract)
Year of foundation: 1969
Tonnes produced on average each year: 300, of which 110 are used for Tonkin's Currency Creek wines
Location: Currency Creek
Area: 48 ha
Soils: deep sand about 4–5 metres deep over clay
Varieties planted: White—chardonnay, riesling, sauvignon blanc, semillon; Red—cabernet sauvignon, gamay, pinot noir, shiraz
Leading wine: Currency Creek Shiraz
Notes: No wines have been tasted recently. Cellar door sales: 7 days 10am–5pm. There is a restaurant and six accommodation units.

SOUTHERN FLEURIEU PENINSULA

The discovery and the naming of this part of the South Australian coast as the Fleurieu Peninsula is another example of Anglo-French cooperation in the exploration of southern Australia. The principal players in this maritime drama of 1802 were, of course, Lieutenant Matthew Flinders aboard *Investigator* and Captain Nicolas Baudin on *Geographe*. They had met in nearby Encounter Bay. Flinders named the area 'Cape Jervis' after Lord St Vincent, whose family name was Jervis. More enduringly, Baudin named it 'Fleurieu' after his sponsor Charles de Fleurieu, a minister of Marine in Napoleon's government. Only the tip of the Peninsula has retained the name 'Cape Jervis'.

For many centuries, however, prior to the arrival of Baudin and Flinders, the general area was occupied by two Aboriginal tribes, the Kaurna and the Ngarrundjeri peoples, who were later decimated by sickness and conflict after contact with white sealers and early settlers.

In 1855 an early settler, Robert Norman, by profession a dentist, purchased land on the coast near Yankalilla and began to build the town of Normanville the following year. A man of piety and obvious practicality, he first built several churches and two hotels. These were followed by a blacksmith's forge, a police station and a school. By 1860 the district had a population of 2000. Surrounding Normanville and Yankalilla were excellent pastoral and agricultural lands. Soon wheat, reputed to be the best in South Australia, was the chief crop of the district and there were three flour mills in operation. Normanville soon became a port for shipments of wheat and other produce to the eastern colonies. By 1870 two breweries had joined the flour mills, as well as prize sheep and cattle studs in the surrounding countryside. Dairying also became an important industry and later in the 1930s pine forest plantations replaced much of the native bushland. Mining also, at first for copper, lead and silver and later for limestone, opened up the region.

Though as in most of rural Australia, early settlers planted a few vines if only to see what happened, the first serious viticulturist of the region was Buxton Laurie, ancestor of the Laurie family of the Adelaide Hills, who arrived in South Australia in 1848. He later settled on Southcote near Port Elliot and by 1866 was producing over 6700 litres of wine. By 1876 the Southcote vineyards at Port Elliot extended over 180 hectares. The vineyard was later destroyed by massive bushfires in the late 19th century. There were also several other vineyards flourishing at this time but by the end of the 19th century, viticulture and winemaking in the region was in decline and would not be revived until the 1970s, when Sanderson's Trafford Hill vineyard was established. Today there are over 530 hectares of vines in the region and the vine area is still growing.

Location: latitude 35°22'S, longitude 138°27'E, Myponga in the north of the region is about 50 km south south-west of Adelaide. Further south within the region are the towns of Normanville, Yankalilla, Rapid Bay, Victor Harbour and Port Elliot (which forms part of the boundary between it and the Currency Creek region).
Elevation: the region rises from sea level to over 300 m (tops of ranges), but about two-thirds of it lies between 75 and 300 m.

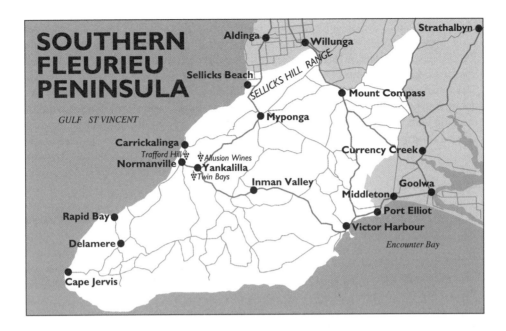

Topography and soils: Southern Fleurieu is an undulating area consisting of coastal plains, hills, slopes, valleys and ranges. Indeed the southern Mount Lofty Ranges are a natural boundary for the east of the region, as is the Sellick range in its north.

There is a wide variety of soils but in general the soils fall into two groups. 1) ironstone gravelly loams on the highlands from Mount Compass to Parawa and 2) sandy loams over the remainder. Both types are well-suited to viticulture in that they are adequately moisture-retentive, drain reasonably well, have good aeration and are stable and non-eroding.

Climate: Myponga MJT 19°C, MAR 10.45°C, HDD 1299 (cut off at 19°C but not otherwise adjusted), AR 758.6 mm (Oct–Apr 260 mm), RH 54% (9am Jan) 44% (3pm Jan), AI na, SH na. Victor Harbour MJT 19.8°C, MAR 8.3°C, HDD 1648 (cut off at 19°C but not otherwise adjusted), AR 535 mm (Oct–Apr 204 mm), RH 68% (9am Jan) 58% (3pm Jan), AI na, SH na

The Southern Fleurieu Peninsula has a variable Mediterranean climate. Myponga at an altitude of 216 metres with its dry summer and wet winter is cool at an HDD of 1299, whereas Victor Harbour at sea level is more typically Mediterranean with a warm HDD of 1648 and a lower rainfall, only 40% of which falls during the growing season. The region therefore would seem suitable for all grape varieties apart from those which prosper only in very cool conditions.

Winds are predominantly maritime, cooling vineyard areas in the afternoons, reducing frost risk to very low and susceptibility to mildews.

Though there are no irrigation schemes serving the region, private bores and dams are used for drip irrigation. In some areas such as Yankalilla, Normanville, Delamere and Victor Harbour, mains water may be utilised to ensure the establishment of young vineyards.

Harvest time: shiraz, early–mid March to early April; cabernet sauvignon, late March, early April

Principal grape varieties: White—riesling; Red—cabernet sauvignon, shiraz

Total area: (2000) 530 ha

Major wine styles: It is rather early to say but red wine styles will most likely be dominant due not only to market but also climatic forces. Allusion Wines is experimenting with a very interesting Shiraz-Viognier red.

Leading wineries and vineyards: Allusion Wines, Trafford Hill.

Allusion Wines R85

Smith Hill Road, Yankalilla, SA 5203
Ph/Fax 08 8558 3333, Email
allusion@dove.net.au

Owners: Steve and Wendy Taylor
Chief winemakers: Steve Taylor and Peter Fraser
Year of foundation: vineyard 1990, cellar door 1996
Tonnes crushed on average each year: 10
Location: Yankalilla
Area: 3 ha
Soils: various soils but chiefly sandy loam over coffee rock and gravel
Varieties planted: White—sauvignon blanc, semillon, viognier; Red—cabernet sauvignon, shiraz
Leading wines: Allusion Semillon-Sauvignon Blanc, Viognier, Cabernet Sauvignon, Shiraz-Viognier
Notes: Allusion is a small family-owned business, whose great forte is its Shiraz-Viognier blend, a la Cote Rotie, a smooth stylish red which is well worth tasting. Cellar door sales: weekends and public holidays 11am–5pm or at other times by appointment.

Trafford Hill R83

Lot 1 Bower Road, Normanville, SA 5203
Ph 08 8558 3595

Owners: Irene and John Sanderson
Chief winemaker: John Sanderson
Year of foundation: 1996
Tonnes crushed on average each year: 5

Location: Normanville
Area: 2 ha
Soils: sandy loam over limestone and ironstone clay deposits
Varieties planted: White—riesling; Red—cabernet sauvignon, grenache, shiraz
Leading wines: Trafford Hill Family Reserve Blend (Red), Riesling
Notes: John Sanderson was at time of writing the president of the Southern Fleurieu Peninsula Winegrapegrowers and Winemakers Association, an enthusiastic group devoted to promoting the local region, which has the much larger McLaren Vale as its northern neighbour. One white and one red is usually made. The reds are well-structured and fruity. Cellar door sales by appointment.

Twin Bays NR

Martin Road, Yankalilla, SA 5203
Ph 08 8267 2844, Fax 08 8239 0877,
Email twinbays@merlin.net.au

Owners: Bruno and Ginny Giorgio
Chief winemaker: Bruno Giorgio, Allan Dyson (contract)
Year of foundation: 1989
Tonnes produced on average each year: 10 (some fruit is also purchased from local growers)
Location: Yankalilla
Area: 1.2 ha
Soils: clayey loams over a limestone base
Varieties planted: White—riesling; Red—cabernet sauvignon, malbec, shiraz

Leading wines: Twin Bays Riesling, Liqueur Riesling, Shiraz, Cabernet

Notes: Twin Bays is a pretty spot, located on a ridge between Rapid and Lady Bays (hence the name of the vineyard). I have not tasted its wines but it has secured bronze awards at the Adelaide and Cowra Wine Shows. Local olive oils and wine vinegars are also available. Cellar door sales: weekends and public holidays 10am–5pm.

❦ THE PENINSULAS ZONE

If the success of Boston Bay Wines is any guide, the Southern Eyre Peninsula would seem to be ideal for classification as a wine region. Its topography is gently undulating. Its soils are typical of the majority of quality Australian vineyard regions, varying from terra rossa over limestone to sandy clayey loams to buckshot gravels over limestone. Its climate is temperate—Mediterranean with a moderating maritime influence.

Climate: MJT 20°C, MAR na, HDD raw 1722 (1583 cut off and adjusted for latitude, daily temperature range and vine sites), AR 486 mm (Oct–Apr 161 mm), RH 53%, AI na, SH 7.5 (Gladstones)
Leading winery: Boston Bay Wines

Boston Bay Wines R88

Lincoln Highway, Port Lincoln, SA 5606
(about 6 km north of Port Lincoln)
Ph/Fax 08 8684 3637,
Email bbw@camtech.net.au

Owners: Graham and Mary Ford and family
Chief winemaker: (contract)
Year of foundation: 1984
Tonnes crushed on average each year: 45
Location: Port Lincoln, Southern Eyre Peninsula
Area: 7.5 ha
Soils: brown sandy loam over clay over limestone
Varieties planted: White—chardonnay, riesling; Red—cabernet sauvignon, merlot, shiraz
Leading wines: Boston Bay Riesling, Cabernet Sauvignon, Merlot, Shiraz
Notes: Boston Bay seems like a slightly warmer version of Medoc, with well-drained soils, a strong maritime influence, and cabernet sauvignon and merlot. There are even whales who slosh past Boston Bay, interrupting the pruning. The wine strengths here are red, especially the Cabernet Sauvignon. Show results demonstrate a consistent silver and bronze standard. Cellar door sales: 11.30am–4.30pm weekends, public holidays and school holidays.

Delacolline Estate NR

Whillas Road, Port Lincoln, SA 5606
Ph 08 8682 4571, Fax 08 8683 4195,
Email ifletch@pl.camtech.net.au

Owner: Ian Fletcher
Chief winemaker: Andrew Mitchell (contract)
Year of foundation: 1984
Tonnes crushed on average each year: 30
Location: Port Lincoln
Area: 5 ha
Soils: gravelly red soils over clay and some sandy limestone country
Varieties planted: White—chardonnay, riesling, sauvignon blanc, semillon; Red—cabernet sauvignon, merlot, shiraz
Leading wine: Delacolline Estate Semillon-Sauvignon Blanc
Notes: Delacolline Estate, Port Lincoln's other winery, is 5 km from the sea and at an elevation of 160 m. Cellar door sales: weekends and public holidays 1.30pm–4pm.

❦ LOWER MURRAY ZONE

This is a large arid stretch of land, extending from the Victorian border west to the foothills of the Mount Lofty Ranges. Its lifeblood is the water of the River Murray. It has one wine region, Riverland.

RIVERLAND REGION

The region was first discovered by Charles Sturt in 1830 when he sailed down the Murrumbidgee, into the Murray River (which he named) and on to Lake Alexandrina and its confluence with the sea in Encounter Bay. As a horticultural and viticultural area, it began with the establishment of an irrigation area at Renmark by the Chaffey Brothers in 1887 (see Murray–Darling region). Similar small irrigation settlements were started along the river during the 1890s and in the years following until the First World War. Viticulture had also commenced at this time and, in 1910, Angove's established a distillery at Renmark and a winery at Lyrup three years later. They were followed by Chateau Tanunda (the Adelaide Wine Company) which, in 1914, erected a distillery. This was sold in 1916 on the liquidation of the Adelaide Wine Co to what was to become the Renmark Growers Co-operative. Thomas Hardy & Sons built two wineries in 1915–16 (one at Waikerie, the other at Murray View) and there were the beginnings of the Berri Co-operative in 1918. The years after the First World War brought soldier settlement blocks, much more planting and increased production as South Australia enjoyed a boom in strong red and fortified wines. As in the early days of the Murray–Darling region, there was an emphasis on distillation and the doradillo variety was widely planted. By 1927 the quantity of Riverland fruit produced outstripped that of the Barossa Valley for the first time.

Though the Great Depression brought considerable hardship, the region was fortunate in that there was a continuing demand for brandy and fortified wines, which, due to beer shortages, continued through the Second World War. In the 1950s, vineyard development in the region continued. Orlando planted at Ramco in 1952. By 1958 when it became clear that the pendulum of public taste was swinging back to lighter table wines, the Berri Co-operative constructed a winery intended entirely for that purpose. Other large vineyards were established at that time, such as Seppelt near Qualco and Yalumba at Oxford Landing. By the 1970s and 1980s, wine casks (soft pack) had made an indelible mark on the wine industry and many millions of litres of Riverland wine were employed to fill them. These days, with the emphasis on bottled table wines, the region produces many varietal table wines of good quality and of particularly good value, as well as its traditional brandies and fortifieds, though in much smaller quantity than previously.

Location: latitude 34°27'S, longitude 140°36'E about 200 km north-east of Adelaide
Elevation: 10–20 m (River valley terraces), 35–50 m (Mallee country above)
Topography and soils: The region consists of gently undulating Mallee Highlands and

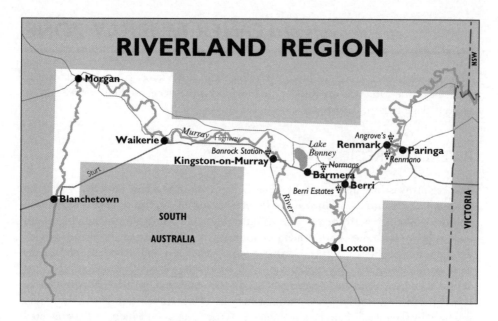

dissected river valley terraces of various heights. The terrace soils are grey and brown clays frequently lying above layers of coarse sand where sandbars and sandhills previously existed. Such soils are present in Renmark, Cobdogla and Lyrup.

The Mallee Highlands are constituted by a series of discontinuous east–west parallel sand dunes. Soils here are chiefly deep red sands or loamy sands with moderate calcium carbonate content about 0.5 to 1 metre deep. On the flatter areas and in the depressions of the Mallee, the soils are of heavier texture to sandy clay loams, and heavier often overlying layers of calcium carbonate at a depth of half a metre. Such soils often contain shallow water tables which require the construction of tile drains to remove effluent, which is pumped into evaporation basins. The Highland soils occur in Berri, Waikerie and Loxton. The soils are normally deficient in nitrogen and zinc; the former can be corrected by the growth of cover crops, the latter by the use of foliar sprays.

Climate: Riverland MJT 23°C, MAR 13.2°C, HDD raw 2084, AR 274 mm (Oct–Mar) 130 mm, RH 51% (9am), AI 510 mm, SH 9.6 (Dry & Smart). Berri MJT 23°C, MAR na, HDD raw 2144, 1745 (cut off and adjusted for latitude and daily temperature range), AR 269 mm (Oct–Apr 139 mm), RH 24% (3pm) (Gladstones), AI na, SH 9.4. Though the Riverland is undoubtedly a hot area, it is the coolest of all Australian fully-irrigated regions during ripening. All vineyards are irrigated, about 80% by sprinkler or drip and the balance by flood, though flood is slowly disappearing, as all new vineyards must be under micro or drip irrigation. Viticultural problems which may be encountered include downy and powdery mildew, though increasing use of trickle irrigation may counter the onset of downy mildew to some extent. In addition normal spray regimes are employed. Other pests in certain areas include nematodes, which may reduce yields, and light brown apple moth.

Harvest time: chardonnay third week of February, shiraz first week of March, cabernet sauvignon mid-March.

Major varieties: 1996 (over 500 ha planted) White—chardonnay, muscat gordo blanco, sultana; Red—cabernet sauvignon, grenache, shiraz
Total area: (1996) c13 400 ha (including table grapes, drying and all-purpose varieties)
Major wine styles: Chardonnay, a reputation established and maintained by Renmano. This is a wine which has changed in style considerably in the past decade from a hugely oaked ripe almost fat style to something much more lean and almost fine, very good considering the warmth of the area. Angove also produces a reliable range of varietal wines as well as a very fine aged Brandy, St Agnes Seven Star XO. Otherwise current drinking bottled and soft pack table wines.
Leading winery: Kingston Estate

Angove's   **R78**

Bookmark Avenue, Renmark, SA 5341
Ph 08 8580 3100, Fax 08 8580 3155,
Email angoves@angoves.com.au

Owners: Angove family
Chief winemaker: Jane Gillham
Year of foundation: 1886
Tonnes crushed on average each year: 17 000, virtually all of which are used for Angove's wines and brandies
Locations: (winery and distillery) Renmark, (vineyards) Renmark and Paringa
Area: 512 ha (Nanya Vineyard, Paringa 480 ha; Anchorage Vineyard, Renmark 32 ha)
Soils: alluvial red sandy loam with underlying limestone areas
Varieties planted: White—chardonnay, chenin blanc, colombard, doradillo, grenache blanc, palomino, riesling, sauvignon blanc, semillon, sylvaner, traminer, trebbiano; Red—cabernet sauvignon, carignan, grenache noir, malbec, merlot, petit verdot, pinot noir, ruby cabernet, rubired, shiraz
Leading wines: Classic Reserve range, Stonegate range, Butterfly Ridge range
Notes: Angove is a producer of good quality table wines at reasonable prices. St Agnes 7 Star XO Brandy is arguably Australia's best. Cellar door sales: Renmark Mon–Fri 9am–5pm, closed weekends. Cellar door outlet also at Angove's original cellars at Tea Tree Gully, 20 km north-east of Adelaide, 9am–5pm.

Banrock Station (vineyard and cellar door only)   **R81**

Holmes Road, Kingston on Murray, SA 5331
Ph 08 8583 0299, Fax 08 8583 0235

Owner: BRL Hardy Ltd
Chief winemaker: Linley Schultz (Renmano)
Year of foundation: small plantings in 1955, vastly extended in 1995–96
Tonnes produced on average each year: estimated at 4000 (in addition, other fruit is purchased from local growers)
Location: Kingston on Murray
Area: 240 ha
Soils: Mallee highland soils, sand or sandy loams over limestone
Varieties planted: White—chardonnay, crouchen, doradillo, muscadelle, riesling, sauvignon blanc, semillon; Red—cabernet sauvignon, grenache, malbec, merlot, petit verdot, rubired, tinta cao, tinta molle, touriga
Leading wines: Banrock Station premium range (Unwooded Chardonnay, Verdelho, Merlot, Shiraz), Banrock Station range (Semillon-Chardonnay, Chardonnay, Shiraz-Cabernet, Cabernet-Merlot), Sparkling Wines
Notes: This vineyard produces large quantities of fruit made at Renmano into competent reds and whites. Cellar door sales: 7 days 10am–5pm.

Berri Estates (winery, distillery and cellar door only) NR

Sturt Highway, Berri, SA 5343
Ph 08 8582 0300, Fax 08 8583 2224

Owner: BRL Hardy Ltd
Chief winemaker: Paul Kassebaum
Year of foundation: 1918
Tonnes crushed on average each year: not disclosed but believed to be in excess of 70 000
Location: Berri (no vineyards owned)
Leading wines: Brentwood range of table wines, Hardy Black Bottle Brandy
Notes: Though it was once the leader of table wine production in the region and has a Jimmy Watson trophy to its credit, it was a long time ago. These days Berri Estates is a producer of bulk wine and soft-pack material. Cellar door sales: daily 10am–5pm.

Kingston Estate R82

Sturt Highway, Kingston on Murray, SA 5331
Ph 08 8583 0500, Fax 08 8583 0304

Owners: Moularadellis family
Chief winemaker: Bill Moularadellis
Year of foundation: 1979
Tonnes crushed on average each year: 18 000
Location: Kingston on Murray
Area: 200 ha
Soils: shallow loam to sandy loam over limestone
Varieties planted: White—chardonnay; Red—cabernet sauvignon, merlot, petit verdot, shiraz
Leading wines: Kingston Estate Merlot, Petit Verdot
Notes: For this region, Kingston Estate is a medium to large winery with a small to medium sized vineyard, most of which is not yet bearing. Its wines are widely exported and are of excellent quality for their price. No cellar door sales.

Mildara Blass Qualco NR

Qualco, SA

Owner: Mildara Blass Ltd
Chief winemaker: Chris Hatcher
Year of foundation: 1960
Tonnes crushed on average each year: 950
Location: Qualco
Area: 84 ha
Soils: deep red sand over limestone
Varieties planted: White—chardonnay, riesling; Red—cabernet sauvignon, shiraz
Leading wines: a contributor to Mildara Blass' commercial table wines
Notes: The former DA Tolley vineyard was acquired when Mildara Blass bought DA Tolley a few years ago. These days the fruit forms part of lower priced bottled wines in the Mildara Blass ranges. No local cellar door sales.

Normans Murray Valley Winery NR

Lone Gum Winery, Nixon Road, Monash, SA 5342
Ph 08 8583 5255, Fax 08 8583 5444

Owner: Normans Wines Limited (in receivership)
Chief winemaker: Peter Fraser
Year of foundation: 1994
Tonnes crushed on average each year: 20 000 (all purchased from growers)
Location: Monash (winery)
Area: no vineyards owned
Leading wines: Normans' Lone Gum range of Chardonnay, Shiraz-Cabernet and Merlot
Notes: The Lone Gum Winery is the engine room for Normans middle and lower range labels. Cellar door sales: Mon–Fri 9am–4.30pm.

Orlando (vineyard only) NR

Qualco Road, Sunlands, SA 5322

Owner: Orlando Wyndham Pty Ltd
Chief winemaker: Phil Laffer

Year of foundation: 1952
Tonnes produced on average each year: 2500
Location: Ramco
Area: 140 ha
Soils: discontinuous east–west parallel sand
dunes of loamy sands with lower areas of
shallower heavy-textured soils of sandy clay
loam overlying calcium carbonate (calcrete)
Varieties planted: White—chardonnay, muscat
gordo blanco, sauvignon blanc, semillon, white
frontignac; Red—ruby cabernet, shiraz
Leading wines: Jacobs Creek Shiraz-Cabernet
(part), Shiraz (part), Cabernet (part)
Notes: Ramco contributes to Jacobs Creek
Shiraz-Cabernet, Shiraz and Cabernet. No local
cellar door sales.

Renmano (winery and cellar door only) NR

Sturt Highway, Renmark, SA 5341
Ph 08 8586 6771, Fax 08 8586 5939

Owner: BRL Hardy Ltd
Chief winemaker: Linley Schultz
Year of foundation: Adelaide Wine Co 1914,
Renmark Growers Co-op 1916
Tonnes crushed on average each year: not
disclosed but believed to be over 20 000
Location: Renmark
Area/Soils/Varieties planted: no vineyards are
owned by BRL Hardy
Leading wines: Renmano range, Lauriston
range
Notes: A large producer of wine cask reds and
whites. Cellar door sales: daily 10am–5pm.

Southcorp NR

Waikerie, SA 5330

Owner: Southcorp Wines
Chief winemaker: John Duval

Years of foundation: winery 1915, vineyards
Markaranka 1969
Tonnes crushed on average each year: not
disclosed but estimated at 4500
Location: Waikerie (winery), Markaranka
(vineyard), Nildottie (leased vineyard)
Area: Markaranka 149.75 ha, Nildottie
17.35 ha (leased)
Soils: red sands over calcrete
Varieties planted: White—chardonnay, muscat
gordo blanco; Red—cabernet sauvignon,
sangiovese, shiraz
Leading wines: lower priced bottled and soft-
pack throughout the group
Notes: For Southcorp, Riverland is an area of
massive production which finds its way into
soft-pack wines and lower priced bottles, both
still and sparkling of many Southcorp brands.
No local cellar door sales.

Yalumba (vineyard only) 80

Waikerie Cadell Road, Oxford Landing,
SA 5321

Owner: S Smith & Son Pty Ltd
Chief winemaker: Brian Walsh
Year of foundation: 1958
Tonnes produced on average each year: 4250
Location: Oxford Landing
Area: 261 ha
Soils: deep red sand over limestone
Varieties planted: White—chardonnay,
sauvignon blanc, viognier; Red—cabernet
sauvignon, merlot, shiraz
Leading wines: Oxford Landing Chardonnay,
Sauvignon Blanc, Cabernet-Shiraz
Notes: Though Oxford Landing is theoretically
the basement door of the Yalumba edifice, it is
always of good quality and well-priced. Its
Chardonnay is one of the benchmark products
of the region. No local cellar door sales.

✤ Chardonnay, Brian Croser and the Adelaide Hills

It is probably correct to say that the commercial exploitation of chardonnay began throughout Australia about 1980, when sufficient chardonnay vines had been planted to satisfy (in a very small way) a growing demand which, later that same decade, became almost insatiable. Before that time it was really a phenomenon of the Hunter Valley where it had been 'discovered' in the late 1960s by the late Murray Tyrrell. It was successfully fermented in barrel (a traditional Burgundian technique) in 1973, a year that should perhaps be commemorated as the date of introduction of modern Chardonnay technique to Australia.

Since 1980, with the assistance of Burgundian experience (where, after all, chardonnay probably originated), and with the objective of achieving greater complexity in Australian Chardonnay, our winemakers have shown their characteristic cleanliness and skill and have left few chardonnay stones unturned. For barrel fermentation and maturation, there have been flirtations with many types of French Oak, Nevers, Limousin, Allier and Vosges, not to mention American and German, as well as more exotic kinds such as Yugoslav, Hungarian, Portuguese and even (in the late 1990s) Russian. Then there came into vogue various degrees of wood-charring, light-, medium- and heavy-toast. Then it was realised that it was not perhaps the type of oak or the charring that was ultimately important, but the quality and the seasoning of the wood and perhaps even the skill of the French coopers. So we sought out the coopers who made the barrels for the Burgundians. During this time of oak experimentation, many other technical developments occurred in chardonnay making: skin contact, malolactic fermentation, low sulfurs, no sulfurs, oxidative handling, non-oxidative handling, maturation on still and stirred lees, whole bunch pressing, early bottling, late bottling and, in the last few years, unwooded chardonnay with or without malolactic fermentation.

As all these technical advances continued, chardonnay came to be planted in every wine-growing region in Australia and virtually everywhere it has been planted it has succeeded, for chardonnay is, in Brian Croser's words, 'a very forgiving variety'. If Murray Tyrrell may be termed the modern 'discoverer' of Australian chardonnay, Brian Croser must at least be its patron saint. He is certainly the modern pioneer of the viticultural possibilities of the Piccadilly Valley in particular and the Adelaide Hills region in general. Croser, who has made over 20 chardonnay vintages, long ago realised that great chardonnay was made in the vineyard, not necessarily the winery.

In 1996, Croser revealed what he considered to be the essential factors of site selection for great Australian chardonnay. The soil, aspect and climatic requirements of the site were, he contended, as follows:

- the slope must be free-draining of both air (to prevent frost) and moisture (to avoid 'wet feet') in the vines
- the soil should be of a bright red or white colour, which is light reflective in nature
- the soil should be old (in the geological sense) and of moderate fertility so that the

vine spends its time ripening a moderate crop rather than trying to ripen an excessive crop or to produce excessive foliage. New volcanic soils are to be avoided

- the slope should be as steep as is manageable, facing to the north-east (in Australia, the aspect most favourable in harnessing and maximising the early morning sunlight hours to ripen chardonnay, while protecting it from the extremes of cold southerly and extremely hot or cold westerly or hot northerly winds
- the climate should be Mediterranean (i.e. a wet, cold winter and a dry summer of moderate humidity)
- the region should be cool enough to delay ripening into mid to late autumn, conditions favouring retention of grape acidity and the development of the fine but intense aromatics that typify great chardonnay
- such sites are likely to occur in a cool region of 900 to 1250 degree days (few sites in Australia are as cool as 900—perhaps a HDD of 1000 is more realistic).

Croser was convinced that such sites are found only in 'cool' regions, where chardonnay bud-burst, flowering, veraison (the colouring and ripening of the grapes) are as late as possible in their cycle and harvest is close to autumn leaf fall, but within that area, the 'distinguished site' will be the warmest (a 'hot spot').

In addition, there are ten other viticultural and meteorological criteria which that 'hot spot' must have in order to become distinguished.

1 steep hillside rows which maximise sunlight intensity, such rows being oriented north–south for even ripening on both sides of the vine
2 a close spacing of the vineyard to spread the vineyard's natural spacing of shoots
3 a vertical canopy for full interception of sunlight
4 leaf stripping from just above the fruiting zone when the vine has stopped growing (usually about a month before veraison) to allow sunlight penetration and ventilation to the fruit
5 protection from wind to limit the amount of water sucked through the vine (to replenish dehydration)
6 cool flowering conditions to achieve natural crop control at a level of 6–9 tonnes per hectare (to achieve small bunches consisting of large and small berries, which is extremely important, for small berries ripen more easily and give a higher skin to juice flavour. In this way, what the French call 'millerandage' and the Australians 'hen and chicken' can be beneficial.)
7 vines of ten years' age or more to achieve full root exploitation of the soil and provide old wood carbohydrate storage
8 a summer dry enough to stop the vine growing and to induce some stress (but not too much)
9 a long, cool air, sunny, dry autumn during which the grapes mature completely before the onset of rain
10 the uniqueness, conferred by a discrete, obviously different location.

Such were Croser's conclusions after a visit to Burgundy, based on a comparison he made between his own Piccadilly Valley vineyards and the hill of Aloxe-Corton in the Cote de Beaune. So we may ask what sort of Chardonnays such an Australian vineyard site is likely to produce. Fine-textured wines of intense aromatics and great finesse that most certainly need years in bottle to develop ultimate complexity. Where in Australia are such vineyard sites to be found? Some already exist in the Adelaide Hills, the Yarra Valley and northern Tasmania. Others are still to be located, maybe at altitude, the Snowy Mountains and Central Tablelands of New South Wales or perhaps much closer to sea-level in southern Victoria or the far south-east of South Australia or the south-west of Western Australia.

In his chardonnay making, Brian Croser is very fortunate in that he has a number of quality 'sites' from which to select his raw material. Such a number of quality sites within one region increases vastly the number of options that a maker of chardonnay has at vintage time.

It is common knowledge that the modern chardonnay maker never makes only one wine. Depending upon the resources of chardonnay fruit (whether from different vine-yards within the same sub-region, region, wine zone, State or perhaps all of Australia), there is a multitude of options. As regards parts of the final wine, the maker may direct that the fruit be picked at varying stages of ripeness; it may be crushed or be subject to whole bunch ferment; it may be left in contact with skins; the juice may be clarified; it may be left on 'solids'. It may be fermented anaerobically or subject to a degree of oxi-dation. At what temperature has the must been fermented? What degree of sulfuring has it had? After fermentation in tank or in new or older oak, it may be stored in stainless steel or matured in that same barrel or barrels. And the maturation oak itself, as pointed out above, may be new or older and have many different national provenances or even diverse origins within the same country (as witness the different types of French oak with their variations of flavour). And what of the imprint of the cooper? What degree of 'toasting' has the oak undergone? Has the wine undergone malolactic fermentation? And indeed what length of maturation and what treatment within that period of maturation has the wine experienced? Have its 'lees' been still or stirred? Has it been 'cleaned up' and taken totally off 'lees'? Has its sulfur been adjusted or is it virtually sulfur-free? As you will readily appreciate, depending on resources, the winemaker may finish with forty or fifty different chardonnays, all in varying quantities—lots of detail with which to complete the big picture or a miniature if desired. But in either case the dominant feature of that picture will be complexity, in the greatest possible degree that the winemaker can achieve in the regional or sub-regional wine, through tasting, monitoring and differenti-ating quality at several stages during the winemaking and maturation process. Fairly soon, the 'top' components for the final wine or wines will emerge and will then be subject to the final dab of the brush, a slight oak adjustment perhaps here and there, some parts to spend a little more time in oak and some to come out and remain in stain-less steel for a while. The final blending will take place some time thereafter. And there are still other decisions to be made. Will it be filtered prior to bottling? How long should it remain in bottle prior to release? Such attention to minutiae has made Australian winemakers sought-after the world over.

And what of the rest of the wine? There may be a second Chardonnay label avail-able for some further part of it, but what is rejected will be sold or blended with another variety or varieties to form a lower-priced and lesser-quality wine. Such is present-day Chardonnay.

MOUNT LOFTY RANGES ZONE

The broad uplands of South Australian viticulture. An important zone containing old and new wine regions—the Adelaide Hills and the Clare Valley.

ADELAIDE HILLS REGION

By 1830, what is today the Adelaide coast and its hinterland of steep hills had become quite well-known to explorers and sealers and the first inland explorations had begun to take place. In that year Charles Sturt navigated the Murray River to its mouth in Lake Alexandrina and Captain Barker climbed Mount Lofty the following year. After settlement of the coastal plain in 1836, early colonists, both Anglo-Celt and German, wasted little time in heading for the hills behind what was to become the city of Adelaide. By 1844, the Hills' first wines began to appear, made in all probability by Walter Duffield who, in 1848, became South Australia's first wine exporter by shipping a case of his wine, now famous as the 'Echunga hock', to Queen Victoria. By 1871, the Hills region was reportedly producing over 700 000 litres of wine from a vineyard area of 536 ha. From then on, the region went into a slow but persistent decline, though not due, as in some other Australian areas, to phylloxera. This time the causes were most probably the lack of consistent quality, the rise of the prohibition movement, non-existence of export markets and over-supply of local ones, and a gradual change in public taste in favour of fortified wines and big reds. By 1910, however, viticulture had become a minor economic activity and by 1930 had ceased altogether. In the half-century following, the region became highly regarded for its fruit and vegetables, for which there was a much more constant demand from nearby Adelaide than there had ever been for wine.

Although Leigh and Jan Verrall of Glenara made their first plantings at Upper Hermitage in 1971, the viticultural renaissance of the Adelaide Hills was due to one man, who was conscious of the history of the region and ever confident in its suitability for the making of sparkling and delicate table wines. Brian Croser built his first winery, Petaluma, and planted his surrounding vineyards at Piccadilly in the late 1970s. From then on a second rush to the Hills swiftly gained momentum. Today there are over eleven cellar door sales facilities in the region. In this most scenically attractive region, it is to be noted that present planning restrictions wisely confine future winery size to a maximum crush of 500 tonnes, because of environmental considerations and the endemic shortage of water in the region.

Location: latitude 34°56'S, longitude 138°45'E, about 14 km directly east of Adelaide, a long narrow swathe of land on a north–south axis, located in the southern Mount Lofty Ranges, about 75 km long and 20 km wide
Elevation: averaging about 400 m with peaks at 730 m and gullies at 350 m
Topography: the main feature is the southern Mount Lofty Ranges which run north–south through the central west of the wine region. West-facing are a series of

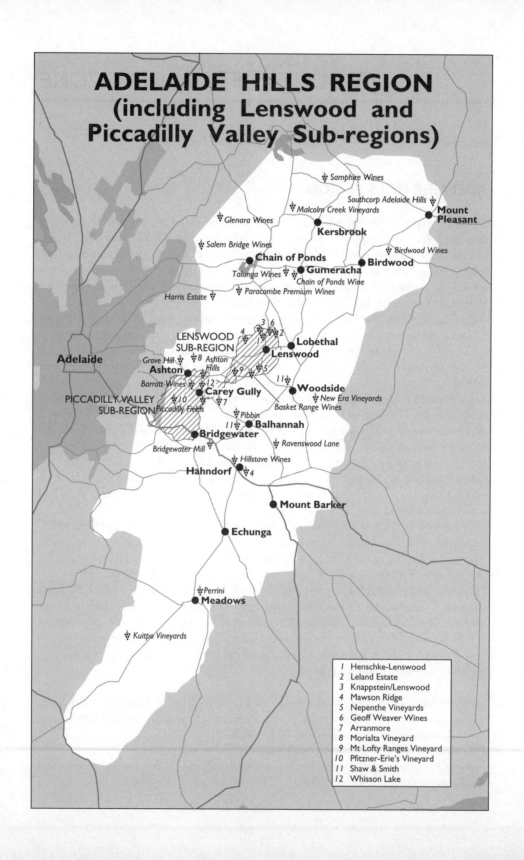

ADELAIDE HILLS REGION
(including Lenswood and Piccadilly Valley Sub-regions)

Samphire Wines

Southcorp Adelaide Hills

Malcolm Creek Vineyards

Mount Pleasant

Glenara Wines

Kersbrook

Salem Bridge Wines

Birdwood Wines

Chain of Ponds

Gumeracha

Birdwood

Talunga Wines

Chain of Ponds Wine

Harris Estate

Paracombe Premium Wines

3 6

4 2

LENSWOOD
SUB-REGION

1

Lobethal

Lenswood

Grove Hill

8 Ashton
Hills

Adelaide

Ashton

9 5

Barratt Wines

12

11

Woodside

PICCADILLY VALLEY
SUB-REGION

Carey Gully

7

New Era Vineyards

10

Piccadilly Fields

Basket Range Wines

Pibbin

11

Balhannah

Bridgewater

Bridgewater Mill

Ravenswood Lane

Hillstave Wines

Hahndorf

4

Mount Barker

Echunga

Perrini

Meadows

Kuitpo Vineyards

1	Henschke-Lenswood
2	Leland Estate
3	Knappstein/Lenswood
4	Mawson Ridge
5	Nepenthe Vineyards
6	Geoff Weaver Wines
7	Arranmore
8	Morialta Vineyard
9	Mt Lofty Ranges Vineyard
10	Pfitzner-Erie's Vineyard
11	Shaw & Smith
12	Whisson Lake

steep scarps or tiers, ultimately descending to the Adelaide plain, but ascending to summits at the centre and then east of the peaks, more gentle slopes on the descent to the east. The whole area is undulating with local peaks and fertile gullies.

Soils differ greatly throughout the region with variations occurring both north–south and east–west. In the north of the wine region, the underlying rock is Aldgate Sandstone, upon which there have developed yellow, gritty clays and dark grey sandy loams. In the creeks and gullies, there are alluvial deposits and deep schistic clays with dark red-brown loams. In the centre are bedrocks of Torrens Sandstone on which there are skeletal grey and yellow podsols with alluvial deposits in the gullies and on the creek flats, while to the south and east there are meadow podsols. Most country is free-draining.

Climate: Belair (western foothills) MJT 20.4°C, MAR na, HDD raw 1727, 1625 (cut off and adjusted for latitude and daily temperature range), AR 755 mm (Oct–Apr 282 mm), RH 51% (3pm Jan), AI na, SH 8.2. Stirling (high Hills) MJT 17.7°C, MAR na, HDD raw 1183, 1213 (as adjusted for latitude, daily temperature range and vine sites), RH 52% (3pm Jan), AI na, SH 8.3. Mount Barker (eastern foothills) MJT 18.8°C, MAR na, HDD raw 1433, 1337 (cut off and adjusted for latitude, daily temperature range and vine sites), RH 39% (3pm Jan), AI na, SH 8.1. The Adelaide Hills region has basically a Mediterranean climate with variations in some micro-climates due to altitude. There are three basic areas with the coolest and wettest vineyard sites in the high Hills north and north-east of Stirling (1121 mm annual rainfall) about as far north as Uraidla and as far north-east as Lenswood. The warmest and driest areas are in the western foothills (Belair, 755 mm annual rainfall) and in the northern part of the region (north of Gumeracha), though the eastern foothills (Mount Barker) are also warm and dry (781 mm annual rainfall). The whole region has a maritime influence due to weather changes from the west and south-west. It is cold and sometimes bleak in winter with some higher areas receiving occasional dustings of snow. Often cold even in January, it can be generally described as a cool area. Rainfall is between 750 mm and 1200 mm depending on location, the western (highest) edge of the high Hills being normally the wettest. Most falls are in winter and spring; about 15% falls in summer, but is unreliable. Supplementary irrigation is essential, especially when establishing vine-yards. Drip or micro-spray irrigation is by bore water from extremely local aquifers or water from private surface dams, though the latter are now being restricted due to the fact that the region is a watershed for the Adelaide metropolitan area. Salinity is gener-ally not a problem but some bores do return unacceptably saline water.

Spring frosts after budburst are a difficulty on the bottoms of valleys and on river flats with some growers retarding pruning in an attempt to avoid frost damage. Birds too present problems because of the relatively small size of vineyards and their prox-imity to orchards and forests.

The growing season sees budburst (depending on variety) from mid-September to mid-October, flowering mid to late November and veraison mid to late February.

Harvest time: late March to early May, though occasionally earlier, with auslese pickings extending into late May

Principal grape varieties: White—chardonnay, riesling, sauvignon blanc, semillon; Red—cabernet sauvignon, merlot, pinot noir, shiraz (increasingly respected, especially in the southern and northern areas of the Adelaide Hills, see entry on Kuitpo Vineyards). However, as the ever-efficient Adelaide Hills Wine Region Inc informs me, virtually the whole ampelographical catalogue is now planted somewhere in those Hills. Here are just a few others: White—pinot gris, traminer, verdelho, viognier; Red—cabernet franc, gamay, grenache, lagrein, malbec, meunier, mourvedre (mataro), nebbiolo, petit verdot, sangiovese, saperavi, tannat, tempranillo, zinfandel.

There seems little doubt however that the principal varieties planted, especially chardonnay, sauvignon blanc and pinot noir, are eminently suited to the cooler higher parts of the Hills (growers in those parts should plant nothing else and if possible graft over cabernet sauvignon and later-ripeners to chardonnay and pinot); while later ripeners such as cabernet sauvignon, shiraz and petit verdot do need lower warmer Hill climes for success. I await with very great interest more gamays, for a soft fruity non-extractive 'Beaujolais' style is a personal favourite.

Total area: (est) 2000 ha

Principal wine style: The Adelaide Hills region is arguably the leading quality region in Australia for Chardonnay. Usually, its wines are beautifully structured, aromatic, long-palated and crisp-finishing with very good cellaring capacity.

Leading wineries and vineyards: Ashton Hills, Petaluma, Penfolds Adelaide Hills, Shaw & Smith, Henschke Lenswood, Hillstowe, Knappstein Lenswood, Geoff Weaver Wines, Chain of Ponds, Ravenswood Lane, Leland Estate, Pibbin, Barratt, Nepenthe, Mount Lofty Ranges, Whisson Lake.

Arranmore R85

Rangeview Road, Carey Gully, SA 5142
Ph 08 8390 3034, Fax 08 8390 0005,
Email arranmore@camtech.net.au

Owners: John and Meredith Venus
Chief winemaker: John Venus
Year of foundation: 1998
Tonnes produced on average each year: 3
Location: Carey Gully, Piccadilly Valley
Area: 2 ha, only 0.3 ha being in production at time of writing
Soils: fairly heavy clay loams on a fairly gentle east-facing slope
Varieties planted: White—chardonnay, sauvignon blanc; Red—pinot noir
Leading wine: Arranmore Black Pinot
Notes: John and Meredith Venus already have an Adelaide Hills Wine Show bronze medal to their credit for a vigorous Black Pinot. The white varieties planted should also perform well. Cellar door sales: phone or fax first.

Irregular opening at weekends. At other times by appointment.

Ashton Hills R91

Tregarthen Road, Ashton, SA 5137
Ph/Fax 08 8390 1243

Owners: Peter Van Rood and Stephen George
Chief winemaker: Stephen George
Year of foundation: 1982
Tonnes crushed on average each year: 21
Location: Ashton, Piccadilly Valley
Area: 3 ha
Soils: shallow sandy clay loam over well-draining ancient sandstone
Varieties planted: White—chardonnay, riesling; Red—cabernet franc, merlot, pinot noir
Leading wines: Ashton Hills Pinot Noir, Riesling, Chardonnay, Obliqua (a red blend of the 'Bordeaux' varieties), Sparkling (Salmon Brut, Blanc de Blanc)
Notes: A vineyard with stunning views from its

ridge-top over the Piccadilly Valley, Ashton Hills has become well-known for its very fine Pinot Noir and also its Riesling. Its Chardonnay also is of excellent Adelaide Hills style, as is its Blanc de Blanc sparkler. A winery not to miss. Cellar door sales: weekends and public holidays 11am–5.30pm. At other times by appointment.

Barratt R86

Collins Road, Summertown, SA 5141
Ph/Fax: 08 8390 1788

Owners: Lindsay and Carolyn Barratt
Chief winemaker: Jeffrey Grosset (contract)
Year of foundation: 1993
Tonnes crushed on average each year: 14, but production is increasing
Location: Summertown, Piccadilly Valley
Area: 8.9 ha, consisting of two vineyards (Uley 5.5 ha and Bonython 3.4 ha)
Soils: Uley, ranging from sandy loam at top to light clay over sandstone at bottom; Bonython, sandy loam
Varieties planted: (Uley) White—chardonnay, sauvignon blanc; Red—pinot noir. (Bonython) White—none; Red—merlot, pinot noir
Leading wines: Barratt Chardonnay, Pinot Noir
Notes: Barratt wines are produced only from estate-grown fruit and have won many totally justified awards for Pinot Noir at the Adelaide Hills Wine Show over recent years. The Chardonnay is excellent also. No cellar door sales but there is mail order to PO Box 204, Summertown, SA 5141.

Basket Range R84

Blockers Road, Basket Range, SA 5138
Ph 08 8390 1515, Fax 08 8390 0499

Owners: Philip and Mary Broderick
Chief winemaker: Philip Broderick
Year of foundation: 1980
Tonnes crushed on average each year: 6
Location: Basket Range
Area: 2 ha

Soils: sandy loam over sandstone, acidic
Varieties planted: White—none; Red—cabernet franc, cabernet sauvignon, malbec, merlot, petit verdot
Leading wine: Basket Range Cabernet Blend
Notes: Basket Range is a very small vineyard concentrating its resources on a Bordeaux-style red. No cellar door sales. Wine sales by mail order to above address.

Birdwood Estate NR

Mannum Road, Birdwood, SA 5234
Ph 08 8263 0986

Owners: Oli and Susan Cucchiarelli
Chief winemaker: Oli Cucchiarelli, but not on site
Year of foundation: 1980 (first wine 1988)
Tonnes crushed on average each year: 20, all of which are made into wine, with half used for Birdwood Estate wines
Location: Birdwood
Area: 10 ha
Soils: sandy loams over yellow clay
Varieties planted: White—chardonnay, riesling, sauvignon blanc; Red—cabernet franc, cabernet sauvignon, merlot
Leading wines: Birdwood Estate Chardonnay, Cabernet Sauvignon
Notes: No cellar door sales. Sales by mail order to PO Box 194, Birdwood, SA 5234.

Chain of Ponds R87

Main Road, Gumeracha, SA 5233
Ph 08 8389 1415, Fax 08 8336 2462

Owners: Amadio family
Chief winemaker: Caj Amadio
Year of foundation: vineyards 1985, winery 1993
Tonnes crushed on average each year: 1600, of which 110 are used for Chain of Ponds wines
Location: Gumeracha
Area: 153 ha. There are two vineyards—Gumeracha part owned by the Amadio family

(85 ha) and Kersbrook, wholly owned by the Amadio family (68 ha)

Soils: both vineyards, heavy brown loams over permeable clay over weathered bluestone

Varieties planted: White—chardonnay, riesling, sauvignon blanc, semillon, viognier; Red—cabernet sauvignon, grenache, merlot, mourvedre, nebbiolo, pinot noir, sangiovese, shiraz

Leading wines: Chain of Ponds Chardonnay, Cabernet Sauvignon 'Amadeus', Shiraz 'Ledge'

Notes: Chain of Ponds is a highly awarded winery that has received a great press since its inception in the mid 1990s. It is worth every award and every word of praise it has received. Its Chardonnay is never less than excellent and usually outstanding. Cellar door sales: daily 10.30am–4.30pm.

Glenara NR

126 Range Road North, Upper Hermitage, SA 5131
Ph 08 8380 5277, Fax 08 8380 5056,
Email glenara@senet.com.au

Owners: LE and JL Verrall
Chief winemaker: Trevor Jones (contract)
Year of foundation: vineyard 1971, winery 1988
Tonnes crushed on average each year: 90
Location: Upper Hermitage
Area: 12 ha
Soils: dark brown loam over red clay over siltstone

Varieties planted: White—chardonnay, riesling, sauvignon blanc; Red—cabernet franc, cabernet, sauvignon, merlot, meunier, pinot noir, shiraz

Leading wines: Glenara Adelaide Hills, Cabernet Sauvignon, Pinot Noir, Merlot, Shiraz, Sauvignon Blanc

Notes: Glenara has been in the Verrall family for over 70 years, though a vineyard only since 1971. Recently it has been approved as an organic vineyard by the Organic Vignerons

Association of Australia and all vintages since 1993 have been certified as organically grown. Cellar door sales: by appointment only.

Geoff Weaver Wines (formerly Stafford Ridge) (vineyard only) R88

Stafford Road, Lenswood, SA 5240
Ph 08 8272 2105, Fax 08 8271 0177,
Email weaver@adelaide.on.net

Owners: Geoff and Judy Weaver
Chief winemaker: Geoff Weaver
Year of foundation: 1982
Tonnes crushed on average each year: 75
Location: Lenswood (vineyard)
Area 11.7 ha
Soils: acid, podsolic sandy loam and clay, well-drained over sandstone and quartzite

Varieties planted: White—chardonnay, riesling, sauvignon blanc; Red—cabernet sauvignon, merlot, pinot noir

Leading wines: Geoff Weaver Chardonnay, Sauvignon Blanc, Cabernet-Merlot

Notes: Formerly chief winemaker at Hardy's, since 1992 Geoff Weaver has concentrated his considerable energies on his vineyard at Stafford Ridge. His whites, a tropical deep-flavoured Sauvignon Blanc and a complex multi-layered Chardonnay, are remarkably fine, while his Cabernet-Merlot is superb in riper years. There are no cellar door sales, but mail order is possible c/- 2 Gilpin Lane, Mitcham, SA 5062.

Grove Hill NR

120 Old Norton Summit Road, Norton Summit, SA 5136
Ph/Fax 08 8390 1437

Owner: Marguerite Giles
Chief winemaker: Dave Powell (contract)
Year of foundation: 1978
Tonnes crushed on average each year: 10
Location: Norton Summit

Area: 2 ha
Soils: clay loam, acidic
Varieties planted: White—chardonnay, riesling;
Red—pinot noir
Leading wines: Grove Hill Chardonnay, Pinot
Noir
Notes: Grove Hill is a close-planted vineyard,
located on a property owned for over 150
years by the Giles family. At about 400 metres
in altitude, it has its own very cool
microclimate. Its riesling is not irrigated and
other varieties are irrigated only when
absolutely necessary. No cellar door sales.

Harris Estate R84

Paracombe Road, Paracombe, SA 5132
Ph/Fax 08 8380 5353

Owners: Trevor and Sue Harris
Chief winemaker: Trevor Harris
Year of foundation: 1975
Tonnes produced on average each year: 14
Location: Paracombe
Area: 2.5 ha
Soils: medium loam topsoils above clay
Varieties planted: White—chardonnay;
Red—cabernet sauvignon, shiraz
Leading wines: Harris Estate Shiraz, Cabernet
Sauvignon
Notes: Paracombe is one of the older
established areas of the Adelaide Hills and the
Harris Estate shiraz vines, being originally
planted in the early 1960s, must now be
amongst the veterans of the Adelaide Hills.
Like most golden oldies, they substitute style
and elegance for the brash enthusiasm of
youth.

Henschke Lenswood
(vineyard only) R88

Cnr Coldstore and Croft Roads,
Lenswood, SA 5240
Ph 08 8564 8223, Fax 08 8564 8294,
Email henschke@dove.net.au

Owners: Stephen and Prue Henschke
Chief winemaker: Stephen Henschke,
(viticulturalist) PM Henschke
Year of foundation: 1981
Tonnes crushed on average each year: 64
Location: Lenswood
Area: 13 ha
Soils: schisty sandy loam with shale fragments,
well drained
Varieties planted: White—chardonnay,
riesling; Red—cabernet sauvignon, merlot,
pinot noir
Leading wines: Henschke Lenswood Green's
Hill Riesling, Croft Chardonnay, Giles Pinot
Noir, Abbot's Prayer (a red blend from the red
varieties other than pinot noir)
Notes: If ever any doubt is expressed about the
suitability of the Lenswood region for
superlative reds, simply utter 'Abbott's Prayer'
and any such doubts are instantly allayed. The
Giles Pinot Noir is always complex and
interesting, while the Croft Chardonnay and
the Green's Hill Riesling are never less than
excellent. No cellar door sales at Lenswood.
Wines are available for sale at Henschke,
Keyneton (See Eden Valley region).

Hillstowe R88

104 Main Road, Hahndorf, SA 5245
Ph 08 8388 1400, Fax 08 8388 1411,
Email wines@hillstowe.com.au

Owner: Banksia Wines Pty Limited
Chief winemaker: Chris Laurie
Year of foundation: Carey Gully vineyard,
Lenswood sub-region, 1984; Hahndorf cellar
door, 1995; Mount Torrens winery, 1997
Tonnes crushed on average each year: 160, of
which 140 are used for Hillstowe wines
Location: Hahndorf (cellar door), Mount
Torrens (winery), Carey Gully, (vineyard)
Area: 16.5 ha
Soils: ancient weathered podsols
Varieties planted: White—chardonnay, pinot
gris, sauvignon blanc; Red—merlot, pinot noir

Leading wines: Hillstowe Udy's Mill Chardonnay, Udy's Mill Pinot Noir, Sauvignon Blanc, Lenswood 'The Pinch Row' Merlot, Lenswood Pinot Gris

Notes: For simple unalloyed excellence, Hillstowe Udy's Mill Chardonnay is incomparable. The Pinot Noir is also extremely good. Hillstowe is an obligatory destination on any wine tour of the Adelaide Hills. Do not miss it. Cellar door sales: 7 days 10am–5pm. Lunch is also available.

Knappstein Lenswood Vineyards (formerly Lenswood Vineyards) (vineyard only) R88

Crofts Road, Lenswood, SA 5240
Ph 08 8389 8111, Fax 08 8389 8553,
Email admin@knappsteinlenswood.com.au

Owners: Tim and Annie Knappstein
Chief winemaker: Tim Knappstein (the wines are not made on site, but under Tim Knappstein's supervision and control at Knappstein Wines in Clare, except for Pinot Noir, which is made at Nepenthe Vineyards, Lenswood)
Year of foundation: 1981
Tonnes crushed on average each year: 130, the best of which are used for Knappstein Lenswood wines, the balance being sold as bulk wine. It is anticipated that the crop will rise to 200 tonnes by 2002
Location: Lenswood
Area: 26.67 ha
Soils: old soils; duplex, grey-brown and red-brown loam over crumbly clay subsoils with sandstone over quartz gravel, generally of low fertility
Varieties planted: White—chardonnay, sauvignon blanc, semillon; Red—cabernet sauvignon, malbec, merlot, pinot noir
Leading wines: Knappstein Lenswood Pinot Noir, Chardonnay, Sauvignon Blanc
Notes: This is one of the most exciting vineyards of the new sub-region of Lenswood, which is

rapidly gaining a reputation for Chardonnay and Pinot Noir excellence and proving that only in exceptionally warm and long growing seasons are the high sites of Lenswood suitable for cabernet sauvignon. Unfortunately there are no cellar door sales, but tours of the vineyard may be arranged by appointment.

Kuitpo Vineyards (Geoff Hardy Wines) R85

Tynan Road, Kuitpo, SA
Ph 08 8323 8125, Fax 08 8323 7766,
Email wine@pertaringa.com.au

Owner/chief winemaker: Geoff Hardy
Year of foundation: vineyard 1987
Tonnes produced on average each year: 200, of which less than 50 are used for Kuitpo Vineyard wines (the rest of the fruit is sold)
Location: Kuitpo
Area: 30 ha
Soils: old podsolic duplex, gravelly, quartzite
Varieties planted: White—chardonnay, sauvignon blanc; Red—cabernet franc, cabernet sauvignon, merlot, pinot noir, shiraz
Leading wines: Geoff Hardy Kuitpo Cabernet, Shiraz, Sauvignon Blanc
Notes: Geoff Hardy's 1993 Kuitpo Shiraz was the winner of the inaugural Qantas Great Australian Shiraz Challenge, a remarkable achievement for a cool-area Shiraz. It is necessary, however, to restrict shiraz to a low crop in Kuitpo to ripen it fully. Cellar door sales are at Pertaringa (see McLaren Vale region) Mon–Fri 9am–5pm, long weekends 10am–5pm. Closed ordinary weekends.

Leland Estate (vineyard only) R87

Neudorf Road, Lenswood, SA 5240
Ph 08 8389 6928

Owners: Adam, Jessie and Robb Cootes
Chief winemaker: Robb Cootes
Year of foundation: 1986

Tonnes crushed on average each year: 40, half of which are used for Leland Estate wines
Location: Lenswood
Area: 2.5 ha close planted
Soils: red-brown earth, duplex, podsolic
Varieties planted: White—chardonnay, sauvignon blanc; Red—pinot noir
Leading wines: Adele Sparkling, Neudorf Sauvignon Blanc, Neudorf Pinot Noir
Notes: The Leland Estate is now producing wines of great quality. Adele is a fine example of a top Adelaide Hills sparkler, while the red Pinot Noir is usually rich velvety and soft-finishing. Regrettably there are no cellar door sales. Sales by mail c/- PO Lenswood.

Malcolm Creek Vineyard R85

Bonython Road, Kersbrook, SA 5231
Ph/Fax 08 8389 3235

Owners: RL and EM Tolley
Chief winemaker: RL Tolley at Barossa Vintners
Year of foundation: 1982
Tonnes crushed on average each year: 10
Location: Kersbrook
Area: 2 ha
Soils: schistic loam over clay
Varieties planted: White—chardonnay; Red—cabernet sauvignon
Leading wines: Malcolm Creek Cabernet Sauvignon, Chardonnay
Notes: What do winemakers do when they retire from winemaking? Make wine! The wines are supple and stylishly Adelaide Hills. In addition, they always have some bottle age. Cellar door sales: weekends and public holidays 11am–5pm.

Mawson Ridge NR

24 Main Street, Hahndorf, SA 5245
Ph/Fax 08 8388 1288

Owners: Raymond and Madeleine Marin
Chief winemaker: (contract)

Year of foundation: vineyard 1993, cellar door 1998
Tonnes crushed on average each year: 14
Location: Lenswood (vineyard), Hahndorf (cellar door)
Area: 4 ha
Soils: heavy loam over shale, highly acidic
Varieties planted: White—chardonnay, pinot gris, sauvignon blanc; Red—cabernet franc, merlot, pinot noir
Leading wines: Mawson Ridge Chardonnay, Sauvignon Blanc, Pinot Noir
Notes: Sited high in the Lenswood sub-region (indeed Dr Ray Marin believes that at 550 in altitude, it is the highest in the region), Mawson Ridge should produce some exceptional whites and reds from pinot noir. However, merlot and cabernet franc may prove more difficult to ripen. Cellar door sales are at Hahndorf, open daily. There is also a restaurant and a gallery.

Morialta Vineyard (vineyard only) R85

195 Norton Summit Road, Norton Summit, SA 5136
Ph 08 8390 1061, Fax 08 8390 1585

Owner: a syndicate of Adelaide businessmen
Chief winemaker: Jeffrey Grosset (contract)
Year of foundation: vineyard 1989
Tonnes produced on average each year: 180, of which 3 are presently crushed for Morialta Vineyard wines
Area: 11 ha
Soils: variable from rock with a minimal topsoil cover in the higher areas to dark loamy topsoil over heavy clay in the lower parts
Varieties planted: White—chardonnay, sauvignon blanc; Red—cabernet sauvignon, merlot, pinot noir, shiraz
Leading wine: Morialta Vineyard Chardonnay
Notes: First developed as a mixed farm and orchard in the 1850s, Morialta at one time exported wine to London, but though a few

vines survived until the 1950s, the bulk of the vineyard had gone by the turn of the 20th century. The current vineyard was first planted in 1989, with most varieties very suitable for the area except perhaps for cabernet sauvignon, but in Jeffrey Grosset's skilled winemaking hands, the other varieties should make first class wines. No cellar door sales as yet, but they are available by mail order.

Mt Lofty Ranges Vineyard (vineyard only) R86

Harris Road, Lenswood, SA 5240
Ph 08 8389 8339, Fax 08 8369 8349,
Email mtlofty@box.net.au

Owners: Alan Herath and Jan Reed
Chief winemaker: Peter Leske (contract)
Year of foundation: 1992
Tonnes produced on average each year: 50, half of which is used for Mt Lofty Ranges wines
Area: 5 ha
Soils: red earths with quartz, sandstone and ironstone outcrops
Varieties planted: White—chardonnay, riesling, sauvignon blanc; Red—pinot noir
Leading wines: Mt Lofty Ranges Vineyard Riesling, Pinot Noir
Notes: Lenswood, and the Mt Lofty Ranges Vineyard in particular, seem like excellent places for Riesling, as its 1999 won top gold at the Adelaide Hills Wine Show and its 2000 version of the same was equally good. This is another Lenswood vineyard with a lot of promise for the future. Cellar door sales: weekends and public holidays 11am–5pm. There is also mail order.

Nepenthe Vineyards R86

Vickers Road, Lenswood, SA 5240
Ph 08 8431 7588, Fax 08 8431 7688,
Email plimpus@nepenthe.com.au

Owners: Twedell family
Winemaker: Peter Leske
Year of foundation: 1994

Tonnes crushed on average each year: 500, all of which are used for Nepenthe wines (other contract crushing and winemaking is carried out at other permitted sites)
Location: Lenswood (winery and vineyards)
Area: 70 ha
Soils: predominantly low fertility duplex, shallow (about 60 cm deep) and slightly acidic topsoils over shale/schist with some quartz and gravel. An old horticultural site that contributes to low fertility
Varieties planted: White—chardonnay, pinot gris, riesling, sauvignon blanc, semillon; Red—cabernet franc, cabernet sauvignon, malbec, merlot, pinot noir, tempranillo, zinfandel
Leading wines: Nepenthe Chardonnay, (Wooded and Unwooded), Sauvignon Blanc, Riesling, Pinot Noir, The Fugue (a blend of the Bordeaux varieties mentioned above)
Notes: Nepenthe was only the second winery with full crushing facilities to be built in the Adelaide Hills (the first was Petaluma in 1979). All its whites are excellent and its Merlot-based 'Fugue' is a harmonious intricacy of varietal themes. There are no cellar door sales, but distribution is widespread throughout the eastern states and South Australia. Sales also by mail order.

New Era Vineyard R83

Pfeiffer Road, Woodside, SA 5244
Ph/Fax 08 8389 7562

Owner: Patricia Wark
Chief winemaker: (contract)
Year of foundation: 1988
Tonnes produced on average each year: 135, about 2 of which are used for New Era wines
Location: Woodside
Area: 12.5 ha
Soils: alluvial deposits of rich deep sandy loams about 30 cm deep
Varieties planted: White—chardonnay; Red—cabernet sauvignon, merlot, shiraz

Leading wines: New Era Gold Cabernet
Sauvignon
Notes: New Era Vineyard is contracted to
Mildara Blass and is the source of the Wolf
Blass Cabernet Merlot. Wine produced under
its own label is made by Paracombe. No cellar
door sales. Sales by mail order to PO Box 239,
Woodside, SA 5244.

Paracombe Premium Wines   **R85**

Paracombe Road, Paracombe, SA 5132
Ph 08 8380 5058, Fax 08 8380 5488

Owners: Paul and Kathy Drogemuller
Chief winemaker: Paul Drogemuller (reds);
Petaluma contract (sparkling, whites); Tim
Adams (white wine consultant)
Year of foundation: 1983
Tonnes crushed on average each year: 90, of
which 40 are used for Paracombe wines
Location: Paracombe
Area: 13.3 ha
Soils: variable from brown sandy loam and
ironstone over clay and quartz rock to brown
loam over buckshot gravel and yellow pipe clay
Varieties planted: Whites—chardonnay,
sauvignon blanc; Red—cabernet franc,
cabernet sauvignon, merlot, pinot noir, shiraz
Leading wines: Paracombe Sauvignon Blanc,
Cabernet Franc, Chardonnay
Notes: Situated in the Adelaide Hills above the
Torrens Valley north-east of Adelaide,
Paracombe makes its own reds on site and its
whites in Clare where Tim Adams is
consultant. It regularly exhibits at local wine
shows (Adelaide Hills, Royal Adelaide) and
consistently wins show awards at bronze and
silver level, with a smattering of golds and the
occasional trophy. This is a winery of
consistently high standards. Though there are
no cellar door sales, there is a mailing list and
an annual wine release day (usually the last
Sunday in October) on which mailing list
members can taste and purchase wines. Mail
order is available throughout the year.

Perrini Estate Winery   **NR**

Bower Road, Meadows, SA 5201
Ph/Fax 08 8388 3210

Owners: A and CI Perrini
Chief winemaker: Tony Perrini
Year of foundation: 1997
Tonnes produced on average each year: 15,
increasing as the vines mature
Location: Meadows
Area: 2.82 ha
Soils: friable black topsoils 20–60 cm deep
with some clay over limestone
Varieties planted: White—none; Red—cabernet
sauvignon, merlot, shiraz
Leading wine: Perrini Estate Shiraz
Notes: This is a new and growing family-
owned winery in Meadows. For the time being
until the Meadows vineyard comes into full
bearing, McLaren Vale fruit is being purchased
to blend with the estate-grown material. I have
no knowledge of the wines, though there are
two whites and four reds. Cellar door sales:
Wed–Sun 10am–5pm including public
holidays.

Petaluma   **R90**

Spring Gully Road, Piccadilly, SA 5151
(winery, not open to the public)
Mount Barker Road, Bridgewater,
SA 5155 (sales)
Ph 08 8339 4122, Fax 08 8339 5253,
Email petaluma@petaluma.com.au
(winery and sales)
Ph 08 8339 3422, Fax 08 8339 5311,
Email bridgewatermill@petaluma.com.au

Owner: Lion Nathan
Chief winemaker: Brian Croser
Years of foundation: label 1976; first Piccadilly
Valley vineyard, 1978; Piccadilly Valley winery,
1979; Bridgewater Mill label, 1986
Tonnes crushed on average each year: not
disclosed but estimated at 600 from Adelaide
Hills vineyards owned, leased and managed by

Petaluma, all of which are used for Petaluma and Bridgewater Mill wines
Location: Piccadilly (winery), Bridgewater Mill (restaurant and champenisation facility), Piccadilly Valley and Mount Barker (vineyards)
Area: 75 ha (Piccadilly Valley 60 ha, Mount Barker 15 ha)
Soils: Piccadilly Valley, variable from clay loams and clay over shales and siltstone and sandstone; Mount Barker, sandy clay loams over schist
Varieties planted: White—chardonnay, sauvignon blanc, viognier; Red—pinot noir, shiraz
Leading wines: Petaluma Chardonnay (sourced solely from the Piccadilly Valley sub-region); Petaluma Viognier, Petaluma Shiraz (each is sourced from the western flank of Mount Barker in the Adelaide Hills); Tiers Chardonnay (sourced entirely from the Tiers vineyard adjacent to the Petaluma winery); 'Croser' (a vintage sparkling wine, made by the traditional method, usually 50/50 Pinot Noir-Chardonnay, though these proportions may be varied according to the year) (sourced entirely from the Piccadilly Valley sub-region)
Notes: Petaluma is the fount of modern winemaking both in the Adelaide Hills and Australia as a whole. Since its erection in 1979, the Piccadilly winery has seen a steady stream of postgraduate winemaking talent flow out to the Australian wine industry and indeed the world. The inspiration for this has been Brian Croser, who has devoted his professional career to ensuring that Petaluma has only one standard—the highest. Croser was drawn to the Hills in his search for a region to make the finest of Australian sparkling wine. No one can deny that in the making of 'Croser', he has succeeded brilliantly. In the course of so doing, he has made excellent table wines from other regions under the Petaluma label, a riesling from Clare and excellent reds from Coonawarra, and two more recent wines Shiraz and Viognier from the Mount Barker area. It is, however, his

Chardonnay that has created the benchmark by which all other Australian Chardonnays are judged. Yet Croser himself, with the release of 'Tiers' a few years ago, has set the Chardonnay bar even higher. Cellar door sales at Bridgewater Mill, daily 9.30am–5pm. There is also an excellent restaurant open daily for lunch except Tuesdays and Wednesdays.

Pfitzner-Eric's Vineyard (vineyard only) R84

Spring Gully Road, Piccadilly, SA
Postal Address: C/- John Pfitzner, 6B 39–45 Jeffcot Street, North Adelaide, SA 5006
Ph/Fax 08 88267 5404,
Email pfitzner@camtech.net.au

Owner: Pfitzner family
Chief winemaker: Petaluma (contract)
Year of foundation: vineyard 1983, label 1996
Tonnes produced on average each year: 50, about half of which are used for Pfitzner-Erics Vineyard wines
Area: 5.5 ha
Soils: very old friable free-draining loams with a strip of ironstone running through the vineyard
Varieties planted: White—chardonnay, sauvignon blanc; Red—merlot, pinot noir
Leading wines: Pfitzner-Erics Vineyard Chardonnay, Pinot Noir
Notes: Adjoining Petaluma's Tiers Vineyard, Eric's Vineyard shares the same glorious 'European' views across the Piccadilly Valley. With the reds and yellows of the beeches and poplars and the dark greens of the pines, one doubts that one is in Australia and imagines the autumn golds of Burgundy. The Chardonnay vines here are almost as old as those of Petaluma and produce an excellent full-bodied yet elegant style. There are no cellar door sales but mail order is available from the above address.

Pibbin R86

Greenhill Road, Balhannah,
SA 5242
Ph 03 8420 6363, Fax 03 8420 6399,
Email pibbin@pibbin.com.au

Owners: Pibbin Wines
Chief winemaker: Roger Salkeld
Year of foundation: vineyard 1986, winery and
cellar door 1991
Tonnes crushed on average each year: 26
Location: (winery, cellar door and vineyard)
Balhannah, (other vineyard) Verdun
Area: 7.9 ha (Balhannah 5.1 ha, Verdun
2.8 ha)
Soils: Balhannah, a gravel and clay loam
western slope; Verdun, free-draining loam over
ironstone gravel, north-facing
Varieties planted: (Balhannah) White—viognier;
Red—merlot, pinot noir. (Verdun)
White—none; Red—pinot noir
Leading wine: Pibbin Pinot Noir
Notes: Pibbin operates two quite different
vineyards, 9 kilometres apart. At Balhannah,
pinot and viognier vines are densely planted
1.8m x 1.5m, with the merlot more open at
2.5m x 1.8m. Vineyard faces west. Verdun is
also closed spaced with a northern aspect and
is sometimes susceptible to spring frosts. Pinot
noir is the principal variety and its wine is rich
and flavoursome, though merlot, planted in
1997, now has a substantial presence at
Balhannah. No cellar door sales.

Piccadilly Fields R83

185 Piccadilly Road, Piccadilly, SA 5151
Ph 08 8370 8800, Fax 08 8370 8717,
Email picf@camtech.net.au

Owners: Virgara family, Sam Virgara and
syndicates of investors
Chief winemaker: Sam Virgara
Year of foundation: first vineyard 1984, label
1989
Tonnes crushed on average each year: 2000, of

which about 30 are used for Piccadilly Fields
wines
Location: Piccadilly Valley
Area: Total area 176 ha consisting of Schocroft
Road (vineyard) 8 ha; Chapel Valley 10 ha;
Udy's Road (two vineyards) 6 ha and 4 ha;
Cemetery 6 ha; Uraidla 2 ha; Balhampton
(vineyard) 30 ha; Bluestone (vineyard) 40 ha;
Glendeahl (vineyard) 30 ha; Charlies Patch
29 ha; Harris Road, Lenswood 1 ha; Kumnick
Hill 10 ha.
Soils: Bluestone Vineyard, soils generally
consist of clay loams over weathered granite
bases; Piccadilly Valley vineyards, Lenswood
and Glendeahl, clay loams over sandstone and
quartz, Balhampton and Charlies Patch, clay
loams over broken slate
Varieties planted: White—chardonnay, pinot
gris, sauvignon blanc, viognier; Red—cabernet
sauvignon, gamay, merlot, pinot noir
Leading wines: Piccadilly Fields Chardonnay,
Sauvignon Blanc, Merlot-Cabernet Sauvignon,
Pinot Noir, Gamay
Notes: Though Piccadilly Fields (with 176 ha of
vineyards in the Adelaide Hills) has arguably the
largest vineyard area in the region, it is not yet
a label that is widely encountered in Australia,
most of its production being sold to other
winemakers. Of the wines available in Australia,
my pick is the Piccadilly Fields Chardonnay. No
cellar door sales. Mail order sales available.

Ravenswood Lane
(vineyard only) R87

Ravenswood Lane, Hahndorf, SA 5245
Ph 08 8388 1250, Fax 08 8388 7233,
(mob) 0419 862 811,
Email thelane@olis.net.au

Owners: John and Helen Edwards
Chief winemakers: (reds) Stephen Pannell,
Robert Mann; (whites) Glen James and Robert
Mann (contract)
Year of foundation: 1993
Tonnes crushed on average each year: 200, of

which 50 are used for Ravenswood Lane wines and the balance for a joint venture label Starvedog Lane (the Edwards family and BRL Hardy, see below)

Location: Hahndorf (vineyard)

Area: 28 ha

Soils: John Edwards, a pragmatic man, not usually given to exaggeration or indeed exasperation, describes the vineyard soils as 'absolute crap over exquisite red clay' or more seriously 'sandy loam over porous red clay and granitic sand over rock'

Varieties planted: White—chardonnay, pinot gris, sauvignon blanc, semillon, viognier; Red—cabernet sauvignon, merlot, shiraz

Leading wines: Ravenswood Lane Reunion Shiraz, Beginning Chardonnay, Gathering Sauvignon Blanc

Notes: Ravenswood Lane at 425 m in altitude is about 50 m lower than vineyards in the Piccadilly Valley. Accordingly, though Chardonnay here is crisp and fine-boned and Sauvignon Blanc exhibits classical gooseberry flavours, it is also an excellent red area, being slightly warmer and brighter than Piccadilly. John Edwards is particularly excited about his Shiraz. All wines will be available at cellar door and, in time, at fine restaurants throughout Australia. No cellar door sales. Orders by phone or fax, or by mail to PO 326, Hahndorf, SA 5245.

Starvedog Lane R83

C/- Ravenswood Lane as above

Starvedog Lane is a new Adelaide Hills label resulting from a joint venture (which began in 1999), between John and Helen Edwards and BRL Hardy. John Edwards is responsible for the style of the wines with BRL Hardy carrying out the making, marketing and sales. Presently about 500 tonnes of Adelaide Hills fruit is processed for wines made under this label. With the exception of meunier (used for a sparkling wine), the varieties used are the

same as those for the Ravenswood Lane label, but not necessarily of Ravenswood Lane origin. The wine range presently consists of Starvedog Lane Shiraz, Cabernet, Chardonnay, Sauvignon Blanc, Sparkling.

Salem Bridge Wines (vineyard only) NR

Salem Bridge Road, Lower Hermitage, SA 5131

Ph/Fax 08 8380 5240

Owner: Barry Miller and Tracy Scott

Chief winemaker: Barry Miller

Year of foundation: 1989, first wines made 1994

Tonnes crushed on average each year: 120, of which about 12 are used for Salem Bridge wines

Location: Lower Hermitage

Area: 16 ha

Soils: shallow sandy soils over clay or rock

Varieties planted: White—none; Red—cabernet franc, cabernet sauvignon, durif, merlot, shiraz

Leading wines: Salem Bridge Cabernet Franc, Cabernet Sauvignon, Shiraz

Notes: Salem Bridge is a grapegrower making a small part of its crop into its own wine. Its Cabernet Franc has won bronze awards at Royal Hobart and the Adelaide Hills Wine Shows. No cellar door sales. Sales by mail order to RSD 126, Houghton, SA 5131.

Samphire Wines and Pottery NR

Cnr Watts Gully Road and Robertson Road, Kersbrook, SA 5231

Ph 08 8389 3183, Email samphire@senet.com.au

Owners: Tom and Rosie Miller

Chief winemaker: Tom Miller

Year of foundation: vineyard 1978, first vintage 1982

Tonnes crushed on average each year: 3

Location: Watts Gully

Area: 0.3 ha
Soils: alluvium of deep clay (weathered schist) on a base of coarse grained schist and gneiss
Varieties planted: White—riesling; Red—none
Leading wine: Miller's Samphire Riesling
Notes: Adjacent to the picturesque Heysen trail, tiny Samphire is located near the northern boundary of the Adelaide Hills region, not far from Eden Valley. Hence Tom Miller's understandable affection for riesling. Cellar door sales: daily 9am–6pm, but ring ahead. Wines may be sold out.

Shaw and Smith   R89

Lot 4 Jones Road, Balhannah, SA 5242
Ph 08 8398 0500, Fax 08 8398 0600,
Email shawandsmith@shawandsmith.com

Owners: Shaw and Smith Pty Ltd
Chief winemaker: Martin Shaw
Year of foundation: 1989
Tonnes crushed on average each year: 500, of which 400 are used for Shaw and Smith wines
Location: Balhannah (winery and vineyard), Woodside (vineyard)
Area: 34.8 ha consisting of Woodside 28 ha, Balhannah 6.8 ha
Soils: Each property has red and brown sandy loam with some clay over schist
Varieties planted: (Woodside) White—chardonnay, sauvignon blanc; Red—merlot. (Balhannah) White—riesling; Red—pinot noir
Leading wines: Shaw and Smith Sauvignon Blanc, Unoaked Chardonnay, Reserve Chardonnay, Incognito (Merlot)
Notes: Shaw and Smith is a wine duo of all the talents—the consummate winemaking of Martin Shaw and the unerring palate of Michael Hill-Smith MW. The result is a regional wine range of brilliance. Of the styles to be drunk young, there is the Unoaked Chardonnay, fresh and full of fruit, and also the Sauvignon Blanc, zingy and alive in the mouth, while the Reserve Chardonnay made with restraint and elegance needs only patience and 4–5 years in the bottle

to reveal an almost 'Burgundian' complexity. There is also a very stylish Merlot and to come a Riesling and perhaps a Pinot Noir. No formal cellar door sales, but visits and functions can be arranged by appointment.

Southcorp Adelaide Hills (vineyard only)   R90

North East Road, Mount Pleasant, SA 5235

Owner: Southcorp Wines
Chief winemaker: John Duval
Year of foundation: 1981
Tonnes produced on average each year: not disclosed but estimated at 700
Location: Partalunga Vineyard, Mount Pleasant
Area: 69.8 ha
Soils: Sand over sandy loam, podsolics not dissimilar to Leo Buring Eden Valley soils
Varieties planted: White—chardonnay, sauvignon blanc; Red—cabernet sauvignon
Leading wines: Partalunga is also a part source of the excellent Yattarna and Adelaide Hills Chardonnays
Notes: Planted in 1981 by Seppelt (then family owned), the Partalunga vineyard, the only vineyard owned by Southcorp in this region, built an excellent reputation for its Chardonnay, which after infrequent appearances, was discontinued in 2001, its grapes being utilised partly for the prestigious Yattarna and Adelaide Hills Chardonnays. Cellar door sales: at Penfolds Nuriootpa. No local cellar door sales.

Talunga Wines   R83

Adelaide Mannum Road, Gumeracha, SA 5233
Ph 08 8389 1222, Fax 08 8389 1233,
Email talunga@hotmail.com

Owners: di Cesare and Scaffidi families
Chief winemaker: Vince Scaffidi and contract
Year of foundation: vineyard 1981, winery 1988

Tonnes crushed on average each year: 1000, of which 25 are used for Talunga label purposes
Location: Gumeracha
Area: 65 ha
Soils: shaley loams
Varieties planted: White—chardonnay, riesling, sauvignon blanc, semillon, verdelho; Red—cabernet franc, cabernet sauvignon, gamay, grenache, merlot, nebbiolo, pinot noir, sangiovese, shiraz
Leading wines: Talunga Shiraz, Chardonnay, Sangiovese-Merlot
Notes: This is a large vineyard with a considerable production, most of which is sold to other winemakers. The wine standards are good and there is an emphasis on some increasingly popular Italian varieties such as sangiovese. Cellar door sales: Wed–Sun and public holidays 10.30am–5pm. There is also a restaurant.

Whisson Lake
(vineyard only)   **R86**

Gully Road, Carey Gully, SA 5142
Ph 08 8390 1303, Fax 08 8390 3822,
Email trigpoint@olis.net.au

Owners: Mark Whisson and Bruce Lake
Chief winemaker: David Powell (contract)
Year of foundation: vineyard 1985, first wine made 1989
Tonnes produced on average each year: 30, of which 4 are used for Whisson Lake Pinot
Location: Carey Gully
Area: 5.6 ha
Soils: orange-yellow clays (old podsols) over schist/gneiss about 0.8 m deep. A very steep and elevated vineyard having an east-north-east aspect
Varieties planted: White—none; Red—pinot noir
Leading wine: Whisson Lake Pinot Noir
Notes: Whisson Lake is a small yet mature vineyard, what the French might term a 'monocru'. Most of its fruit is sold, but a small amount of Pinot Noir is made, a rare single variety single vineyard wine. There are no cellar door sales, but there is mail order to PO Box 91, Uraidla, SA 5142.

Lenswood Sub-region

The Adelaide Hills were settled soon after the foundation of South Australia in 1836 and from as early as 1844 in Echunga there was a history of winemaking. Such was not the case with Lenswood (formerly called Jerry's Flat), where from 1861 early agricultural activities were horticulture, market gardening and grazing and, later, dairying. Orcharding, however, remained the major activity and by 1982 the area produced 95% of South Australia's apples. Yet even before 1982 interest in orcharding was diversifying to cherries, flowers and, of course, vines.

Inspired by Brian Croser's planting of a vineyard in the Piccadilly Valley in the late 1970s, the interest in producing wine spread rapidly to other areas in the Hills and especially Lenswood where Tim Knappstein planted a commercial vineyard in 1981. He was soon followed by Stephen Henschke and Geoff Weaver in the following year. The first Lenswood grapes were produced in 1985 and since then Lenswood wines have been conspicuous winners in local and national wine shows with Chardonnay, Pinot and Sauvignon Blanc leading the varietal charge. In 1997, Nepenthe, the sub-region's first winery, began operation. An important factor in the development of Lenswood was the involvement of experienced winemakers and wine show judges, such as Tim Knappstein, Geoff Weaver and Stephen Henschke, in the achievement of high professional standards of winemaking, a participation which has added a final gloss to the polish of the sub-region. Lenswood is a sub-region of significant quality.

Location: latitude 34°57'S, longitude 138°48'E, about 25 km east of Adelaide, its boundaries are contours, set at a base elevation of 400 m, extending to an upper altitude of 560 m

Elevation: 400–560 m. Such boundaries exist because there is no country in the sub-region above 560 m and grape-growing conditions in the valleys below 400 m are distinctly different.

Topography and soils: part of the South Mount Lofty Ranges, running north-east to south-west, the Lenswood sub-region consists of a range of hills, its boundaries being wholly situated within the catchment of the Onkaparinga River. The Lenswood vineyards are generally planted east-facing close to the tops of the hills to benefit from more mild and even-temperature conditions and to avoid the potential frost problems of the valleys. Suitable slopes are limited in availability and much of the region is very steep and afforested by old eucalypt woodland.

The soils are podsolic with a leached sandy loam topsoil between 1 and 1.5 metres deep over a subsoil of generally yellow clay. They are characterised by (a) low fertility, important in restraining the vigour of the vine, a restraint in turn critical in the production of quality fruit, and (b) good water-holding capacity in the clays with restricted release, giving the vines a slow but steady supply of water ensuring constant but moderate activity.

Climate: MJT 19.3°C, HDD 1350, MAR na, AR 920 mm, RH na, AI na, SH na. Lenswood is a cool and wet sub-region, cooler and wetter in fact than all the rest of the Adelaide Hills region except the Piccadilly Valley. It has a low diurnal range of temperatures and such cool but even temperatures yet sufficient warmth in most years allow all but the latest-ripening grape varieties to ripen. Importantly its rainfall during March and April is low again enabling ripening and the prevention of rots and mildews.

Irrigation is required but only sparingly, as water stress during the growing season is low and such irrigation is obtained from private dams and from bores. However, official approval is now required to drill bores or construct dams and is also required for the clearing of native vegetation.

Harvest time: sauvignon blanc and pinot noir third week of March to second week of April; chardonnay first to third week of April; cabernet sauvignon third week of April to first week of May

Principal grape varieties: White—chardonnay, sauvignon blanc; Red—pinot noir

Total area: na

Major wine styles: Chardonnay, Sauvignon Blanc, Pinot Noir

Wineries and vineyards within the sub-region: The following winery and vineyards using their own labels were situated within the Lenswood sub-region at the time of writing: Geoff Weaver Wines, Basket Range, Henschke-Lenswood, Hillstowe, Knappstein Lenswood, Leland Estate, Lenswood Vineyards, Mawson Ridge, Mt Lofty Ranges Vineyard, and Nepenthe Vineyards and Winery. See above for individual notes.

Piccadilly Valley Sub-region

Dominated by the summit of Mount Lofty, so called by Matthew Flinders when commanding HMS *Investigator* in 1802, the Piccadilly Valley was first settled in 1837. Early on it was called The Tiers, a name now commemorated by a premium single-vineyard chardonnay made by Petaluma.

Quite presciently, Robert Cock, one of the first explorers and settlers in the district, remarked in 1838 that its hillsides 'seemed well-adapted for vineyards'. However, its first industry was timber-getting, the local stringybark being considered ideal for basic fencing and bush dwellings. Such logging operations were the beginning of the township of Crafers, named after one David Crafer, who opened the Norfolk Arms Hotel there in 1839. Timber-getting continued, though small farms soon sprang up. To encourage access to the area, the construction of the Great Eastern (Mount Barker) Road was begun in 1841 and Cox's Creek Village (near the present town of Bridgewater) was founded soon after. This road, however, was not considered satisfactory, being replaced by a new Mount Barker Road in 1851, which passed through the present-day towns of Stirling, Aldgate and Bridgewater and was the precursor of the modern South-Eastern Freeway. Subdivision of Stirling followed during the 1850s, though sales were slow due to the poor quality of the land. To the north, however, around present-day Piccadilly and Summertown, the country was of greater fertility and towards the end of the 19th century began to be used for horticulture and market gardening. These activities continued well into the 20th century.

Save for the 19th century vineyard of Brooklyn at Summertown, there is little or no evidence of widespread viticultural activity before the 1980s. In the 19th century, popular belief held that viticulture was suitable only for warmer sites and the Piccadilly Valley, mostly settled by Anglo-Celts without a native wine tradition, was most likely considered too cold for that purpose and in any case Adelaide was a close and prosperous market for the fruit and vegetables that grew so well in the area.

In the modern era, grape growing began in the 1970s. By 1978 Brian Croser was planting Petaluma to chardonnay and pinot noir for the making of still and sparkling table wines. The sub-region began to boom in the 1980s, with Stephen George planting at Ashton Hills in 1981, Piccadilly Fields being commenced in 1984, and the Woodshill Vineyard being established in 1987–88. Chardonnay and pinot noir have remained the dominant plantings. This sub-region is bounded by the sub-region of Lenswood to the east and north-east.

Location: latitude 34°58'S, longitude 138°47'E, the Piccadilly Valley is located about 18 km south-east of Adelaide
Elevation: elevation varies from about 400 m to 710 m (the summit of Mount Lofty)
Topography and soils: the base rocks of the sub-region are very old, being of the palaeo-proterozoic era and mostly consisting of quartz-mica-feldspar schists and gneisses, overlain by Basket Range sandstone, Woolshed flat shale, the Castambul Formation siltstone and Stonyfell quartzite.

Its topographies and soils are variable, being recently described as having three dominant landforms BC, BA and AC. The BC presence is categorised as 'low hills formed on sandstones with surface ironstone. The main soils are sandy loam over brown clay on rock and loam over orange clay on rock'. BA and AC occur with equivalent frequency. BA is described as 'low hills and slopes formed on medium to coarse grained sandstones with chief soils of sandy loam over brown clay, shallow loamy sand on rock'. AC is depicted as 'low hills and hills of the high rainfall inner ranges, the soils of which are loam over brown clay on rock'.

Of more infrequent occurrence are landforms CA, DB, SC and BB. CA is 'rolling to steep low hills and slopes formed on coarse grained sandstones with main soil of stony sand over clayey sand grading to yellow sandy clay on rock'. DB is 'low hills to hills in the high rainfall inner ranges with main soil being loam over orange to brown friable clay forming on shale'. Stringybark forest is a typical vegetation. SC has drainage depressions and lower slopes on coarse-grained alluvium with main soil of gravelly loamy sand over yellow, red and grey clay. BB comprises rocky hillslopes formed on coarse-grained sandstones with main soil of shallow stony coarse sands on rock.

Climate: climate information is complicated by the fact that the weather recording station at Stirling was closed in 1985 and moved to Mount Lofty. So two sets of data are given, one current for 22 years until 1985, the more recent only since 1991 at Mount Lofty. Stirling (until 1985) MJT 18.65°C, HDD 1260 (cut off at 19°C where necessary but not adjusted for latitude, altitude, daily temperature or vine sites), MAR na, AR 1118.2 mm (Oct to Apr 425.9 mm), RH 64% (9am) and 50% (3pm), AI na, SH 1771 (Gladstones). Mount Lofty from 1991 MJT 16°C, HDD 898.4 (cut-offs were unnecessary here but no other adjustments were made), MAR na, AR 1225.6 mm (Oct–Apr 470 mm), RH 76% (9am) and 62% (3pm), AI na, SH na. Other rainfall information: Ashton (65 years to 1998) AR 1054.5 mm (Oct–Apr 388 mm). Uraidla (108 years to 1998) AR 1087.1 mm (Oct–Apr 379.9 mm).

Though the sub-region is quite close to St Vincents Gulf (about 15 kilometres in a direct line), it is considered to have a climate that is continental rather than maritime, because of the intervening Mount Lofty Range. It is obviously a very cool viticultural area and its boundary approximates the 1000 mm average rainfall line, which means that Piccadilly Valley fruit can virtually be grown without supplementary irrigation. However, supplementary irrigation, sourced from wells of high quality water, is necessary when establishing vineyards and is an obvious insurance factor even in the Piccadilly Valley for the occasional drought years.

Generally, the sub-region has few disease problems, provided the usual spray regimes are adhered to. Netting for protection from birds seems to be unnecessary, nor are other bird-scaring devices employed.

Harvest time: chardonnay, mid to late April, generally varying because of aspect, topography, soil type and 'cultural control', i.e. vine management. This last factor is an amalgam of pruning regime, the amount of irrigation, crop loads and canopy manipulation and is very variable.

Principal grape varieties: White—chardonnay, riesling; Red—pinot noir, meunier, gamay, merlot, cabernet sauvignon. Chardonnay seems to be the premium variety of the sub-region and totally suited to it.

Total area: na

Major wine styles: Chardonnay, Sparkling

Wineries and vineyards within the sub-region: Arranmore, Ashton Hills, Barratt Wines, Petaluma, Pfitzner-Eric's Vineyard, Piccadilly Fields and Whisson Lake

Gumeracha, which has a substantial vineyard area and a slightly warmer climate than either of the above sub-regions, may well be the next area to apply for sub-regional status in the Adelaide Hills region.

❦ Riesling

From the mid-1980s Riesling struggled with Chardonnay for white supremacy. By the early 1990s it had definitely been vanquished and Chardonnay was king. But then fashion, forever fickle, threw out a line to Riesling and restored it to a certain favour. After all it was cheaper, wasn't it? And it was pretty good really! And anyway, most consumers were becoming much more conscious of red. So it may now be confidently asserted that the future of Australian Riesling is quite secure and will definitely remain so if vintages such as 2000 can be replicated with a certain frequency.

Riesling has often been described as the archetypal 'continental' grape variety. Is this description justified? The table compares the three Australian areas mentioned with Geisenheim in the Rheingau, another 'classic' riesling area.

		Geisenheim		Clare Valley	Eden Valley*	Mount Barker (WA)
Altitude		100 m		398 m	450 m	253 m
Effective degree	Apr	23	Oct	143	72	120
days	May	171	Nov	225	140	175
	June	265	Dec	279	211	244
	July	279	Jan	279	258	279
	Aug	279	Feb	252	235	252
	Sep	182	Mar	279	225	277
	Oct	26	Apr	156	110	210
	Total	1225		1613	1251	1557
Average rainfall (mm)						
April–Oct		333	Oct–April	245	243	285
Nov–Dec		185	May–Sept	387	415	471
Total		518		632	658	756
Relative humidity						
(3pm)		56%**		37%**	44%**	54%**
Sunshine hours		1333		1870	1764	1518
Continentality***		11.8		8.5	7.2	5.7

   * Eden Valley degree days not adjusted for vine sites.

  ** All relative humidity averaged over the growing season.

*** In this instance, not the difference between the mean January temperature and the mean July temperature, but the difference between daily mean temperature averaged from October to April and daily mean temperatures averaged for the other five months of the year in Australia. In the northern hemisphere, the relevant months are of course reversed.

Note: All statistics are after Gladstones, *Viticulture and Environment*.

As is commonly said, there are lies, damned lies and statistics. Certainly from the continentality aspect, Geisenheim is much more 'continental'. It warms very quickly from April to May, much more speedily than October to November in any Australian site mentioned. It is also the coolest site in degree day terms with fewest sunshine hours. As well, it has the highest relative humidity and the highest growing season rainfall. Among the Australians, Clare is by far the warmest in degree day terms with the greatest number of sunshine hours. (But see the Clare regional entry—the Clare HDD may be distorted or at least not representative of the Clare regional areas where riesling is grown.) Clare is also the driest, both in annual rainfall and in relative humidity with the highest Australian 'continentality'. Eden Valley is the highest site of the four and, of the Australians, the coolest and second driest. As for Mount Barker, it has a relative humidity of 54% (approaching that of Geisenheim), the least 'continentality' and is relatively warm, yet with the second lowest number of sunshine hours. So there is no statistical consistency overall (perhaps one should not expect it), but there are similarities in degree days between Geisenheim and Eden Valley, for both areas can produce rieslings which have been described as 'steely' and which mature slowly. Indeed the only factors in common between Clare and Eden Valley are similar altitudes, a high continentality (in Australian terms) and low humidities. Are these factors the climatic reasons for classic Australian riesling?

John Vickery, now of Richmond Grove in the Barossa Valley and a renowned maker of Australian riesling, thinks not. His experience of the riesling of both areas extends over 40 years and to him, humidity-stressed vines give concentrated but not better flavours. In his opinion, there are indeed differences between Clare and Eden Valley rieslings, but they are primarily brought about by soil divergencies, not climate. He prefers to use fruit that is not moisture-stressed. In Clare, he sees citrus characters in riesling, brought about by Clare's alluvial red-brown soils, which sit over a marly limestone subsoil. In Eden Valley, the sandy, schisty, less fertile soils give riesling a more aromatic floral and spice character. He fully understands the misapprehensions of some writers who allege that Eden Valley rieslings are sometimes 'improved' by a non-disclosed and substantial addition of traminer, but knows that such allegations are quite wrong.

So the differences in Australian rieslings cannot be attributed to climatic factors alone. The differences in the wines are as usual the product of a multitude of other things, with soils, climate and winemaking technique all playing interactive roles.

WINERY WITHIN THE MOUNT LOFTY RANGES ZONE BUT NOT WITHIN A REGION

Macaw Creek   🍇 **R87**

Main North Road, Rhynie, SA
(about 5 km south of the town)
Ph/Fax 08 8847 2237, Mob 0418 890 203,
Email hooper@capri.com.au

Owners: Rod and Miriam Hooper and family
Chief winemaker: Rod Hooper
Year of foundation: vineyard 1992, cellar door 1998
Tonnes produced on average each year: 20
Locations: Macaw Creek, Gilbert Valley
Area: 10 ha planted (2.5 ha in full production)
Soils: terra rossa (red clay loam over deep powdery limestone), biscay (black cracking clay over red clay) and limestone and terra rossa shale (red clay loam over shale/slate)
Varieties planted: White—riesling, semillon, viognier; Red—cabernet sauvignon, grenache, malbec, petit verdot, shiraz

Leading wines: Macaw Creek Shiraz-Cabernet Reserve, Grenache-Shiraz, Riesling
Notes: Rod Hooper is a winemaker of Australian and world-wide experience, having spent vintages in Germany, California and France as well as some years in every winemaking state of Australia except Victoria and Tasmania. The Macaw Creek vineyard has an aura of history about it, being in the 1880s the location of Wooroora, which in the latter years of the 19th century was the third largest winery in the Clare/Gilbert Valley area. Macaw Creek reds, like those of Clare further north, are generous in flavour, yet tight in structure and mature well. Definitely worth investigating. Cellar door sales: Sundays and public holidays 11am–4pm.

CLARE VALLEY REGION

The early history of the Clare region is a little obscure. Perhaps it was Mr Hill—who named the Hutt River but about whom not much else is known—who first visited the area, but it is certain that, in May 1839, Edward Eyre, a young man of 24, rode north from Adelaide. Like Blaxland, Wentworth and Lawson in New South Wales a quarter of a century before, he was in search of new pastoral land. He surmounted the Flinders Ranges, reaching as far as the dry Lake Torrens, having passed through what was to become a few years later the village of Clare. In 1840 another Englishman, John Horrocks, like Eyre a pastoralist/explorer, also arrived. He settled Hope Farm in what is now the Clare Valley, named the village of Penwortham after his birthplace in Lancashire and is credited, through the labours of one of his servants, no doubt, with planting the first few vines there. Mount Horrocks commemorates him. In 1841, the Hawker brothers also established their Bungaree station just north of Clare and there too a few vines were planted. The foundation of the town of Clare (or Clareville as it was initially called) must be laid at the feet of an Irishman, Edmund Burton Gleeson, born where else but in County Clare. He had arrived in the district in 1840 and six years later he planned a village near a property of his, Inchiquin. He too was vinously inclined, having subscribed five pounds to Captain Sturt's Vine Association, a sum which gained him over 500 vines which he planted at Inchiquin. But regions and their

CLARE VALLEY REGION

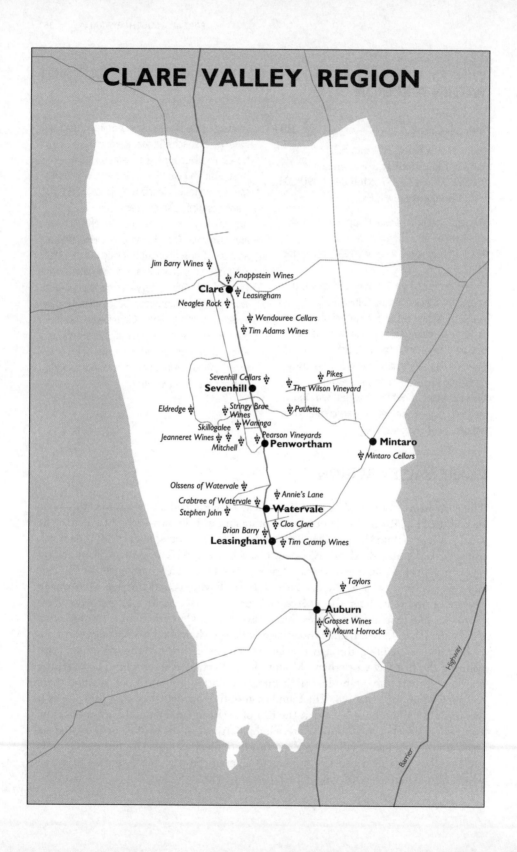

Jim Barry Wines

Knappstein Wines

Clare

Leasingham

Neagles Rock

Wendouree Cellars

Tim Adams Wines

Sevenhill Cellars

Pikes

The Wilson Vineyard

Sevenhill

Eldredge

Stringy Brae Wines

Pauletts

Waninga

Skillogalee

Jeanneret Wines

Pearson Vineyards

Penwortham

Mitchell

Mintaro

Mintaro Cellars

Olssens of Watervale

Annie's Lane

Crabtree of Watervale

Watervale

Stephen John

Clos Clare

Brian Barry

Leasingham

Tim Gramp Wines

Taylors

Auburn

Grosset Wines

Mount Horrocks

Barrier

Highway

villages and vineyards, in order to grow, need an economic imperative and this was provided by the discovery of copper at Burra in 1845. The copper was transported to the sea, not via Adelaide but across country by a road to Port Wakefield in the north of the Gulf of St Vincent, which traversed the countryside south of the settlement at Clare through present-day Mintaro, Watervale, Leasingham and Auburn, all of which, including the small village of Clare, enjoyed a copper-inspired prosperity. This copper boom, while not creating the wave of excitement that was to swamp Australia by the discoveries of gold in the eastern colonies a few years later, certainly provided a solid economic base for the permanence of the area. On the basis of this modest mining prosperity, the Clare district and its more southerly regions grew and when later the copper 'boom' was renewed by discoveries in the late 1850s at Moonta and Wallaroo, the prosperity remained. Though Clare suffered in the economic downturn of South Australia in the 1860s, it would rise again in the 1870s to enjoy the wheat boom of that period by becoming the rural centre for the mid-north wheatfields. There were, however, other influences that would also affect Clare.

Arriving in 1848, seeking respite from religious persecution, the Society of Jesus introduced a religious element into the Clare equation and initially settled near Neagle's Rock, south-west of the town. In 1851, intending to create a Catholic educational and cultural centre in emulation of Rome, the Jesuit Order founded a college south of Clare which they named Sevenhill in imitation of the Seven Hills of the Eternal City. Later the college became a school which educated as many as 450 boys, closing in 1887 due to competition from Adelaide. It was also a seminary for the training of priests. For sacramental purposes, the brothers planted vines in 1852 and dug the first wine cellar in the region. In 1862, building began on the Collegiate Church, which was consecrated in 1875. Unlike school-teaching, however, winemaking was to continue to the present day.

About the same time as the foundation of Sevenhill, a wandering Cornishman, Francis Treloar, who had been modestly successful in a sojourn on the Victorian goldfields, decided to settle near present-day Watervale. He called his property Springvale and he too planted vines in 1853. By the 1890s, after passing through several hands, that property with a considerably enlarged vineyard was renamed Quelltaler by its owners Messrs Buring and Sobels.

The 1890s also saw a general wine boom throughout South Australia, with Clare playing a considerable part. One large and one small winery in particular were to endure to the present decade. The smaller was Birks Wendouree, Australia's first boutique winery. It was dedicated to quality then and remains so. Though it has undergone a change of ownership, it is otherwise unchanged to this day. The Stanley Wine Co was formed to fulfil a need that had been discerned earlier that decade—a winery to crush the many tonnes of grapes which were not subject to contract by the small number of wineries then present in the region. For this purpose the principals, including the outspoken John Christison (owner of the local brewery) had purchased and equipped an old jam factory. It suited well enough, but they continually lamented the vast amounts of money that it was consuming and its lack of return on capital. By 1912 it was under the control of one man, JH Knappstein. It was his family that took the Stanley Wine Co through the thick of the early and mid-twenties boom and the thin of the Great Depression until the next wine boom of the 1960s and ultimate sale by the Knappstein family to the Heinz Co in 1971. Another merger at this time also saw Quelltaler become part of the Melbourne wine distributor Nathan and Wyeth and later Remy Martin.

At this time also, Taylor's, a huge new vineyard and winery complex in Auburn at the southern end of the Clare Valley, was established. For its pains, the Taylor family, a very few years later, felt the anguish of the swing in Australian wine taste from red to white in the mid-1970s. The sale of Stanley paradoxically saw the rise of the Enterprise Wine Co, a venture of Tim Knappstein, in the same old brewery building that had once housed the original venture of John Christison. The wheel had turned full circle.

The 1990s saw Mildara Blass in control of Quelltaler (later to close it down in 1999 and remove winemaking operations to the Barossa Valley), Petaluma in possession of the Tim Knappstein Wines (formerly Enterprise), BRL Hardy owning Stanley (now renamed Leasingham), Taylor's remaining Taylor-made and the hand of God still upon Sevenhill. There are also many large companies with broadacres of vines, but wineries outside the Clare region. In addition there are many smaller winemaker/proprietors (all highly qualified former employees of large wine companies) with their own vineyards of varying sizes and many grower/proprietors with their own labels, who use their winemaking services.

Location: latitude 33°50'S to 34°3'S, longitude 138°42'E to 138°44'E, about 140 km north of Adelaide. The Clare Valley region commences at Auburn in the south (100 km north of Adelaide) and runs further north 40–45 km more, the vineyards ending just north of the town of Clare.

Elevation: 300–550 m

Topography and soils: Part of the northern Mount Lofty Ranges, the Clare Valley region is a central valley (through which the Main North Road passes) running basically south–north. As this valley runs north, it rises to a watershed around Sevenhill, and thereafter the main valley falls with a shallow gradient to the north. The principal townships of the Valley, Leasingham, Watervale, Penwortham, Sevenhill and Clare, all lie along this axis. To the west the regional boundary largely follows the 300 m contour, while between this boundary and parallel with the central valley is the important Skillogalee Valley. Altitudes in this area reach 450–550 m. To the east is an undulating ridge reaching altitudes of 450 m and further east still a more consistent ridge attains 500 m. This ridge incorporates Quarry Hill, Lodge Hill and Stony Point. In the middle of the region, to the east of the main valley, rises the highest point of the region, Mount Horrocks (608 m), which forms the head of the Hill River catchment, while the Camel's Hump Range comprises its right. Auburn, the first town of the Valley as one approaches from the south, lies on the Wakefield River at an altitude of 330 m. Here the country is much flatter, but the hills to the west mark the continuation of the Skillogalee Valley. The soils are quite variable. Red and yellow podsolic (Dr & Dy) soils often prevail on the hillsides, while on the valley floors there are red-brown earths with good water-holding capacity. In addition there are areas of deep friable black soil said to be specially suited to merlot. Subsoils also vary from clay through limestone to slatey shaley rock.

Climate: Bureau of Meteorology Clare PO MJT 21.45°C, MAR 13.3°C, HDD raw 1737, 1576 (cut off at 19°C), AR 632 mm (Oct–Apr 245 mm), RH 47% (9am Jan), 30% (3pm Jan), AI na, SH na. MJT 21.9°C, MAR 13.6°C, HDD raw 1774, AR 634 mm (Oct–Mar 182 mm), RH 47% (9am Jan), AI 426 mm, SH 8.8 (D&S), MJT 21.3, MAR na, HDD raw 1779, 1613 (cut off and adjusted for latitude daily temperature range and vine sites), AR 632 mm (Oct–Apr 245 mm), RH 32% (3pm Jan), AI na, SH 8.8 (Gladstones). The Clare climate is a paradox. The Dry & Smart HDD portrays Clare as a very warm viticultural area. Though Gladstones' HDD is more favourable to the production of the robust red table wines and fine rieslings, which after all are the Clare Valley's forte, he still suggests that his statistics relate to vineyards with a comparable altitude and latitude to that of the weather station. He also suggests that its location might have distorted the true vineyard situation to some extent (it was formerly sited at the post office in an enclosed courtyard on concrete paving in the centre of the town, close to such causes of urban warming as buildings and roads about 398 m in altitude). Thus he seems to imply that most of the region is cooler.

There may be other factors at work. One may be higher altitude, for example, such vineyards as Petaluma's Hanlins Hill Vineyard and others at Penwortham and Polish Hill River are nearly 100 m higher. A second factor is a different, more southerly latitude, for example, Watervale which has a similar altitude to Clare but is 15 km further south. A third may be the incidence of a cooling south-westerly sea breeze. A fourth could be different topographies, some vineyards being located on ridges with free air drainage in all directions, thus offsetting any tendencies to excessive heat. So perhaps the individual differences among the vineyards are the important factors, not any attempt to apply a uniform HDD to an entire region.

Traditionally (that is, pre-1975) viticulture in the Clare Valley was a dryland activity, confined to those areas where rainfall was highest and the vineyard soils sufficiently moisture-retentive (that is, valley bottoms or contour planted hillsides). However, the late 1970s and the 1980s saw the widespread introduction of drippers and the consequent increase in the areas considered suitable for viticulture. The ensuing demand for water witnessed such depletion of both underground and surface water resources that it caused great concern. In 1995 a 12-month moratorium was imposed on new water resource use, followed in July 1996 by a proclamation that limited any greater use of water to 500 kL per annum from proclaimed surface and/or groundwater sources other than for domestic or stock purposes unless a licence was held. Water supplies also had to be metered. Thus vineyards within the proclaimed area must be managed within a limited water budget and therefore crop levels controlled. This of course has a beneficial effect on resultant fruit quality. It is for this reason that the Proclaimed Water Area boundary corresponds to that of the Clare Valley region.

Harvest time: Like other aspects of Clare regional viticulture, these are quite variable. Riesling in warmer areas of the region can ripen as early as the first week of March, but in cooler areas can be as late as mid-April. Shiraz has broadly the same ripening parameters—from second week of March in warmer areas to third week of April in those that are cooler. Cabernet sauvignon ripens from the fourth week of March in warmer locations to the end of April in colder spots.

Principal varieties: shiraz, riesling, cabernet sauvignon, chardonnay, semillon

Principal wine styles: It is an ancient cliché to speak of iron fists within velvet gloves, but regrettably such a cliché does fit Clare Shiraz. A young Clare Shiraz should be redolent of berries and black pepper, a nose which given time changes to ripe berries, but not to leather. Its youthful palate should have a good weight of open berry flavour and a firm but not harsh or extractive structure of tannin and acid. With bottle age the palate should soften and harmonise, retaining a soft and silky berry fruitiness. Again such wines can be aged up to 15 years.

In its best years, a young Riesling from Clare shows marginally tropical aromas which soon change to lime citrus with a light floral overlay and then, after a year or so in bottle, to a very slight 'toast' character. The palate should be fresh, again lime citrusy in flavour but tending after a little time to broader floral-lime flavours. Finishing acidity may be crisp, but should at all times be integrated and not harsh, neither should the wine be too soft and round in the mouth. With bottle age the wine becomes toasty, both on nose and palate, though never giving the impression of tiredness or oxidation. The best Clare Rieslings can live for 8–12 years.

Clare Cabernet Sauvignon is usually bigger and firmer in most respects than Clare Shiraz, having a deep purpley colour, a nose of berries, mint and spice and a similar youthful palate with size, concentration and firmness to match. With age (12–15 years), such reds soften into a velvety harmony of berries and mint, though always giving the impression of ripeness and warmth, albeit with a certain firmness on finish.

Semillon is usually wood-matured, a sophistication that increases harmony and adds distinction. The nose of young wooded Clare Semillon should show ripe lemon and vanilla aromas, its palate will be of similar flavours though revealing a soft fullness that makes such wines excellent drinking after 1–2 years. I have not tasted such wines of any age and am reluctant to recommend any ageing period beyond 2–3 years, as I doubt whether they have the structure of, say, Hunter Semillon in its best years.

Perhaps Chardonnay, a variety often described as 'most forgiving', is at its least lenient in Clare. Not that it always makes bad wine—the excellent Clare Chardonnays of Hardy's and Penfolds prove the contrary—but perhaps it is somehow aware that, standing as it does in the shadow of a great Riesling tradition, it is often undistinguished.

Leading wineries and vineyards: Grossett Wines, Wendouree Cellars, Brian Barry Wines, Petaluma Wines, Knappstein Wines, Leasingham Wines, Mount Horrocks Wines, Sevenhill Cellars, Old Station, Neagle's Rock, Taylors.

Brian Barry (vineyard only)   **R89**

Farrell Flat Road, Clare, SA 5453
PO Box 128, Stepney, SA 5069
Ph 08 8363 6211, Fax 08 8362 0498,
Email bbwines@senet.com.au

Owner: Jud's Hill Nominees Pty Ltd
Chief winemaker: Brian Barry

Year of foundation: 1976
Tonnes crushed on average each year: 150, of which 120 are used for Jud's Hill wines
Location: East Clare
Area: 24 ha
Soils: mainly terra rossa soil over deep limestone
Varieties planted: White—chardonnay, riesling;

Red—cabernet franc, cabernet sauvignon, merlot
Leading wines: Jud's Hill Riesling, Cabernet Sauvignon, Merlot
Notes: Brian Barry is one of Australia's most experienced winemakers and wine judges and now makes his own wines using the facilities of Petaluma. Jud's Hill, 500 m in altitude and planted on red and black loam over limestone, is a typical dry grown Clare vineyard about 1.5 km east of the town. Unusually in this age of mechanisation, all grapes are hand-picked. He is a Clare specialist and his Rieslings are usually amongst the best to be obtained in the region. His reds, both Cabernet Sauvignon and Merlot, are also extremely good. Cellar door sales: weekends at Leasingham Village Cabins and Restaurant, Main North Road, Leasingham. Mail order also available at the above postal address.

Clos Clare NR

Government Road, Watervale, SA 5452
(about 1 km south of town)
Ph/Fax 08 8843 0161,
Email cloclare@capri.net.au

Owner: Noel Kelly
Chief winemakers: Jeffrey Grosset and David Powell (contract)
Year of foundation: 1993
Tonnes crushed on average each year: 16
Location: Watervale (part of the old Leo Buring Florita vineyard)
Area: 2.125 ha
Soils: terra rossa over limestone
Varieties planted: White—riesling; Red—none
Leading wines: Clos Clare Riesling, Shiraz
Notes: Clos Clare is a small vineyard whose Riesling, being made by Jeffrey Grosset, is assured of a certain pedigree. The Clos Clare Shiraz is made from purchased grapes. Cellar door sales: weekends and public holidays 10am–5pm.

Crabtree of Watervale NR

North Terrace, Watervale, SA 5452
Ph 08 8843 0069, Fax 08 8843 0144

Owners: Robert and Elizabeth Crabtree
Chief winemakers: Robert Crabtree and Stuart Bourne
Year of foundation: 1981
Tonnes crushed on average each year: 100
Location: Watervale (winery and vineyard)
Area: 13 ha
Soils: There are three types of soil on the Crabtree vineyard, loam on a limestone and shale base (riesling), a lighter sandy loam (shiraz) and heavier black soils (cabernet sauvignon)
Varieties planted: White—muscat of Alexandria, pedro ximenez, riesling, semillon; Red—cabernet sauvignon, grenache, shiraz, tempranillo
Leading wines: Crabtree of Watervale Riesling, Shiraz-Cabernet Sauvignon
Notes: Robert Crabtree is an experienced Clare vigneron and his Riesling is well in the mainstream of Clare style. Cellar door sales: 7 days 11am–5pm.

Eldredge Vineyards R85

Spring Gully Road, Clare, SA 5453
Ph/Fax 08 8842 3086

Owners: Leigh and Karen Eldredge
Chief winemaker: Leigh Eldredge
Year of foundation: 1992
Tonnes crushed on average each year: 80
Location: Clare, west of Sevenhill (vineyard and cellar door)
Area: 1.5 ha (most of fruit used is purchased from growers)
Soils: sandy loams over gravel and schist
Varieties planted: White—riesling;
Red—cabernet sauvignon, malbec, merlot, sangiovese, shiraz
Leading wines: Eldredge Blue Chip Shiraz, Cabernet Sauvignon, Riesling

Notes: Eldredge has an excellent show record and makes excellent Riesling and Shiraz, two of the specialities of Clare. Cellar door sales: 7 days 11am–5pm. Restaurant also open for lunch, Thurs–Sun and public holidays.

Grosset Wines R93

King Street, Auburn, SA 5451
Ph 08 8849 2175, Fax 08 8849 2292,
Email grosset@capri.net.au

Owner/chief winemaker: Jeffrey Grosset (60%), private growers (balance)
Year of foundation: 1981
Tonnes crushed on average each year: 200, about 140 of which are used for the Grosset labels
Locations: (winery and cellar door) Auburn, (vineyards) Watervale, Polish Hill River Valley, Piccadilly Valley (Adelaide Hills)
Area: 18 ha
Soils: Polish Hill, clay over gravel with underlying shale and slates; Watervale, red loam over limestone; Piccadilly Valley, sandy loam to loamy clay, over shale and some sandstone
Varieties planted: (Clare Valley) White—riesling, semillon; Red—cabernet franc, cabernet sauvignon, merlot. (Adelaide Hills) White—chardonnay, sauvignon blanc; Red—pinot noir
Leading wines: Grosset Polish Hill Riesling, Watervale Riesling, Gaia (red blend). (Adelaide Hills) Piccadilly Pinot Noir. (Clare Valley) Adelaide Hills Semillon-Sauvignon Blanc
Notes: Jeffrey Grosset is a winemaker of excellence, commended internationally for his Rieslings, two wines of well-recognised quality, which emphasise the differences in 'terroir', that Grosset, the artist-winemaker succeeds in expressing: the elegant and (in comparison to Polish Hill River) generous flavours of Watervale Riesling as opposed to the steely minerality of Polish Hill River. He also makes Gaia, a superbly structured Clare red that combines the wealth of blackcurrent richness of Clare cabernet sauvignon with elegant structure of cabernet franc and the soft, plummy generosity of merlot. It has been compared to a young Bordeaux, but such comparisons are odious. It is something quite different—a perfectly ripened Clare cabernet blend showing strength, complexity and elegant style, which can stand quite independently of foreign comparison. It is a red that is uniquely Clare. He also makes another acclaimed white—Piccadilly Chardonnay. Cellar door sales: from the first weekend in September, Wed–Sun 10am–5pm while stocks last.

Howarth's Pycnantha Hill R84

Benbournie Road, Clare, SA 5453
Ph/Fax 08 8842 2137,
Email howarthwj@bigpond.com

Owner: Howarth family
Chief winemaker: Jim Howarth
Year of foundation: 1997
Tonnes produced on average each year: 14, rising to 20 tonnes when in full production
Location: Pycnantha Hill, about 4 km north-west of the town (vineyard and winery)
Area: 2.1 ha, not all in full production
Soils: two main soil types, terra rossa (red-brown earth over limestone marl) and red-clay loam over weathered sandstone
Varieties planted: White—chardonnay, riesling; Red—cabernet sauvignon, shiraz
Leading wines: Howarth's Pycnantha Hill Shiraz, Cabernet Sauvignon, Chardonnay, Riesling
Notes: Pycnantha Hill is a small family owned and operated winery and vineyard, with a near-organic approach to viticulture and traditional winemaking. Production is small and the wines are in the mid-stream of Clare Valley quality. There are no cellar door sales, but there is mail order at PO Box 669, Clare 5453.

Jeanneret Wines R85

Jeanneret Road, Sevenhill, SA 5453
Ph 08 8843 4308, Fax 08 8843 4251,
Email jwines@bigpond.com

Owner: Patricia Jeanneret
Chief winemaker: Ben Jeanneret
Year of foundation: 1994
Tonnes crushed on average each year: 170
(most fruit is purchased from local growers)
Location: Sevenhill
Area: 4 ha
Soils: varying from red clay over limestone to a
rich dark sandy loam
Varieties planted: White—semillon;
Red—cabernet sauvignon, shiraz
Leading wines: Jeanneret Riesling, Semillon,
Cabernet Sauvignon, Shiraz
Notes: Jeanneret is another example of the
increasingly organic approach to Australian
viticulture. Its own vineyards have an 'A'
organic certification and the first organic wine,
a Semillon, was made in 1999. In addition to
the organic approach in viticulture,
winemaking standards are high. Cellar door
sales: Mon–Fri 11am–5pm, weekends and
public holidays 10am–5pm.

Jim Barry Wines R85

Craigs Hill Road, Clare, SA 5453
Ph 08 8842 2261, Fax 08 8842 3752,
Email jimbarry@capri.net.au

Owners: Jim Barry family
Chief winemaker: Mark Barry
Year of foundation: 1959
Tonnes crushed on average each year: 1200, of
which about 700 are used for Jim Barry wines
Location: Clare
Area: 200 ha
Soils: red loam/limestone/alluvial schist/shale
Varieties planted: White—chardonnay, riesling,
sauvignon blanc, semillon; Red—cabernet
sauvignon, malbec, merlot, pinot noir,
sangiovese, shiraz

Leading wines: Jim Barry, The Armagh, McRae
Wood Shiraz, Watervale Riesling
Notes: Peter Barry notices a great demand for
reds these days both at home and overseas
and with styles such as The Armagh and
McRae Wood Shiraz, it is no wonder.
Cellar door sales: Mon–Fri 9am–5pm,
weekends and public holidays 9am–4pm.

Kirribilly NR

Farrell Flat Road, Clare, SA 5453
Ph 08 8842 1233, Fax 08 8842 1556,
Email office@kirribillywines.com.au

Owner: Kirribilly Wines Ltd
Chief winemaker: Richard Rowe
Year of foundation: 1999
Tonnes crushed on average each year: more
than 5000, of which it is forecast that about
1300 tonnes will by 2005 be used for Kirribilly
wines
Location: Clare
Area: no vineyards owned
Leading wines: Kirribilly Clare Valley Riesling,
Shiraz, Cabernet
Notes: Kirribilly is a contract processing winery
in an area historically noted as being chronically
short of wineries. Indeed this was the reason
for the creation of the Stanley winery in the
late 19th century. I have tasted no wines from
Kirribilly but Richard Rowe is a well-respected
former BRL Hardy winemaker who knows the
region well. No cellar door sales.

Knappstein Wines R88

2 Pioneer Ave, Clare, SA 5453
Ph 08 8842 2600, Fax 08 8842 3831,
Email cellardoor@knappsteinwines.com

Owner: Petaluma Limited
Chief winemaker: Andrew Hardy
Year of foundation: 1976
Tonnes crushed on average each year: 1500,
about 1000 of which are used for Knappstein
wines

Locations: (winery and cellar door sales) Clare, (vineyards) East Clare, Watervale

Area: 100.27 ha consisting principally of Knappstein Vineyard (34.4 ha), Yertabulti Vineyard (37.6 ha) (both at East Clare) and Ackland (24.3 ha) at Watervale

Soils: (all vineyards) chiefly red-brown clay over limestone (terra rossa) and red-brown clay over slate

Varieties planted: (Knappstein) White—riesling, sauvignon blanc, traminer; Red—cabernet franc, cabernet sauvignon, merlot. (Yertabulti) White—riesling; Red—cabernet sauvignon, malbec, merlot, shiraz. (Ackland) White—riesling, semillon; Red—cabernet sauvignon, merlot, shiraz

Leading wines: Knappstein Enterprise Shiraz, Hand Picked Riesling, Enterprise Cabernet Sauvignon

Notes: Founded by eminent winemaker and show judge Tim Knappstein, who now makes excellent wines in the Adelaide Hills, the winery was sold to Wolf Blass Wines some years ago and later sold to Petaluma, the present owner. Its wines, now made by Andrew Hardy, a longtime disciple of Brian Croser, are very fine. Its Rieslings are crisp and refreshing and about three times every decade there is a superb Botrytis Riesling. Its reds, both Cabernet Sauvignon and Shiraz in contradistinction to the regional style, tend to elegance rather than weight with great volumes of fruit yet particularly fine-grained tannins. A winery that should be visited. Cellar door sales: weekdays 9am–5pm, Sat 11am–5pm, Sun 11am–4pm.

Leasingham Wines   R88

7 Dominic Street, Clare, SA 5453
Ph 08 8842 2555, Fax 08 8842 3293

Owner: BRL Hardy Limited
Chief winemaker: Kerri Thompson
Year of foundation: 1893
Tonnes crushed on average each year: 4000,

about two-thirds of which are used for Leasingham labels

Locations: Clare (winery and cellar door), with Rogers vineyard 7 km north-east, Provis vineyard 4 km east and Dunn's 4 km south-east of the town; Leasingham (Schobers vineyard 3 km south of the village)

Area: 283 ha consisting of Rogers (96 ha), Provis (65 ha), Dunn's (50 ha), Schobers (72 ha)

Soils: Rogers and Provis, variable soils, predominantly red loam over limestone and slate with some areas of shallow grey soils over slate; Dunn's, predominantly deep terra rossa with small areas of shallow grey soils over grey slate; Schobers, 30 cm of red loam over limestone with shaley slate sections on an exposed wind-swept hill in a rain shadow

Varieties planted: White—principally chardonnay, riesling, semillon; Red—principally cabernet franc, cabernet sauvignon, malbec, merlot, shiraz

Leading wines: Leasingham Classic Clare Cabernet Sauvignon, Shiraz, Sparkling Shiraz, Riesling; Bin Range Leasingham Cabernet-Malbec Bin 56, Shiraz Bin 61, Grenache Bin 45, Riesling Bin 7, Chardonnay Bin 37, Late Picked Riesling Bin 6

Notes: Leasingham winery is the old Stanley winery which was established in the heady South Australian wine boom days of 1893 and was for years owned by the Knappstein family and later by Heinz. After its purchase by BRL Hardy, it dropped the Stanley name some years ago and has since been successfully transformed into a 'boutique' (though it still crushes about 4000 tonnes of grapes a year). It crushes only local fruit and maximises the quality reputation of the Clare region for delicate Rieslings, and massive, almost earth-moving Shiraz and Cabernet reds which, despite their 'size', retain an amazing fruit softness on palate. Quality over the whole range is excellent. Cellar door sales: daily 10am–5pm.

Mildara Annies Lane R85

Quelltaler Road, Watervale, SA 5452

Owner: Mildara Blass
Chief winemaker: Caroline Dunn
Year of foundation: 1853
Tonnes produced on average each year: 1800
Locations: Watervale (cellar door and vineyards), Polish Hill River (vineyard)
Area: 32) ha. The principal vineyards are located at Watervale (170 ha) and in Polish Hill River Valley (140 ha). There are two other small vineyards in the area (totalling 10 ha)
Soils: Red loam over limestone and red loam over slate
Varieties planted: White—chardonnay, riesling, semillon; Red—cabernet franc, cabernet sauvignon, merlot, petit verdot, shiraz
Leading wines: Annies Lane Riesling, Cabernet-Merlot, Shiraz
Notes: Though Mildara Blass has ceased winemaking here, the old bluestone winery (commenced in 1863 and now solidly esconsed on its limestone hill dominating the village) remains a Watervale treasure. The original estate was founded in 1853 by Cornishman John Treloar, who called it Spring Vale, and the vineyards and winery passed through several hands until they were acquired in 1890 by Messrs Hermann Buring and Carl Sobels. They germanicised the name to Quelltaler, which remained as a wine name, though, like the moon, waxing and waning, for another 106 years, until Mildara Blass introduced the brand 'Annies Lane', named after a draywoman called Annie Wayman. The wines, however named, are still sourced from its vineyards and remain very good. Cellar door sales: Mon–Fri 8.30am–5pm, weekends 11am–4pm.

Mintaro Cellars NR

Leasingham Road, Mintaro, SA 5415
Ph 08 8843 9046, Fax 08 8843 9050,
Email mintaro@hotmail.com

Owner/chief winemaker: Peter Houldsworth
Year of foundation: 1984
Tonnes crushed on average each year: 50
Location: Mintaro, about 13 km south-east of Clare
Area: 10 ha
Soils: terra rossa over limestone
Varieties planted: White—riesling; Red—cabernet sauvignon, grenache, shiraz
Leading wines: Mintaro Wines Riesling, Cabernet Sauvignon, Shiraz
Note: This is a small but consistently good performer at regional and state wine shows, whose best product is usually Clare's speciality—Riesling. Cellar door sales: 7 days 9am–5pm.

Mitchell Winery R85

Hughes Park Road, Sevenhill, SA 5453
Ph 08 8843 4258, Fax 08 8843 4340,
Email mitchell@capri.net.au

Owners: Mitchell Clare Pty Ltd
Chief winemaker: Andrew Mitchell
Year of foundation: 1975
Tonnes crushed on average each year: 500
Locations: Sevenhill and Watervale
Area: 75 ha consisting of Sevenhill (8 ha), Watervale (53 ha), Auburn (14 ha, newly planted vineyard, bearing for the first time in 2001)
Soils: Sevenhill, sandy loam over gravelly subsoil; Watervale, red loam over deep crumbly limestone; Auburn, red loam over limestone
Varieties planted: (Sevenhill) White—riesling; Red—cabernet franc, cabernet sauvignon, merlot; (Watervale) White—riesling, semillon; Red—grenache, shiraz. (Auburn) White—riesling; Red—malbec, mataro, petit verdot, shiraz
Leading wines: Mitchell Sevenhill Cabernet Sauvignon, Peppertree Vineyard Shiraz, Watervale Riesling
Notes: Mitchell is one of the leading smaller wineries of the Clare region (indeed with a

crush of 500 tonnes, not so small these days). The Cabernet and Shiraz reds, when young, are rich and robust and age harmoniously. They are typical of the top wines of the region. The Riesling is aromatic and charming, easy to drink when youthful, but with the usual regional ability to age very gracefully. The Auburn vineyard has been planted to traditional Clare varieties (except for petit verdot) and is often cooled in the early evening by a welcome south westerly sea breeze, reviving the vines after a searingly hot summer day. Cellar door sales: 7 days 10am–4pm (as the maker adds, 'when stocks are available').

Mount Horrocks Wines   **R88**

Auburn Railway Station, Auburn, SA 5451
Ph/Fax 08 8849 2243, 08 8849 2243, Email horrocks@capri.net.au

Owner/chief winemaker: Stephanie Toole
Year of foundation: 1982
Tonnes crushed on average each year: 65
Locations: (winery and cellar door) Auburn, (vineyard) Watervale
Area: 10 ha
Soils: partly red loam over limestone and partly fairly poor grey stony marl
Varieties planted: White—chardonnay, riesling, semillon; Red—cabernet sauvignon, shiraz
Leading wines: Mount Horrocks Cordon Cut Riesling, Riesling, Shiraz
Notes: Stephanie Toole has owned the Mount Horrocks label for some years and using her partner Jeffrey Grosset's nearby winery she makes excellent Rieslings, both dry and sweet. In addition she has now made her first Shiraz, a 1996, which, in a search for subtlety and style, has been matured in French oak rather than American. In other times, the railway station was the most important building in town. These days, the trains rarely run on time—or at all. So Stephanie Toole conceived the marvellous idea of making the local station popular again. Her

Auburn refreshment rooms are open for tasting on weekends and public holidays, 11am–5pm. Cellar door sales: weekends and public holidays 10am–5pm. Lunch is also available. But do not try to arrive by train.

Neagles Rock   **R86**

Misery Vineyard, Main North Road, Clare, SA 5453
Ph/Fax 08 8843 4020, Fax 08 8843 4021, Email nrvclare@capri.net.au

Owners: Steve Wiblin and Jane Willson
Chief winemaker: Steve Wiblin and contract
Year of foundation: 1997
Tonnes produced on average each year: 150, about half of which are used for Neagles Rock wines
Locations: Misery Vineyard (cellar door and Georges Restaurant), Clare (4 km south of the town), Home Block Vineyard (south-west edge of the town)
Area: 15 ha consisting of Misery Vineyard (7.5 ha), Home Block (7.5 ha)
Soils: Misery, grey sandy loam over shale; Home, terra rossa over limestone
Varieties planted: White—riesling, semillon; Red—cabernet sauvignon, grenache, sangiovese, shiraz
Leading wines: Neagles Rock Vineyard Cabernet, Riesling, Shiraz, Semillon, Grenache
Notes: What do wine marketers do when they cease working for large wine companies and distributors? Market their own wine! That is exactly what Steve Wiblin and Jane Willson did in 1997 when they established Neagles Rock. This is a new name with a uniformly high standard of reds and whites, very worthwhile exploring on any trip to Clare. Cellar door sales: daily 10am–5pm, except Wed. Georges Restaurant has similar hours, but is open for dinner Friday and Saturday nights 6pm–10pm.

Old Station Vineyard (vineyard only) R86

Watervale, SA 5452
Ph 02 9144 1925, Fax 02 9440 7323,
Mob 0414 441 925

Owners: Bill and Noel Ireland
Chief winemaker: Quelltaler (contract)
Year of foundation: vineyard planted 1926,
wine 1995
Tonnes crushed on average each year: 30
Location: Watervale
Area: 6 ha
Soils: red loam over limestone
Varieties planted: White—riesling;
Red—grenache, shiraz
Leading wines: Old Station Riesling, Shiraz,
Grenache-Shiraz, Free-run Grenache (rosé style)
Notes: This is a 'retirement' occupation for
former Sydney retailer Bill Ireland, who
obviously enjoys his life in wine. No cellar
door sales.

Olssens of Watervale R85

Unnamed road, an extension of North
Terrace, Watervale, SA 5452 (about 3 km
north-west of the village)
Ph/Fax 08 8843 0065

Owners: Kevin and Helen Olssen
Chief winemaker: (contract) with assistance
from Kevin Olssen
Year of foundation: vineyard 1979, label 1994
Tonnes crushed on average each year: 45, of
which about 15 are used for the Olssen label
Locations: Watervale. There is also a joint
venture vineyard at Auburn not yet fully
planted or bearing. Among the newly planted
varieties are malbec, merlot and petit verdot
Area: 5 ha
Soils: variable but chiefly red clay loams over
slatey, shaley rock
Varieties planted: White—riesling, semillon;
Red—caberent franc, cabernet sauvignon,
merlot, shiraz

Leading wines: Olssens of Watervale Riesling,
Cabernet Sauvignon-Cabernet Franc-Merlot,
Semillon
Notes: Yet another of the footsoldiers of
Australian viticulture, this is a small family
owned vineyard whose proprietors are keenly
interested in their region and its quality. Such
vineyards are so essential to the growth and
development of Australian wine and help to
maintain the enthusiasm and momentum of
the Australian wine industry. The reds and
whites are of excellent standard. Cellar door
sales: Mon–Fri, weekends and public holidays
11am–5pm, other times by appointment.

Pauletts Wines R85

Polish Hill River Road, via Sevenhill,
SA 5453
Ph 08 8843 4328, Fax 08 8843 4202

Owners: Neil and Alison Paulett
Chief winemaker: Neil Paulett
Year of foundation: 1983
Tonnes crushed on average each year: 200
Location: Polish Hill River Valley
Area: 10.95 ha
Soils: variable red-brown clayey loam, grey
sandy loam and Biscay over slatey sandstone;
subsoil acidic
Varieties planted: White—chardonnay, riesling,
sauvignon blanc; Red—cabernet sauvignon,
merlot, shiraz
Leading wines: Paulett Riesling, Shiraz,
Cabernet-Merlot
Notes: Neil Paulett is an experienced and skilful
winemaker. He began his winemaking self-
employment in 1983, a year of turmoil for
Clare with bushfires and floods all manifesting
before and during vintage. However, Pauletts is
now firmly established and making excellent
award-winning Riesling and Shiraz which after
all is the mainstream of Clare winemaking.
Cellar door sales: 7 days 10am–5pm, except
Christmas Day and Good Friday.

Pearson Vineyards **NR**

Main North Road, Penwortham, SA 5453
(western side of main road in the village)
Ph 08 8843 4234, Fax 08 8843 4141,
Email pearson@capri.net.au

Owners: Jim and Trish Pearson
Chief winemaker: Jim Pearson
Year of foundation: 1993
Tonnes crushed on average each year: 15, of
which 12 are used for Pearson wines
Location: Penwortham
Area: 2 ha
Soils: clayey-loam soils
Varieties planted: White—riesling, semillon;
Red—cabernet franc, cabernet sauvignon,
malbec
Leading wines: Pearson Vineyards Cabernet
Sauvignon, Riesling
Notes: A small vineyard with a winery
completed in time for 1999 vintage. I have not
tasted its wines. Cellar door sales: daily
11am–5pm.

Penfolds (vineyard only) **NR**

Quarry Road, Clare, SA 5453

Owner: Southcorp Wines
Chief winemaker: John Duval
Year of foundation: 1980
Tonnes crushed on average each year: 1800,
all of which is used for Southcorp wines
Location: Clare
Area: 179.4 ha
Soils: shallow red-brown earth over broken
clay and slate subsoils, red-brown earth clay
loam over clay Biscay on creek flats
Varieties planted: White—chardonnay, riesling,
semillon; Red—barbera, cabernet franc,
cabernet sauvignon, dolcetto, malbec, merlot,
nebbiolo, petit verdot
Leading wines: Penfolds Bottle-Aged Clare
Valley Riesling, Organic White and Red table
Wine (export only) made from the organically
managed blocks

Notes: Three blocks of this vineyard are
cultivated organically (no insecticides are used),
but the former Clare Estate range now seems
to have been discontinued. What will
eventuate, if anything, Southcorp is not yet
saying. No local cellar door sales.

Petaluma (vineyard only) **R88**

Hanlin's Hill, Clare, SA 5453

Owner: Petaluma Limited
Chief winemaker: Brian Croser
Year of foundation: vineyard 1968
Tonnes crushed on average each year: 200
Location: Hanlin's Hill (about 3 km east of
Clare)
Area: 29.7 ha
Soils: red-brown loam over slate
Varieties planted: White—chardonnay, riesling,
sauvignon blanc; Red—malbec, shiraz
Leading wine: Petaluma Riesling
Notes: The quintessential estate white has
come from the same source since the vineyard's
acquisition by Petaluma with never a sign of
being blended with riesling from elsewhere.
Typical of and often the elegant best of its
region. When young it is usually a pale green
colour with an attractive lime-citrus nose and a
crisp refreshing palate, but such a description is
mere generalisation. The wine must be tasted.
It ages well also. The other varieties are usually
blended into the Bridgewater Mill range. No
local cellar door sales.

Pikes Wines **R82**

Polish Hill River Road, Sevenhill,
SA 5453
Ph 08 8843 4370, Fax 08 8843 4353,
Email pikes@capri.net.au

Owners: Pike family
Chief winemaker: Neil Pike
Year of foundation: 1984
Tonnes crushed on average each year: 450
Location: Polish Hill River Valley

Area: 32 ha
Soils: red-brown earth over clay with slate and broken bluestone subsoil, well drained
Varieties planted: White—chardonnay, riesling, sauvignon blanc, semillon; Red—cabernet sauvignon, merlot, pinot noir, sangiovese, shiraz
Leading wines: Pikes Riesling, Shiraz, Chardonnay, Merlot, Sauvignon Blanc, Sangiovese
Notes: Neil Pike produces very good whites (Riesling in particular) and reds (excellent Shiraz), which are typical of the region.
Cellar door sales: 7 days 10am–4pm.

Sevenhill Cellars R87

College Road, Sevenhill, SA 5453
(7 km south of Clare)
Ph 08 8843 4222, Fax 08 8843 4382,
Email 7hillcel@rbe.net.au

Owner: Society of Jesus
Chief winemaker: Brother John May SJ
winemaker John Monten
Year of foundation: 1851
Tonnes crushed on average each year: 500
Location: Sevenhill
Area: 55.31 ha
Soils: red loam over limestone, flinty to shaley soils over clay, sandy clay loams
Varieties planted: White—chardonnay, chenin blanc, crouchen, muscadelle, pedro ximinez, riesling, semillon, traminer, verdelho, white frontignac; Red—cabernet franc, cabernet sauvignon, grenache, malbec, merlot, red frontignac, ruby cabernet, shiraz, touriga
Leading wines: Sevenhill Cellars Cabernet Sauvignon, St Ignatius (a red blend of the 'Bordeaux' varieties), Riesling, Liqueur Tokay, Liqueur Verdelho
Notes: Sevenhill Cellars is the oldest wine establishment in the Clare region and its wines epitomise the spirit of the region. When wineries and distilleries belonging to religious orders are mentioned we imagine cowled

monks hurrying along ivied cloisters with secret formulas. Certainly there are buildings which evoke that atmosphere but, thanks to Brother John May, Sevenhill today is a technically advanced, very modern winery. Its reds in particular are of an excellent standard. This is a Sevenhill institution which should not be missed. Cellar door sales: weekdays 8.30am–4.30pm, Saturdays and public holidays 9am–4pm, closed Sundays, Christmas Day, New Year's Day and Good Friday.

Skillogalee R85

off Hughes Park Road, Sevenhill
via Clare, SA 5453
Ph 08 8843 4311, Fax 08 8843 4343,
Email skilly@capri.net.au

Owners: Dave and Diana Palmer
Chief winemaker: Dave Palmer
Year of foundation: 1976
Tonnes crushed on average each year: 100
Locations: (cellar door and vineyards) Skillogalee Valley, Sevenhill, west of Main North Road, about 8 km south of Clare; (vineyard) Watervale
Area: 25 ha (Sevenhill 19.3 ha, Watervale 5.7 ha)
Soils: Sevenhill, red podsols; Watervale, red loam over limestone
Varieties planted: (Sevenhill) White—riesling, traminer; Red—cabernet franc, cabernet sauvignon, malbec, shiraz. (Watervale) White—chardonnay, riesling; Red—shiraz
Leading wines: Skillogalee The Cabernets, Shiraz, Riesling, Gewurztraminer
Notes: Bounded on the west by the Spring Gully National Park, Skillogalee enjoys a charming setting in its secluded valley at the western end of the Sevenhill area, having a slightly cooler location and a slightly higher rainfall than the valleys to the east. It is a consistent award winner at wine shows, its specialities being those of the region as a whole—flavoursome, full-bodied reds and

good Riesling. It has a restaurant open for lunch, morning and afternoon tea. Cellar door sales: 7 days 10am–5pm.

Stephen John Wines R85

Watervale, SA 5452 (about 1 km west of the Watervale Hotel)
Ph/Fax 08 8843 0105,
Email sjwines@capri.net.au

Owners: Rita and Stephen John
Chief winemaker: Stephen John
Year of foundation: 1994
Tonnes crushed on average each year: 70, of which 60 are used for Stephen John wines
Location: Watervale (vineyard and winery)
Area: 5.5 ha
Soils: rich loam over limestone and slate
Varieties planted: White—chardonnay, pedro ximinez, riesling; Red—cabernet sauvignon, shiraz
Leading wines: Stephen John Watervale Riesling, Clare Valley Shiraz, Estate Reserve Shiraz, Estate Reserve Cabernet Sauvignon
Notes: Stephen John is a member of the well-known Barossa family of coopers and winemakers. In his own right he is an eminent wine judge and a well-known winemaker, formerly employed as chief winemaker at Quelltaler by Mildara Blass. Having realised that perhaps, in the Mildara Blass scheme of things, Quelltaler's days were numbered, Stephen took the road to independence in 1994, having chosen the prestigious Watervale location as his area of practice. His extremely cool vineyard there, 500 m in altitude, has seen snow three times in the past seven years and, like Watervale, favours riesling, yet his reds are very good. Cellar door sales: daily 11am–5pm.

Stringy Brae Wines R78

Sawmill Road, Sevenhill, SA 5453
Ph/Fax 08 8843 4319, Email
stringy@capri.net.au

Owners: Donald and Sally Wilson
Chief winemaker: Andrew Mitchell (contract)
Year of foundation: 1988
Tonnes crushed on average each year: 80, of which 25 are used for Stringy Brae wines
Location: Sevenhill
Area: 8 ha
Soils: an undulating vineyard with variable soils, chiefly loam over clay and loam over limestone and shale
Varieties planted: White—riesling; Red—cabernet sauvignon, shiraz
Leading wines: Stringy Brae Riesling, Shiraz, Cabernet Sauvignon
Notes: Stringy Brae has now opened a new facility, Waldie's Shed, consisting of cellar door sales and tasting, tempting food snacks for wine tasters and a function or conference facility. Cellar door sales: weekends, public holidays and school holidays 10am–5pm.

Taylors Wines R86

Taylors Road, Auburn, SA 5451
Ph 08 8849 2008, Fax 08 8849 2240,
Email wakefld@ozemail.com.au

Owners: Taylors Wines Pty Limited (owned by the Taylor family)
Chief winemaker: Adam Eggins
Year of foundation: 1969
Tonnes crushed on average each year: 4000
Location: Auburn
Area: 550 ha
Soils: red-brown loam over limestone
Varieties planted: White—chardonnay, riesling, semillon, traminer; Red—cabernet sauvignon, pinot noir, shiraz
Leading wines: Taylors Cabernet Sauvignon, Chardonnay, Promised Land Shiraz-Cabernet, Unwooded Chardonnay, St Andrews Riesling, Chardonnay, Cabernet Sauvignon
Notes: Taylors is now a veteran of the Clare region. Its Riesling conforms very pleasantly to Clare quality and its reds, which once tended to be on the lighter side, are these days much

fuller-bodied and very much in the mainstream of Clare style. Cellar door sales: weekdays 9am–5pm, Saturdays and public holidays 10am–5pm, Sundays 10am–4pm, closed Christmas Day and Good Friday.

Tim Adams Wines R85

Warenda Road, Clare, SA 5453
(about 3 km south of the town)
Ph 08 8842 2429, Fax 08 8842 3550,
Email tim@timadamswines.com.au

Owners: Tim Adams, Pam Goldsack, Grant and Jackie Crawley
Chief winemaker: Tim Adams
Year of foundation: 1987
Tonnes crushed on average each year: 400, about 270 of which are used for Tim Adams and other labels
Locations: (winery and cellar door) Clare, 3 km south of the town; (vineyard) Watervale
Area: 16 ha
Soils: red-brown clay loams of variable depth over calcareous limestone
Varieties planted: White—pinot gris, riesling, semillon, viognier; Red—shiraz
Leading wines: Aberfeldy Shiraz, The Fergus, Semillon
Notes: Tim Adams is well-known for Aberfeldy Shiraz, which I have not tasted recently and also for his Semillon. Cellar door sales: weekdays 10.30am–5pm, weekends and public holidays 11am–5pm.

Tim Gramp Wines NR

Mintaro Road, Leasingham, SA 5452
(2 km south of Watervale)
(Office) Ph 08 8431 3338,
(Winery) 08 8843 0199

Owners: Tim and Kathy Gramp
Chief winemaker: Tim Gramp
Year of foundation: 1990
Tonnes crushed on average each year: 150, of which 100 are used for Tim Gramp wines

Location: Leasingham
Area: 2 ha
Soils: brown to red loam over limestone, sandy loam over limestone
Varieties planted: White—riesling; Red—cabernet sauvignon, grenache, shiraz
Leading wine: Tim Gramp Shiraz
Notes: With a name like Gramp, which has five generations of winemaking ancestry in South Australia, what else do you do except make wine! Regrettably I have not tasted any of Tim's recent wines. Cellar door sales: weekends and public holidays 10.30am–4.30pm.

Waninga NR

Hughes Park Road, Sevenhill via Clare, SA 5453
Ph/Fax 08 8843 4395

Owners: Graham and Ethel Mill, Bob Ling, Ken Foggo, Hilary Taylor
Chief winemakers: Tim Adams, Jeffrey Grosset (contract)
Year of foundation: vineyard 1974, first wine, 1989
Tonnes crushed on average each year: 250, of which 25 are used for the Waninga labels
Location: Sevenhill, west of the Main North Road, in the Skilly Hills midway between Sevenhill and Penwortham
Area: 37.5 ha
Soils: red-brown loam over rock and clay with sandy loams elsewhere
Varieties planted: White—chardonnay, chenin blanc, riesling, semillon; Red—cabernet sauvignon, shiraz
Leading wines: Waninga Riesling, Shiraz, Cabernet Sauvignon
Notes: Waninga is a large vineyard supplying fruit to, among others, Tim Adams and Jeffrey Grosset who are its contract winemakers. Its wines are consistent medal winners at the Clare Regional Wine Show. Cellar door sales: weekends, public and school holidays 10am–5pm.

Wendouree Cellars **R90**

Spring Farm Road, Clare, SA 5453
(about 2 km south-east of town)
PO Box 27, Clare, SA
Ph 08 8842 2896

Owners: Liberman family
Chief winemaker: Tony Brady
Year of foundation: 1893, first wine 1895
Tonnes crushed on average each year: 50
Location: Clare
Area: 11.4 ha
Soils: most is red loam over limestone, but
there are small sections of red clay/loam, some
shale and two small vineyards of black alluvial
Varieties planted: White—muscat of
Alexandria; Red—cabernet sauvignon, malbec,
mataro (mourvedre), shiraz
Leading wines: Wendouree Shiraz, Shiraz-
Mataro, Shiraz-Malbec, Cabernet Sauvignon,
Cabernet-Malbec
Notes: In a sense, Wendouree Cellars is
Australia's oldest boutique vineyard. Its wines I
imagine are much the same as they were a
century ago—quintessentially Clare and of
course red, big wines intended for people with
cellars and patience, much the same as people
were a century ago. In the meantime, the Birks
family has come and gone from Wendouree
and Tony and Lita Brady carry the Wendouree
torch and the Birks' tradition, in much the
same way as the Olympic torch is carried,
reverently and with great care. The reds are
still made beautifully and intended for
medium- to long-term cellaring, about
10 years minimum. Cellar door sales by mail
order only.

The Wilson Vineyard **NR**

Polish Hill River, Sevenhill, SA 5453
Ph 08 8843 4310

Owners: Wilson family
Chief winemaker: John Wilson
Year of foundation: 1974
Tonnes crushed on average each year: 85, all
of which are used for Wilson Vineyard wines
Location: Cellar door and vineyards: Polish Hill
River Valley
Area: 12 ha
Soils: acidic red-brown clayey loam over
decomposing slate
Varieties planted: White—chardonnay,
gewurztraminer, riesling, semillon;
Red—cabernet sauvignon, malbec, merlot,
nebbiolo, petit verdot, shiraz, zinfandel
Leading wines: The Wilson Vineyard Gallery
Series Riesling, Gallery Series Cabernet
Sauvignon, Hippocrene, Chardonnay, Zinfandel
Notes: John Wilson is an articulate man who
writes a delightful newsletter and is yet
another of the legion of Australian medical
men bewitched by the vine, an enchantment
which has now lasted for over twenty years.
His vineyard has a whole pharmacopoeia of
grape varieties, but the best of them are—as
usual for Clare—riesling, shiraz and cabernet
sauvignon. He may not agree with me about
the grape varieties, but the Gallery Series
Riesling and Cabernet Sauvignon are
consistently good. Cellar door sales: weekends
between May and October 10am–4pm.

PART IV

WESTERN AUSTRALIA

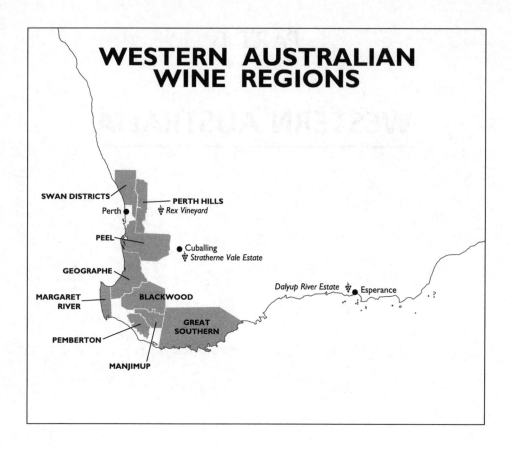

WESTERN AUSTRALIAN WINE REGIONS

SWAN DISTRICTS

PERTH HILLS
Perth
Rex Vineyard

PEEL

Cuballing
Stratherne Vale Estate

GEOGRAPHE

Dalyup River Estate
Esperance

MARGARET RIVER

BLACKWOOD

PEMBERTON

GREAT SOUTHERN

MANJIMUP

❧ EASTERN PLAINS, INLAND AND NORTH OF WESTERN AUSTRALIA

This is a vast area (in fact, all of Western Australia except the temperate south-west) which so far has no wine significance.

❧ WEST AUSTRALIAN SOUTH EAST COASTAL ZONE

This is a long, lonely east-west stretch of the Western Australian coastline beginning near Bremer Bay about 120 km east of Albany, travelling through Esperance (the natural centre of the zone) and ending some 250 km further east (about halfway to the western border of South Australia). At the time of writing, Esperance had applied for but not yet granted wine regional status. There are relatively few vineyards in this zone, but there is no reason why, given sufficient irrigation, there should not be many more.

Dalyup River Estate **NR**

Esperance, WA
Ph/Fax 08 9076 5027,
Email dalyup@wn.com.au

Owners: Tom and Jenny Murray
Chief winemaker: Tom Murray
Year of foundation: 1987
Tonnes crushed on average each year: 15, all of which are used for Dalyup River estate wines
Location: Esperance (35 km west of the town, 7 km off Highway 1)
Area: 3 ha
Soils: silty loam A horizon about 0.8 m deep over clay loam subsoil
Varieties planted: White—chardonnay, riesling, sauvignon blanc; Red—cabernet sauvignon, shiraz
Leading wine: Dalyup River Estate Shiraz
Notes: Though one of the most remote vineyards in Australia, Dalyup River Estate is no mere distraction for occasional tourists, but a serious winery, which goes about the business of winning awards and trophies at wine shows. This Dalyup River has done several times since the mid-90s, capping it all with a trophy for Best Shiraz and Best Dry Red at the Mount Barker Wine Show. But if you want to taste the wine, you will need to go rather a long way. Cellar door sales: weekends and public holidays from late September to Easter 10am–4pm; or from retailers in Esperance or by mail to PO box 1233, Esperance WA 6450.

✾ SOUTH WEST AUSTRALIA ZONE

This is the heartland of Western Australian viticulture. Its cooler areas such as Margaret River produce excellent reds of marvellous fruitiness and high quality whites; those that are warmer make fuller-bodied reds of good character. Currently, this zone comprises four registered wine regions, Great Southern, Margaret River, Geographe and Blackwood Valley, and two more in the offing as a result of the fracture of the proposed former region—Pemberton. These two may be Pemberton (diminished), and Manjimup.

The Great Southern region has four registered sub-regions—Mount Barker, Albany, Porongurups and Frankland River. In addition, a further sub-region is proposed, Denmark. In Margaret River there are also some possible sub-regions, but more about those later.

GEOGRAPHE REGION

The Geographe region was often previously called the South West Coastal Plain, but is now enlarged to encompass the foothills of the Darling Range and the country to its south-east around Donnybrook-Kirup. It is named after Geographe Bay, most of which it fronts, the bay itself deriving its name from one of the two vessels under the command of Nicholas Baudin who explored much of the coast of south-western and southern Australia in the early years of the nineteenth century. The other ship was the *Naturaliste* which gave its name to a cape at the western end of Geographe Bay.

There was little tradition of grape-growing in the region until the inter-war period of the 1920s and 1930s, when small vineyards and wineries were established around the town of Harvey by Italian migrants. With the onset of the Second World War, many of these vignerons were interned and their vineyards fell into neglect, being grazed by dairy cows and never re-established after the war.

The modern viticultural era of the Geographe region began in 1973 when Dr Barry Killerby planted a vineyard at Stratham, 15 km south of Bunbury. He was followed a year later by Dr Peter Pratten, who commenced planting at Capel Vale on the Capel River just west of the town of Capel and in 1976 by Gil Thomas. Soon after a vineyard was established on the South West Highway between Donnybrook and Kirup.

So the region remained until 1995 when Rob Bowen formerly of Capel Vale and Matt Aldridge then of Killerby began to encourage local grape-growing interest by the formation of the Geographe Vignerons Association. As a result, there are now many more young vineyards in the region with one vineyard over 60 ha in extent. There are three major wineries in the region, Capel Vale, Killerby and Willow Bridge Estate, as well as another recently established winery, Donnybrook Valley, and several growers who wish to market some or all of their own grapes as wine under their own label.

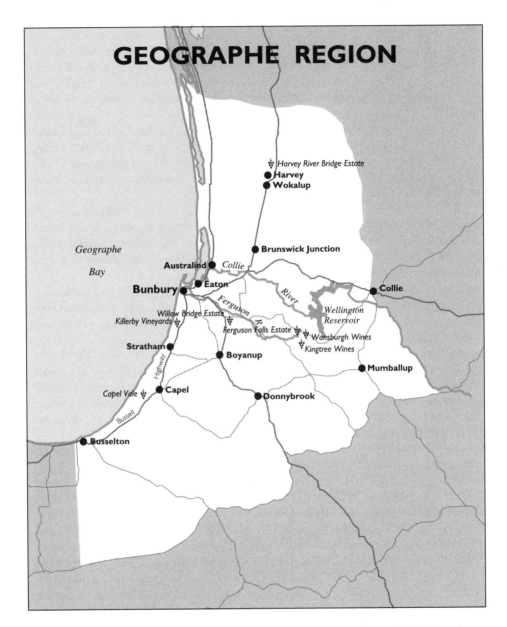

GEOGRAPHE REGION

Location: Bunbury (centre of region) latitude 33°18'S, longitude 115°38'E. Busselton (south-west of region) latitude 33°38'S, longitude 115°22'E. Collie (east of region) latitude 33°21'S, longitude 116°08'E. Wokalup (north of region) latitude 33°08'S, longitude 115°53'E. Bunbury is about 150 km south of Perth.

Elevation: from sea-level to 200 m

Topography and soils: The country rises gradually from the west (the coast) to the east (the Darling Range) about 200–250 m, but rather less so to the south-east and south.

Along the coastal strip and at virtually sea-level is the 'tuart country', characterised by growths of *Eucalyptus gomphocephala* (the tuart gum). This consists of deep yellow sands over limestone. These are well-drained, iron-stained, siliceous sands usually over 2 metres deep. They are suitable for viticulture, but are of low natural fertility and need building up in respect to organic matter. They also often require nutrition as nutrients leach easily.

The major river systems of the region are the Harvey, Collie, Preston and Capel. Along the banks of these rivers are found brown loamy earths and brown sandy earths. These are alluvial, usually over 2 metres deep, well-drained and inherently fertile. Topsoils comprise rich brown loamy sands, sandy loam and loam passing into red or brown clay loamy or clayey subsoil.

As the altitude increases and the slopes and valleys of the Darling Range are reached, there are friable red-brown loamy earths together with brown loamy earths and brown deep loam duplex soils. These are 1–2 metres deep and have formed on the gneiss and granite of the Yilgarn Block. Topsoils here usually consist of sandy loams or loams above clays, which are usually porous and well structured.

Further upwards still on hills and ridges are located loamy gravels and moderately deep sandy gravels. These are lateritic and consist of loamy sands and sandy loams containing 20–80% rounded ironstone gravel above red or yellow-brown clayey subsoils about 50 cm thick.

In the south (adjacent to the Margaret River region) and south-east of the region, the increase in altitude is not so pronounced. Busselton is flat and its soils are poorly drained. Further south, around Chapman's Hill, the soils are often gravelly 'marri' country and suitable for viticulture, while in the south-east in the vicinity of Donnybrook and Kirup, there are gravelly sandy loams very suitable for wine grapes. However, frosts in this locality present a considerable problem.

Climate: Bunbury (centre) MJT 21.2°C, MAR na, HDD raw 1875, 1685 (cut off and adjusted for latitude, daily temperature range and for vine sites), AR 881 mm (Oct–Apr 185 mm), RH 54%, AI na, SH 8.8 (Gladstones). Busselton (south) MJT 20.9°C, MAR na, HDD raw 1779, 1589 (cut off and adjusted for latitude, daily temperature range and vine sites), AR 838 mm (Oct–Apr 179 mm), RH 51% (3pm Jan), AI na, SH 8.4. Donnybrook (south-east) MJT 21.7°C, MAR na, HDD raw 1878, 1657 (cut off and adjusted for latitude, daily temperature range and vine sites), AR 1019 mm (Oct–Apr 221 mm), RH 31% (3pm Jan), AI na, SH 8.6 (Gladstones). Collie (east) MJT 21.6°C, MAR na, HDD raw 1779, 1611 (cut off and adjusted for latitude, daily temperature range and vine sites), AR 988 mm (Oct–Apr 221 mm), RH 34% (3pm Jan), AI na, SH 8.7. Wokalup (north) MJT 22.6°C, MAR na, HDD raw 2057, 1707 (cut off and adjusted for latitude, daily temperature range and vine sites), AR 1010 mm (Oct–Apr 224 mm), RH 41% (3pm Jan), AI na, SH 8.9 (Gladstones).

The climate of the region may be termed Mediterranean, that is, generally warm and dry between October and April with less than a quarter of its annual rainfall occurring during this period. The MJTs become warmer, as a general rule, to the north, east and south-east as one moves inland from Bunbury. Only Busselton is marginally cooler in January.

Around Bunbury, the climate during the growing season is warm, though maritime influences keep temperatures equable. Favourable relative humidities due to sea breezes emanating from the Indian Ocean are also maintained. Frosts are rare.

The area to the south of Busselton, which adjoins the Margaret River region, is Chapman's Hill. Here, the rain shadows of the more southerly Whicher range and the westerly ridge running north–south from Cape Naturaliste to Cape Leeuwin have resulted in a warm, dry and sunny climate not unlike that of the coastal area nearer Bunbury.

South-east of Bunbury around Donnybrook, the locality has good surface water catchments and its climate appears to favour full-bodied red and light fortifieds. Its relative humidity is low, increasing the risk of water stress during ripening but reducing risks of mildew. There is also a frost risk in spring and site selection for vineyards must be carried out very carefully to ensure that there is maximum air drainage.

Inland from Bunbury are the towns of Burekup and Dardanup. Suitable vine sites here for medium- to full-bodied whites and reds appear to be Henty Brook (south-east of Burekup) and the Ferguson Valley and Crooked Brook (south-east of Dardanup). Winter–spring rainfall is generous and reliable and there are good surface water catchments. The locality is also mostly free of frosts. Already in the Ferguson Valley there is an explosion of vineyards, including the largest in the region (presently 60 ha, but planned to extend to 100). As one proceeds north, the region becomes hotter. Wokalup is typical and seems more suited to fortifieds than the more southerly parts, though the cooling and humidifying influences of the prevailing sea breeze still has a beneficial effect.

There are relatively few other viticultural problems, though powdery mildew does occur. It is treated in the usual way by sulfur spray. Insect pests include wingless grasshoppers and garden weevils. Open range guineafowl have proved most effective in reducing their numbers.

Principal varieties: White—chardonnay, verdelho; Red—shiraz, merlot, cabernet sauvignon

Harvest time: chardonnay mid-February to third week of March, shiraz third week of March, cabernet sauvignon fourth week of March, merlot third week of March to first week of April

Total area: 1000 ha

Principal wine styles: What has come from the region so far is largely represented by its largest makers, Capel Vale and Killerby. Capel Vale makes excellent Chardonnays and also very good full-bodied Shiraz reds, though many of these have emanated from Mount Barker. Killerby likewise has made a name for its local reds in recent years. Cabernet Sauvignon, however, produces only adequate wines which lack the tannic fullness and varietal character of Cabernet from, say, Margaret River. Merlot is a variety relatively new to the district, which is showing excellent promise. There is no reason to suppose that Merlot should not become a major wine style of the region.

Leading wines and vineyards: Capel Vale, Killerby.

Capel Vale **R90**

Stirling Estate, Mallokup Road, Capel,
WA 6271
Ph 08 9727 1986, Fax 08 9727 1904

Owners: Dr Peter and Mrs Elizabeth Pratten
Chief winemaker: Nicole Esdaile
Year of foundation: 1975
Tonnes crushed on average each year: 2300
Location: (winery and cellar door) Stirling
Estate, Capel, together with vineyards at
Wellington (Geographe region), Sheldrake
(proposed Pemberton region), Whispering Hill
(Mount Barker, Great Southern region) and
Madrigals (Cowaramup, Margaret River region)
Area: 156 ha consisting of Stirling Estate 7 ha,
Wellington 14 ha, Sheldrake 77 ha,
Whispering Hills 13 ha, Madrigals 45 ha
Soils: Stirling Estate, deep loam over limestone,
('tuart'); Wellington same as Stirling Estate;
Sheldrake, deep karri loams; Whispering Hill,
old 'marri' loams resulting from degraded
Porongurup granite; Madrigals lateritic gravel
Varieties planted: (Stirling Estate)
White—chardonnay, riesling; Red—cabernet
sauvignon, merlot, shiraz. (Wellington)
White—chardonnay; Red—merlot, pinot noir.
(Sheldrake) White—chardonnay, sauvignon
blanc, semillon, verdelho, viognier;
Red—cabernet franc, cabernet sauvignon,
merlot, pinot noir, shiraz. (Whispering Hill)
White—riesling; Red—shiraz. (Madrigals)
White—none; Red—cabernet sauvignon,
nebbiolo, sangiovese.
Leading wines: Capel Vale Frederick
Chardonnay, Whispering Hill Riesling, Howcroft
Merlot Kinnaird Shiraz
Notes: Capel Vale is one of the veterans of the
Geographe region and has grown significantly
in the past decade, having a vineyard presence
in all the leading wine regions of Western
Australia. Its wine quality is consistent and
excellent. No more need be said. Cellar door
sales: 7 days 10am–4pm.

Donnybrook Valley Wines **NR**

Lot 384 South Western Highway,
Newlands, WA 6239
Ph/Fax 08 9731 6349

Owners: Lawrance and Wise families
Chief winemaker: Siobhan Lynch
Year of foundation: 1988
Tonnes crushed on average each year: 80
Location: Donnybrook
Area: 12 ha
Soils: gravelly loams over clay
Varieties planted: White—chardonnay,
colombard, sauvignon blanc, verdelho;
Red—cabernet franc, cabernet sauvignon,
merlot
Leading wines: Wise Vineyards Merlot,
Chardonnay
Notes: All wines are sold under the Wise
Vineyards labels. There are no cellar door sales
(see Wise Vineyards in the Margaret River
region).

Ferguson Falls Estate **NR**

Pile Road, Ferguson Valley via Dardanup,
WA 6236
Ph 08 9728 1083, Fax 08 9278 1616

Owners: Peter and Margaret Giumelli
Chief winemaker: Rob Bowen (contract)
Year of foundation: 1993
Tonnes crushed on average each year: 12 but
increasing
Location: Ferguson Valley via Dardanup
Area: 6 ha (of which 2 ha are not yet
producing)
Soils: lateritic gravels and sandy gravel slopes,
well drained and quite steep
Varieties planted: White—chardonnay,
verdelho; Red—cabernet sauvignon, grenache,
merlot, nebbiolo
Leading wines: Ferguson Falls Cabernet
Sauvignon, Chardonnay
Notes: Ferguson Falls is a small, family owned
vineyard, whose wines I have not tasted. Cellar

door sales: weekends and public holidays
10am–4pm.

Harvey River Bridge Estate R80

Third Street, Harvey, WA 6220
Ph 08 9729 2199, Fax 08 9729 2298,
Email harveyfresh@harveyfresh.com.au

Owner: Harvey Fresh (1994) Ltd
Chief winemaker: Camilla Vote
Year of foundation: 1999
Tonnes crushed on average each year: 400
Location: Harvey (winery)
Area: no vineyards owned
Leading wines: Harvey River Bridge range,
Joseph River range
Notes: This is a new winery at Harvey in the
north of the Geographe region, which
purchases all its fruit from within the region.
Quality is good. Sales by mail order only to
PO Box 223, Harvey, WA 6220.

Killerby Vineyards R85

Minninup Road, Stratham, WA 6230
Ph 08 9795 7222, Fax 08 9795 7835,
Email winemaker@killerby.com.au

Owner: Ben Killerby
Chief winemaker: Paul Boulden
Year of foundation: 1973
Tonnes crushed on average each year: 120
Location: Stratham
Area: 22 ha
Soils: 'tuart', free-draining sandy loam over
limestone
Varieties planted: White—chardonnay,
semillon; Red—cabernet sauvignon, merlot,
shiraz
Leading wines: Killerby Vineyards Shiraz,
Cabernet Sauvignon, Chardonnay
Notes: This is the pioneer of the Geographe
region, or the South West Coastal Plain as the
area was once called, and a maker of good
Chardonnay, Shiraz and Cabernet Sauvignon.
Cellar door sales: 10am–5pm daily.

Kingtree Wines NR

Kingtree Road, Wellington Mills,
WA 6236
Ph 08 9728 3050, Fax 08 9728 3113

Owners: David and Cheryl Rourke
Chief winemaker: Capel Vale (contract)
Year of foundation: 1991
Tonnes crushed on average each year: 30, but
will increase to 45 (about 10 tonnes presently
used for Kingtree's own labels)
Location: Ferguson Valley
Area: 6 ha
Soils: rich, gravel loams, amply watered by a
surface catchment dam, filled by a rainfall of
1000 mm per annum
Varieties planted: White—riesling, sauvignon
blanc; Red—cabernet sauvignon, merlot
Leading wines: Kingtree Sauvignon Blanc,
Riesling, Cabernet Sauvignon-Merlot
Notes: Located on the edge of the Darling
Scarp in the newly booming Ferguson Valley,
Kingtree, though hardly 9 years old, is already
a veteran of the district. There is a guest lodge
that accommodates four couples. Cellar door
sales: weekends 11am–5pm.

Wansbrough Wines NR

Pile Road, Ferguson, WA 6236
Ph 08 9728 3104, Fax 08 9728 3091,
Email brenc@altu.net.au

Owners: Brian and Jan Wansburgh
Chief winemaker: Willespie Wines (contract)
Year of foundation: 1986
Tonnes crushed on average each year: 40, of
which 5 are used for Wansbrough wines
Location: Ferguson Valley
Area: 8 ha
Soils: sandy gravelly lateritic ('marri') loam on
a steep, well-drained slope
Varieties planted: White—chardonnay, riesling,
sauvignon blanc, semillon; Red—cabernet
sauvignon, merlot, shiraz
Leading wines: Wansburgh Sauvignon Blanc,

Semillon, Cabernet-Shiraz
Notes: I have not recently tasted the wines.
Cellar door sales: weekends 11am–5pm.

Willow Bridge Estate **R82**

Gardincourt Drive, Dardanup, WA 6236
Ph 08 9728 0055, Fax 08 9728 0066,
Email wine@willowbridgeestate.com

Owners: Jeff Dewar and family
Chief winemaker: Rob Bowen
Year of foundation: 1997
Tonnes produced on average each year: 250
(vintage 2000), but crop should reach 1100
tonnes when the vineyard is fully planted and
in full bearing

Location: (winery, cellar door and vineyards)
Ferguson Valley
Area: 60 ha (2001) going to 100 ha by 2006
Soils: granitic, gravelly loam over gravelly clay
subsoils
Varieties planted: White—chardonnay, chenin
blanc, sauvignon blanc, semillon;
Red—cabernet sauvignon, shiraz
Leading wines: Willow Bridge Estate Shiraz,
Cabernet Sauvignon, Chardonnay.
Notes: Willow Bridge Estate is large by
Ferguson Valley standards, but it has started
well and should prosper under the experienced
guidance of Rob Bowen. Cellar door sales:
daily 10am–4pm.

MARGARET RIVER REGION

Early exploration of the coasts of the region was carried out by Dutch navigators in the early seventeenth century and more extensive mapping in the early nineteenth century by the British and French (Matthew Flinders in the *Investigator*, Nicolas Baudin in *Geographe* and Freycinet in *Naturaliste*). Hence the names Geographe Bay and Cape Naturaliste. Though there are reports of Margaret River wine being bartered for tea, coffee and bolts of gingham in the 1850s, early history is sketchy. More substantiated is the planting by an Italian farmer, Jimmy Meleri, of 4 hectares of doradillo in 1914. However, Margaret River really sprang to life as a vineyard region as a result of two research reports. Californian viticulturalist Professor Harold Olmo and the Western Australian scientist Dr John Gladstones are the researchers to whom credit is due. Olmo was commissioned by the Western Australian government in 1955 to evaluate the state's wine industry and to advise on its future. As with most reports, the government response was most notable for its absence but finally, in 1962, it resolved to act by planting an experimental vineyard at Forest Hill near Mount Barker in the Great Southern region. Sufficient interest had, however, been aroused in the Margaret River region by Olmo's report to cause Dr John Gladstones of the University of Western Australia to carry out further research in that region in 1965. His enthusiastic report stimulated Perth cardiologist Dr Tom Cullity to plant his Vasse Felix vineyard near Willyabrup in 1967. His first vintage was in 1971 and his vigorous pursuit of the Margaret River vine inspired others. Dr Bill Pannell began to plant Moss Wood in 1970, followed by Dr Kevin Cullen and his wife Di in 1971. In 1978, the region, led by Dr Kevin Cullen, was among the first in Australia to adopt regional certification of wines as a means of improving local wine quality. The region is rightly regarded, with Coonawarra and the Yarra Valley, as one of the three premium cabernet sauvignon areas in Australia.

MARGARET RIVER REGION

1	Abbey Vale Vineyards
2	Amberley Estate
3	Ashbrook Estate
4	Becketts Flat
5	Brookland Valley
6	Clairault
7	Chapman's Creek
8	Cullen Wines
9	Driftwood
10	Evans & Tate
11	Fermoy Estate
12	Deepwoods Estate
13	Happs
14	Hay Shed Hill
15	Howard Park
16	Lenton Brae
17	Moss Brothers
18	Moss Wood Winery
19	Palmer Wines
20	Pierro
21	Ribbon Vale Estate
22	Rivendell Vineyard
23	Sandalford Wines
24	Treeton Estate
25	Vasse Felix
26	Vasse River Wines
27	Willespie
28	Wise Vineyards
29	Woodlands Wines
30	Woody Nook
31	Juniper Estate

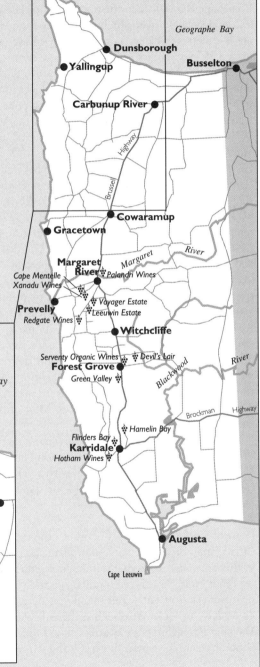

Geographe Bay

Dunsborough

Yallingup

Busselton

Carbunup River

Brussel Highway

Cowaramup

Gracetown

Margaret River

Cape Mentelle
Xanadu Wines

Margaret River

Palandri Wines

Prevelly
Redgate Wines

Voyager Estate
Leeuwin Estate

Witchcliffe

Serventy Organic Wines
Forest Grove

Devil's Lair

Green Valley

Blackwood River

Brockman Highway

Flinders Bay

Hamelin Bay

Karridale
Hotham Wines

Augusta

Cape Leeuwin

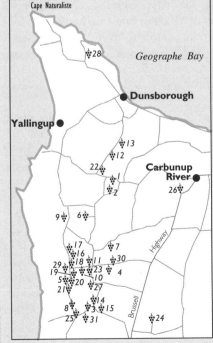

Cape Naturaliste

Geographe Bay

28

Dunsborough

Yallingup

13
12

22

Carbunup River

26

9   6

17
16
7
29 18 11 30
19   23   4
5 20 10
21   27
8   14
25   31   15
24

Brussel Highway

Location: the region south of Perth and west of longitude 115°18'E, approx 33°42'S, about 250 km south-south-west of Perth

Elevation: 90 m

Topography and soils: The dominant feature of Margaret River is a low ridge extending from Cape Naturaliste in the north to Cape Leeuwin in the south consisting of granitic and gneissic rocks over which laterite has formed. It is an undulating region whose soils are 1–2 metres thick and consist of grey-brown gravelly, sandy loams, varying in colour from dark grey to dark red-brown. These surface soils cover pale yellow or brown sub-surface soils which pass into clayey subsoils. Such soils are permeable when moist, but difficult to wet when dry, and are also subject to wind erosion. They are acid to neutral in pH and can be deficient in phosphorus, potassium and calcium.

Climate: (Major centres north to south in the Margaret River region) Yallingup MJT 20°C, MAR na, HDD raw 1664, 1629 (cut off and adjusted for latitude, daily temperature range and vine sites), AR 1083 mm (Oct–Apr 232 mm), RH 55% (3pm Jan), AI na, SH 7.9 (Gladstones). Willyabrup MJT 20.2°C, MAR na, HDD raw 1649, 1601 (cut off and adjusted for latitude, daily temperature range and vine sites), AR 1138 mm (Oct–Apr 253 mm), RH 54% (3pm Jan), AI na, SH 7.8 (Gladstones). Margaret River MJT 20°C, MAR 7.2°C, HDD raw 1597, 1557 (cut off and adjusted for latitude, daily temperature range and vine sites), AR 1192 mm (Oct–Apr 274 mm), RH 53% (3pm Jan), AI na, SH 7.7. Karridale MJT 19.1°C, MAR na, HDD raw 1529, 1507 (cut off and adjusted for latitude and daily temperature range only without adjusted for vine sites), AR 1200 mm (Oct–Apr 294 mm), RH 55% (3pm Jan), AI na, SH 7.2 (Gladstones). A warm but rarely hot climate, maritime in nature, paradoxically regarded as 'cool' because of its long slow ripening season. The reality is that winter in Margaret River is rarely very cold, as witness its mean July temperature of 12.8°C (Dry & Smart). But it is quite often very wet, as a result of which its vines are hardly ever fully dormant, burst their buds very early and then are subject to many spring and early summer dangers, such as strong, salt-bearing winds, which wreak havoc with young chardonnay shoots. Annual rainfall is on average over 1150 mm, approximately 70% falling between April and September. Most of the region is drip irrigated from dams and bores.

Principal varieties: Red—cabernet sauvignon, merlot, shiraz, cabernet franc, pinot noir; White—chardonnay, semillon, sauvignon blanc, chenin blanc, verdelho, riesling

Harvest time: February to mid April with a variation of 3–4 weeks in the maturation of cabernet sauvignon and 2–3 weeks for semillon, depending on location within the region, the north being the earliest

Total area: 3000 ha (2001)

Principal wine styles: Red—Cabernet Sauvignon, Cabernet-Merlot, Shiraz; White—Chardonnay, Semillon, Sauvignon Blanc, Semillon-Sauvignon Blanc, Verdelho. Shiraz in this previously Cabernet-dominant region is growing in popularity among makers, yet Pinot Noir, though often quite soft and palatable, seems rarely to have the classic structure (i.e. soft entry, full middle palate and soft exit from palate) that the better Pinots have in cooler areas such as the Adelaide Hills, Southern Victoria and Tasmania. Margaret River Pinots are evenly palated without a full middle palate and often with a noticeable tannic grip on finish. Of the whites, Sauvignon Blanc and Semillon when blended or when bottled separately show herbaceous and/or tropical characters and are usually racy and refreshing. Chardonnay also can be exceptionally good.

Leading wineries and vineyards: Cullen Wines, Moss Wood, Leeuwin Estate, Cape Mentelle, Pierro, Evans & Tate, Voyage Estate, Devils Lair, Vasse Felix, Sandstone, Brookland Valley, Redjate Winery.

Gladstones' map subregionalising Margaret River Region

Since the registration of Margaret River as a wine region and as knowledge of its micro-climates and soils has increased, the indefatigable Dr John Gladstones has been at work again, producing in 1999 his 'Conceptual Plan for Viticultural Sub-regions of Margaret River'. As the ultimate test for distinctions in sub-regionality is the style of wine produced and as such wine differences are not likely to emerge for decades, Gladstones proposes that perhaps natural drainage basins and their probable climate differences should form the principal basis for creating new sub-regions, together with divergencies in soil type and other landform features. His proposed six sub-regions are (from north to south): Yallingup, Carbunup, Wilyabrup, Treeton, Wallcliffe and Karridale.

Yallingup (generally) consists of the northern part of the Leeuwin–Naturaliste Ridge including the drainage basins of the Gunyulgup, Wyadup and Quininup Brooks. Its southern boundary is the drainage divide between these and the Wilyabrup Brook, as far east as its intersection with the Bussell Highway. Its eastern boundary runs north from there until it reaches the Metricup turn-off, then travels west along this road to the former Metricup Railway siding, then follows the former railway north until it crosses Wildwood Road. (This eastern boundary broadly corresponds to the Duns-borough (Geological) Fault and the related transition between the Cowaramup and Metricup land systems to the west and the flatter Yelverton Shelf to the east.) The boundary is completed by drawing a straight line northwards from this point (Metricup Siding/Wildwood Road) to Central Dunsborough and the coast.

The Yallingup climate is warm and has ample sunshine. It has a very strong maritime influence, being exposed to warm dry winds from the north and east, such winds from the north and north-east being moderated by their passage across Geographe Bay. Cool winds such as those from the south and south-east being correspondingly warmed by their passage across 80 km of land mass.

Its soils are mostly made up of gravelly sands to gravelly loams on the slopes of the Metricup and Wilyabrup land systems together with similar soils on the flatter uplands of the Cowaramup land system.

Carbunup (generally) is that area of land east of the Yallingup sub-region having as its northern boundary the shore of Geographe Bay east almost to Busselton, and its western boundary the eastern boundary of Yallingup sub-region, its eastern boundary being line of longitude 115°18'E, while its southern boundary follows the southern boundary of certain officially surveyed lots (i.e. lots 2576, 2574, 2685, 2684, 2692, 2677, 2676, 2675 and 2671), which in turn corresponds closely with the transition from the Yelverton Shelf in the north to the Treeton Hills system in the south.

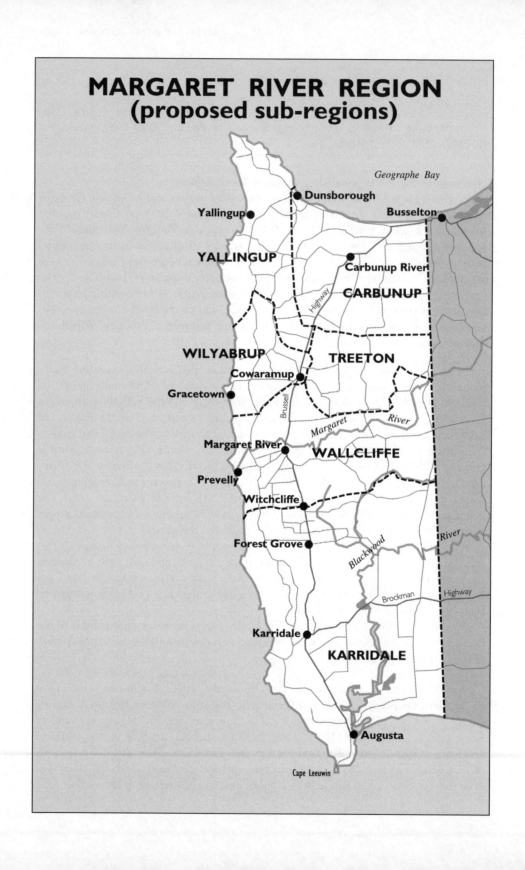

The Carbunup climate is relatively maritime, but is cut off from the south by the Whicher Range and from the West by the Leeuwin–Naturaliste Ridge, thus making this part of the sub-region warmer and drier than the rest.

In Carbunup, there are two distinctive land systems absent elsewhere in the Margaret River region. These are the Abba series of flat coastal sands and alluvial soils up to about 40 metres altitude and the very gently sloping Yelverton Shelf fringing them inland up to about 80 metres altitude. Soils here are mainly gravelly sands and duplex soils. Only better-drained soils and those having at least some fertility are suitable for viticulture, but such country is reasonably extensive in area and good supplies of bore water are available.

Wilyabrup (generally) is the combined area of the drainage basins of the Wilyabrup and Cowaramup Brooks, which drain westwards into the Indian Ocean. Together with the western environs of the town of Margaret River, it is also the most renowned viticultural area of the Margaret River region.

In climate it is similar to Yallingup but is less directly exposed to warmer north and north-east winds. There is a tendency for diurnal east–west air convection cells to form during summer due to the lie of the land, but it is too far north for southerly influences to dominate. Its soils are similar to those of Yallingup but with a higher proportion of those gravelly loams that have proved so successful for viticulture during the past 30 years. If sub-regionality is required within Margaret River, Wilyabrup is the archetypal sub-region. It has proved itself beyond the shadow of a doubt.

Treeton is the smallest of the proposed sub-regions. It is also subject to two difficulties: first, viticulture there is limited and, second, on the primary basis of drainage basins, it should be part of Carbunup. However, it does not share Carbunup's soils or flatter topography, being undulating. Rainfall is also higher and it is slightly cooler because of altitude and latitude. In these respects it may be similar to Wilyabrup, but it has a different drainage basin. So where does all this leave Treeton? In limbo perhaps, until its viticultural potential is proved. Gladstones suggests that these sub-regions may be revisited (i.e. altered) by the Geographical Indications authorities at some future time, but this may be difficult as the GI Board does not appear to have the power to alter regional or sub-regional boundaries once they are finally registered.

Wallcliffe Centred upon the region's principal town and namesake, Margaret River, Wallcliffe comprises three drainage basins, Ellen Brook, Boodjidup Brook and Margaret River itself, all of which flow west into the Indian Ocean.

Its climate is cooler and subject to greater southerly influences, because of its more southerly location and its partial shielding from the north by the Whicher Range. Its soils are similar to those of Yallingup and Wilyabrup, but have a greater proportion of loam formed from the granite-gneiss country rock found mainly in the Margaret River Valley.

Again Gladstones raises the question of the lands such as Rosa Brook to the east of the Bussell Highway. Should these be included or excluded? Gladstones favours inclusion, but with his option for a later revisiting. The same point mentioned above (of regulatory power to alter boundaries once these are finally registered) again arises. But

Wallcliffe certainly deserves sub-regionality if only because of Leeuwin Estate and Cape Mentelle.

Karridale is the largest of the proposed sub-regions and consists of all the Southern Margaret River area which drains into the Lower Blackwood River. Climatically, it is separate from the rest of the Margaret River region, as it is fully exposed to the south coastal south-east winds in summer with warm northerly and north-easterly winds resulting from more northerly heat-waves only occasionally altering this pattern. These cool breezes naturally funnel up the valleys of the Blackwood and its subsidiary brooks, the Chapman and Upper Chapman. The result is an air barrier between them and the more northerly Margaret River Valley. This barrier is noticeable as clouds coming from the south tend to dissipate around Witchcliffe, which is on the drainage ridge between the Chapman and Boodjidup Brooks.

Karridale has some viticultural soils in common with its northern neighbours, but also has two others of its own. a) Calgarup sands i.e. deep outwash deposits on moderate intermediate and lower slopes draining south and east towards the Upper Chapman and Chapman Brooks and the Blackwood River. Surface soil is a yellow slightly loamy sand passing into yellow clayey sand at 60 cm deep and draining freely. Such soils are characterised by natural vegetation of jarrah-marri-banksia and, in places where the soil is heavier, by vigorous marri. b) The second soil is a brownish karri sand occurring on the lowest, east-facing slopes of the Leeuwin–Naturaliste Ridge from Augusta in the south to the old Karridale townsite and beyond in the north. Gladstones concludes that such soils are undoubtedly suitable for viticulture.

Such is Gladstones' proposal. It is logically based and unassailable on climatic and geographical grounds. But are such grounds the only factors of distinction that sub-regions must have? It may, however, be subject to other criticisms. Firstly, the legal point mentioned. The GI Board seems to have no power to 'revisit' wine regions and sub-regions once such are finally registered. It may be that in the future the Board may be given such power, but this may require a legislative amendment to its Act. A further criticism may well be 'marketability' (i.e. the lack of knowledge by the market of the names chosen for these sub-regions). Margaret River has been a familiar name to winebuffs for at least 20 years, and Wilyabrup, home of Cullens, Moss Wood, Pierro etc. is certainly well-known by the market. Perhaps Yallingup is also becoming known outside the Margaret River region, but the others? Even Wallcliffe, home of such wineries as Leeuwin Estate, Cape Mentelle, Xanadu (names that helped make Margaret River world-famous), is a name that scarcely hangs from winelovers' lips. So perhaps the proponents of sub-regionality should not rush into registration until they are recognisable by the market as wine producers of quality. Sub-regionality is useless if the producers of the sub-region use only the regional name. This may mean that perhaps only Wilyabrup, Yallingup and 'Wallcliffe' under a name more identifiable with 'Margaret River' be registered as sub-regions. The rest can always use 'Margaret River' regional status for some years to learn whether they can produce wines of sub-regional distinctiveness.

Abbey Vale   R83

392 Wildwood Road, Yallingup, WA 6282
Ph 08 9755 2277, Fax 08 9755 2286,
Email: info@abbeyvale.com.au

Owners: McKay family
Chief winemaker: Kevin McKay, Dorham Mann
(consultant)
Year of foundation: 1986
Tonnes crushed on average each year: 600
Location: Yallingup
Area: 84 ha
Soils: ironstone gravel (laterite) about 60 cm
deep over friable clay subsoil. There are also
some areas of sandy topsoil of variable depth.
The ironstone provides excellent drainage
Varieties planted: White—chardonnay,
sauvignon blanc, semillon, verdelho;
Red—cabernet sauvignon, malbec, merlot,
shiraz
Leading wines: Abbey Vale Cabernet Merlot,
Merlot, Verdelho, Sauvignon Blanc,
Chardonnay
Notes: Bill McKay has literally careered around
the world—as an engineer working in Uganda
for the British Foreign Office, the owner of a
private electronics business, which was later
taken over by another company, a stint in
Canada, then five years' study to qualify as a
clinical psychologist. He then moved to
Western Australia and finally to Margaret River,
where his son, Kevin, had become interested in
viticulture. As grapegrowers, the McKays first
sold their fruit to Houghtons, reserving a little
for their own label, then the study bug hit Bill
again and he enrolled in a summer course in
brewing at UC Davis, later to establish the
Moonshine brewery at Abbey Vale. After all
this, Abbey Vale may be an anti-climax, but
the whites are accessible and full of flavour.
Cellar door sales: each day 10.30am–5pm.

Amberley Estate   R83

Thornton Road, Yallingup, WA 6282
Ph 08 9755 2288, Fax 08 9755 2171

Owner: Amberley Estate Pty Ltd
Chief winemaker: Eddie Price
Year of foundation: 1986
Tonnes crushed on average each year: 1300,
including production from Amberley Estate
vineyards and fruit purchased from growers
Location: Yallingup
Area: 31.5 ha
Soils: gravelly loams, 'marri' country
Varieties planted: White—chardonnay, chenin
blanc, sauvignon blanc, semillon;
Red—cabernet franc, cabernet sauvignon,
merlot, shiraz
Leading wines: Amberley Estate Cabernet
Sauvignon, Semillon, Shiraz
Notes: Amberley Estate is a medium sized
Margaret River winery of very good quality
producing wines in the midstream of Margaret
river style. There is also a restaurant.
Cellar door sales: each day 10am–4.30pm,
except Christmas Day and Good Friday.

Aquila Estate see Swan Districts Region

Ashbrook Estate   R81

Harman's Road South, Willyabrup,
WA 6284
PO Box 320, Cowaramup, WA 6284
Ph 08 9755 6262, Fax 08 9755 6290,
Email ashbrook@netserve.net.au

Owners: Devitt family
Chief winemakers: Tony and Brian Devitt
Year of foundation: 1975
Tonnes crushed on average each year: 120
Location: Willyabrup
Area: 17 ha
Soils: gravelly red loam (laterite gravel)
Varieties planted: White—chardonnay, riesling,
sauvignon blanc, semillon, verdelho;
Red—cabernet franc, cabernet sauvignon,
merlot, petit verdot, shiraz
Leading wines: Ashbrook Estate Chardonnay
(wooded), Semillon, Verdelho, Cabernet Merlot

Notes: Full but fresh Margaret River flavours epitomise the whites, while the red is a complex stylish Cabernet Merlot. Cellar door sales: each day 11am–5pm.

Beckett's Flat R80

Beckett Road off Bussell Highway, Metricup, WA
Ph 08 9755 7402, Fax 08 9755 7344,
Email bfwinery@bigpond.com

Owner: Bill and Noni Ilic
Chief winemaker: Belizar Ilic
Year of foundation: 1992
Tonnes produced on average each year: 100, of which 60 are used for Beckett's Flat wines
Location: Metricup
Area: 14 ha
Soils: gravelly and sandy loams
Varieties planted: White—chardonnay, sauvignon blanc, semillon, verdelho; Red—cabernet sauvignon, merlot, shiraz
Leading wines: Beckett's Flat Cabernet Sauvignon, Chardonnay
Notes: Beckett's Flat is a consistent winner of silver snd bronze awards at local wine shows. Cellar door sales: daily 10am–6pm.

Brookland Valley R85

Caves Road, Willyabrup, WA 6284
Ph 08 9755 6250, Fax 08 9755 6214,
Email brookland@brooklandvalley.com.au

Owners: BRL Hardy (50%), Malcolm Jones (25%) and an investor wishing to remain unnamed (25%)
Chief winemakers: Peter Dawson and Larry Cherubino
Year of foundation: 1984
Tonnes crushed on average each year: 125
Location: Wilyabrup
Area: 23 ha
Soils: chiefly shallow loam over gravel ('marri'), deep sand, deep alluvial loams
Varieties planted: White—chardonnay, sauvignon blanc; Red—cabernet franc, cabernet sauvignon, merlot, shiraz
Leading wines: Brookland Valley Sauvignon Blanc, Chardonnay, Cabernet Sauvignon-Merlot, Merlot, Shiraz, made only from original Brookland Valley Estate Vines. Verse1, a second label, includes Semillon-Sauvignon Blanc, Chardonnay, Cabernet Merlot and Shiraz
Notes: Brookland Valley is highly regarded for its whites and also its very supple Cabernet Sauvignon-Merlot. Cellar door sales: each day 10am–5pm. There is also a restaurant, Flutes Café.

Cape Mentelle R91

Off Wallcliffe Road, Margaret River, WA 6285
Ph 08 9757 3266, Fax 08 9757 3233,
Email info@capementelle.com.au

Owner: Veuve Clicquot Ponsardin
Chief winemaker: John Durham
Year of foundation: 1970
Tonnes crushed on average each year: 700, to which are added a further 800 purchased from local growers
Location: Margaret River
Area: 125 ha
Soils: lateritic gravels over permeable clays derived from decomposed granite
Varieties planted: White—chardonnay, sauvignon blanc, semillon; Red—cabernet sauvignon, merlot, shiraz, zinfandel
Leading wines: Cape Mentelle Cabernet Sauvignon, Shiraz, Flinders Vineyard Cabernet Merlot
Notes: Now one of the veteran estates of the Margaret River region and, like its Cabernet Sauvignons which are made to last 15–20 years and twice winners of the Jimmy Watson trophy, ageing magnificently. Highly regarded also for its Shiraz and a stylishly tangy Semillon Sauvignon. Though wholly owned by Veuve Clicquot Ponsardin of Reims, it is still very much under the day-to-day direction of its

founder, David Hohnen. That direction remains unswerving in its continued search for even greater quality. Cellar door sales: each day 10am–4.30pm, except Good Friday and Christmas Day.

Chapman's Creek NR

Yelverton Road, Willyabrup, WA 6280
Ph 08 9755 7545, Fax 08 9755 7571

Owner: Tony Lord
Chief winemaker: contract
Year of foundation: 1992
Tonnes crushed on average each year: 100
Location: Willyabrup
Area: 10 ha
Soils: sandy gravelly loam
Varieties planted: White—chardonnay, chenin blanc, sauvignon blanc, semillon;
Red—cabernet sauvignon, merlot
Leading wines: Chapman's Creek Unoaked Chardonnay, Chardonnay, Merlot, Cabernet Merlot
Notes: This is the vineyard of former *Decanter* editor, Tony Lord. I have not tasted the wines recently. Cellar door sales: daily 10.30am–4.30pm.

Clairault R83

Henry Road, Willyabrup, WA 6280
Ph 08 9755 6225, Fax 08 9755 6229,
Email clairault@cclairaultwines.com.au

Owners: Matin family
Chief winemakers: Peter Stark
Year of foundation: 1976
Tonnes crushed on average each year: 500
Location: (Winery, vineyard and cellar door) Willyabrup
Area: 22.6 ha
Soils: yellow-brown gravelly sandy loams
Varieties planted: White—riesling, sauvignon blanc, semillon; Red—cabernet franc, cabernet sauvignon, merlot, nebbiolo, petit verdot, sauzao, shirax, tempranillo, touriga

Leading wines: Clairault Reserve (a blend of Cabernet Sauvignon, Cabernet Franc and Merlot), Sauvignon Blanc
Notes: Clairault (formerly Cape Clairault) changed hands recently, though continuity remains in winemaking in Peter Stark's hands. As usual the Reserve and Sauvignon Blanc are very good. Cellar door sales: each day 10am–5pm.

Cullen Wines R93

Caves Road, Cowaramup, WA 6284
Ph 08 9755 5277, Fax 08 9755 5550

Owners: Cullen family
Chief winemaker: Vanya Cullen
Year of foundation: 1971
Tonnes crushed on average each year: 275
Location: Cowaramup
Area: 30 ha
Soils: lateritic gravel
Varieties planted: White—chardonnay, chenin blanc, sauvignon blanc, semillon;
Red—cabernet franc, cabernet sauvignon, merlot, petit verdot, pinot noir
Leading wines: Cullen Cabernet Sauvignon-Merlot, Chardonnay, Pinot Noir, Sauvignon Blanc-Semillon
Notes: In an age of drip irrigation, Cullen's holds to traditional dry-land viticulture. As Di Cullen points out, the region receives over 1150 mm of rain each year, so drip irrigation is probably unnecessary. The Cullen philosophy is one of absolute wine quality and Vanya Cullen was Winemaker of the Year in 2000. Under her skilled direction, the winemaking goes from strength to strength. Cullen Cabernet Sauvignon-Merlot and Chardonnay are outstanding. Cellar door sales: each day 10am–4pm. Lunch is also available.

Deep Woods Estate R83

Commonage Road, Yallingup, WA 6282
Ph/Fax 08 9756 6066,
Email gould@netserv.net.au

Owners: Malcolm and Margaret Gould
Chief winemaker: Ben Gould, Candy Jonnson
(consultant)
Year of foundation: vineyard 1987, winery and
cellar door 1998
Tonnes produced on average each year: 130
Location: Yallingup
Area: 14.9 ha
Soils: gravelly loam
Varieties planted: White—chardonnay,
sauvignon blanc, semillon, verdelho;
Red—cabernet franc, cabernet sauvignon,
merlot, shiraz.
Leading wines: Deep Woods Estate Semillon-
Sauvignon Blanc, Cabernet Sauvignon,
Verdelho
Notes: Deep Woods Estate is yet another story
of the investor becoming a keen grower, and,
taking it further, becoming a vintner. The
wines are solidly in the midstream of Margaret
River quality. Cellar door sales: Wed–Sun and
public holidays 11am–5pm

Devil's Lair Wines R87

Rocky Road, Witchcliffe, WA 6285
Ph 08 9757 7573, Fax 08 9757 7533

Owner: Southcorp Wines
Chief winemaker: Stuart Pym
Year of foundation: 1981
Tonnes crushed on average each year: 676
Location: Witchcliffe
Area: 89 ha
Soils: gravelly loams, undulating country
Varieties planted: White—chardonnay,
sauvignon blanc, semillon; Red—cabernet
franc, cabernet sauvignon, merlot, petit verdot,
shiraz
Leading wines: Devil's Lair Chardonnay,
Margaret River (predominantly a Cabernet
Sauvignon blend), Fifth Leg White and Fifth
Leg Red
Notes: Renowned for its stylish Margaret River
red and for its Chardonnay, Devil's Lair
regrettably has no cellar door sales, but mail
order c/- PO Box 212, Margaret River, WA
6285 is available.

Driftwood Estate NR

Lot 13, Caves Road, Yallingup,
WA 6282
Ph 08 9755 6323, Fax 08 9755 6343

Owners: Tom and Helen Golopoulos
Chief winemakers: Barney Mitchell
Year of foundation: 1989
Tonnes crushed on average each year: 150
Location: Yallingup
Area: 18.8 ha
Soils: variable, rich loams to gravelly loams to
gritty sandy soils over ironstone and clay
Varieties planted: White—chardonnay, chenin
blanc, sauvignon blanc, semillon, verdelho;
Red—cabernet sauvignon, merlot, shiraz
Leading wines: Driftwood Estate Shiraz,
Semillon, Cabernet Sauvignon, Chardonnay
Notes: A moderate-sized Yallingup estate,
which crushes its own fruit only, Driftwood is
known for its whites, but they have not come
my way recently. Cellar door sales: each day
11am–4.30pm. There is also an award-winning
restaurant.

Evans & Tate R89

Cnr Metricup and Caves Roads,
Willyabrup, WA 6280
Ph/Fax 08 9755 6244,
Email ct@evansandtate.com.au

Owner: Evans & Tate Ltd
Chief winemaker: Steve Warne
Year of foundation: 1971
Tonnes crushed on average each year: 2600
Locations: Willyabrup (cellar door and
vineyard); Jindong (winery and vineyard)

Area of vineyards owned or managed: 409 ha, consisting of Redbrooks (26 ha), Jindong (86 ha), Lionel's (107 ha), Alexanders (127 ha), Oakfield (55 ha) and Yungarra Estate (8 ha)
Soils: Redbrook, lateritic gravel; Lionel's, Jindong, Oakfield, 'abba' fertile, red-orange light sandy loams with a low clay content over ironstone; Alexanders, gravel and sandy loam over ironstone; Yungarra, gravelly loam over clay, lateritic
Varieties planted: (Redbrook)
White—chardonnay, semillon; Red—cabernet sauvignon, merlot, shiraz. (Lionel's)
White—chardonnay, sauvignon blanc, semillon; Red—cabernet sauvignon, shiraz. (Jindong)
White, Red—same as Lionel's. (Alexanders)
White—none; Red—cabernet sauvignon, grenache, merlot, nebbiolo, zinfandel. (Oakfield) White, Red—same as Lionel's. (Yungarra) White—semillon; Red—cabernet sauvignon, merlot
Leading wines: Redbrook Semillon, Chardonnay, Margaret River Classic, Verdelho, Sauvignon Blanc-Semillon, Shiraz, Gnangara Shiraz, Chardonnay
Notes: Evans & Tate is renowned for its marvellous Redbrook Semillon, an elegant nectar of lemony fragrance and supple, ever so slightly herbaceous, palate. Steve Warne, appointed as chief winemaker in September 2000, carries the Redbrook Semillon baton, so ably handled by former chief Brian Fletcher. Another notable wine from this maker is Margaret River Shiraz. Cellar door sales: daily 10.30am–4.30pm.

Fermoy Estate NR

Metricup Road, Willyabrup, WA 6280
Ph 08 9755 6285, Fax 08 9755 6251,
Email fermoy@fermoy.com.au

Owner: Hulsbergen family
Chief winemaker: Michael Kelly
Year of foundation: 1985
Tonnes crushed on average each year: 360, of which 300 are used for Fermoy Estate wines
Location: (Winery, cellar door and vineyard) Willyabrup
Area: 14 ha
Soils: lateritic gravelly loam
Varieties planted: White—chardonnay, chenin blanc, sauvignon blanc, semillon; Red—cabernet franc, cabernet sauvignon, malbec, merlot
Leading wines: Fermoy Estate Cabernet Sauvignon, Semillon, Merlot, Chardonnay
Notes: I have not tasted Fermoy's wines recently. Cellar door sales: 7 days 11am–4.30pm.

Flinders Bay Vineyard (vineyard only) R83

Off Wilson Road, Karridale, WA 6288
Ph 08 9757 6281, Fax 08 9757 6353,
Sales 0414 441 925

Owners: Winecorp Pty Ltd (Bill and Noel Ireland 50%, Alastair Gillespie 25%, Colleen Gillespie 25%)
Chief winemaker: Whites—Vasse Felix, (contract), Cabernet, Sandstone (contract), Shiraz and Merlot Quelltaler winery, Watervale. Martin Shaw (consultant)
Year of foundation: vineyard 1995
Tonnes crushed on average each year: vines not yet in full bearing. Vintage 2000 yielded 290 tonnes. In that year 350 tonnes were used to produce Flinders Bay wines, 60 tonnes being purchased from local growers
Location: Karridale
Area: 51 ha
Soils: mostly red lateritic gravel with some areas of sandy loam over clay, on the whole well-drained
Varieties planted: White—chardonnay (3 clones), sauvignon blanc, semillon; Red—cabernet sauvignon, malbec, merlot, shiraz
Leading wines: Flinders Bay Pericles (a Sauvignon Blanc Semillon blend), Agincourt (a Cabernet Malbec Merlot blend)

Notes: The Flinders Bay dream is slowly but surely being realised. The wines are now in production and tasting well. What is more important from the vignerons' point of view, they are selling, both at home and overseas. Regrettably there are no cellar door sales yet, but there is at least a phone number.

Green Valley Vineyard NR

Sebbes Road, Forest Grove, WA 6286
Ph/Fax 08 9757 7510,
Email greenvly@ca.com.au

Owners: Ed and Eleonore Green
Chief winemaker: Keith Mugford (contract)
Year of foundation: 1979
Tonnes crushed on average each year: 40 increasing to 80 by vintage 2002
Location: Forest Grove
Area: 8 ha
Soils: lateritic gravel ('marri'), sandy and also 'karri' loam
Varieties planted: White—chardonnay, chenin blanc, colombard, muller-thurgau, riesling; Red—cabernet sauvignon, merlot, shiraz
Leading wines: Green Valley Cabernet Sauvignon, Chardonnay, Shiraz
Notes: Green Valley is a consistent winner of silver and bronze awards at local and interstate wine shows, though the wines have not come my way recently. Cellar door sales: weekends and public holidays 10am–6pm, at other times by appointment.

Hamelin Bay R84

(vineyard) Five Ashes Vineyard, 116 McDonald Road, Karridale, WA 6288 (winery and cellar door) Brockman Highway, Karridale, WA 6288
Ph/Fax 08 9758 5555,
Email hbwines@ibm.net

Owners: Richard and Roslyn Drake-Brockman
Chief winemaker: Phil Tubb
Year of foundation: 1992

Tonnes crushed on average each year: 200
Location: Karridale
Area: 25.4 ha
Soils: brown gravelly sandy loams, known locally as 'Forest Grove' soils
Varieties planted: White—chardonnay, sauvignon blanc, semillon; Red—cabernet sauvignon, merlot, shiraz
Leading wines: Hamelin Bay Chardonnay, Sauvignon Blanc, Hamelin Bay Cabernet Sauvignon, Hamelin Bay Shiraz
Notes: Karridale may well be proposed as a sub-region of Margaret River region. It is a very cool maritime area in the far south of the region. Cellar door sales: daily 10.30am–4pm.

Happs R79

Commonage Road, Dunsborough, WA 6281
Ph 08 9755 3300, Fax 08 9755 3846,
Email happs@happs.com.au

Owner: Happs Pty Ltd
Chief winemakers: Erl Happ and Frank Kittler
Year of foundation: 1978
Tonnes crushed on average each year: 270
Locations: Dunsborough (winery, cellar door and two vineyards); Karridale (vineyard)
Area: 36.97 ha consisting of Dunsborough 7.08 ha and Karridale 29.89 ha
Soils: Dunsborough, 'Mungite' sand 'Jarrah' soil sandy gravelly overlying kaolinitic clay. Karridale, sandy gravels, felspathic-quartzey with a pink tint
Varieties planted: White—chardonnay, chenin blanc, furmint, marsanne, muscadelle, sauvignon blanc, semillon, verdelho, viognier; Red—bastardo, cabernet franc, cabernet sauvignon, carignan, cinsaut, gamay, graciano, grenache, malbec, merlot, mourvedre, muscat, nebbiolo, petit verdot, pinot noir, sangioves, shiraz, souzao, tempranillo, tinta cao, touriga
Leading wines: Happ's Merlot, Cabernet-Merlot, Viognier, Chardonnay, Marrimee

Margaret River White, PF Red (preservative free) and PF White (preservative free)

Notes: As may be seen from the list of varieties planted, Erl Happ has an intense interest in varieties and their distinctive flavours and the wines made reflect this interest. The Karridale vineyard is 60 km south of Dunsborough, is approaching full bearing and is much cooler. Merlot seems the pick of Erl's wines. Cellar door sales: 7 days 10am–5pm.

Hay Shed Hill NR

Harman's Mill Road, Willyabrup,
WA 6280
Ph 08 9755 6234, Fax 08 9755 6305,
Email hayshed@highway1.com.au

Owners: Barrington Wine Co Ltd
Chief winemaker: Peter Stanlake
Year of foundation: 1988
Tonnes crushed on average each year: 250
Location: Willyabrup
Area: 17 ha
Soils: chiefly lateritic gravel with some loam over clay and sand pockets
Varieties planted: White—chardonnay, sauvignon blanc, semillon; Red—cabernet sauvignon, pinot noir
Leading wines: Hayshed Hill Cabernet Sauvignon, Chardonnay
Notes: I have not tasted the wines recently. Cellar door sales: daily 10.30am–5pm.

Hesperos Wines NR

36 Elva St, Margaret River, WA 6285
Ph/Fax 08 9757 3302,
Email hesperos@highway1.com.au

Owners: Jurg Muggli and Sandra Hancock
Chief winemaker: Jurg Muggli
Year of foundation: 1993
Tonnes crushed on average each year: 20, all of which are purchased locally
Location: Margaret River (sales but no cellar door), Witchcliffe (vineyard)

Area: 6 ha not yet bearing
Soils: gravelly loams
Varieties planted: White—none; Red—cabernet franc, cabernet sauvignon, merlot
Leading wines: Hesperos Shiraz, Sauvignon Blanc
Notes: Hesperos is the boutique winemaking operation of Swiss winemaker Jurg Muggli and Sandra Hancock, which commenced in 1993 and has made wine each vintage since. It is now expanding. Its vineyard was planted in September 2001 in the cool Witchcliffe area. I have not tasted its wines, but as I know Muggli's devotion to quality from his Xanadu wines, they are certain to be superior. No cellar door sales.

Hotham Wines R82

Brockman Highway, Karridale, WA 6288
Ph 08 9758 5999, Fax 08 9758 5988,
Email HothamValley2@bigpond.com

Owner: Hotham Wines Ltd
Chief winemaker: James Pennington
Year of foundation: 1986 (at Wandering)
Tonnes produced on average each year: 1420, of which 800 are used for Hotham Estate wines
Locations: Winery, vineyard and cellar door: Karridale. Vineyard: Alexandra Bridge. Bridgeland Vineyard: Margaret River. Cellar door winery and Vineyard Yallingup. Vineyard, winery and cellar door: Wandering vineyard only (Central Western Australian Zone)
Area: 151 ha consisting of Karridale Vineyard 36 ha, Wildwood vineyard 6 ha, Bridgeland Vineyard 97 ha, Wandering Vineyard 12 ha
Soils: Wandering, gravelly loam over clay; Karridale, gravelly loam to pure sand; Bridgeland, variable from gravelly loam through clay loam to gravelly sand; Wildwood, gravelly loam, unirrigated
Varieties planted: (Karridale)
White—chardonnay, sauvignon blanc, semillon; Red—cabernet sauvignon, shiraz. (Bridgeland)

White—same as Karridale; Red—cabernet franc, cabernet sauvignon, merlot, shiraz. (Wildwood) White—chardonnay, chenin blanc, sauvignon blanc, semillon; Red—cabernet franc, cabernet sauvignon, pinot noir, merlot. (Wandering) White—chardonnay, chenin blanc, riesling, semillon; Red—cabernet franc, cabernet sauvignon, merlot, zinfandel.
Leading wines: Hotham Valley Estate Chardonnay, Cabernet Sauvignon-Merlot, Semillon-Sauvignon Blanc, Shiraz.
Notes: With public company status and a healthy capital injection as a result, Hotham Wines has left the comparative backblocks of the Central Western Australia Zone, (though it retains its Wandering vineyard and winery) and has arrived in the viticultural 'big smoke' of Margaret River, buying the former Wildwood vineyard and cellar door at Yallingup, a new winery at Karridale and planting a substantial vineyard at Bridgelands in the Rosa Brook area of the region. At Wandering it has been renowned for its excellent Semillon. As for its other wines, none have yet been tasted. Cellar door sales: Wildwood daily 10am–5pm, Karridale daily 11am–5pm.

Juniper Estate (formerly Wright's Winery) R84

Harman's Road South, Cowaramup, WA 6284
Ph 08 9755 9000, Fax 08 9755 9100, Email juniperestate@ozemail.com.au

Owners: Roger Hill and Vivian Booker
Chief winemaker: Mark Messenger
Year of foundation: 1973 as Wrights, 1998 as Juniper Estate
Tonnes crushed on average each year: 70, to which 30 tonnes purchased locally are added to meet the requirements of Juniper Estate wines
Location: (Winery, cellar door and vineyard) Cowaramup
Area: 11 ha (2.5 ha not yet fully bearing)

Soils: an undulating vineyard with variable soils rising from red loam over clay to gravelly lateritic loam over clay
Varieties planted: White—chardonnay, riesling, semillon; Red—cabernet franc, cabernet sauvignon, malbec, merlot, petit verdot
Leading wines: Juniper Estate Semillon, Cabernet Sauvignon
Notes: Juniper Estate is the new image of the old Wright's Wines, purchased from the Wright family in 1998. The new winemaker, Mark Messenger, was formerly assistant winemaker at Cape Mentelle. So there are encouraging credentials, as are the Junpier Estate wines. Cellar door sales: daily 10am–5pm. Cheese platters are available.

Leeuwin Estate R90

Stevens Road, Margaret River, WA 6285
Ph 08 9757 6253, Fax 08 9757 6364, Email info@leeuwinestate.com.au

Owners: Horgan family
Chief winemaker: Robert Cartwright
Year of foundation: 1975
Tonnes crushed on average each year: 600
Location: Margaret River
Area: 120 ha
Soils: old granite derived lateritic gravel—'marri-jarrah' for red, 'marri-karri' for white
Varieties planted: White—chardonnay, riesling, sauvignon blanc; Red—cabernet sauvignon, pinot noir and small areas of malbec and petit verdot
Leading wines: Leeuwin Estate Art Series Chardonnay, Cabernet Sauvignon, Riesling, Pinot Noir, Sauvignon Blanc, Prelude Chardonnay, Classic Dry White, Cabernet-Merlot, Siblings Sauvignon Blanc-Semillon
Notes: The showplace of Margaret River, Leeuwin Estate has an obsession—quality. Its Art Series Chardonnay in particular is a benchmark for the Australian style. An excellently structured white that matures well, even when released, as it usually is, at four

years of age. It is aromatically rich but elegant, with a palate that matures into a fig-peach ripeness without fatness. The Art Series Cabernet Sauvignon is also a magnificent red, maturing into a complex leafy, berry, pencilly oak complexity that can often be mistaken for Bordeaux. Cellar door sales: 10am–4.30pm each day. There is also a restaurant open daily for lunch and Saturday evening for dinner.

Lenton Brae Estate NR

Caves Road, Willyabrup, WA 6284
Ph 08 9755 6255, Fax 08 9755 6268,
Email lentonbrae@netserve.net.au

Owners: Bruce and Jeanette Tomlinson
Chief winemaker: Edward Tomlinson
Year of foundation: 1982
Tonnes crushed on average each year: 120
Location: Willyabrup
Area: 10 ha
Soils: gravelly loam, 'marri' country
Varieties planted: White—chardonnay, sauvignon blanc, semillon; Red—cabernet franc, cabernet sauvignon, merlot, petit verdot
Leading wines: Lenton Brae Chardonnay, Cabernet-Merlot, Margaret River (a blend of cabernet sauvignon, merlot and petit verdot)
Notes: I have not tasted Lenton Brae wines recently. Cellar door sales: daily 10am–6pm.

Moss Brothers R82

Lot 1 Sussex Location 341
Caves Road, Willyabrup, WA 6280
Ph 08 9755 6270, Fax 08 9755 6298,
Email mbv@mossbrothers.com.au

Owners: Moss family
Chief winemaker: David Moss
Year of foundation: 1984
Tonnes crushed on average each year: 23 (some fruit purchased from growers in the district)
Location: Willyabrup
Area: 7 ha

Soils: sandy loam over clay, lateritic gravels over clay
Varieties planted: White—chardonnay, sauvignon blanc, semillon; Red—cabernet franc, cabernet sauvignon, merlot, pinot noir
Leading wines: Moss Brothers Cabernet-Merlot, Semillon
Notes: Moss Brothers is located in the premium area of Wilyabrup or Willyabrup (the spelling seems optional). This is good red country and Cabernet-Merlot blends excel. The Moss Brothers Cabernet-Merlot is one of them. Cellar door sales: daily 10am–5pm.

Moss Wood Winery R92

Metricup Road, Willyabrup, WA 6280
Ph 08 9755 6266, Fax 08 9755 6303,
Email mosswood@mosswood.com.au

Owners: Clare and Keith Mugford
Chief winemaker: Keith Mugford
Year of foundation: 1969
Tonnes crushed on average each year: 80
Location: Willyabrup
Area: 10 ha
Soils: gravelly loam about 1–2 metres deep over clay
Varieties planted: White—chardonnay, semillon; Red—cabernet franc, cabernet sauvignon, merlot, petit verdot, pinot noir
Leading wines: Moss Wood Cabernet Sauvignon, Semillon, Chardonnay, Pinot Noir
Notes: Moss Wood is another very famous Margaret River winery, for many years owned by Dr Bill Pannell, like Keith Mugford a talented winemaker-proprietor. The most famous wines here are the Semillon in the whites—elegant and stylish like most Margaret River Semillons—and the Cabernet Sauvignon. Though Margaret River is rather warm for the variety, Keith Mugford also makes a light and very flavoursome Pinot Noir. Cellar door sales by appointment.

Palandri Wines R82

Bussell Highway, Margaret River,
WA 6285
Ph 08 9755 5711, Fax 08 9755 5722,
Email info@palandri.com.au

Owner: Palandri Wines Ltd
Chief winemaker: Tony Carapetis
Year of foundation: 1998
Tonnes produced on average each year: with
the exception of fruit from the former Rosa
Brook estate, all fruit is presently purchased
from growers, as the Palandri vineyard in
Frankland River is not yet bearing
Location: Margaret River (winery (with a 1500
tonne capacity) and cellar door), Rosa Brook
and Frankland River (vineyards)
Area: 225 ha consisting of Rosa Brook
(Margaret River region) 15 ha, Frankland River
(Great Southern region) 210 ha. A further
block of 140 ha in Frankland River was planted
in 2001
Soils: Rosa Brook, deep sandy loam varying to
deep sandy gravel loam over clay; Frankland
River, multi-layered soils with a gravelly loam
topsoil, 1–2 m of red clay beneath and a
deeper layer of white clay. About 50 cm down
the clay becomes impervious with an
increasing water holding (and, so far as the
vines are concerned, water-logging) capacity,
that obliges such water to be 'farmed' through
drains and holding dams and pumped back
uphill for later irrigation use. It is imperative
that such water does not run into a river or
creek, otherwise it will bring salt up with it.
Such layers of clay prevent penetration by vine
roots and it is therefore necessary to rip the
clay pan to allow the roots to penetrate deeper
into the ground. In this respect Palandri faces
the same problem faced by Houghton some
years ago at its Netley Brook vineyard which
is obviously similar country i.e. local rivers
and creeks being too salty could not be
used for irrigation. The Palandri vineyards
are drip-irrigated

Varieties planted: (Rosa Brook)
White—chardonnay, sauvignon blanc, semillon;
Red—cabernet franc, cabernet sauvignon,
merlot, shiraz. (Frankland River)
White—chardonnay, riesling, sauvignon blanc,
semillon; Red—cabernet franc, cabernet
sauvignon, malbec, merlot, shiraz
Leading wines: Palandri Aurora Cabernet-
Shiraz, Chardonnay
Notes: Palandri Wines is a new middling–large
wine company with a substantial vineyard in
Frankland River, the new Great Southern wine
sub-region and also a Margaret River vineyard,
the former Rosabrook Estate. I have tasted no
regional or sub-regional wines from this
company (none have yet been released), as its
vineyards in Frankland River are not yet fully
bearing and it has just purchased Rosabrook
Estate. The wines tasted were harmonious
current-drinking blends of various Western
Australian sources but predominantly
Frankland River and Margaret River. Cellar door
sales: daily 11am–4.30pm. There is also a
restaurant.

Palmer Wines R83

Caves Road, Willyabrup, WA 6280
51 Road, Cowaramup, WA 6284
Ph 08 9755 4767, Fax 08 9755 4107

Owners: Helen and Steve Palmer
Chief winemaker: Bernard Abbot (contract)
Year of foundation: 1977
Tonnes crushed on average each year: 160, of
which 100 are used for Palmer wines
Location: Willyabrup
Area: 20 ha
Soils: red gravel loams over clay
Varieties planted: White—chardonnay,
sauvignon blanc, semillon; Red—cabernet
sauvignon, merlot, shiraz
Leading wines: Palmer Merlot, Chardonnay,
Cabernet Sauvignon, Shiraz
Notes: The Palmer vineyard is in the heartland
of Willyabrup. Its wines, especially the

Cabernet Sauvignon, have great suppleness on the palate. Cellar door sales by appointment.

Pierro Margaret River Vineyards R90

Caves Road, Willyabrup, WA 6280
Ph 08 9755 6220, Fax 08 9755 6308

Owner/chief winemaker: Dr Mike Peterkin
Year of foundation: 1980
Tonnes crushed on average each year: 250
Location: Willyabrup
Area: 8 ha (Pierro), 8 ha (Fire Gully)
Soils: lateritic gravelly loam over friable clay subsoils
Varieties planted: (Pierro) White—chardonnay, sauvignon blanc, semillon; Red—cabernet franc, cabernet sauvignon, malbec, merlot, petit verdot, pinot noir. (Fire Gully) White—chenin blanc, sauvignon blanc, semillon, viognier; Red—cabernet sauvignon, merlot, shiraz
Leading wines: Pierro Chardonnay, Cabernets, Semillon-Sauvignon Blanc. There is also a second range of wines, Fire Gully
Notes: Mike Peterkin is a winemaking medical practitioner, renowned for Pierro Chardonnay, one of the best examples of the variety anywhere in Australia, a lively semillon-sauvignon blanc blend and a supple and stylish cabernet, made from the classic Bordeaux brotherhood, cabernet sauvignon, cabernet franc, merlot and petit verdot. Cellar door sales: each day 10am–5pm.

Redgate Wines R85

Boodjidup Road, Margaret River, WA 6285
Ph 08 9757 6488, Fax 08 9757 6308, info@redgatewines.com.au

Owner: WW Ullinger
Chief winemaker: Andrew Forsell
Year of foundation: 1977
Tonnes crushed on average each year: 200

Location: Margaret River
Area: 20 ha
Soils: light lateritic gravel varying to sand in the valley
Varieties planted: White—chardonnay, chenin blanc, sauvignon blanc, semillon; Red—cabernet franc, cabernet sauvignon, merlot, pinot noir, shiraz
Leading wines: Redgate Chardonnay, Sauvignon Blanc Reserve, Chenin Blanc, Cabernet Sauvignon, Cabernet Franc, Shiraz, Pinot Noir
Notes: Redgate is by Margaret River standards quite an old-established winery with a good reputation for its herbaceous Sauvignon Blanc, its Shiraz and its Cabernet Sauvignon, both reds of firmer style. Cellar door sales: each day 10am–5pm.

Ribbon Vale Estate R82

Lot 5 Caves Road, Willyabrup, WA 6280
Ph 08 9755 6272, Fax 08 9755 6337

Owner: Moss Wood
Chief winemaker: Michael Davies (contract)
Year of foundation: 1977
Location: Willyabrup
Area: 7 ha
Soils: lateritic gravel overlying kaolinised granite gneiss
Varieties planted: White—chardonnay, sauvignon blanc, semillon; Red—cabernet franc, cabernet sauvignon, merlot
Leading wines: Ribbon Vale Sauvignon Blanc, Merlot
Notes: Ribbon Vale is so named not only because it has delightful views over the Willyabrup valley but primarily because of its shape, 185 m wide and 1.3 km long. Fresh Sauvignon Blanc, lemony herbaceous Semillon and plummy Merlot are the hallmarks of this estate. Cellar door sales: weekends and public holidays 10am–5pm.

Rivendell Vineyard NR

Wildwood Road, Yallingup, WA 6282
Ph 08 9755 2090, Fax 08 9755 2301

Owners: Mark and Wendy Standish
Chief winemakers: Mark Standish and contract
Year of foundation: 1987
Tonnes crushed on average each year: 40
Location: Yallingup
Area: 4 ha plus a contract grower
Soils: lateritic gravel 'marri' country
Varieties planted: White—sauvignon blanc,
semillon; Red—cabernet franc, cabernet
sauvignon, merlot, shiraz
Leading wines: Rivendell Cabernets, Semillon-
Sauvignon Blanc, Verdelho
Notes: This is a family-run vineyard and cellar
door, whose wines I have not recently tasted.
Cellar door sales: each day 10.30am–5pm.

Sandalford Wines NR

Metricup Road, Willyabrup, WA 6284
Ph 08 9755 6213, Fax 08 9755 6284

Owner: Sandalford Wines Pty Ltd
Chief winemaker: Paul Boulden
Year of foundation: 1973 (Margaret River
vineyard)
Tonnes crushed on average each year: 500
Location: Willyabrup
Area: 120 ha
Soils: lateritic gravel 'marri' country
Varieties planted: White—chardonnay, chenin
blanc, riesling, sauvignon blanc, semillon,
verdelho; Red—cabernet sauvignon, shiraz
Leading wines: Sandalford Margaret River
Sauvignon blanc, Verdelho, Mount Barker-
Margaret River Shiraz, Mount Barker-Margaret
River Cabernet Sauvignon, Mount Barker
Cabernet-Merlot
Notes: Unusually Sandalford does not have a
straight Margaret River red, preferring to blend
in Mount Barker fruit, but from vintage 2001 a
change is planned. If Margaret River Cabernet
or Shiraz stands up to be counted then a

Margaret River red, either Cabernet or Shiraz
will be released. Cellar door sales: daily
10am–5pm.

Sandstone R86

Caves and Johnson Roads, Willyabrup,
WA 6280
Ph 08 9755 6271, Fax 08 9755 6292

Owners: Jan and Mike Davies and partners
Chief winemakers: Jan and Mike Davies
Year of foundation: 1988
Tonnes crushed on average each year: 15
Location: Willyabrup
Area: 14 ha
Soils: lateritic gravel, 'jarrah-marri' country
Varieties planted: White—semillon;
Red—cabernet sauvignon
Leading wines: Sandstone Semillon, Cabernet
Sauvignon
Notes: The Davies specialise in two varietal
wines, Semillon and Cabernet Sauvignon, each
entirely satisfactory. No cellar door sales.

Serventy Organic Wines NR

Valley Home Vineyard, Rocky Road,
Witchcliffe, WA 6286
Ph/Fax 08 9757 7534,
Email serventy@netserve.net.au

Owners: Peter Serventy
Chief winemaker: Peter Serventy
Year of foundation: 1984
Tonnes crushed on average each year: 20
Location: Witchcliffe
Area: 6 ha
Soils: 'Karri' loam over gravel
Varieties planted: White—chardonnay;
Red—pinot noir, shiraz
Leading wines: Serventy Chardonnay, Pinot
Noir, Shiraz
Notes: An organic vineyard, certified A Level
Organic. Cellar door sales: Fri–Sun and public
holidays 10am–4.30pm.

Treeton Estate NR

North Treeton Road, Cowaramup,
WA 6284
Ph 08 9755 5481, Fax 08 9755 5051,
Email treeton@netserv.net.au

Owner/chief winemaker: David McGowan
Year of foundation: vineyard 1987, first wine
1991
Tonnes crushed on average each year: 60
Location: Cowaramup
Area: 9.1 ha
Soils: pebbly lateritic loam
Varieties planted: White—chardonnay, chenin
blanc, sauvignon blanc; Red—cabernet
sauvignon, shiraz
Leading wine: Treeton Estate Shiraz
Notes: This is a small family-operated winery
whose wines I have not recently seen. Cellar
door sales: 7 days 10am–6pm.

Vasse Felix R87

Cnr Caves and Harmans South Roads,
Willyabrup, WA 6280
Ph 08 9755 5242, Fax 08 9755 5425,
Email info@vassefelix.com.au

Owner: Vasse Felix Pty Ltd (a part of the
Heytesbury group)
Chief winemaker: Clive Otto
Year of foundation: 1967
Tonnes crushed on average each year: 1800
Location: Cowaramup (winery, cellar door and
vineyard), Jindong (vineyard)
Area: 170 ha consisting of Cowaramup 15 ha,
Jindong 155 ha
Soils: Cowaramup, lateritic gravelly loam over a
clay base; Jindong, 55 ha east side of creek,
bleached white sands about 1 m deep to
gravelly loams (planted to whites); Jindong,
100 ha west side of creek, sandy loams 2–3 m
deep (planted to reds)
Varieties planted: White—chardonnay, riesling,
sauvignon blanc, semillon; Red—cabernet franc,
cabernet sauvignon, malbec, merlot, shiraz

Leading wines: Vasse Felix Cabernet Sauvignon,
Shiraz, Cabernet-Merlot, Merlot and a super
premium range, Heytesbury red (a Cabernet
blend), Heytesbury white (Chardonnay)
Notes: Vasse Felix is where the Margaret River
wine story began in 1967 when Dr Tom Cullity
planted his first vines. By the early 1970s it had
become famous for its Cabernet Sauvignon.
These days it belongs to Heytesbury, a
company belonging to Janet Holmes a Court,
and its range is considerably expanded. The
pick is the Heytesbury range. Cellar door sales:
7 days 10am–4pm. A restaurant is open daily
from 10.30am–4pm.

Vasse River Wines NR

Bussell Highway, Carbunup, WA 6280
Ph/Fax 08 9755 1111

Owners: Credaro family
Chief winemaker: Robert Credaro
Year of foundation: 1988
Tonnes crushed on average each year: 350, of
which 55 are used for Vasse River wines
Location: Carbunup
Area: 45 ha
Soils: red gravelly loam over clay
Varieties planted: White—chardonnay,
semillon, verdelho; Red—cabernet sauvignon,
merlot, shiraz
Leading wines: Vasse River Cabernet Merlot,
Chardonnay
Notes: Vasse River is a family-operated vineyard
and winery whose wines I have not tasted.
Cellar door sales: daily 10am–5pm.

Voyager Estate R88

Steven's Road, Margaret River, WA 6285
Ph 08 9757 6358, Fax 08 9757 6405,
Email voyager@highway1.com.au

Owner: Michael Wright
Chief winemaker: Cliff Royle
Year of foundation: 1978
Tonnes crushed on average each year: 500

Location: Margaret River
Area: 73 ha
Soils: variable, sandy loam, gravelly loam, clay gravel
Varieties planted: White—chardonnay, chenin blanc, marsanne, sauvignon blanc, semillon; Red—cabernet franc, cabernet sauvignon, grenache, malbec, merlot, petit verdot, shiraz
Leading wines: Voyager Estate Chardonnay, Cabernet Sauvignon-Merlot, Shiraz-Grenache
Notes: In only a decade, Voyager Estate has become one of the showplaces of the region. Its Chardonnay is consistently excellent, while the Cabernet Sauvignon-Merlot is one of the most stylish reds of the region. Cellar door sales: summer daily 10am–5pm. Winter daily 11am–5pm.

Willespie R84

Harman's Mill Road, Willyabrup, WA 6280
Ph 08 9755 6248, Fax 08 9755 6210, Email willespie@netserv.net.au

Owners: Kevin and Marian Squance
Chief winemaker: Kevin Squance
Year of foundation: 1976
Tonnes crushed on average each year: 150
Location: Willyabrup (winery, cellar door and vineyard), Dawson Gully, Calloorup (vineyard)
Area: 28 ha consisting of Willyabrup 20 ha, Dawson Gully, Calloorup 8 ha
Soils: Willyabrup, chiefly gravelly loam over clay, loam over clay; Calloorup, yellow sandy gravel and surface rock over clay subsoil
Varieties planted: (Willyabrup) White—riesling, sauvignon blanc, semillon, verdelho; Red—cabernet sauvignon, merlot. (Dawson Gully, Calloorup) White—none; Red—cabernet sauvignon, merlot, shiraz
Leading wines: Willespie Cabernet Sauvignon, Cabernets, Merlot, Shiraz, Verdelho, Semillon-Sauvignon Blanc
Notes: Now one of the older Willyabrup vineyards, Willespie has always made very

good full-bodied Cabernet Sauvignon and fresh whites. Now the red range has been extended to include a Cabernets blend, a Merlot and a Shiraz. Cellar door sales: 7 days 10.30am–5pm.

Wise Vineyards NR

Eagle Bay Road, Meelup, WA 6281
Ph 08 9756 8098, Fax 08 9755 3979, Email cellar@wisewine.com.au

Owner: Ron Wise
Chief winemakers: Andy Coppard and Amanda Kramer; Bruce Dukes (consultant)
Year of foundation: 1986
Tonnes crushed on average each year: 600
Location: Meelup (winery, cellar door and vineyard), Margaret River (Bramley Vineyard), Donnybrook (Geographe Region) (winery and vineyard)
Area: 49 ha consisting of Meelup 28 ha, Margaret River 6 ha, Donnybrook 15 ha
Soils: Meelup, gravelly loams over clay; Margaret River, richer loam over clay; Donnybrook, sand over clay
Varieties planted: (Meelup) White—chardonnay, chenin blanc, sauvignon blanc, semillon; Red—cabernet sauvignon, merlot, pinot noir, sangiovese, shiraz. (Bramely Vineyard) White—chardonnay; Red—cabernet sauvignon, merlot, shiraz. (Donnybrook) White—chardonnay, sauvignon blanc, semillon, verdelho; Red—merlot
Leading wines: Wise Vineyards Chardonnay, Bramley Cabernet Sauvignon, Donnybrook Merlot
Notes: A change of emphasis is taking place at Wise Vineyards, with Bramley Individual Vineyard Cabernet Sauvignon being made for the first time in 2001 to join the Donnybrook Merlot. Cellar door sales: daily 10am–5pm. There is also a restaurant with scenic views over Geographe Bay.

Woodlands Wines R86

Caves Road, Willyabrup, WA 6280
Ph 08 9755 6226 (winery),
Fax 08 9274 6421

Owners: David and Heather Watson
Chief winemaker: David Watson
Year of foundation: vineyard 1973, winery 1979
Tonnes crushed on average each year: 30, of which 10 are used for Woodlands wines (production should increase to 65 tonnes by 2003)
Location: Willyabrup
Area: 10 ha (5 ha of old non-irrigated vines and 5 ha bearing for the first time in 2001)
Soils: red-brown gravelly loam over clay with a southerly aspect
Varieties planted: White—chardonnay; Red—cabernet franc, cabernet sauvignon, malbec, merlot, pinot noir
Leading wine: Woodlands Cabernet-Merlot, Cabernet Sauvignon
Notes: Another veteran of the region, Woodlands is at the heart of Willyabrup's best cabernet country and its Cabernets are sometimes astounding in their quality. To date production has been small, but is planned to be increased by 2003. Cellar door sales: weekends by appointment.

Woody Nook NR

Metricup Road, Metricup, WA 6284
Ph/Fax 08 9755 7547,
Email woodynook@highway1.com.au

Owners: Jane and Peter Bailey, Neil Gallagher
Chief winemaker: Neil Gallagher
Year of foundation: 1982
Tonnes crushed on average each year: 65
Location: Metricup
Area: 8 ha
Soils: lateritic gravelly loam over clay
Varieties planted: White—chardonnay, chenin blanc, sauvignon blanc, semillon, verdelho; Red—cabernet franc, cabernet sauvignon, merlot, shiraz
Leading wines: Woody Nook Gallaghers Choice (a Cabernet Sauvignon), Classique (a white blend)
Notes: A small Margaret River winery whose wines I have not recently seen. Cellar door sales: 7 days 10am–4.30pm. There is also a restaurant, 'The Nookery'.

Xanadu Wines (formerly Chateau Xanadu) R84

Terry Road, Margaret River, WA 6285
Ph 08 9757 2581, Fax 08 9757 3389,
Email chxanadu@netserv.net.au

Owners: Chateau Xanadu Wines Ltd
Chief winemaker: Glen Goodall and contract
Year of foundation: 1977
Tonnes crushed on average each year: 1400
Locations: Margaret River (winery, cellar door and vineyard), Rosa Brook (vineyard), Kudarup (vineyard)
Area: 129.6 ha consisting of Lagan Estate (Margaret River), 16.92 ha, Rosa Brook vineyard 68.39 ha and Jindawarra vineyard (Kudarup) 44.29 ha
Soils: Margaret River and Rosa Brook, lateritic gravel 'marri' country; Jindawarra vineyard (Kudarup) sandy gravels and sandy loams about three quarters of a metre deep over clay, well-drained
Varieties planted: (Margaret River) White—chardonnay, sauvignon blanc, semillon; Red—cabernet franc, cabernet sauvignon, merlot. (Rosa Brook) White—semillon; Red—cabernet franc, cabernet sauvignon, merlot, shiraz. (Kudarup) White—chardonnay, viognier; Red—cabernet sauvignon, merlot, petit verdot, pinot noir, shiraz
Leading wines: Xanadu Cabernet Sauvignon, Secession (a blend of semillon and sauvignon blanc)
Notes: Xanadu is an expanding publicly listed company. Its wine range is consistently good. Cellar door sales: every day 10am–5pm.

GREAT SOUTHERN REGION

Albany, the largest city in the Great Southern region, is also the oldest settlement in Western Australia, being founded on Christmas Day 1826. The suitability of the region for vines was assessed much later, thanks largely to the pioneering report of Professor Olmo in 1955, made for the Western Australian government, further work by John Gladstones in 1963 (see the introduction to Margaret River) and the ongoing enthusiasm shown by Bill Jamieson, the Western Australian state viticulturalist at that time. Its vineyard beginnings are generally acknowledged to have commenced in 1965 with the planting of the first cuttings at Forest Hill on land leased to the Western Australian Department of Agriculture by local farmers, Tony and Betty Pearse. The initial plantings of a little over a hectare each of riesling and cabernet sauvignon were unsuccessful due to excessive spring rainfall. Notwithstanding that setback, the vines were replanted the following year and succeeded. Its first wines in 1972 were pretty much a family affair, the riesling being made by Dorham Mann at Sandalford, and the cabernet at Houghton's in 1972 by his father Jack, the doyen of the Western Australian wine industry, then making his 51st and last vintage before retirement. About the same time (1967), John Roche, an Adelaide businessman, was planting one hectare each of cabernet and riesling on his Frankland River property, Westfield. Local grazier Tony Smith also caught the mood by planting his Bouverie vineyard near Denbarker with a hectare of cabernet sauvignon and one of shiraz in 1968. The Roche plantings today form a very small part of the Houghton Wine Co Frankland River Vineyard and those of Smith form a fraction of the Plantagenet vineyard.

In 1975, Plantagenet made its first wines at Mount Barker and the region was firmly established, there being seven vineyards in operation between Mount Barker and Frankland River. Soon after, vineyards in the Porongurups area were being developed, as well as others around Denmark. Today the region is highly regarded for its Rieslings and Shiraz though Pinot Noir is also quite successful.

Location: Albany latitude 35°02'S, longitude 117°42'E, about 400 km south-east of Perth; Mount Barker latitude 34°36'S, longitude 117°38'E, about 350 km south-east of Perth

Elevation: from sea-level to about 400 m in fairly uniform gradients. The Porongurups apart, the region is gently undulating.

Topography and soils: Topographically, from Albany and the southern coast, the region climbs gently northward to the plateau of the Yilgarn Rock in the west and in the east traverses another slightly rising plain of tertiary sediments to the Porongurups and Stirling Ranges in the north. Its soils seem nicely divided by the north–south passage of the Albany Highway. To the west are sandy gravels on mainly Precambrian granites and gneisses while to the east and south of the Stirlings are deep sand, sand over gravel and sand over clay on chiefly tertiary siltstones and spongolites.

As in other parts of south-western Australia, the soils are generally divided into 'marri' and 'karri' depending on the prevalent tree, 'marri' being gravelly, sandy, lateritic soils and 'karri' heavier, clayey loams with much less, if any, gravel.

Drainage of the western part is by way of the Frankland, Kent, Denmark, Sleeman and Hay Rivers. Between the rivers, the plateau country is poorly drained. To the east

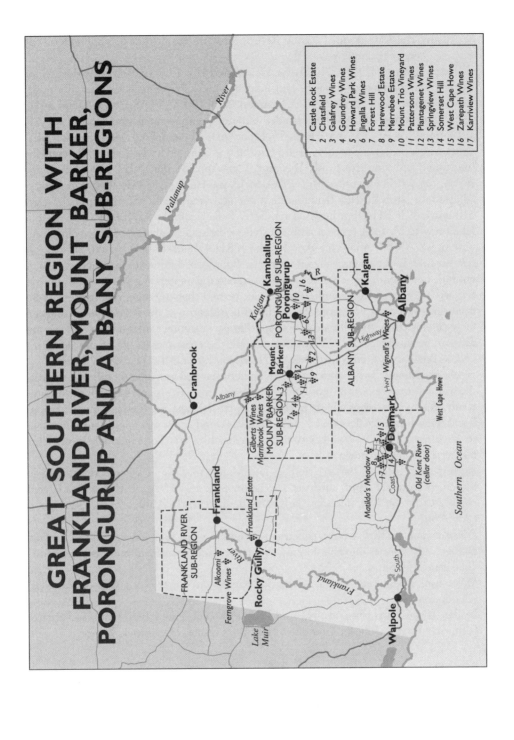

GREAT SOUTHERN REGION WITH FRANKLAND RIVER, MOUNT BARKER, PORONGURUP AND ALBANY SUB-REGIONS

1   Castle Rock Estate
2   Chatsfield
3   Galafrey Wines
4   Goundrey Wines
5   Howard Park Wines
6   Jingalla Wines
7   Forest Hill
8   Harewood Estate
9   Merrebee Estate
10 Mount Trio Vineyard
11 Patersons Wines
12 Plantagenet Wines
13 Springview Wines
14 Somerset Hill
15 West Cape Howe
16 Zarepath Wines
17 Karriview Wines

of Albany, the Kalgan and Pallinup Rivers do drain this district to some extent but drainage here is generally poor.

Climate: Albany MJT 19°C, MAR na, HDD raw 1495, 1533 (cut-off and adjusted for latitude, daily temperature range and vine sites), AR 800 mm (Oct–Apr 303 mm), RH 54% (3pm Jan), AI na, SH 7.9. Denmark MJT 18.7°C, MAR na, HDD raw 1471, 1461 (cut-off and adjusted for latitude, daily temperature range and vine sites), AR 1012 mm (Oct–Apr 354 mm), RH 65% (3pm Jan), AI na, SH 6.6. Mount Barker MJT 19°C, MAR na, HDD raw 1440, 1488 (cut-off and adjusted for latitude, daily temperature range and vine sites), AR 756 mm (Oct–Apr 285 mm), RH 49% (Jan 3pm), AI na, SH 7.1. Porongurups MJT 19°C, MAR na, HDD raw 1441, 1446 (cut-off and adjusted for latitude, daily temperature range and vine sites), AR 748 mm (Oct–Apr 310 mm), 49% RH (3pm Jan), AI na, SH 7.1. Rocky Gully MJT 19.8°C, MAR na, HDD raw 1530, 1494 (cut-off and adjusted for latitude, daily temperature range and vine sites), AR 687 mm (Oct–Apr 215 mm), RH 43% (3pm Jan), AI na, SH 7.6 (all Gladstones). In such a large region there are slight local differences in temperature and rainfall, but overall the climate is Mediterranean, experiencing warm, dry summers and wet winters. As a generalisation, it can be said that the more one moves inland from the south coast, the more the moderating influence of the sea is reduced and the more 'continental' the climate becomes (that is, in summer inland temperatures are warmer, in winter, colder). As for the rainfall, the coastal areas are of course wetter and, as one moves from west to east and from south to north, the rainfall declines.

As the Mount Barker area sits on an ancient sea-bed and areas of salt still exist in the soil, salinity presents its problems for irrigation from rivers and bores. Surface water is run off into local dams which, in times of water shortage, are used for drip irrigation. Local hazards include damage by birds, kangaroos and emus, where vineyards are close to large tree plantations and national parks (such as the Porongurups). Frosts after budburst are not unknown.

Harvest time: (Mount Barker) riesling late March to early April, chardonnay early March, shiraz early April, cabernet sauvignon early to mid-April. (Frankland River) riesling early April, chardonnay early March, shiraz early April, cabernet sauvignon early April.

Principal varieties: Red—shiraz, cabernet sauvignon, pinot noir, cabernet franc, merlot, malbec; White—riesling, chardonnay, sauvignon blanc, semillon, traminer, verdelho
Total area 2150 ha
Major wine styles: Red—Shiraz, Cabernet Sauvignon, Pinot Noir; White—Riesling, Chardonnay
Leading wineries and vineyards: Howard Park, Alkoomi, Forest Hill, Frankland Estate, Ferngrove Estate, Gilberts, Goundrey, Harewood Estate, Marribrook Wines.

Alkoomi **R88**

Wingeballup Road, Frankland, WA 6396
Ph 08 9855 2229, Fax 08 9855 2284

Owners: Merv and Judy Lange and family
Chief winemaker: Michael Staniford

Year of foundation: 1971
Tonnes crushed on average each year: 1000
Location: Frankland River
Area: 70 ha
Soils: free draining gravel over clay, 'marri' country

Varieties planted: White—chardonnay, riesling, sauvignon blanc; Red—cabernet sauvignon, merlot, malbec, cabernet franc, shiraz
Leading wines: Alkoomi Sauvignon Blanc, Riesling, Chardonnay, Cabernet Sauvignon, Shiraz
Notes: Alkoomi is one of the veterans of the once remote Frankland River area. Its excellent Sauvignon Blanc is usually a pungent reminder of the variety at its tart and refreshing best. Its Riesling is delightfully delicate and varietally correct. Its reds, particularly its Cabernet Sauvignon, are deep-flavoured and age well up to 10 years and sometimes longer. If you are in the Great Southern region, Alkoomi must be visited. Its wine quality is superb. Cellar door sales: daily 10am–5pm.

Castle Rock Estate R83

Porongurup Road, Porongurup, WA 6324
Ph 08 9853 1035, Fax 08 9853 1010,
Email diletti@castlerockestate.com.au

Owners: Angelo and Wendy Diletti
Chief winemaker: Robert Diletti
Year of foundation: vineyard 1983, winery 2001
Tonnes crushed on average each year: 80
Location: Porongurup
Area: 12 ha (3 of which are not yet in full bearing)
Soils: an undulating vineyard with red loam over clay on its higher slopes and gravelly loam over tight clay on its lower parts
Varieties planted: White—chardonnay, riesling, sauvignon blanc; Red—cabernet franc, cabernet sauvignon, merlot, pinot noir
Leading wines: Castle Rock Riesling, Cabernet Sauvignon, Pinot Noir, Chardonnay, Great Southern White (a blend)
Notes: Castle Rock Estate instituted its new winery in 2001, a promising vintage in its sub-region. Angelo Diletti has long specialised in the elegant Riesling style of the Porongurup sub-region. The Cabernet Sauvignon here is also extremely good. Cellar door sales: Mon–Fri

10am–4pm, weekends and public holidays 10am–5pm.

Chatsfield Wines R82

O'Neill Road, Mount Barker, WA 6324
Ph/Fax 08 9851 1704,
Email chats@omninet.net.au

Owner: Dr Ken Lynch
Chief winemaker: Rob Lee
Year of foundation: 1976 as Waterman's, renamed Chatsfield in 1985
Tonnes crushed on average each year: 110
Location: Mount Barker
Area: 16 ha
Soils: gravelly loam over clay
Varieties planted: White—chardonnay, gewurztraminer, riesling; Red—cabernet franc, shiraz
Leading wines: Chatsfield Shiraz, Cabernet Franc, Chardonnay, Riesling
Notes: With some vines now over 20 years old, Chatsfield is one of the quiet quality performers of the Great Southern region. It produces rich Shiraz reds, often medal winners, delicate Rieslings and Traminers and a refreshing sometimes Chinon-like Cabernet Franc. Cellar door sales: Tue–Sun and public holidays 10.30am–4.30pm.

Ferngrove Wines R85

Ferngrove Road, Frankland WA 6396
Ph 08 9855 2378, Fax 08 9855 2367,
Email info@franklandvalley.com.au

Owner: Ferngrove Vineyards Ltd
Chief winemaker: (contract)
Year of foundation: 1997
Tonnes produced on average each year: 3000, of which 2500 are used for Ferngrove Vineyards Estate wines.
Location: Frankland
Area: 425 ha consisting of three vineyards at Frankland (155 ha, 70 ha and 60 ha) and one at Mount Barker (140 ha)

Soils: all vineyards are basically 'marri' gravelly loams

Varieties planted: White—chardonnay, riesling, sauvignon blanc, semillon, verdelho; Red—cabernet franc, cabernet sauvignon, malbec, merlot, pinot noir, shiraz

Leading wines: Ferngrove Vineyards Estate Riesling, Shiraz

Notes: Ferngrove is a very large new estate at Frankland River with another substantial vineyard at Mount Barker. When fully bearing, it will be easily the biggest in the Great Southern region. Cellar door sales: daily 9am–5pm.

Forest Hill R87

Muir Highway, Mount Barker, WA 6324
Ph 08 9851 2096, Fax 08 9755 5425,
Email info@foresthillvineyard.com.au

Owner: Tim Lyons
Chief winemakers: Clive Otto and Will Shields (contract)
Year of foundation: 1965
Tonnes crushed on average each year: 250, of which 100 are used for Forest Hill wines
Location: Mount Barker
Area: 90 ha
Soils: gravelly loams over clay, 'marri' country, undulating country
Varieties planted: White—chardonnay, riesling, sauvignon blanc, traminer; Red—cabernet franc, cabernet sauvignon, malbec, merlot, shiraz
Leading wines: Forest Hill Chardonnay, Riesling, Cabernet Sauvignon
Notes: It is very pleasing to acknowledge that after more than 35 years in the making, the Forest Hill Vineyard has at last come of age. Under the energetic direction of owner Tim Lyons, and with a core vineyard of mature vines, it is producing an excellent range of whites and reds, including a Chardonnay, a Riesling and a Shiraz which should not be missed. Cellar door sales: Wed–Sun 10am–4pm.

Frankland Estate R86

Frankland Road, Frankland, WA 6396
Ph 08 9855 1544, Fax 08 9855 1549,
Email franklandestatewines@bigpond.com

Owners/chief winemakers: Barrie Smith and Judi Cullam
Year of foundation: 1988
Tonnes crushed on average each year: 300
Location: Frankland
Area: 30 ha
Soils: duplex soils of gravel and loam about a metre deep over a clay subsoil
Varieties planted: White—chardonnay, riesling; Red—cabernet franc, cabernet sauvignon, malbec, merlot, petit verdot, shiraz
Leading wines: Frankland Estate Olmo's Reward (a red blend made from the 'Bordeaux' varieties mentioned above), Isolation Ridge (Shiraz)
Notes: Famous for its two reds, Olmo's Reward (named in tribute to Professor Olmo) and Isolation Ridge, Frankland Estate also has a very aromatic and elegant Riesling. Cellar door sales and tasting by appointment.

Galafrey Wines R83

Quangellup Road, Mount Barker, WA 6324
Ph 08 9851 2022, Fax 08 9851 2324,
Email galafrey@wn.com.au

Owners: Ian and Linda Tyrer
Chief winemaker: Ian Tyrer
Year of foundation: 1975
Tonnes crushed on average each year: 230 (some fruit is purchased from local growers)
Location: Mount Barker
Area: 12 ha
Soils: gravelly loam over clay
Varieties planted: White—chardonnay, muller-thurgau, riesling; Red—cabernet sauvignon, cabernet franc, merlot, pinot noir, shiraz
Leading wines: Galafrey Riesling, Cabernet Sauvignon, Art Label White (a blend), Art Label Red (a blend)

Notes: Ian Tyrer makes a good Mount Barker Riesling which is always worth tasting. Cellar door sales: daily 10am–5pm.

Gilberts Wines **R86**

Albany Highway, Kendenup, WA 6323
Ph 08 9851 4028, Fax 08 9851 4021,
Email gilberts@rainbow.agn.net.au

Owners: Jim and Beverley Gilbert
Chief winemakers: Gavin Berry and Gordon Parker (contract)
Year of foundation: 1985
Tonnes crushed on average each year: 40
Location: Albany Highway, 18 km north of Mount Barker
Area: 8.4 ha
Soils: gravelly loam over clay, 'marri' country
Varieties planted: White—chardonnay, riesling; Red—cabernet sauvignon, shiraz
Leading wines: Gilberts Riesling, Chardonnay, Shiraz
Notes: Jim and Beverley Gilbert run a mixed farm north of Mount Barker and their vineyard is very much a hands-on operation. Their leading wines, in particular Shiraz and Riesling, are amongst the best of the region. Cellar door sales: 7 days 10am–5pm.

Goundrey Wines **R85**

'Langton', Muir Highway, Mount Barker, WA 6324
Ph 08 9851 1777, Fax 08 9851 1997,
Email info@goundreywines.com.au

Owners: Jack Bendat and family
Chief winemaker: David Martin
Year of foundation: 1975
Tonnes crushed on average each year: 2700, all of which are used for Goundrey and Fox River wines
Location: Langton, Mount Barker
Area: 175 ha
Soils: gravelly loam over clay with some granitic and sandy areas
Varieties planted: White—chardonnay, riesling, sauvignon blanc, semillon; Red—cabernet sauvignon, merlot, pinot noir and shiraz
Leading wines: Goundrey Reserve Chardonnay, Riesling, Sauvignon Blanc, Cabernet Sauvignon, Shiraz Goundrey range, Fox River range
Notes: Goundrey is one of WA's larger wine companies, having a crush of nearly 3000 tonnes. It is also a prolific winner of silver and bronze show awards, which points to a consistently high rather than a stratospheric standard. Shiraz is the strength here. Cellar door sales: Mon–Sat 10am–4.30pm, Sun 11am–4.30pm.

Harewood Estate **R85**

Scotsdale Road, Denmark, WA 6333
Ph 08 9840 9078, Fax 08 9840 9053,
Email grahare@bigpond.com

Owners: Keith and Margie Graham
Chief winemaker: Michael Kerrigan (contract)
Year of foundation: 1988
Tonnes crushed on average each year: 100, of which 10 are used for Harewood wines
Location: Denmark
Area: 9 ha
Soils: well-drained friable 'karri' loams
Varieties planted: White—chardonnay; Red—pinot noir
Leading wines: Harewood Chardonnay, Pinot Noir
Notes: Harewood has equal areas of chardonnay and pinot noir, sells most of its fruit, but does retain sufficient to make an excellent Chardonnay and a Pinot Noir of good structure. No cellar door sales. Tasting by appointment only.

Howard Park R89

Denmark Winery, Scotsdale Road,
Denmark, WA 6333
Ph 08 9848 2345, Fax 08 9848 2064,
Email hpw@denmarkwa.com.au
Leston Park Winery, Willyabrup, WA
Ph 08 9755, 9988, Fax 08 9755 9048

Owners: Jeff and Amy Burch
Chief winemakers: Michael Kerrigan and James
Kellie
Year of foundation: Denmark 1986, Willyabrup
vineyard 1996, winery 2000
Tonnes crushed on average each year: each
winery is capable of crushing 1000 tonnes.
Production in the year 2000 was 1500 tonnes,
all of which were used for the Howard Park
and Madfish Bay wines
Locations: Denmark, (winery and cellar door),
Willyabrup (winery, vineyard and cellar door)
Area: Willyabrup 50 ha
Soils: Leston Park, loamy gravels about a metre
deep over friable clays; Denmark, no vineyards
owned
Varieties planted: White—chardonnay;
Red—cabernet franc, cabernet sauvignon,
shiraz
Leading wines: Howard Park Riesling,
Chardonnay, Cabernet-Merlot. The Madfish
Bay range. Two other wines were released in
2001, 'Scotsdale' (wine of the Denmark area)
and 'Leston' (for wine of Willyabrup)
Notes: Like many Western Australian wineries,
Howard Park has expanded into the Margaret
River region, which is also a popular tourist
and holiday destination as well as being WA's
premium wine-growing region. Expansion
there may be, but the quality of all three
Howard Park wines has not been stretched. It
remains extremely high, the Chardonnay and
Cabernet-Merlot brilliant. Either winery should
be high on any visiting list. Cellar door sales:
Denmark daily 10am–4pm, Willyabrup daily
10am–5pm.

Jingalla Wines R83

Bolganup Dam Road, Porongurup,
WA 6324
Ph/Fax 08 9853 1023,
Email jingallawine@wn.com.au

Owners: Geoff and Nita Clark, Barry and
Shelley Coad
Chief winemaker: John Wade (contract)
Year of foundation: 1979
Tonnes crushed on average each year: 50
Location: Porongurup
Area: 9 ha
Soils: pea gravel, 'marri' country, and some red
'karri' loams deep granitic and ironstone
'jarrah' country
Varieties planted: White—riesling, semillon,
verdelho; Red—cabernet sauvignon, shiraz
Leading wines: Jingalla Riesling, Cabernet
Sauvignon
Notes: Located on the northern slopes of the
spectacular Porongurup Range at 450 m
altitude, Jingalla is ideally suited to produce
excellent Rieslings, which it does consistently.
Cellar door sales: 7 days 10.30am–5pm.

Karriview Wines R88

Roberts Road, Denmark, WA 6333
Ph 08 9840 9381, Fax 08 9855 1549

Owners: Frankland Estate, Richard Manser and
Jane Barblet
Chief winemakers: Howard Park and
Elizabeth Smith
Year of foundation: 1986
Tonnes crushed on average each year: 18
Location: Denmark
Area: 2 ha
Soils: 'karri' loam but with some gravel 'marri'
country over clay
Varieties planted: White—chardonnay;
Red—pinot noir
Leading wines: Karriview Chardonnay, Pinot
Noir
Notes: With ultra-close spacing of vines,

Karriview's crop is very low in quantity but high in quality, highlighting the promise of Denmark as a high-quality cool area for the cultivation of chardonnay and pinot noir. At 1000 cases in all, the wines will always be scarce but well worth seeking out, especially now that the highly-respected Frankland Estate is part-proprietor. Cellar door sales: weekends, school and public holidays 11am–4pm.

Marribrook Wines R85

Albany Highway, 16 km north of
Mount Barker, WA 6324
Ph 08 9851 4651, Fax 08 9851 4652

Owners: Denis and Faye Brooks
Chief winemaker: Gavin Berry and Gordon Parker (contract)
Year of foundation: 1990
Tonnes crushed on average each year: 54, of which 35 are used for Marribrook wines
Location: (vineyard) Frankland, (vineyard and cellar door) Albany Highway, Mount Barker, 16 km north of the town
Area: 5.3 ha
Soils: gravelly sandy clay loam 20–30 cm deep over clay subsoil
Varieties planted: White—chardonnay, marsanne, sauvignon blanc, semillon;
Red—cabernet franc, cabernet sauvignon, malbec, merlot
Leading wines: Marribrook Marsanne, Reserve Chardonnay, Cabernet Merlot
Notes: Marribrook produces the only Marsanne in the West and, as in the East, it generally matures into a strawy-honeysuckle smoothness on palate. Cellar door sales: Wed–Sun and public holidays 10.30am–4.30pm.

Matilda's Meadow NR

Hamilton Road, Denmark, WA 6333
Ph 08 9848 1951, Fax 08 9848 1957

Owners: Don Turnbull and Pamela Meldrum-Turnbull

Chief winemaker: Brenden Smith (contract)
Year of foundation: 1990
Tonnes crushed on average each year: 50, of which 20 are used for Matilda's Meadow wines
Location: Denmark
Area: 6.8 ha
Soils: 'karri' loam
Varieties planted: White—chardonnay, sauvignon blanc, semillon; Red—cabernet franc, cabernet sauvignon, pinot noir, shiraz
Leading wines: Matilda's Meadow Chardonnay, Pinot Noir, Cabernet Sauvignon, Semillon-Sauvignon Blanc
Notes: No wines have been recently tasted. Cellar door sales: Wed–Mon 10am–5pm. There is also a restaurant.

Merrebee Estate R82

Lot 3339, St Werburgh's Road, Mount
Barker, WA 6324
Ph 08 9851 2424, Fax 08 9851 2425,
Email merrebee@ozware.com

Owner: Merilyn Basell
Chief winemaker: Brenden Smith (contract)
Year of foundation: 1985
Tonnes crushed on average each year: 40
Location: Mount Barker
Area: 10 ha
Soils: sandy gravelly loams over clay, 'marri' country
Varieties planted: White—chardonnay, riesling; Red—cabernet franc, cabernet sauvignon, merlot, shiraz
Leading wines: Merrebee Estate Chardonnay, Shiraz, Riesling
Notes: Merrebee Estate has recently added a further area of 6 ha to its vineyard, planting the two cabernets, sauvignon and franc, and also merlot. It is anticipated that the crop will double by 2005. The strengths here are those of Mount Barker as a whole, Riesling and Shiraz, but the 'Bordeaux' varietal blend should be very palatable in a few years. Cellar door sales: weekends and public holidays

10am–4pm excluding Good Friday and
Christmas Day.

Mount Trio Vineyard R82

Cnr Castle Rock and Porongurup Roads,
Porongurup, WA 6324
Ph 08 9853 1136, Fax 08 9853 1120

Owners: Gavin Berry and Gill Graham
Chief winemaker: Gavin Berry
Year of foundation: 1989 first Porongurup
vineyard, 1999 second Porongurup vineyard
Tonnes produced on average each year: 12
(Mount Trio uses about 40 tonnes of grapes
for its own wine purposes)
Location: Porongurup
Area: 8.1 ha
Soils: first vineyard, gravelly loams; second
vineyard, rocky ironstone, an old gravel pit, of
low fertility
Varieties planted: White—chardonnay, riesling;
Red—merlot, pinot noir, shiraz
Leading wines: Mount Trio Pinot Noir,
Chardonnay
Notes: Mount Trio is a home away from home
for Plantagenet winemaker, Gavin Berry. As at
Plantagenet, Pinot Noir shows up very well.
Cellar door sales by appointment.

Old Kent River R83

Turpin Road, Rocky Gully, WA 6397
Ph 08 9855 1589, Fax 08 9855 1660

Owners: Mark and Debra Noack
Chief winemaker: Michael Staniford (contract)
Year of foundation: 1985
Tonnes crushed on average each year: 90, of
which 50 are used for Old Kent River wines
Locations: (vineyard) Rocky Gully, (vineyard and
cellar doors sales) South Coast Highway,
Denmark
Area: 14 ha consisting of Rocky Gully vineyard
12 ha, Denmark vineyard 2 ha
Soils: silt, loam and gravel
Varieties planted: White—chardonnay,

sauvignon blanc; Red—cabernet sauvignon,
pinot noir, shiraz
Leading wine: Old Kent River Pinot Noir,
Chardonnay, Shiraz
Notes: The Noacks are proud of their Pinot
Noir, and so they should be. It is a consistent
wine show performer, regularly winning silver
and bronze awards and the occasional gold
and even a trophy as in Adelaide in 1999.
Cellar door sales: Denmark Wed–Sun
9.30am–5.30pm.

Pattersons R83

St Werburgh's Road, Mount Barker,
WA 6324
Ph/Fax 08 9851 2063,
Email patwine@omninet.net.au

Owners: AF and SM Patterson
Chief winemaker: Plantagenet Wines (contract)
Year of foundation: 1982
Tonnes crushed on average each year: 30
Location: Mount Barker
Area: 6.5 ha
Soils: red sandy loam over granite and grey
granitic sandy loam over granite (unusual in this
area as most soils are 'marri' gravelly loams)
Varieties planted: White—chardonnay;
Red—pinot noir, shiraz
Leading wines: Pattersons Chardonnay, Pinot
Noir, Shiraz
Notes: Traditionally, Pattersons have produced
generously flavoured Chardonnays, but more
recently the baton has been passed to Pinot
Noir with four gold awards and three trophies
at the excellent Mount Barker Wine Show.
Cellar door sales: Sat–Wed 10am–5pm.
At other times by appointment.

Plantagenet Wines R83

Albany Highway, Mount Barker,
WA 6324
Ph 08 9851 2150, Fax 08 9851 1839,
Email planwine@rainbow.agn.net.au

Owner: Lionel Samson Pty Ltd
Chief winemaker: Gavin Berry
Year of foundation: 1974
Tonnes crushed on average each year: 1400
Locations: (winery and cellar door) Mount
Barker, (vineyards) Crystal Brook, Narrikup;
Wyjup, Denbarker; Bouverie, Denbarker;
Rosetta, Mount Barker (2002)
Area: 88 ha consisting of Crystal Brook 64 ha,
Wyjup 17 ha, Bouverie 7 ha (Rosetta 40 ha is
to be planted in 2002)
Soils: All vineyards have 'marri' soils
(i.e. gravelly loams)
Varieties planted: (Crystal Brook)
White—chardonnay; Red—cabernet franc,
cabernet sauvignon, merlot, pinot noir, shiraz.
(Wyjup) White—chardonnay, riesling;
Red—cabernet sauvignon, shiraz. (Bouverie)
White—chardonnay; Red—cabernet
sauvignon, pinot noir, shiraz
Leading wines: Riesling, Chardonnay, Cabernet
Sauvignon, Shiraz
Notes: Plantagenet is one of the pioneers
of the Great Southern and one of the larger
producers of the region. It is renowned for
its Shiraz and Cabernet Sauvignon. It also
makes a stylish Pinot Noir. Cellar door
sales: Mon–Fri 9am–5pm, weekends
10am–4pm.

Somerset Hill NR

891 McLeod Road, Denmark, WA 6333
Ph 08 9840 9388, Fax 08 9840 9394,
Email somerset@wn.com.au

Owners: Graham and Lee Upson
Chief winemaker: Brenden Smith (contract)
Year of foundation: 1995
Tonnes produced on average each year: 75, of
which 30 are used for Somerset Hill wines
Location: Denmark
Area: 10.5 ha
Soils: varying from deep 'karri' loams to
ironstone gravel 'marri' into grey sandy loams
Varieties planted: White—chardonnay,

sauvignon blanc, semillon; Red—merlot,
pinot noir
Leading wines: Somerset Hill Chardonnay,
Semillon-Sauvignon Blanc, Pinot Noir
Notes: A vineyard soon to be in full-bearing,
which is starting to win awards for its whites
and Pinot Noir at regional wine shows. Cellar
door sales: daily 11am–5pm.

Springviews NR

Woodlands Road, Porongurup, WA 6326
Ph 08 9853 2088, Fax 08 9853 2098

Owners: Andy and Alice Colquhoun
Chief winemaker: Howard Park (contract)
Year of foundation: 1987
Tonnes crushed on average each year: 37, of
which 6 are used for Springviews wines
Location: Porongurup
Area: 4 ha
Soils: old gravelly loams over yellow clay, acidic
Varieties planted: White—chardonnay, riesling;
Red—cabernet sauvignon
Leading wines: Springviews Chardonnay,
Riesling, Cabernet Sauvignon
Notes: This is a small vineyard making wine
from each variety grown, none of which I have
tasted. Cellar door sales: daily 10am–5pm.

West Cape Howe NR

Lot 42, South Coast Highway, Denmark,
WA 6333
Ph 08 9848 2959, Fax 08 9848 2903,
Email wchowe@denmarkwa.net.au

Owners: Brenden and Kylie Smith
Chief winemaker: Brenden Smith
Year of foundation: 1997
Tonnes crushed on average each year: 40, all
of which are used for West Cape Howe wines.
There are plans to increase production to 150
within a few years. Many more tonnes are
crushed, as this winery has a capacity of 1000
tonnes and acts as a contract-making facility
for 19 vineyards

Location: Denmark
Area: 2.4 ha
Soils: na
Varieties planted: White—chardonnay, sauvignon blanc, viognier; Red—shiraz
Leading wines: West Cape Howe Semillon-Sauvignon Blanc, Chardonnay, Late Picked Riesling, Shiraz, Cabernet Sauvignon
Notes: West Cape Howe is at this stage primarily a contract winemaking establishment. I have not tasted its wines. Cellar door sales: daily 10am–5pm.

Wignall's Wines R84

Lot 5384 Chester Pass Road, Albany, WA 6330
Ph 08 9841 2848, Fax 08 9842 9003

Owners: Bill, Patricia and Robert Wignall
Chief winemaker: Ben Kagi
Year of foundation: 1982
Tonnes crushed on average each year: 90 (production will exceed 100 tonnes after vintage 2001)
Location: Albany (7 km north-east of town)
Area: 22 ha
Soils: varying from sand to heavy loam. The more vigorous varieties are planted on less fertile soils to control vigour and to channel growth into fruit production. Other vineyards are planted on gravelly, sandy soils over friable clays, allowing good drainage and good root growth
Varieties planted: White—chardonnay, sauvignon blanc; Red—pinot noir, cabernet sauvignon, merlot, shiraz
Leading wines: Wignall's Pinot Noir and Chardonnay
Notes: Bill Wignall could be said to have established Great Southern's reputation for Pinot Noir. In good years, they are soft fleshy wines of opulent flavour and always worth

drinking. Wignals are also fully committed to BIFS (a new acronym standing for 'biologically integrated farm systems'), which in plain English simply means that the grape-grower/winemaker does everything in his power to reduce chemical use in the growth and making of his products. As an example of Wignall's commitment to this idea, Bill points out that no chemical insecticides have been used since 1988 and that green tree frogs are thriving in the vineyard canopy. As this is arguably Western Australia's best pinot vineyard, let us hope that the frogs drink only water. Cellar door sales: 7 days noon–4pm.

Zarephath Wines R80

Moorialup Road, East Porongurup, WA 6331
Ph/Fax 08 9853 1152,
Email christcr@iinet.net.au

Owner: The Christ Circle Inc. (a Roman Catholic Benedictine Community)
Chief winemaker: Brenden Smith (contract)
Year of foundation: 1994
Tonnes produced on average each year: 17 (production is growing and is expected to reach 50 tonnes by 2003)
Location: East Porongurup
Area: 9 ha
Soils: varying from gravelly soils with some clay to sandy loam
Varieties planted: White—chardonnay, riesling; Red—cabernet sauvignon, merlot, pinot noir, shiraz
Leading wines: Zarephath Riesling, Pinot Noir
Notes: It is very early days yet for Zarephath vineyard, but its Riesling shows promise and according to Brother Laurence Etheredge the Pinot Noir (not tasted) is 'sensational'. Cellar door sales: weekends and public holidays: 10am–4pm or by appointment.

Mount Barker Sub-region

This was the first sub-region in Australia to secure recognition.

Topography, soils and climate: The sub-region is located on the Plantagenet plateau with the Mount Barker hill at its centre. It varies in altitude from 180 to 250 m above sea-level. It is gently undulating and is distinguished from the other winegrowing areas of the Great Southern region—Frankland River, Denmark, Porongurups and Albany— by its comparatively poor 'marri' soils, that is, lateritic gravelly sandy loams or sandy loams directly derived from granite rock. Good drainage and soil warmth are their major contribution to the well-being of the vine. Vineyards are planted chiefly on the tops and sides of the hills, avoiding the valley bottoms because of increased salinity. For the same reason, irrigation dams have not been built in such valleys. These dams have tended to be constructed so they can be fed from road catchments.

The climate of the sub-region is classified as Mediterranean with the majority (471 mm) of its annual rainfall (756 mm) falling between May and September. HDD for vineyard sites is 1488. Sunshine hours are 1518 and 3pm relative humidity is 54%. During the growing season, the most likely month for frosts to occur is October and this risk increases as one travels from south to north. There is also an increase in sunshine hours and a decrease in rainfall and relative humidity in the same direction.
Harvest time: Here is a further point of distinction of Mount Barker from its co-occupants of the Great Southern region. Typical dates for early and late maturity of the Mount Barker crop are second week of March for chardonnay and pinot noir, last week of April for cabernet sauvignon. Areas to the south such as Albany and Denmark have budburst and harvest two weeks earlier, while the Porongurups harvest two weeks later.
Total area over 2000 ha
Principal wine styles: Those two great 'continental' grape varieties, shiraz and riesling, have most definitely distinguished themselves at Mount Barker, though how their 'Mount Barker' qualities are distinct *per se* from the qualities of the rieslings and shiraz from Frankland River or the Porongurups is difficult to say and would certainly require very precise tasting from a panel of experts. But this observation apart, the Rieslings of Mount Barker usually have an intensely appealing 'lime-citrus' character on nose and palate and an ability to age which rivals those of the Eden and Clare Valleys. Shiraz too has its distinctions, being related more to the spicy Rhone Valley style than to the heavier berry and black-pepper warm area wines of McLaren Vale and the Barossa Valley.

Wine producers utilising Mount Barker fruit and present in the sub-region are Chatsfield, Forest Hill, Galafrey, Gilberts, Goundrey, Houghton, Merrebee Estate, Patterson and Plantagenet (see individual entries).

Albany Sub-region

Though most of the credit for the early exploration of the southern Australian coast is due to Matthew Flinders and the French navigators Baudin and Freycinet, the inhabitants of Albany have certainly not forgotten the contribution of Captain George

Vancouver who, in 1791, discovered and named such local features as King George Sound, Princess Royal Harbour and Oyster Harbour. Vancouver, who had sailed with Cook on his second and third voyages to the Pacific, was also responsible for the discovery and naming of Vancouver, British Colombia.

On Christmas Day, 1826, Major Edmund Lockyer, who had been despatched from Sydney, arrived at King George Sound in the brig *Amity* to claim the western part of the Australian continent for Great Britain. On his small square rigger, he brought with him 29 soldiers, 23 convicts, a surgeon, ship's captain and crew as well as six months' provisions. On 21 January 1827, he duly raised the Union Jack and called his settlement Fredericks Town, a name later changed to Albany. After the founding of the Swan River Colony in 1829, civilian government eventually came to Albany in 1831, when the first magistrate, Alexander Collie, was appointed.

Besides the usual occupation of land for grazing, Albany was associated with whaling from its earliest days. Whaling ceased in 1978, but the whaling station remains as the world's largest whaling museum. Though it was common knowledge in the area that grapes grew well in Albany, the sub-region's first commercial vineyard, Redmond, did not appear until 1974. Its grapes were sold to Plantagenet. In 1982, Bill Wignall planted his King River vineyard. Its first vintage in 1985 was a tremendous success, the Pinot Noir receiving a gold medal at an interstate capital city wine show and the Chardonnay winning the SGIO trophy as WA's Best Table Wine. Such success, however, did not enthuse the local public and it was not until the mid-1990s that, in line with the growth of general Australian interest in vineyards, more vineyards began to be planted in the sub-region.

There is one operating winery and cellar door sales outlet within the sub-region, the highly regarded Wignall's Wines.

Topography and soils: The sub-region has been described as an area of 'sands and laterite on elongate crests' (CSIRO Groundwater Research 1979–1982) with intervening valleys lying on sedimentary rock that is not suitable for viticulture due to this fact and to poor drainage. Its geographical formations are chiefly Precambrian granites and gneisses and its basic soils are sandy gravels overlying a layer of laterite rock of varying thickness, which it is necessary to deep-rip for viticultural purposes. Below the laterite is a clay or clay loam, which has good rooting characteristics. The soils, however, have been modified by history. As the prevailing summer wind is easterly, the western slopes of the area have less sand in their soil profiles, while the eastern slopes have correspondingly more. Sites suitable for viticulture within the sub-region need to be carefully selected as drainage is restricted and this means that the areas suitable for viticulture are confined mostly to the slopes. Irrigation is available only from private water harvesting, which is usually by means of rainfall run off into dams. The elevation of the sub-region varies from 14–40 m.

Climate: For details, see the notes on the Great Southern region. Generally, however, the climate of the sub-region is quite uniform, though rainfall in the west, adjacent to the coast, is slightly higher than the east, and temperature is marginally lower closer to the coast than further inland due to sea breezes. Generally the climate can be described as Mediterranean with moist but cool rather than cold winters, and warm dry summers. Diurnal variation of temperature is generally slight once more due to maritime winds (the Albany Doctor, as such breezes are called locally). A further factor in this slight diurnal variation is the release from rocks after sunset of heat stored during sunlight hours. The particular virtue of the sub-region is that the middle of the day in summer is optimal for photosynthesis, a balance of reasonable humidity and reasonable heat ensuring that the leaf stomata of the vines do not close, but remain active with consequent efficient and satisfactory ripening.

Harvest time: Harvest usually commences early in March with pinot noir, followed 7–10 days later by chardonnay and then sauvignon blanc. Cabernet sauvignon usually ripens mid-April.

Principal wine styles: Because of the justifiable devotion of Bill Wignall to pinot noir, Wignall's King River Pinot Noir has created the red wine reputation of the sub-region. Chardonnay, however, is not far behind and regularly wins trophies and gold medals. Other promising varieties are sauvignon blanc and cabernet sauvignon. An increasing amount of shiraz is now being grown in the sub-region.

Porongurup Sub-region

This is a further sub-region of the Great Southern Region. Its name is a corruption of the Aboriginal word Purringorep and means place of the spirits. It was formally settled about 1859, but in practice had been used by squatters for sheep grazing since about 1830, a practice that has continued to the present day. However, in the intervening 160 years, more and more farmers moved into the area with the consequence that pastoral activities expanded to include cattle, both for beef and dairying, as well as a variety of horticultural pursuits including orcharding, vegetable growing and very recently viticulture.

Interest in viticulture grew slowly but positively after the publication of the favourable viticultural reports of Harold Olmo and John Gladstones in the 1950s and 60s, the first vineyard in the sub-region, Bolganup, being planted to 2 ha of cabernet sauvignon in 1974. Others soon followed with the initial planting of the present Millinup Wines vineyard, being made to 1 ha of riesling in 1978. The following year Jingalla Wines was established with a vineyard of 3 ha, as was Karrivale with 1 ha of riesling vines. In the 1980s, vineyard expansion continued albeit in a restrained and careful way. 1983 saw the beginning of the Castle Rock Estate, and 1985 the commencement of Springviews. Since then, in common with the general Australian trend of the early 1990s, there has been a proliferation of smaller vineyards. There are two wineries within the sub-region, Porongurup Winery, which makes the wines of its four owners but currently has no cellar door sales, and Castle Rock Winery, the new facility of the Diletti family.

Topography and soils: The area has been described by John Gladstones as 'a small, isolated, range of intrusive granite'. The dominant feature of the sub-region is the Porongurup Range, a series of large, bare, granite knobs crowding one upon the other over a length of 12 km and a width of 3 km. The height of the range is about 600 m. The highest point is the Devils Slide at 670 m. These granite domes constitute the National Park. Most of the vineyards are planted on the northern slopes below the knobs at about 300 m in altitude on 'karri' loams as the soils derived from the weathered granite are commonly known. These are quite deep and lie above a clay subsoil. This sub-region differs from that of Mount Barker in that the Mount Barker soils are lateritic gravelly loams known as 'marri', and from the Albany sub-region where the soils are commonly sandy loams. The area has excellent air drainage.

Climate: Climatic data for this sub-region has been mentioned in the general notes concerning the regional climate of the Great Southern, but it is worth noting that, according to Gladstones, the sub-region develops a thermal zone '[i.e. a layer of warm night air] that sits above the inversion or fog boundary that caps the dense cold air that settles on the valley bottoms' because of 'its isolated and projecting hills'. Therefore it has less temperature variability and extremes during the ripening period. Rainwater from the granite slopes is usually run off into dams and most vineyards are drip-irrigated.

Harvest time: Harvesting usually begins about the middle of March and extends until the end of April, with individual varieties ripening one to two weeks later than their counterparts in the Mount Barker sub-region.

Principal wine styles: The main varieties grown in the sub-region are riesling, chardonnay, verdelho, cabernet sauvignon, shiraz, pinot noir, merlot, cabernet franc and semillon. The major wine style from a national point of view is probably Riesling, a reputation gained from the early styles of Castle Rock, though Cabernet also can be excellent.

Growers with cellar door sales facilities within the sub-region are Castle Rock (also with a winery), Jingalla Wines, Springviews and Zarephath Wines.

Frankland River Sub-region

First settled in the 1850s, the Frankland River district was first farmed to sheep and cattle. In the 1890s, as a gold boom swept Western Australia, fruit was grown on some properties to supply the goldfields. Later, after the Second World War, the large grazing blocks of 30 000 acres, surveyed in the late 1890s, were subdivided into much smaller general farming lots of 1200–1500 acres for the Soldier Settlement Scheme. With the advent of this scheme, population grew and the Frankland River community developed.

Its viticultural beginnings can be attributed to former State Government viticulturalist, Bill Jamieson, who shortly after the Second World War, during an extended stay in Victoria and South Australia (where he studied viticulture at Roseworthy), met the legendary Maurice O'Shea. O'Shea told him that if he was to begin again, he would, basing his judgments on climate and topography, choose not the Hunter Valley, but the Great Southern.

In 1955, as State Government viticulturalist, Jamieson commissioned the eminent Californian viticulturalist Harold Olmo to study the State's dried fruit industry and also the table wine potential of the Great Southern. Olmo's report held the Frankland River area in high regard. In the early 1960s, the State Government, wishing to decentralise the State's dried fruits industry, failed to find suitable sites for this purpose and so turned its attention to table wine. A committee set up to investigate table wine found no call for it in 1961 and so deferred decision until a further request for action was made by the Premier, Sir Charles Court, in 1964. Then the committee began to investigate more thoroughly. Jamieson and another member, Jack Mann, were 'caught' digging holes on the Forest Hill property of the Pearse family, west of Mount Barker. The soil samples taken were found to be suitable for viticulture and so a trial block of 4 ha was leased from the Pearses for ten years beginning in 1965. The planting was initially a disaster, as heavy rains gave the vine cuttings an incurable dose of wet feet, but the next year saw the successful establishment of riesling and cabernet sauvignon. This vineyard however, though nearby, is not within the Frankland River sub-region.

The first vines within the sub-region were planted in 1968 on 'Westfield', a Netley Brook property belonging to the Roche family of Adelaide. This vineyard is now Houghton's Netley Brook vineyard. In 1971 the first vines were planted on Merv and Judy Lange's property, 'Alkoomi', a vineyard and winery which during the next 30 years established the quality of the sub-region. By the end of the 1980s, there were over 200 ha of vineyard in the Frankland River district. By the year 2000 the region had grown substantially. Cellar door sales facilities within the sub-region can be found at Alkoomi, Ferngrove, and Frankland Estate. Old Kent River, though within the sub-region, has cellar door sales at Denmark.

Topography and soils: The sub-region consists of gently undulating country, which forms the catchments of four rivers, the Frankland, Gordon, Kent and Tone. With the exception of several individual hills, the sub-region and its vineyards are contoured between 200–300 m. Geologically, the sub-region is on the south-west extremity of the Yilgarn Block and is adjacent to the Albany–Fraser Mobile. To the east is the Stirling Range and to the south the Beardmore range. The area has typical granite-gneiss outcrops with remnant laterite capping. Its soils are the typical 'marri' gravel, associated with laterite ridges, and often adjoin rich red soils which are in turn typical of the granite country. Such soils are superimposed at a constant depth upon orange non-reactive clays. Such evenness of soil makes large areas suitable for viticulture.

Climate: Frankland River vineyards MJT 19.9°C, MAR 13.6°C, HDD 1558 (cut off at 19°C, but not otherwise adjusted), AR 614 mm (Oct–Apr 203.5 mm), RH 59% 9am Jan, 39% 3pm Jan, AI na, SH na. The Frankland River sub-region is an extension of the Great Southern Mediterranean climate, i.e. warm, dry summers and cool but by no means cold, wet winters. Rainfall generally declines across the sub-region from west to east. Due to the salinity of the rivers and the soils in the valley bottoms, irrigation is not generally practised unless water is available from 'water-farming', a system involving many kilometres of drains, catchment and holding dams and expensive pumping systems (see above), or from holding dams constructed on mid-slopes or from roaded catchment dams. The sub-region's comparatively dry growing season reduces the incidence of powdery mildew and fungus diseases and as yet downy mildew has not appeared in the sub-region. Frankland River experiences no maritime influences with the exception of the 'Albany Doctor', an evening breeze which causes a reduction of the temperature about 2 degrees on average below other sub-regions within the Great Southern region.

Harvest time: All major varieties, e.g. chardonnay, riesling, shiraz and cabernet sauvignon, ripen from mid-March to mid-April.

Principal wine styles: In whites, Frankland Estate and Alkoomi have established delightfully delicate Riesling styles. Alkoomi also makes exceptionally good 'tropical-fruit' Sauvignons Blancs, while Chardonnays are also very successful. In reds, Cabernet

Sauvignon and its associated 'Bordeaux' varieties do extremely well and subtle Shiraz reds from such vineyards as Isolation Ridge have also proved top-notch.

PEMBERTON REGION (INTERIM REGISTRATION)

Timber and apples were perhaps the first claims to fame of the Pemberton and Manjimup areas. Like the other cooler areas of South Western Australia wine zone, Pemberton owes a great debt of gratitude to Dr John Gladstones for his pioneering viticultural studies of this region, as well as those of Margaret River and the Great Southern. Until Gladstones' work in the 1960s, little was known of Pemberton's potential for viticulture, but Gladstones, noting the similarity between the mean temperatures and sunlight hours of Manjimup and Bordeaux, made the confident prediction that 'the wines produced from the appropriate grape varieties should be very much in the mainstream of Bordeaux styles'.

Thus the Western Australian Department of Agriculture, imbued with the same spirit of experimentation that saw the founding of the Forest Hill vineyard in 1965, established a successful pilot vineyard midway between Pemberton and Manjimup in 1977. During the 1980s many commercial plantings occurred, seven of them in excess of 20 ha, and in 1988 the Pemberton Vignerons' Association was formed. By 1990, the first wines from Pemberton were being produced and in the ensuing vintage, the first wines from the nearby Manjimup area came on to the market. It was originally planned that there should be one region, but there was some dispute as to its proper name. Some favoured 'Pemberton', some favoured 'Warren Valley' and at a meeting of the Pemberton Vignerons' Association in October 1994, the name 'Pemberton' was found to be preferred by a majority of the vignerons, but this did not prove to be a lasting solution. More recently it has been decided that there should be two adjoining regions. However, debate continues and the matter has not been finally resolved.

Location: The town of Pemberton stands on latitude 34°27'S, longitude 116°01'E, about 280 km virtually due south of Perth. It is linked to other south-western wine regions by the South West Highway (from Albany and Walpole) and by the Vasse Highway (from Margaret River and Busselton). Northcliffe is also a part of the region.
Elevation: Pemberton, about 171 m above sea-level with vineyards 60–200 m. Northcliffe about 100 m above sea-level, with its vineyards 100–120 m.
Topography and soils: Pemberton is an undulating region rising from an altitude of about 100 m in the south to about 200 m in its north. Local soils are 'karri' loams, that is, those which have carried karri trees. The 'karri' loams are formed from gneissic rock, though outcrops of 'marri' soil occur on some of the higher slopes throughout the area. On the 'karri' loams also, viticulturalists need to be on guard against excess vine vigour.

Gravel content, much sought-after in this region for its drainage and soil-warming capabilities, is sometimes as high as 60% in the 'marri' soil and much lower or nil in the 'karri' loam. Subsoil is usually medium clay. Appropriate viticultural soils are characterised by good drainage with low to moderate water-holding capacity. Irrigation is generally, though by no means universally, practised.

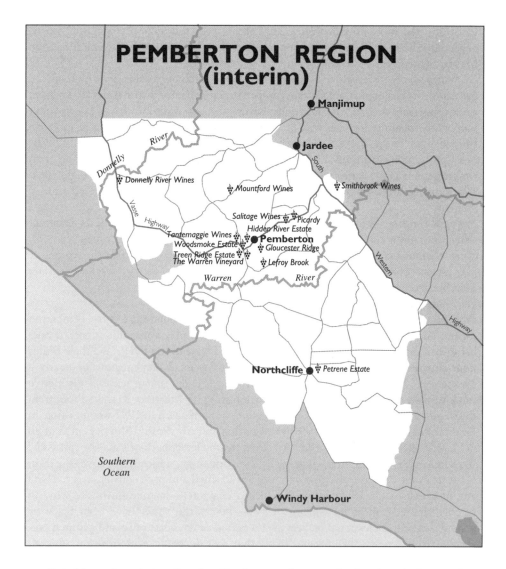

Suitable red varieties for the Pemberton district which, though lower than Manjimup, is cooler include pinot noir and meunier, but not varieties ripening later than merlot. Cabernet sauvignon in this location seems to require a very warm exposure in order to ripen completely.

Climate: Pemberton MJT 19.2°C, MAR na, HDD raw 1403, 1421 (cut-off and adjusted for latitude, daily temperature range and vine sites), AR 1255 mm (Oct–Apr 361 mm), RH 48%, AI na, SH 6.7 (Gladstones). The Southern Ocean is the major influence on the region's climate, though its influences are tempered somewhat by the altitude of suitable viticultural sites. The regional climate can be described as Mediterranean, warm but rarely hot summers and cool, wet winters. Annual rainfall varies throughout the region from about 1255 mm (Pemberton) to about 1400 mm (Northcliffe).

Generally, the more proximate the Southern Ocean, the more precipitation can be expected. The bulk (72%) of the annual rainfall occurs within the five months from May to September.

Water supply for irrigation is usually from large catchment dams, for which official permission is required, though some properties are permitted to irrigate direct from adjoining rivers such as the Donnelly River and Lefroy Brook. In addition, water supply for irrigation purposes may be permitted from bores. Rivers in the region with the exception of the Warren are largely unaffected by salinity. Birds (particularly silver-eyes) are a problem in any location where native flowering gums bloom later than early-ripening grape varieties. Alternative food supplies and netting are the only solution. Nematodes may also occur in certain places, but are not considered a major problem.

Principal varieties: White—chardonnay, sauvignon blanc, verdelho; Red—cabernet sauvignon, pinot noir, merlot, cabernet franc (in descending order of area planted). Some chardonnay and pinot noir is used as sparkling wine base outside the region.

Harvest time: chardonnay, early–mid-March; pinot noir, late February; merlot, mid–late March; cabernet sauvignon, mid–late April

Total area: 800 ha

Principal wine styles: It is rather early to speculate on the wine future of the Pemberton region, but Pinot Noir and Chardonnay will certainly play a prominent part, if only because of the personalities present in the region. I have tasted Pinots and some Shiraz from this region and the adjacent Manjimup (Warren Valley) region for nearly a decade and I first detected what I thought was a particular *goût de terroir*, a distinctive smokiness on nose and palate in 1993, when tasting (at Margaret River) a Pinot from the Pemberton region made by Keith Mugford. I saw it again in 1997 when tasting an Eastbrook Pinot and finally in 1999 when tasting an early Picardy Shiraz. Dan Pannell of Picardy offered one explanation. Ash from nearby forest burn-offs may be carried by the wind and, prevented from escaping by low-lying mists, subsequently cover the fruit, but if this were the case, all other varieties would smell and taste equally smoky. There are, of course, other explanations for such a character—maturation of the wine in heavily charred oak or mercaptan are two—but as the wines have been made by several different professional makers over a period of ten years or so and matured presumably in different oaks, it seems likely that *goût de terroir* or more accurately *goût d'atmosphere* is the only logical explanation. At least that seemed like a good theory and was my opinion until Ely Jarvis of Cape Mentelle, who is familiar with the Manjimup region through her making of the Fonty's Pool wines, suggested that the 'smoke' would not be tasted in whites because they were usually taken off skins quickly, whereas reds were often left to 'cold soak' on skins before fermentation and to macerate on skins afterwards, thereby providing plenty of opportunity to 'smoke' the resulting red. So does the character result from burn-offs or from the soils? Or perhaps from both? This question may provide an opportunity for further research. Of other varieties verdelho seems to impress as a fresh young white style and sauvignon blanc is another variety of promise. As to cabernet sauvignon, perhaps the verdict is still awaited.

Leading wineries and vineyards: Salitage, Picardy, Smithbrook, Gloucester Ridge

Bracken Ridge Estate (vineyard only) NR

Roche Road, Pemberton, WA 6260
Ph 08 9776 0016, Fax 08 9776 0017

Owner: Bracken Ridge Holdings Pty Ltd
Year of foundation: 1996
Tonnes crushed on average each year: vineyard not yet in bearing
Location: Pemberton
Area: 63.06 ha (planted 1996), 28 ha (planted 1997)
Soils: 'karri' and 'marri' loams
Varieties planted: White—chardonnay, sauvignon blanc, semillon, verdelho; Red—cabernet sauvignon, merlot, pinot noir, shiraz
Leading wines: no present plans to produce wine under a Bracken Ridge label
Notes: Bracken Ridge is presently one of the larger vineyards of the Pemberton region, but has no intention at the present time of erecting a winery or having any cellar door facilities.

Donnelly River Wines NR

Vasse Highway, Pemberton, WA 6260
Ph 08 9776 2052, Fax 08 9776 2053,
Email drw@karriweb.com.au

Owners: Matt and Anne Harsley
Chief winemaker: Blair Meiklejohn
Year of foundation: 1986
Tonnes crushed on average each year: 250
Location: Peerabeelup
Area: 11.5 ha
Soils: rich alluvial loam
Varieties planted: White—chardonnay, sauvignon blanc, semillon; Red—cabernet sauvignon, merlot, pinot noir, shiraz
Leading wines: Donnelly River Chardonnay, Cabernet Sauvignon, Pinot Noir
Notes: Donnelly River is another farming diversification story, where a property purchased with retirement in mind by former owner George Oldfield not only became a vineyard but also the site of the region's first winery. Cellar door sales: 7 days 9.30am–4.30pm.

Gloucester Ridge R84

Burma Road, Pemberton, WA 6260
Ph 08 9776 1035, Fax 08 9776 1390,
Email gridge@karriweb.com.au

Owners: Don and Sue Hancock and Trevor Kitchner
Chief winemaker: Brenden Smith (contract)
Year of foundation: 1985
Tonnes crushed on average each year: 200 (other fruit is produced from local growers)
Location: Pemberton
Area: 6.5 ha
Soils: deep gravelly loam
Varieties planted: Whites—chardonnay, sauvignon blanc; Red—cabernet franc, cabernet sauvignon, merlot, pinot noir
Leading wines: Gloucester Ridge Chardonnay, Pinot Noir, Cabernet Sauvignon
Notes: Two of the pioneers of the Pemberton region, Don and Sue Hancock, are now solidly established and successful vignerons close to Pemberton town. Gloucester Ridge is a consistent silver and bronze award winner at local and interstate wine shows. Cellar door sales: daily 10am–5pm. There is also a restaurant.

Hidden River Estate NR

Millineaux Road, Pemberton, WA 6260
Ph 08 9776 1437, Fax 08 9776 0189,
Email goldring@mns.net.au

Owners: Phil and Sandy Goldring
Chief winemaker: Brenden Smith (contract)
Year of foundation: 1994
Tonnes crushed on average each year: 17, with a further 10 tonnes purchased from local growers
Location: Pemberton
Area: 3 ha

Soils: medium 'karri' loam over clay (the vineyard is planted on a north-facing slope)
Varieties planted: White—chardonnay (Gin Gin clone); Red—shiraz
Leading wines: Hidden River Estate Premium Wooded Chardonnay, Basket Press Shiraz
Notes: I have not tasted any wines from this vineyard. Cellar door sales: Wed–Sun 9am–4pm, closed in August.

Lefroy Brook NR

Glauder Road, Pemberton, WA 6260
Ph 08 9386 8385

Owners: Holt family
Chief winemaker: Peter Fimmel (contract)
Year of foundation: 1982
Tonnes crushed on average each year: 6
Location: Pemberton
Area: 1.2 ha
Soils: 'karri' loam
Varieties planted: White—chardonnay; Red—pinot noir
Leading wines: Lefroy Brook Chardonnay, Pinot Noir
Notes: Patrick Holt is the pioneer of the Pemberton region. His vineyard is 15 years old and the beneficiary of a wealth of experience of the habits of silver-eyes and kangaroos. As a result, the vineyard is now permanently netted and kangaroo-proof. Patrick is also a Burgundy enthusiast. It shows in the varieties planted, the close spacing of the vineyard, the lack of irrigation and certainly in the wine style. There are no cellar door sales. Mail order available from PO Box 185, Pemberton, WA 6260.

Mountford Wines R83

Bamess Road, Pemberton, WA 6260
Ph/Fax 08 9776 1345,
Email mountfrd@karriweb.com.au

Owners: Andrew and Sue Mountford
Chief winemaker: Andrew Mountford
Year of foundation: 1987

Tonnes crushed on average each year: 135, of which 65 are used for Mountford wines
Locality: West Pemberton
Area: 6 ha
Soils: 'karri' loams, well-drained
Varieties planted: White—chardonnay, sauvignon blanc; Red—cabernet franc, cabernet sauvignon, malbec, merlot, pinot noir
Leading wines: Sauvignon Blanc, Chardonnay, Pinot Noir
Notes: Andrew Mountford is very much a hands-on winemaker. The winery, cafe and gallery were constructed from hand-made mud-bricks with local timber hewn by his own hands. All this and his own wine and cider, too. Andrew shows his wines at Western Australian wine shows and has been deservedly successful, his major prize being an SGIO wine award, made in 1992 for the best Pemberton white. Cellar door sales: 7 days 10am–4pm.

Petrene Estate NR

Muirillup Road, Northcliffe, WA 6262
Ph/Fax 08 9776 7145

Owners: Peter Hooker and Irene Wilson
Chief winemaker: (contract)
Year of foundation: 1994
Location: Northcliffe
Area: 2 ha
Soils: deep gravelly loam ('karri') over clay loam or light clay
Varieties planted: White—chardonnay, sauvignon blanc; Red—pinot noir
Leading wine: Petrene Chardonnay
Notes: No wines have been tasted. Cellar door sales: weekends, school and public holidays 10.30am–4pm.

Picardy R86

Cnr Eastbrook Road and Vasse Highway, Pemberton, WA 6260
Ph 08 9776 0036, Fax 08 9776 0245

Owners: Pannell family
Chief winemakers: Dan Pannell, Bill Pannell
Year of foundation: 1993
Tonnes crushed on average each year: 60
Location: Pemberton
Area: 8 ha
Soils: lateritic gravel on a ridge, well-drained
Varieties planted: White—chardonnay
(4 Burgundian clones 76, 95, 96 and 277);
Red—cabernet franc, cabernet sauvignon,
malbec, merlot, pinot noir (clones 114, 115,
277, OSV12 and a clone of pinot tordu,
imported to Western Australia over 60 years
ago), shiraz (a second generation selection
made by John Kosovich from a Swan Valley
clone)
Leading wines: Picardy Chardonnay, Pinot Noir,
Merlot-Cabernet (a blend of the 'Bordeaux'
varieties mentioned above), Shiraz
Notes: Bill Pannell has had a long and
distinguished wine career. He founded Moss
Wood over 30 years ago, sold it in 1985 to
Keith Mugford and, because he is a lover of
Burgundies, joined a syndicate of Australian
investors to purchase an interest in the
Domaine de la Pousse d'Or in Volnay in the
Cote de Beaune. The syndicate later
purchased land in Pemberton and developed
Smithbrook Estate. When he also sold his
interest in this syndicate in 1992, he
purchased the present land, of which the
Picardy Vineyard forms part. As one would
expect, considering Bill's sympathies, it is
planted partly to pinot noir and to
chardonnay, but present also are shiraz and
the Bordeaux red varieties with the exception
of petit verdot. The Picardy vineyard is not yet
fully mature, but early Chardonnays and
Pinots Noirs bode well for the future. Tasting
is by appointment only. There are no cellar
door sales. Mail order is available from PO Box
1063, Manjimup, WA 6258.

Salitage Wines **R87**

Vasse Highway, Pemberton, WA 6260
Ph (winery cellar door) 08 9776 1771,
Fax 08 9776 1195,
Email salitage@salitage.com.au

Owners: John and Jenny Horgan
Chief winemaker: Patrick Coutts
Year of foundation: 1989, winery erected in
1994
Tonnes crushed on average each year: 200
Location: Pemberton
Area: 20 ha
Soils: deep ironstone gravelly soils
Varieties planted: White—chardonnay,
sauvignon blanc; Red—cabernet franc, cabernet
sauvignon, merlot, petit verdot, pinot noir
Leading wines: Chardonnay, Pinot Noir and
a second range
Notes: Salitage shares what is rapidly
becoming known as the 'Pemberton Ridge', a
long, low hill of lateritic gravel ('marri' country)
about 12 km north-east of Pemberton. It is a
hilltop site with excellent air drainage to avert
frost-risk and good ripening aspect. It is also
drip irrigated to prevent moisture stress. Until
recently Salitage has been the quality pace-
setter for the region and its wines remain of
very high standard, but as the Pemberton
Ridge is shared also by Picardy, its prominent
position may now be under challenge. When
its vines are mature, superb wines are
expected. Cellar door sales: 7 days 10am–4pm.

Smithbrook Wines **R85**

Smith Brook Road, Pemberton, WA 6260
Ph 08 9772 3557, Fax 08 9772 3579,
Email smithbrk@karriweb.com.au

Owners: Petaluma Ltd and Stimson Lane Inc
Chief winemaker: Michael Symons
Year of foundation: 1988
Tonnes crushed on average each year: 550, of
which 220 are used for Smithbrook wines
Location: Pemberton

Area: 60 ha
Soils: 'karri' loam and 'marri' loam
Varieties planted: White—chardonnay, sauvignon blanc, semillon; Red—cabernet franc, cabernet sauvignon, merlot, petit verdot
Leading wines: Smithbrook Sauvignon Blanc, Cabernet Sauvignon, Chardonnay, Merlot
Notes: Smithbrook has a very strong quality-oriented proprietorship and uses only the best of its own crop for wines made for its own labels. Of these a tropical 'passionfruit' Sauvignon Blanc is an excellent example of the richer style, while its Merlot is elegantly styled with prominent berry and plum fruit. A winery will be erected in the near future. Cellar door sales by appointment.

Tantemaggie Wines (vineyard only) NR

Lot 1 Kemp Road, Pemberton, WA 6260
Ph 08 9776 1164, Fax 08 9776 1810

Owners: Pottinger family
Chief winemaker: (contract)
Year of foundation: 1987
Tonnes crushed on average each year: 250, of which 6 are used for Tantemaggie wines
Location: Pemberton
Area: 20 ha
Soils: 'karri' loam to gravel
Varieties planted: White—chardonnay, sauvignon blanc, semillon, verdelho; Red—cabernet sauvignon
Leading wines: Tantemaggie Cabernet Sauvignon, Verdelho
Notes: Once more, the Pottingers are making a small amount of wine under their own label. Regrettably, I have not been able to taste either. Cellar door sales by appointment.

The Warren Vineyard NR

Conte Road, Pemberton, WA 6260
Ph/Fax 08 9776 1115,
Email annew@karriweb.net.au

Owner: Anne Wandless
Chief winemaker: Harmans Ridge Estate (Bernard Abbot) (contract)
Year of foundation: 1985
Tonnes crushed on average each year: 6
Location: Pemberton
Area: 1.5 ha
Soils: 'karri' loam
Varieties planted: White—none grown, but some white is made from purchased local fruit; Red—cabernet franc, cabernet sauvignon, merlot
Leading wines: Warren Vineyard Cabernet Sauvignon, Merlot, Cabernet-Merlot
Notes: Anne Wandless owns and manages a typical, small, 'karri' loam vineyard close to the heart of Pemberton. It is non-irrigated and fertilised organically as she believes in maximum natural flavour. Her reds are usually 4–5 years old before release, but are rarely seen outside the region. Cellar door sales are available by appointment.

Treen Ridge Estate NR

Packer Road, Pemberton, WA 6260
Ph 08 9776 1131, Fax 08 9775 1176

Owners: Molly and Barry Scotman
Chief winemaker: Andrew Mountford (contract)
Year of foundation: 1992
Tonnes crushed on average each year: 8
Location: Pemberton
Area: 1.75 ha
Soils: sandy gravelly soils ('karri' loam)
Varieties planted: White—riesling, sauvignon blanc; Red—cabernet sauvignon, shiraz
Leading wine: Treen Ridge Shiraz
Notes: Treen Ridge has a very good north-easterly aspect, on 'karri' and 'marri' country between the Warren National Park and the Treen Forest. Cellar door sales: weekends 10am–5pm.

Woodsmoke Estate   **NR**

Lot 2 Kemp Road, Pemberton, WA 6260
Ph/Fax 08 9776 0225

Owners: Rod and Carmel Liebech
Chief winemaker: Julie White
Year of foundation: 1992
Tonnes crushed on average each year: 20, of
which 10 are used for Woodsmoke Estate wines
Location: Pemberton
Area: 2.25 ha

Soils: 'marri' and 'karri' loams
Varieties planted: White—sauvignon blanc,
semillon; Red—cabernet franc, cabernet
sauvignon
Leading wines: Woodsmoke Estate Semillon,
Cabernet Sauvignon, Cabernet Franc,
Sauvignon Blanc
Notes: No wines recently tasted. Cellar door
sales: daily 10.30am–4pm.

MANJIMUP REGION (INTERIM REGISTRATION)

From a regional historical perspective, the Warren Valley region and the Pemberton
region have much in common. Perhaps Pemberton has a slight claim to seniority in
wine production but only by one vintage—1990 as opposed to 1991. Where they differ
is primarily in soil type and climate and that after all is what regional identity is about.

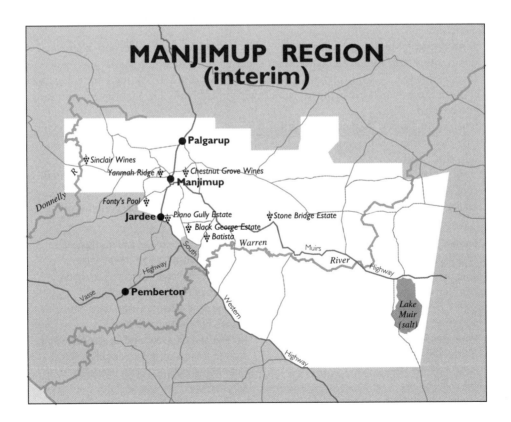

Location: Manjimup latitude 34°14'S, longitude 116°09'E, about 255 km south-east of Perth

Elevation: 279 m with vineyards from 200–300 m

Topography and soils: This area is an undulating region which rises in altitude up to 300 m to the north of Manjimup. The principal type of soil is that which carried 'marri' trees ('marri' soils). The 'marri' soils are gravelly, lateritic sandy loams and gravelly loams. The gravel content of 'marri' soils is much prized because of its draining and soil-warming capabilities. Around Manjimup in warmer exposures, such soils are suitable for varieties such as cabernet sauvignon, but not for later-ripening varieties. There is also a second type of soil called 'karri' loam and the transition from 'marri' to 'karri' occurs south of Manjimup, midway to Pemberton.

Climate: Manjimup MJT 19.2°C, MAR na, HDD raw 1441, 1482 (cut-off and adjusted for latitude, daily temperature range and vine sites), AR 1055 mm (Oct–Apr 288 mm), RH 42% (3pm Jan), AI na, SH 7.2 (Gladstones). Though slightly warmer than Pemberton, Warren Valley can nevertheless be termed a cool temperate region with more than two-thirds of its annual rainfall occurring between May and September. Viticultural dangers occur largely from frost in the north of the region (Manjimup and north). Birds present problems where native trees flower later than the ripening of early grape varieties. An increasing body of local opinion now prefers 'marri' soils for viticulture, regarding 'karri' soils as giving rise to wines which are light in flavour and a little characterless.

Principal varieties: White—chardonnay, sauvignon blanc, verdelho; Red—cabernet sauvignon

Harvest time: (Manjimup) chardonnay early to mid-March, sauvignon blanc mid-March, pinot noir similar to chardonnay, cabernet sauvignon late April

Area: Estimated 270 ha, but an extensive new vineyard is planned by a leading Western Australian wine company which will probably double Manjimup's vineyard area by 2005

Principal wine styles: As with Pemberton it is too early to speculate about the major wine styles which will eventuate. In good sites cabernet sauvignon should ripen quite well, along with other 'Bordeaux' red varieties, though perhaps there should be a reservation about petit verdot. As for whites, chardonnay, sauvignon blanc and verdelho seem adequately suited to the region.

Leading wineries and vineyards: Chestnut Grove, Stone Bridge Estate, Fonty's Pool

---

Batista   🍇 NR

Franklin Road, Middlesex, WA 6260
Ph/Fax 08 9772 3530

Owners: Bob and Grace Peruch
Chief winemaker: Bob Peruch
Year of foundation: 1993
Tonnes crushed on average each year: 20
Location: Middlesex
Area: 3.5 ha
Soils: low yielding gravel and 'marri' red soils, well-drained with gravel and quartz texture
Varieties planted: White—chardonnay; Red—cabernet franc, cabernet sauvignon, merlot, pinot noir, shiraz
Leading wines: Batista Shiraz, Cabernet-Merlot, Pinot Noir, Sparkling
Notes: Batista is a low yielding vineyard, which adds concentration of flavour to Bob Peruch's Pinot Noir and Shiraz. Cellar door sales: by appointment.

Black George Pemberton Estate NR

Black Georges Road, Middlesex, WA 6260
Ph 08 9772 3569, Fax 08 9772 3102

Owners: Wilson family
Chief winemaker: Shelley Wilson
Year of foundation: 1991
Tonnes crushed on average each year: 110
Location: Middlesex
Area: 12 ha
Soils: deep gravelly loam over clay, well-drained
Varieties planted: White—chardonnay, sauvignon blanc, verdelho; Red—cabernet franc, merlot, pinot noir
Leading wines: Black George Estate Pinot Noir, Cabernet-Merlot, Verdelho, Captain's Reserve Chardonnay
Notes: Black George Vineyard is situated on a mixture of soils, part sandy gravel and part deep 'karri' loam, typical of the region which is so water-retentive that Doug Wilson does not irrigate. He feels it to be unnecessary with a rainfall of 1200 mm per year. He believes that 'if the vine is in balance and not stressed, then maximum flavour is achieved'. The Wilsons are a fully independent winemaking family, having a 250-tonne winery in the charge of Shelley Wilson, one of the increasing numbers of talented female Australian winemakers. Cellar door sales: each day 10.30am–4.45pm.

Chestnut Grove R89

Chestnut Grove Road off Perup Road (8 km east of Manjimup), WA 6258
Ph 08 9772 4345, Fax 08 9772 4543,
Email winery@chestnutgrove.com.au

Owners: Kordic family
Chief winemaker: Kim Horton
Year of foundation: 1988, winery 1999
Tonnes crushed on average each year: 140
Location: Manjimup
Area: 18.2 ha
Soils: gravelly loam over clay and coffee rock, 'jarrah' country
Varieties planted: White—chardonnay, sauvignon blanc, semillon, verdelho; Red—cabernet sauvignon, merlot, petit verdot, pinot noir, shiraz
Leading wines: Chestnut Grove Verdelho, Pinot Noir, Merlot, Cabernet-Merlot, Sauvignon Blanc, Chardonnay
Notes: Chestnut Grove is a vineyard that has fully explored verdelho and found just how suitable this region is for it. Most of the trophies and gold awards made to Chestnut Grove have been for this variety, but its Pinot Noir and Merlot have also performed very well. Cellar door sales: Mon–Sat 10am–4pm, Sunday by appointment.

Fonty's Pool (vineyard only) R84

Fonty's Pool Farm, Seven Day Road, Manjimup, WA 6258 (about 10 km south-west of the town)

Owners: a joint venture between Cape Mentelle Wines and Fonty's Pool Farm Pty Ltd
Chief winemaker: Eloise Jarvis
Year of foundation: vineyard 1989, joint venture 1998
Tonnes produced on average each year: 850, of which 100 are presently used for Fonty's Pool wines. It is anticipated that vineyard production will grow to 1000 tonnes by 2003, while the quantity of fruit used for Fonty's Pool wines will increase to 400 tonnes during the next few years
Location: (vineyard) Manjimup, (cellar door) Cape Mentelle, Margaret River
Area: 110 ha (75 ha in full production and 35 ha of young vines between 1 and 4 years old)
Soils: predominantly deep free-draining karri loam; however some of the best blocks of pinot noir, chardonnay and shiraz are grown on marri/jarrah ironstone gravelly loam

Varieties planted: White—chardonnay, sauvignon blanc, semillon, viognier; Red—cabernet franc, cabernet sauvignon, pinot noir, shiraz

Leading wines: Fonty's Pool Chardonnay, Pinot Noir, Shiraz

Notes: Fonty's Pool is a very interesting joint venture between one of Western Australia's leading wineries and a large established Manjimup vineyard. The reds tasted (Pinot Noir and Shiraz) showed a dominant but not unpleasant smoky character both on nose and palate; the white, a Chardonnay, was more neutral on nose and palate showing no 'smoke' at all. (See my notes on *gout de terroir* above—Manjimup also is heavily forested.) Cellar door sales: see Cape Mentelle, Margaret River.

Piano Gully Estate NR

Piano Gully Road, Manjimup, WA 6258
Ph/Fax 08 9316 0336,
Email info@pianogully.com.au

Owners: George and Antoinette Lewkowski
Chief winemaker: Michael Staniford (contract)
Year of foundation: 1987
Tonnes crushed on average each year: 50
Location: Manjimup
Area: 6 ha
Soils: 'karri' loam
Varieties planted: White—chardonnay, sauvignon blanc, verdelho; Red—cabernet sauvignon, pinot noir, shiraz
Leading wines: Piano Gully Chardonnay, Pinot Noir, Cabernet Sauvignon
Notes: I have not recently tasted its wines but a silver medal for a Chardonnay made at the 2000 Sheraton Wine Awards struck the right chord. Cellar door sales: weekends by appointment.

Sinclair Wines R82

Glenoran Springs Vineyard, Graphite Road, Glenoran, WA 6258
(close to One Tree Bridge)
Ph (vineyard) 08 9772 1406,
(HO) 08 9335 6318, Fax 08 9421 1191,
Email sinclairwines@bigpond.com

Owners: John Healy and Darelle Sinclair
Chief winemaker: Brenden Smith (contract)
Year of foundation: 1994
Tonnes crushed on average each year: 35, of which about 30 are used for Sinclair wines
Location: Glenoran (about 17 km west of Manjimup)
Area: 5 ha
Soils: red gravelly loams with 30% to 65% gravel content in the topsoil. The vineyard is established on steep slopes at 300 m in altitude. Predominant trees are karri, red gum and blackbutt
Varieties planted: White—chardonnay, sauvignon blanc, semillon; Red—cabernet franc, merlot, shiraz, cabernet sauvignon
Leading wines: Sinclair Cabernet Sauvignon, Chardonnay, Sauvignon Blanc
Notes: Sinclair Wines has been a consistent winner of silver and bronze awards at capital city and smallmaker wine shows recently. Cellar door tastings by appointment made at home phone.

Stone Bridge Estate R84

Holleys Road, Manjimup, WA 6258
Ph 08 9773 1371, Fax 08 9773 1309,
Email: shooker@gidgenet.com.au

Owners: Sid and Susan Hooker
Chief winemaker: Kate Hooker
Year of foundation: vineyard 1990, first wine produced 1996
Tonnes produced on average each year: 55
Location: Manjimup
Area: 9 ha
Soils: marri gravel

Varieties planted: White—chardonnay, malvasia, sauvignon blanc, semillon; Red—cabernet franc, cabernet sauvignon, malbec, merlot, pinot noir, sangiovese, shiraz

Leading wines: Stone Bridge Estate Cuvee, Cabernet-Merlot, Semillon-Sauvignon Blanc

Notes: An impressive new entrant to the ranks of Manjimup makers, Kate Hooker of Stone Bridge, Champagne-trained, has begun with an excellent Cuvee of Pinot Noir and Chardonnay. Good also are her Semillon-Sauvignon Blanc and Cabernet-Merlot blends, the latter showing the slight smokiness that is often carried by the reds of the Forest regions (i.e. Manjimup and Pemberton). Cellar door sales: by appointment.

Yanmah Ridge **NR**

Yanmah Road, West Manjimup, WA 6258
Ph 08 9772 1301, Fax 08 9772 1501, Email info@yanmahridge.com.au

Owners: Nicholas family
Chief winemaker: Peter Nicholas, John Wade (consultant)
Year of foundation: 1987
Tonnes crushed on average each year: 190, of which 50 are used for Yanmah Ridge wines. The balance of fruit grown is presently sold but may in time be used for Yanmah Ridge wines
Location: West Manjimup
Area: 26 ha
Soils: red gravelly loam, 'marri-jarrah' country
Varieties planted: White—chardonnay, sauvignon blanc, semillon; Red—cabernet franc, cabernet sauvignon, merlot, meunier, pinot noir, sangiovese
Leading wines: Yanmah Ridge Sauvignon Blanc, Chardonnay, Cabernet-Merlot, Merlot, Karrimont (a sparkling)
Notes: Yanmah Ridge uses no residual herbicides or chemical pesticides. A new winery was erected in time for 2001 vintage. Cellar door sales: by appointment.

BLACKWOOD VALLEY REGION

The Blackwood Valley region has followed a familiar Australian rural path: exploration in the 1830s and 1840s, settlement a decade later, grazing and wool production in the later nineteenth century and then timber milling, which still continues in a small way. The area is also known for its development of subterranean clover at Dwalganup in the 1930s. Orcharding was also widespread in Boyup Brook about this time, but receded in the 1960s due to the salination of the Blackwood River and to poor returns. This area remains a rich mixed farming district but again poor economic returns have obliged some farmers to diversify by planting vineyards. Again there are problems due to the salinity of the Blackwood River, so local farmers use surface run-off water, collected in contour banks and dams for this purpose.

The urban centre of the region is Bridgetown, about 30 km west of Boyup Brook. It has a slightly higher rainfall than Boyup Brook, but a similar mixed farming economy. Orcharding still survives here in places as does local tin mining. About 50 km to the west of Bridgetown is Nannup, another mixed farming and grazing community where there are several grapegrowers and a thriving timber milling industry.

The wine history of the region is very recent, dating from 1978 when local farmer Max Fairbrass felt the region might be suitable because of table grapes grown years before by his grandfather. Max planted a 3-hectare vineyard of riesling, semillon, sauvignon

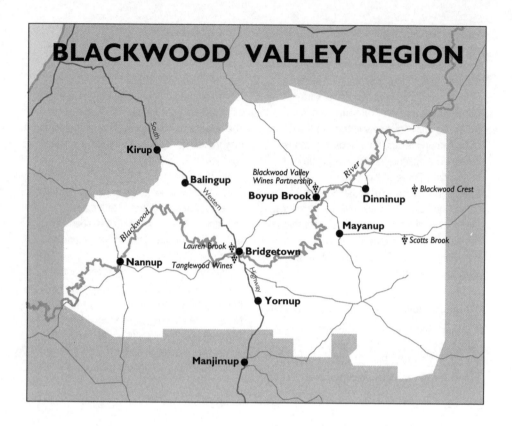

blanc, cabernet sauvignon and shiraz. He was followed in 1987 by Brian and Kerry Walker at Scotts Brook.

The region expanded rapidly at the end of the 20th century and by the year 2005 should be producing in excess of 3000 tonnes.

Location: Bridgetown latitude 33°57'S, longitude 116°07'E, about 212 km south-south-east of Perth

Elevation: Bridgetown 154 m, but the region as a whole varies between 100 m (Nannup) and 340 m (parts of Boyup Brook)

Topography and soils: Most of the area is part of the Darling Plateau Systems, consisting of narrow plateau remnants and moderately incised valleys. Soils here are gravelly on the divides with yellow soils and red earths on valley slopes. Around Bridgetown and part of Nannup are deeply incised valleys with red and yellow earths, rocky outcrops on slopes and narrow alluvial terraces.

Climate: Bridgetown MJT 20.6°C, MAR na, HDD raw 1578, 1492 (cut-off and adjusted for latitude, daily temperature range and vine sites), AR 856 mm (Oct–Apr 219 mm), RH 36%, AI na, SH 7.9 (Gladstones). The Blackwood Valley region has dry summer months and a high winter rainfall. Temperatures are not excessive and it can be called a cool region.

Within the region, rainfall becomes greater as one approaches the coast, the area around Boyup Brook receiving 600–700 mm per annum, Bridgetown 800–900 mm and Nannup 1000–1100 mm. In the Bridgetown–Kirup locality, suitable vine sites (good gravelly loamy soils and good potential for water catchment) do exist but in the past the region has been downgraded by some writers because of an extreme risk of spring frosts due to low humidity, wide temperature variability and poor air drainage.

Max Fairbrass, the third generation of his family in the region, whose Blackwood Crest vineyard is near Boyup Brook some way to the north-east of Bridgetown, remembers many more frosts in his youth and feels that the region is becoming warmer. He has recently backed that judgment by planting more vineyard area. Boyup Brook, higher and drier than Bridgetown with possibly better air drainage, is proving a popular grape-growing area, but even here frost remains a risk and certainly should be taken into account if a vineyard site is being selected. Further west around Nannup, both climatic and soil conditions appear similar to the south-western part of the Geographe region and this area also should be quite suitable for viticulture.

Principal varieties: chardonnay, cabernet sauvignon, shiraz

Harvest time: chardonnay late February to early March, shiraz mid-March, cabernet sauvignon late March to early April

Principal wine styles: It is too soon for any pronouncement, but medium to full-bodied reds made from cabernet sauvignon and shiraz are likely to be prominent

Leading winery: Lauren Brook

Blackwood Crest **NR**

Chambers Road, Boyup Brook, WA 6244
Ph/Fax 08 9767 3029

Owners: Max and Roslynne Fairbrass
Chief winemaker: Max Fairbrass
Year of foundation: 1976
Tonnes crushed on average each year: 50, of which about 15 are used for Blackwood Crest wines
Location: East Boyup Brook
Area: 8 ha
Soils: loamy gravelly soils, typical red gum 'marri' country
Varieties planted: White—chardonnay, riesling, sauvignon blanc, semillon; Red—cabernet sauvignon, pinot noir, shiraz
Leading wines: Blackwood Crest Shiraz, Cabernet Sauvignon
Notes: Max Fairbrass is the pioneer of the region. He feels that the area is 'red' country

and shiraz is a very good variety for the region, but he has not neglected whites. Cellar door sales: 10am–5pm each day.

Blackwood Valley Wine Partnership **NR**

Dwalganup Vineyard, Dwalganup Road and Clark Vineyard, Wagner Road, Boyup Brook, WA 6244
Ph 08 9765 1169, Fax 08 9765 1340

Owners: Blackwood Valley Wine Partnership
Chief winemaker: Ferngrove Winery (contract)
Tonnes produced on average each year: 800, of which 350 tonnes are used for premium bulk wine for sale to the industry
Location: Boyup Brook
Area: 85 ha
Soils: deep loamy gravels over clay (vineyards are planted on gentle slopes with good airflow as a frost prevention measure)

Varieties planted: White—chardonnay, sauvignon blanc; Red—cabernet sauvignon, shiraz
Leading wines: bulk Cabernet Sauvignon
Notes: The partnership is a grower of grapes and a producer of bulk wine for sale to the industry. No cellar door sales.

Lauren Brook R81

Lot 54, Eedle Terrace, Bridgetown, WA 6255 (on the Blackwood River 1.5 km from the centre of town)
Ph 08 9761 2676, Fax 08 9761 1879, Email laurenbrook@bigpond.com.au

Owner: Lauren Brook Winery Pty Ltd
Chief winemaker: Stephen Bullied
Year of foundation: 1993
Tonnes crushed on average each year: 15
Location: Bridgetown (the company owns no vineyards)
Leading wine: Lauren Brook Unwooded Chardonnay
Notes: Lauren Brook is the only winery in Bridgetown, though with the pace of vineyard development in the region generally, it may not remain so for long. Cellar door sales: school holidays, public holidays, weekends and festivals 11am–4pm; at other times Thurs–Sun 11am–4pm.

Scotts Brook NR

Scotts Brook Road, Boyup Brook, WA 6244
Ph 08 9765 3014, Fax 08 9765 3015, Email goodwine@mns.net.au

Owners: Brian and Kerry Walker, Ian Robinson
Chief winemaker: contract

Year of foundation: 1987
Tonnes crushed on average each year: not disclosed but 8.5 tonnes are used for Scotts Brook wines
Location: Boyup Brook
Area: 17.2 ha
Soils: gravelly loam over clay
Varieties planted: White—chardonnay, riesling, sauvignon blanc, semillon; Red—cabernet sauvignon, pinot noir, shiraz
Leading wines: Scotts Brook Cabernet Sauvignon, Chardonnay
Notes: After Blackwood Crest, Scotts Brook is the second most senior vineyard in the Blackwood Valley. No wines have been recently tasted. Cellar door sales: weekends by appointment.

Tanglewood Vines NR

Greenbushes, Boyup Brook Road, Bridgetown, WA 6255
Ph 08 9764 4051, Email twv@iinet.net.au

Owners: Hamish and Caroline Hume
Chief winemaker: (to be appointed)
Tonnes produced on average each year: 2001 was the first crop
Location: Bridgetown
Area: 4.35 ha
Soils: gravelly loams with good drainage
Varieties planted: White—none; Red—cabernet sauvignon, merlot
Leading wines: very likely a Cabernet-Merlot red
Notes: It's early days yet for Tanglewood Vines, which picked its first crop in 2001.

❦ CENTRAL WESTERN AUSTRALIA ZONE

This is a large area of country with few vineyards as yet. It seems 'continental' in nature with hot summers and cold winters. It contains no wine region at present.

Hotham Valley Estate (see Margaret River Region)

Rex Vineyard (vineyard only) **NR**
Beaufort, WA
Ph/Fax 08 9384 3210

Owners: Peter and Gillian Rex
Chief winemaker: Julie White (contract)
Year of foundation: 1991
Tonnes produced on average each year: 16, of which 8 are used for Rex Vineyard wines
Location: Arthur River, Beaufort
Area: 2 ha
Soils: gravelly loamy soils
Varieties planted: White—chardonnay; Red—cabernet sauvignon, merlot, shiraz
Leading wines: Rex Vineyard Cabernet Sauvignon-Shiraz-Merlot (a red blend), Unwooded Chardonnay, Elvira (sparkling wine made by the traditional method)

Notes: No wines have been tasted. Cellar door inquiries may be directed to the above phone/fax no.

Stratherne Vale Estate **NR**
Campbell St, Cuballing, WA 6312
Ph 08 9881 2148, Fax 08 9881 3129

Owners: Gordon and Janette Suckling
Chief winemaker: James Pennington (contract)
Year of foundation: 1980
Tonnes crushed on average each year: 5
Location: Cuballing
Area: 2 ha
Soils: a light red, sandy, clayey loam
Varieties planted: White—none; Red—cabernet sauvignon, merlot, shiraz
Leading wine: Stratherne Vale Red (a blend of the red varieties mentioned above)
Notes: A very small local vineyard with sales only to local bottle shops. No cellar door sales.

❦ GREATER PERTH ZONE

This zone is the cradle of Western Australian viticulture, comprising the Swan Districts wine region, renowned for its fortifieds and rich white wines, and also the much newer and higher Perth Hills region. There is also a proposed Peel wine region located in the southern coastal area of the Zone.

PEEL REGION

Although the region has been settled since time immemorial by aborigines of the Pindjarup dialect group of the Noongar people, the first European settlement occurred soon after the settlement of the Swan River Colony (Perth) in 1829. Under a settlement scheme organised by Mr Thomas Peel, three ships of settlers migrated to areas of land along the coastline from south of Fremantle to Western Australia's Murray River. The fertile soils and grassy plains near Pinjarra attracted those interested in grazing and cropping while some settled near Mandurah for fishing and other activities. In 1846 a lead, silver and zinc mine was established near the present-day Mundijong town site, and this was a portent of other mining activities to occur in the region in the late 20th century. Later in the 19th century, timber-getting and broadacre mixed wheat and sheep farming were important agricultural activities in the east of the region and with the development of railways, timber was transported to Perth for use throughout the colony and for export to the United Kingdom, where hardwood was much in demand for street-paving. The railway also led to the development of Mundijong, Waroona and Dwellingup, which were to become service centres for the timber industry. In other areas of the region, such as Waroona, dairying had assumed a degree of importance by 1930. After World War II, there was a marked increase not only in dairying but also in horticultural production, but from the 1970s onwards Western Australia enjoyed a minerals boom and extractive industries such as mining of large deposits of mineral sands, bauxite and gold have flourished in the region and provide the largest contribution to the regional economy. Today the economic centre of the region is the city of Mandurah. Other centres are Serpentine in the north, Pinjarra and Dwellingup in the central west, Waroona in the south west and Boddington and Wandering in the east.

Though there was a vineyard established near Pinjarra in 1857, which flourished for over 40 years and produced a gold medal for its proprietor at the Melbourne Centenary Exhibition, it was uprooted by the owner's widow in 1898. There was further viticultural activity by Italian migrant families in the towns of Waroona and Harvey in the 1930s, but this was curtailed by the internment of Italians after the commencement of World War II. The first substantial viticultural development within the region occurred in 1976 with the establishment of the first vineyards of Peel Estate by Will Nairn. This was followed by the planting of Baldivis Estate in 1982 and Hotham Valley Estate, near Wandering, by James Pennington in 1982. Since then the region has seen steady growth. Today the region has 138 hectares under vine and a further 71 hectares are planned for the near future.

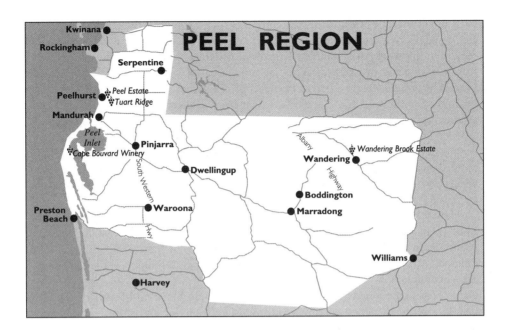

Location: Mandurah latitude 32°30'S, longitude 115°46'E, 62 km south of Perth on the coast of the Indian Ocean; Wandering latitude 32°41'S, longitude 116°40'E, in the east of the region about 125 km south-east of Perth

Elevation: The region rises in altitude from the Indian Ocean coast (sea level) to its highest point, Mount Saddleback near Boddington, 575 m

Topography and soils: The region is generally flat to undulating, except for the steep rise of the Darling Scarp and isolated outcrops such as Mount Saddleback. Its soils vary from the typical 'tuart' sands of the coast through sandy fluvial sediments on the plains near Waroona/Dwellingup to moderately deep yellow duplex soils and loams with stone and gravel (marri-jarrah country) from Boddington to Wandering. The majority of vineyards are on northern or western facing slopes at elevations between 5 m at Baldivis and 290 m near Wandering.

Climate: Mandurah Park MJT 23.1°C, MAR 10.15°C, HDD 1802 (cut off at 19°C but otherwise not adjusted), AR 878 mm (Oct–Apr 173.6 mm), RH 53% (9am Jan), 45% (3pm Jan), AI na, SH na. Wandering comparison MJT 22.75°C, MAR 13.05°C, HDD 1739 (cut off at 19°C but otherwise not adjusted), AR 617 mm (Oct–Apr 156.4mm), RH 50% (9am Jan), 26% (3pm Jan), AI na, SH na.

The Peel region has a warm to hot Mediterranean climate (i.e. warm–hot summers and cool, wet winters). Its coastal summer temperatures are moderated by cooling sea breezes during the afternoon and warm nocturnal easterly winds, which narrow the diurnal temperature range and provide optimal berry development, helping also to prevent mildews and other fungal diseases. Inland the diurnal temperature variation is wider, being about 11°C at Baldivis, up to 14°C on the Darling Scarp at Dwellingup and over 15°C on the Darling Plateau at Boddington.

Rainfall increases from the coast to the Darling Scarp and then decreases to the east at Wandering, but as befits a Mediterranean climate is quite low throughout the region during spring and summer. Irrigation, which is necessary during the growing season, is effected by drippers. The various sources of water are as follows. *Coastal Plain*: The ground water resources of the Coastal Plain are substantial and water may be drawn from several aquifers by bore. The chief aquifers are the Superficial, Leederville, Yarragadee and Cockleshell Gully formations. *Waroona*: Areas between Waroona and Yarloop have access to the South West Irrigation Scheme and land owners in this district have shares in the scheme, each share carrying with it the right to one megalitre of water per annum. Such shares pass with the sale of the land. *Wandering*: Owners of lands east of the Darling Scarp must harvest water run-off into dams for irrigation use.

Hail risk is minimal throughout the region and while frost risk is low near the coast, increasing substantially in areas of poor air drainage and in the east of the region (Boddington and Wandering) because of high diurnal temperature variation.

Principal varieties: White—chardonnay, chenin blanc, semillon, verdelho; Red—cabernet sauvignon, merlot, shiraz

Harvest time: chardonnay mid–late February, sauvignon blanc mid-February, semillon mid–late February, cabernet sauvignon mid-March, merlot and shiraz early to mid-March.

Total area: (2000) 138.7 ha

Principal wine styles: Lighter styles of white and red from the tuart country of the coastal plains; (further inland) full-bodied whites made from chenin blanc, chardonnay, semillon or verdelho or perhaps a blend of all four; ripe red styles from cabernet sauvignon, merlot or shiraz, or again perhaps a blend of all three; fortifieds (if market conditions ever become favourable)

Leading wineries and vineyards: Peel Estate, Cape Bouvard Winery

---

Cape Bouvard Winery   **R84**

Lot 1 Mt John Road, Mandurah,
WA 6210
Ph/Fax 08 9739 1360

Owners: Garry and Sally Greirson
Chief winemaker: Garry Greirson
Year of foundation: vineyard 1987
Tonnes produced on average each year: 40
Location: Mandurah
Area: 3.4 ha, consisting of Mandurah vineyard 1 ha and Donnybrook vineyard 2.4 ha, close planted
Soils: Mandurah, tuart country (deep yellow-brown sand over limestone), alkaline; Donnybrook, rich alluvial loam with lateritic gravel (marri)
Varieties planted: White—chardonnay, chenin blanc, sauvignon blanc, semillon; Red—cabernet sauvignon, shiraz
Leading wines: Cape Bouvard Chardonnay, Tuart Shiraz
Notes: Cape Bouvard does not show its wines. It does not usually have enough quantity. Its Shiraz is made in the traditional way by 'pigeage', which results in a soft medium full red. Its Chardonnay has been well reviewed by *Winestate* and awarded 4.5 stars. Cellar door sales: daily 10am–5pm. Light lunches are available.

Peel Estate **R87**

Fletcher Road, Baldivis, WA 6210
Ph 08 9524 1221, Fax 08 9524 1625

Owner/chief winemaker: Will Nairn
Year of foundation: 1974
Tonnes crushed on average each year: 100
Location: Baldivis
Area: 16 ha
Soils: 'tuart' country, typical deep free-draining
sand over a limestone base
Varieties planted: White—chardonnay, chenin
blanc, verdelho; Red—cabernet franc, cabernet
sauvignon, merlot, shiraz, souzao, tinta
amarella, tina cao, touriga, zinfandel
Leading wines: Peel Estate Wood Matured
Chenin Blanc, Shiraz
Notes: Peel Estate is well known for its soft
and spicy oak-matured Chenin Blanc and
generously flavoured reds. Cellar door sales:
7 days 10am–5pm.

Tuart Ridge **NR**

344 Stakehill Road, Baldivis, WA 6171
Ph/Fax 08 9524 1445,
Email: pfranz@southwest.com.au

Owner/chief winemaker: Phil Franzone
Year of foundation: 1996
Tonnes produced on average each year: 40
Location: Baldivis
Area: 5 ha
Soils: 'tuart' soils (i.e. deep well-drained sands
over limestone)
Varieties planted: White—chardonnay,

verdelho; Red—cabernet sauvignon, grenache,
merlot, shiraz
Leading wines: none yet available, but will be
all varietal (2001 was first vintage)
Notes: Early days yet for Phil Franzoni and Tuart
Ridge. Cellar door sales: weekends 10am–4pm.

Wandering Brook Estate **NR**

Wandering North Road, Wandering,
WA 6308
Ph/Fax 08 9884 1064

Owners: Laurie and Margaret White
Chief winemaker: Paul Radikovich
Year of foundation: 1989
Tonnes crushed on average each year: 50, of
which 20 are used for the Wandering Brook
label
Location: Wandering
Area: 11.5 ha
Soils: gravel and coarse rock all over clay
sloping down to heavy red and grey loam
Varieties planted: White—chardonnay, chenin
blanc, sauvignon blanc, verdelho;
Red—cabernet sauvignon, merlot, shiraz
Leading wines: Wandering Brook Verdelho,
Unwooded Chardonnay, Chardonnay,
Cabernet Sauvignon
Notes: Wandering Brook has established
medal-winning wine standards as local show
results prove, but despite this, according to
Laurie White, sales remain slow. Cellar door
sales: weekends 10am–6pm, weekdays by
appointment, open for morning and afternoon
teas and light lunches.

SWAN DISTRICTS REGION

Settlement of the Swan River colony took place in 1829. From the very first years of settlement, the alluvial flats of the Swan River district were found to be suitable for cereal crops and by 1833 over 500 acres were in cultivation to wheat, barley, oats and maize. In 1830 the townsite of Guildford at the junction of the Swan and Helena Rivers was established. Crops grown on the alluvial soil were carted to Guildford and transported by barge along the Swan to Perth and Fremantle.

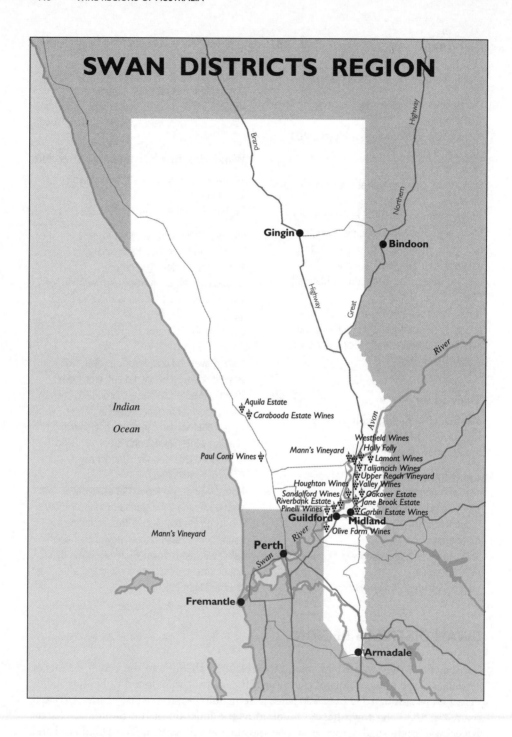

SWAN DISTRICTS REGION

From that time also there was a great interest in the vine, with records of plantings existing as early as 1834 and a wine cellar being dug even earlier by Thomas Waters. Two of the Swan Valley land grants made about that time, Houghton and Sandalford, are today household names in Western Australian viticulture. A large proportion of the early settlers were middle and upper class Anglo-Celtic gentry unused to physical labour, as were other owners of large tracts of land who were retired Army and Navy officers. The result was a substantial shortage of labour in the Swan River colony and so, in 1850, the penal system, never employed in the colony of South Australia and hardly tolerated in Victoria, was introduced into Western Australia. All Western Australian public buildings, roads and bridges after that time and until the cessation of the system were erected by convict labour. Such convicts were frequently given tickets-of-leave and therefore gained employment quite readily as labourers.

Though by 1860 there are records of 400 acres of vines, producing 90 000 litres of wine and nearly 20 tonnes of dried fruit, the founder of the commercial Western Australian wine industry must be said to be Dr John Ferguson who purchased the Houghton Estate in 1859, erecting a wine cellar and expanding the vineyard. By 1885, the York railway had been completed, indirectly causing the eclipse of Guildford as the major trading and transport centre of the Swan. This was because of the decision to site the southern terminus of the railway five kilometres east of Guildford at what is today the major business centre of the region—Midland Junction.

How sparsely would Australia have been populated were it not for goldrushes! As in the eastern colonies of Victoria and New South Wales 40 years earlier, there was an explosion of population caused by the rush to the 'eastern' goldfields of Western Australia in the 1880s and 1890s. It was a rush which came at an opportune time, for it prevented Western Australia experiencing the worst effects of the bank crashes of the early 1890s in the eastern colonies. As the fields declined, many 'diggers' returned to the countryside closer to Perth with money to purchase land. The result was the subdivision of many larger estates in the Swan region and the creation of many small farms, including vineyards. This was a trend accelerated by the end of the First World War and the need to settle returned servicemen. Immigration from central and southern Europe also increased in the 1920s and many of the immigrants brought with them viticultural skills. From about this time good markets for table, drying and, to a lesser extent, wine grapes were established.

By the late 1930s over 2400 hectares of table, drying and wine grapes existed in the Swan Valley, about half of them owned by southern European migrants. Many are still run by their descendants. Though vineyards were chiefly grown for table and drying grapes, the wine industry also thrived. Important names at this time were Houghton, which commenced the production of its famous 'White Burgundy' in the late 1930s, Valencia and Swanville. The area under vine peaked in the 1940s and thereafter declined due to uncertainties in the dried fruit and wine market and also to urban pressures, but this decline now appears to have been arrested.

Until the 1980s, the Swan Valley area, its climate greatly favouring the production of fortified wines, was dotted with small wineries mostly owned by Yugoslav and Italian migrant families who made basic fortified wine, sold in bulk to customers who brought their own containers. But with the swing in public taste to fresher styles of table wine, bulk sales of fortified are becoming more difficult and the wineries formerly making fortifieds are themselves offering a wider range of table wines.

Today, due to the proximity of the city of Perth, the Swan Valley wine industry has limited opportunity for expansion, which has swung from the east to the north, Moondah Brook at Gin Gin. In addition there are vineyards at Bindoon and Chittering, though due to their altitude, these areas may become part of the proposed wine region of Perth Hills. The region as proposed falls into three sub-areas: the Valley floor (the area north from Guildford); Moondah Brook and Lennards Brook; and Wanneroo and the northern beaches.

Location: Guildford latitude 31°53'S, longitude 116°01'E, about 15 km north-east of Perth

Elevation: 8 m with most Valley plantings less than 60 m above sea-level

Topography and soils: The Swan Districts region is relatively flat to slightly undulating with several distinct types of soils. In its northern coastal strip (around Wanneroo) there is the typical 'tuart' country (deep free-draining sands over limestone). To the east as the Darling Scarp is approached there is the drainage basin of the Swan and here, on its western perimeter, the Valley is flat with coastal sands grading to deep reddish sandy loams forming the river terraces. These young alluvial soils are quite suitable for viticulture. Fringing these soils are grey-brown sands overlying clays, while between this area and the gravelly sands adjacent to the Scarp, there are poorly drained soils much less suited to viticulture.

Climate: (1) Guildford MJT 24.1°C, MAR na, HDD raw 2396, 1826 (adjusted for latitude and daily temperature range, but not for vine sites), AR 865 mm (Oct–Apr 220 mm), RH 40% (3pm Jan), AI na, SH 9.2 (Gladstones).

The Swan Valley is a very hot area, tending to favour the production of fortified wines and drying grapes, especially currants. It is cooled in summer generally from noon onwards by a south-west sea breeze, famous in cricketing circles as the Fremantle Doctor, and as the Valley extends to the north-east it is naturally favoured by this breeze. However, rich full-bodied whites and reds can be made, but they generally lack the freshness and fruit qualities of cooler areas. If such grapes are not stressed during ripening, they make up in body and softness what they lack in fruit freshness. If stressed, the reds become porty and jammy and generally lack structure. The whites, generally more successful, are made from verdelho, chenin blanc and chardonnay. So the Swan Valley vigneron, if intent on making finer styles of table wines, generally hopes for a cooler than average vintage.

In the northern part of the region around Gin Gin (Moondah Brook and Lennards Brook), the vineyard elevations are slightly higher, thus compensating in heat factors for the higher latitude. The Fremantle Doctor has a very beneficial effect here, too. As exemplified by the Houghton Moondah Brook table wines, the fruit grown there has always proved to be of very high quality.

(2) Wanneroo (Perth Obs) MJT 23.5°C, MAR na, HDD raw 2264, 1815 (adjusted for latitude and daily temperature range but not for vine sites), AR 883 mm (Oct–Apr 176 mm), RH 43% (3pm Jan), AI na, SH 9.2 (G).

This is the coastal strip of the Swan Districts region. Its predominant soil is 'tuart', deep sand over limestone, a frequently occurring soil type from Yanchep (north of Wanneroo) south as far as Bunbury and Busselton. It is arguable that on the basis of this soil type there should be a Western Australian 'South West Coastal' region, but it would be disparate in location and its climate would not be uniform. During its growing season, Wanneroo would seem to be fractionally cooler than other parts of Swan Districts, being favoured by strong south-west sea breezes. From my own experience of Paul Conti's Shiraz reds, its styles are lighter and softer, and this may result from the combination of lighter soils and slightly cooler climate.

In the Swan Districts region water for irrigation presents difficulties. Traditionally water has been sourced from bores as the Swan River was tidal and saline as far as Upper Swan. Shallow bores (less than 100 m in depth) have become saline in recent years and access to deeper reserves is tightly regulated due to urban demand. Most of the traditional Swan Valley vineyards are dry-grown, but growers with access to the Leederville aquifer (deeper than 100 m) enjoy good quality water which is rather high in iron content.

In the north of the region around Gin Gin, high quality water is available from Moondah Brook and is sufficient to irrigate over 90 ha of vines, whereas on the coast water can be sourced from shallow bores (less than 100 m in depth), but because of pressure from urbanisation, many vineyards are dry-grown.

Harvest time: chardonnay and verdelho mid-February, chenin blanc and shiraz late February, cabernet sauvignon first week of March

Principal varieties: In its youth chenin blanc shows appley, citrusy and tropical characters and is the leading variety of the Swan Districts region, dominating the plantings here. In this hot climate, whether on its own or in a blend, it produces rich and luscious wine which responds well to bottle age (such as Houghton White Burgundy, of which chenin was traditionally a part) and is often not at its best until 5–7 years old. It may be wooded or unwooded.

Verdelho, when vinified as a table wine, displays sherbety aromas and flavours when young. It is normally not oaked as it is considered to be an aromatic variety. With bottle age it becomes more complex, displaying honeysuckle and tropical characters. It can also be used as a dessert wine, as it commonly was until about 1970.

Chardonnay is as successful in the Swan Districts as in any other hot area of Australia, producing typically peachy aromas and flavours which are sometimes a little 'hot'.

Major wine styles: See principal varieties (above). Historically one style stands out above all others of the region and that is Houghton White Burgundy, a full-bodied white blend usually blended from 50% chenin blanc, 15–20% chardonnay, 15% muscadelle and smaller percentages of semillon and verdelho.

Leading wineries and vineyards: Houghton, Sandalford

Aquila Estate R80

85 Carabooda Road, Carabooda,
WA 6033
Phone 08 9561 8166, Fax 08 9561 8177,
Email aquila@pertwa.com.au

Owners: Washer family
Chief winemaker: Andrew Spencer-Wright
(contract)
Year of foundation: 1993
Tonnes crushed on average each year: 350
Location: Carabooda. No vineyards are owned,
but fruit is purchased from Blackwood Valley
and Margaret River and varieties purchased
include chardonnay, chenin blanc, sauvignon
blanc and semillon in whites and cabernet
sauvignon, merlot, pinot noir and shiraz in
reds Leading wines: Aquila Estate Cabernet
Sauvignon, Chardonnay, Flame (a light red
blend)
Notes: If you wish to identify Aquila, it is the
winery in Carabooda Road next to the avocado
plantation. I have located Aquila in Swan
Districts because of the location of its winery
and its proximity to Perth (Carabooda is a 30
minute drive to the north of the city). The fruit
for its wines originates in Blackwood Valley
and Margaret River and is either trucked to the
winery from these regions overnight or
crushed and settled and the juice tankered to
the winery. The strength here is Cabernet
Sauvignon. Cellar door sales are planned for
late 2001 but ring ahead.

Carabooda Estate Wines NR

297 Carabooda Road, Carabooda,
WA 6033
Ph/Fax 08 9407 5283,
Email carabooda@aol.com.au

Owners: Terry and Simonne Ord
Chief winemaker: Terry Ord
Year of foundation: 1979
Tonnes produced on average each year: 20
Location: Carabooda

Area: 3 ha
Soils: 'tuart' sands
Varieties planted: White—chardonnay,
sauvignon blanc; Red—cabernet sauvignon,
shiraz
Leading wine: Carabooda Estate Cabernet
Sauvignon
Notes: Carabooda Estate is a 'tuart' sands
vineyard, which is likely to produce supple
reds, though nothing has been tasted.
Cellar door sales: daily 10am–6pm.

Garbin Estate Wines NR

209 Toodyay Road, Middle Swan,
WA 6056
Ph/Fax 08 9274 1747,
Email binwine1@bigpond.com

Owners: Garbin family
Chief winemaker: Peter Garbin; Andrew
Spencer-Wright (consultant)
Year of foundation: 1956
Tonnes crushed on average each year: 50
Locations: Middle Swan (vineyard and cellar
door), Gin Gin (vineyard)
Area: 27.5 ha consisting of Middle Swan
2.5 ha, Gin Gin 25 ha
Soils: Middle Swan sandy clay, Gin Gin red
loam with intermixed gravel
Varieties planted: White—chardonnay, chenin
blanc, semillon, verdelho; Red—cabernet
sauvignon, merlot, shiraz
Leading wines: Garbin Estate Chardonnay,
Cabernet Sauvignon-Merlot, Chenin, Shiraz
Notes: Good standards are kept here. The
show results show chiefly bronze awards with
good wine magazine reviews, but there are
also the occasional trophy and gold and silver
at the local Swan Valley show. Cellar door
sales: daily 10.30am–5.30pm.

Holly Folly **NR**

649 Campersic Road, Baskerville,
WA 6056
Ph/Fax 08 9296 2043

Owners: Peter, Liz and Alison Hollingworth
Chief winemaker: Peter Hollingworth
Year of foundation: 1995
Tonnes produced on average each year: 4,
of which 2 are used for Holly Folly wines
(the vineyard is not yet fully bearing)
Location: Baskerville
Area: 6 ha
Soils: Loton gravel and Oakover gravel, alluvial
Varieties planted: White—chardonnay, chenin
blanc, marsanne, verdelho, viognier;
Red—grenache, merlot, petit verdot
Leading wines: Holly Folly Barrel Fermented
Verdelho, Traditional Method Sparkling,
Marsanne, Viognier, Light Red
Notes: There is both tradition and innovation
at Holly Folly. The emphasis on whites and the
planting of chenin blanc and verdelho are
traditional, the planting of white varieties such
as viognier and marsanne quite innovative.
Certainly as the vines mature, there will be
interesting whites. No cellar door sales.
Sales by mail order.

Houghton Wines **R86**

Dale Road, Middle Swan, WA 6056
Ph 08 9274 5100, Fax 08 9250 3872,
Email corporate@brlhardy.com.au

Owner: BRL Hardy Ltd
Chief winemaker: Larry Cherubino
Year of foundation: 1836
Tonnes crushed on average each year: not
disclosed but estimated at 5000 tonnes, all of
which are used for Houghton wines or related
brands
Locations: Middle Swan (vineyards only at
other locations)
Area: 455.8 ha consisting of 60 ha (Houghton
Middle Swan), 142 ha (Moondah Brook, Gin

Gin) 90 ha (Netley Brook, Frankland River),
other contracted vineyards 73 ha (Omrah,
Mount Barker) and 90.8 ha (Pemberton)
Soils: Middle Swan, sand (called locally 'Herne
Hill' sand) about 20 cm deep over clay;
Moondah Brook, deep sands, called locally
'Gin Gin' sands; Netley Brook, 'karri' loam;
Omrah, Mount Barker, 'marri', gravelly loams
over clay; Pemberton, 'karri' loam
Varieties planted: (Middle Swan)
White—chardonnay, chenin blanc, sauvignon
blanc, semillon, verdelho; Red—none.
(Moondah Brook) White—chardonnay, chenin
blanc, muscadelle, verdelho; Red—cabernet
sauvignon, shiraz. (Netley Brook)
White—chardonnay, riesling, semillon,
verdelho; Red—cabernet sauvignon, malbec,
merlot, pinot noir, shiraz. (Omrah)
White—chardonnay, sauvignon blanc;
Red—cabernet sauvignon, shiraz. (Pemberton)
White—chardonnay, sauvignon blanc,
verdelho; Red—cabernet sauvignon, merlot,
pinot noir
Leading wines: Moondah Brook range,
Houghton range, Crofters range
Notes: Once by far the largest winery in the
west, but about to be challenged in the next
few vintages by several in Margaret River,
Houghton is the production centre for all BRL
Hardy's Western Australian fruit wherever it
originates. Except for Moondah Brook, which
makes fine reds, its wines are mostly multi-
regional WA blends. Cellar door sales: daily
10am–5pm.

Jane Brook Estate **R81**

229 Toodyay Road, Middle Swan,
WA 6056
Ph 08 9274 1432, Fax 08 9274 1211,
Email janewine@highway1.com.au

Owners: David and Beverley Atkinson
Chief winemaker: Julie White
Year of foundation: 1972
Tonnes crushed on average each year: 220

Locations: (vineyard, winery and cellar door sales) Middle Swan, (vineyard) Margaret River
Area: 45 ha consisting of 15 ha (Middle Swan vineyard), 30 ha (Margaret River vineyard)
Soils: Middle Swan, sandy gravel over clay; Margaret River, gravelly loam
Varieties planted: (Middle Swan) White—chardonnay, chenin blanc, sauvignon blanc, verdelho; Red—cabernet franc, cabernet sauvignon, merlot, shiraz. (Margaret River) White—sauvignon blanc; Red—cabernet sauvignon
Leading wines: Jane Brook Pemberton Swan Valley Sauvignon Blanc, James Vineyard Verdelho, James Vineyard Chardonnay, Mountjoy Cabernet-Merlot
Notes: Jane Brook Estate has a consistent award-winning record at wine shows, especially at the Swan Valley Wine Show where it won three trophies, a gold and four silvers in 1999. Cellar door sales: daily noon–5pm.

Lamont Wines NR

Bisdee Road, Millendon, WA 6056
Ph 08 9296 4485, Fax 08 9296 1663

Owner: Corin Lamont
Chief winemaker: Mark Warren
Year of foundation: 1978
Tonnes crushed on average each year: 90 (in addition to the vineyard production, fruit is purchased from local growers)
Location: Millendon
Area: 5 ha
Soils: sandy loams to gravelly loams
Varieties planted: White—muscadelle, navera, verdelho; Red—cabernet sauvignon, shiraz
Leading wine: Lamont Family Reserve (red)
Notes: In Perth, Lamont is a name synonymous with wine and food quality. Not only is there a restaurant at the winery, but there are also a take-away food shop and catering service in the city and another restaurant on the waterfront at East Perth. Corin Lamont is the

daughter of the late Jack Mann, for many years chief winemaker at Houghton, whose winemaking philosophy, shared by his daughter, favoured full-flavoured table and fortified wines. Cellar door sales: Wed–Sun 10am–5pm.

Mann's Vineyard NR

105 Memorial Avenue, Baskerville, WA 6056
Ph/Fax 08 9296 4348

Owners: Dorham and Sally Mann
Chief winemaker: Dorham Mann
Year of foundation: 1988
Tonnes crushed on average each year: 9
Location: Baskerville
Area: 3 ha
Soils: red alluvial soil on a high river terrace
Varieties planted: White—none; Red—cabernet sauvignon
Leading wine: Mann (a sparkling cabernet sauvignon made by the Champagne method)
Notes: Located on a high bank with scenic views of the Valley, the Mann cuverie is owned by former Sandalford winemaker and expert adviser to the WA industry Dorham Mann. It makes just one wine—a sparkling cabernet sauvignon. Cellar door sales: daily 10am–5pm.

Moondah Brook (see Houghton Wines)

Oakover Estate NR

14 Yukich Close, Middle Swan, WA 6056
Ph 08 9274 0777, Fax 08 9274 0788, Email Graeme_Yukich@poyntons.com.au

Owners: Mark, Graeme and Kim Yukich
Chief winemaker: Julie White (contract)
Year of foundation: 1990
Tonnes produced on average each year: 400, of which 40 are used for Oakover Estate wines
Location: Middle Swan
Area: 42 ha

Soils: loam and clay
Varieties planted: White—chardonnay, chenin
blanc, verdelho; Red—shiraz
Leading wines: Oakover Estate Chardonnay,
Verdelho, Shiraz
Notes: For the area, this is quite a large
vineyard, and one which sells most of its fruit.
No wines have been tasted. Cellar door sales:
Fri–Sun 11am–5pm.

Olive Farm Wines NR

77 Great Eastern Highway, South
Guildford, WA 6055
Ph 08 9277 2989, Fax 08 9277 6828

Owner/chief winemaker: Ian Yurisich
Year of foundation: 1829
Tonnes crushed on average each year: 70
Location: South Guildford (winery and cellar
door), Upper Swan (vineyard)
Area: 14 ha
Soils: deep alluvial loam on a clay base
Varieties planted: White—chardonnay, chenin
blanc, gewurztraminer, sauvignon blanc,
semillon, verdelho; Red—cabernet sauvignon,
cabernet franc, pinot noir, merlot, shiraz
Leading wines: Olive Farm Chardonnay,
Cabernet-Shiraz-Merlot
Notes: Though it has not been continuously
used as such, Olive Farm can justly claim to be
the oldest wine cellar still in use in Australia.
Cellar door sales: Mon–Fri 10am–5.30pm,
weekends 11am–3pm.

Paul Conti Wines NR

529 Wanneroo Road, Woodvale,
WA 6026
Ph 08 9409 9160, Fax 08 9309 1634,
Email conti@eepo.com.au

Owners: Paul and Anne Conti
Chief winemaker: Paul Conti
Year of foundation: 1948
Tonnes crushed on average each year: 150,
which includes grapes purchased

Location: (winery, cellar door) Woodvale;
(vineyards) Woodvale, Mariginiup, Carabooda
Area: 23 ha
Soils: all three vineyards, 'tuart' sands (i.e. deep
free-draining sands over limestone)
Varieties planted: White—chardonnay, chenin
blanc, muscat gordo blanco, sauvignon blanc;
Red—cabernet sauvignon, grenache, pinot
noir, shiraz
Leading wines: Paul Conti The Tuarts
Chardonnay, Mariginiup Shiraz
Notes: Paul Conti is one of the top makers of
this area which, as noted above, is quite
different in its soils to the rest of the Swan
region. Except for some of the larger, better-
resourced wineries, his wines have more finesse
and suppleness than most of their colleagues in
the Swan, yet age well over 3–5 years. It is
noteworthy also that, in the 1970s, he made
some of the earliest wines from the Mount
Barker sub-region. Cellar door sales: Mon–Sat
9.30am–5.30pm, closed Sundays.

Pinelli Wines NR

30 Bennett St, Caversham, WA 6055
Ph 08 9279 6818, Fax 08 9377 4259

Owners: Pinelli family
Chief winemaker: Robert Pinelli
Year of foundation: 1979
Tonnes crushed on average each year: 180
Locations: (vineyard, winery) Caversham;
(vineyard) Middle Swan
Area: 2.8 ha (Caversham), 5.2 ha (Middle
Swan)
Soils: swan loam and alluvial red clay
Varieties planted: White—chenin blanc,
chardonnay, semillon, verdelho; Red—cabernet
sauvignon, merlot, shiraz
Leading wines: Pinelli Chardonnay, Chenin
Blanc, Cabernet Sauvignon
Notes: Pinelli is another Swan winemaker
making the transition from bulk wines to
specialised table wines and, by its show results,
making an excellent job of it. At the Royal

Perth Wine Show, Pinelli has won one gold, three silvers and 15 bronzes in several show outings. Cellar door sales: Coversham 7 days 10am–5pm.

River Bank Estate NR

126 Hamersley Road, Caversham, WA 6055
Ph 08 9377 1805, Fax 08 9377 2168, Email rjb@vianet.net.au

Owners: Robert Bond and Lyn Amery
Chief winemaker: Robert Bond
Year of foundation: 1992
Tonnes crushed on average each year: 65, but it is anticipated that the crop will rise to 200 tonnes by 2005
Location: Caversham
Area: 13 ha
Soils: alluvial gravels and clays
Varieties planted: White—chardonnay, chenin blanc, verdelho; Red—cabernet franc, cabernet sauvignon, grenache, merlot, pinot noir, shiraz, zinfandel
Leading wines: RiverBank Estate Cabernet, Verdelho
Notes: No wines have been tasted. Cellar door sales: weekends and public holidays 10am–5pm.

Sandalford Wines R83

3210 West Swan Road, Caversham, WA 6055
Ph 08 9274 5922, Fax 08 9274 2154, Email sandalford@sandalford.com

Owners: Peter and Debra Prendiville
Chief winemaker: Paul Boulden
Year of foundation: 1840
Tonnes crushed on average each year: 600 (from Caversham and surrounds), but a further 1200 tonnes are crushed from the company's vineyard in Margaret River (qv) and two other contracted vineyards in Mount Barker and Frankland River

Location: Caversham
Area: 25 ha Caversham vineyard, 54 ha Landsdale (contract), 82 ha Frankland River (contract)
Soils: Caversham, alluvial and grey clay over white clay
Varieties planted: White—chenin blanc, semillon, verdelho; Red—cabernet sauvignon, shiraz
Leading wines: Sandalford Sandalera (a fortified dessert wine), Caversham Chenin-Verdelho, Caversham Cabernet-Shiraz (fruit from Caversham accounts for about 60% of the Caversham range)
Notes: Sandalford is one of Western Australia's older and larger vineyards, founded by the Roe family in 1840 and owned by it for many years. Its strengths are reds and fortified (Sandalera), though it has a full range of table wines. Cellar door sales: daily 10am–5pm. There is also a restaurant and access by boat to its vineyard on the Swan River.

Talijancich Wines NR

26 Hyem Road, Herne Hill, WA 6056
Ph 08 9296 4289, Fax 08 9296 1762, Email james@taliwine.com.au

Owners: James and Hilda Talijancich
Chief winemaker: James Talijancich
Year of foundation: 1932
Tonnes crushed on average each year: 150 (includes fruit purchased from outside growers)
Location: Herne Hill
Area: 6 ha
Soils: sandy gravel on a clay base
Varieties planted: White—muscadelle, semillon, verdelho, viognier; Red—graciano, grenache, shiraz
Leading wines: Talijancich Julian James White Liqueur (a blend of muscadelle, verdelho and semillon), Julian James Red Liqueur (basically shiraz with small quantities of grenache and cabernet), Voices Dry White (a premium blend of chardonnay, chenin and semillon), Grenache, Shiraz

Notes: Over the years Talijancich has built up a deserved reputation for the production of high quality fortified wines. Cellar door sales: Sun–Fri 11am–5pm, closed Sat.

Upper Reach Vineyard **NR**

77 Memorial Ave, Baskerville, WA 6056
Ph 08 9296 0078, Fax 08 9296 0278,
Email upperreach@ozemail.com.au

Owners: D & L Pearse and N & H Pearse
Chief winemaker: Dorham Mann (contract)
Year of foundation: 1996
Tonnes produced on average each year: 80, of which 30 are used for Upper Reach wines
Location: Baskerville
Area: 10 ha
Soils: rich river loams
Varieties planted: White—chardonnay, verdelho; Red—cabernet sauvignon, merlot, shiraz
Leading wines: Upper Reach Unwooded Chardonnay, Reserve Chardonnay, Shiraz, Cabernet Sauvignon
Notes: It is early days yet for Upper Reach, but its owners obviously enjoy their chosen life, and have planned well. Cellar door sales: weekends and public holidays 11am–5pm.

Valley Wines **NR**

352 Lennard Street, Herne Hill, WA 6056
Ph 08 9296 4416, Fax 08 9296 1147,
Email zannino@iinet.net.au

Owners: Charlie and Sally Zannino
Chief winemaker: Charlie Zannino
Year of foundation: 1973
Tonnes produced on average each year: 75
Location: Herne Hill
Area: 16 ha
Soils: sandy gravel at the foothills of the Darling Ranges

Varieties planted: White—chardonnay, chenin blanc, pedro ximenes; Red—grenache, shiraz
Leading wines: ValleyWines Shiraz, Grenache
Notes: Wine is available in 25-litre containers for home bottling. Cellar door sales: daily 8am–6pm.

Westfield Wines **NR**

180 Memorial Ave, Baskerville, WA 6056
Ph/Fax 08 9296 4356

Owner/chief winemaker: John Kosovich
Year of foundation: 1922
Tonnes crushed on average each year: 90
Location: Baskerville; Manjimup/Warren Valley Bronze Wing vineyard
Area: 5.6 ha at Baskerville and 5.2 ha at Bronze Wing
Soils: Baskerville, alluvial sandy gravelly clay; Bronze Wing, deep gravelly loam, jarrah-marri country, well-drained over light gravelly clay
Varieties planted: (Baskerville)
White—chardonnay, chenin blanc, riesling, semillon, verdelho;
Red—cabernet sauvignon, merlot, shiraz.
(Bronze Wing) White—chardonnay, verdelho; Red—cabernet franc, cabernet sauvignon, merlot, shiraz
Leading wines: Westfield Bronze Wing Chardonnay, Verdelho, Merlot, Shiraz. Westfield (Swan Valley) Chardonnay, Verdelho, Cabernet Sauvignon, Liqueur Muscat
Notes: Westfield Wines is a consistent producer of wines of quality. At the Perth Wine Show it has twice (1996 and 1997) been most successful exhibitor in the 'under 300 tonnes produced' category. It also produces Chardonnays of complexity and style as well as that Swan Valley speciality, Liqueur Muscat. Cellar door sales: 7 days 10am–4pm.

PERTH HILLS REGION

As a wine region, the Perth Hills extends from Bindoon in the north of the Darling Scarp to the Serpentine reservoir in the south. It is neatly divided into two by the Great Eastern Highway. Bindoon and the Chittering Valley are the most important viticultural sectors of the northern part, while Kalamunda and Mundaring are the commercial centres of the southern part and around these towns are the vineyards most proximate to the city of Perth (except, of course, for those of the Swan Valley).

The area now called Kalamunda was first settled in 1839 when Benjamin Robbins began farming nearby. Timber-getting from the local jarrah forests also became a thriving industry later in the nineteenth century and during the first half of the twentieth, but the town itself was not founded until the year of Federation, 1901. About two years later, during the construction of the Mundaring Reservoir on the Helena River to supply water to Kalgoorlie 600 km away, the town of Mundaring was also established. In addition to timber-getting, early settlers noticed the fertility of the region's valleys and lower slopes and the abundance of water and so, in the early twentieth century, a fruit and vegetable growing industry thrived. The end of the First World War also saw returned soldiers settled on smallholdings and they too mostly turned to horticulture.

The first vineyard and winery in the southern part of the region was established in the 1880s and produced wine for almost 60 years until the winery was burnt down in 1945. The original Darlington Vineyard gave its name to a railway siding which ultimately became a town. There were also vines planted at Kalamunda at the turn of the century.

The modern era of viticulture in the region began in 1969 with the foundation of the Woodthorpe Vineyard near Parkerville. The vineyard is planted on 'marri' country and, now over a quarter of a century old, is the veteran vineyard of the Perth Hills. Woodhenge Vineyard in the Bickley Valley followed, being planted in 1974. At the present time there are more than 17 vineyards planted to wine grapes in the southern part of Perth Hills.

Location: Kalamunda latitude 31°59'S, longitude 116°03'E about 30 km east of Perth
Elevation: 100 m (western boundary of the region) to 405 m, with vineyard sites located between 150 and 400 m in the southern part of the region, while in the northern part (Bindoon) vineyards are situated between 100 and 200 m in altitude
Topography and soils: The region forms a strip of undulating country between the coastal plain and the low rainfall wheat belt of Western Australia. Briefly it can be described as the northern and central parts of the Darling Scarp. Natural vegetation is jarrah and red gum hardwood forest. Vineyard soils fall into two main groups. On hilltops and upper slopes, there are gravels with medium to light loam content, whereas the valleys consist of mostly loams and alluvial soils. On the lower slopes, both types are present. All soils overlie white granitic quartz clays at depths from half a metre to three metres.

The natural fertility of these soils is low and needs to be assisted by artificial fertiliser. However, where soils have previously been planted to orchards, which were

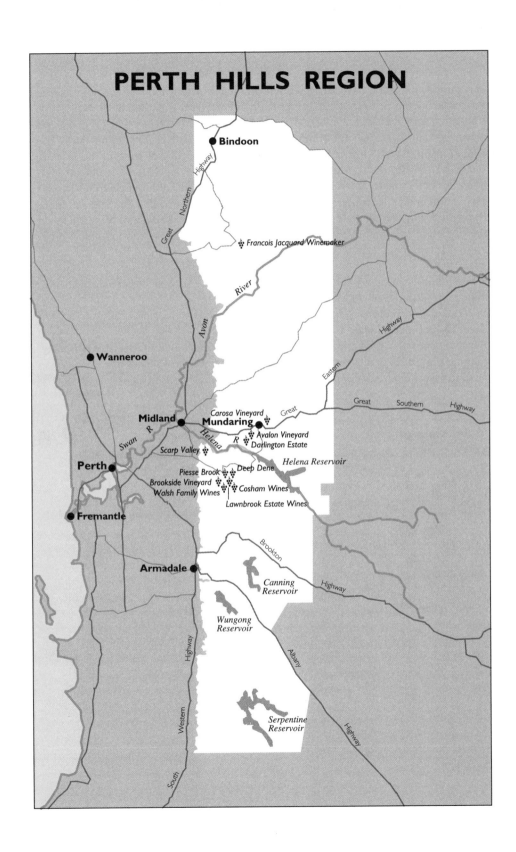

PERTH HILLS REGION

Bindoon

Francois Jacquard Winemaker

River

Avon

Great Northern Highway

Wanneroo

Midland

Carosa Vineyard

Mundaring

Scarp Valley

Avalon Vineyard

Darlington Estate

Helena

R

Helena Reservoir

Great

Great Southern Highway

Eastern Highway

Deep Dene

Piesse Brook

Brookside Vineyard

Walsh Family Wines

Cosham Wines

Lawnbrook Estate Wines

Perth

Swan

R

Fremantle

Armadale

Brookton

Canning Reservoir

Highway

Albany

Wungong Reservoir

Serpentine Reservoir

Highway

Western

South

usually heavily fertilised, such soils are quite fertile. Overall, because of the underlying clay subsoil, soils tend to retain good moisture levels throughout the growing season, thus reducing but not eliminating completely the need for irrigation at that time.

Climate: Kalamunda MJT 23.3°C, MAR 11.6°C, HDD 1769 (cut-off at 19°C but not otherwise adjusted), AR 1069 mm (Oct–Apr 220 mm), RH 55% (9am Jan). The climate of the Perth Hills is typically Mediterranean (cool wet winters and hot dry summers). Within the southern part of the region, however, there is significant variation in microclimate. Within deep or elevated valleys, sub-zero temperatures (frosts) are commonplace in winter and spring and, because of its elevation, temperatures throughout the year are lower than in the adjoining hot coastal plain. Nevertheless it must be classified as a hot area. Irrigation is from dams and bores on individual properties. Hungry birds can also present problems when grapes ripen before the native gums flower.

Harvest time: chardonnay last week of February, shiraz last week of February, cabernet sauvignon second week of March.

Principal varieties: cabernet sauvignon, shiraz, chardonnay, pinot noir

Area: 75 ha (not including Bindoon and Chittering)

Principal wine styles: too early to be dogmatic but soft medium to full-bodied reds made from merlot, shiraz and cabernet sauvignon appear to be most successful

Leading winery and vineyard: Francois Jacquard Winemaker, Deep Dene

---

Avalon Vineyard   **NR**

1605 Bailey Road, Glen Forrest,
WA 6071
Ph 08 9298 8049,
Email lindup@primus.com.au

Owners: Geoff Lindup
Chief winemaker: Rob Marshall (contract)
Year of foundation: 1986
Tonnes produced on average each year: 8, of which 3 are used for Avalon's own labels
Location: Glen Forrest
Area: 2 ha
Soils: gravel and loam on a south-facing slope
Varieties planted: White—chardonnay, semillon; Red—cabernet sauvignon, merlot
Leading wines: Avalon Cabernet-Merlot, Cane-cut Semillon
Notes: Geoff Lindup is very pleased by a best red award for his Cabernet-Merlot at a recent Perth Hills wine show. Cellar door sales by appointment.

Brookside Vineyard   **NR**

Aldersyde Road, Bickley, WA 6076
Ph 08 9291 8705, Fax 08 9291 5316

Owners: Lorna and Lionel Penketh
Chief winemaker: Darlington Estate (contract)
Year of foundation: 1984
Tonnes crushed on average each year: 6
Location: Bickley
Area: 0.5 ha
Soils: gravelly loam with some clay
Varieties planted: White—chardonnay; Red—cabernet sauvignon
Leading wines: Brookside Chardonnay, Cabernet Sauvignon, Methode Champenoise
Notes: This is a small family-run Perth Hills vineyard. Cellar door sales: weekends and public holidays 11am–5pm. There is also bed and breakfast accommodation.

Carosa Vineyard NR

310 Houston Street, Mount Helena,
WA 6082
Ph 08 9572 1603, Fax 08 9572 1604

Owners: Jim and Carole Elson
Chief winemaker: Jim Elson
Year of foundation: 1984
Tonnes crushed on average each year: 15
Location: Mount Helena
Area: 2 ha, but not yet fully bearing
Soils: deep sandy loam over clay, sandy loams
over soft 'coffee' rock
Varieties planted: White—chardonnay, riesling,
semillon; Red—cabernet sauvignon, merlot,
pinot noir, shiraz
Leading wines: Carosa Cabernet-Merlot, Pinot
Noir, Classic Dry White, Chardonnay
Notes: A small vineyard and winery to which
former Seppelt winemaker Jim Elson is
devoting his retirement. Cellar door sales:
weekends and public holidays 11am–5pm,
otherwise by appointment.

Cosham Wines NR

101 Union Road, Carmel, WA 6076
Ph 08 9293 5424, 08 9293 5459,
Fax 08 9293 5062,
Email cosham@highway1.com.au

Owners: Rod, Maxinne and Anthony Sclanders
Chief winemaker: Jane Brook (contract)
Year of foundation: 1989
Tonnes crushed on average each year: 17
Location: Carmel
Area: 2 ha
Soils: gravelly loam on quite a steep slope,
close-planted vines, running east–west
Varieties planted: White—chardonnay;
Red—cabernet sauvignon, merlot, pinot noir,
with small quantities of cabernet franc, petit
verdot and shiraz
Leading wines: Cosham Cabernet-Merlot, Pinot
Noir, Chardonnay, Methode Champenoise
Notes: A small family vineyard with a consistent

bronze award standard at smaller wine shows.
Cellar door sales: weekends and public holidays
10am–5pm. At other times by appointment.

Darlington Estate NR

Lot 39 Nelson Road, Darlington,
WA 6070
Ph 08 9299 6268, Fax 08 9299 7017

Owners: Balt and Francesca van der Meer
Chief winemaker: John Griffiths
Year of foundation: 1983
Tonnes crushed on average each year: 45,
about 30 of which are used for Darlington
Estate wines
Location: Darlington
Area: 8 ha
Soils: well-drained loams on terraced slopes
Varieties planted: White—chardonnay,
sauvignon blanc, semillon; Red—cabernet
sauvignon, merlot, shiraz
Leading wines: Darlington Estate Chardonnay,
Cabernet Sauvignon, Shiraz
Notes: Darlington Estate is now one of the
veterans of the Perth Hills and has enjoyed
great show success over the years. Cellar door
sales: Thurs–Sun noon–5pm. There is a
restaurant open between the same hours and
for dinner Fri–Sat from 7pm.

Deep Dene R84

27 Glenisla Road, Bickley, WA 6076
Ph/Fax 08 9293 0077,
Email info@deepdenewines.com.au

Owner: Deep Dene Pty Ltd
Chief winemaker: Peter Fimmel
Year of foundation: 1994
Tonnes crushed on average each year: 45, of
which 25 are used for Deep Dene wines
Location: Bickley
Area: 5 ha
Soils: gravelly loam on a steep slope
Varieties planted: White—none; Red—pinot
noir, shiraz

Leading wines: Deep Dene Brut Blanc de Noir, Pinot Noir

Notes: After many years at Hainault Vineyard for Perth Hills veteran, Peter Fimmel, Deep Dene is a new challenge for him and his fellow shareholders. Its priority is sparkling wine and it aims to produce 4000 cases per year. Cellar door sales by appointment.

Francois Jacquard Winemaker R86

130 Townshend Road, Subiaco, WA 6008
Ph/Fax 08 9380 9199,
Email jacwine@q-net.net.au

Owner/chief winemaker: Francois Jacquard
Year of foundation: 1997
Tonnes crushed on average each year: 30
Location: Chittering Valley
Area: 4 ha
Soils: 'terra dura', Francois Jacquard's own concept of the soils of his vineyard in the Chittering Valley, which are: i) (mid-slope and river flat) gravelly chocolate loam, a deep soil of medium vigour, suited to cabernet sauvignon and shiraz; ii) (high-slope facing north to north-west) a light gravelly-rocky clay on granitic subsoil, interspersed with some decomposed schist, a soil of medium to low vigour, good for cabernet sauvignon, shiraz, merlot, viognier and chardonnay; iii) (top ridge soil where the white gum meets the jarrah) a decomposed pea-gravel of lateritic formation with a slightly acidic pH of 6.6, sometimes simply called ironstone, very poor in fertility, lacking trace elements and with poor water retention. This country is very low-yielding and most fitted for chardonnay.
Varieties planted: White—chardonnay, sauvignon blanc, semillon, viognier; Red—cabernet sauvignon, merlot, shiraz
Leading wines: Francois Jacquard Chardonnay, Shiraz, Cabernet Sauvignon, Viognier
Notes: Francois Jacquard is a vigneron with a mission and that is to make wines in his own style and from his own terroir, i.e. terra dura,

roughly translated as hard earth, which means not so much that it is difficult to cultivate, but simply that when it is combined with the local climate, it is mean and, if mistakes have been made, unforgiving. This meanness is exacerbated by the winemaker's conscious efforts to cut down on water and fertiliser and to reduce the number of bearing canes. From this you may take it that he does not make wines in the mainstream Australian 'fruity' style. All the wines tasted were extremely interesting, including a 'honey and straw' Viognier, which almost shrieked 'Condrieu' to me. Perhaps, however, the most fascinating was an older Reserve Chardonnay which had become rich and complex, but by no means 'fat' or oxidised. Love them or hate them, his wines are the expressions of an individual style. There will also be a Shiraz of the Cote Rotie mould (i.e. 5% viognier added). No cellar door sales, but sales are available by mail or email.

Lawnbrook Estate Wines   NR

101 Loaring Road, Bickley,
WA 6076
Ph/Fax 08 9291 8425

Owners: Wiebe and Judi Tieleman
Chief winemaker: Stephen Murfitt (contract)
Year of foundation: 1984
Tonnes crushed on average each year: 5
Location: Bickley
Area: 1.8 ha
Soils: heavy valley bottom loam
Varieties planted: White—chardonnay, semillon; Red—cabernet sauvignon, merlot, pinot noir
Leading wines: Lawnbrook Estate Pinot Noir, Merlot
Notes: Wiebe Tieleman is enthusiastic about his Pinot Noir and also about the inclusion of his on-site restaurant (The Packing Shed) in *Gourmet Traveller*'s top 600 restaurants in Australia. Cellar door sales: Fri–Sun and public holidays 10am–5pm.

Piesse Brook NR

226 Aldersyde Road, Bickley, WA 6076
Ph/Fax 08 9293 3309

Owners: Dianne Bray and Ray Boyanich
Chief winemakers: Dianne Bray and Ray
Boyanich, Mike Davies (consultant)
Year of foundation: 1974
Tonnes crushed on average each year: 28
Location: Bickley
Area: 4 ha
Soils: former orchard land with a variety of
soils, gravelly clay loam on the slope and rich
red loam on the flat
Varieties planted: White—chardonnay;
Red—cabernet sauvignon, merlot, shiraz
Leading wines: Piesse Brook Shiraz, Merlot,
Cabernet-Merlot
Notes: Piesse Brook Shiraz is a regular gold
medal winner at local wine shows. Cellar door
sales: Sat 1pm–5pm, Sun and public holidays
10am–5pm except February–March when sales
are by appointment.

Scarp Valley NR

6 Robertson Road, Gooseberry Hill,
WA 6076
Ph 08 9454 5748

Owners: Bob and Doris Duncan
Chief winemaker: contract

Year of foundation: 1978
Tonnes crushed on average each year: 0.5
Location: Gooseberry Hill
Area: 0.1 ha
Soils: granitic soils, trickle irrigation
Varieties planted: White—none; Red—shiraz
Leading wine: Scarp Valley Hermitage
Notes: This is a minute family-operated
vineyard with no cellar door sales.

Walsh Family Winery NR

90 Walnut Road, Bickley, WA 6076
Ph/Fax 08 9291 7341

Owners: Walsh family
Chief winemaker: Celine Rousseau (contract)
Year of foundation: 1995
Tonnes produced on average each year: 15, of
which 6 are used for Walsh Family wines
Location: Bickley
Area: 4 ha
Soils: gravelly loams (the vineyard having both
northerly and southerly aspects)
Varieties planted: White—gewurztraminer;
Red—shiraz
Leading wines: Walsh Family Gewurztraminer,
Shiraz
Notes: This is a small family-operated vineyard
whose wines I have not tasted. Cellar door
sales: daily 9am–5pm.

PART V

NEW SOUTH WALES

NEW SOUTH WALES WINE REGIONS

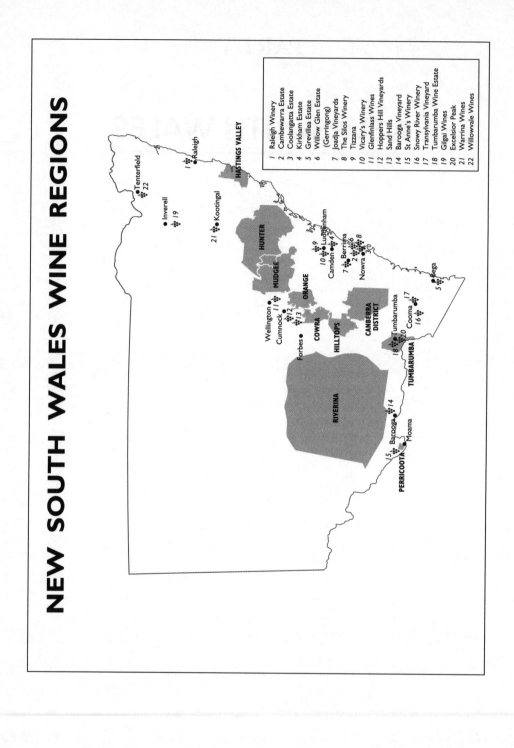

1 Raleigh Winery
2 Cambewarra Estate
3 Coolangatta Estate
4 Kirkham Estate
5 Grevillea Estate
6 Willow Glen Estate
  (Gerringong)
7 Joadja Vineyards
8 The Silos Winery
9 Tizzana
10 Vicary's Winery
11 Glenfinlass Wines
12 Hoppers Hill Vineyards
13 Sand Hills
14 Barooga Vineyard
15 St Anne's Winery
16 Snowy River Winery
17 Transylvania Vineyard
18 Tumbarumba Wine Estate
19 Gilgai Wines
20 Excelsior Peak
21 Warrina Wines
22 Willowvale Wines

Tenterfield
22

Raleigh
1

HASTINGS VALLEY

Inverell
19

Kootingal
21

HUNTER

Ludenham
4

MUDGEE

Berrima
2 6
Nowra 3

Camden
7

9
10

8

Bega
5

ORANGE

Wellington
Cumnock 11
12
13

CANBERRA
DISTRICT

Forbes

COWRA

HILLTOPS

Tumbarumba
17

Cooma
16

20

18

RIVERINA

TUMBARUMBA

14

Barooga
15

Moama

PERRICOOTA

This is a very large portion of New South Wales, stretching westwards from the Lachlan River at Forbes to the South Australian border near Cockburn, south-west from Forbes to the Murray River near Jingellic, and north-west along the Murray River to its junction with the South Australian border.

It is dry and hot and would be very arid were it not for the four big rivers, the Murray, the Darling, the Murrumbidgee and the Lachlan and their associated irrigation schemes. The zone includes four wine regions, Murray–Darling (see Victoria), Swan Hill (see Victoria), Riverina and Perricoota.

Barooga Vineyard
(vineyard only)

Barooga, NSW 3644

Owner: Southcorp Wines
Chief winemaker: Paul Lapsley
Year of foundation: 1921
Tonnes crushed on average each year: not disclosed but estimated at 4000
Location: Barooga in southern New South Wales across the Murray from Cobram in Victoria
Area: 420 ha consisting of Tarn Pirr 240 ha, Windarra 53 ha, Barooga 32 ha and about 95 ha of newly planted areas not yet fully bearing

Soils: variable, deep sand to clay sand, fairly typical alluvial terrace soils
Varieties planted: White—chardonnay, chenin blanc, semillon; Red—cabernet sauvignon, merlot, nebbiolo, pinot noir, sangiovese, shiraz
Leading wines: various premium and semi-premium red, white and sparkling wines. Nothing however carries the name 'Barooga' as an area of origin
Notes: Barooga is an important source of chardonnay and other fruit suitable for sparkling wine production. Such fruit is processed at Great Western. Other fruit finds its way into the Lindeman's Bin range made at Karadoc, while the balance is made at Nuriootpa. There are no local cellar door sales.

PERRICOOTA REGION

The wine region of Perricoota is centred on Moama in New South Wales, immediately across the Murray River from the larger and better-known town of Echuca in Victoria. Its name dates from 1840 when former convict James Malden, one of the region's first squatters, named his property Perricoota. His rival Henry Hopwood, also a former convict, was one of the first squatters on what was to become the Victorian side of the river, founding Echuca and later planting one of the first vineyards in the area in 1858. By 1860–1870, the larger 'stations' on the New South Wales side of the river began to be subdivided and smaller farm holdings became the norm. Though grazing and wool growing remained a major use for these lands, crops such as wheat were successfully cultivated. To transport such products to market, the riverboat trade began to grow and Echuca at this time became the largest inland port in Australia.

Hopwood's vineyard in due course became the centre of an Echuca wine business, which flourished for a few years until his death in 1868. A further vineyard venture at Kanyapella 30 km east of Echuca also thrived briefly but, for lack of permanent irrigation, it failed because of recurrent droughts. In modern times the vinous history of the general Echuca area began in 1972 when Dr Peter Tisdall planted at Picola to the east of Echuca and purchased an old dairy in Echuca which he subsequently converted into a winery in 1978. The venture, under the supervision of John Ellis as its first winemaker, proceeded well through the 1980s but struck difficulties during the early 1990s and was sold ultimately to Mildara Blass who closed it in 1997. The region's first winery is St Anne's.

Location: Moama latitude 36°8'S, longitude 144°50'E about 200 km north-north-west of Melbourne
Elevation: 94 m
Topography and soils: A typical Australian inland riverine landscape of flat terrain and remnants of river red gum forests. Its soils are generally red clay loams of good texture and fair to good moisture-holding capacity. Phosphorus levels are low, but those of potassium and sulfur high. Soil pH is moderately acidic (5.6), tending alkaline at depth. The soils of the region respond well to humus build-up and moderately deep chisel tillage to overcome hard pans caused by shallow ploughing in the past. Effects detrimental to productivity can be remedied by applications of gypsum, animal manure and nitrogenous fertilisers.
Climate: Echuca (Aerodrome) MJT 22.9°C, MAR 17.15°C, HDD raw 2006, AR 432.2 mm (Oct–Apr 222 mm), RH 50% (9am Jan), 28% (3pm Jan), AI na, SH na. (Moama) MJT 22.5°C, MAR na, HDD na, AR 476 mm (Oct–Apr na), RH na, AI na, SH na. A generally hot area but cooler than Murray–Darling and Swan Hill regions to the north-west. Frosts and equinoctial winds can cause problems during spring.
Harvest time: chardonnay late February early March, shiraz mid-March, cabernet sauvignon late March to early April.
Principal varieties: White—chardonnay; Red—cabernet sauvignon, merlot, shiraz
Total area: (2000) 740 ha
Principal wine styles: too early to predict but there will probably be white and red table wines of good quality.

St Anne's   **NR**

Cnr Perricoota Road and 24 Lane, Moama, NSW 2731 and at Western Highway, Myrniong, Vic 3341 (Moama) Ph 03 5480 0099, Fax 03 5480 0077, Email stannes@ozsky.net

Owners: McLean family
Chief winemaker: Richard McLean

Year of foundation: Moama, 1995 vineyards, 1999 winery; Myrniong, 1971 vineyard
Tonnes crushed on average each year: 2000, about half of which is used for St Anne's wines
Location: Moama, Myrniong (vineyard)
Area: 168 ha consisting of 160 ha (Moama) and 8 ha (Myrniong, Ballarat)
Varieties planted: White—chardonnay, gewurztraminer, riesling, sauvignon blanc, semillon; Red—cabernet franc, cabernet

sauvignon, durif, grenache, malbec,
mourvedre, petit verdot, shiraz
Leading wines: (Moama) St Anne's
Chardonnay, Cabernet, Shiraz, fortifieds.
(Myrniong) Riesling, Chardonnay, Cabernet,
fortifieds

Notes: St Annes is a new winery (built in
1999), for a new wine region. The wines of
each vineyard are made and marketed
separately and I have not tasted the wines of
either. There is a restaurant at Western
Highway, Myrniong.

RIVERINA REGION

The Riverina wine region incorporates the Murrumbidgee Irrigation Area and is the second largest wine-producing region in Australia and by far the largest in New South Wales. It was discovered in 1817 by the explorer John Oxley, who succinctly described it as 'a country, which for bareness and desolation has no equal'. Its early settlement was by squatters and pastoralists who soon had reason to dispute Oxley's pessimistic conclusion, for it produced good quality wool and excellent grain. It became so popular among pastoralists that by 1848 there was scarcely any land left unsettled along the Lachlan and Murrumbidgee Rivers. As an agricultural area, it received a further fillip from the Victorian and New South Wales goldrushes of the next decade, as much of its meat and wheat went to feed hungry diggers to the east and the south. The name Riverina, derived from the the adjective 'riverine', came into use as early as 1857. After the rushes, many thousands of sheep and cattle were grazed on the country adjacent to the rivers on the saltbush of the hinterland and the region became solidly prosperous. Grazing today remains an important industry in the general region.

The Riverina's first small irrigation experiment, doubtless inspired by the successes of the Chaffey brothers ten years before in Victoria and South Australia, occurred in 1899 when Samuel McCaughey established North Yanko Station on the Murrumbidgee near Yanko. His aim was to drought-proof family grazing properties and he established an extensive channel and pumping system for this purpose. He later strongly supported official irrigation schemes, which had their beginning in 1908. By July 1912, the first official scheme was open. The region's first vines were planted at Hanwood in the following year by the legendary 'JJ' McWilliam, who had purchased one of the first blocks (although irrigation had not reached it at the time of planting and he was obliged to have the vines watered by hand). Such was the enthusiasm for irrigated land that, by the outbreak of the First World War in August of the following year, some 622 farms covering 9700 ha were in operation. In 1917 McWilliam's Hanwood winery was erected.

The cessation of the war saw an expansion of the Irrigation Scheme, a rush of soldier settlement and in addition the first of the European immigrant families. There were of course more wineries, beginning with Penfolds in 1919. In 1924, Vittorio de Bortoli arrived and purchased land near Bilbul, erecting his winery in 1928. In 1930, Rossetto followed suit. However, not everything was rosy. Inexperience in irrigation procedures, the Great Depression, collapsing prices and subsequent financial failures during the 1930s caused many difficulties here as in other parts of Australia between growers and winemakers.

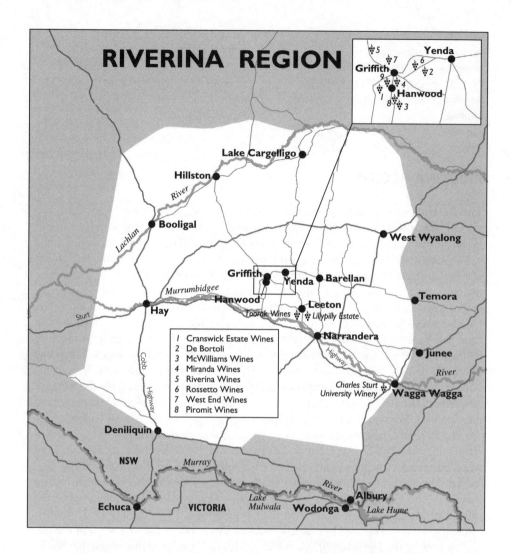

RIVERINA REGION

5
7   Yenda
Griffith   6
9   2
4   Hanwood
1
8   3

Lake Cargelligo ●
Hillston ●
River
Lachlan
● Booligal
● West Wyalong
Murrumbidgee
Griffith ●   Yenda ●   ● Barellan
Hanwood   ● Temora
Sturt   Hay ●   Leeton ●
Toorak Wines   Lillypilly Estate
● Narrandera
Cobb   Highway   ● Junee
River
Charles Sturt   ●
University Winery   Wagga Wagga ●
Highway

	Cranswick Estate Wines
1	Cranswick Estate Wines
2	De Bortoli
3	McWilliams Wines
4	Miranda Wines
5	Riverina Wines
6	Rossetto Wines
7	West End Wines
8	Piromit Wines

Deniliquin ●

NSW   Murray

VICTORIA   Lake   Albury
Echuca ●   Mulwala   Wodonga ●   Lake Hume
Lake   River

In 1933 the NSW Wine Grapes Marketing Board was set up. It continues its work at the present time. In the years prior to the Second World War the wine industry recovered, fortified wine exports increased and there was somewhat of a return to the prosperous days of the 1920s. It was in this period (1939) that Miranda opened its winery. The war, however, though it all but prevented wine export, was no death-blow to the wine industry. There were two armies, ours and the American, in training in Australia. Both had customary soldiers' thirsts and, though the majority preferred beer, wine certainly filled the bill in its absence.

After the end of the Second World War and for the next 30 years, there was a stream of Italian immigration to the region and several of its wine companies date their foundation from this time—West End in 1945, Toorak Wines in 1964, Riverina and Casella both in 1969. In the 1960s the region also saw the development of the wine engineering company A&G Enterprises, which developed the world famous Potter Fermenter. In 1977 there was also a major advance in oenological and viticultural education, when the Riverina College of Advanced Education (today the Charles Sturt University) set up Australia's second wine school at Wagga Wagga. At this time also, there was a significant change in the nature of the varietal composition of the region's vineyards, a swing away from fortified and distilling varieties to premium table wine cultivars, especially white.

Today, as well as wine grapes, the region is an important producer of grain, rice, vegetables and fruit crops. Its area under vine totals about 10 000 hectares, only 70% of which is currently bearing. Though its chief vineyards are centred on Leeton and Griffith, other irrigated areas throughout the region are experiencing a viticultural surge. There are vineyards at Wagga Wagga to the south-east, Jerilderie and Coleambally to the south and Hay and Hillston to the west. In addition, other vineyards are being established at Deniliquin, Narrandera, Darlington Point and Lake Cargelligo. As well as viticulture, emigration has left its cultural imprint on the region. About 25% of the population of the area is either Italian or of Italian descent.

Location: Griffith latitude 34°10'S, longitude 146°2'E. Centred on the city of Griffith, the Riverina wine region is located on the south-western plains of New South Wales, about 650 km south-west of Sydney

Elevation: Winegrowing areas within the region vary from 90 to 230 m above sea-level. Important centres are: Griffith 136 m, Leeton 140 m, Hay 94 m, Hillston 123 m and Wagga 221 m

Topography and soils: The south-western plains of New South Wales are alluvial, resulting from the actions of ancient streams, emanating from the Great Dividing Range and bringing with them remnant soils, clays and gravels from that range. The Riverina region is a generally flat area of land. Its soils are principally red-brown earths with a loamy surface horizon 10–35 cm deep above a reddish-brown clay containing lime at a depth of 70 cm. Most of these red-brown earth deposits have subsequently been elevated above the general plain level and are found around lower hill slopes and river ridges. They are generally free-draining and many contain limestone rubble.

Land to the east, south and west of Griffith is generally flat containing red-brown earths varying from duplex soils in the horticultural areas to heavy cracking clays on the flood plains. To the north-west there are patches of Mallee (high calcium) soils.

Some soils are subject to waterlogging and, where this occurs, so does salinity in areas of impeded drainage, which causes salts to accumulate in the topsoil. Such soils can be reclaimed by redesigning farm drainage in conjunction with land-forming and tile-drainage.

Climate: Griffith (CSIRO) MJT 23.85°C, MAR 13.25°C, HDD (Oct–Apr) 1734, (cut off at 19°C but otherwise not adjusted), AR 406.3 mm (Oct–Apr 225 mm), RH 48% (9am Jan), 30% (3pm Jan), AI na, SH 9.1 (daily Oct–Apr). Leeton MJT 24.6°C, MAR na, HDD raw (Sept–Mar) 2162, AR 430 mm, RH 54.3% (9am av Oct–Mar), 34.6% (3pm av Oct–Mar). Hay MJT 25.1°C, MAR na, HDD raw (Sept–March) 2302, AR 365 mm, RH 53% (9am av Oct–Mar), 31.4% (3pm av Oct–Mar). Hillston MJT 25.6°C, MAR na, HDD raw (Sept–March) 2404, AR 361 mm, RH 50.7% (9am av

Oct–Mar), 31.3% (av Oct–Mar). Wagga MJT 23.7°C, HDD raw (Sept–Mar)1890, AR 570 mm, RH 59.6% (av Oct–Mar), 37.3% (av Oct–Mar).

The region, as characterised by its high mean January temperatures, is very hot. Its annual rainfall is low but is spread evenly throughout the year. With the onset of autumn, temperatures cool and light showers occur, causing mists and an increase in relative humidity, ideal conditions for the spread of botrytis cinerea (noble rot).

Needless to say, irrigation is essential for the survival and growth of vineyards within the region. Good quality water for this purpose is drawn from the Murrumbidgee River at Berembed Weir 40 km east of Narrandera. It is directed through the main irrigation canal to a system of secondary channels, which reticulate low salinity water to about 3000 farms in the region entirely by gravity. A similar irrigation scheme operates in the Coleambally area, while grapegrowers in the Hillston and Hay districts pump directly from the Lachlan and Murrumbidgee Rivers. Traditionally, flood and furrow irrigation was used in the vineyards, though more recently environmental concerns have seen a move to undervine and drip irrigation, especially in recently planted vineyards. About one-fifth of all irrigation is now by drip.

Across the region, viticultural practices are generally uniform. Vines are trained high on a single or double foliage wire. Row width is 3.5 m with vines 2–3 m apart, resulting in a planting density of 1200 to 1500 vines per hectare. The region is phylloxera-free but prone to nematode infestation with the result that most new growers now take the precaution of planting on resistant rootstock. About a third of the region is mechanically pruned and the remainder hand-pruned to two bud spurs, though doubtless the mechanisation will increase as the region grows. The regime of quality water reliably supplied, long hours of sunshine, better clones and selection of virus-free planting material have ensured increasing quantities of adequately ripened grapes, which these days are mechanically harvested, often in the cool of the night, to preserve quality further.

Viticultural problems are few, though unusually high rainfall during the growing season may cause outbreaks of downy mildew. As mentioned, natural climatic conditions often favour the development of noble rot among semillon grapes. This is generally encouraged after the picking of white and red varieties for dry winemaking. *Harvest time*: chardonnay late February, semillon (dry style) late February to early March, merlot and shiraz mid March, cabernet sauvignon late March, semillon (botrytis affected) April

Principal varieties: (in order of quantity produced over 3000 tonnes, 1997 vintage) White—semillon, chardonnay, trebbiano, colombard, muscat gordo blanco; Red—shiraz, cabernet sauvignon

Total area: 10 000 ha (1997)

Principal wine styles: Botrytised Semillons of superb quality, fit to match the best in the world, and fortified wines of very good quality (more rarely these days because of depressed market conditions for such wines). With the advent of responsible, controlled drip irrigation and consequent higher fruit quality, there has also been a tremendous improvement in the last few years in the standards of red winemaking, especially in Cabernet Sauvignon and Merlot. Otherwise the region makes average to good quality varietal table wines likely to be found among cheap to medium priced bottles, mostly of a style suitable and recommended for current drinking.

Leading wineries and vineyards: Westend Wines, McWilliams Wines, Charles Sturt University Winery, Piromit Wines, Riverina Wines.

Casella Wines NR

Wakely Road, Yenda, NSW 2681
Ph 02 6968 1346, Fax 02 6968 1196,
Email johns@casellawine.com.au

Owners: Casella family
Chief winemaker: Alan Kennett
Year of foundation: 1969
Tonnes crushed on average each year: 15 000, of which 2000 come from the Casella vineyards (5000 tonnes are used for Casella wines)
Location: Yenda
Area: 285 ha
Soils: red-brown earths
Varieties planted: White—caverdella, chardonnay, colombard, gewurztraminer, marsanne, sauvignon blanc, semillon, verdelho, viognier; Red—cabernet sauvignon, dolcetto, durif, merlot, petit verdot, sangiovese, shiraz, tempranillo
Leading wines: Carramar Estate range, Casella Wines range
Notes: Casella was formerly a producer of bulk wines but is now making the transition to bottled varietals and blends, intended initially for the markets of the eastern seaboard and for export. The caverdella variety is unique to Casella, but perhaps DNA testing will one day show its true colours. No cellar door sales.

Charles Sturt University Winery R84

Charles Sturt University, Boorooma Street, Wagga Wagga, NSW 2650
Ph 02 6933 2435, Fax 02 6933 2107,
Email csuwinery@csu.edu.au

Owner: Charles Sturt University
Chief winemaker: Greg Gallagher
Year of foundation: 1977
Tonnes crushed on average each year: 500, of which 320 are used for Charles Sturt University labels
Location: Wagga Wagga
Area: 21 ha
Soils: basically loamy clay
Varieties planted: White—chardonnay, gewurztraminer, muscat gordo blanco, palomino, pinot gris, riesling, sauvignon blanc, semillon, viognier; Red—barbera, cabernet franc, cabernet sauvignon, dolcetto, merlot, nebbiolo, pinot noir, shiraz, tinta cao, touriga
Leading wines: Charles Sturt Reserve Cabernet, Chardonnay, Shiraz, Pinot Gris, Pinot-Meunier-Chardonnay (a sparkling wine)
Notes: Charles Sturt University Winery exists to train Australian winemakers of the future in all aspects of Australian winemaking. Its labour force, from planting and cultivation of its vines to winemaking maturation and bottling, is drawn entirely from students. As is to be expected at an Australian university which educates the winemakers of the future, its vineyard contains a whole catechism of cultivars to make many different but commercial styles of wine. In the modern manner, to assist in paying its own way, the winery has become fully commercial, raising its production from about 3000 cases in 1991 to 20 000 in 2000. Its wines are blends chiefly from New South Wales wine regions, Hilltops, Tumbarumba, Gundagai, Cowra and its own vineyard. Its standards are high, especially in Chardonnay. They need to be, for the future of the Australian wine industry and its increasing export sales depends upon high quality. It has won many trophies, gold medals and other awards for its wines since its inception.
Cellar door sales: 7 days 11am–5pm.

Cranswick Estate Wines   R81

Walla Avenue, Griffith, NSW 2680
Ph 02 6962 4133, Fax 02 6962 2888,
Email info@cranswick.com.au

Owner: Cranswick Premium Wines Pty Ltd
Chief winemaker: Andrew Schulz
Year of foundation: 1931
Tonnes crushed on average each year: 1200
Location: Griffith
Area: 250 ha
Soils: red-brown earths
Varieties planted: White—chardonnay,
colombard, gewurztraminer, marsanne;
Red—cabernet sauvignon, grenache, merlot,
shiraz
Leading wines: Cocoparra Vineyard
Chardonnay, Marsanne, Semillon, Cabernet
Sauvignon, Shiraz
Notes: A highly successful, predominantly
export-oriented winemaking enterprise has
resulted from the executive 'buy-out' several
years ago of the Cinzano interests in this
property by Graham Cranswick Smith. Wines
are light-bodied and chiefly of current drinking
quality. Cellar door sales: 7 days 10am–4pm.

De Bortoli   R82

De Bortoli Road, Bilbul, NSW 2680
Ph 02 6964 9444, Fax 02 6964 9400

Owners: De Bortoli family
Chief winemaker: Darren De Bortoli
Year of foundation: 1928
Tonnes crushed on average each year: 48 000
(includes fruit purchased from growers),
amount used for De Bortoli wines not
disclosed
Locations: Bilbul and Nericon (vineyard)
Area: 300 ha
Soils: derived in part from ancient stream beds,
the sandy loam soils vary in colour and
structure from red sandy earths to brown clay
loams
Varieties planted: White—chardonnay, chenin
blanc, colombard, gewurztraminer, muscat of
Alexandria, riesling, sauvignon blanc, semillon;
Red—cabernet franc, cabernet sauvignon,
grenache, malbec, merlot, pinot noir, shiraz
Leading wines: De Bortoli Noble One Botrytis
Semillon, Black Noble (a dessert wine made
from botrytised grapes, then fortified and
matured in wood for many years), the Deen
de Bortoli range of table wines, Chardonnay,
Durif, Shiraz, Sauvignon Blanc, Cabernet
Sauvignon, Verdelho
Notes: As well as a high quality location in the
Yarra Valley, De Bortoli now has an
international reputation for its aptly named
Noble One, made entirely at Bilbul. Though the
table wines are pleasant current drinking, the
outstanding wine here is Noble One, a
botrytised Semillon which has achieved
international fame for its luscious sweetness.
It is an incomparable wine. Cellar door sales:
Bilbul Mon–Sat 9am–5pm, Sun 9am–4pm,
public holidays 10am–4pm.

Lillypilly Estate   R82

Farm 16, Lillypilly Road, Leeton,
NSW 2705
Ph 02 6953 4069, Fax 02 6953 4980,
Email info@lillypilly.com

Owner: P & A Fiumara and Sons Pty Ltd
Chief winemaker: Robert Fiumara
Year of foundation: 1982
Tonnes crushed on average each year: 150
(this will increase as a new vineyard comes into
bearing)
Location: Leeton
Area: 30 ha
Soils: red-brown earths
Varieties planted: White—chardonnay,
gewurztraminer, muscat of Alexandria, riesling,
sauvignon blanc, semillon; Red—barbera,
cabernet sauvignon, petit verdot, shiraz
Leading wines: Lillypilly Estate Tramillon (a
blend of gewurztraminer and semillon), Noble
Riesling, Noble Harvest (botrytised styles of

various varieties and occasionally botrytised white blends), Fortifieds

Notes: This small almost 'boutique' producer by Riverina standards, has built up an excellent reputation for quality over the years, first with its Tramillon blend and more recently with a range of 'noble' (botrytised) whites. Cellar door sales: Mon–Sat 10am–5.30pm, Sun by appointment.

McWilliam's Wines R86

(*i*) Jack McWilliam Road, Hanwood, NSW 2680
Ph 02 6963 0001, Fax 02 6963 0002, Email mcwines@mcwilliams.com.au

Owner: McWilliam's Wines Pty Ltd
Chief winemaker: Jim Brayne
Year of foundation: 1912
Tonnes crushed on average each year: not disclosed but estimated at 19 000
Location: Hanwood
Area: 500 ha
Soils: Riverina clay loams
Varieties planted: White—chardonnay, riesling, sauvignon blanc, semillon, traminer; Red—cabernet sauvignon, merlot, pinot noir, red frontignan, ruby cabernet, shiraz, touriga, tyrian
Leading wines: McWilliams have a three-tiered range: (1) the Regional Collection, consisting of regional whites and reds such as Coonawarra Cabernet and Riverina Tyrian (Tyrian is a very promising cabernet hybrid, which produces a greater quality red than ruby cabernet); (2) the Hanwood range (Chardonnay, Semillon-Chardonnay, Verdelho, Sauvignon Blanc, Shiraz, Cabernet Sauvignon, Merlot, Pinot Chardonnay Brut, Sparkling Shiraz); and (3) the Inheritance range.
Notes: This was the first winery in the region erected in 1917 and is now the producer of many millions of litres of Riverina wine and in addition the wines of Barwang in the Hilltops region. The wine ranges (Hanwood and Inheritance) produced from local grapes are good standard whites and reds, usually quite suitable for current drinking. Hanwood's superior products are its botrytised Semillons and old Fortifieds, especially Muscat and Sherries. Cellar door sales Mon–Sat 9am–5pm, Sun closed.

(*ii*) Doug McWilliam Road, Yenda, NSW 2681 (winery only)
Ph 02 6968 1001, Fax 02 6968 1312, Email mcwines@mcwilliams.com.au

Owner: McWilliam's Wines Pty Ltd
Chief winemaker: Jim Brayne
Year of foundation: 1922
Leading wines: see McWilliam's Hanwood
Notes: The Yenda winery is a production facility only, storing and preparing wine for bottling. It is not open to the public.

Miranda Wines (winery only) R78

57 Jondaryan Avenue, Griffith, NSW 2680
Ph 02 6962 3000, Fax 02 6962 6944, Email info@mirandawines.com.au

Owners: Sam, Jim and Lou Miranda
Chief winemaker: Garry Wall
Year of foundation: 1939
Tonnes crushed on average each year: 30 000, all sourced from local growers
Location: Griffith
Leading wines: Mirrool Creek range Chardonnay, Durif
Notes: Like other Riverina makers, Miranda has in the past decade expanded into other regions (see King Valley, Barossa Valley). Its Riverina wines are good quality current drinking but the highlight here is usually a Botrytised Semillon, which I have not recently tasted. Cellar door sales: 7 days 10am–4pm.

Piromit Wines R83

113 Hanwood Avenue, Hanwood
NSW 2680
Ph 02 6963 0200, Fax 02 6963 0277

Owner: Piromit Wines Pty Ltd
Chief winemakers: Dominic Piromalli and
Pat Mittiga
Year of foundation: 1997
Tonnes crushed on average each year: 1000
Location: Hanwood
Area: 40 ha
Varieties planted: White—chardonnay,
colombard, sauvignon blanc, semillon,
verdelho; Red—cabernet sauvignon, merlot,
shiraz
Leading wines: Piromit Verdelho, Cabernet
Sauvignon
Notes: Piromit is a comparatively new name to
the Riverina region, but one which deserves
to succeed, if wine quality is any true indicator
of success. Cellar door sales: by appointment
during business hours Mon–Fri. Sales also by
mail order.

Riverina Wines R83

700 Kidman Way, Griffith, NSW 2680
Ph 02 6962 4122, Fax 02 6962 4628,
Email RivWines@webfront.net.au

Owner: Riverina Wines Pty Ltd
Chief winemaker: Sam Trimboli
Year of foundation: 1969
Tonnes crushed on average each year: 35 000
(and growing), about one-third of which is
used for Riverina Wines' own labels
Locations: (winery and cellar door) Griffith,
(vineyards) Thargobang and Yenda
Area: 1100 ha
Soils: variable from heavy loam to light clay
Varieties planted: White—chardonnay, chenin
blanc, gewurztraminer, marsanne, sauvignon
blanc, semillon, verdelho; Red—barbera,
cabernet sauvignon, durif, merlot, pinot noir,
ruby cabernet, shiraz

Leading wines: Riverina 1164 range, Warburn
Estate range (Durif, Shiraz, Cabernet-Merlot,
Verdelho, Chardonnay)
Notes: The vineyards here are very much state-
of-the-art, employing as they do the ultimate
in high-tech equipment to ensure maximum
quality production, while balancing this with
environmental considerations. Drip irrigation,
soil moisture monitoring, recycling of all
drainage water and the use of soft, non-
drifting pesticides are all important steps in this
direction. All this meticulous attention to detail
in the vineyard shows in the quality of the
wines and the show success which they enjoy.
Cellar door sales: 7 days 9am–5.30pm.

Rossetto Wines NR

Farm 576 Rossetto Road, Beelbangera,
NSW 2680
Ph 02 6966 0288, Fax 02 6966 0298,
Email rossetto@ozemail.com.au

Owner: Mrs Bianca Rossetto
Chief winemaker: Eddy Rossi
Year of foundation: 1930
Tonnes crushed on average each year: 11 000,
about 5000 of which are used for Rossetto's
own labels
Location: Beelbangera
Area: 10 ha
Soils: red-brown earths
Varieties planted: White—chardonnay,
semillon; Red—shiraz
Leading wines: Rossetto Mitchell Brooke range,
Promenade range, Silky Oak range
Notes: Rossetto is a once traditional Riverina
winemaker, which recently has been thinking
outside the square. It has realised the strengths
of its region, e.g. Botrytised Semillons and
fortified styles, and also its weaknesses, lack of
fruit truly suitable for finer styles of table wine.
While it has not purchased vineyards in other
regions, it has purchased fruit, which it uses to
very good effect in its Mitchell Brooke range
and has continued with its own regional

strengths. It is a consistent winner of silver and bronze awards at local and interstate wine shows. Cellar door sales: Mon–Sat 9am–5pm.

Toorak Wines NR

Toorak Road, Leeton, NSW 2705
Ph 02 6953 2333, Fax 02 6953 4454

Owners: Frank and Vincent Bruno and family
Chief winemaker: Robert Bruno
Year of foundation: 1965
Tonnes crushed on average each year: 4000, of which about 3200 are used for Toorak wines
Location: Leeton
Area: 160 ha
Soils: a range of sandy and clay soils
Varieties planted: White—chardonnay, colombard, muscat gordo, sauvignon blanc, semillon; Red—cabernet sauvignon, merlot, shiraz
Leading wines: Willandra Estate Chardonnay, Botrytis Semillon, Tooraks Liqueur Muscat
Notes: The strength here is, as with the rest of the region, Botrytis Semillon. Cellar door sales: Mon–Sat 9am–5pm.

Westend Wines R88

Braynes Road, Griffith, NSW 2680
Ph 02 6964 1506, Fax 02 6962 1673,
Email westend@webfront.net.au

Owners: William and Lena Calabria
Chief winemakers: William Calabria and James Ceccato
Year of foundation: 1945
Tonnes crushed on average each year: 1600, of which 940 are used for Westend wines
Location: Griffith, Hanwood (vineyard)
Area: 51 ha
Soils: red-brown earths
Varieties planted: White—chardonnay, semillon; Red—cabernet sauvignon, merlot, shiraz
Leading wines: Three Bridges range including Cabernet Sauvignon, Merlot, Chardonnay, Shiraz and Botrytis Semillon
Notes: Excellent Cabernet and Merlot reds are Westend's forte. Botrytis Semillon is also top class. Cellar door sales: Mon–Fri 9am–5pm, Sat 9am–3pm.

❦ Semillon

All the statistics tell us that chardonnay is still king of the whites. But there are encouraging signs of a growth in popularity of semillon, that variety which in the last decade of the 20th century retailers complained of as being boring and neutral (and therefore hard to sell). Perhaps semillon became boring through too much multi-regional blending which, though designed to reduce the price so that retailers would find it easier to sell, destroyed any regional personality the wine would otherwise have had. So semillon has been blended with other varieties, either chardonnay, where it makes a soft commercial common white or sauvignon blanc, where a livelier style usually results. It is fair to say that such a blend, whether a Sauvignon-Semillon or a Semillon-Sauvignon Blanc, is only as good as its regional origins. The most successful of these blends emanate from Margaret River and are noteworthy for their vivacity on nose and palate; unfortunately these blends are not cheap. So I suppose the message is that the personality of the region dominates such blends. A boring region might produce an equally boring blend. So long live Margaret River and its Sauvignons Blancs-Semillons or Semillons-Sauvignons Blancs!

Regional influences, however, take us only so far. Other factors such as growing conditions (*terroir*) and style of viticulture can easily influence a style of semillon.

In moderately warm regions, such as Margaret River, semillon ripens mid-season and can assume grassy, tangy, sauvignon-like characters, as a natural function of its growing conditions. Its vines produce lots of foliage, creating shaded green berries and, in turn, methoxypyrazines (grassy, vegetative, capsicum-like characters) in the fruit. Here makers such as Moss Wood have tamed the naturally grassy characters of the region by the use of Scott-Henry trellising (which opens out the canopy thus reducing its density), by trimming and then leaf-plucking semillon as necessary and ripening the fruit to 13° Be. Such wine is then matured in stainless steel though 'batonage' (oak slats) are sometimes used during fermentation. This way, Keith Mugford of Moss Wood tries to mitigate the 'green' characters of Semillon, though he concedes that there is always a 'modicum' in Margaret River Semillon. The green vegetative style of semillon still appears occasionally on its own, though most makers in that region prefer to blend it with sauvignon blanc.

In warmer regions such as the Hunter Valley, it ripens early mid-season, has lemony, vanillan-lanolin (not derived from American oak) aromas and tends to neutrality (but not boredom) in flavour. It is here that the winemaker may seek to add further complexity to the wine by malolactic fermentation and/or barrel-ferment and maturity in American oak, unless—and here again the Hunter Valley region is an example—Semillon has a reputation for maturing well in bottle.

With age, the young tangy styles of Semillon assume cooked vegetative characters which are extremely unpleasant after about four years and so should be drunk while young and fresh. American oaked Semillons at any age usually reveal strong vanillan aromas and flavours that can be initially attractive unless the wood is overdone on palate. They do not always mature with great harmony, the oak often becoming dominant and the ripe semillon fruit becoming 'fat'. The non-oaked styles of the

Hunter usually grow in lemon-toast complexity in bottle, often for a decade or more, and it is on this very distinctive character that the reputation of the Hunter as a Semillon producer is based.

Why do Hunter Semillons mature so distinctively? Possibly it is a function of the comparative lack of vigour and lower yield which semillon has on the rather poor sandy creek flats where it is mostly grown (its canopies are comparatively thin compared with Margaret River) and its growing climate, though quite hot, never seems as sunny or as dry as say Margaret River in summer. There is often a high humidity and even a slight cloud cover, which often halts semillon-ripening at about 11° Be and frequently the ripening phase thereafter does not seem to restart. Such fruit is fermented slightly oxidatively with low sulfurs, the result being a wine with lemony-strawy aromas and a neutral palate with minimal grassy characters, even sometimes with a minute amount of residual sugar, upon which the wine may 'live' during an extended bottle maturation. History has amply demonstrated that such styles may improve in bottle for up to 15 years and in some cases (as witness the Karl Stockhausen's Lindemans Semillon styles of 1970) even longer. Perhaps today, the wine-drinking public is just not patient enough.

❦ CENTRAL RANGES ZONE

Containing some of the higher and therefore cooler vineyard sites in New South Wales, this is an area of great interest, extending as it does from Lithgow just to the west of the Blue Mountains to Forbes on the Lachlan River. The zone encompasses the wine regions of Mudgee, Orange and Cowra.

Glenfinlass Wines NR

Elysian Farm, Parkes Road, Wellington, NSW 2820 (about 8km south of the town)
Ph 02 6845 2221, 02 6845 2011, Fax 02 6845 3329

Owners: Brian and Nyasa Holmes, Robert Woods
Chief winemaker: Brian Holmes
Year of foundation: 1968
Tonnes crushed on average each year: 8, all used for Glenfinlass labels
Location: Wellington
Area: 2.6 ha
Soils: chiefly old alluvial soils of limestone origins
Varieties planted: White—sauvignon blanc; Red—cabernet sauvignon, shiraz
Leading wines: Glenfinlass Shiraz, Sauvignon Blanc, Cabernet Sauvignon
Notes: This is an old established vineyard with cellar door sales: Sat 10am–4pm.

Hoppers Hill Vineyards NR

Googodery Road, Cumnock, NSW 2867
Ph 02 6367 7270

Owners: Bob and Pat Gilmour
Chief winemaker: Bob Gilmour
Year of foundation: 1978
Tonnes crushed on average each year: 6
Location: Cumnock
Area: 2 ha
Soils: The vineyard has heavy clay soils and is situated on a westerly slope with good air drainage. It is not irrigated

Varieties planted: White—sauvignon blanc; Red—cabernet franc, merlot
Leading wines: Hoppers Hill Cabernet Franc-Merlot
Notes: Bob Gilmour is a Pomerol and St Emilion enthusiast, hence the choice of red grape varieties for his vineyard. No pesticides or systemic sprays are used in the vineyard and all wines are made without added sulphur. Cellar door sales by appointment only.

Sand Hills NR

Sand Hills Road, Forbes, NSW 2871 (about 6 km east of Forbes)
Ph 02 6852 1437, Fax 02 6852 4401, Email sandhill@westserv.net.au

Owner: John Saleh
Chief winemaker: Jill Lindsay, Woodonga Hill (contract)
Year of foundation: 1920
Tonnes crushed on average each year: 10
Location: Forbes
Area: 3.6 ha
Soils: sand to sandy clay
Varieties planted: White—chardonnay, colombard, semillon; Red—cabernet sauvignon, mataro, merlot, pinot noir, shiraz
Leading wines: Sand Hills Chardonnay, Shiraz-Cabernet, Cabernet-Shiraz, Pinot Noir
Notes: Once Sand Hills had a definite emphasis on fortifieds. These days, in accord with modern market conditions, the emphasis is very definitely on table wines which regularly win bronze awards. Cellar door sales: Mon–Sat 9am–5pm, Sun noon–5pm.

COWRA REGION

Within a few years of the crossing of the Blue Mountains in 1813, large tracts of central New South Wales had been explored. In 1815 George Evans discovered the Lachlan River near its junction with the Belubela. Three years later, John Oxley and Allan Cunningham also came that way. In the late 1820s, they were followed by the inevitable squatters searching for grazing land and so, like much of the rest of the Central Ranges zone of New South Wales, the early history of Cowra is pastoral. The town which had its beginnings in the 1840s derives its name from the Aboriginal word *coura* meaning 'rocks', a reference to a ford across the Lachlan close to the town. Later in the nineteenth century, dairying became common and cereal crops such as wheat and barley were also planted. Indeed one of the earliest buildings in the town is the old Mill dating from 1861, now used as a cellar door outlet and restaurant by Windowrie. Orchards and undoubtedly vineyards were also a feature of the district.

In the New South Wales agricultural census of 1879, Cowra is shown as producing 3000 gallons (13 500 litres) of wine and, in 1893 in the *Cowra Free Press*, reference is made to a vineyard planted on James Ousby's farm 'with four kinds of wine grapes, Red Hermitage and Tokay being the principal varieties', and the wine made from these varieties being 'pronounced excellent'.

The modern history of the Cowra vine begins in 1972 when, in a bid for agricultural diversification, Allan Mitchell planted a small experimental vineyard on his property on the banks of the Lachlan, downstream of Cowra. In the same year a larger project was planned by an American company on slopes adjacent to the river south of the town. This was purchased by Sydney-based businessman Tony Gray and planting commenced in 1973. By 1975, a total of 36 ha, mostly of the 'new' chardonnay variety, had been planted. The region first came to prominence in winemaking terms in the late 1970s when eminent winemaker and now Australia's leading vigneron, Brian Croser, made his first Petaluma Chardonnays (1977–79) from Cowra fruit while he was senior lecturer-winemaker at the Charles Sturt University at Wagga. In 1981 the initial Tony Gray vineyard was sold to Rothbury Estate, which began making what proved to be a very successful series of Cowra Chardonnays.

Later in the 1980s, a second vigorous phase of vine-planting ensued when, in 1987, near the village of Billimari north-west of the town, the Windowrie vineyard was commenced. The following year, the 'Cooraminta' vineyard of 220 ha was developed by Orlando-Wyndham, 5 km upstream of Cowra. Today, these two areas to the south and the north-west of the town are the centres of vinegrowing in the region. Today there is one fully equipped winery (Windowrie) and three smaller wineries in the region and one crushing plant.

Location: Cowra latitude 33°50'S, longitude 148°41'E, about 230 km due west of Sydney
Elevation: 300 m. The region has an upper contour boundary of 400 m altitude, which conforms to the catchment area of the upper Lachlan. Most vineyards in the region are presently planted on undulating terrain between 250 and 350 metres in altitude.
Topography and soils: The valley of the Lachlan is filled with a deep alluvium varying

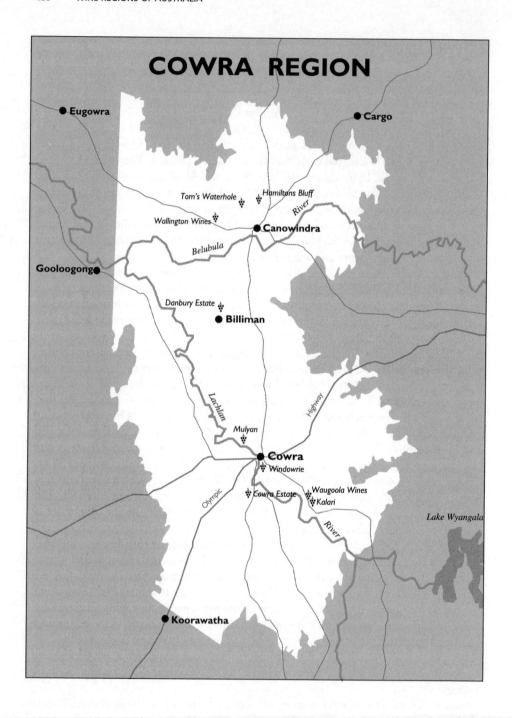

COWRA REGION

Eugowra

Cargo

Tom's Waterhole

Hamiltons Bluff

River

Wallington Wines

Canowindra

Belubula

Gooloogong

Danbury Estate

Billiman

Lachlan

Mulyan

Highway

Cowra
Windowrie

Olympic

Cowra Estate

Waugoola Wines
Kalari

Lake Wyangala

River

Koorawatha

in depth from 40 m near Cowra to 70 m just outside the Wine Region near Gooloogong. This consists of interbedded clays, sands, silts and gravels. The Belubela Valley similarly has alluvium but only as deep as 24 m. Within the Lachlan Valley, river terraces occur along the river on both banks. The Valley's western edge is defined by a sandstone ridge, while its eastern side is bounded by a series of gently undulating to rolling hills of Cowra granodiorite and, to the near north of Billimari, Canowindra porphyry. To the north-east of Canowindra, on the regional boundary, there are outcrops of limestone, the landscape there consisting of undulating hills with occasional steep slopes.

Generally the soils of the Cowra vineyards consist of siliceous sands on the crests of slopes, red podsols on the mid slopes and red-brown earths on the lower slopes. The red podsols are moderately permeable with moderate fertility and neutral pH. The red-brown earths are stable, well-drained soils with moderate permeability but low fertility.

Around Canowindra, there are non-calcic brown soils on the upper slopes with yellow and brown solodics in natural drainage lines. These soils are moderately permeable with limited drainage in the subsoil and are of low fertility.

From the south of the region (north of Koorawatha) through Morongla and north to Billimari, there is gently undulating country. The soils here are non-calcic brown soils on the hill crests with yellow podsols and yellow solodics on the middle and lower slopes. Such soils have moderate permeability, low fertility and are moderately erodible with poor drainage in the yellow solodics.

On the flood plains of the Lachlan and Belubela Rivers, the river terraces are comprised of non-calcic brown soils and red-brown earths, while the river flats consist of alluvial loams. Both soils are moderately to highly permeable and of low erodibility. The contrast is in fertility, the terrace soils having low to moderate fertility, the alluvial loams being highly fertile.

Climate: Cowra PO MJT 24°C, MAR 16.05°C, HDD 1705 (cut off at 19°C, but not otherwise adjusted), AR 613 mm (Oct–Apr 283 mm), RH 51% (9am Jan), 36% (3pm Jan) AI na SH na. Cowra Airport MJT 23.25°C, MAR 15.3°C, HDD 1705 (cut off at 19°C but not otherwise adjusted), AR 624 mm (Oct–Apr 367 mm), RH 58% (9am Jan), 33% (3pm Jan) AI na SH na. Cowra is a hot region, its MJT and raw HDD being comparable with those of Riverina to the west. On this basis, the region would seem to be well suited to full-bodied table wines and indeed fortified styles should these ever recover market favour. Its Chardonnay can only be described as full-bodied, generous in flavour and suitable for early consumption (6 months to 2 years from vintage) in normal years. Its table wine reds chiefly made from cabernet sauvignon and merlot have similar characteristics to its Chardonnay. Nearly 60% of its annual rainfall falls during the growing season and the usual spray precautions against mildews should be taken. It is also prone to frosts during September, when early and mid-season varieties are at budburst. As in the Orange region, great care should be taken with site selection to ensure free air drainage.

All vineyards within the region are irrigated. The entire region is within the Lachlan Catchment Area and both the Lachlan and Belubela Rivers are regulated streams within this catchment area. Rights to irrigate from these are held by owners of adjoining lands on either 'low' or 'high' security allocations. The former are reduced by some percentage in some seasons, perhaps even down to nothing if the storage dams are low in spring, while the latter are reduced only to 70% in the driest of circumstances. Obviously for vinegrowing purposes high security allocations are preferred to low.

The waters of the Lachlan and its tributary, the Abercrombie, are stored by the Wyangala Dam which has a capacity of 1.25 million megalitres, about half of which is available to irrigators in times of full allocation, while the waters of the Belubela are held by the Carcoar Dam, much smaller in capacity at 23 000 megalitres for irrigation purposes. However, many irrigators here also have access to underground aquifers via bores.

At the present time the total allocation available for irrigators on both rivers is limited by the Murray–Darling system cap, set at 1993–94 usage levels on the Lachlan itself. There is an embargo on the issue of new licences though trade in existing licences is permitted within the Lachlan system, allowing adequate allocation of water to meet viticultural needs.

The quality of water from both rivers and from underground bores extracted within a few kilometres of these rivers is generally excellent.

Harvest time: chardonnay first week of March, cabernet sauvignon first week of April
Principal varieties: White—chardonnay; Red—no varieties yet appear to be outstanding, though merlot shows promise
Total area: na
Principal wine styles: Chardonnay
Leading wineries and vineyards: Rothbury Estate, Windowrie, Waugoola Wines

Cowra Estate NR

Boorowa Road, Cowra, NSW 2794
Ph 02 6342 1136, Fax 02 6342 4286,
Email cowraestate@ozemail.com.au

Owner: John Geber
Chief winemaker: Simon Gilbert (contract)
Year of foundation: 1973
Tonnes produced on average each year: 1000, of which 500 are used for Cowra Estate wines
Location: Cowra
Area: 80 ha
Soils: red podsolic soils
Varieties planted: White—chardonnay, gewurztraminer, riesling, sauvignon blanc; Red—cabernet franc, cabernet sauvignon, petit verdot, merlot, pinot noir, shiraz, tempranillo
Leading wines: Cowra Estate Chardonnay, Cabernets-Merlot
Notes: This is Cowra's oldest established vineyard and is responsible conjointly with Rothbury Estate for the Chardonnay reputation

of the region. Cellar door sales: Tues–Sun 10am–4pm.

Danbury Estate NR

Billimari, Canowindra, NSW 2804 or
PO Box 605, Cowra, NSW 2794
Ph 02 6341 2204, Fax 02 6341 4690,
Email middo@westserv.net.au

Owner: Jonathan Middleton
Chief winemaker: Peter Howland (contract)
Year of foundation: 1996
Tonnes produced on average each year: 90
Location: Billimari
Area: 8.5 ha
Soils: red-brown fine sandy loam and also clay loam
Varieties planted: White—chardonnay; Red—none
Leading wine: Danbury Estate Chardonnay
Notes: Danbury Estate is a new vineyard,

planted to chardonnay, the proven performer of the region. Its first vintage, 1998, won gold at the Australian Boutique Wine Awards. Cellar door sales at Quarry Restaurant at Cowra Estate.

Hamiltons Bluff R81

Longs Corner Road, Canowindra, NSW 2804
Ph 02 6344 2079, Fax 02 6344 2165, Email hambluff@netconnect.com.au

Owners: the Andrews family
Chief winemaker: Andrew Margan (contract)
Year of foundation: 1995
Tonnes produced on average each year: 500, of which about 20 are used for Hamiltons Bluff wines
Location: Canowindra
Area: 42 ha
Soils: red sandy clay loam over bedrock of decomposed granite
Varieties planted: White—chardonnay, semillon; Red—cabernet sauvignon, sangiovese, shiraz
Leading wines: Hamilton's Bluff Methode Champenoise, Canowindra Grossi range
Notes: Hamiltons Bluff is a bright new light on the Cowra horizon. Its Canowindra Grossi Unwooded Chardonnay 1998 was selected for service on Qantas first class international and domestic wine lists. The 2000 Chardonnay has also been successful, winning gold at the Cowra Wine Show. The Canowindra Grossi range is named after a local fish fossil discovery. Cellar door sales: weekends and public holidays 10am–4pm.

Kalari NR

120 Carro Park Road, Cowra, NSW 2794
Ph/Fax 02 6342 1465, Email kalari@westserv.net.au

Owners: Valto and Pamela Heikkinen and Bob and Carmel Clark

Chief winemakers: Jill Lindsay and John Reynolds (contract)
Year of foundation: 1995
Tonnes crushed on average each year: 150, of which about 20 are used for Kalari wines
Location: Cowra
Area: 12 ha
Soils: red earths, sandy loam with 20–30% clay
Varieties planted: White—chardonnay, semillon, verdelho; Red—cabernet sauvignon, merlot, shiraz
Leading wines: Kalari Dry and Semi-sweet Verdelho, Shiraz, Fortelho (a fortified Verdelho)
Notes: Kalari is another newly founded vineyard with an emphasis on Verdelho, including a fortified Verdelho, a style for which the region may be eminently suited. Cellar door sales: Fri–Mon, public holidays 10am–4pm.

Mulyan R82

North Logan Road, Cowra, NSW 2794
Ph 02 6342 1336, Fax 02 6341 1015, Email mulyan@westserv.com.au

Owners: Jenni and Peter Fagan
Chief winemaker: Simon Gilbert (contract)
Year of foundation: 1994
Tonnes produced on average each year: 400, of which 40 are used for Mulyan wines
Location: Cowra
Area: 44 ha
Soils: alluvial red soils over soils
Varieties planted: White—chardonnay, viognier; Red—shiraz
Leading wines: Mulyan Chardonnay, Bushrangers Bounty Chardonnay
Notes: From asparagus, tomatoes and sweet corn in the 1940s to wine grapes in the 1990s, the Fagan family has always been keen to seek out new diversification opportunities. Chardonnay as elsewhere in the region, is the pick here. Cellar door sales: by appointment during the week; weekends and public holidays 10am–5pm.

Richmond Grove
(vineyard only)   NR
Reids Flat Road, Cowra, NSW 2794

Owner: Simeon Wines Ltd
Chief winemaker: Phil Laffer
Year of foundation: 1989
Tonnes crushed on average each year: 4000,
all of which are used for Orlando, Richmond
Grove and Wyndham wines
Location: Cowra
Area: 315 ha
Soils: alluvial sandy loams on river flats, red
podsolics on slopes
Varieties planted: White—chardonnay,
sauvignon blanc, semillon, verdelho;
Red—cabernet franc, cabernet sauvignon,
malbec, merlot, pinot noir, ruby cabernet,
shiraz
Leading wines: Richmond Grove Cowra
Chardonnay and parts of many other wines of
the Orlando Wyndham group
Notes: This is the former Orlando Wyndham
vineyard, sold to Simeon Wines in 1994 but
still managed by Orlando Wyndham. All the
fruit is purchased by Orlando Wyndham and
continues to form an important part of the
wines mentioned. Richmond Grove
Chardonnay is the only single wine of origin
from this vineyard. No cellar door sales.

Rothbury Estate
(vineyard only)   R85
Boorowa Road, Cowra, NSW 2794

Owner: Mildara Blass
Chief winemaker: Neil McGuigan
Year of foundation: Cowra Vineyard 1973
Tonnes crushed on average each year: 400
Location: Cowra
Area: 47 ha
Soils: sandy loams over clay
Varieties planted: White—chardonnay,
sauvignon blanc; Red—none
Leading wine: Rothbury Cowra Chardonnay

Notes: This is the home of a ready drinking,
generously flavoured Chardonnay which
placed Cowra firmly on the wine map. No
local cellar door sales.

Tom's Waterhole Wines   NR
'Felton', Longs Corner Road, Canowindra,
NSW 2804
Ph 02 6344 1819, Fax 02 6344 2172,
Email tomswaterhole@aol.com.au

Owner: Graham Timms
Chief winemaker: Graham Kerr
Year of foundation: 1995
Tonnes produced on average each year: 20
and increasing
Location: Canowindra
Area: 5 ha (2 ha not yet bearing)
Soils: red decomposed alluvial soils over basalt
and limestone
Varieties planted: White—chardonnay (not yet
bearing), semillon; Red—cabernet sauvignon,
merlot, shiraz
Leading wines: Tom's Waterhole Cabernet
Sauvignon, Semillon, Shiraz, Humpers dry red
(a red blend)
Notes: This is another new Cowra producer.
I have not tasted its wines. Cellar door sales:
weekends and public holidays 10am–4pm.

Wallington Wines   NR
'Nyrang Creek', Eugowra Road,
Canowindra, NSW 2804
Ph 02 6344 7153, Fax 02 6344 7105,
Email nyrang@westserv.net.au

Owners: Anthony and Margaret Wallington
Chief winemaker: Murray Smith (contract),
Arrowfield (chardonnay, contract)
Year of foundation: 1992
Tonnes produced on average each year: 150,
of which about 30 are used for Wallington
wines
Location: Canowindra
Area: 16 ha

Soils: dark brown red loam
Varieties planted: White—chardonnay,
semillon; Red—cabernet franc, cabernet
sauvignon, grenache, mourvedre, petit verdot,
pinot noir, tempranillo
Leading wines: Wallington Shiraz-Cabernet,
Chardonnay
Notes: Following a policy of low-input
irrigation, Wallington limits production to
8–10 tonnes per hectare and since 2000 has
its own winery. Chardonnay is obviously a
strength here as a Wallington Chardonnay has
been used at receptions at the Australian
Embassy in Washington. Cellar door sales:
open first weekend in the month and public
holidays. At other times by appointment.

Waugoola Wines R84

Cultowa Road, Canowindra, NSW 2804
Ph 02 6342 1435,
Email casey@windowrie.com.au

Owner: Casey and Laura Proctor
Chief winemaker: Rodney Hooper (contract)
Year of foundation: 1996
Tonnes produced on average each year: 35, of
which about 20 are used for Waugoola wines
Location: Carro Park Road, Cowra
Area: 6.5 ha. consisting of Cultowa Road
(4 ha) and Carro Park (2.5 ha)
Soils: red clay loam over clay
Varieties planted: White—chardonnay;
Red—grenache, merlot, shiraz
Leading wines: Cuttowa Shiraz, Carro Park
Chardonnay, Shiraz
Notes: A small family-owned vineyard with
well made Shiraz and Chardonnay. Cellar door
sales: weekends 10am–6pm or by
appointment at other times.

Windowrie R85

Windowrie Road, Canowindra,
NSW 2804
(winery) Ph 02 6344 3598,
Fax 02 6344 3597,
(h) Ph 02 6344 3264, Fax 02 6344 3227,
Email windowrie@windowrie.com.au

Owners: O'Dea family
Chief winemakers: Stephen Craig, Rodney
Hooper (consultant)
Year of foundation: 1988
Tonnes produced on average each year: 2400,
of which about 700 are crushed for
Windowrie's own labels
Location: (vineyard and winery) Canowindra,
(cellar door sales) The Mill, Cowra
Area: 200 ha
Soils: sedimentary, a red loam (about 0.75 m
deep) overlying a red clay loam over red clay
Varieties planted: White—chardonnay,
sauvignon blanc, semillon, verdelho;
Red—cabernet franc, cabernet sauvignon,
grenache, merlot, petit verdot, pinot noir,
sangiovese, shiraz
Leading wines: Windowrie Estate Shiraz,
Chardonnay; The Mill Shiraz, Chardonnay,
Merlot, Cabernet-Merlot, Sangiovese,
Sauvignon Blanc; Platinum Series Chardonnay,
Cabernet Sauvignon
Notes: Windowrie is now the biggest winery in
the Cowra region and is rapidly expanding
with exports to south-east Asia and Europe
and distribution to the eastern states and
South Australia. Windowrie produces the usual
generously flavoured style of Chardonnay for
which Cowra is famous. Cellar door sales: daily
10am–6pm The Mill, Vaux St, Cowra.

MUDGEE REGION

The region's first settlers, George and Henry Cox, reached Mudgee in February 1822. It was obvious from the first that its inhabitants intended that their settlement should have a decent start in life, as the early town planner, Robert Hoddle, was engaged to design the layout of the 'town' in 1823. (He used a grid pattern that he was obviously fond of, for he used a similar plan for Melbourne 14 years later.) Official municipal status was slower in arrival, the 'village' being officially gazetted in 1838 and not until 1860 did it officially become a 'town'. Until that time it had been the centre of a predominantly pastoral neighbourhood (though Adam Roth, an early German settler, had planted vines on his property, Craigmoor, in the 1850s). A great spurt of growth occurred with the discovery of gold at nearby Gulgong and all around Mudgee in the 1860s and 1870s, when the area's population soared to over 20 000. After this bout of gold fever, it was its flat fertile pastures, not gold, that continued to be Mudgee's mainstay. Perhaps Mudgee's outstanding citizen, though he was scarcely known at the time he lived there, was the poet Henry Lawson. Time makes hearts and memories grow fonder and Lawson is of blessed memory in modern Mudgee.

In the 1840s New South Wales was extremely short of skilled agricultural labour. Sir William Macarthur (son of the notorious John), one of Australia's most famous vignerons of the middle of the nineteenth century, convinced the New South Wales and British governments that this shortage could be remedied by importing indentured agricultural labourers from Europe. A number of German labourers applied and were allotted to various settlers. Once their period of service had expired they were free either to stay or return to Germany. Most stayed. Adam Roth was such a man who, in the 1850s, after service with Macarthur, found his way to Mudgee and began wine production in 1858. Roth and his large family remained in the area (indeed by 1880 there were 13 wineries, six of which were operated by Roth and his sons) and other German emigrants were attracted to it with the result that, for the next 30 years, the Mudgee area became the largest German settlement in Australia outside the Barossa Valley. However, what was a thriving Mudgee wine industry by 1890 was seriously affected by the bank crashes in the eastern Australian colonies two to three years later. Mudgee's wineries never quite recovered and by the mid-1960s there were only two wineries, Jack Roth at Craigmoor and Alf Kurtz.

The red wine boom and the town's relatively short distance from Sydney gave added impetus to the minute Mudgee wine industry at this time. New capital flowed to the region from wine-interested professionals from Sydney. New vineyards were planted and new wineries erected in this 'nest in the hills'. Important at that time and of continuing importance are the Roberts' family winery at Huntington and, slightly later, the Transfield company's Montrose winery. Another who soon followed was Ian MacRae at Miramar. By the end of the 1970s Mudgee was booming. In 1978, Mudgee was one of the first Australian wine areas to adopt a wine certification of origin scheme, when the Society for the Appellation of the Wines of Mudgee was formed. It was a voluntary system whereby winemakers could for a few cents per bottle apply to have their wines (made from grapes grown solely within the defined Mudgee area) awarded the mark of the Society and carry the entitlement 'Certified Mudgee Appellation Wine' on their

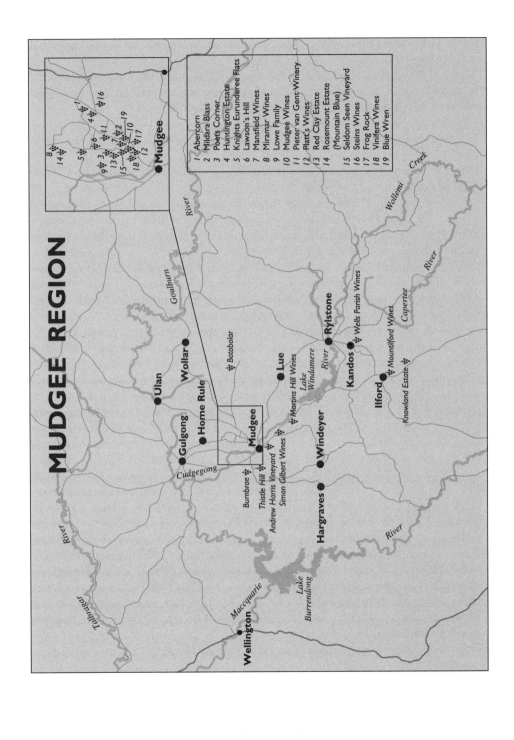

MUDGEE REGION

1 Abercorn
2 Mildara Blass
3 Poets Corner
4 Huntington Estate
5 Knights Eurunderee Flats
6 Lawson's Hill
7 Mansfield Wines
8 Miramar Wines
9 Lowe Family
10 Mudgee Wines
11 Pieter van Gent Winery
12 Platt's Wines
13 Red Clay Estate
14 Rosemount Estate
 (Mountain Blue)
15 Seldom Seen Vineyard
16 Steins Wines
17 Frog Rock
18 Vinifera Wines
19 Blue Wren

labels. This scheme no longer operates, having been superseded by the Geographical Indications system.

Today the Mudgee area has attracted the attention of the 'big battalions', with the major presence of Orlando Wyndham and to a lesser extent Mildara Blass and Rosemount. It has 17 working wineries and numerous cellar door outlets.

Location: Mudgee (town) latitude 32°35'S, longitude 149°35'E, about 261 km northwest of Sydney

Elevation: (town) 454 m. The vineyards of the region are located between 470 and 1080 m in altitude.

Topography and soils: The region is an important transitional area between the western slopes of the Great Divide and the central tablelands and western plains. It is the most northerly region of the Central Ranges Wine Zone, its principal town being Mudgee (located in the valley of the Cudgegong River, a tributary of the Macquarie). The valley is dominated to its east, south and south-west by the Great Dividing Range, while in the immediate vicinity of the town there are low to medium-sized hills to its north, north-west and north-east, the country rising again on the road back through the Goulburn Ranges to Muswellbrook and the Hunter Valley.

Its soils are chiefly hard red duplex (Dr 2) and hard mottled yellow duplex (Dy 3), though there are some red massive earths (Gn 2). Beneath about half a metre of topsoil, there is a subsoil of clay and gravel, in turn overlying Ordovician sandstone, slate, phyllite and limestone. Such soils are moderately permeable and well drained. They are also moderately fertile but often low in nitrogen and phosphorus.

Climate: MJT 22.9°C, MAR 15°C, HDD raw 2055, AR 668 mm (Oct–Mar 361 mm), RH 63% (9am Jan), AI 303 mm, SH 8 (D&S). Cf MJT 23.3°C, MAR na, HDD raw 2085, 1617 (cut-off and adjusted for latitude, daily temperature range and vine sites), AR 667 mm (Oct–Apr 405 mm), RH 42% (3pm Jan), AI na, SH 9.1 (Gladstones). Local MJT 23.25°C, MAR 15.4°C, HDD raw 2075, AR 669 mm (Oct–Apr 405 mm), RH 63% (9am Jan), 39% (3pm Jan), AI na, SH na. The warm climate favours the production of full-bodied reds and whites and would favour fortifieds, market conditions permitting. Like the rest of the regions in the Central Ranges zone, there is a substantial frost risk where air drainage is poor. So vineyard sites need careful selection. There is also a risk of hail during the growing season (during Spring 1997, the region did suffer such damage). Most vineyards are drip irrigated from surface dams, collected from rainwater run-off and from bores. There is also some availability from the Cudgegong River.

Harvest time: generally late February to early April, in paricular chardonnay in late February, shiraz and semillon first to second week of March, cabernet sauvignon late March to early April

Principal varieties: White—chardonnay, semillon; Red—shiraz, cabernet sauvignon, merlot

Total area: 4500 ha

Principal wine styles: Ripe full-bodied reds, especially Shiraz, which cellar well over 4–5 years and sometimes longer. Comparisons are odious, but there is a slight similarity to the reds of Clare in South Australia which is at a similar altitude and only a degree of latitude further south

Leading wineries and vineyards: Rosemount Estate, Andrew Harris Wines, Poets Corner, Huntington Estate, Simon Gilbert Wines, Blue Wren Vineyard.

Abercorn **NR**

Cassilis Road, Mudgee, NSW 2850
Ph 02 6373 3106, Fax 02 6373 3108

Owners: Timothy and Constance Stevens
Chief winemaker: Tim Stevens
Year of foundation: 1972, first wine 1997
Tonnes crushed on average each year: 75
Location: Mudgee
Area: 10 ha
Soils: sand over clay
Varieties planted: White—chardonnay;
Red—cabernet sauvignon, shiraz
Leading wines: Abercorn Unwooded
Chardonnay, Chardonnay, Shiraz, Shiraz-Cabernet
Notes: Timothy and Constance Stevens intend that Abercorn's wines be of premium quality. The vineyard is one planted by Craigmoor and is now quite mature. I have tasted no wines from Abercorn recently. Cellar door sales: Thurs, Fri, Sat, Mon 10.30am–5pm, Sun 10.30am–3pm.

Andrew Harris Vineyards **R86**

Sydney Road, Mudgee, NSW 2850
Ph 02 6373 1213, Fax 02 6373 1296,
Email ahv@andrewharris.com.au

Owners: Andrew and Debbie Harris
Chief winemaker: Frank Newman
Year of foundation: 1991
Tonnes crushed on average each year: 1500, of which 260 are used for Andrew Harris labels
Location: Mudgee
Area: 110 ha
Soils: red to brown loam over gravelly clay
Varieties planted: White—chardonnay, riesling, sauvignon blanc, semillon, verdelho;
Red—cabernet sauvignon, merlot, petit verdot, shiraz, zinfandel
Leading wines: Andrew Harris The Vision

(a Shiraz and Cabernet Sauvignon blend), Reserve Cabernet Sauvignon, Reserve Shiraz, Reserve Cabernet-Merlot, Reserve Chardonnay, Shiraz, Premium Cabernet Sauvignon, Chardonnay, Verdelho, Semillon, Merlot
Notes: The Andrew Harris reds are among the best in the region, particularly The Vision. These are dark, powerful wines which have enjoyed spectacular show success over the years. The pity of it is that there are no present cellar door sales. These are not planned till at least 2002.

Blue Wren Vineyard (formerly Britten's Wines) **R83**

Cassilis Road, Mudgee, NSW 2850
Ph 02 6372 6205, Fax 02 6372 6206,
Email winesales@bluewrenwines.com.au

Owners: James and Diana Anderson
Chief winemaker: Simon Gilbert Wine Services (contract)
Year of foundation: vineyard 1985
Tonnes crushed on average each year: 50
Location: Mudgee
Area: 15 ha consisting of two vineyards, Mudgee 7 ha, Cooyal 8 ha
Soils: Mudgee sandy loams over basalt clays; Cooyal, red basalt over limestone clay
Varieties planted: White—chardonnay, semillon, verdelho; Red—cabernet sauvignon, merlot, shiraz
Leading wines: Blue Wren Merlot, Semillon, Cabernet
Notes: Blue Wren is a new maker in the Mudgee region, having commenced only in 1999. Fortunately it had its own established vineyard as a source of fruit and after only two vintages in 2000 it had won a gold, silver and bronze award for its wines in local shows. Its Merlot appears to be the strength here, but its Shiraz is also very good. Cellar door sales:

Thurs–Mon 10am–4pm. There is also a café and restaurant.

Botobolar NR

89 Botobolar Road, Mudgee, NSW 2850
Ph 02 6373 3840, Fax 02 6373 3789,
Email botolobar@winsoft.net.au

Owners: Kevin and Trina Karstrom
Chief winemaker: Kevin Karstrom
Year of foundation: 1971
Tonnes crushed on average each year: 95
Location: Mudgee
Area: 25 ha
Soils: yellow podsolic heavy clay loam
Varieties planted: White—chardonnay, crouchen, marsanne; Red—cabernet sauvignon, mourvedre, pinot noir, shiraz
Leading wines: Botobolar The King (a red blend of Cabernet-Shiraz-Mourvedre), Shiraz, Chardonnay, Marsanne
Notes: Botobolar is a member of the National Association of Sustainable Agriculture Australia and as such is an organic vineyard. There are two preservative-free wines and others conventionally made. Cellar door sales: Mon–Sat 10am–5pm, Sun and public holidays 10am–3pm.

Burrundulla Vineyards NR

Castlereagh Highway, Mudgee, NSW 2850
Ph 02 6372 1620, Fax 02 6372 4058

Owners: Burrundulla Pty Ltd
Chief winemaker: no wine currently made
Year of foundation: 1994
Tonnes produced on average each year: 400, all sold. Vineyards are not yet fully bearing but about 600 tonnes is anticipated when the vineyard is in full production
Location: Mudgee
Area: 61.2 ha
Soils: A free-draining red loam over friable red clay

Varieties planted: White—chardonnay, semillon; Red—cabernet sauvignon, merlot, shiraz
Leading wines: Burrundulla Cabernet Sauvignon-Shiraz, Chardonnay
Notes: At this stage, Burrundulla is primarily a grapegrower, but winemaking is envisaged for the future. No cellar door sales.

Frog Rock Wines (formerly Tallara) NR

Lawson Farm, Edgell Lane, Mudgee, NSW 2850
Ph 02 6372 2408, Fax 02 6372 6924

Owner: Tinobah Pty Ltd
Chief winemaker: Simon Gilbert (contract)
Year of foundation: 1973
Tonnes produced on average each year: 300, of which 50 are used for Frog Rock wines
Location: Mudgee
Area: 55 ha
Soils: browny-red loams
Varieties planted: White—chardonnay, semillon; Red—cabernet sauvignon, chambourcin, merlot, shiraz
Leading wines: Frog Rock Cabernet Sauvignon, Shiraz
Notes: This long-established grower has recently changed its name from Tallara to Frog Rock. It uses a small amount of its production for the Frog Rock label. I have not tasted its wines. Cellar door sales: weekends 10am–4pm.

Huntington Estate R85

Cassilis Road, Mudgee, NSW 2850
Ph 02 6373 3825, Fax 02 6373 3730,
Email huntwine@lisp.com.au

Owners: Bob and Wendy Roberts
Chief winemaker: Susie Roberts
Year of foundation: 1969
Tonnes crushed on average each year: 300
Area: 43 ha
Soils: varied soils but chiefly red to sandy clay

loams over clay and limestone
Varieties planted: White—chardonnay,
semillon; Red—cabernet sauvignon, grenache,
merlot, pinot noir, shiraz
Leading wines: Huntington Estate Shiraz,
Cabernet Sauvignon, Cabernet
Sauvignon-Merlot, Semillon
Notes: Huntington is one of the oldest wineries
in the region and has created an envied
reputation for its wines, especially its reds. But
Huntington is not all wine. There is also the
outstanding Huntington Music Festival, held
every year in November–December. Of a fine
range of full-bodied reds, the Shiraz is usually
the longest-lived and always worth cellaring
for several years. Its Cabernet Sauvignon-
Merlot is also consistently good. Cellar door
sales: Mon–Fri 9am–5pm, Sat 10am–5pm,
Sun 10am–3.30pm.

Knights Eurunderee Flats Winery NR

655 Henry Lawson Drive, Eurunderee
via Mudgee, NSW 2850
Ph 02 6373 3954, Fax 02 6373 3750

Owners: Peter and Maria Knights
Chief winemaker: Peter Knights
Year of foundation: 1985
Tonnes crushed on average each year: 25, of
which 20 are used for Knights Eurunderee Flats
wines
Location: Eurunderee
Area: 5 ha
Soils: red-grey clay loam on a clay base
Varieties planted: White—muscat gordo
blanco, riesling, sauvignon blanc, semillon;
Red—merlot, muscat hamburgh, shiraz
Leading wines: Eurunderee Flats Shiraz, Merlin
Rouge (light red), Knight Vines Round Table
Tawny Port
Notes: There is a range of reds, whites and
fortifieds here, none of which I have tasted.
Cellar door sales: Sun–Fri 10am–4pm,
Sat 10am–5pm.

Knowland Estate Wines NR

Mount Vincent Road, Running Stream,
NSW 2850
Ph 02 6358 8420, Fax 02 6358 8423

Owner: Peter R Knowland and Associates
Pty Ltd
Chief winemaker: Peter Knowland
Year of foundation: 1990
Tonnes crushed on average each year: 15
Location: Running Stream
Area: 4 ha
Soils: basalt
Varieties planted: White—gewurztraminer,
pinot gris, sauvignon blanc; Red—pinot noir
Leading wines: Knowland Estate Pinot Noir,
Sauvignon Blanc
Notes: At 1080 m in altitude, Knowland Estate
is one of the highest vineyards in Australia, an
extremely cool environment for the sauvignon
blanc and pinot noir planted there. Peter
Knowland has tried later ripening varieties
such as cabernet sauvignon and merlot, but
the ripening season at Knowland Estate is just
too short. Cellar door sales by appointment.

Lawsons Hill Estate NR

574 Henry Lawson Drive, Mudgee
NSW 2850
Ph 02 6373 3953, Fax 02 6373 3948

Owners: Jose and June Grace
Chief winemaker: contract
Year of foundation: 1985
Tonnes crushed on average each year: 50
Location: Mudgee
Area: 8.5 ha
Soils: clayey loams to red basalt on a clay base
Varieties planted: White—chardonnay, chenin
blanc, gewurztraminer, riesling, verdelho;
Red—cabernet sauvignon, gamay, malbec,
merlot, pinot noir
Leading wines: Lawsons Hill Merlot, Cabernet
Sauvignon, Cabernet-Merlot
Notes: At the time of writing the property was

being sold. Cellar door sales: Mon, Thurs–Sat 10am–4.30pm, Tues–Wed by appointment, Sun and public holidays 10am–4pm.

Lowe Family Wines NR

Tinja Lane, Mudgee, NSW 2850
Ph 02 6372 0800, Fax 02 6372 0811

Owners/chief winemakers: David Lowe and Jane Wilson
Year of foundation: vineyard 1974, winery 1999
Tonnes crushed on average each year: 120
Location: Mudgee
Area: 16.3 ha
Soils: red basalt over quartzy red clay over limestone
Varieties planted: White—chardonnay; Red—barbera, merlot, sangiovese, shiraz, zinfandel
Leading wines: Lowe Family Semillon (made from purchased fruit), Chardonnay, Orange Red (a cabernet sauvignon, cabernet franc and merlot blend), Merlot (Hunter-Mudgee), Shiraz (Hunter)
Notes: David Lowe and Jane Wilson operate two wineries, one at Mudgee, the other at Peppers Creek in the Hunter Valley. At Mudgee, fruit from the high quality Orange region is also purchased and blended but what David and Jane most cherish are the unirrigated, untrellised bush vines on their Mudgee vineyard. I have seen no recent Lowe Family wines. Cellar door sales at Mudgee by appointment.

Mansfield Wines NR

Eurunderee Road, Mudgee, NSW 2850
Ph 02 6373 3871, Fax 02 6373 3708

Owner: Ian McLellan
Chief winemaker: (contract)
Year of foundation: 1975
Tonnes crushed on average each year: 40
Location: Mudgee

Area: 6.8 ha
Soils: red basalt over clay
Varieties planted: White—chardonnay, sauvignon blanc, white frontignac; Red—black muscat, cabernet sauvignon, merlot, touriga, zinfandel
Leading wines: Mansfield White Frontignac, Chardonnay, Cabernet-Merlot
Notes: This long-established winemaker shows regularly at the Mudgee Show, winning silver, bronze, and the occasional gold award. Cellar door sales: daily 10am–5pm.

Martins Hill Wines NR

Sydney Road, Mudgee, NSW 2850
(16 km south of Mudgee)
Ph/Fax 02 6373 1248

Owners: Michael Sweeney and Jan Kenworthy
Chief winemaker: (contract)
Year of foundation: 1985
Tonnes crushed on average each year: 12
Location: Martins Hill, Mudgee
Area: 2 ha
Soils: Silurian aged acid volcanic
Varieties planted: White—sauvignon blanc; Red—cabernet sauvignon, pinot noir, shiraz
Leading wines: Martins Hill Sauvignon Blanc, Cabernet Sauvignon
Notes: Martins Hill is an organically grown vineyard and typical of the enthusiastic revival of winegrowing in the Central Ranges of New South Wales. Cellar door sales: none. Sales by mail order.

Mildara Blass
(formerly Augustine Wines) R83

George Campbell Drive, Mudgee, NSW 2850
Ph 02 6372 3880, Fax 02 6372 2977

Owner: Mildara Blass Ltd
Chief winemaker: Neil McGuigan
Year of foundation: 1918
Tonnes crushed on average each year: 620

Location: Mudgee
Area: 55 ha
Soils: brown sandy loam over clay subsoils,
fertile, friable and well-drained
Varieties planted: White—chardonnay,
gewurztraminer, semillon; Red—aleatico,
cabernet sauvignon, merlot, pinot noir, shiraz
Leading wines: Rothbury regional labels
including Mudgee Shiraz and Mudgee
Cabernet Merlot
Notes: This is one of the veteran vineyards of
Mudgee, having been founded by Dr Fiaschi in
1918. These days its grapes form part of the
Rothbury regional range of wines. Cellar door
sales: Fri–Tues 10am–4pm.

Miramar Wines **R81**

Henry Lawson Drive, Mudgee,
NSW 2850
Ph 02 6373 3874, Fax 02 6373 3854

Owners: Ian MacRae and others
Chief winemaker: Ian MacRae
Year of foundation: 1977
Tonnes crushed on average each year: 350, of
which about 150 are used for Miramar wines
Location: vineyard, winery and cellar door sales
at Eurunderee, Mudgee (about 12 km north of
the town); Eljamar vineyard, Mudgee (about
5 km north of the town)
Area: 35 ha
Soils: very variable but generally clay loam over
deep friable clays
Varieties planted: White—chardonnay, riesling,
sauvignon blanc, semillon; Red—cabernet
sauvignon, merlot, pinot noir, shiraz
Leading wines: Miramar Shiraz, Chardonnay,
Semillon, Cabernet-Merlot
Notes: Ian MacRae is one of the veterans of
Mudgee winemaking and the winner of many
trophies at the Mudgee Show. His wines are
certainly worth a detour. Cellar door sales:
7 days 9am–5pm.

Mountilford Winery **NR**

2 km off the Sydney Road, at Ilford
50 km south of Mudgee
Ph/Fax 02 6358 8544

Owners: Helen and Don Cumming
Chief winemaker: Don Cumming
Year of foundation: 1976
Tonnes crushed on average each year: 48, of
which 28 are used for Mountilford wines
Location: Ilford
Area: 7 ha
Soils: loam and shale over grey clay
Varieties planted: White—gewurztraminer,
pinot gris, riesling, sylvaner; Red—cabernet
sauvignon, shiraz
Leading wines: Mountilford Pinot Gris, Riesling,
Cabernet Sauvignon, Shiraz
Notes: At 950 m altitude, Mountilford is a
long-established family vineyard and one of
the highest vineyards before Orange, where
there are several higher. Cellar door sales:
7 days 10am–4pm.

Mudgee Wines **NR**

280 Henry Lawson Drive, Mudgee,
NSW 2850
Ph 02 6372 2258

Owners: David and Lendy Conway
Chief winemaker: David Conway
Year of foundation: 1963
Tonnes crushed on average each year: 8
Location: Mudgee
Area: 12 ha
Soils: clay on limestone
Varieties planted: White—chardonnay,
gewurztraminer, riesling, trebbiano;
Red—black muscat, cabernet sauvignon,
pinot noir, shiraz
Leading wines: Mudgee Wines Cabernet
Sauvignon, Shiraz, Chardonnay
Notes: Mudgee Wines has recently changed
hands. Henceforth customary commercial
viticultural and winemaking practices will be

followed. Cellar door sales: Thurs–Mon 10am–5pm, Tues–Wed by appointment, open 7 days during school holidays.

Pieter van Gent Winery and Vineyard NR

141 Black Springs Road, Mudgee, NSW 2850
Ph 02 6373 3807, Fax 02 6373 3910

Owners: Pieter and Sheila van Gent
Chief winemakers: Pieter van Gent and Philip van Gent
Year of foundation: 1979
Tonnes crushed on average each year: 150
Location: Mudgee
Area: 14 ha
Soils: clayey loam
Varieties planted: White—chardonnay, muller-thurgau, semillon, verdelho; Red—cabernet sauvignon, muscat a petits grains rogue, shiraz
Leading wines: Pieter van Gent Pipeclay Port, White Port; Sundance Soft Red and White Matrix (a red blend of two varieties and two years and two oaks); Matador Shiraz
Notes: I have tasted nothing from this winery recently. Cellar door sales: Mon–Sat 9am–5pm, Sun 11am–4pm.

Platt's Wines R82

cnr Cassilis Road and Henry Lawson Drive, Mudgee, NSW 2850
Ph 02 6372 7041, Fax 02 6372 7043,
Email platt@lisp.com.au

Owners: Barry and Marina Platt
Chief winemaker: Barry Platt
Year of foundation: 1984
Tonnes crushed on average each year: 180
Location: cellar door sales Mudgee, vineyard Gulgong
Area: 8 ha (fruit is also purchased locally)
Soils: red basalt above a shaley clay
Varieties planted: White—chardonnay,

gewurztraminer, semillon; Red—cabernet sauvignon, shiraz
Leading wines: Platt's Chardonnay, Cabernet Sauvignon
Notes: Platt's Wines is now located in the newly restored Fairview Winery, originally built in 1895 by a son of Adam Roth. Cellar door sales: 7 days 9am–5pm. There is also a cafe and a guesthouse with three bedrooms.

Poets Corner Winery (formerly Craigmoor and Montrose) R86

Henry Lawson Drive, Mudgee, NSW 2850 (winery but no cellar door sales)
Craigmoor Road, Mudgee, NSW 2850 (cellar door sales and restaurant)
Ph 02 6373 3853, Fax 02 6373 3795

Owner: Orlando Wyndham Group Pty Ltd
Chief winemaker: James Manners
Year of foundation: Craigmoor 1858, Montrose 1974, Poets Corner 1999
Tonnes produced on average each year: 2500, all of which are used for Poets Corner and Orlando Wyndham wines
Area: 250 ha consisting of Montrose vineyards (Montrose and Oakfield) 110 ha, Craigmoor vineyards 70 ha and Stony Creek 70 ha
Soils: Montrose, clay loam changing to reddish ironstone on tops of hills; Craigmoor, reddish ironstone with some clay loam; Stony Creek, red gravelly loams, well-drained
Varieties planted: (Montrose) White—chardonnay, gewurztraminer, riesling, sauvignon blanc, semillon; Red—cabernet sauvignon, pinot noir, shiraz. (Oakfield) White—riesling, semillon, verdelho, white frontignac; Red—barbera, cabernet franc, cabernet sauvignon, chambourcin, nebbielo, sangiovese, shiraz
Leading wines: Poets Corner PC and Henry Lawson ranges, Montrose range, Craigmoor range
Notes: Poets Corner is a brand name that has

lent its name to a winery, an ex-winery and a cellar door outlet for Orlando Wyndham. The poet in question is of course Henry Lawson. The winery is Montrose (whose cellar door closed in 1999), and the ex-winery (now cellar door outlet, restaurant and wine museum) is Craigmoor, founded in 1858. The Group's wines, now made solely from Mudgee fruit, are marketed under the Poets Corner PC, Henry Lawson, Montrose and Craigmoor labels. Cellar door sales: Mon–Fri 9am–4pm, weekends 10am–4pm.

Red Clay Estate NR

269 Henry Lawson Drive, Mudgee, NSW 2850
Ph/Fax 02 6372 4596,
Email redclay@lisp.com.au

Owners: Ken Heslop and Annette Bailey
Chief winemaker: Ken Heslop
Year of foundation: vineyard 1988, winery 1997
Tonnes crushed on average each year: 30
Location: Mudgee, vineyard Gulgong
Area: 5 ha consisting of Mudgee vineyard 2.5 ha and Gulgong 2.5 ha
Soils: Mudgee, heavy red to brown clay; Gulgong, orange-red clays
Varieties planted: White—chardonnay, sauvignon blanc, white frontignac; Red—cabernet sauvignon, merlot, muscat, shiraz
Leading wines: Red Clay Cabernet-Merlot, Chardonnay, Sauvignon Blanc
Notes: A vineyard established on typical Mudgee clay with reds of bronze medal standard. Cellar door sales: Fri–Mon 10am–5pm.

Rosemount (vineyards only) R90

Henry Lawson Drive, Mudgee, NSW 2850

Owner: Southcorp Wines
Chief winemaker: Andrew Koerner

There are three Rosemount vineyards in Mudgee, all located on Henry Lawson Drive.

(i) Mountain Blue

Year of foundation: 1953
Tonnes produced on average each year: not disclosed but estimated at 160
Area: 18 ha
Soils: red-brown loam, clays, over red clay subsoil
Varieties planted: White—none; Red—cabernet sauvignon, shiraz
Leading wine: Mountain Blue Shiraz-Cabernet

(ii) Hill of Gold

Year of foundation: 1973
Tonnes produced on average each year: not disclosed but estimated at 1100
Area: 120 ha
Soils: red-brown loam, clays, over red clay subsoil; on hill patches quartz and slate subsoils
Varieties planted: White—chardonnay, sauvignon blanc; Red—cabernet franc, cabernet sauvignon, merlot, pinot noir, shiraz
Leading wines: Hill of Gold range

(iii) Cumbandry

Henry Lawson Drive, Gulgong

Year of foundation: 1997
Tonnes produced on average each year: not yet in full production
Area: 550 ha, of which 192 ha are bearing, 358 ha are non-bearing (as at 2001)
Soils: red clay loams over quartzite shaly gravels
Varieties planted: White—chardonnay, riesling, traminer; Red—barbera, cabernet sauvignon, shiraz, merlot, nebbiolo
Leading wines: contributor to Rosemount Diamond label range or better

Notes: Under Philip Shaw's skilled direction, both Mountain Blue and Hill of Gold vineyards produced brilliant Shiraz and Shiraz-dominant reds. No local cellar door sales.

Seldom Seen Vineyard NR

'Honey Haven', cnr Hill End and
Gulgong Roads, Mudgee, NSW 2850
Ph 02 6372 0839, Fax 02 6372 1055

Owner: Seldom Seen Vineyard Pty Ltd
(vineyard leased)
Chief winemaker: Barry Platt
Year of foundation: 1987
Tonnes crushed on average each year: 75
Location: Mudgee
Area: 17.8 ha
Soils: red-brown basalt to a depth of half a metre over a gravelly clay subsoil
Varieties planted: White—chardonnay, gewurztraminer, semillon; Red—none
Leading wines: Seldom Seen Barrel Fermented Chardonnay, Wooded Semillon, Unwooded Chardonnay, Unwooded Semillon
Notes: Unusually for Mudgee, this is an all-white vineyard, not a red vine in sight. The wines, however, have won awards at the Mudgee Show. Cellar door sales: daily 9am–5pm.

Simon Gilbert Wines R84

1320 Castlereagh Highway, Apple Tree
Flat via Mudgee, NSW 2850
Ph 02 6373 1245, Fax 02 6373 1350,
Email sgwsmudg@winsoft.net.au

Owner: Simon Gilbert Wines Ltd
Chief winemaker: Simon Gilbert
Year of Foundation: 1999
Tonnes produced on average each year: the vineyard not yet fully bearing. In addition fruit is purchased from growers in many quality Australian regions including McLaren Vale, the Hunter Vally and Orange. All production is used for Simon Gilbert wines.

Location: Apple Tree Flat, 16 kms south of Mudgee
Area: 40 ha
Soils: There are three types of soils: i) a very steep north-facing hillside with a loamy, rocky topsoil less than 10cms deep overlying shaly rock planted to shiraz and sangiovese; ii) a valley to the west of the winery with red loamy clay with some fragments of shale, overlying a friable clay planted to merlot, cabernet sauvignon, petit verdot and zinfandel; and iii) a gentle slope of sandy loam opposite the winery containing river pebbles overlying permeable clay, planted to chardonnay, barbera, cabernet sauvignon, merlot, and sangiovese
Varieties planted: White—chardonnay; Red—barbera, cabernet sauvignon, merlot, petit verdot, sangiovese, shiraz, zinfandel
Leading wines: The wines from this vineyard will form the basis of the Simon Gilbert flagship Mudgee range, but presently only Shiraz is in production
Notes: Simon Gilbert is a descendant of one of South Australia's first vignerons, Joseph Gilbert and in his own right is a widely experienced and skilful winemaker. Until the construction of the winery at Apple Tree Flat, Simon has been a consultant and contract winemaker to many small wineries in central New South Wales and the Hunter Valley. That practice will continue.

From the new winery at Apple Tree Flat, two wine ranges will be widely marketed: 'Simon Gilbert' consisting of quality varietal wine from the top regions for each variety including a Mudgee Shiraz, and 'Simon Gilbert Card Series', described simply as 'premium Australian wines at value for money prices'. Cellar door sales from late 2001

Steins Wines NR

Pipeclay Lane, Mudgee, NSW 2850
Ph 02 6373 3991, Fax 02 6373 3709

Owners: RS and LM Stein
Chief winemaker: Robert Stein
Year of foundation: 1976
Tonnes crushed on average each year: 75
Location: Mudgee
Area: 8 ha
Soils: brown-grey loam with a clay subsoil
Varieties planted: White—chardonnay,
gewurztraminer, riesling, semillon; Red—black
muscat, cabernet sauvignon, shiraz
Leading wines: Stein's Chardonnay, Shiraz and
a wide range of fortifieds including a Vintage
Port and a Liqueur Muscat
Notes: Steins wines is a prolific winner of gold,
silver and bronze awards at the Mudgee Show.
Cellar door sales: 7 days 10am–4.30pm.

Thistle Hill Vineyard   R80

McDonalds Road, Mudgee, NSW 2850
Ph 02 6373 3546, Fax 02 6373 3540,
Email robertsn@winsoft.net.au

Owners: Robertson family
Chief winemaker: David Robertson (until his
death in late 2001)
Year of foundation: 1976
Tonnes crushed on average each year: 60
Location: Mudgee
Area: 11 ha
Soils: basalt over ironstone 0.6 m deep,
permeable to about 4 m and some red clay
subsoil
Varieties planted: White—chardonnay, riesling;
Red—cabernet sauvignon, pinot noir
Leading wines: Thistle Hill Pinot Noir, Cabernet
Sauvignon
Notes: This vineyard is classified as Grade A
Organic by the National Association of
Sustainable Agriculture in Australia. Over the
years Thistle Hill has built up an excellent
reputation for its Cabernet Sauvignon, and its
Chardonnay is never far behind. It also exhibits
with great success at the Mudgee Wine Show.
Cellar door sales: 7 days 9am–5pm. There are
also picnic and barbecue facilities and a 3-
bedroom cottage for rental.

Vinifera Wines   NR

194 Henry Lawson Drive, Mudgee,
NSW 2850
Ph/Fax 02 6372 2461

Owners: Tony and Debbie McKendry
Chief winemaker: Stephen Dodd (contract)
Year of foundation: 1994
Tonnes crushed on average each year: 80, of
which 25 are used for Vinifera's wines
Location: Mudgee
Area: 7.5 ha
Soils: yellow duplex loams, toposoil 0.4 m
deep, slightly alkaline
Varieties planted: White—chardonnay,
semillon; Red—cabernet sauvignon,
tempranillo
Leading wines: Vinifera Tempranillo, Cabernet
Sauvignon
Notes: Tony and Debbie McKendry are very
interested in Spanish varietals and in Rioja style
and hope one day to use manzuelo, graciano
and garnacha with their tempranillo to
reproduce this style. Cellar door sales: daily
10am–5.30pm.

Wells Parish Wines   NR

Bylong Valley Way, Kandos, NSW 2848
Ph 02 6379 4168, Fax 02 6379 4996,
Email trounson@winsoft.net.au

Owners: Richard and Rachel Trounson
Chief winemakers: Pieter and Philip Van Gent
(contract)
Year of foundation: 1995
Tonnes produced on average each year: 100,
of which 10 are used for Wells Parish wines
Location: vineyard only at Kandos
Area: 16 ha
Soils: sandy loam over clay
Varieties planted: White—chardonnay,
verdelho; Red—cabernet sauvignon, merlot,
petit verdot, shiraz
Leading wines: Wells Parish Chardonnay,
Cabernet Sauvignon
Notes: This is a new vineyard in the Kandos

area of Mudgee, which has already had show success with a gold and two silvers for Chardonnay and awards also for its Cabernet

Sauvignon. Sales by mail order and from retail outlets.

ORANGE REGION

It is common knowledge now among vignerons that if you wish to grow cool-climate grapes, you either seek a high latitude or a high altitude. That may explain the popularity of southern Victoria and Tasmania on the one hand and places like Stanthorpe and Orange on the other. Other pieces of pragma are pome and stone fruit—if they grow well and ripen slowly, then grapes often follow their example. Most of the areas mentioned have grown apples and peaches extremely well and it is not their fault if they are now being supplanted there by growers seeking better returns from the wine grape.

Orange was named in 1828 by Major Mitchell, Surveyor-General of New South Wales, after Prince William of Orange (did the House of Orange ever use any other Christian name? This one was a rather loose cannon who had fought in the Peninsular War). It had been discovered by another famous Surveyor-General of New South Wales, John Oxley, in 1820 and was proclaimed a village in 1846. Like much of central New South Wales and Victoria, it enjoyed a goldrush in 1851 and thereafter grew rapidly, settling down into solid agricultural prosperity for the rest of the century. In the last 100 years, it has been a thriving horticultural centre and table grapes were once an important product. Orange was also on the shortlist for consideration as our Federal capital, but was rejected because of a shortage of water (a problem that still plagues the inhabitants of Orange and its surrounds, but more of this later). Today, Orange remains a leading grower of horticultural products (apples, pears, peaches, cherries, plums and nectarines). The table grapes have declined in importance and today their place is being taken by wine grapes. Other products are beef, lamb and wool. Gold also remains on the agenda with the opening of Australia's largest open-cut goldmine at Cadia.

The wine history of the region began as recently as the early 1980s, but nearby Molong had been the subject of trial plantings by the late Graham Gregory on behalf of the New South Wales Department of Agriculture more than 30 years before. The pioneers of the region were the Doyles of Bloodwood, the Swansons of Cargo Road Wines and Highland Heritage Estate. In 1988 Philip Shaw of Rosemount Estate also developed a major vineyard. By 1995, there were 150 hectares of vines, but this area has since been virtually tripled by the establishment of the Little Boomey Vineyard of 277 hectares. By 1996 the vineyard area of the region was over 570 hectares with only about 75 hectares of bearing vines. These yielded some 700 tonnes in 1996, most of which were vinified in the Hunter Valley.

Location: latitude 33°19'S, longitude 149°03'E, about 270 km west-north-west of Sydney
Elevation: 922 m with vineyards ranging in altitude from 600 m to 1100 m
Topography and soils: The region is hilly and undulating, a relatively young uplifted topography caused by the volcanic activity of Mount Canobolas, its dominant feature.

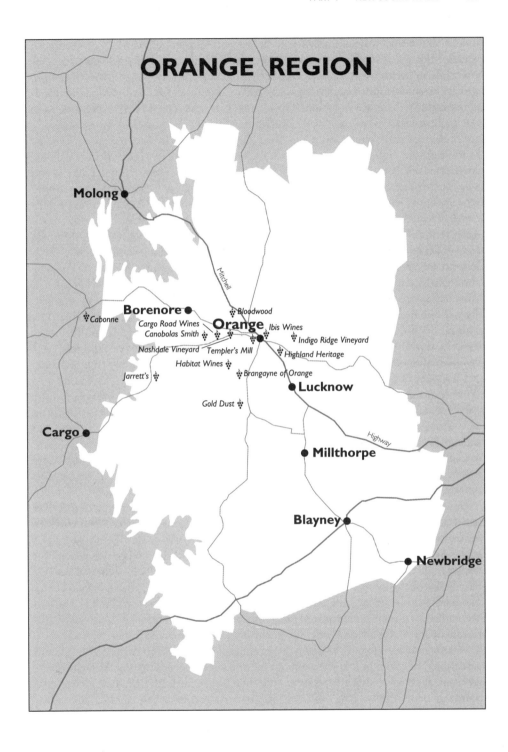

ORANGE REGION

Molong

Borenore

Cabonne

Bloodwood

Cargo Road Wines
Canobolas Smith

Orange

Ibis Wines

Indigo Ridge Vineyard

Nashdale Vineyard Templer's Mill

Highland Heritage

Habitat Wines

Brangayne of Orange

Jarrett's

Lucknow

Gold Dust

Mitchell

Cargo

Highway

Millthorpe

Blayney

Newbridge

Indeed this extinct volcano might well be in John Gladstones' words 'a projecting or isolated' hill, a factor which—together with, say, excellent air drainage—may prove its vineyards to be 'the very best'. Basalt rock is common in the area of the mountain, which also shows limestone outcrops from 600 m altitude. Such outcrops underlie much of the country of higher elevation. The region is also the source of tributary streams to the Lachlan and Macquarie Rivers, which run west into the Murray–Darling system.

There are four main soil types used for viticulture in the region as follows. Kraznozems are deep, well-drained clay soils derived from tertiary basalt material. These are located adjacent to Mount Canobolas and extend for a radius of about 10 km and even further towards Millthorpe. These soils, usually found at higher elevations overlying limestone, are quite fertile and promote strong vine vigour. Red earths/red-brown earths are older, gradational soils of red-brown clay loam over redder light clays. Such soils are slightly acid, well-drained and of medium to high fertility. Red podsols/brown podsols are duplex soils of red-brown to brown loam over medium to heavy clay. These soils are generally shallower, are of lower fertility and only moderate vigour. They are also slightly acid in nature. *Terra rossa*, though rarer in the region, are present in isolated areas in its west and lie above hard limestone outcrops. They have a more neutral pH, are well-drained and are excellent for viticulture, provided that water is available.

Climate: Orange Agricultural College (University of Sydney) MJT 19.45°C, MAR 14.25°C, HDD (Oct–Apr) 1243, (cut off at 19°C but otherwise not adjusted), AR 946 mm (Oct–Apr 520 mm), RH (9am Jan), 66% (3pm Jan 50%). AI 103 mm, SH (Oct–April av) 8.7.

Orange might be viewed as a viticultural 'layer-cake', with varieties favouring warmer climes at, say, 500–600 m, cultivars preferring slightly cooler conditions at 700–800 m and so on, as one ascends, to varieties such as pinot noir on the very top layer and presumably chardonnay of differing styles being produced at each level. This notion is, of course, fanciful but Orange certainly does seem to have a capacity for climatic and therefore varietal versatility within its boundaries. Altitude, however, poses its own problems—low relative humidity and low concentration of carbon dioxide.

Its annual rainfall, varying within the region from 750 to 915 mm (more than half of which falls during the October–April growing season) is generous enough and needs to be, for the Orange region lies within the Murray–Darling basin of New South Wales and until recently there was a complete embargo on the issue of irrigation licences within this area, that is, except from dams and bores in existence before 1995. Now the Water Act has liberalised this situation slightly in that every landholder may without licence retain in a dam and use for any purposes up to 10% of run-off from his own land, calculated according to a prescribed formula. As regards amounts of water in excess of this, governmental deliberations are still proceeding with snail-like celerity in respect of the issue.

The region has a frost risk during spring and again from mid to late autumn, so great care should be taken in the selection of vineyard sites by ensuring that such sites have good air drainage and do not face south, thereby avoiding the chill factors of cold southerly or south-westerly winds. Strong easterly winds during summer sometimes cause canopy roll and problems with flowering. The very presence of a mountain such as Mount Canobolas of about 1400 m in altitude ensures that Orange weather changes quickly with snow and sleet a possibility virtually at any time of the year. Hail is also possible in certain areas. Powdery mildew can be a problem, but is controlled by systemic spraying early in the season and later by sulfur.

Harvest time: this varies with altitude. Chardonnay at 850 m late March, at 900 m mid April, at 960 m early May. Cabernet Sauvignon at 850 m second to third week of April, at 900 m third week of April, at 960 m early May.

Principal varieties: White—chardonnay, sauvignon blanc, riesling and others; Red—cabernet sauvignon, shiraz, merlot, pinot noir, cabernet franc and others

Total area: (2001) 1300 ha

Principal wine styles: From the varieties planted and my tastings to date, Orange is undoubtedly a region of light to medium-bodied fruit-driven whites of style and elegance and medium- to full-bodied reds which are fruit-dominant and well balanced. Orange Chardonnay and Orange Cabernet will be wines of national importance in the next twenty years.

Leading wineries and vineyards: Rosemount, Bloodwood, Canobolas Smith, Ibis, Highland Heritage, Habitat, Indigo Ridge, Cargo Road

Bloodwood **R85**

4 Griffin Road, Orange, NSW 2800
Ph 02 6362 5631, Fax 02 6361 1173,
Email sdoyle@bloodwood.com.au

Owner: Bloodwood Pty Ltd
Chief winemaker: Stephen Doyle
Year of foundation: 1983
Tonnes crushed on average each year: 65, of which 40 are used for Bloodwood wines
Location: Orange (3.5 km west of the city on the road to Molong)
Area: 8.61 ha
Soils: friable, red, gravelly, loamy topsoil, tending to be acid (the vineyard is located on the mid slopes of a free-standing north and easterly facing headland between 810 and 845 m above sea level)
Varieties planted: White—chardonnay, riesling; Red—cabernet franc, cabernet sauvignon, malbec, merlot, pinot noir, shiraz
Leading wines: Bloodwood Chardonnay, Riesling, 'Schubert' (a white blend), Cabernet Sauvignon, 'Maurice' (a red blend)
Notes: By Australian standards, Bloodwood is very cool, often receiving two or three snowfalls a year, which does assist subsoil moisture retention. As well, the vineyard is

irrigated in times of drought stress by what Stephen Doyle describes as 'the judicious use of supplemental water harvested from the slopes of Bloodwood'. Chardonnay and Cabernet Sauvignon of elegant rather than beefy style are the highlights here. Cellar door sales by appointment.

Brangayne of Orange **R82**

49 Pinnacle Road, Orange, NSW 2800
Ph 02 6365 3229, Fax 02 6365 3170,
Email brangayne@netwit.net.au

Owner: Brangayne Pty Ltd
Chief winemaker: Simon Gilbert (contract)
Year of foundation: 1994
Tonnes crushed on average each year: 300, of which 60 are used for Brangayne wines
Location: Orange (about 10 km south-west of the town)
Area: 26 ha
Soils: volcanic loam
Varieties planted: White—chardonnay, sauvignon blanc; Red—cabernet sauvignon, merlot, pinot noir, shiraz
Leading wines: Brangayne of Orange Tristan (a red blend), Pinot Noir, Reserve Chardonnay
Notes: There are two vineyards here, one high,

the other higher. Like the rest of Orange, they both have extremely cool climate conditions. The vineyard's strengths are Chardonnay and Tristan, the red blend of Cabernet Sauvignon, Merlot and Shiraz, and both are in the usual elegant Orange mode. Cellar door sales by appointment.

Cabonne Vintners R82

Cudal–Cargo Road, Cudal, NSW 2884
Ph 02 6364 2273, Fax 02 6364 2388,
Email quondong@cabonneltd.com.au

Owners: Cabonne Vintners Pty Ltd
Chief winemaker: Jon Reynolds
Year of foundation: Little Boomey vineyard 1995, Angullong and Wirrilla vineyards 1998, winery, Cabonne Vintners 1998
Tonnes produced on average each year: only the Little Boomey vineyard is near full production, but forward estimates equate to a production of 12 500 tonnes by 2004. It is presently estimated that about 80% of this amount will be used for Cabonne's own labels and/or bulk wine
Location: Little Boomey (18 km north-east of Molong), Angullong, (Panuara, near Millthorpe), Wirrilla (Jugiong, near Gundagai)
Area: 869 ha consisting of Little Boomey 503 ha, Angullong 186 ha, Wirrilla 180 ha
Soils: Little Boomey, basalt and shale with some limestone, well-drained with good depth and fertility; Angullong, volcanic origin with excellent depth, good aeration and drainage, top 30–40 cm red-brown loam, changing to a sandier clay shale at 1 m in depth; Wirrilla, predominantly earthy and gritty sands of granitic origin, well-drained and granitic in nature
Varieties planted: White—chardonnay, marsanne, riesling, roussanne, sauvignon blanc, semillon, verdelho; Red—cabernet sauvignon, grenache, merlot, mourvedre, shiraz
Leading wines: Reynolds, intended to be international brand with three ranges—

Landscape (2nd tier range of white and reds); Little Boomey (bottom tier 1st), Portrait (2nd label); no ultra premium label yet released
Notes: Cabonne by any standards is an ambitious project with vast areas of vineyards. It does have vineyards in and close to the Orange region (as well as a winery in nearby Cudal), so I have positioned it here, but equally it could be placed in the Central Ranges Zone. No cellar door sales yet.

Canobolas Smith R85

Boree Lane, off Cargo Road, Orange, NSW 2800
Ph/Fax 02 6365 6113,
Email canobolas.smith@netwit.net.au

Owners: Smith family
Chief winemaker: Murray Smith
Year of foundation: 1986
Tonnes crushed on average each year: 45, of which 40 are used for Canobolas Smith labels
Location: Orange
Area: 8 ha
Soils: tertiary basalt soils derived from Mt Canobolas (an extinct volcano)
Varieties planted: White—chardonnay, sauvignon blanc, semillon; Red—pinot noir, cabernet sauvignon, cabernet franc, shiraz
Leading wines: Alchemy (a red blend), Chardonnay (barrel-fermented)
Notes: From his purposely unirrigated vineyard at 800 m in altitude, Murray Smith produces some of the leading wines of the Orange region, handcrafted wines such as Alchemy and a complex barrel-fermented Chardonnay. Murray is a minimalist, that is minimal use of herbicides and no insecticides at all. Cellar door sales: weekends and public holidays 11am–5pm.

Canobolas Vineyard *(vineyard only)* R87

Forbes Road, Orange, NSW 2800
(10 km west of Orange opposite Mount Canobolas)

Owners: Philip Shaw, Oatley family and Southcorp wines
Year of foundation: 1989
Tonnes produced on average each year: 350, all of which are used for Rosemount wines
Location: Borenore
Area: 100 ha, of which 60 are currently bearing
Soils: limestone basalt shaley, wind blown soils
Varieties planted: White—chardonnay; Red—cabernet sauvignon, pinot noir, merlot, shiraz
Leading wines: Rosemount Orange Chardonnay, Shiraz, Cabernet Sauvignon
Notes: This is the source of Rosemount's exciting Orange Cabernet and Shiraz, excellent wines which are adding immeasurably to the reputation of the region. There are no local cellar door sales.

Cargo Road Wines **R83**

Cargo Road, Fernlidster, Orange, NSW 2800 (12 km from Orange on the Cargo Road)
Ph 02 6365 6100, Fax 02 6365 6001, Email cargo@ix.net.au

Owner: James Sweetapple
Chief winemakers: James Sweetapple, Rob Crawford (contract)
Year of foundation: 1983
Tonnes crushed on average each year: 35, but will increase to 60 when new plantings come into bearing
Location: Orange (with café and gallery)
Area: 8 ha including new plantings
Soils: deep red volcanic soils
Varieties planted: White—gewurztraminer, riesling, sauvignon blanc, Red—cabernet sauvignon, merlot, zinfandel
Leading wines: Cargo Road Gewurztraminer, Sauvignon Blanc, Riesling, Merlot, Cabernet-Merlot, Zinfandel
Notes: Amongst the reds, Merlot is excellent. The aromatic whites are also very good. Cellar door sales: weekends 11am–5pm.

Gold Dust **NR**

South Park, Forest Reefs, NSW 2796
Ph 02 6366 5168, Fax 02 6361 9165

Owners: John and Jacqui Corrie
Chief winemaker: Jon Reynolds (contract)
Year of foundation: 1992
Tonnes crushed on average each year: 50, of which 20 are used for Gold Dust wines
Location: Forest Reefs
Area: 8 ha
Soils: kraznozems
Varieties planted: White—chardonnay, riesling; Red—pinot noir
Leading wine: Gold Dust Riesling
Notes: Gold Dust is located in the foothills of Mount Canobolas and, at 900 m in altitude, it has a lofty location similar to most other Orange vineyards. The vineyard is frost-free and well drained. The vineyard's first wine was a riesling, good enough at its first showing to win a bronze medal in Perth. Cellar door sales: phone ahead.

Habitat Wines **R86**

Old Canobolas Road, Orange, NSW 2800, (13 km south-west of Orange)
Ph/Fax 02 6365 3294

Owner: Susan Sanders
Chief winemaker: Phil Stevenson
Year of foundation: 1989
Tonnes crushed on average each year: 20, of which 15 are used for Habitat wines
Location: vineyard only at Old Canobolas Road; cellar door sales at Ibis Wines (qv)
Area: 2.5 ha
Soils: deep red/black fertile basalt soils from the extinct volcano of Mount Canobolas
Varieties planted: White—pinot gris, sauvignon blanc; Red—merlot, pinot noir
Leading wines: Habitat Pinot Noir, Merlot
Notes: At 1050 m above sea-level, Habitat is one of the highest vineyards in Australia. Its speciality is Pinot Noir, of good colour and

structure, bearing a strong resemblance to the Pinots of Southern Victoria, which proves that in New South Wales it is necessary to grow pinot noir at a good altitude (perhaps always at 1000 m or more). The Pinot Noir is worth a special trip, while the Merlot is generously plummy and soft on palate. Cellar door sales: see Ibis Wines.

Highland Heritage Estate R85

Mitchell Highway, Orange, NSW 2800
Ph 02 6361 3612, Fax 02 6362 6183,
Email daquino@netwit.net.au

Owner: D'Aquino brothers
Chief winemaker: John Hordern (contract)
Year of foundation: 1983
Tonnes crushed on average each year: 20
Location: Orange
Area: 20 ha
Soils: granite loam
Varieties planted: White—chardonnay, riesling, sauvignon blanc; Red—merlot, pinot noir, shiraz
Leading wines: Highland Heritage Estate Sauvignon Blanc, Chardonnay
Notes: Highland Heritage is one of the older established vineyards of Orange. Its specialities are Sauvignon Blanc and Chardonnay. Cellar door sales: daily 9am–5pm.

Ibis Wines R86

Kearneys Drive, Orange, NSW 2800
Ph 02 6362 3257, Fax 02 6362 5779,
Email ibiswines@bigpond.com

Owner/chief winemaker: Philip Stevenson
Year of foundation: vineyard 1988, winery 1998
Tonnes crushed on average each year: 8, to which 6 are added to make up 14 (being the amount required for Ibis wines)
Location: Orange (5 km north of the city)
Area: 1.5 ha
Soils: grey podsolic soils producing good vigour

Varieties planted: White—chardonnay, riesling; Red—cabernet franc, cabernet sauvignon, pinot noir, shiraz
Leading wines: Ibis Pinor Noir, Cabernet Sauvignon
Notes: At 906 m, Ibis is another high altitude Orange vineyard. As at Habitat, which Phillip also makes, the Pinot Noir is very good, but so are the other reds. An essential winery stop if you are anywhere near Orange. Cellar door sales: weekends and public holidays 11am–5pm, at other times by appointment.

Indigo Ridge R84

Icely Road, Orange, NSW 2800
Ph/Fax 02 6362 1851

Owners: Paul Bridge and Trish McPherson
Chief winemaker: Jon Reynolds (contract)
Year of foundation: 1995
Tonnes crushed on average each year: 35, of which 10 are used for Indigo Ridge wines
Location: Orange
Area: 4 ha (a further 2 ha are to be planted)
Soils: volcanic and varied including red earths, yellow/brown podsols and gravelly yellow loam with andesite, slate, luff, greywalke and limestone
Varieties planted: White—sauvignon blanc; Red—cabernet sauvignon
Leading wines: Indigo Ridge Sauvignon Blanc, Cabernet Sauvignon
Notes: Paul Bridge was one of the architects of the Orange Region Geographical Indication. The Indigo Sauvignon Blanc is crisp and flavourful. The Cabernet Sauvignon shows a berry flavoured elegance typical of this cool area. Cellar door sales: weekends by appointment.

Jarretts of Orange R82

Springvale Vineyard, Cargo Road, Orange NSW 2800 (25 km west of the city)
Ph 02 6364 3118, Fax 02 6364 3048

Owners: Pip and Justin Jarrett
Chief winemaker: Mark Davidson (contract)
Year of foundation: 1997
Tonnes produced on average each year: the vineyard is not yet in full bearing, but it is hoped to produce 140 tonnes, of which about 60 will be used for Jarretts' own wines
Location: Orange
Area: 16 ha
Soils: red and yellow podsols over a shale base
Varieties planted: White—chardonnay, marsanne, sauvignon blanc; Red—cabernet sauvignon, merlot
Leading wines: Chardonnay, Sauvignon Blanc
Notes: The Jarretts have an excellent show record after only a few vintages, especially for Chardonnay. The record includes a trophy for Best Chardonnay at the Canberra Regional wine show and several silvers and bronzes at other shows close to the region. Tasting confirms the judges' opinions. Mail order is available through fax no. Wine is also available through licensed outlets in Orange.

Nashdale Vineyard **NR**

Borenore Lane, Nashdale, NSW 2800
Ph 02 6365 2463, Fax 02 6361 4495

Owner: Edward Fardell
Chief winemaker: Mark Davidson (contract)
Year of foundation: 1982
Tonnes produced on average each year: 30, of which 20 are used for Nashdale wines
Location: Nashdale
Area: 10 ha
Soils: rich volcanic loam
Varieties planted: White—chardonnay, riesling, sauvignon blanc; Red—cabernet sauvignon, pinot noir
Leading wine: Nashdale Chardonnay
Notes: I have tasted no wines from this vineyard. Cellar door sales: weekends 2pm–6pm.

Templer's Mill **R82**

University of Sydney, Orange,
Leeds Parade, Orange 2800
Ph 02 6360 5590, Fax 02 6360 5698,
Email templersmill@orange.usyd.edu.au

Owner: The University of Sydney
Chief winemaker: Jon Reynolds
Year of foundation: vineyard 1994, first wine 1997
Tonnes produced on average each year: 150, of which 30 are used for Templer's Mill wines
Location: Leeds Parade, Orange
Area: 19.4 ha
Soils: red earths, deep, well-drained, red-brown clay loams over light clay (chardonnay) varying to gravelly red and yellow earths, also well-drained, moderately fertile and 1 m in depth
Varieties planted: White—chardonnay, sauvignon blanc; Red—cabernet sauvignon, merlot, shiraz
Leading wines Templer's Mill Chardonnay, Cabernet Sauvignon, Sauvignon Blanc, Shiraz
Notes: Formerly called the Orange Agricultural College, this establishment is now the Faculty of Rural Management within the University of Sydney, devoted to farm development, diversification and 'winegrape enterprise'. This last branch of learning is the raison d'etre for Templer's Mill. Its vineyard provides viticultural management training for the wine and grape industry in vineyard planning, irrigation, plant protection strategies, management and sustainable viticulture. As for its wines, its Chardonnays and reds are of good standard. Cellar door sales: Mon–Fri 9am–4pm and on other special occasions.

❦ HUNTER VALLEY ZONE

This is a wine zone, only slightly larger than its component wine region—Hunter.

HUNTER REGION

Hunter Valley or Hunter? Except for the Newcastle metropolitan area and some coastal strips, wine zone and wine region seem identical, yet the logic of it lies in the boundaries of the Hunter catchment area. As yet, there is only one sub-region, Broke Fordwich (which for its uniqueness among the rest of the Hunter relies on its more fertile soils and its slightly warmer climate), though it is inevitable that more will come into existence sooner rather than later. As to what the sub-regions will be, logic, geographic separation, the concentration of wineries and vineyards, soil types and common usage might postulate simply Lower and Upper, as in the Medoc. It has been suggested, however, that old parish names such as Pokolbin and Rothbury or districts such as Lovedale and Mount View might be used. Certainly Pokolbin is one of Australia's best-known wine names.

The Hunter is Australia's oldest viticultural area, yet its principal city, Newcastle, had its origins because of coal deposits, noticed by Lieutenant Shortland in 1797. In 1804, it became both a convict depot for recalcitrants and a coal mine. A decade later, agricultural development began on the fertile alluvial flats of the Lower Hunter Valley to the west of Newcastle and, by 1832, there were about 6 hectares of vineyards on the river flats north and west of present-day Maitland. They were shared among ten settlers and it is not exactly known who was first to plant, though an educated guess might lead us to James Kelman, the brother-in-law of James Busby, Australia's apostle of viticulture. Famous names of this period included George Wyndham, James King and, a little later, Dr Henry Lindeman. The winegrowers soon divorced themselves from other agricultural interests, especially the pastoralists, and became quite skilful in political lobbying, pressing their cause for the immigration of skilled labour with local and British authorities. By 1847, the Hunter Valley Vineyard Association was set up. Settlement of the Pokolbin region in the southern part of the Lower Hunter commenced in the mid-1850s as ancestors of wine families prominent today, such as Tyrrell and Drayton, planted their first vineyards.

To the north-west, settlement of the Upper Hunter began in the 1820s and its first vineyard, the original 'Rosemount', was established in 1864 by Carl Brecht, a German shepherd, a demeaning description of a man with great winemaking talent.

Following the bank crashes of the 1890s, however, the region became economically depressed until coal was once more discovered in the first decade of the twentieth century near present-day Cessnock. Such depression was not to leave the Hunter wine industry for 70 years. The industry disappeared altogether in the Upper Hunter and gradually slid into virtual oblivion in the Lower, despite the efforts of the immortal winemaker Maurice O'Shea. By 1956, vineyard area had declined to 489 hectares.

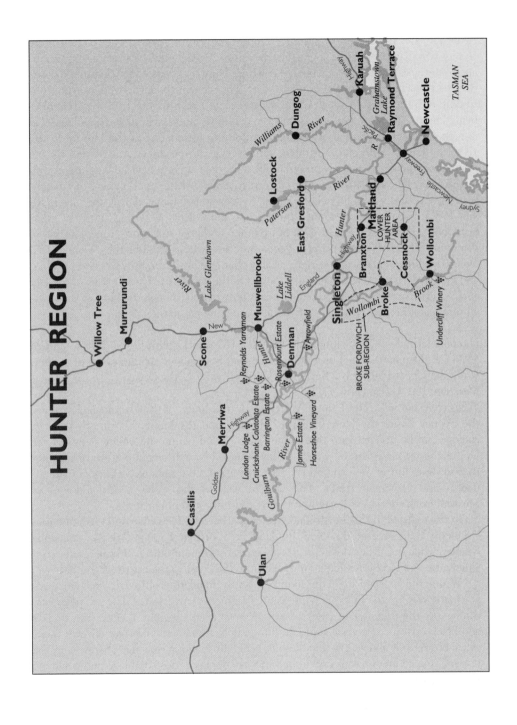

A decade later popular enthusiasm for Hunter red was increasing, due to the culture change wrought by post-war migration, the efforts of wine publicists such as Len Evans and to enthusiasts such as Dr Max Lake, whose Hunter cabernet vineyard in 1963 was the first new Hunter planting for many years. The red wine boom arrived in 1968, continuing into the 1970s, though changing its colour to white, much to the chagrin of many Hunter shiraz growers. It was a boom due in its later stages to the popularisation of a then obscure grape variety called chardonnay, introduced to the Hunter in the 1830s by James Busby. Its Australian renaissance can be directly attributed to one Hunter winemaker, the late Murray Tyrrell, a devotee of French white burgundies who instinctively felt, and was later proved correct, that a 'white pinot' variety in a neighbouring vineyard was in fact chardonnay. As mentioned above, during the late 1970s and 1980s, the Hunter continued on the ups and downs of the big-dipper of grape fashion and economics. Due to lack of irrigation and poor soil, most of its plantings of shiraz and other reds were entirely uneconomic and, where possible, these were grafted over to a more popular white variety, usually chardonnay. If not, they were grubbed out and vineyards once more became paddocks. On the whole, the Hunter story of the late 1980s and early 1990s has been one of steady growth and, though the Hunter is no viticultural paradise, reports of its early demise are quite premature.

Location: latitude 32°60'S, longitude 151°20'E (Cessnock), latitude 32°20'S longitude 150°60'E (Denman). The Lower Hunter vineyards are about 165 km north of Sydney, while the Upper Hunter is a further 70 km north-west of the Lower.
Elevation: 100–180 m (Lower), 120–240 m (Upper)
Topography and soils: The Hunter Valley sits at the limits of three geological systems, the Sydney Basin, the New England Fold Belt and the Hunter Thrust System. Its geology can be divided into three main parts. Flood plains and valley slopes of the Upper Hunter have created a wide valley bounded by a dissected plateau of resistant triassic strata in the west and on the east by rugged mountainous country of Carboniferous and Devonian strata. The eastern wall of the valley south and east of Muswellbrook consists of lower and less rugged hills of Permian strata.

In the south of the Valley, around Cessnock, there are Devonian and Carboniferous sediments indicative of the New England Fold Belt and rough Triassic sandstone country, while the Valley floor consists of Permian sediments, made of shales, tuffs, conglomerates and sandstone, extending west from the coast to the centre of the Valley.

Within the vineyard areas, the country is gently undulating, although some vineyards at Mount View south of Pokolbin are planted on more elevated sites. The soil types vary throughout the region. The vineyard soils, formed from alluvium, include brown clays and black earths, red podzols and lateritic podzols, formed on old river terraces, non-calcic brown soils and yellow solodic soils, generally found in drainage channels. In the Lower Hunter, vineyard soils vary from friable red duplex to deep friable loams, while the soils of Upper Hunter vineyards are well drained, moderately fertile, black silty loams and red duplex soils, moderately acid to alkaline and also well drained.
Climate: Cessnock MJT 22.7°C, MAR 12.8°C, HDD raw 2070, AR 740 mm (Oct–Apr 530 mm), RH 58% (9am Jan), AI na, SH 7.3 (D&S). Cf MJT 23.8°C, MAR na, HDD raw 2327, 1812 (cut-off and adjusted for latitude, daily temperature range and vine

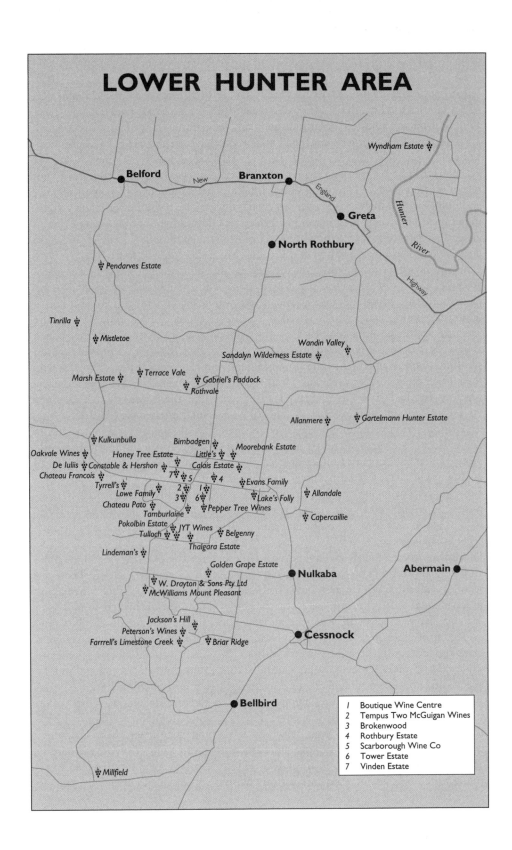

LOWER HUNTER AREA

Wyndham Estate

Belford
Branxton
New England
Greta

Hunter River
Highway

North Rothbury

Pendarves Estate

Tinrilla
Mistletoe

Wandin Valley

Sandalyn Wilderness Estate

Marsh Estate
Terrace Vale
Gabriel's Paddock
Rothvale

Allanmere
Gartelmann Hunter Estate

Kulkunbulla
Bimbadgen
Moorebank Estate

Oakvale Wines
Honey Tree Estate
Little's

De Iuliis
Constable & Hershon
Calais Estate

Chateau Francois
7 5   4

Tyrrell's
2 1
Evans Family

Lowe Family
3 6
Lake's Folly
Allandale

Chateau Pato
Pepper Tree Wines

Tamburlaine
Capercaillie

Pokolbin Estate
JYT Wines

Tulloch
Belgenny

Lindeman's
Thalgara Estate

Golden Grape Estate

Nulkaba
Abermain

W. Drayton & Sons Pty Ltd
McWilliams Mount Pleasant

Jackson's Hill

Peterson's Wines

Farrrell's Limestone Creek
Briar Ridge
Cessnock

Bellbird

1	Boutique Wine Centre
2	Tempus Two McGuigan Wines
3	Brokenwood
4	Rothbury Estate
5	Scarborough Wine Co
6	Tower Estate
7	Vinden Estate

Millfield

sites), AR 746 mm, (Oct–Apr 493 mm), RH 47% (3pm Jan), AI na, SH 7.8 (G). Jerry's Plains MJT 23.6°C, MAR na, HDD 2358, AR 635 mm (Oct–Apr 423 mm), RH 47% (9am Jan), AI na, SH 8.2 (G). Cf Scone MJT 24.6°C, MAR na, HDD raw 2380, 1772 (cut-off and adjusted for latitude and daily temperature range but not vine sites), AR 634 mm (Oct–Apr 419 mm), RH 40% (3pm Jan), AI na, SH 8.5 (Gladstones). Muswellbrook MJT 22.3°C, MAR 12.7°C, HDD 2170, AR 620 mm (Oct–Apr 400 mm), RH 75% (9am Jan), AI na, SH 7.5 (HV Vineyard Assn). This warm to hot region is often described as a sub-humid climatic zone, its summers being typically hot and humid with a high cloud cover, especially noticeable in the Lower Hunter. Rain, sometimes very heavy, is common just before and during harvest and a 'good year' is generally characterised by a dry summer. Average annual rainfall (Cessnock 740 mm) decreases as one moves away from the coast (Muswellbrook 620 mm). The region is generally frost-free during the growing season and birds do not constitute a major problem. Chief disease factors are downy mildew for which a spray program commences in mid-Spring and, during wet to very wet years, bunch rot. Hail also occurs during the spring and summer months. The heat of the Hunter Valley during the ripening season is often tempered by the light afternoon cloud cover, mentioned above. This factor—when accompanied by the fact that the ratio of growing season sunshine hours as opposed to the total of effective day degrees is low—explains why the Hunter produces soft, medium- to full-bodied whites and reds and cannot grow satisfactory fortified styles as compared with areas like the Swan though the raw HDDs are very similar (Cessnock av daily SH 7.3, Guildford av daily SH 9.2).

Drip irrigation is commonly employed in the region, though water resources in the Lower Hunter are generally restricted to farm storage dams and occasional bores, while properties in the Upper Hunter adjacent to rivers have access to a good supply of quality water. Here, too, farm storage dams are important.

Harvest time: The region's normally high temperatures generally result in an early, comparatively uniform and short vintage period, commencing in late January for cultivars such as gewurztraminer and pinot noir and finishing in early March for varieties like cabernet sauvignon.

Principal varieties: Though varietal fashion often decrees the planting of certain grape varieties, the Hunter's most suitable grape varieties have long been settled. These are semillon and shiraz. Of the rest, only chardonnay, as responsive to skilful winemaking in warm areas as it is in cool, has made the grade. Pinot noir in this region makes an ordinary dry red except in very special years and cabernet sauvignon exhibits only average fruit characters and is very reliant on wood for any complexity. Sauvignon blanc produces quite fat and soft wines without the vibrant varietal life of cooler areas, while riesling rarely achieves the concentrated lime citrus characters so sought-after by makers and consumers alike. Perhaps only merlot needs further consideration.

The Semillon of the Lower Hunter is one of the world's unique wines, often starting life as a comparatively low-alcohol neutral white (sometimes as low as 10.5% Alc v/v) and then with 5–10 years cellar age developing magnificent toasty characters on nose and palate, while retaining sufficient acidity still to be lively in the mouth. Shiraz, too, from good years in the Lower Hunter displays soft berry flavours when young which become more savoury with increasing bottle age and after 5–10 years in bottle exhibit definite regional characters of earth and leather, complex traits which make a very rewarding bottle. Chardonnay, however, reacts similarly in the Hunter to any other warm Australian area. Subject to rare exceptional years, it can be drunk at 6–9 months of age and should not be kept longer than three years from vintage. Otherwise that rich nutty flavour becomes flabby and oxidised.

Total area: 1900 ha (Lower Hunter), 1050 ha (Upper Hunter)

Leading wineries and vineyards: Rosemount Estate, Brokenwood, Lindemans, Tyrrells, J.Y. Tulloch, McWilliams Mount Pleasant, McGuigan Wines, Meerea Park, Briar Ridge, Pepper Tree Wines, Scarborough, Rothbury Estate

Allandale R84

Lovedale Road, Pokolbin via Maitland, NSW 2321
Ph 02 4990 4526, Fax 02 4990 1714,
Email wines@allandalewinery.com.au

Owner: Villa Villetri Wines Pty Ltd
Chief winemaker: Bill Sneddon
Year of foundation: 1978
Tonnes crushed on average each year: 250
Location: Lovedale
Area: 7 ha
Soils: sandy loam over clay
Varieties planted: White—chardonnay, semillon; Red—pinot noir
Leading wine: Allandale Chardonnay
Notes: Allandale is a low-profile winery but by no means an unknown boutique. It specialises in Chardonnay, which is usually of the generously drinkable Hunter mould. It grows less than 20% of its fruit requirements and, like many Hunter wineries of its size, has spread its intake of fruit to encompass areas other than the Hunter Valley. In Allandale's case, fruit is sourced also from Mudgee and the Hilltops districts. Cellar door sales: Mon–Sat 9am–5pm, Sun 10am–5pm.

Allanmere R82

Lovedale Road, Lovedale, NSW 2320
Ph 02 4930 7387, Fax 02 4930 7900,
Email winemasters@allanmere.com.au

Owners: Greg Silkman, Gary Reed, Ray Donald, 1st Wine Fund (a publicly listed company)

Chief winemakers: Greg Silkman
Year of foundation: 1985
Tonnes crushed on average each year: 40, to which 200 are added by purchase to fulfil requirements for the Allanmere labels
Location: Lovedale
Area: 4 ha
Soils: loam about 40 cm over clay
Varieties planted: White—chardonnay; Red—none
Leading wine: Allanmere Durham Chardonnay
Notes: Allanmere is a successful Hunter boutique, established some years ago by Dr Newton Potter and presently partly owned by experienced Hunter maker, Greg Silkman. Chardonnay quality is excellent. Cellar door sales: 7 days 10am–5pm.

Arrowfield NR

Denman Road, Jerry's Plains, NSW 2330
Ph 02 6576 4041, Fax 02 6576 4144,
Email arrowine@hunterlink.net.au

Owners: Hokuriko Coca-Cola Bottlers Co and Peter Helene
Chief winemaker: Blair Duncan
Year of foundation: 1969
Tonnes crushed on average each year: 1500
Location: Jerry's Plains
Area: 58 ha
Soils: coarse chocolate brown sandy loam interspersed with clay, deep and free-draining but not fertile
Varieties planted: White—chardonnay,

sauvignon blanc, semillon; Red—cabernet franc, cabernet sauvignon, merlot, pinot noir, ruby cabernet, shiraz
Leading wines: Arrowfield Show Reserve range (which includes Chardonnay, Cabernet Sauvignon, Shiraz and Semillon)
Notes: Arrowfield was prophetically named, as it was destined to undergo the 'slings and arrows of outrageous fortune' in its very first decade. It narrowly missed the Hunter red boom of the 1960s and early 1970s, then was faced with the white boom of the mid-1970s, having virtually an entirely red vineyard. It also suffered from the poor economics of Hunter winegrowing at that time and soon entire vineyards of shiraz were being top-grafted if possible, or uprooted if not. Since then quite a few changes of ownership have occurred, but its winemaking has been consistent and dedicated to quality, which is maintained to the present time. Its Show Reserve range of wines is often very impressive, as it has chosen to buy select parcels of fruit from other regions. Cellar door sales: 7 days 10am–5pm.

Barrington Estate NR

Yarraman Road, Wybong, NSW 2333
Ph 02 6547 8118, Fax 02 6547 8039,
Email yarraman@brooknet.com.au

Owner: a private company
Chief winemaker: Stephen Hagan
Year of foundation: 1960
Tonnes crushed on average each year: 900, of which 600 are used for Barrington Estate wines
Location: Wybong
Area: 160 ha
Soils: light sandy loam, heavy black loam, red podsols
Varieties planted: White—chardonnay, gewurztraminer; Red—chambourcin, merlot, shiraz
Leading wines: The Barrington Estate Yarramaan Road range (Chardonnay, Shiraz),

Barrington Estate Pencil Pine range (Gewurztraminer, Chambourcin)
Notes: This is a vineyard with a considerable history. It began life as Penfolds Wybong Estate in 1960 with a young Brian McGuigan at the winemaking helm. Its ensuing life was unfortunate. Though there was quality in some of the early wines, there was little irrigation in the vineyard and many grape varieties were planted on unsuitable soils. Overall it proved an economic disaster for Penfolds and perhaps was the telling factor in their decision to leave the Hunter Valley in 1978 after a presence there of more than 70 years. It fell to the succeeding owner, Rosemount, to make effective use of the large winery on the site and a much reduced vineyard until 1992 when the winery became a storage facility. It was purchased by the Blom family in 1994 and Barrington Estate was established. Cellar door sales: daily 10am–5pm.

Belgenny Vineyard R82

De Beyers Road, Pokolbin, NSW 2321
No cellar door phone,
Email douglas@belgenny.com.au

Owners: Norman Seckold and Dudley Leitch
Chief winemaker: contract
Year of foundation: 1991
Tonnes produced on average each year: 100
Location: Pokolbin
Area: 13.5 ha
Soils: red podsolic soils over clay
Varieties planted: White—chardonnay, semillon; Red—merlot, shiraz
Leading wines: Belgenny Shiraz, Merlot, Partners Reserve Chardonnay
Notes: A new name in the Pokolbin area with its cellar door recently opened. Its chief white is an excellent Partners Reserve Chardonnay. Its semillon and reds have also gained wine show awards from time to time. Cellar door sales: late 2001, until then, cellar door sales are at Small Winemakers Centre, McDonalds Road, Pokolbin.

Bimbadgen Estate NR

Lot 21 McDonalds Road, Pokolbin,
NSW 2320
Ph 02 4998 7585, Fax 02 4998 7732,
Email office@bimbadgen.com.au

Owner: Mulpha Pty Ltd
Chief winemaker: Kees Van de Scheur
Year of foundation: 1972 (as Bimbadgen
 since 1996)
Tonnes crushed on average each year: 1000, of
which 850 are used for Bimbadgen wines
Location: Pokolbin
Area: 88 ha
Soils: loam over clay, infertile
Varieties planted: White—chardonnay,
semillon, verdelho; Red—cabernet sauvignon,
pinot noir, shiraz
Leading wines: Bimbadgen Semillon, Verdelho,
Shiraz
Notes: Bimbadgen is yet another incarnation
of the McPherson winery erected in 1972,
which has passed through three
proprietorships between times. It is now
Bimbadgen—may fortune shine upon it!
Cellar door sales: daily 10am–5pm. There is
also a restaurant.

Briar Ridge R85

Mount View Road, Mount View
via Cessnock, NSW 2325
Ph 02 4990 3670, Fax 02 4990 7802,
Email indulge@briarridge.com.au

Owners: John Davis and Mildara Blass
Chief winemaker: Neil McGuigan (Mildara
Blass), Adrian Lockhart (site winemaker)
Year of foundation: 1972
Tonnes crushed on average each year: 350, of
which 250 are used for Briar Ridge wines
Location: Mount View
Area: 70 ha
Soils: red loam over limestone
Varieties planted: White—chardonnay,
sauvignon blanc, semillon, traminer, verdelho,

viognier; Red—cabernet sauvignon, merlot,
pinot noir, shiraz
Leading wines: Briar Ridge Signature range
including Semillon, Chardonnay, Shiraz and
Cabernet-Merlot and The Reserve Red (Shiraz)
Notes: Some changes have taken place
recently at Briar Ridge. Neil McGuigan has
taken over responsibility for winemaking at the
Mildara Blass Rothbury Estate, while retaining
his position as Chief winemaker at Briar Ridge.
Mildara Blass has also purchased his equity in
Briar Ridge. All this is comparatively
unimportant. The important thing is that
winemaking responsibility remains the same, as
does the high wine quality. Importantly too for
Semillon and Shiraz styles, winemaker
emeritus, Karl Stockhausen, remains as
consultant. Cellar door sales: Mon–Sat
9.30am–5pm, Sun 10am–5pm.

Brokenwood Wines R90

McDonalds Road, Pokolbin, NSW 2320
Ph 02 4998 7559, Fax 02 4998 7893,
Email graveyard@brokenwood.com.au

Owner: Brokenwood Wines Pty Ltd
Chief winemaker: Iain Riggs
Year of foundation: 1970
Tonnes crushed on average each year: 1000
Location: Pokolbin
Area: 20 ha consisting of Graveyard 16 ha and
Cricket Pitch 4 ha, and also a vineyard in
Cowra of 37 ha
Soils: Pokolbin, dry loam over clay, known
locally as Pokolbin red podsols; Cowra, sandy
loam, well-drained, over clay
Varieties planted: (Graveyard)
White—chardonnay; Red—shiraz. (Cricket
Pitch) White—semillon; Red—cabernet
sauvignon, merlot. (Cowra)
White—chardonnay, sauvignon blanc, semillon;
Red—none
Leading wines: Brokenwood Graveyard Shiraz,
Hunter Valley Semillon
Notes: Brokenwood is the vineyard of which

the author was one of three founding partners in 1970. It began to change from its 'hobby' status in 1975, when an adequate winery was built to accommodate what was hoped to be 20–30 tonnes of fruit. That hope was never fulfilled, at least not from the original Brokenwood vineyard. The change continued in 1978 when what was to be called the Graveyard Vineyard was purchased from the then large Hunter company, Hungerford Hill. The company was at that time very much concerned, along with many other Hunter producers, by the financial problems created by the poor economics of, and the poor public response to, Hunter Valley Shiraz. At Brokenwood, new partnership equity had been progressively introduced since the mid-1970s and with it came new enthusiasm from those doctors, geologists, marine biologists and company executives who so willingly devoted their weekends to vineyard and winery activity. In 1982, a trickle of white wine was made and when Iain Riggs joined Brokenwood late in that year to supervise the construction of a 200-tonne winery and all wine production thereafter, Brokenwood ceased to be a hobby. Since then, wine production has increased substantially and Brokenwood wine horizons, never limited solely to the Hunter Valley, have expanded to become national. It is fair to say that national respect for Brokenwood now justifies those national horizons. Its wine portfolio concentrates on quality. From the Hunter there is Graveyard Shiraz, an estate wine totally restricted to its Graveyard Vineyard origin and not only to origin but to ultimate quality as well (in poor Hunter years—and they happen all too often—Graveyard Shiraz is declassified and does not appear). There is also Hunter Valley Semillon, iconoclastic in that, when young, it is fresh and lemony in aroma, avoiding the neutrality of many young Hunter Semillons, but, like the best of its breed, maturing well over 6–10 years to a nutty, honeyed excellence. In the first edition of this

book, I declined to rate Brokenwood, because I had (and still have) an ongoing commitment to and equity in it, but on this occasion I have decided that merit should be acknowledged where it exists. Hence the above rating. Cellar door sales: daily 10am–5pm.

Calais Estates NR
Palmers Lane, Pokolbin, NSW 2320
Ph 02 4998 7654, Fax 02 4998 7813

Owners: Richard and Susan Bradley
Chief winemaker: Adrian Sheridan
Year of foundation: 1973 as Wollundry, 1986 as Calais Estates
Tonnes crushed on average each year: 350
Location: Pokolbin
Area: 10 ha but to be extended to 19 by late 2001
Soils: volcanic soil on hills, light sandy loam over yellow clay
Varieties planted: White—chardonnay, semillon; Red—cabernet sauvignon, chambourcin, durif, shiraz
Leading wines: Calais Estates Chambourcin, Reserve Chardonnay
Notes: Ownership changed in June 2000. No wines recently tasted. Cellar door sales: daily 9am–5pm.

Capercaillie R84
Londons Road, Lovedale, NSW 2325
Ph 02 4990 2904, Fax 02 4991 1886,
Email capercaillie@hunterlink.com.au

Owners: Alasdair and Patricia Sutherland
Winemaker: Alasdair Sutherland
Year of foundation: 1975 (vineyard planted by former owner, Ben Dawson)
Tonnes required on average each year: 90, of which 30 are produced by Capercaillie vineyard
Location: Lovedale
Area: 5.25 ha
Soils: grey sandy loams overlying white and yellow clays

Varieties planted: White—chardonnay, gewurztraminer; Red—chambourcin, petit verdot
Leading wines: Capercaillie Chardonnay, Semillon, Shiraz
Notes: Now a veteran Hunter hand, Alasdair Sutherland began Capercaillie in 1995. Alasdair, a vastly experienced winemaker, was for many years at the cutting edge of Chardonnay development in the Hunter. He is also a skilled maker of Semillon, while his reds are also extremely good. There are no poor wines at Capercaillie. Go and see for yourself! Cellar door sales: Mon–Sat 9am–5pm and Sun 10am–5pm.

Catherine Vale NR

656 Milbrodale Road, Bulga, NSW 2330
Ph/Fax 02 6579 1334,
Email catherinevale@hotmail.com

Owners: Bill and Wendy Lawson
Chief winemaker: Horseshoe Wines (contract)
Year of foundation: 1993
Tonnes crushed on average each year: 50, of which 15 are used for Catherine Vale wines
Location: Bulga
Area: 4.5 ha
Soils: sandy loam over clay
Varieties planted: White—chardonnay, semillon, verdelho; Red—barbera, dolcetto
Leading wines: Catherine Vale Chardonnay, Semillon, Semillon-Chardonnay
Notes: No wines recently tasted. Cellar door sales: weekend and public holidays 10am–4pm, other times by appointment.

Chateau Francois NR

Broke Road, Pokolbin, NSW 2321
Ph 02 4998 7548, Fax 02 4998 7805

Owner/chief winemaker: Dr Don Francois
Year of foundation: 1969
Tonnes crushed on average each year: 5
Location: Pokolbin

Area: 2.4 ha
Soils: sandy, clayey soils
Varieties planted: White—semillon; Red—pinot noir, shiraz
Leading wines: Chateau Francois Shiraz Noir, Semillon, Sparkling Pinot Noir
Notes: Chateau Francois was designed originally as a one-man winery with assistance from friends at crucial times of the year. It still functions according to plan. In the shadow of the Brokenback Range and protected from southerly weather, the vineyard is beautifully sited on a north-facing slope with extensive views over the Hunter Valley and the distant Barrington Tops. Don's Semillon is one of the more reliable traditionally made whites of the Valley. Cellar door sales: weekends by appointment.

Chateau Pato R83

Thompson's Road, Pokolbin, NSW 2320
Ph 02 4998 7634, Fax 02 4998 7860,
Email chateaupato@hotmail.com

Owner: Helen Paterson
Chief winemaker: Nicholas Paterson
Year of foundation: 1980
Tonnes crushed on average each year: 5
Location: Pokolbin
Area: 2.5 ha
Soils: red volcanic loams, black loams
Varieties planted: White—chardonnay; Red—pinot noir, shiraz
Leading wine: Chateau Pato Shiraz
Notes: Chateau Pato was founded by the late David Paterson, 'Pato' to his many friends. He was a very popular media personality and a great enthusiast for the Hunter and its wines. Chateau Pato Shiraz, well-made by David's son, Nicholas, continues his memory. Cellar door sales by appointment.

Cockfighters Ghost (vineyard only)   R82

331 Milbrodale Road, Broke, NSW 2330
Ph 02 9667 1662, Fax 02 9667 1442,
Email info@harbridgewines.com.au

Owner: David Clarke
Chief winemakers: Neil McGuigan (contract) as
to Semillon, Chardonnay and Shiraz; Phil Ryan
(contract) as to Verdelho, Unwooded
Chardonnay and Coonawarra Cabernet
Sauvignon; John Wade assists in Pinot Noir
Year of foundation: unknown but believed to
be a soldier-settlement block originally planted
about 1920
Tonnes crushed on average each year: 90
Location: Broke
Area: 10 ha
Soils: alluvial sandy loam
Varieties planted: White—chardonnay,
semillon; Red—shiraz
Leading wines: Cockfighters Ghost
Chardonnay, Semillon, Shiraz, Premium Reserve
Cabernet Sauvignon (Coonawarra)
Notes: Cockfighters Ghost is not a second
label of Poole's Rock as is sometimes thought,
but a stand-alone brand with its own
supporting vineyard. It also employs a trio of
talented winemakers in its cause. There is
also in its range a Coonawarra Cabernet
Sauvignon. No cellar door sales, but the
wines may be purchased at the Broke
Village Store.

Constable & Hershon   NR

1 Gillards Road, Pokolbin, NSW 2320
Ph/Fax 02 4998 7887,

Owners: Constable and Hershon families
Chief winemaker: Neil McGuigan (contract)
Year of foundation: 1982
Tonnes crushed on average each year: 45
Location: Pokolbin
Area: 7 ha
Soils: red volcanic soils

Varieties planted: White—chardonnay,
semillon; Red—cabernet sauvignon, merlot,
shiraz
Leading wines: Constable & Hershon
Unwooded Chardonnay, Semillon, Shiraz
Notes: This is a boutique vineyard set beside
eight hectares of gardens (of which there are
four, one 'secret' and others of roses, herbs
and sculptures). The vineyard whites have
performed impressively in recent Hunter Valley
and Hunter Valley boutique wine shows, but
I have not tasted them. Cellar door sales:
7 days 10am–5pm.

Cruickshank Calatoota Estate   R81

2656 Wybong Road, Wybong,
NSW 2333
Ph 02 6547 8149, Fax 02 6547 8144,
Email johnc@nobbys.net.au

Owner: John HF Cruickshank
Chief winemaker: John Cruickshank
Year of foundation: 1973
Tonnes crushed on average each year: 120
Location: Wybong
Area: 10.3 ha
Soils: alluvial with some sandy loams
Varieties planted: White—none; Red—cabernet
franc, cabernet sauvignon, shiraz
Leading wines: Cruickshank Calatoota
Cabernet Sauvignon Show Reserve, Cabernet
Sauvignon Pressings
Notes: Calatoota relies entirely on its own fruit
and has one of the larger cabernet plantings in
the Hunter Valley. The Cabernet styles vary
from lighter free-run to fuller-bodied wines
and interestingly there is also a Cabernet Rose.
Cellar door sales: 7 days 9am–5pm.

De Iuliis Vineyards   R81

21 Broke Road, Pokolbin, NSW 2321
(between Tyrrells and Oakvale)
Ph 0407 701 369, Fax 02 4968 8192,
Email dewine@wareng.com.au

Owners: De Iuliis family
Chief winemakers: Michael de Iuliis and David Hook (contract)
Year of foundation: 1990
Tonnes crushed on average each year: 100
Location: vineyard Keinbah, Rothbury; winery and cellar door Pokolbin
Area: 17 ha
Soils: heavy clay loam, acidic, some cracking clays (Biscay)
Varieties planted: White—chardonnay, semillon, verdelho; Red—merlot, shiraz
Leading wines: De Iuliis Shiraz, Verdelho, Methode Champenoise
Notes: A brand new winery and cellar door sales area was erected during 2001. Wine standards are good. Cellar door sales: phone ahead.

Drayton Family Wines R84

Bellevue Winery, Oakey Creek Road, Pokolbin, NSW 2320
Ph 02 4998 7513, Fax 02 4998 7743, Email drink@draytonswines.com.au

Owners: W Drayton & Sons Pty Ltd
Chief winemaker: Trevor Drayton
Year of foundation: 1853
Tonnes crushed on average each year: 1500
Location: Pokolbin
Area: 100 ha, consisting of two vineyards, Oakey Creek and Bellevue
Soils: sandy alluvial loam over clay on Oakey Creek. Slightly heavier loam again over clay by the winery at Bellevue
Varieties planted: White—chardonnay, semillon, verdelho; Red—cabernet sauvignon, merlot, shiraz
Leading wines: Drayton Semillon, Chardonnay, William Shiraz, Merlot
Notes: With Tyrrells, Draytons is one of the ancestral wineries of the Hunter Valley and will celebrate its sesquicentenary in 2003. Of its wine range, its Chardonnay has been very reliable over the years and Trevor Drayton reports that its Merlot is keenly sought after.

Cellar door sales: Mon–Fri 8am–5pm, weekends 10am–5pm.

Drews Creek Wines NR

558 Wollombi Road, Broke, NSW 2330
Ph/Fax 02 6579 1062, Email drews.creek.wines@hunterlink.net.au

Owners: Graeme Gibson and Jennifer Burns
Chief winemaker: David Lowe (contract)
Year of foundation: 1992
Tonnes crushed on average each year: 50, of which 5 are used for Drews Creek wines
Location: Wollombi (vineyard and cellar door sales)
Area: 7 ha
Soils: alluvial flat, mountain wash (rocky, pebbly) soils
Varieties planted: White—chardonnay; Red—merlot, sangiovese
Leading wine: Drews Creek Merlot
Notes: Graeme Gibson is an energetic lawyer-winegrower, who was largely responsible for the creation of the Broke Fordwich sub-region of the Hunter. Somewhat away from Hunter tradition, Graeme's choice of grape varieties for Drews Creek includes merlot and sangiovese. There is not a semillon or shiraz vine in sight. However, vive la difference. The Merlot, made by David Lowe, appears to be the strength here, but I have not tasted it. Cellar door sales by appointment.

Evans Family NR

Lot 157 Palmers Lane, Pokolbin, NSW 2321
Ph 02 4998 7333, Fax 02 4998 7798, Email evansfamilywines@bigpond.com.au

Owner: Len Evans Holdings Pty Ltd
Chief winemaker: Keith Tulloch (contract)
Year of foundation: 1976, first wine 1980
Tonnes crushed on average each year: 20
Location: Pokolbin
Area: 6 ha

Soils: oxidised basalt on limestone, sandy clay soils

Varieties planted: White—chardonnay; Red—gamay, pinot noir

Leading wine: Evans Family Chardonnay

Notes: The winner of *Decanter*'s Wineman of the Year award in 1997, Len Evans is the larger than life character of Australian wine. His almost modest vineyard in the Hunter Valley testifies to his broader sphere of loyalty. He is no mere Hunter spokesman. He is a man of national concept, rather than local detail, very much preferring the big picture to the domestic miniature. Perhaps this is why the Evans Family Vineyard is not quite as well known as it should be. Its Chardonnay is always worthwhile seeking out for its consistently good quality in all years. Cellar door sales at Toby Evans Antiques, Broke Road, Pokolbin.

Farrell's Limestone Creek Vineyard R82

Mount View Road, Mount View via Cessnock, NSW 2325
Ph 02 4991 2808, Fax 02 4991 3414

Owners: John and Camille Farrell
Chief winemaker: Neil McGuigan (contract)
Year of foundation: 1980
Tonnes crushed on average each year: 58
Location: Mount View
Area: 8 ha
Soils: red loam over limestone
Varieties planted: White—chardonnay, sauvignon blanc, semillon, verdelho; Red—cabernet franc, cabernet sauvignon, merlot, pinot noir, shiraz
Leading wines: Limestone Creek Chardonnay, Semillon, Shiraz
Notes: This is a small family vineyard, beautifully sited on a hillside in the picturesque Mount View district. In the past, it has exhibited with some success at local wine shows. Its leading wines are of good regional standard. Cellar door sales: daily 10am–5pm.

Gabriel's Paddocks Vineyard (formerly Sutherland Wines) NR

Deaseys Road, Pokolbin, NSW 2321
Ph 02 4998 7650, Fax 02 4998 7603

Owner: Anderson family
Chief winemaker: Greg Silkman (contract)
Year of foundation: 1979
Tonnes produced on average each year: 100
Location: Pokolbin
Area: 13.6 ha
Soils: red clay
Varieties planted: White—chardonnay, chenin blanc, semillon; Red—cabernet sauvignon, merlot, pinot noir, shiraz
Leading wines: Gabriels Paddocks Shiraz, Chenin Blanc, Pinot Noir
Notes: Nothing tasted since the winery changed hands 2 years ago. Cellar door sales: Thurs–Mon 9am–5pm. Homestead and cottage available for rental.

Gartelmann Hunter Estate R84

Lovedale Road, Lovedale, NSW, 2321
Ph 02 4930 7113, Fax 02 4930 7114,
Email sales@gartelmann.com.au

Owners: Jorg and Jan Gartelmann
Chief winemaker: Gary Reed (contract), David Lowe (contract)
Year of foundation: 1970
Tonnes produced on average each year: 90
Location: Lovedale
Area: 16 ha
Soils: volcanic clay over limestone (shiraz), variable clay soils (other varieties)
Varieties planted: White—chardonnay, chenin blanc, semillon; Red—merlot, muscat, shiraz
Leading wines: Gartelmann Shiraz, Chardonnay, Semillon, Sparkling White
Notes: Excellent Semillon and Shiraz here with a good show record at local wine shows. Cellar door sales: daily 10am–5pm.

Glenguin Wine Company R84

River Oaks Vineyard
Lot 8 Milbrodale Road, Broke,
NSW 2330
Ph/Fax 02 6579 1011

Owners: Tedder family
Chief winemaker: Robin Tedder MW
Year of foundation: 1988
Tonnes crushed on average each year: 60
Location: vineyard Broke; cellar door sales
Boutique Wine Centre, Broke Road, Pokolbin
Area: 17 ha
Soils: deep red weathered basalt and pebbley
clay, overlain in parts by alluvial sandy loam
Varieties planted: White—chardonnay,
semillon; Red—shiraz, tannat
Leading wines: Glenguin Old Broke Block
Semillon, River Terrace Chardonnay, School
House Block Shiraz, Orange Vineyard Merlot,
Griffith Botrytised Semillon
Notes: Glenguin has an excellent reputation
for Hunter Semillon and Shiraz and has
recently spread its wings to include an
Orange Merlot and a Griffith Botrytis
Semillon in a very interesting range.
Cellar door sales: daily.

Golden Grape Estate NR

Oakey Creek Road, Pokolbin, NSW 2320
Ph 02 4998 7588, Fax 02 4998 7730

Owner: Golden Grape Estate Pty Ltd
Chief winemaker: contract
Year of foundation: vineyard 1853; as Golden
Grape Estate 1985
Tonnes produced on average each year: 45
Location: Pokolbin
Area: 13 ha
Soils: red podsols over clay
Varieties planted: White—chardonnay,
semillon, verdelho; Red—merlot, muscat,
shiraz
Leading wines: Golden Grape Premium
Chardonnay, Semillon, Verdelho, Connoisseur

Selection range (Merlot, Shiraz, Botrytis,
Mount Leonard)
Notes: Golden Grape Estate has been resident
in the Valley since 1985, succeeding the old
Happy Valley winery of the late Barry Drayton.
In addition to its cellar door outlet and
restaurant, there is a wine museum and a gift
shop. I have not recently tasted its wines.
Cellar door sales: daily 10am–5pm.

Honeytree Estate Wines R80

16 Gillards Road, Pokolbin, NSW 2320
Ph/Fax 02 4998 7693,
Email honeytree@bigpond.com

Owners: Henk and Robyn Strengers
Chief winemaker: (contract)
Year of foundation: 1970
Tonnes crushed on average each year: 50
Location: Pokolbin
Area: 9.6 ha
Soils: rich red volcanic soils over clay
Varieties planted: White—clairette, semillon;
Red—cabernet sauvignon, shiraz
Leading wines: Honeytree Estate Shiraz,
Cabernet Sauvignon, Clairette
Notes: Honeytree Estate has a consistent
record of wine show results for Shiraz and
Cabernet Sauvignon. Interestingly, it also
makes that very late ripening white variety
Clairette into a pleasant fresh white. Cellar
door sales: Fri–Mon 9am–5pm, Tues–Thurs by
appointment.

Hope Estate
(formerly Hill of Hope) R81

Cobcroft Road, Broke, NSW 2330
Ph 02 6579 1161, Fax 02 6579 1373,
Email hope@hunterlink.net.au

Owner: Michael Hope
Chief winemaker: Peter Howland
Year of foundation: 1996
Tonnes crushed on average each year: 600
Location: Broke

Area: 68 ha, consisting of winery block 25 ha, Hope Estate 30 ha, Troon vineyard 13 ha
Soils: Hope Estate, alluvial sandy loam with spots of clay; winery, rich red basalt over clay; Troon, alluvial sandy loam
Varieties planted: White—chardonnay, semillon, verdelho; Red—cabernet sauvignon, merlot, pinot noir, shiraz
Leading wines: Hope Estate Chardonnay, Shiraz
Notes: Michael Hope is a vigneron in a hurry. Not only has he created a large Hunter Valley estate in only five years, but he has also acquired the famous Macedon vineyard of Virgin Hills and a vineyard at Donnybrook in the Geographe region of Western Australia as well. His Hunter wines have received consistent praise from overseas writers, especially the influential *Wine Spectator*. Winemaker Peter Howland, whose winemaking experience includes spells in Italy and Margaret River, is attempting to break the Australian mould of stereotyped clean fruit characters and introduce more complexity into whites and reds by fermentation on wild yeasts and solids in some whites and whole berry ferment in Shiraz. Cellar door sales: daily 10am–4.30pm.

Horseshoe Vineyard NR

Horseshoe Road, Horseshoe Valley
via Denman, NSW 2328
Ph 02 6547 3528, Fax 02 6547 3548,
Email horseshoe@hunterlink.net.au

Owner: Anthony Hordern & Sons Pty Ltd
Chief winemaker: John Hordern
Year of foundation: 1969
Tonnes crushed on average each year: 45
Location: Horseshoe Valley via Denman
Area: 10 ha
Soils: red earth over clay
Varieties planted: White—chardonnay, semillon; Red—shiraz
Leading wines: Horseshoe Vineyard Semillon, Chardonnay
Notes: John Hordern began his winemaking career with one advantage at least—mature vines. His first vintage was in 1986 and since then he has specialised in whites, semillon particularly. Cellar door sales: weekends and public holidays 10am–4pm.

Hungerford Hill NR

Formerly an independent producer of Hunter and Coonawarra wines, Hungerford Hill owned its own winery and sales complex at the Hungerford Village at the corner of Broke and McDonalds Roads, Pokolbin. It was purchased by Seppelt (then part of South Australian Brewing) in the late 1980s for its Coonawarra vineyards and its winery was later sold to Brian McGuigan Wines Ltd. It now exists only as a Southcorp brand for the marketing of regional red and white wines of New South Wales origin.

Jackson's Hill Vineyard NR

Mount View Road, Mount View
via Cessnock, NSW 2325
Ph 02 4990 1273, Fax 02 4991 3233

Owners: Michael and Pamela Winbourne
Chief winemaker: Michael Winbourne
Year of foundation: 1984
Tonnes crushed on average each year: 19
Location: Mount View
Area: 3 ha
Soils: red basalt soils up to a metre deep over broken down limestone, at least 6–8 m deep
Varieties planted: White—semillon; Red—cabernet franc, cabernet sauvignon
Leading wines: Jackson's Hill Cabernet Franc, Cabernet Sauvignon, Semillon
Notes: Jackson's Hill is a typical small Hunter winery. It does not irrigate, therefore production is not large. It uses only its own fruit, which is vinified on the premises. It is spectacularly situated above Cessnock on the scenic Mount View range. Cellar door sales: Thur–Mon 10am–5pm.

James Estate R81

951 Rylstone Road, Sandy Hollow,
NSW 2333
Ph 02 6547 5168, Fax 02 6547 5164

Owner: David James
Chief winemaker: Peter Orr
Year of foundation: 1971 (as Serenella), 1998
James Estate
Tonnes crushed on average each year: 1250,
expected to increase to 2500 by 2005
Location: Sandy Hollow
Area: 96 ha
Soils: sandy loams over clay, red loams
Varieties planted: White—chardonnay, riesling,
semillon, sylvaner, verdelho; Red—cabernet
franc, cabernet sauvignon, merlot, petit verdot,
pinot noir, shiraz
Leading wines: James Estate Reserve range,
Compass range, Sundara range
Notes: Founded as Serenella in 1971, the
property was sold to its present owner in 1998
and renamed James Estate. The Estate has a
substantial vineyard and in addition has other
vineyards contracted to it. Since the change of
ownership, its Reserve range has performed
solidly at local and interstate wine shows.
Reserve Chardonnay is the highlight. Cellar
door sales: 7 days 10am–4pm.

JYT Wine Co NR

De Beyers Road, Pokolbin, NSW 2320
Ph 02 4998 7528, Fax 02 4998 7370,
Email jytwine@hunterlink.net.au

Owners: Jay and Julie Tulloch
Chief winemaker: Jay Tulloch
Year of foundation: 1997
Tonnes produced on average each year: 30
Location: Pokolbin
Area: 3 ha
Soils: red soils of the favoured type eroded
from the Brokenback Range
Varieties planted: White—chardonnay,
semillon, verdelho; Red—sangiovese, shiraz

Leading wines: 2002 will be the first full
vintage (vineyard is not yet in full bearing)
Notes: This is a new venture, now come to
fruition, for Jay Tulloch, who retired from
Southcorp Wines in 1996. The vineyard has
mature white vines, but the reds are new and
not yet fully bearing. Cellar door sales: daily
10am–5pm.

Kulkunbulla R83

Corner Broke and Hermitage Roads,
Pokolbin, NSW 2320
Ph (vineyard) 02 4998 7358,
Fax 02 9898 0200,
Email wines@kulkinbulla.com.au

Owner: Kulkunbulla Pty Ltd
Chief winemaker: Rhys Eather (contract)
assisted by Gavin Lennard
Year of foundation: 1996
Tonnes required each year for Kulkunbulla
wines 60, of which 35 are produced on
average each year by the Kulkunbulla vineyard
Location: Pokolbin (the old Brokenback
vineyard)
Area: 7 ha
Soils: red sandy loam to brown sand
Varieties planted: White—chardonnay,
semillon; Red—none
Leading wines: Kulkunbulla Chardonnay,
Semillon, Unwooded Chardonnay, Reserve
Chardonnay, Reserve Semillon
Notes: Kulkunbulla is a reinvention of part of
the old Brokenback vineyard of Rothbury
Estate. Highlights are its Reserve Chardonnay
and Semillon. Sales are presently by mail order
to PO Box 6265 Silverwater DC, NSW 1811.

Lake's Folly R83

Broke Road, Pokolbin, NSW 2321
Ph 02 4998 7507, Fax 02 4998 7322,
Email folly@ozemail.com.au

Owners: Peter Fogarty
Chief winemaker: Rodney Kempe

Year of foundation: 1963
Tonnes crushed on average each year: 65
Location: Pokolbin
Area: 12 ha
Soils: volcanic red basalt over limestone on the hill; sandy loam over clay on the creek flat
Varieties planted: White—chardonnay; Red—cabernet sauvignon, merlot, petit verdot, shiraz
Leading wines: Lake's Folly Chardonnay, Cabernets (a blend of cabernet sauvignon, petit verdot, shiraz and merlot)
Notes: In 1963, Dr Max Lake, after leaving no sod unturned in his search for good Hunter Valley 'dirt' (never an easy task), decided on a south-east facing block across the Broke Road from McWilliam's famous Rose Hill vineyard. The Folly, as his friends soon called it, was the first new winery and vineyard established in the Hunter Valley last century and remains Australia's most famous boutique. It became, as Max intended, instantly famous for its Cabernet Sauvignon, a variety which is never really favoured by Hunter Valley conditions. Early Folly Cabernet Sauvignons had a certain 'Bordeaux' flair about them, possibly due to new small oak with which most red consumers of the time, including myself, had little acquaintance, but some of them were criticised for their disparity of fruit and oak. Whatever the criticisms, just or unjust, the Folly Cabernet Sauvignon (or Cabernets, as it has now become) remains an Australian icon. The Folly is now equally famous for its Chardonnay. Cellar door sales: Mon–Sat 10am–4pm. Saturdays only when wine is available. Closed Sundays.

Latara (vineyard only) NR

McDonalds Road, Pokolbin, NSW 2320
Ph 02 9231 4708, Fax 02 9221 5290
(vineyard) Ph 02 4998 7320

Owners: Ken Boorman, Bill Harrison, Ross Homard and Tom Taylor

Chief winemaker: Ian Riggs (contract), David Hook (contract)
Year of foundation: 1978
Tonnes produced on average each year: 45, of which 5 are retained for Latara wines
Location: Pokolbin
Area: 6 ha
Soils: low yielding red clay
Varieties planted: White—chardonnay, semillon; Red—cabernet sauvignon, shiraz
Leading wine: Latara Semillon
Notes: The Latara vineyard is the source of fruit for Brokenwood Semillon. No cellar door sales.

Lindemans Hunter River Winery R88

McDonalds Road, Pokolbin, NSW 2320
Ph 02 4998 7684, Fax 02 4998 7324

Owner: Southcorp Wines
Chief winemaker: Patrick Auld
Year of foundation: 1870
Tonnes crushed on average each year: not disclosed but estimated at 600
Location: Pokolbin
Area: 52 ha (Ben Ean and Steven Vineyards)
Soils: Ben Ean, red fertile loamy soils; Steven, dark brown clay loams over shaley limestone
Varieties planted: White—semillon; Red—shiraz
Leading wines: Lindemans Hunter River range Semillon, Chardonnay, individual vineyard releases such as Steven Shiraz and more rarely these days older Classic Release wines
Notes: Lindeman and the Hunter Valley is one of the historic wine associations of Australia. The company was founded by Dr Lindeman at Cawarra near Gresford in the Hunter Valley in 1843 and has had a continuous presence in the Valley since that time. The move to Pokolbin took place about 1912 when the Lindeman family purchased the Ben Ean vineyard from John McDonald who had established it in 1870. It is renowned for its Semillon whites, which often age magnificently

and its soft-palated welcoming Shiraz reds, which also mature extremely well. Cellar door sales: daily 10am–4.30pm.

Little's Winery R83

Lot 3 Palmers Lane, Pokolbin, NSW 2320
Ph 02 4998 7626, Fax 02 4998 7867, Email littleswinery@bigpond.com

Owners: Little and Kindred families
Chief winemaker: Suzanne Little
Year of foundation: 1983
Tonnes crushed on average each year: 200, of which 170 are used for Little's wines
Location: Pokolbin
Area: 46 ha
Soils: red and brown podsolic clay loam
Varieties planted: White—chardonnay, marsanne, semillon; Red—cabernet sauvignon, pinot noir, shiraz
Leading wines: Little's Chardonnay, Semillon, Shiraz
Notes: This is a small to medium-sized Hunter winery with a good reputation for Chardonnay. Cellar door sales: 7 days 10am–4.30pm.

London Lodge Estate NR

Golden Highway, Gungal, NSW 2333
Ph/Fax 02 6547 6122

Owner: Robert James Lloyd
Chief winemaker: Garry Reid (contract)
Year of foundation: 1987
Tonnes produced on average each year: 60
Location: Gungal
Area: 20 ha
Soils: black marly soils
Varieties planted: White—chardonnay; Red—cabernet sauvignon, pinot noir, shiraz
Leading wines: London Lodge Estate Cabernet Sauvignon, Chardonnay, Shiraz
Notes: I have had no recent tastings of London Lodge Estate wines, but the vineyard is a consistent winner of bronze awards at the

Hunter Valley Wine Show. Cellar door sales: daily 8am–9pm.

Lowe Family Wine Company NR

Peppers Creek Winery, cnr Broke Road and Ekerts Lane, Pokolbin, NSW 2320
Ph/Fax 02 4998 7121

Owners: David Lowe and Jane Wilson
Chief winemakers: David Lowe (white), Jane Wilson (red)
Year of foundation: 1996
Tonnes crushed on average each year: 40
Locations: Pokolbin
Area: 1 ha
Soils: poor clay soils
Varieties planted: White—none; Red—merlot
Leading wines: Lowe Family Unwooded Semillon, Unwooded Chardonnay, Chardonnay
Notes: David Lowe and Jane Wilson now operate from Peppers Creek winery on Ekerts Lane, Pokolbin and also in Mudgee. Whites are strong here. Cellar door sales: daily 10am–5pm. Closed Tuesdays.

Margan Family Winemakers R84

1238 Milbrodale Road, Broke, NSW 2330
Ph/Fax 02 6579 1317, Email marganfw@hunterlink.net.au

Owners: Andrew and Lisa Margan
Chief winemaker: Andrew Margan
Year of foundation: 1991
Tonnes crushed on average each year: 800, of which 500 are used for Margan Family wines
Location: Broke
Area: 26 ha consisting of four vineyards (Broke, 3 vineyards, 22 ha; Belford 4 ha)
Soils: Broke, sandy alluvial loams to red volcanic basalt over sand; Belford, alluvial loams
Varieties planted: White—chardonnay, semillon, verdelho; Red—barbera, cabernet sauvignon, merlot, shiraz
Leading wines: Margan Family Semillon,

Botrytis (Semillon), Shiraz

Notes: According to Andrew Margan, two trophies won at the Sydney Show have helped the cause immeasurably, but this young winemaker has always been close to the top of his profession. Cellar door sales: Hermitage Road, Belford Thurs–Mon 10am–5pm.

Marsh Estate NR

Deasey's Road, Pokolbin, NSW 2321
Ph 02 4998 7587, Fax 02 4998 7884

Owner/Chief winemaker: Andrew Marsh
Year of foundation: 1978
Tonnes crushed on average each year: 140
Location: Pokolbin
Area: 28 ha
Soils: red volcanic loam on the hillside, sandy soils on the creek flat and a mixture of both in between
Varieties planted: White—chardonnay, semillon; Red—cabernet sauvignon, merlot, shiraz
Leading wines: Marsh Estate Chardonnay, Sauternes (botrytised Semillon)
Notes: Since 1978, former pharmacist Peter Marsh has built a true wine estate in every sense of the word. It uses only its own (unirrigated) fruit and all wine is made there, including a luscious botrytised Semillon. Cellar door sales: Mon–Fri 10am–4.30pm, weekends 10am–5pm.

McGuigan Wines (formerly Brian McGuigan Wines) R86

Cnr McDonalds and Broke Roads, Pokolbin, NSW 2320
Ph 02 4998 7400, Fax 02 4998 7401,
Email mcguigan@onaustralia.com.au

Owner: Brian McGuigan Wines Ltd
Chief winemaker: Peter Hall
Year of foundation: 1992
Tonnes crushed on average each year: 4000
Locations: (Lower Hunter) Pokolbin—Hunter Ridge 32 ha, winery block 3 ha. (Central Hunter Valley) Broke Fordwich—Spring Mountain 42 ha, Saxonvale 72 ha, Yellowrock 17.2 ha. (Upper Hunter) Richmond Grove 112 ha, Denman 56 ha
Area: 334.2 ha
Soils: (Lower Hunter) Hunter Ridge—red podsols, sandy loam and yellow clay; Winery Block— red podsols over clay. (Broke Fordwich) Saxonvale—deep red loam, alluvial sand; Spring Mountain—chiefly sandy loam; Yellowrock—fertile sandy loam. (Upper Hunter) Denman—rich black alluvial loam; Richmond Grove—sandy loam
Varieties planted: White—chardonnay, semillon, verdelho; Red—cabernet sauvignon, merlot, shiraz
Leading wines: McGuigan Wines Personal Reserve and Shareholders range
Notes: The McGuigan Winery crushes about 4000 tonnes of fruit from its extensive Hunter Valley vineyards. This however constitutes only about a quarter of the crush throughout Australia, as its vineyard resources throughout Australia are very large. At the top of its range, quality is very good. Cellar door sales: daily 9am–5pm.

McWilliam's Mount Pleasant R87

Marrowbone Road, Pokolbin, NSW 2321
Ph 02 4998 7505, Fax 02 4998 7761,
Email mcwines@mcwilliams.com.au

Owner: McWilliam's Wines Pty Ltd
Chief winemaker: Phillip Ryan
Year of foundation: 1880
Tonnes crushed on average each year: 1600, of which 900 are used for Mount Pleasant wines
Locations: (winery, vineyards and cellar door sales) Mount Pleasant, Pokolbin; (vineyards) Middle Creek, Lovedale, Rosehill
Area: 130 ha
Soils: Mount Pleasant, dark brown basaltic loam over limestone; Lovedale and Middle Creek, grey alluvial sandy loam and light clay;

Rosehill, red basaltic loam over limestone
Varieties planted: White—chardonnay, montils, semillon, verdelho; Red—cabernet franc, cabernet sauvignon, merlot, pinot noir, shiraz, tyrian
Leading wines: Mount Pleasant Elizabeth, Lovedale Semillon, Old Paddock and Old Hill Shiraz, Maurice O'Shea Chardonnay, Shiraz
Notes: Mount Pleasant carries on a marvellous Hunter tradition. Founded in 1880, it was owned in the 1920s and 1930s by that doyen of the Hunter Valley, the much revered Maurice O'Shea. He sold a half-share in the winery and vineyard to its present owners, the McWilliam family, in 1932, but retained his winemaking and managerial position. During the 1940s and until his death in 1956, he made some legendary reds, which are still spoken of in awe. McWilliam's is the last of the Hunter wineries to release a mature semillon, 'Elizabeth', at 5 years of age. Facilities include restaurant, picnic area and winery tours daily at 11am. Cellar door sales: 7 days 10am–4.30pm.

Meerea Park R86

Broke Road, Pokolbin, NSW 2320
mob 0417 699 3310, Fax 02 4930 7100,
Email MeereaPark@hunterlink.net.au

Owners: Eather family
Chief winemaker: Rhys Eather
Year of foundation: 1991
Tonnes crushed on average each year: 150
Locations: (vineyard) Corinda Ridge Belford (not yet bearing); (cellar door sales) Boutique Wine Centre, Broke Road, Pokolbin
Area: 2.5 ha
Soils: sandy loam over clay, partially alluvial
Varieties planted: White—semillon; Red—none
Leading wines: Meerea Park Alexander Munro Shiraz, Chardonnay, Semillon
Notes: The Eather family has its roots deep in the Hunter, having settled at Broke originally in 1826. Though it has only a small area of

vineyard at the present time, it is well-known for Alexander Munro Shiraz, the current star in its wine range. Cellar door sales as above, daily 9.30am–4.30pm.

Millfield R82

Lot 341 Mount View Road, Millfield, NSW 2325
Ph 02 4998 1571, Fax 02 4998 0172,
Email millfieldwines@bigpond.com.au

Owners: David and Sue Lowes
Chief winemaker: David Fatches
Year of foundation: 1997
Tonnes produced on average each year: 80
Location: Millfield
Area: 12.5 ha, consisting of three vineyards, Pokolbin, Mount View and Broke-Fordwich
Soils: Broke, alluvial river flats sandy grey loams, planted to chardonnay; Mount View, volcanic black cracking clay (biscay) planted to semillon; Pokolbin, red loamy clay over limestone planted to shiraz and the other reds
Varieties planted: White—chardonnay, semillon; Red—cabernet sauvignon, merlot, shiraz
Leading wines: Millfield Chardonnay, Semillon, Rose, Shiraz
Notes: A new entrant to Hunter winemaking and well regarded for its Semillon. Cellar door sales: Fri–Sat 10am–4pm.

Mistletoe Wines R80

771 Hermitage Road, Pokolbin, NSW 2320
Ph 02 4998 7770, Fax 02 4998 7792,
Email mistletoe@hunterlink.net.au

Owners: Ken and Gwen Sloan
Chief winemaker: John Reynolds (contract)
Year of foundation: 1989
Tonnes crushed on average each year: 30
Location: Pokolbin
Area: 4 ha
Soils: primarily shallow clay over siltstone/fine

sandstone with some volcanic shaley material in part of one block of semillon
Varieties planted: White—chardonnay, semillon; Red—shiraz
Leading wines: Mistletoe Semillon, Shiraz
Notes: Mistletoe has a solid wine show record with one trophy, four silvers and 16 bronzes since 1996. Cellar door sales: Fri–Mon 10am–6pm.

Moorebank Estate NR

Palmers Lane, Pokolbin, NSW 2320
Ph 02 4998 7610, Fax 02 4998 7367,
Email moorebank@ozemail.com.au

Owners: Debra Moore and Ian Burgess
Chief winemakers: Iain Riggs (Brokenwood), Gary Reed, both by contract
Year of foundation: 1977
Tonnes crushed on average each year: 25
Location: Pokolbin
Area: 5 ha
Soils: cracking clays on the top of the hill with sandy alluvial loam on the creek flat
Varieties planted: White—chardonnay, gewurztraminer, semillon; Red—merlot
Leading wines: Moorebank Traditional Hunter Semillon, Barrel Fermented Chardonnay, Merlot
Notes: One of the prides of Moorebank is its 130-year-old ironbark press, these days in retirement as no wine is made on site. Its Chardonnay and Semillon are very reliable and its 100% Merlot is quite a rare red among the more usual Shiraz of the Lower Hunter Valley. Cellar door sales: Fri–Mon 10am–4pm, otherwise by appointment.

Mount Broke Estate NR

Mount Broke, Adams Peak Road, Broke, NSW 2330
Ph/Fax 02 6579 1313,
Email jo@mtbrokewines.com.au

Owners: Phil and Jo McNamara
Chief winemaker: contract

Year of foundation: 1997
Tonnes produced on average each year: 17, but the vineyard is not yet fully bearing (about 10 tonnes are used for Mount Broke's own wines)
Location: Broke
Area: 9.2 ha
Soils: River Bank blocks, deep alluvial soils, black loam; Dairy Block, red volcanic soils (weathered dolorite); Black Pine Ridge, weathered conglomerate
Varieties planted: White—semillon, verdelho; Red—barbera, cabernet sauvignon, merlot, shiraz
Leading wines: Mount Broke River Bank Shiraz, Verdelho, Black Pine Ridge Merlot
Notes: Founded only in 1997, Mount Broke is scarcely in bearing, but the first crop of Shiraz managed a bronze medal at Hunter Smallmakers Show. There is a café, 'The Cow', and cellar door sales weekends and public holidays 10am–5pm. I have not tasted its wines.

Mount Eyre Vineyards NR

1325 Broke Road, Broke, NSW 2330
Ph 0438 683 973, Fax 02 9591 2245,
Email mteyre@email.com

Owners: Drs Aniello and Eve Iannuzzi; Mr Theo and Mrs Soula Tsironis
Chief winemakers: Dan Crane (contract)
Year of foundation: vineyards 1970
Tonnes crushed on average each year: 230, of which 100 are used for Mount Eyre wines
Location: Broke
Area: 24 ha
Soils: alluvial sandy loam to loamy clay
Varieties planted: White—chardonnay, semillon; Red—cabernet franc, cabernet sauvignon, shiraz
Leading wines: Mount Eyre Chardonnay, Semillon, Semillon-Chardonnay
Notes: No wines have been tasted. No cellar door sales. Sales by mail order to the above address.

Nightingale Wines R79

1239 Milbrodale Road, Broke, NSW 2330
Ph 02 6579 1499, Fax 02 6579 1477,
Email gail@nightingalewines.com.au

Owners: Gail and Paul Nightingale
Chief winemaker: Andrew Margan (contract)
Year of foundation: 1997
Tonnes produced on average each year: 60
Location: Broke
Area: 12 ha
Soils: river flat sandy loam
Varieties planted: White—chardonnay,
verdelho; Red—cabernet sauvignon,
chambourcin, merlot, shiraz
Leading wines: Nightingale Verdelho, Shiraz,
Cabernet Sauvignon, Merlot
Notes: From young vine material, Nightingale
Wines has won bronze medal awards at the
Hunter Valley and Rutherglen wine shows,
which is a promising beginning for a young
vineyard. Cellar door sales Wed–Sun
10am–4pm. Light lunches are served on
weekends.

Oakvale Wines R81

Broke Road, Pokolbin, NSW 2320
Ph 02 4998 7520, Fax 02 4998 7747,
Email info@oakvalewines.com.au

Owners: Richard and Mary Owens
Chief winemaker: Cameron Webster
Year of foundation: Oakvale 1893 as Elliott's,
Milbrovale Vineyard 1995
Tonnes crushed on average each year: 200
Locations: winery, vineyard and cellar door
Pokolbin; vineyard Broke
Area: 47 ha consisting of Oakvale, 13 ha and
Broke, 34 ha
Soils: Oakvale, sandy alluvial soils over a light
clay base; Broke, red alluvial sandy loam
Varieties planted: (Broke) White—chardonnay,
semillon, verdelho; Red—pinot noir,
sangiovese, shiraz. (Oakvale)
White—chardonnay; Red—shiraz

Leading wines: Oakvale Peach Tree
Chardonnay, Peppercorn Shiraz, Milbrovale
Reserve Seven Stones Semillon, Owens Family
Verdelho
Notes: The Owens family has now
amalgamated its two vineyards, Milbrovale
Estate and Oakvale, though the wines in the
premium ranges in top years are kept separate.
The Owens Family Verdelho struck gold at the
2000 Sydney Wine Show. Other wines have
won silvers. Cellar door sales: Broke Road,
Pokolbin, daily 9am–5pm. There is also a
bookshop and a delicatessen.

Pendarves Estate R81

110 Old North Road, Belford, NSW 2335
Ph 02 6574 7222, Fax 02 9970 6152

Owners: Philip and Belinda Jill Norrie
Chief winemaker: Monarch Winemaking
Services
Year of foundation: 1986
Tonnes crushed on average each year: 130
Location: Belford
Area: 20 ha
Soils: clay on limestone
Varieties planted: White—chardonnay,
sauvignon blanc, verdelho; Red—chambourcin,
malbec, merlot, pinot noir, shiraz
Leading wines: Pendarves Verdelho,
Chardonnay, Merlot-Malbec
Notes: Philip Norrie is a busy medical
practitioner, author and protagonist for the
therapeutic qualities of wine, when consumed
in moderation. His Pendarves vineyard sits atop
the Belford Dome (a local outcrop of limestone
beneath a clayey topsoil). The area has long
been famous in Hunter wine lore. In the
middle of the 20th century, Elliott's Semillons,
also from Belford, became quite famous. Cellar
door sales: weekends 11am–5pm.

Pepper Tree Wines R85

Halls Road, Pokolbin, NSW 2320
(winery)
Audrey Wilkinson Vineyard, Oakdale,
De Beyers Road, Pokolbin (vineyard)
Ph 02 4998 7539, Fax 02 4998 7746,
Email ptwinery@peppertreewines.com.au

Owner: Pepper Tree Wines Pty Ltd
Chief winemaker: Chris Cameron
Year of foundation: 1993
Tonnes crushed on average each year: 1000, of
which 200 are used for Pepper Tree wines
Location: Pokolbin
Area: 40 ha
Soils: red volcanic loam over limestone, black
alluvial
Varieties planted: White—chardonnay,
gewurztraminer, semillon, verdelho;
Red—cabernet sauvignon, malbec, merlot,
shiraz
Leading wines: Pepper Tree Chardonnay,
Cabernet Sauvignon, Shiraz
Notes: Pepper Tree Wines is a medium-sized
Hunter winery of quality. Its Reserve
Chardonnay and Cabernet Sauvignon are
among the best in the Valley and, in addition,
it sometimes has an excellent Coonawarra
Cabernet. Cellar door sales: weekdays
9am–5pm, weekends 9.30am–5pm.

Peterson's Wines NR

Mount View Road, Mount View,
NSW 2325
Ph 02 4990 1704, Fax 02 4991 1344

Owners: Peterson family
Chief winemaker: Gary Reed
Year of foundation: Mount View 1971;
Mudgee 1996; Armidale 1999
Tonnes crushed on average each year: 550, of
which 150 is produced from the Hunter Valley
and 400 from the Peterson's Mudgee vineyard.
About 225 tonnes of fruit are used for

Peterson's wines each year
Locations: Mount View (winery, vineyard and
cellar door sales); Mudgee and Armidale
(vineyards)
Area: 75 ha consisting of Mount View 25 ha,
Mudgee 42 ha and Armidale 8 ha
Soils: Mount View, red volcanic loam and black
alluvial and sandy loams; Mudgee, soils varying
from red loam over dolerite through grey river
sediment over dolerite to moraine; Armidale,
red basalt loams
Varieties planted: (Mount View)
White—chardonnay, semillon, viognier;
Red—muscat, pinot noir, shiraz. (Mudgee)
White—none; Red—cabernet sauvignon,
chambourcin, durif, malbec, merlot, shiraz,
zinfandel. (Armidale) White—riesling,
sauvignon blanc, semillon; Red—cabernet
sauvignon, merlot, shiraz
Leading wines: Peterson's Chardonnay,
Semillon, Shiraz
Notes: Peterson's Chardonnays are rarely less
than very good and new red plantings at
Mudgee and Armidale should add a great deal
of red variety to the Peterson's products. No
recent tastings. Cellar door sales: Mon–Sat
9am–5pm, Sun 10am–5pm.

Pokolbin Estate NR

McDonalds Road, Pokolbin, NSW 2321
Ph 02 4998 7524, Fax 02 4998 7765

Owners: Richard Friend and John Hindman
Chief winemakers: Neil McGuigan (contract),
Trevor Drayton (contract)
Year of foundation: 1980
Tonnes crushed on average each year: 36
Location: Pokolbin
Area: 12 ha
Soils: poor clay soil, graduating to grey sandy
soils over clay on the creek flat
Varieties planted: White—riesling, semillon;
Red—shiraz
Leading wines: Pokolbin Estate Semillon, Shiraz

Notes: Nothing recently tasted from this extremely low-yielding vineyard. Cellar door sales: each day 10am–6pm.

Poole's Rock (vineyard only)   **R83**

229 Wollombi Road, Broke, NSW 2330
Ph 02 9667 1662, Fax 02 9667 1442,
Email info@harbridgewines.com.au

Owner: David Clarke
Chief winemaker: Phil Ryan (contract)
Year of foundation: 1988
Tonnes crushed on average each year: 50
Location: Broke
Area: 12 ha, comprising two adjoining vineyards, Poole's Rock, 5 ha and the recently acquired Simon Whitlam Wollombi Brook Vineyard, 7 ha
Soils: deep sandy alluvial loam
Varieties planted: (Poole's Rock)
White—chardonnay; Red—none. (Simon Whitlam Wollombi Brook Vineyard)
White—chardonnay, semillon; Red—none
Leading wine: Poole's Rock Chardonnay
Notes: The recent acquisition of the former Simon Whitlam Wollombi Brook vineyard should allow a substantial increase in production of the popular Poole's Rock Chardonnay. When young, it is usually an elegant style, but like most Hunter Chardonnays tends to become rather plump after 2 to 3 years. No cellar door sales but Poole's Rock Chardonnay may be purchased at the Broke Village Store.

Reynolds Yarraman   **R82**

Yarraman Road, Wybong, NSW 2333
Ph 02 6547 8127, Fax 02 6547 8013,
Email contact@reynoldswine.com.au

Owners: Cabonne Ltd
Chief winemaker: Jon Reynolds
Year of foundation: 1967
Tonnes crushed on average each year: 400, of which 200 are produced by the Reynolds Yarraman vineyard

Location: Wybong
Area: Wybong 20 ha, Orange 40 ha
Soils: Wybong, red sandy loams on the valley slopes and dark medium clay soils on the valley floor that have evolved from rich basalt soils higher up the Wybong Valley
Varieties planted: (Wybong)
White—chardonnay, semillon, traminer; Red—shiraz, sangiovese, tempranillo. (Orange)
White—chardonnay, riesling, sauvignon blanc; Red—cabernet sauvignon, merlot, pinot noir, sangiovese
Leading wines: Reynolds Yarraman Semillon, Shiraz
Notes: Important things have been happening recently to Reynolds Yarraman. Firstly it has been purchased by the new Central Ranges wine giant, Cabonne Ltd. Secondly Jon Reynolds has become chief winemaker and a substantial shareholder in that operation. However, the Reynolds Hunter winery will remain. Cellar door sales: Mon–Sat 10am–4pm, Sun and public holidays 11am–4pm.

Rosemount Estate   **R89**

Rosemount Road, Denman, NSW 2328
Ph 02 6549 6400, Fax 02 6549 6499,
Email mail@rosemountestates.com.au

Owner: Southcorp Wines
Chief winemaker: Andrew Koerner
Year of foundation: 1969
Tonnes crushed on average each year: not disclosed, but estimated Hunter production at 5000
Locations: Denman; vineyards at Giant's Creek, Yarrawa and Roxburgh
Area: 400 ha Hunter vineyards (see also Langhorne Creek, Mudgee, Orange, McLaren Vale and Coonawarra)
Soils: Giant's Creek, weathered sandstone over pebbly grey clay; Yarrawa, alluvial gravel over brown clay; Denman, alluvial river bed; Roxburgh, terra rossa over broken limestone

Varieties planted: White—(Roxburgh) chardonnay, semillon; (Giant's Creek) chardonnay, semillon; (Yarrawa) sauvignon blanc; (Denman) chardonnay, gewurztraminer, semillon; Red—none

Leading wines: Roxburgh Chardonnay, Giant's Creek Chardonnay

Notes: Rosemount Estate is one of the success stories of Australian winemaking. An Upper Hunter grower, it pioneered the renaissance of winemaking in that area in the early 1970s. It surmounted the difficulties of the mid-1970s by anticipating the white wine boom (its Rhine Riesling and Traminer-Rieslings introduced many Australians to white wine) and was prominent in the development and promotion of the ensuing surge of Australian chardonnay (introducing at least one New South Wales politician to it). Since then it has become a national winemaking company, expanding its vineyard interests in New South Wales to Mudgee and Orange and then to South Australia, where it now has vineyards in McLaren Vale, Langhorne Creek and Coonawarra. Its Hunter whites (such as Roxburgh Chardonnay) have always commanded more respect than its reds, but red wines from other regions such as its Balmoral Shiraz and Coonawarra Reserve Cabernet are worthy of the highest respect, while its blended reds show great consistency. Rosemount Estates was recently purchased from the Oatley family by Southcorp Wines. Cellar door sales: Mon–Sat 10am–4pm, Sun 10.30am–4pm.

Rothbury Estate   **R85**

Broke Road, Pokolbin, NSW 2320
Ph 02 4998 7555, Fax 02 4998 7870

Owner: Mildara Blass Ltd
Chief winemaker: Neil McGuigan
Year of foundation: 1968
Tonnes crushed on average each year: 4000, increasing to 5500 by 2003
Locations: Pokolbin (winery block and

Brokenback vineyard); Denman, Cowra, Mudgee (vineyards)

Area: Brokenback and Pokolbin 40 ha, Denman 80 ha, Mudgee 60 ha

Soils: Brokenback, red sandy loam to brown sand; Pokolbin, shallow clay over shaley clay; Denman, heavy black alluvial loam and red friable loams, quite deep; Mudgee, clay loam half-metre deep to red clay

Varieties planted: (Brokenback, Pokolbin and Denman) White—chardonnay, sauvignon blanc, semillon; Red—cabernet sauvignon, merlot, pinot noir, shiraz. (Mudgee) White—chardonnay, semillon, traminer; Red—shiraz, cabernet sauvignon, pinot noir, merlot, aleatico

Leading wines: Rothbury Estate Brokenback Semillon, Chardonnay, Shiraz

Notes: With the enthusiastic Neil McGuigan at the winemaking helm and no shortage of cash in the bank, Rothbury Estate is well set for the challenges of the 21st century. The wines have always been good. What they will now receive is some McGuigan pizazz. Cellar door sales: 7 days 9.30am–4.30pm. There is also a café.

Rothvale   **R84**

Deasy's Road, Pokolbin, NSW 2320
Ph/Fax 02 4998 7290, Email
RothvaleHunterHabit@bigpond.com.au

Owner/chief winemaker: Max Patton
Year of foundation: 1997
Tonnes produced on average each year: 85 and increasing to about 150
Location: Pokolbin
Area: 20 ha
Soils: various, from red clay over limestone (terra rossa) to sandy loams on a clay base
Varieties planted: White—chardonnay, semillon; Red—cabernet sauvignon, shiraz
Leading wines: Rothvale Chardonnay, Shiraz
Notes: Rothvale in recent vintages has built up an excellent reputation for Chardonnay. Cellar door sales: daily 10am–5pm.

Ryan Family Wines (formerly Broke Estate on Monkey Place Creek) **R81**

Broke Road, Broke, NSW 2330
Ph/Fax 02 6579 1065,
Email wryan@ryanwines.com.au

Owner: Ryan family
Chief winemaker: Matthew Ryan and Monarch Winemaking Services (contract)
Year of foundation: 1988
Tonnes produced on average each year: 220
Locations: Broke, Whittingham (vineyard)
Area: 25 ha
Soils: Broke, rich fertile river flat loam; Whittingham, rich, heavy black clay
Varieties planted: White—chardonnay, sauvignon blanc, semillon; Red—cabernet franc, cabernet sauvignon, shiraz
Leading wines: Broke Estate Cabernet Sauvignon, Chardonnay, Semillon, Lacrima Angelorum (Angel's Tear)
Notes: An interesting array of table wines including an attractive cordon-cut sweet style that shows slight botrytis (Lacrima Angelorum). Cellar door sales: weekends and public holidays 10am–5pm.

Sandalyn Wilderness Estate **NR**

Wilderness Road, Rothbury, NSW 2321
Ph/Fax 02 4930 7611,
Email sandalyn@hunterlink.net.au

Owner: Sandra and Lindsay Whaling
Chief winemaker: contract
Year of foundation: 1988
Tonnes crushed on average each year: 60
Location: Rothbury
Area: 8 ha
Soils: red-brown loam over friable clay
Varieties planted: White—chardonnay, semillon, verdelho; Red—pinot noir, shiraz
Leading wines: Sandalyn Pinot Noir, Verdelho, Chardonnay-Verdelho Traditional Method (sparkling)

Notes: I have tasted no wines recently from this vineyard. Cellar door sales: 7 days 10am–5pm.

Scarborough Wine Co **R85**

Gillards Road, Pokolbin, NSW 2320
Ph 02 4998 7563, Fax 02 4998 7786

Owners: Ian and Merralea Scarborough
Chief winemaker: Ian Scarborough
Year of foundation: 1987
Tonnes produced each year on average: 100
Locations: vineyard, winery and cellar door sales Pokolbin; vineyard at the old Lindeman's Sunshine site, now being replanted at Rothbury
Area: 10 ha
Soils: deep friable red loam over a soft limestone base (terra rossa) and sandy creek flat soils
Varieties planted: White—chardonnay; Red—pinot noir
Leading wine: Scarborough (Yellow Label) Chardonnay
Notes: Ian Scarborough is not only a very skilled winemaker, but also an admirer of Burgundy wines. He makes two Chardonnays (one in the fuller-bodied barrel-fermented style, the other in a more austere 'Chablis' mould with only partial malolactic fermentation). There is also a Pinot Noir. Cellar door sales: 7 days 9am–5pm.

Tamburlaine **R82**

McDonalds Road, Pokolbin, NSW 2321
Ph 02 4998 7570, Fax 02 4998 7763,
Email sales@tamburlaine.com.au

Owner/chief winemaker: Mark Davidson
Year of foundation: 1966
Tonnes crushed on average each year: 1000
Location: Pokolbin
Area: 122 ha consisting of Pokolbin 30 ha; Borenore, Orange 92 ha
Soils: Pokolbin, shallow clay loam over clay; Borenore, red volcanic loams
Varieties planted: (Pokolbin)

White—chardonnay, semillon, verdelho;
Red—cabernet sauvignon, chambourcin,
shiraz. (Borenore) White—chardonnay, riesling,
sauvignon blanc; Red—cabernet franc,
cabernet sauvignon, merlot, shiraz
Leading wines: Tamburlaine Chapel
Chardonnay, Shiraz. (Hunter) Tamburlaine
Orange Sauvignon Blanc, Riesling, Merlot,
Cabernet Sauvignon
Notes: Tamburlaine is yet another vineyard
founded by a doctor, Lance Allen, who sold it
in 1985. Since then, Mark Davidson has made
Tamburlaine one of the Hunter's leading
smaller labels. Tamburlaine also has its major
vineyard in the very promising Central Ranges
region of Orange. The wine strengths in the
Hunter are Chapel Reserve Chardonnay and
Shiraz, Orange Chardonnay and Merlot.
Cellar door sales: 7 days 10am–5pm.

Tempus Two R79

Hermitage Road, Pokolbin, NSW 2320
Ph 02 4998 7521, Fax 02 4998 7796,
Email tempus.two@bigpond.com

Owner: McGuigan Wines
Chief winemaker: Peter Hall
Year of foundation: 1996
Tonnes crushed for brand on average each
year: 450
Location/Area/Soils: see McGuigan Wines
Varieties used for brand: White—chardonnay,
semillon, verdelho; Red—cabernet sauvignon,
merlot, shiraz
Leading wines: Tempus Two Broke Vineyard
Chardonnay, Hunter Valley Shiraz
Notes: Tempus Two is a consistent winner of
silver and bronze awards with occasional golds
and trophies at international, national and
regional wine exhibitions. A brand of
McGuigan Wines, it uses the vast vineyard
resources of that company to produce regional
wines of good, albeit not outstanding, quality.
Cellar door sales at Hunter cellars, Pokolbin,
daily 10am–5pm.

Terrace Vale NR

Deasy's Road, Pokolbin, NSW 2321
Ph 02 4998 7517, Fax 02 4998 7814,
Email wines@terracevale.com.au

Owner: Paul Batchelor
Chief winemaker: Alain Leprince
Year of foundation: 1971
Tonnes crushed on average each year: 200, of
which 100 are used for Terrace Vale wines
Location: Pokolbin
Area: 37 ha
Soils: sandy loam on flat over sandstone and
clay rising to old podsolic soils over clay
Varieties planted: White—chardonnay,
sauvignon blanc, semillon, traminer;
Red—cabernet sauvignon, merlot, pinot noir,
shiraz
Leading wines: Terrace Vale Chardonnay,
Semillon, Shiraz
Notes: This is one of the older established
boutique wineries of the Hunter Valley with a
good reputation for its Chardonnays. Cellar
door sales: 7 days 10am–4pm.

Thalgara Estate NR

De Beyers Road, Pokolbin, NSW 2320
Ph 02 4998 7717, Fax 02 4998 7774

Owner/chief winemaker: Steve Lamb
Year of foundation: 1987
Tonnes crushed on average each year: 50
Location: Pokolbin
Area: 8 ha
Soils: red podsols over clay, and smaller areas
of limestone
Varieties planted: White—chardonnay,
semillon; Red—shiraz
Leading wine: Thalgara Estate Shiraz
Notes: Thalgara these days seems to be
concentrating on the Hunter Valley's most
important red variety, Shiraz. It is a
concentration that is often rewarded. Nothing
recently tasted. Cellar door sales: 7 days
10am–5pm.

Tinonee Vineyard NR

1273 Milbrodale Road, Broke, NSW 2330
Ph 02 6579 1308, Fax 02 9719 1833,
Email tonymears@msn.com.au

Owners: Robyn and Tony Mears
Chief winemaker: Andrew Margan (contract)
Year of foundation: 1997
Tonnes crushed on average each year: not yet in full bearing, but 9 tonnes were picked in vintage 2000
Location: Broke
Area: 8 ha
Soils: red volcanic basalt planted to most of the reds; the whites and some of the chambourcin and durif are planted in sandy loam
Varieties planted: White—chardonnay, verdelho; Red—chambourcin, durif, merlot, shiraz
Leading wines: Tinonee Verdelho but the reds are expected to be prominent on maturity of the vines
Notes: Tinonee is a small family vineyard with Verdelho the only wine available at time of writing. Cellar door sales: Sundays and public holidays 11am–4pm; occasionally on Saturdays, but ring ahead.

Tintilla Estate NR

725 Hermitage Road, Pokolbin, NSW 2320
Ph 02 6574 7093, Fax 02 6574 7094, mob 0411 214 478,
Email thelusbys@bigpond.com

Owners: Robert and Mary Lusby
Chief winemaker: contract
Year of foundation: 1993
Tonnes crushed on average each year: 55, of which 45 are crushed for Tintilla Estate wines
Location: Pokolbin
Area: 10 ha
Soils: red clay on limestone with alluvial sandy soils on the flat
Varieties planted: White—semillon on the alluvial flat; Red—merlot, sangiovese, shiraz on the red clay hillside
Leading wines: Tintilla Estate Shiraz, Sangiovese
Notes: Tintilla Estate is now producing and Shiraz and Sangiovese are showing up amongst the reds. Regrettably, I have tasted neither. Cellar door sales: weekends 10.30am–5pm and until 6pm in summer. At other times by appointment.

Tower Estate NR

Cnr Broke Road and Halls Road, Pokolbin, NSW 2320
Ph 02 4998 7989, Fax 02 4998 7919,
Email sales@towerlodge.com.au

Owner: a consortium (Len Evans, Chairman)
Chief winemaker: Dan Dineen
Year of foundation: 1999
Tonnes crushed on average each year: 200, of which 150 are used for Tower Estate wines
Location: Pokolbin
Area: 3 ha (vines not yet bearing)
Soils: acidic, salty, poor
Varieties planted: White—chardonnay; Red—shiraz
Leading wine: Tower Estate Adelaide Hills Chardonnay, Coonawarra Cabernet Sauvignon
Notes: Tower Estate is a glitzy Hunter address, with a small vineyard, not bearing at time of writing. Its winemaking object is to produce the tops from the better Australian regions, which with Dan Dineen's skilful winemaking and his Chairman's strict supervision, will most likely be achieved. Cellar door sales: 7 days 10am–6pm.

JY Tulloch & Son Pty Ltd R87

Glen Elgin, De Beyers Road, Pokolbin, NSW 2320
Ph 02 4998 7580, Fax 02 4998 7226

Owner: Southcorp Wines
Chief winemaker: Pat Auld
Year of foundation: purchased 1895

Tonnes crushed on average each year: not disclosed, but estimated at 50
Location: Pokolbin
Area: 8 ha
Soils: red volcanic loam over friable clay
Varieties planted: White—none; Red—shiraz
Leading wines: Tulloch Verdelho, Unoaked Chardonnay, Hector of Glen Elgin (Shiraz), Cabernets
Notes: Tulloch was once a family-owned vineyard and in the 1960s perhaps the most prestigious name in the Hunter Valley. Alas, that is long gone. After the Tulloch family sold Glen Elgin in 1966, it went through many hands and at times was promoted as a national brand. Under Southcorp ownership, it is again solely a Hunter brand and at the present time is Hunter winemaking headquarters for Lindemans, Tullochs and the Hungerford Hill brand. Cellar door sales: daily 10am–4.30pm.

Tyrrells Vineyards Pty Ltd R88

Ashmans, Broke Road, Pokolbin, NSW 2321
Ph 02 4993 7000, Fax 02 4998 7723, Email admin@tyrrells.com.au

Owner: Tyrrells Vineyards Pty Ltd
Chief winemaker: Andrew Spinaze
Year of foundation: 1858
Tonnes crushed on average each year: 3700 (Pokolbin and Scone)
Locations: Pokolbin and Scone (NSW); other vineyards are at Heathcote (Vic), McLaren Vale and Penola (SA)
Area: 185 ha (Pokolbin and Scone)
Soils: Pokolbin, light sandy alluvial soil, red clay over chocolate loam over limestone; Scone, light sandy soil, some gravel
Varieties planted: (Pokolbin) White—chardonnay, semillon, trebbiano; Red—cabernet sauvignon, pinot noir, shiraz. (Scone) White—chardonnay, semillon, traminer; Red—cabernet sauvignon

Leading wines: Tyrrell's Vat 1 Semillon, Vat 47 Chardonnay, Vat 9 Shiraz
Notes: A lover of Burgundy style, Murray Tyrrell, who died in the year 2000, saw and presided over Tyrrells' expansion from a small family-owned Pokolbin winery to a national winemaking undertaking. In the 1970s, he was responsible for the burgeoning popularity of chardonnay, making his first white from that variety in the inauspicious Hunter vintage of 1971. This tiny beginning led to the chardonnay boom of the 1980s and 1990s. The white wines of Australia have never been the same since the famous Vat 47 Chardonnay of 1973. Even though the Hunter Valley climate rarely favours that variety, he has espoused pinot noir also with hardly less success, his 1976 wine winning an international award at the Gault-Millau Wine Olympics in 1979. In the pursuit of quality and complexity, Tyrrells have, in the 1990s, expanded into Victoria and South Australia. Doubtless growth will continue. Cellar door sales: Mon–Sat 8am–5pm, closed Sundays.

Undercliff Winery NR

Yango Creek Road, Wollombi, NSW 2325
Ph/Fax 02 4998 3322, Email finewines@undercliff.com.au

Owners: Peter and Lesley Chase
Chief winemaker: David Carrick (contract)
Year of foundation: 1994
Tonnes crushed on average each year: 14
Location: Wollombi
Area: 2.5 ha
Soils: black alluvial (river flat) soils
Varieties planted: White—semillon; Red—muscat, shiraz
Leading wines: Undercliff Semillon, Shiraz
Notes: A small winery in the south of the region with its mainstay varieties, Semillon and Shiraz as its chief wines. There are also local paintings and pottery on display. Cellar door

sales: Wed–Fri 11am–3pm, weekends and public holidays 10am–4pm.

Vinden Estate Wines   NR

Lot 17 Gillards Road, Pokolbin, NSW 2320
Ph 02 4998 7410, Fax 02 4998 7421,
Email finewines@vindenestate.com.au

Owner: Vinden Estates Pty Ltd
Chief winemaker: John Baruzzi (contract) assisted by Guy Vinden
Year of foundation: 1998
Tonnes produced on average each year: not yet fully bearing. All fruit produced is used for Vinden Estate wines
Location: Pokolbin
Area: 2.8 ha
Soils: red volcanic soils over clay
Varieties planted: White—none; Red—merlot, shiraz
Leading wines: Vinden Estate Chardonnay, Semillon, Shiraz
Notes: A relatively new winery in Gillards Road, which has several good winery addresses (notably Scarborough Estate). As it has no whites planted, Vinden Estate buys in its chardonnay and semillon fruit. In Guy Vinden's words, it rarely 'pursues the wine show path', but it has had some success with a silver and a bronze. Cellar door sales: daily 10am–5pm.

Wandin Valley Estate   R83

Wilderness Road, Rothbury, NSW 2321
Ph 02 4930 7317, Fax 02 4930 7814,
Email jamesdavern@talent.com.au

Owners: James and Philippa Davern
Chief winemaker: Sarah Kate Wilson, Karl Stockhausen (consultant)
Year of foundation: 1973 as Millstone Vineyard, 1993 as Wandin Valley Estate
Tonnes required each year: 100, of which 50 are produced by the Estate
Location: Lovedale

Area: 9 ha
Soils: red volcanic clay planted to reds, grey black sandy alluvial loam for whites
Varieties planted: White—chardonnay; Red—cabernet sauvignon, malbec, merlot, ruby cabernet, shiraz
Leading wines: Wandin Valley Estate Reserve Chardonnay, Bridie's Shiraz, Riley's Reserve, Cabernet Sauvignon
Notes: James Davern has enjoyed a winning touch, firstly as owner of an extremely successful Hunter winery and also as a top television producer. The winery, now under the control of Sarah Kate Wilson, has won over 150 show awards in the past decade and has a good reputation for Chardonnay. There is also a village cricket ground and pavilion, the Café Crocodile, several four bedroom self-contained villas and a function centre suitable for corporate occasions, wine dinners and weddings. Cellar door sales: 7 days 10am–5pm.

Wyndham Estate   R87

Dalwood Road, Dalwood, NSW 2335
Ph 02 4938 3444, Fax 02 4938 3422

Owner: Wyndham Estate Pty Ltd
Chief winemaker: Brett McKinnon
Year of foundation: 1971 (by Brian McGuigan), 1828 (by George Wyndham)
Tonnes crushed on average each year: 500
Location: Dalwood; Pokolbin (vineyard)
Area: 80 ha consisting of Dalwood 40 ha and Pokolbin 40 ha
Soils: Dalwood alluvial sandy loams; Pokolbin, red podsolic soils
Varieties planted: White—chardonnay, riesling, semillon, verdelho; Red—cabernet sauvignon, merlot, shiraz
Leading wines: Wyndham Estate Hunter Valley Show Reserve Semillon, Shiraz
Notes: The cradle of Australian winemaking, this estate was founded by George Wyndham in 1828 and vines were certainly being grown

there by 1832. It continued as a leading Hunter Valley vineyard for the next 60 years until it fell on hard times in the 1890s, a fact which caused a correspondent of the *Maitland Mercury* to lament that 'the departed glory of Dalwood is a thing to be deplored'. In the early twentieth century, it was purchased by Penfolds, who remained there over 60 years, before moving to Dalwood Estate in the upper Hunter Valley. Then in 1970, the property was sold to the McGuigan family and soon after became Wyndham Estate. During the 1970s and 1980s, it grew rapidly until taken over by

Orlando in 1990. Under the tutelage of Brian McGuigan, its wines became very consistent and keenly priced but were never outstanding, a policy which continues to the present time. On a smaller scale, however, policies are changing. After being closed for some years as an operating winery, Dalwood now specialises in small batches of the traditional wine specialities of the Lower Hunter Valley, shiraz and semillon, which are excellent at the top level. Cellar door sales: Mon–Sat 9am–5pm, Sun 10am–5pm.

Broke Fordwich Sub-region

The first thirty years of the sub-region's history are identical to those of the Hunter region. However, in 1820, following John Howe's explorations north of Windsor, the areas south and west of present-day Singleton saw its first settlers along the Upper Hunter and Goulburn Rivers. An early settler in the sub-region was John Blaxland, brother of Gregory, who had been born in Fordwich, Kent, and arrived in Sydney in 1805 on the suggestion, it is said, of Sir Joseph Banks. Blaxland had been granted over 2000 ha of land, mostly in the Broke area. Fordwich Homestead, from which Blaxland pursued his pastoral interests, was built in 1829 and was also allowed to be used for Anglican church services and as the local school. Prior to the First World War, the area was used mostly for grazing, though by 1910 the larger estates had begun to be sub-divided. After that war, the area became subject to the Fordwich Soldiers Settlement Scheme and vines were first planted in the sub-region by some of those returned soldiers from 1920 on. However, the blocks were small and uneconomic. When the Great Depression of 1929 decimated the wine industry in the early 1930s, the vine blocks were sold mostly to Tullochs, who had commenced purchasing them as early as 1922. The last of the vine-growing soldier-settlers of Fordwich sold his block to the Elliott family in 1940. These blocks remained under vine and in the ownership of the Tulloch and Elliott families until 1965 in the case of the Tullochs and slightly later in the case of the Elliotts. By this time, the red wine boom of the late 1960s was in full swing and other vineyards were planted there. There were no wineries in the sub-region until the Saxonvale winery and vineyards were established in the early 1970s. All fruit from Fordwich, as the grapegrowing area was called in those days, was previously transported to Pokolbin for vinification. Yet, despite the skill of its early winemakers, Mark Cashmore and Alasdair Sutherland, and the success of its Chardonnays, the company encountered financial difficulties throughout its short history and its assets finally passed into the ownership of Wyndham Estate. Its winery was closed in 1988 but was reopened recently as the Hope Estate, making its first vintage there in 1997. During this time other large companies such as Lindemans also

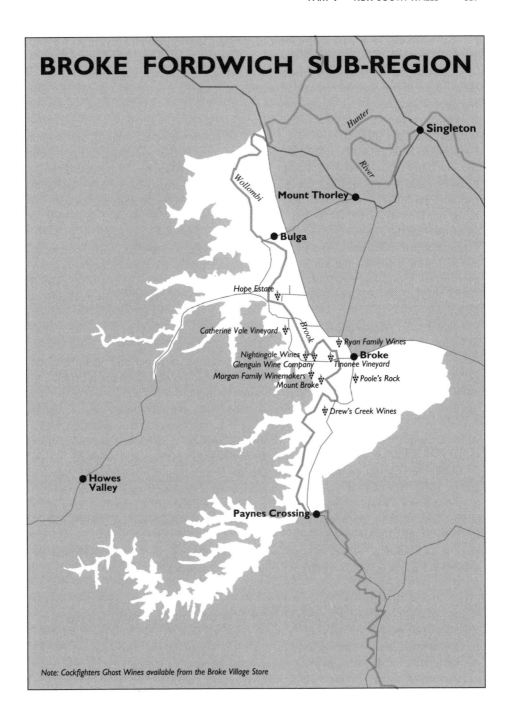

BROKE FORDWICH SUB-REGION

Hunter

Singleton

River

Wollombi

Mount Thorley

Bulga

Hope Estate

Brook

Catherine Vale Vineyard

Ryan Family Wines

Nightingale Wines

Broke

Glenguin Wine Company

Tinonee Vineyard

Morgan Family Winemakers

Poole's Rock

Mount Broke

Drew's Creek Wines

Howes
Valley

Paynes Crossing

Note: Cockfighters Ghost Wines available from the Broke Village Store

planted extensive vineyards in the sub-region and McWilliam's also had plans for substantial vineyards. They too have moved on from the sub-region.

Today Broke Fordwich is a sub-region of reborn enthusiasm paying little heed to the reverses of the past. May that enthusiasm be justified and the mistakes of the past not be repeated.

Location: latitude 32°46'S, longitude 151°5'E. The sub-region is about 20 km west of Pokolbin in what might be called the Central Hunter Valley and is defined as part of the catchment area of the Wollombi Brook, falling within the Shire of Singleton below the 200 m contour line. It is of irregular shape and situated on the left and right banks of the Brook, commencing about 15 km south of Broke. It abuts the Brook, as it flows north-west for about 35 km, ending near Warkworth about 5 km from its juncture with the Hunter River.

Topography and soils: Apart from the Brokenback Range, the terrain is gently undulating with vineyard sites varying in altitude from virtually sea-level to nowhere more than 200 m. Most of its vineyards are planted on sandy loam, loam or clay loam of good depth. Such soils are moderately acid, permeable and well drained with moderate to high fertility.

Climate: It is an undeniably warm sub-region with MJT 23.75°C. Its annual rainfall is 647 mm with about two-thirds of this (428 mm) falling during the growing season (October to April). Like the Lower Hunter, it enjoys the ameliorating light cloud cover which accompanies the summer afternoon sea breeze, but this sea breeze can often be blocked by the Brokenback Range, which possibly explains the higher summer temperatures. As in the Lower Hunter, heavy rain at vintage causing direct damage to fruit and consequent attacks of bunch rot (botrytis) can create problems both as regards quantity and quality. Spraying for downy mildew is necessary from October to February. There is also a danger of hail during spring and summer.

Other than by natural rainfall, most vines in the sub-region are watered by drip irrigation, either by water taken directly from Wollombi Brook or from storage dams filled from the Brook. Water may also be taken from under the bed of the Brook by spear points. Bore water of good quality is also used, but water bores require a licence from the New South Wales Government.

Harvest time: Vintage is generally about two weeks later than the Lower Hunter for corresponding varieties (i.e. from mid-February to late March).

One of the distinguishing factors of Broke Fordwich viticulture as opposed to Lower Hunter viticulture generally is that about 90% of the vineyards in the sub-region are of a Scott-Henry type and most of the remainder rely on vertical shoot positioning for canopy management. Also because of the extra vigour of the vines caused by the greater fertility of the sub-region's soils, rows are generally planted further apart than in other areas of the Hunter region. An average vineyard spacing would be 3-metre row width with vines 1.8 m apart. Production is also greater with yields about double those of the Lower Hunter.

Now all of this might lead a casual observer to conclude that Broke Fordwich is just another sub-region devoted to producing maximum quantity at the expense of quality.

This is not the case, provided that the vines are not overcropped and the crop carried can ripen properly. It has been contended that the Chardonnays of the Broke Fordwich sub-region have a particular sub-regional melony flavour mainly because of the fertility of the soil, while Chardonnays from the Lower Hunter have a peachy character mainly because of the less fertile nature of the soil. Such statements must be treated with caution and are unfortunate because soil fertility or infertility in itself has little to do with flavour production. The development of flavourants (i.e. pigments, flavours and aromas) is the product of the vine's ripeness, metabolism and climatic factors. Warmth and soil structure (e.g. soil warmth and drainage) are much more relevant. This is not to say that a skilled palate might not notice some flavour or aromatic differences between Broke and Pokolbin Chardonnays, but they would certainly not be due to soil fertility or lack of it.

It has also been contended that in Semillon, the Broke Fordwich sub-region produces lemony citrus characters as opposed to the Semillon of the Lower Hunter which shows more of a lanolin or soapy character. Lemony citrus characters in semillon are of course not peculiar to Broke Fordwich. They exist in most other warm areas, such as the Barossa Valley, Clare and certainly the Lower Hunter. Again this cannot be the product of soil fertility or lack of it. Flavour production, and therefore differences between areas, is more the product of the vine's ripeness metabolism which in turn is due to climate and factors other than soil fertility.

In regard to red wines and in particular cabernet sauvignon, it is also argued that the Broke Fordwich sub-region produces intense flavour and colour in this variety. This argument may be based on the 1993 vintage, a very abnormal year for the Hunter Valley and one of very late ripening for most varieties including cabernet sauvignon. Such relatively cool, late-ripening and dry years rarely occur in the Hunter Valley. I have noticed, however, in over 30 years of tasting Hunter Cabernet Sauvignon that cool, dry, rather late-ripening Hunter years certainly show cabernet sauvignon picked off relatively young vines at its varietal best (*viz* Lake's Folly Cabernet Sauvignon 1967, Brokenwood Cabernet Sauvignon 1975). Yet cool, dry years are very much the exception there. Wet, humid years (e.g. 1971, 1978, 1984, 1988, 1989) and hot drought years (1977, 1981, 1991) are predominant. When Hunter cabernet sauvignon vines become older (about 6–7 years of age), they seem to lose the innate vibrant berry character of the variety and become much more regional and leathery in nature. All of this goes to show that shiraz in most years is a much more suitable variety for the Hunter Valley as a whole than cabernet sauvignon.

Vineyards and wineries within the Broke Fordwich sub-region contained in this book are: Catherine Vale Vineyard, Cockfighters Ghost, Drews Creek, Glenguin Wines, Hope Estate, Margan Family, Milbrovale Estate (see Oakvale), Mount Broke Estate, Mount Eyre Vineyards, Nightingale Wines, Poole's Rock, Ryan Family Wines and Tinonee Vineyard.

SOUTH COAST ZONE

This is a long and narrow strip of land commencing on the central coast of New South Wales and proceeding south along the coastline to the Victorian border. The zone extends west as far as the Blue Mountains, includes the Sydney Metropolitan area, the old wine area of Camden, the Southern Highlands, the Shoalhaven Valley and the Bega Valley. Its southern parts seem more favoured for viticulture due principally to drier climates and less humidity.

At the time of going to print, the Southern Highlands area has applied for registration as a wine region.

Climate: Bega MJT 20.7°C, MAR na, HDD raw 1817, 1630 (cut-off and adjusted for latitude, daily temperature range and vine sites), AR 871 mm (Oct–Apr 547 mm), AI na, SH 7.9 (Gladstones).

Leading winery and vineyard: Coolangatta Estate, Grevillea Estate.

Cambewarra Estate — NR

520 Illaroo Road, Cambewarra,
NSW 2540
Ph/Fax 02 4446 0170

Owner: Louise Cole
Chief winemaker: Tamburlaine (contract)
Year of foundation: 1991
Tonnes crushed on average each year: 35, of which 30 are used for Cambewarra Estate wines
Location: Cambewarra
Area: 6.5 ha
Soils: alluvial topsoil, clay subsoil
Varieties planted: White—chardonnay, verdelho; Red—cabernet sauvignon, chambourcin
Leading wines: Cambewarra Estate Verdelho, Chardonnay, Cabernet Sauvignon, Chambourcin
Notes: Cambewarra continues its wine show successes with trophies for Verdelho and Cabernet Sauvignon and the first gold in Australia awarded for Chambourcin, as well as a high silver for Chardonnay at the Sydney show. Cellar door sales: weekends and school holidays 10am–5pm.

Coolangatta Estate — R81

Coolangatta Village, 1335 Bolong Road,
Shoalhaven Heads, NSW 2535
Ph 02 4448 7131 Fax 02 4448 7997,
Email coolangatta@shoalhaven.net.au

Owner: Bishop family
Chief winemaker: Tyrrells (contract)
Year of foundation: 1988
Tonnes produced on average each year: 55
Location: Shoalhaven Heads
Area: 7 ha, including new plantings 3 ha
Soils: upper slopes brown loam over a shale base; lower slopes well-drained sandy loam
Varieties planted: White—chardonnay, sauvignon blanc, semillon, verdelho; Red—cabernet sauvignon, chambourcin, merlot, sangiovese, shiraz
Leading wines: Coolangatta Estate Alexander Berry Chardonnay, Verdelho, Semillon, Chambourcin, Cabernet-Shiraz
Notes: This is a restoration of an original convict-built settlement dating from 1822 and one of the first settlements on the South Coast of New South Wales. Its originators were Alexander Berry and Edward Wollstonecraft, early Sydney merchants who gave their names to several parts of Sydney's lower North Shore

and were among that area's first settlers also. Wine quality is good, especially in whites. Cellar door sales: 10am–5pm daily, closed Christmas Day. There is also a restaurant.

Grevillea Estate **R80**

Buckajo Road, Bega, NSW 2550
Ph 02 6492 3006, Fax 02 6492 5330,
Email grevillea@acr.net.au

Owner/chief winemaker: Nicola Collins
Year of foundation: 1980
Tonnes crushed on average each year: 70, all of which are used for Grevillea Estate and Collina wines
Location: Bega
Area: 6.4 ha
Soils: almost half and half granite soils and decomposed shale
Varieties planted: White—chardonnay, gewurztraminer, riesling, sauvignon blanc; Red—cabernet sauvignon, merlot, shiraz
Leading wines: South Coast Cabernets, Grevillea Estate Grosses Creek Merlot
Notes: Grevillea Estate is a working vineyard within a working dairy farm. All its wines are estate-grown, made, matured, bottled and labelled. There are some good reds here, especially South Coast Cabernets and Grosses Creek Merlot. Cellar door sales: daily 9am–5pm, except Jul–Aug 10am–4pm. Sales also at Sydney St, Mogo NSW.

Joadja Vineyards **NR**

Cnr Greenhills and Joadja Roads, Berrima, NSW 2577
Ph/Fax 02 4878 5236,
Email joadjal@hinet.net.au

Owners: Kim Moginie and Frances Moginie
Chief winemaker: Kim Moginie
Year of foundation: 1983
Tonnes crushed on average each year: 50
Location: Berrima
Area: 6.5 ha

Soils: rich basalt soils
Varieties planted: White—chardonnay, sauvignon blanc; Red—cabernet sauvignon, malbec
Leading wines: Joadja Vineyards Sauvignon Blanc, Cabernet-Malbec
Notes: The winery is located in the wet, cool Southern Highlands area south-west of Sydney, which now has many new small vineyards, which are yet to be proved. Cellar door sales: 7 days 10am–5pm.

Kirkham Estate **NR**

3 Argyle St, Camden, NSW 2570
Ph/Fax 02 4655 7722

Owners: Stan Aliprandi and Leif Karlsson
Chief winemaker: Stan Aliprandi
Year of foundation: 1993
Tonnes produced on average each year: 50
Area: 10 ha
Soils: very deep alluvial soils of low pH, rich
Varieties planted: White—chardonnay, semillon, verdelho; Red—cabernet sauvignon, merlot, petit verdot, pinot noir, shiraz
Leading wines: Kirkham Estate Shiraz, Cabernet, Chardonnay
Notes: Kirkham Estate is located in one of Australia's oldest wine regions, the Camden Valley, most famous perhaps for John Macarthur, who bred Australia's first merino sheep at Camden Park and founded its wool industry. More renowned in wine at Camden Park was his son Sir William Macarthur. Kirkham Estate therefore has some history to live up to, though I have not tasted any wines. Cellar door sales: daily 10am–5pm.

The Silos Winery **NR**

Princes Highway, Jaspers Brush, NSW 2535 (about 6.4 km south of Berry)
Ph 02 4448 6082, Fax 02 4448 6246,
Email thesilos@thesilos.com

Owners: Kate Khoury and Gaynor Sims
Chief winemaker: Bevan Wilson

Year of foundation: 1985
Tonnes crushed on average each year: 20
Location: Jaspers Brush
Area: 4.5 ha
Soils: a mix of clay and shale
Varieties planted: White—chardonnay, sauvignon blanc, semillon; Red—cabernet sauvignon, malbec, merlot, shiraz
Leading wines: The Silos Oaked Chardonnay, Merlot
Notes: Located in a century-old dairy, The Silos is a popular landmark in a well-known tourist area of the South Coast of New South Wales. The Oaked Chardonnay has proved successful at the Cowra wine show, but I have not tasted any wine from this winery. Cellar door sales: Wed–Mon 10am–5pm. There is also a bookshop, restaurant and self-contained guest accommodation.

Tizzana NR

518 Tizzana Road, Ebenezer, NSW 2756
Ph 02 4579 1150, Fax 02 4679 1216,
Email enquiries@tizzana.com.au

Owners: Peter and Caroline Auld
Chief winemaker: Peter Auld
Year of foundation: 1887
Tonnes crushed on average each year: less than 5
Location: Ebenezer
Area: 3 ha
Soils: light sandy loams, pH just a little acid
Varieties planted: White—none; Red—aleatico, cabernet sauvignon, petit verdot, shiraz
Leading wines: Rosso di Tizzana, Waterloo Shiraz, Sackville Tawny, Vintage Port
Notes: Dr Thomas Fiaschi was an Italian-Australian surgeon who practised for many years in Australia, always extolling the medical benefits of wine. Tizzana was Dr Fiaschi's original winery, erected in 1887. I have not tasted the wines. Cellar door sales: weekends and public holidays noon–6pm, at other times by appointment.

Vicary's Winery NR

Northern Road, Luddenham, NSW 2745
Ph 02 4773 4161, Fax 02 4773 4411

Owner/chief winemaker: Chris Niccol
Year of foundation: 1923
Tonnes crushed on average each year: 30
Location: Luddenham
Area: 5 ha
Soils: heavy clay
Varieties planted: White—chardonnay, gewurztraminer; Red—none
Leading wines: Vicary's Chardonnay, Cabernet-Merlot, Semillon
Notes: Chris Niccol shows his wines at the Hunter and Cowra Shows and over the last decade has won a commendable number of medals (5 trophies and 100 medals). Cellar door sales: Mon–Fri 9am–5pm, weekends 10am–5pm.

Willow Vale Estate NR

11 Willow Vale Road, Gerringong, NSW, 2534
Ph 02 4234 0975, Fax 02 4234 4477

Owners: Brian and Narelle Jackson
Chief winemaker: Bevan Wilson
Year of foundation: 1998
Tonnes produced on average each year: 2001 was first vintage, but 120 tonnes are scheduled for vintage 2003
Location: Gerringong
Area: 13.5 ha
Soils: mostly red basalt and clay loam
Varieties planted: White—arneis, chardonnay, verdelho; Red—cabernet sauvignon, chambourcin, merlot, ruby cabernet, sangiovese, shiraz
Leading wines: too early to predict
Notes: With a vineyard of 13.5 ha in extent, Willow Vale Estate is arguably one of the largest in the South Coast wine zone, but it is early days yet to predict wine styles or for that matter quality. At the time of writing, both winery and cellar door sales area were in course of erection.

SOUTHERN NEW SOUTH WALES ZONE

A generally elevated zone extending from the southern boundary of the Central Ranges Zone (Cowra) to the Murray River at Jingellic. It is primarily a cool area except for the relatively warm Hilltops Region. It includes the wine regions of Canberra District, Hilltops and Tumbarumba. At the time of going to print, the Gundagai area has applied for registration as a wine region.

Snowy River Winery ❧ NR
Rockwell Road, Berridale, NSW 2628
Ph 02 6456 5041, Fax 02 6456 5005

Owner: Manfred Plumecke
Chief winemaker: Roger Harris (contract)
Year of foundation: 1984
Tonnes crushed on average each year: 27
Location: Berridale
Area: 3.2 ha
Soils: decomposed granite, very thin topsoil
Varieties planted: White—muller thurgau, riesling, siegerrebe, sylvaner; Reds—none
Leading wines: Snowy River Riesling, Noble Riesling, Siegerrebe
Notes: Located in a very cool area, literally within a stone's throw of the Snowy River, the vineyard, entirely planted with 'German' varieties, well suited to the cold surrounds, is irrigated by pumping from the river. The wine styles are understandably floral and aromatic (i.e. 'Germanic'), tending to sweetness. For Manfred Plumecke that is ideal, for occasionally (just occasionally) conditions are suitable for making eiswein (in June of course, not December). There are no local reds, it is simply too cold. Cellar door sales: Summer, Wed–Sun 10am–5pm; winter, public holidays and school holidays, daily 10am–5pm.

Transylvania Vineyard ❧ NR
Monaro Highway, Cooma, NSW 2630
(15 km north of the town)
Ph 02 6452 4374, Fax 02 6452 6281

Owners: Peter and Maria Culici
Chief winemaker: Peter Culici
Year of foundation: 1988
Tonnes crushed on average each year: 25
Location: Monaro plains north of Cooma
Area: 14 ha
Soils: part is red loamy topsoil, part granitic; the vineyard is irrigated from sweet bore water
Varieties planted: White—chardonnay, gewurztraminer, muscadelle, sauvignon blanc; Red—cabernet sauvignon, merlot, pinot noir
Leading wines: Culici Chardonnay, Cabernet Sauvignon-Merlot, Pinot Noir
Notes: I have driven along the Monaro Highway for 40 years and never expected to see a vineyard here, but most expectations prove ill-founded and this was just another one. This vineyard is very high at 860 m and would see snow several times a year. Its vines are very interesting too, with a rather cold aspect, planted facing west away from the morning sun. The reason is that, in its first few minutes of rising, the sun causes great damage to plants facing it which have been frosted during the night and very early morning. So the Transylvanian vines have extra time to adjust to any frost effect with the result that such damage may not be as severe. Nevertheless, its immediate environment is extremely cool and the vineyard soils may not warm as quickly as with an eastern or north-eastern aspect. Still, there are different approaches in viticulture as in most things. I am informed that its cabernet sauvignon can reach 14° Be in potential alcohol. Cellar door sales: 9am–5pm daily.

CANBERRA DISTRICT REGION

As a winegrowing region, Canberra District is a creature of government, centred on and named after Australia's capital, though more than half of it is located outside the capital's boundaries, in New South Wales to its north-west, north, north-east and east. Many of its vignerons have worked for the Federal government and its agencies during their professional lives. It does not presently have a large area under vine, only about 400 ha, but its winegrowers are an enthusiastic group, conscious of the quality of their region and its growing reputation amongst the Canberra populace, all of whom live within a 45 minute drive of any of its growing number of wineries, which at the end of the year 2000 numbered 24.

As a winegrowing area it dates only from the early 1970s, though there is evidence that, about 130 years ago, there were wineries in the Yass district of New South Wales in the north of the present region, the last of these closing in the early years of the twentieth century. Today, there are numerous wineries in the region, the principal wine-growing sites being close to the villages of Bungendore, Hall and Murrumbateman.

Location: latitude 35°20'S, longitude 149°10'E, the region is around Canberra and about 280 km south-west of Sydney

Elevation: 500–800 m

Topography and soils: The region consists of four basic rock groups, Ordovician iso-clinally folded sediments, acid volcanic rocks, granite and Devonian sandstone. Its north-west section, the vineyards around Murrumbateman and Wallaroo, is undulating country with open flat valleys of porphyry-derived soils. East of the Yass River, the terrain rises to the 'Cullarin Horst', a dissected plateau on sedimentary rocks. Here are located some of the higher altitude vineyards of the region. The country continues to rise in the east of the region. Around Lark Hill, above Bungendore, the soils are clayey loam on shale. Separate soil information is given below in respect of individual vineyard sites.

Climate: Canberra Airport MJT 20.35°C, MAR 14.85°C, HDD 1381 (cut off at 19°C but otherwise not adjusted), AR 630 mm (Oct–Apr 405 mm), RH 62% (9am Jan), 37% (3pm Jan), SH (daily av Oct–Apr) 8.75 AI na. Canberra District is a dry area and drip irrigation from surface dams and bores is necessary to prevent vine stress as relative humidity is low and consequently its evaporation rate is quite high (average mean daily evaporation rate Oct–Apr 6.3 mm). It has a mild rather than extremely cool climate, yet should suit varieties such as pinot noir, except in very warm years, and is certainly too cool in most years for late ripening Mediterranean varieties such as grenache and mourvedre. As for those cultivars in between (the majority), it is quite satisfactory.

Climatic hazards include spring frosts (as are common through most of the Central and Southern Tablelands and the Monaro district of New South Wales), though such frosts are often not widespread in the Canberra District, but limited as usual to sites of poor air drainage. Birds are also a danger, but netting is an effective countermeasure.

Harvest time: late March (traminer, pinot noir, chardonnay) to early May (cabernet sauvignon)

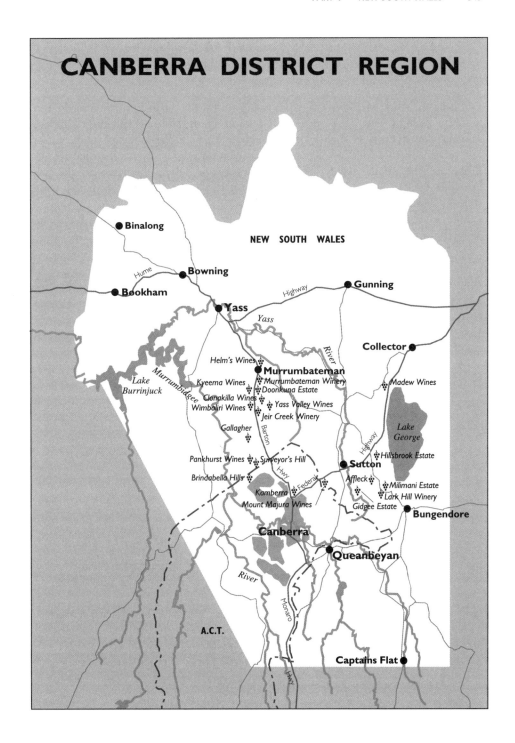

CANBERRA DISTRICT REGION

NEW   SOUTH   WALES

● Binalong

Hume

● Bowning

● Bookham

● **Yass**

Yass

● **Gunning**

Highway

Collector ●

River

Helm's Wines 🍇

● **Murrumbateman**

Kyeema Wines 🍇   🍇 Murrumbateman Winery
Clonakilla Wines 🍇   🍇 Doonkuna Estate
Wimbaliri Wines 🍇   🍇 Yass Valley Wines
🍇 Jeir Creek Winery

🍇 Madew Wines

*Lake
Burrinjuck*

Murrumbidgee

Gallagher 🍇

Barton

*Lake
George*

Pankhurst Wines 🍇 Surveyor's Hill

Brindabella Hills 🍇

Hwy

Federal

🍇 Hillsbrook Estate

● **Sutton**

Affleck 🍇

Highway

🍇 Milimani Estate
🍇 Lark Hill Winery

Kamberra 🍇
Mount Majura Wines

Gidgee Estate 🍇

● **Bungendore**

Canberra

● **Queanbeyan**

River

Monaro

A.C.T.

Hwy

Captains Flat ●

Principal varieties: White—chardonnay, riesling, sauvignon blanc, semillon; Red—cabernet sauvignon (needs a warm exposure and is not suited to higher altitudes in the region), merlot, pinot noir, shiraz
Total area: 400 ha
Principal wine styles: Merlot—a very promising variety for this region when made into a subtly plummy and fresh medium-full style. Pinot Noir—excellent in 'Indian summer' slow-ripening or slightly cooler Canberra years. It does not show at its best in hot years. Cabernet-Merlot—generally good when Merlot performs its usual role of filling out the middle palate. Shiraz—shows savoury olive characters in the few examples seen by the writer. Promising but yet to be proved. Other principal wine styles—Chardonnay, Riesling, Sauvignon Blanc
Leading wineries and vineyards: Lark Hill, Brindabella Hills, Kyeema Wines, Kamberra Wine Tourism Complex, Clonakilla Wines, Jeir Creek, Pankhurst Wines

Affleck R79

154 Millynn Road, Bungendore,
NSW 2621
Ph 02 6236 9276, Fax 02 6236 9090,
Email wine@affleck.com.au

Owners: Ian and Susie Hendry
Chief winemaker: Ian Hendry
Year of foundation: 1976
Tonnes crushed on average each year: 6
Location: Bungendore
Area: 3 ha
Soils: poor shaley hillside country with little topsoil, possibly due to water erosion over many years
Varieties planted: White—chardonnay, sauvignon blanc, semillon; Red—cabernet sauvignon, merlot, muscat, pinot noir, shiraz
Leading wines: Affleck Pinot Noir, Chardonnay
Notes: Affleck is a very small vineyard and winery crushing only its own fruit and run by family and friends. Pinot Noir and Chardonnay are of good quality. Cellar door sales: daily 9am–5pm. Barbecue facilities and light lunches available.

Brindabella Hills R88

156 Woodgrove Close via Wallaroo Road,
Hall, ACT 2618
Ph 02 6230 2583, Fax 02 5230 2023,
Email BrindabellaHills@bigpond.com

Owners: Roger and Faye Harris
Chief winemaker: Roger Harris
Year of foundation: 1986
Tonnes crushed on average each year: 90, of which about 35 are used for the Brindabella Hills labels, 25 tonnes being produced by Brindabella Hills
Location: Hall
Area: 3.5 ha
Soils: red and orange duplex soils (Dr and Dy); sandy loams over gravelly clay on decomposed porphyric lignumbrite; colluvial silty clay loam over coarse sands and gravels; low clay content, free draining; low natural nutrition and pH
Varieties planted: White—chardonnay, riesling, sauvignon blanc, semillon; Red—cabernet franc, cabernet sauvignon, merlot, shiraz
Leading wines: Brindabella Hills Chardonnay, Sauvignon Blanc Semillon, Cabernet Blend, Riesling
Notes: Distinguished research scientist Dr Roger Harris is also a qualified winemaker, and an extraordinarily good one at that. Wine

highlights here are many, especially Chardonnay, Riesling and Sauvignon Blanc-Semillon. Roger Harris also has a deft touch with Cabernet and makes a fine Merlot. Certainly worth a detour on any trip to Canberra. With wines such as these, it is no wonder that Brindabella Hills is a consistent award winner at local and interstate wine shows. Cellar door sales: weekends and public holidays 10am–5pm, otherwise by appointment.

Clonakilla Wines **R85**

Crisps Lane off Gundaroo Road, Murrumbateman, NSW 2582
Ph 02 6227 5877, Fax 02 6251 1938, Email jtokirk@clonakilla.com.au

Owner: Dr John TO Kirk
Chief winemaker: Timothy P Kirk
Year of foundation: 1971
Tonnes crushed on average each year: 50
Location: Murrumbateman
Area: 3 ha
Soils:red kandosol (a sandy clay loam derived from volcanic rock)
Varieties planted: White—chardonnay, riesling, sauvignon blanc, semillon, viognier;
Red—brown muscat, cabernet franc, cabernet sauvignon, merlot, pinot noir, shiraz
Leading wines: Clonakilla Shiraz-Viognier, Riesling, Viognier
Notes: Clonakilla has established a very good reputation for its Shiraz-Viognier blend. Indeed, its Viognier white is also excellent. Cellar door sales: daily 11am–5pm.

Doonkuna Estate **R77**

Barton Highway, Murrumbateman, NSW 2582
Ph 02 6227 5885, Fax 02 6227 5085, Email wine@doonkuna.com.au

Owners: Barry and Maureen Moran
Chief winemaker: Malcolm Burdett

Year of foundation: 1973
Tonnes crushed on average each year: 60, increasing to 200 when recently planted vines come into full bearing
Location: Murrumbateman
Area: 20 ha, 16 of which have been recently planted
Soils: black humus on a clay base
Varieties planted: White—chardonnay, riesling, sauvignon blanc, semillon; Red—cabernet franc, cabernet sauvignon, merlot, pinot noir, shiraz
Leading wines: Doonkuna Estate Riesling, Chardonnay, Cabernet Sauvignon-Merlot, Cian (a sparkling white made from Pinot Noir and Chardonnay by the traditional method)
Notes: Doonkuna is an old established Canberra winery now in the middle of a development phase. Cellar door sales: daily 11am–4pm.

Gallagher Estate **R82**

Dog Trap Road, Murrumbateman, NSW 2582
Ph 02 6254 9957, Fax 02 6278 3654, Email gallwine@dynamite.com.au

Owners: Greg and Libby Gallagher
Chief winemaker: Greg Gallagher
Year of foundation: 1995
Tonnes crushed on average each year: 50
Location: Murrumbateman
Area: 2 ha
Soils: decomposed granitic sandy loam over clay
Varieties planted: White—chardonnay; Red—shiraz
Leading wines: Gallagher Estate Chardonnay, Shiraz
Notes: Greg Gallagher was at Taltarni in western Victoria for many years and currently is winemaker at Charles Sturt University, Wagga. His Shiraz is the strength here. There are no cellar door sales, sales being made by mail order or by retail.

Gidgee Estate NR

441 Weeroona Drive, Wamboin,
NSW 2621
Ph 02 6236 9506, Fax 02 8236 9070,
Email GIDGEE@bigpond.com

Owners: Kay Brett and Cheryl Lane
Chief winemakers: White—David Madew;
Red—Andrew McEwin (contract)
Year of foundation: 1996
Tonnes produced on average each year: 3
Location: Wamboin
Area: 1 ha
Soils: mainly clay
Varieties planted: White—chardonnay, riesling;
Red—cabernet sauvignon, cabernet franc,
merlot
Leading wines: Gidgee Estate Riesling,
Chardonnay, Ensemble (a blend of the three
red varieties)
Notes: Gidgee Estate is a very small vineyard
with a production of only 300 cases. No wines
have been tasted. Cellar door sales: most
weekends noon–4pm but ring ahead.
Otherwise by appointment.

Helm Wines R84

Butts Road, Murrumbateman, NSW 2582
Ph 02 6227 5953, Fax 02 6227 0207,
Email khelm@enternet.com.au

Owners: Ken and Judith Helm
Chief winemaker: Ken Helm (consultant Gerry
Sissingh)
Year of foundation: 1973
Tonnes crushed on average each year: 100
Location: Murrumbateman
Area: 2.5 ha owned, 15 ha under contract
Soils: good alluvial soils varying to poor quartzy
hillside soils over white pipe-clay subsoil
Varieties planted: White—chardonnay, riesling;
Red—cabernet sauvignon, merlot
Leading wines: Helm Wines Cabernet-Merlot,
Riesling, Non-oaked Chardonnay
Notes: A former CSIRO researcher, Ken Helm is

one of the pioneers of the Canberra region,
making his twenty-fifth vintage in 2001. Helm
Wines has an excellent show record and very
good Cabernet-Merlot is made here. Cellar
door sales: daily 10am–5pm, closed Wed and
Thurs.

Hillbrook Estate NR

Doust Road, Geary's Gap, NSW 2621
Ph 02 6236 9455, Fax 02 6280 7933

Owners: Adolf and Lavina Zanzerl
Chief winemakers: Dr David and Sue
Carpenter (contract), David Madew (contract)
Year of foundation: 1994
Tonnes produced on average each year: 23
Location: Geary's Gap
Area: 6.5 ha
Soils: clay loams, rocky
Varieties planted: White—chardonnay, riesling,
sauvignon blanc; Red—cabernet sauvignon,
merlot, pinot noir, shiraz
Leading wines: Hillbrook Estate Riesling,
Chardonnay, Merlot, Pinot Noir
Notes: No wines have been tasted. Cellar door
sales: weekends and public holidays
10am–5pm.

Jeir Creek Wines R85

Gooda Creek Road, Murrumbateman,
NSW 2582
Ph 02 6227 5999, Fax 02 6227 5900,
Email rob@jeircreekwines.com.au

Owners: Rob and Kay Howell
Chief winemaker: Rob Howell
Year of foundation: 1984
Tonnes crushed on average each year: 60,
increasing to 100 by the year 2002
Location: Murrumbateman
Area: 8.9 ha
Soils: quartz porphyry (decomposed granite)
based
Varieties planted: White—chardonnay, riesling,
sauvignon blanc; Red—cabernet sauvignon,

merlot, muscat de frontignan, pinot noir, shiraz
Leading wines: Jeir Creek Riesling, Sauvignon
Blanc, Cabernet-Merlot, Shiraz, Merlot, Botrytis
Semillon-Sauvignon Blanc
Notes: Jeir Creek is a flourishing winery run by
enthusiastic husband and wife team Rob and
Kay Howell. There are excellent whites and
reds here including savoury 'olive and white
pepper' Shiraz styles and a very fine
apricot/citrus 'sticky' (made from botrytised
semillon and sauvignon blanc). Cellar door
sales: Fri–Sun and public holidays 10am–5pm.

Kamberra Wine Tourism Complex **R86**

Cnr Northbourne Ave and Flemington
Road, Lyneham, ACT 2602
Ph 02 6262 2333, Fax 02 6262 2300,
Email kamberra@brlhardy.com.au

Owner: BRL Hardy Ltd
Chief winemaker: Peter Dawson
Year of foundation: 2000
Tonnes crushed on average each year: First
vintage crushed at the Kamberra winery was
2001. The crush will increase as vineyards
come on stream. There are also many contract
growers
Locations: (winery, small vineyard and cellar
door sales) Lyneham. (vineyard) Holt
Area: 82 ha (vineyard is at Holt within the ACT
and was planted in two stages, being
completed in 2001)
Soils: Holt Stage1, loamy clay topsoil over clay,
almost pipeclay; Stage 2, 50 cm of light clay
loam over a heavier loam over a light clay
subsoil
Varieties planted: White—chardonnay, riesling,
sauvignon blanc, semillon, viognier;
Red—cabernet sauvignon, merlot, shiraz
Leading wines: There are two price ranges, the
premium Kamberra range and a lesser priced
Meeting Place range. The Kamberra range
includes Chardonnay, Pinot Sparkling,
Cabernet Sauvignon and Shiraz; the Meeting

Place range includes Riesling, Verdelho,
Sauvignon Blanc-Semillon, Chardonnay, Pinot
Noir and Shiraz-Cabernet
Notes: BRL Hardy have constructed an
impressive 'gateway' to the Canberra District
wine region. Its wine-making facility is
presently only a crushing and fermenting plant
but will ultimately become a fully-equipped
winery. It already has a large cellar door
complex and a small vineyard. More
importantly it has some excellent regional
wines. In the vineyard, BRL Hardy has made a
strong commitment to shiraz and viognier as
very suitable varieties for this region. Cellar
door sales: daily 10am–5pm.

Kyeema Wines **R87**

Scrubby Lane off Barton Highway,
Murrumbateman, NSW (vineyard and
winery)
43 Shumack St, Weetangera, ACT 2614
(Head Office and postal address)
Ph 02 6254 7557, Fax 02 6254 7336,
Mob 0407 913 912,
Email kyeema@spirit.com.au

Owner/chief winemaker: Andrew McEwin
Year of foundation: 1985
Tonnes produced on average each year: 40, of
which 20 are used for Kyeema wines
Location: Murrumbateman
Area: 4 ha
Soils: granitic soils derived from Ordovician
granite
Varieties planted: White—chardonnay;
Red—cabernet sauvignon, merlot, shiraz
Leading wines: Kyeema Shiraz, Merlot,
Cabernet-Merlot
Notes: Kyeema has a proud wine show record,
especially with its Shiraz and Merlot, which are
indeed worth seeking out. There are no cellar
door sales. Sales by mail and Email from postal
and, email addresses.

Lark Hill Winery R90

RMB 281 Bungendore Road, Bungendore,
NSW 2621
Ph/Fax 02 6238 1393,
Email larkhill@dynamite.com.au

Owners: Dave and Sue Carpenter
Chief winemaker: Sue Carpenter
Year of foundation: 1978
Tonnes crushed on average each year: 120
Location: Bungendore
Area: 5 ha
Soils: poor shallow clayey soils over shale and
slate rock
Varieties planted: White—chardonnay, riesling,
sauvignon blanc; Red—merlot, pinot noir
Leading wines: Lark Hill Chardonnay,
Sauvignon Blanc, Pinot Noir, Cabernet-Merlot,
Methode Champenoise, Exultation Cabernet
Notes: Lark Hill powers on. Its Pinots are
magnificent, especially in slightly cooler years
such as 1997 and 1999, its Chardonnays only
marginally less so. However the climate at Lark
Hill has proved too cold overall for cabernet
sauvignon, so it has been removed from the
vineyard. To fill this void, exceptional parcels
of cabernet fruit are purchased and on
occasion they are exalted into Exultation, a
super-premium range, which may include any
of the Lark Hill varietals, provided they are of
superb quality. Cellar door sales: 7 days
10am–5pm, except Tuesdays by appointment
only.

Madew Wines R84

'Westering', Federal Highway,
Lake George, NSW 2581
Ph 02 4848 0026,
Email drink.madew@madewwines.com.au

Owners: David Madew Snr, David and Romilly
Madew
Chief winemaker: David Madew
Year of foundation: 1994
Tonnes crushed on average each year: 60

Location: Lake George
Area: 8 ha
Soils: gravel wave banks of Lake George over
clay base and also black soil over clay
Varieties planted: White—chardonnay, pinot
gris, riesling; Red—merlot, pinot noir, shiraz
Leading wines: Madew Riesling, Merlot, Shiraz,
Pinot Noir
Notes: Merlot is the pick here, showing
delightfully fresh plummy characters. There is
also a very new restaurant, with extensive views
over the flat expanse of plain that once was
Lake George and may be once more, God
willing! Cellar door sales: Wed–Sun 11am–5pm.

Milimani Estate Wines R81

92 The Forest Road, Bungendore,
NSW 2621
Ph 02 6238 1421, Fax 02 6238 1424,
Email milimani@milimani.com.au

Owners: Mary, David and Rosemary Preston
Chief winemaker: Dr David and Sue Carpenter
(contract)
Year of foundation: 1989
Tonnes produced on average each year: 9
Location: Bungendore
Area: 4 ha
Soils: thin shaley soils
Varieties planted: White—chardonnay,
sauvignon blanc; Red—cabernet franc, merlot,
pinot noir
Leading wines: Milimani Pinot Noir,
Chardonnay, Sauvignon Blanc
Notes: A small family-owned vineyard making
pleasant Pinot Noir. Cellar door sales: most
weekends and public holidays, but ring ahead.
Otherwise by appointment.

Mount Majura Wines R82

RMB 314 Majura Road, Majura,
ACT 2609
Mob 0403 355 682, Fax 02 6262 4288,
Email fvande01@postoffice.csu.edu.au

Owners: a Sydney-based partnership
Chief winemaker: Frank van de Loo, Roger
Harris (consultant)
Year of foundation: 1988
Tonnes produced on average each year: 10,
but new plantings will see this increase to 90
by vintage 2004
Location: Mount Majura
Area: 9.4 ha
Soils: red clay loam rich in iron, containing
metamorphosed limestone as well as
ironstone-like material; vineyard has north-
easterly and south-easterly aspects
Varieties planted: White—chardonnay, pinot
gris, riesling; Red—cabernet franc, cabernet
sauvignon, merlot, pinot noir, shiraz, tempranillo
Leading wines: Mount Majura Chardonnay,
Pinot Noir, Cabernet Franc-Merlot
Notes: Mount Majura has a consistent local
wine show record of winning silver and bronze
awards with an occasional gold and trophy.
Pinot and Chardonnay are obviously suited to
the site and promise well for the future. There
are no present cellar door sales, but they are
planned for the future. Sales by mail order.

Murrumbateman Winery **R79**

Barton Highway, Murrumbateman,
NSW 2582 (3 km south of the village)
Ph 02 6227 5584, Fax 02 6227 5987

Owners: Michael Marriman, Reg Shaw, Bill
Carson and Duncan Leslie
Chief winemaker: Duncan Leslie
Year of foundation: 1972
Tonnes crushed on average each year: 30
Location: Murrumbateman
Area: 2.52 ha
Soils: fine clay soils on a pipe-clay and granite
base
Varieties planted: White—chardonnay,
sauvignon blanc; Red—cabernet sauvignon,
shiraz
Leading wines: Murrumbateman Sauvignon
Blanc, Cabernet-Merlot-Shiraz

Notes: One of the first Canberra District
wineries to be established, Murrumbateman
has a licensed restaurant and function centre
available for parties. Cellar door sales:
10am–5pm daily, except Tuesdays and
Wednesdays.

Pankhurst Wines **R83**

Old Woodgrove, Woodgrove Close, Hall,
NSW 2618
Ph/Fax 02 6230 2592,
Email pankhurst@ozemail.com.au

Owners: Christine and Alan Pankhurst
Chief winemaker: Sue Carpenter (contract)
Year of foundation: 1986
Tonnes crushed on average each year: 50, of
which 25 are used for Pankhurst wines
Location: Hall
Area: 4.7 ha
Soils: weathered granite soils of good depth,
which retain moisture well
Varieties planted: White—chardonnay,
sauvignon blanc, semillon; Red—cabernet
sauvignon, merlot, pinot noir
Leading wines: Pankhurst Cabernet-Merlot,
Pinot Noir, Chardonnay
Notes: Excellent Pinot here as one would
expect when made by Sue Carpenter. Cellar
door sales: Sun and public holidays
10am–5pm, at other times by appointment.

Surveyors Hill Winery **R81**

215 Brooklands Road via Wallaroo Road,
Hall, ACT 2618
Ph 02 6230 2046, Fax 02 6230 2048

Owners: Leigh Hobba, Denise McFayden and
Glenys London
Chief winemaker: Roger Harris (contract)
Year of foundation: 1986
Tonnes produced on average each year: 85, of
which 20 are used for Surveyors Hill wines
Location: Hall
Area: 9.9 ha

Soils: porphyric lignumbrite, coarse sandy soils of volcanic derivation with poor water retention
Varieties planted: White—chardonnay, riesling, sauvignon blanc, semillon; Red—cabernet franc, cabernet sauvignon, merlot, pinot noir, shiraz, touriga
Leading wines: Surveyors Hill Sauvignon Blanc, Riesling, Cabernet Sauvignon
Notes: There are good wines here, even, unusually, a dry Touriga Rose. There is also bed and breakfast accommodation. Cellar door sales: weekends and public holidays 10am–5pm, at other times by appointment.

Wimbaliri Wines R81

Barton Highway, Murrumbateman, NSW 2582 (3 km south of the village)
Ph/Fax 02 6227 5921

Owners: John and Margaret Andersen
Chief winemaker: John Andersen
Year of foundation: 1988
Tonnes produced on average each year:12
Location: Murrumbateman
Area: 2.2 ha
Soils: decomposed granite with patches of gravel, clays varying from yellow to a more fertile deep red
Varieties planted: White—chardonnay; Red—cabernet sauvignon, cabernet franc, merlot, pinot noir, shiraz

Leading wines: Wimbaliri Cabernet-Merlot, Pinot Noir, Chardonnay
Notes: A small family owned vineyard and winery making good Cabernet-Merlot and Pinot Noir. Cellar door sales: weekends 11am–5pm, at other times by appointment.

Yass Valley Wines R79

Crisps Lane, Murrumbateman, NSW 2582
Ph/Fax 02 6227 5592,
Email yasswine@cyberone.com.au

Owners: Mick Withers and Anne Hillier
Chief winemaker: Mick Withers
Year of foundation: 1979
Tonnes crushed on average each year: 15
Location: Murrumbateman
Area: 2.8 ha
Soils: heavy clay loams with a thin sandy A horizon, tending to be boron-deficient, sometimes zinc-deficient and very acidic
Varieties planted: White—chardonnay, riesling, semillon, traminer, verdelho; Red—aleatico, barbera, merlot, shiraz
Leading wines: Yass Valley Riesling, Cabernet Sauvignon-Merlot, Traminer, Shiraz
Notes: This is a mature vineyard as regards its riesling and traminer plantings which were made in 1979. Cellar door sales: Wed–Sun and public holidays 11am–5pm.

HILLTOPS REGION

The region was first settled in the 1820s after Hamilton Hume's exploration of the Yass district in 1821 had opened it up for squatting. However, as squatting was illegal until 1830, there are no records of settlements or settlers until that year. The first settlements within the region were near the present-day towns of Boorowa, Harden and Young. Its population was greatly increased in 1856 by a local epidemic of mid-nineteenth century gold fever, a contagion which in 1861 provoked the inter-racial riots between Chinese and European diggers at Lambing Flat (present-day Young). Inevitably the luckier diggers bought land within the region to graze sheep and cattle.

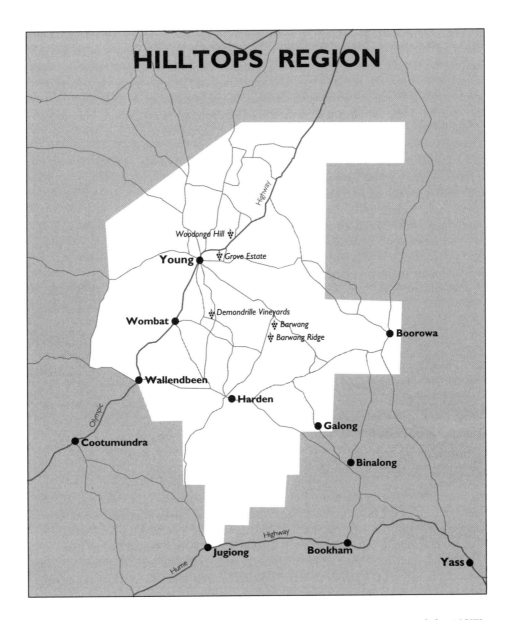

HILLTOPS REGION

However, the age of closer settlement was at hand and the passing of the NSW Lands Act of 1861, which provided for smaller blocks, led to more intensive farming. The arrival of the railway in 1877 was also of great assistance to an area which was, by that time, primarily agricultural. By the 1890s, orcharding had commenced in the region and first-quality crops of apples, pears, quinces, grapes and cherries were consigned to the Sydney markets. Orcharding continued to expand after WWI and the region was still more closely settled by returning soldiers after the passing of the Soldier Settlement Acts. Today the Young area is still famous for its cherries.

The region dates its wine history from 1860 with the arrival at the 'Three Mile Rush' of Nichole Jasprizza, a Croatian from Dalmatia. Like the wisest of those who rushed to the goldfields, Jasprizza did not intend to mine but to supply the miners with food and beverages by growing fruit and vegetables and making wine. He settled on a property near Young known as Summer Hill. He evidently prospered, for 20 years later he sponsored the immigration of three of his nephews, Tony, Valdo and Andrew Cunich, who brought with them—as was the fashion of emigrants from winegrowing countries—vine cuttings. In this case, it was a muscat type, known as snowy muscat from Yanyana in Dalmatia. Grapes were planted in three locations, Jasprizza's Summer Hill property, opposite Summer Hill on the Old Monteagle Road and at Cherry Grove on the Boorowa Road near Young. Some of the original vines exist today. The orchard and vineyard plantings of Jasprizza and his nephews continued to expand until the early years of the twentieth century and reached 240 hectares in extent. Grapegrowing continued until the 1940s when it began to be unprofitable due to labour shortages and increasing costs. In 1960 the old vineyards, by that time neglected, were grubbed out and more profitable cherries and stone fruit planted in their place.

Yet vineyards did not depart the district for long. In 1969, Peter Robertson of 'Barwang', perhaps with the intention of 'diversifying'—a popular rural concept in those days—but probably inspired by the report of the late Graham Gregory recommending the region for viticulture—planted an eight-acre vineyard on his property, having propagated cuttings obtained from McWilliam's at Griffith. He chose cabernet sauvignon, shiraz, riesling and semillon. His intention was to sell the fruit to McWilliam's. But fate in an unusual form stepped in—the fruit fly. Robertson's first vintage, in 1974, coincided with an outbreak of fruit fly in the district and quarantine restrictions prevented its sale to Griffith. Nor was he any luckier in attempting to sell his fruit in the Hunter Valley. So in six weeks, he set up a winery and made his first vintage. Beginner's luck or not, his first Cabernet Sauvignon won a silver medal at the National Wine Show in Canberra. He continued winemaking at Barwang until 1988 when he sold the property to McWilliam's. Meanwhile, others had been following in Robertson's footsteps. In 1973, the Moppity Park vineyard was established, followed in 1979 by Hercynia Vineyard (now Demondrille Vineyards) and Nioka Ridge (since renamed Barwang Ridge). It was also about this time that Cartobe Vineyard (now called Castle's Creek) was planted. To complete the list, Woodonga Hill was established in 1986.

Though there have been grapes within the region for well over 100 years, its name is much more recent, being devised in 1983 by Andrew Birks, then a lecturer in wine science at Charles Sturt University. Today there are three wineries and many vineyards in the region.

Location: latitude 34°20'S, longitude 148°18'E (Young), 34°34'S, 148°21'E (Harden), about 360 km west-south-west of Sydney
Elevation: Young 440 m, Harden 431 m
Topography and soils: As its name suggests, the region is hilly and undulating. It is located around the formation known as the Young Granites, which run in a north–south direction between Young in the north, Harden in the centre and Jugiong in the extreme south of the region and stretch eastwards as far as Galong. There are

small areas of Aeolian (wind-blown) soils around Young and Harden but the chief soils found in these areas are red duplex and red earths. In the east of the region and on its boundaries to the north of Boorowa are found rather sandy soils, formed by the Wyangala Granites found in this part of the region. These tend to salinity because they were once part of an ancient seashore.

Climate: Young (Post Office) MJT 22.95°C, MAR 15.85°C, HDD 1619 (cut off at 19°C but otherwise not adjusted), AR 653.5 mm (Oct–Apr 355.3 mm), RH 63% (9am Jan), 32% (3pm Jan), AI na, SH na. Harden (Bundarbo Street) MJT 22.45°C, MAR 15.65°C, HDD 1572 (cut off at 19°C but otherwise not adjusted), AR 612.8 mm (Oct–Apr 348.4 mm), RH 56% (9am Jan), 36% (3pm Jan), AI na, SH na.

Hilltops is undoubtedly a warm region, and would be suited for the production of fortified wines if market conditions were favourable. As they are not, Hilltops is certainly suited for the production of full-bodied reds (see Principal wine styles below). More than half its annual rainfall falls during the growing season, the rainfall increasing in the more rugged eastern parts of the region.

Vineyards are commonly drip-irrigated from private dams or bores, but of course there are restrictions on the use of irrigation within the Murray–Darling basin of which the Hilltops Region forms part. Such restrictions confine water use to 1994 levels. These restrictions are based on the rules that no dam larger than 10 megalitres may be installed for irrigation purposes, no area larger than 10 hectares may be irrigated from such a dam, and dams may not be installed on a designated water course. What constitutes a designated water course is decided by officers of the NSW Land and Water Resources Department. Further, no new licences are presently being issued for the use of water from water courses. There have also been instances of restrictions on the use of bore water within the Lachlan River basin. The standard of bore water used for drip irrigation should also be checked regularly, but is usually of sound quality, especially if taken from higher areas.

Water apart, there are no real problems in the Hilltops Region except birds, which are effectively deterred by electronic means. Mildews and botrytis can be controlled by the usual spray methods and frost presents no difficulties if the vineyard sites have been chosen on slopes and ridges with good air drainage.

Harvest time: Chardonnay is harvested at the end of March and early April, riesling early April, and sauvignon blanc and semillon at the end of March. Pinot noir is picked at the end of March, shiraz and merlot mid-April, and cabernet sauvignon at the end of April.

Principal varieties: White—chardonnay, sauvignon blanc, semillon, traminer; Red—cabernet sauvignon, merlot, shiraz

Total area: na

Principal wine styles: It is really early days to determine the definitive wine styles of the Hilltops Region. The Cabernet Sauvignon and Shiraz reds of Barwang, which are full-bodied, moderately but not overtly fruity and well balanced by sufficient tannin and acid, are presently the benchmark reds of the region, which will become noteworthy for such reds in the future. Hilltops would also suit fortified wines, should these ever return to market favour, and perhaps also finer styles of sweet botrytised whites, though I doubt whether it will ever achieve the lusciousness of areas such as Griffith.

Barwang Ridge Vineyard NR

1 Barwang Road, Young, NSW 2594
(20 minutes east of the town)
Ph/Fax 02 6382 6363,
Email hansenhilltops@yol.net.au

Owner: Peter Hansen.
Chief winemaker: Greg Gallagher (contract)
Year of foundation: 1979
Tonnes produced on average each year: 45, all
of which is used for Hansen Hilltops wines
Location: Young
Area: 4.87 ha
Soils: deep red weathered granite, not too rich
Varieties planted: White—chardonnay, riesling,
semillon; Red—cabernet sauvignon, cabernet
franc, malbec, merlot, shiraz
Leading wines: Hansen Hilltops Riesling,
Cabernet Sauvignon, Shiraz
Notes: Barwang Ridge has a commendable
show record at smaller regional shows,
including a trophy for Riesling at the Canberra
Regional Show. Cellar door sales: Fri–Mon
10am–6pm

Barwang (vineyard only) R86

Barwang Road, Young, NSW 2594

Owner: McWilliam's Wines Pty Ltd
Chief winemaker: Jim Brayne
Year of foundation: 1969
Tonnes crushed on average each year: not
disclosed but all is used by McWilliams Wines
Location: Barwang, Harden
Area: 115 ha
Varieties planted: White—chardonnay,
semillon; Red—cabernet sauvignon, merlot,
shiraz
Leading wines: Barwang Chardonnay,
Cabernet Sauvignon, Shiraz and, occasionally
in very good years, Semillon
Soils: decomposed reddish granite soils on a
clay base
Notes: The first and biggest producer in the
Region, Barwang was founded in 1969 by the

late Peter Robertson who sold it in 1988 to
McWilliam's. Its wines are typical of the firm
but full-flavoured styles of the region and are
produced expertly at Griffith by Jim Brayne.
Barwang Cabernet Sauvignon and Shiraz are
of excellent quality. There is a winery on site,
but it is used only for crushing purposes. There
are no local cellar door sales.

Demondrille Vineyards NR

Prunevale Road, Prunevale via Harden
NSW 2587
Ph 02 6384 4272, Fax 02 6384 4292,
Email demondrille@bigpond.com.au

Owner: Robert Provan
Chief winemaker: Mark Davidson (contract)
Year of foundation: 1979
Tonnes crushed on average each year: 25
Location Prunevale
Area: 9.1 ha including 3.6 ha non-bearing
Soils: red sandy loam over clay aeolian
Varieties planted: White—chardonnay, riesling,
sauvignon blanc, semillon, traminer;
Red—aleatico, cabernet sauvignon, merlot,
pinot noir, shiraz
Leading wines: Demondrille Vineyards Tin Shed
Riesling, Stan Dessert Wine (a blend of
aleatico, traminer, frontignac, semillon),
Purgatory (a pinot noir rose), The Dove
Sauvignon Blanc-Semillon, The Raven Shiraz,
Black Rose Cabernet-Merlot, Bloodline Pinot
Noir, Precious Botrytised Riesling
Notes: Demondrille has an eclectic selection of
wines, none of which I have recently tasted.
Cellar door sales: weekends 10.30am–5pm,
open public holidays, closed Christmas Day,
Boxing Day and Good Friday. Luncheon by
appointment.

Grove Estate R80

Boorowa Road, Young, NSW 2594
Ph 02 6382 6999, Fax 02 6382 4527,
Email grove.estate@yol.net.au

Owners: Brian Mullany, Mark Flanders and John Kirkwod
Chief winemaker: Greg Silkman (contract)
Year of foundation: 1989
Tonnes produced on average each year: 300, of which 60 are used for Grove Estate wines
Location: Young
Area: 30 ha
Soils: red podsols over granulated granite subsoil
Varieties planted: White—chardonnay, semillon; Red—barbera, cabernet sauvignon, merlot, petit verdot, sangiovese, shiraz, zinfandel
Leading wines: Grove Estate Murrango Way Chardonnay, Partners Cabernet Sauvignon, Cellar Block Shiraz, Hilltops Semillon, Hilltops Zinfandel
Notes: With a blue-gold award at the top 100 exhibition for its Partners Cabernet and a trophy for its Semillon as top white at the Cool Area Wine show at Murrumbateman, Grove Estate makes typically rich Cabernet and Shiraz reds as well as good whites. Cellar door sales: weekends 10am–5pm.

Lindsays Woodonga Hill (formerly Woodonga Hill) NR

Cowra Road, Young, NSW 2594
Ph/Fax 02 6382 2972,
Email lindsays@yol.net.au

Owner: Woodonga Hill Pty Ltd
Chief winemaker: Jill Lindsay
Year of foundation: 1978
Tonnes crushed on average each year: 80
Location: Young
Area: 10 ha
Soils: Burrengong series 1,2,3 deep red soils with a clay base
Varieties planted: White—chardonnay, gewurztraminer, riesling, sauvignon blanc, semillon; Red—cabernet franc, cabernet sauvignon, gamay, shiraz, touriga
Leading wines: Lindsays Woodonga Hill Riesling, Cabernet Sauvignon, Shiraz
Notes: Woodonga Hill shows regularly at local shows, particularly Canberra Regional, Cowra and Rutherglen. Its Cabernet and Shiraz Reds are consistent winners of silver and bronze awards. Cellar door sales: 7 days 9am–5pm.

TUMBARUMBA REGION

The rumbling echo 'Tumbarumba' is indeed onomatopoeic, being the sound, according to local folklore, of the reverberations from hollow 'sounding grounds' associated with the basalt rock formations within the higher parts of the region.

The first inhabitants were the Wolgalu aboriginal people who migrated through the region in late summer, feasting on the multitude of Bogong moths in the area. The first Europeans to see the region were the Australian-born Hamilton Hume and the Englishman William Hovell, who left Hume's property at Gunning, north of present-day Canberra, in 1824 on their journey of exploration to Westernport Bay. They missed Westernport Bay, but did discover Port Phillip and ended their journey near Geelong. As usual the explorers were followed by the graziers with their sheep and cattle. Soon Yass and Canberra were being grazed and by the middle of the 1830s their stock had arrived in the open uplands of the Murray. By the 1850s, an epidemic of gold fever erupted in the Snowy Mountains and the town of Tumbarumba was born. After the epidemic, the area concentrated on timber-getting from its vast Alpine Ash forests and a hardwood timber industry was established, though snow-lease grazing continued until the 1960s. Later in the 1920s, softwoods were planted to consolidate the timber industry in the region and at this time also the railway reached the town. Thereafter until the 1950s, the region relied on timber-getting and grazing.

A major economic spur for the region in the 1950s and 1960s was the construction of the massive Snowy Mountains Hydro-Electric Scheme. Many more people, mostly migrants from Europe after the Second World War, came to the area; many access roads were built and at least one permanent town, Khancoban, was established.

Wine has come late to the region, its first vineyards being established in 1983 by Frank and Christine Minutello and Ian and Juliet Cowell (now Juliet Cullen). The varieties planted, chardonnay and pinot noir, were primarily intended for sparkling wine, though small areas of other whites, sauvignon blanc and pinot gris, were also established. Early vintages were sold to Rosemount, who at that time seemed intent on establishing sparkling wines in their portfolio. However, Rosemount did not persist, removing its sparkling wine equipment to its Upper Hunter base in 1986. At this point, Seppelt's former chief winemaker, Ian McKenzie, enters Tumbarumba wine history and Seppelts, now part of Southcorp, proceeded to buy Tumbarumba grapes for sparkling wine purposes from 1987 onwards. In 1994, Southcorp purchased the original Cowell/Cullen vineyard, at the same time changing the vineyard emphasis somewhat from all sparkling to sparkling and table whites. Since then, other winemakers such as BRL Hardy and Charles Sturt University have become interested in the region.

By 1997, about 310 ha of vineyards had been established around Tumbarumba, shared amongst 28 vineyards. There is a crushing plant but no wineries within the region, all local wines being made outside the region by contract. There are three licensed cellar door outlets.

Location: Tumbarumba PO latitude 32°46'S, longitude 148°01'E, about 375 km south-west of Sydney and virtually the same distance north-east of Melbourne

Elevation: The region, though with areas in the upper Murray catchment as low as 250 m above sea level, is mostly above the 300 m contour line and occupies the undulating country between the edge of the Riverina plain and the higher parts of the Australian Alps. Closer to the town of Tumbarumba, elevations of between 500 and 750 metres are found, with the vineyard areas generally between 550 and 700 metres.

Topography and soils: The soils of the region are derived from the rock of the three geological formations forming the western parts of the main range of the Australian Alps. These are 1) sedimentary material giving rise to shallow shale and siltstone related soils. These occur in the western parts of the region and deepen as one progresses east into the higher parts. 2) granitic soils stemming from the higher parts where granite-based material is predominant, and 3) smaller areas of basalt-based soils originating from an older overlying basalt cap.

These differentiate the hill country of the region from its lower northern and western areas, where material deposited from the higher country by mountain streams dominates the open valleys and plains.

Climate: Tumbarumba PO MJT 20°C, MAR 14.85°C, HDD 1241 (cut off at 19°C, but otherwise not adjusted), AR 986 mm (Oct–Apr 492 mm), RH 62% (9am Jan), 39% (3pm Jan), AI na, SH na.

The region has all the characteristics of an alpine climate with an MAR of 14.85°C and a quite generous rainfall fairly evenly spread between the growing and non-growing season. It can of course be considered as the western foothills and lower slopes of the Snowy Mountains, having deep valleys and differences in elevation which may result in differences in air drainage and other climatic factors. Its growing season is short and the region as a whole is cool, inclining to very cool, limiting the varieties which may successfully be ripened to pinot noir and meunier amongst reds and pinot gris, gewurztraminer, sauvignon blanc and chardonnay amongst whites.

There are no irrigation schemes within the region, which relies on private surface dams to collect run-off.

Harvest time: chardonnay, late March to mid April; pinot noir same; sauvignon blanc early April; pinot noir for sparkling wine base mid to late March

Principal Varieties: White—chardonnay, sauvignon blanc; Red—pinot noir.

Total area: (2000) 600 ha

Principal wine styles: Sparkling, Chardonnay, Pinot Noir, Sauvignon Blanc, Merlot

Excelsior Peak
(vineyard only)
 R84

Jingellic Road, Tumbarumba, NSW 2653
Ph/Fax 02 6948 5102

Owner/chief winemaker: Juliet Cullen
Year of foundation: 1994
Tonnes produced on average each year: 80, of which 10 are used for Excelsior Peak wines
Location: Tumbarumba
Area: 10 ha
Soils: granitic sandy loam
Varieties planted: White—chardonnay, viognier; Red—meunier, pinot noir, sangiovese
Leading wines: Excelsior Peak Pinot Noir, Chardonnay, Methode Champenoise, Excellent Pinot Noir
Notes: Excellent Pinot Noir. No cellar door sales. Mail order to PO Box 269, Tumbarumba, NSW 2653.

Tumbarumba Wine Estates
(vineyards only)
 R83

PO Box 190 Tumbarumba, NSW 2653
Ph/Fax 02 6948 8326

Owners: a consortium organised by Frank Minutello

Chief winemaker: Roger Harris (contract)
Year of foundation: 1989
Tonnes produced on average each year: 300, of which about 20 are used for Tumbarumba Wine Estates labels
Location: Tumbarumba
Area: 25 ha
Soils: predominantly basalt
Varieties planted: White—chardonnay, sauvignon blanc; Red—cabernet sauvignon, merlot, pinot noir, shiraz
Leading wines: Tumbarumba Wine Estates Cabernet-Merlot, Chardonnay, Sauvignon Blanc, Pinot Chardonnay Methode Champenoise
Notes: Tumbarumba Wine Estates exhibits at local wine shows and has a consistent record of silver and bronze awards. There are no cellar door sales, but mail order is available from PO Box 190, Tumbarumba, NSW 2653.

Tumbarumba Wine Growers
(vineyards only)
 NR

'Sunnyside', Albury Close, Tumbarumba, NSW 2653
Ph/Fax 02 6948 3055

Owners: Mal Barclay, George Martin, Bruce Wright, Robert Parkes

Chief winemaker: (contract)
Year of foundation: 1996
Tonnes produced on average each year: not
disclosed but estimated at 250, of which 10
are used for Tumbarumba Wine Growers labels
Location:Tumbarumba
Area: 25.1 ha
Varieties planted: White—chardonnay, riesling,
sauvignon blanc; Red—pinot noir
Leading wines: Black Range Pinot Noir,
Chardonnay, Pinot Chardonnay (sparkling).
There is also a George Martin range.
Notes: No wines have been tasted. Cellar door
sales: weekends and public holidays:
noon–4.30pm, but ring ahead.

❧ NORTHERN RIVERS ZONE

This zone is constituted by the north coastal area of New South Wales, extending from the coast just to the north of Newcastle to the Queensland border, and westwards to the Great Divide. It is generally warm, wet and humid and because of these features, it is not particularly suited to viticulture. However, the wines of the Hastings River wine region have been quite successful, especially the Chardonnays.

Raleigh Winery **NR**

Queen Street, Raleigh, NSW 2454
Ph 02 6655 4388, Fax 02 6655 4265

Owner/chief winemaker: Lavinia Dingle
Year of foundation: 1982
Tonnes crushed on average each year: 11
Location: Raleigh
Area: 1.5 ha
Soils: the vineyard is situated on an alluvial flood plain, which is nevertheless quite well-drained
Varieties planted: White—gewurztraminer, riesling, semillon; Red—cabernet franc, pinot noir, shiraz
Leading wines: Raleigh Semillon-Chardonnay, Pinot Noir Rouge (a rose style), Shiraz-Cabernet, Gewurztraminer-Riesling, Ruby Port, Brandy Liqueur Creme
Notes: A small vineyard in what might be otherwise termed banana country. However the wines are shown regularly and have won three bronze medals at the Royal Hobart Show. Cellar door sales: 7 days 10am–5pm, closed Christmas and Good Friday.

HASTINGS VALLEY REGION

Situated at the mouth of the Hastings River, the urban centre of the region is Port Macquarie, which was established as a penal settlement in 1821. The area's first vines are believed to have been planted as early as 1837 by Henry Fancourt White, a Colonial Assistant Surveyor. From that time and until the 1890s, viticulture, probably using a mixture of vitis vinifera and hybrid varieties, prospered in the region and by 1890 there were 33 wineries and vineyards. Shortly thereafter, bank crashes shook all the colonial economies of eastern Australia, and the Hastings River wine industry wound down, to disappear entirely between the First and Second World Wars. A small number of vineyards, however, persisted until about 1950, their produce being used for fresh fruit and jam-making. The modern era of Hastings Valley winemaking began in 1980 when John Cassegrain planted his first vineyard.

Location: latitude 31°30'S, longitude 152°53'E, 400 km north north-east of Sydney
Elevation: most vineyards are situated within 15 km of the coast and planting elevations vary between 10 and 50 m in altitude
Topography and soils: The region slopes gently upwards from the coast towards the west. Its soils vary from areas of deep red kraznozems and alluvial red soils to red podsolics on the tops of coastal ridges and yellow podsols at the bottom of such ridges. As the

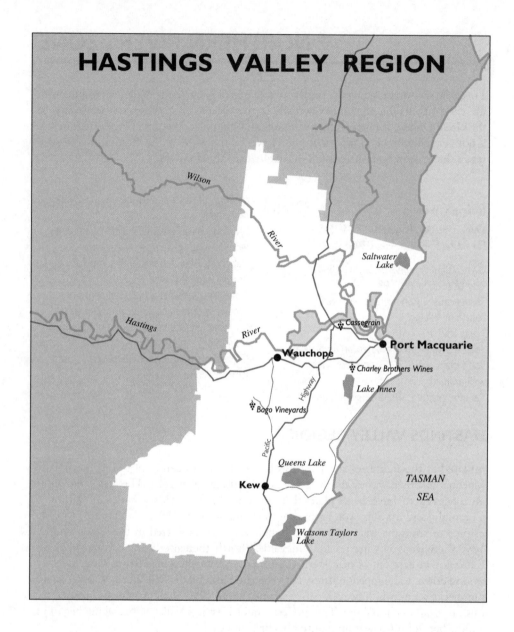

HASTINGS VALLEY REGION

soil type changes, so do drainage capacities. The kraznozems and alluvial soils have excellent drainage, while the red podsols drain reasonably well. The poorest of all in drainage are the yellow podsols, which require careful attention in this respect.

Climate: Port Macquarie MJT 21.9°C, MAR 8.45°C, HDD (Sept–Feb raw) 1695, AR 1515 mm (Sept–Feb 740.3 mm), RH 77.8% (9am Jan). The Hastings Valley has a very warm and humid maritime climate. Even allowing for the fact that its vintage usually commences late in January and is complete about five weeks later, almost half of its annual rainfall occurs during the growing season. Prevailing breezes in summer are north-easterly, cooling the vineyards in the afternoon and evening but also increasing humidity. Due to the frequency of rain during the growing season, the vineyards within the region are generally not irrigated but strict attention therefore must be paid to anti-fungal sprays.

Harvest time: one of the earliest regions in Australia generally commencing vintage in late January and finishing in early March

Principal varieties: White—chardonnay, semillon, sauvignon blanc, verdelho; Red—chambourcin, pinot noir, cabernet sauvignon, cabernet franc, shiraz, merlot. It is to be noted that chambourcin is a vinifera hybrid, which shows great resistance to moulds.

Total area: (2000) 180 ha

Principal wine styles: Cassegrain is the largest winery in the region and by its recent show results must be judged the success of the region's wines. In its whites, Chardonnay has enjoyed reasonable success, mostly at a show standard of silver and bronze medals, but with the occasional gold, while Semillon has also won a modicum of similar medals. In the reds, Cabernet Merlot blends have performed almost as well as Chardonnay. Chambourcin and Shiraz also have won bronze awards. As a general rule the Region's reds are medium-bodied with good vinosity and style.

Bago Vineyards (formerly Broken Bago Vineyards) NR

Milligan's Road, Wauchope, NSW 2446
Ph/Fax 02 6585 7099,
Email bagowine@nor.com.au

Owners: Jim and Kay Mobbs
Chief winemaker: Jim Mobbs (smaller volumes of white and red), contract (larger volumes)
Year of foundation: 1985
Tonnes crushed on average each year: 120, of which 25 are used for Bago wines
Location: Wauchope
Area: 10 ha
Soils: chocolate alluvial soils on the flats, red kraznozems on the ridges
Varieties planted: White—chardonnay, verdelho; Red—cabernet sauvignon, chambourcin, merlot, pinot noir
Leading wines: Bago Vineyards Sparkling Pinot Noir-Chardonnay, Chambourcin, Merlot-Chambourcin
Notes: Bago is a vineyard specialising in the grape variety chambourcin, which tolerates the high humidity of this region. I have not tasted its wines. Cellar door sales: daily 11am–5pm, closed Christmas Day. There is also a music festival held in March each year and a jazz festival held in June.

Cassegrain NR

764 Fernbank Creek Road,
Port Macquarie, NSW 2444
Ph 02 6583 7777, Fax 02 6584 0354,
Email info@cassegrainwines.com.au

Owners: Cassegrain family
Chief winemaker: John Cassegrain
Year of foundation: 1980
Tonnes crushed on average each year: 650, of which 550 are used for Cassegrain wines
Location: Port Macquarie
Area: 94 ha
Soils: kraznozems, red and yellow podsols
Varieties planted: White—chardonnay, semillon; Red—cabernet franc, cabernet sauvignon, chambourcin, malbec, merlot, pinot noir, shiraz

Leading wines: There are three wine ranges: Premium Selection, Five Mile Hollow Selection, Cassegrain range

Notes: In an often warm and humid climate, Cassegrain wines are of a consistent quality, regularly winning silver and bronze awards and more occasionally golds and trophies at capital city and regional wine shows. Cellar door sales: daily 9am–5pm. Closed Christmas Day and Boxing Day. There is also a restaurant, open for morning and afternoon teas and lunch.

Charley Brothers NR

The Ruins Way, Port Macquarie, NSW 2444
Ph 02 6581 1332, Fax 02 6581 0391

Owner: Charley Brothers Pty Ltd
Chief winemaker: John Cassegrain (contract)
Year of foundation: 1988
Tonnes crushed on average each year: 38, about 15 of which are used for Charley Brothers' wines

Location: Port Macquarie
Area: 10 ha
Soils: red and yellow podsols
Varieties planted: White—chardonnay, semillon; Red—cabernet sauvignon, pinot noir, shiraz
Leading wines: Charley Brothers Semillon, Cabernet-Merlot
Notes: Inneslake, the property on which the vineyard is situated, saw vines in the 1840s and other types of fruit in the years since. In 1988, Bob and Jim Charley, influenced by the Cassegrain family, decided to replant to vines. Though the wines are no longer shown, there were early successes in the form of bronze and silver medals at the Hunter Valley Wine Show in the early 1990s. I have not tasted the wines, but they are certain to be well made under John Cassegrain's direction. Cellar door sales: Mon–Fri 1pm–5pm, weekends and public holidays 10am–5pm.

NORTHERN SLOPES ZONE

A large area stretching from the north of Central Ranges Wine Zone and the Hunter Valley Wine Zone to the Queensland border. Its south-eastern boundary is the escarpment of the Liverpool Ranges. Its western boundary is generally the Newell Highway, running as far north as the Queensland border at Goondiwindi and then along the border as far east as Kyogle. It includes all the New South Wales territory south of the Granite Belt in Queensland, which seems already to be overflowing with vines into the Tenterfield and Glen Innes areas of New South Wales. Other areas such as Armidale already have young vineyard plantings, but frosts may present problems in respect of ill-chosen sites.

Gilgai Wines NR

Tingha Road, Gilgai, NSW 2360
Ph 02 6722 1204, Fax 02 6722 1932

Owner/chief winemaker: Keith Whish
Year of foundation: 1968
Tonnes crushed on average each year: 8
Location: Tingha near Inverell
Area: 6 ha
Soils: old decomposed red laterite
Varieties planted: White—sauvignon blanc, semillon, riesling, trebbiano; Red—cabernet sauvignon, grenache, malbec, mataro, pinot noir, shiraz
Leading wines: Gilgai Pinot-Malbec, Pinot Noir, Chandelier White Port, Old Courthouse Port
Notes: An old established vineyard owned and run by Dr Keith Whish. Cellar door sales: Mon–Sat 10am–6pm, Sun noon–6pm.

Warrina Wines NR

Back Road, Kootingal, NSW 2352
Ph 02 6760 3985, Fax 02 6765 5746

Owners: David and Susan Nicholls
Chief winemaker: David Nicholls
Year of foundation: 1989
Tonnes produced on average each year: 25
Location: Kootingal
Area: 2.5 ha
Soils: red clay loam

Varieties planted: White—chardonnay, sauvignon blanc; Red—cabernet sauvignon, shiraz
Leading wines: winemaking commenced in 2001
Notes: A small family-owned vineyard, which has made wine occasionally until 2001 when regular winemaking began. Cellar door sales: weekends 10am–4pm.

Willowvale Wines NR

Black Swamp Road, Tenterfield, NSW 2372
Ph 02 6736 3589, Fax 02 6736 3753, Email Willowvale_Wines@bigpond.com.au

Owners: John and Lyn Morley
Chief winemaker: (reds) John Morley, (whites) contract
Year of foundation: 1994
Tonnes produced on average each year: 17
Location: Tenterfield
Area: 2 ha
Soils: decomposed granite, slightly acidic
Varieties planted: White—chardonnay; Red—cabernet sauvignon, merlot
Leading wines: Willowvale Chardonnay, Cabernet
Notes: A small winery with handmade reds, Willowvale has won show awards in the past two years. Cellar door sales: daily 10am–5pm.

WESTERN PLAINS ZONE

An extensive area of western and north-western New South Wales. The Lachlan River west of Forbes forms the boundary between Big Rivers and Western Plains, while the Newell Highway and the Parkes–Cootamundra railway line delineate the border between the Central Ranges and the other two. There are a growing number of vineyards but no wine regions within the Western Plains Zone.

PART VI

QUEENSLAND AND
NORTHERN TERRITORY

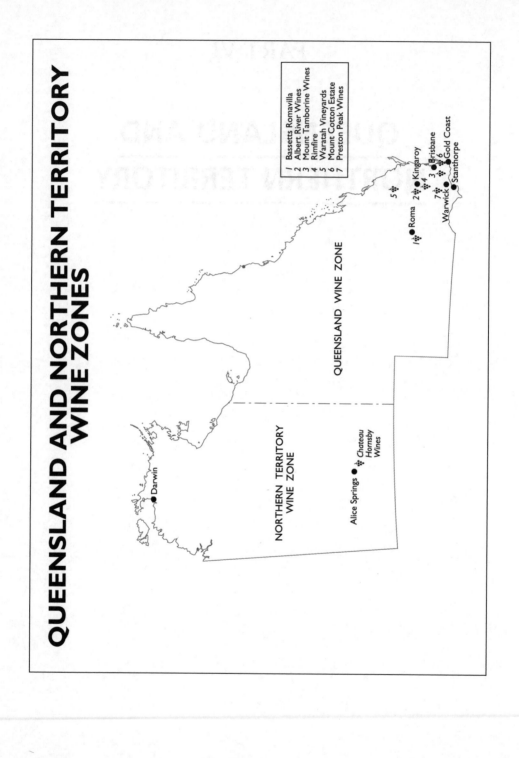

QUEENSLAND AND NORTHERN TERRITORY WINE ZONES

1 Bassetts Romavilla
2 Albert River Wines
3 Mount Tamborine Wines
4 Rimfire
5 Waratah Vineyards
6 Mount Cotton Estate
7 Preston Peak Wines

QUEENSLAND WINE ZONE

NORTHERN TERRITORY WINE ZONE

Alice Springs ● Chateau Hornsby Wines

Darwin ●

Roma
Kingaroy
Brisbane
Gold Coast
Warwick
Stanthorpe

❦ QUEENSLAND ZONE

It is fair to say that Queenland's wine history began when a 23-year-old Cornishman, Samuel Bassett, who had during his peregrinations worked for his uncle at East Maitland in the Hunter Valley, planted a few hundred vines near Roma in central Queensland in 1863. From this small beginning in a most unlikely and arid spot, Bassett's venture thrived. By 1900, Romavilla, as the estate was called, extended to 180 hectares. Most of the wine was fortified and this favoured contemporary market trends, although white and red table wines appear to have been offered and irrigation was introduced. Bassett even sent his son William to learn winemaking from Leo Buring. Bassett family ownership continued until 1973, the wine styles remaining largely unchanged. The winery still exists today, though production is much smaller.

Albert River Wines NR

1/117 Mundoolun Connection Road,
Tamborine, Qld 4270
Ph 07 5543 6622, Fax 07 5543 6627,
Email info@tamborinehouse.com.au

Owners: David and Janette Bladin
Chief winemaker: Peter Scudamore-Smith
(contract)
Year of foundation: 1997
Tonnes crushed on average each year: 60
Location: Tamborine, about 45 minutes from
Brisbane and the Gold Coast
Area: 10 ha
Soils: rich river loam over sandstone; vines are
dry-grown
Varieties planted: White—chardonnay,
viognier; Red—cabernet sauvignon, merlot,
shiraz
Leading wines: Albert River Private Reserve
Shiraz, Shiraz-Cabernet-Merlot, Private Reserve
Chardonnay
Notes: A recently established winery close to
Brisbane and the Gold Coast. No wines have
been tasted. Cellar door sales: daily
10am–4pm. There is also a restaurant.

Bassetts Romavilla Winery NR

Northern Road, Roma, Qld 4455
(just north of the town)
Ph/Fax 07 4622 1822,
Email romawine@bigpond.com

Owners: David and Joy Wall
Chief winemakers: David and Richard Wall
Year of foundation: 1863
Tonnes crushed on average each year: 35
Location: Roma
Area: 10 ha
Soils: sandy loams on the edge of the flood
plain of the Bungil Creek
Varieties planted: White—chenin blanc,
crouchen, riesling, syrian, voignier; Red—black
cluster, black, red and white muscat, merlot,
shiraz
Leading wines: There is a wide selection of
fortifieds, dry whites and dry reds
Notes: Founded in 1863, Romavilla is the oldest
winery in Queensland and a repository of grape
varieties in existence at that time, two of which
are black cluster (a red) and syrian (a white).
Wisely, this winery still concentrates on fortified
wine styles, for which it has won multitudes of
show awards over the years. There are also, of
course, white and red table wines. Cellar door
sales: weekdays 8am–5pm, Sat 9am–noon and
2pm–4pm, closed Sundays.

Mount Cotton Estate NR

850 Mount Cotton Road, Mount Cotton,
Qld 4185
Ph 07 3206 2999, Fax 07 3206 0900,
Email wines@mountcottonestate.com

Owner: Sirromet Wines Pty Ltd
Chief winemakers: Adam Chapman, Alain
Rousseau and Craig Stevenson
Year of foundation: 1998
Tonnes produced on average each year: 600
Location: Mount Cotton (winery); Ballandean
(vineyard)
Area: 100 ha (Ballandean)
Soils: decomposed granite about 0.5 to 1
metre deep, over a layer of grey and white clay
0.4 metres deep over old hard granite.
Varieties planted: White—chardonnay,
sauvignon blanc, semillon, viognier;
Red—cabernet franc, cabernet sauvignon,
merlot, pinot noir, shiraz
Leading wines: Rather early to say, as the
company's vineyard is extremely young. The
premium Mount Cotton Estate Reserve range
presently consists of Chardonnay, Shiraz, a
Sparkling wine and a sweet wine called 'Finito'.
Although some interstate wine is currently
used, this will change when the company's
Ballandean vineyard comes into full bearing.
Cellar door sales: 7 days 10am till late.

Mount Tamborine Vineyard and Winery NR

32 Hartley Road, North Tamborine,
Qld 4272
Ph 07 5545 3506, Fax 07 5545 3311,
Email sales@mttamborinewinery.com.au

Owners: AD & RS Hart
Chief winemaker: Colin Williams
Year of foundation: 1991
Tonnes produced on average each year: 10
Location: North Tamborine
Area: 2.5 ha (an associated vineyard is located
in the Granite Belt region)

Soils: volcanic clay loam
Varieties planted: White—none; Red—cabernet
franc, merlot
Leading wines: Mount Tamborine Sparkling
Merlot, Sparkling Red
Notes: No wines have been tasted. Cellar door
sales: 7 days 10am–4pm.

Preston Peak R78

Old Wallangarra Road, Devil's Elbow,
Wallangarra, Qld 4383
Ph 07 4684 3480, Fax 07 4684 3154
(cellar door sales) 31 Preston Peak Lane,
Preston, Qld 4352
Ph 07 4630 9499

Owners: Ashley Smith and Kym Thumpkin
Chief winemaker: Philippa Hambleton and
Rod Macpherson
Year of foundation: 1994
Tonnes crushed on average each year: 50
Locations: Devil's Elbow (Granite Belt) and
Preston (near Toowoomba)
Area: 10 ha consisting of Preston 2 ha and
Devil's Elbow 8 ha
Soils: At 860 m in altitude, the Devil's Elbow
vineyard has typical free-draining granite-
derived soils. The Preston vineyard is terraced
on a steep rocky east-facing slope and lower in
altitude at 640 m.
Varieties planted: (Devil's Elbow) White—
chardonnay, sauvignon blanc, white muscat;
Red—cabernet sauvignon, merlot, petit verdot,
shiraz. (Preston) White—viognier;
Red—nebbiolo, petit verdot, shiraz
Leading wines: Preston Peak Reserve
Chardonnay, Reserve Shiraz
Notes: Preston Peak has won several silver and
bronze awards for its reds. Cellar door sales
only at Preston Peak Toowoomba: Wed–Fri
11am–3pm, Weekends 10am–5pm.

Rimfire **R79**

via Bismarck St, Maclagan, Qld 4352
Ph 07 4692 1129, Fax 07 4692 1260,
Email rimfire@onaustralia.com.au

Owners: Connellan family
Chief winemaker: Tony Connellan
Year of foundation: 1992
Tonnes crushed on average each year: 76, of
which 70 are used for Rimfire wines
Location: Maclagan
Area: 12 ha
Soils: chocolate brown brigalow scrub soils
Varieties planted: White—chardonnay,
colombard, marsanne, muscat blanc a petits
grains, taminga, verdelho; Red—cabernet
sauvignon, cabernet franc, ruby cabernet,
sangiovese, shiraz, tarrango, touriga nacional
Leading wines: Rimfire Chardonnay, Verdelho,
Shiraz, Cabernet Franc
Notes: A not so small family-owned winery,
whose wines hold much promise for such a
northerly latitude. Cellar door sales: 7 days
10am–5pm. There is also a café.

Waratah Vineyard and Winery **NR**

Gladstone Road, Mungungo, via Monto
Qld 4630
Ph/Fax 07 4166 5161, Email
braelin@powerup.com.au

Owners: Max Lindsay, Lynette Tucker, David
and Pamela Bray
Chief winemaker: Peter Scudamore-Smith
(contract)
Year of foundation: 1998
Tonnes required for average annual crush: 15,
of which 10 are produced in the Waratah
vineyard on average each year
Location: Mungungo
Area: 4 ha
Soils: alluvial river flats over gravel
Varieties planted: White—chardonnay,
semillon, verdelho, viognier; Red—merlot,
shiraz, petit verdot
Leading wines: Three Moon Creek Queensland
White Blend, Chardonnay, Shiraz
Notes: No wines tasted. Cellar door sales: daily
10am–5pm.

THE GRANITE BELT REGION (INTERIM REGISTRATION)

It is believed that the first semi-permanent settlers of the Granite Belt region were the Kambuwal Aboriginal tribe, who migrated from the coastal belt to hunt native game when they found that seafood supplies in summer were insufficient.

Though the convict settlement of Moreton Bay was established in Northern New South Wales in 1824, it was not until 1842 that Governor Gipps allowed free settlement within a radius of 85 kilometres (50 miles) of the penal colony. In 1827, however, the explorer Allan Cunningham journeyed from Tamworth to the Darling Downs (which he named in honour of Governor Ralph Darling), crossing the present-day NSW–Queensland border near Beebo, about 100 km south-south-west of the future town of Stanthorpe. On his return to Tamworth, he investigated what is now the Granite Belt. As usual, the explorers were pursued by the graziers and pastoral development followed in the Granite Belt and Darling Downs areas. In 1840 a further Cunningham discovery located a gap in the escarpment separating the coastal strip from the hinterland, and so Cunningham's Gap proved a relatively easy route from the Moreton Bay settlement to the Darling Downs and the Granite Belt. By 1844 four large pastoral leases covered parts of the present-day wine region. In 1859 the colonies of New South Wales and Queensland were separated, the border stretching west across

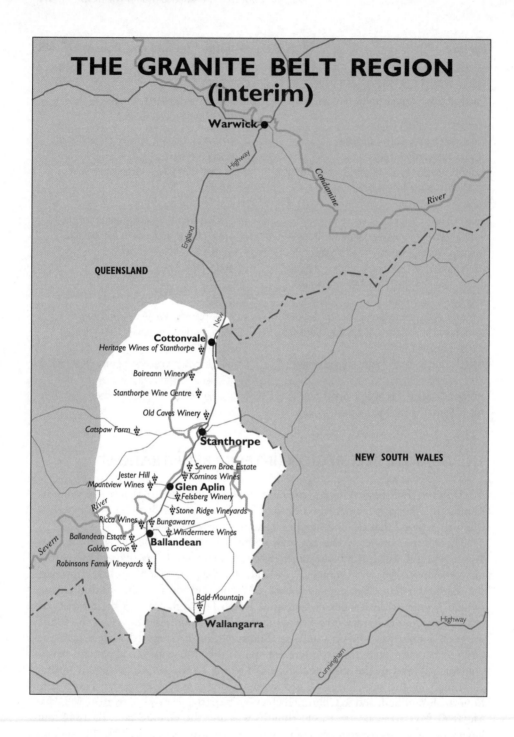

THE GRANITE BELT REGION
(interim)

Warwick

QUEENSLAND

Cottonvale
Heritage Wines of Stanthorpe

Boireann Winery

Stanthorpe Wine Centre

Old Caves Winery

Catspaw Farm

Stanthorpe

NEW SOUTH WALES

Severn Brae Estate
Jester Hill   Kominos Wines
Mountview Wines   Glen Aplin
Felsberg Winery

Stone Ridge Vineyards

Ricca Wines   Bungawarra
Ballandean Estate   Windermere Wines
Golden Grove   Ballandean

Robinsons Family Vineyards

Bald Mountain

Wallangarra

the coastal strip, running south of the MacPherson range and then across the Great Divide before turning south near present-day Stanthorpe and running west once more, close to the Severn River. By this time there was a mining boom in the areas to the north and west of the Granite Belt, but it was tin, not gold, that attracted new settlers to the region. There was also a spurt of railway construction from 1867 onwards, which came too late for the tin boom but did assist the fruit and vegetable industry which succeeded it.

Throughout the temperate parts of Australia, the early pastoralists usually planted vine cuttings as soon as they established a permanent homestead. The early 'Queenslanders' were certainly no different. Vines were grown for fresh fruit and in all probability small quantities of wine were made, though the squatters universally believed that there was much more money in wool. By the 1870s significant orcharding and table grape production had commenced in the southern Granite Belt region, grapes being forwarded to Brisbane in 1872; and by 1875 the Border Agricultual Horticultural and Mining Society was formed with classes for wine competition at its exhibitions. In 1877, an Act of Parliament was passed to prevent the spread of phylloxera, though too late to protect the Brisbane metropolitan area, which remains a designated phylloxera area. By the 1890s, a small local wine industry was most likely in existence, as there are recorded warnings of the disastrous effects that southern States' competition would have when intercolonial tariffs were abolished after Federation. These dire predictions probably proved correct as there is little mention of a Granite Belt wine industry after Federation. In the 1920s, the first Italian emigrants came to Australia and many settled in Queensland, some purchasing abandoned soldier settlement blocks and planting orchards and table grapes in the Granite Belt, while others worked on the sugar cane plantations in the northern parts of the State. Soon the local wine industry redeveloped as bulk wines made from excess table grapes were shipped from the Granite Belt to the canefields. This industry continued for the next 50 years and to some extent still persists. However, by the mid 1960s the red wine boom throughout Australia had extended to Queensland and an interest in more conventional wine grape varieties was developing. By the early 1970s, the first wine grape vineyards were coming into bearing and in 1974 Angelo Puglisi made the region's first wine grape red, a Shiraz. Since then many wineries have opened in the region, with the result that there were 23 licensed cellar door operations in the year 2000 in the Granite Belt.

Location: Stanthorpe Horticultural Research Station (north of the region) latitude 28°37'S, longitude 151°57'E, about 180 km south-west of Brisbane. Wallangarra PO (south of the region) latitude 28°55'S, longitude 151°56'E, about 200 km south-west of Brisbane

Elevation: 872 m. Its vineyards are located between 700 m (west of Ballandean) and over 1000 m (east of Ballandean on the Eukey Road); Wallangarra 877 m

Topography and soils: The region is an elevated, slightly undulating plateau and has two dominant rock types: granites and granodiorites on the one hand, and on the other, a hardened metamorphic rock erroneously called 'traprock'. These give rise respectively to two soils: coarse granitic sands, which in turn produce acid to slightly acidic podsolic soils of low to moderate fertility; and shallow, clayey brown soils, again of low to moderate fertility.

Climate: Stanthorpe Horticultural Research Station MJT 20.65°C, MAR 12.85°C, HDD 1611 (cut off at 19°C but otherwise not adjusted), AR 784 mm (Oct–Apr 550 mm), RH 69% (9am Jan), 56% (3pm Jan), AI na, SH na. Wallangarra PO MJT 20.6°C, MAR 12.65°C, HDD 1602 (cut off at 19°C but otherwise not adjusted), AR 782 mm (Oct–Apr 547.5 mm), RH 65% (9am Jan), na (3pm Jan), AI na, SH na.

The Granite Belt is an area of high elevation, but unlike other similar Australian areas, is moderately warm and quite wet during its growing season, over two-thirds of its annual rainfall occurring between October and April. This of course increases relative humidity and reduces drought stress but increases the risk of mildews and rots.

The region is prone to hailstorms, particularly during the early part of the growing season. Average expectancy appears to be once or more often per season. Most apple orchards are protected by hail netting. A further recurring pattern seems to be that the closer the site is to the Great Divide, the greater the likelihood of hail.

Frosts too present problems, occurring from mid-April to late October. Snow also falls occasionally in the region.

At present grape vines derive their water from natural rainfall, instream weirs, off-stream water storages and gully dams. Some of these water facilities require Government licensing, but a new dam is planned for the Severn River at Fletcher within the wine region.

Birds, both local and imported (starlings, silvereyes, currawongs and parrots), pose a major problem for winegrowers during ripening. This problem is minimised by the use of netting and scare guns.

Principal varieties: White—chardonnay, semillon, sauvignon blanc, verdelho; Red—shiraz, cabernet sauvignon, merlot

Harvest time: Chardonnay first to second week of March; shiraz fourth week of March, first week of April; cabernet sauvignon: first to second week of April

Principal wine styles: Chardonnay, Shiraz

Total area: 370 ha (2000)

Leading wineries and vineyards: Ballandean Estate, Robinson Family Vineyards, Stone Ridge Vineyards.

Bald Mountain NR

Cnr Old Wallangarra Road and Hickling Lane, Wallangarra, Qld 4383
Ph 07 4684 3186, Fax 07 4684 3433

Owners: Denis and Jackie Parsons
Chief winemaker: John Cassegrain (contract)
Year of foundation: 1985
Tonnes crushed on average each year: 70
Location: Wallangarra
Area: 7 ha

Soils: granite-derived gravel about 3 m deep, free-draining
Varieties planted: White—chardonnay, sauvignon blanc; Red—cabernet sauvignon, shiraz
Leading wines: Bald Mountain Sauvignon Blanc, Chardonnay, Shiraz, Cabernet Sauvignon
Notes: No wines recently tasted. Cellar door sales: 7 days 10am–4pm.

Ballandean Estate R85

Sundown Road, Ballandean, Qld 4382
Ph 07 4684 1226, Fax 07 4684 1288,
Email enquiries@ballandean-estate.com.au

Owner: Puglisi family
Chief winemakers: Dylan Rhymer and Ian Henderson
Year of foundation: 1970
Tonnes crushed on average each year: 250
Location: Ballandean
Area: 32 ha consisting of Ballandean 20 ha and Bellevue 12 ha
Soils: Ballandean, shallow decomposed granite, not fertile and in need of careful management; Bellevue, orange decomposed granite, quite coarse
Varieties planted: (Ballandean) White—chardonnay; Red—none
Leading wines: Ballandean Estate
Notes: Angelo Puglisi made the region's first winegrape red in 1974 and both he and the region have come a long way since, so far in fact that Ballandean was most successful exhibitor in the 1997 National Small Winemakers Show. Wine quality is consistently good. Cellar door sales: 7 days 9am–5pm. There is also a café.

Boireann Winery R80

Donnelly's Castle Road, The Summit, Qld 4377
Ph/Fax 07 4683 2194

Owners: Peter and Therese Stark
Chief winemaker: Peter Stark
Year of foundation: 1995
Tonnes crushed on average each year: 5
Location: The Summit
Area: 1 ha
Soils: deep decomposed granite sand
Varieties planted: White—none; Red—barbera, cabernet franc, cabernet sauvignon, merlot, mourvedre, nebbiolo, petit verdot, shiraz
Leading wines: Boireann Shiraz-Grenache-

Mourvedre, Cabernet Sauvignon, Cabernet Sauvignon-Cabernet Franc-Merlot
Notes: Boireann is a fairly recent arrival on the Granite Belt scene and in 2001 began to show its wines. It is an all red vineyard with three current wines, a Cabernet Sauvignon, a 'Rhone' and a 'Bordeaux' blend. Cellar door sales: Fri–Tues 10am–4pm.

Bungawarra NR

Bents Road, Ballandean, Qld 4382
Ph/Fax 07 4684 1128

Owner: Jeff Harden
Chief winemaker: Bruce Humphery-Smith (contract)
Year of foundation: 1973
Tonnes crushed on average each year: 20
Location: Ballandean
Area: 5.5 ha
Soils: a heavy sandy granitic loam, deep and well-drained
Varieties planted: White—chardonnay, gewurztraminer, semillon; Red—cabernet sauvignon, malbec, muscat hamburgh, shiraz
Leading wines: Bungawarra Foundation (unwooded) Chardonnay, Paragon (a shiraz cabernet blend), Traminer, Liqueur Muscat
Notes: A vineyard which is now mature on typical Ballandean crushed granite soils. Cellar door sales: 7 days 10.30am–4.30pm.

Catspaw Farm NR

MS 312 Texas Road, Stanthorpe, Qld 4380
Ph 07 4683 6229, Fax 07 4683 6386,
Email catspaw@halenet.com.au

Owners: Chris and Leonie Whitfort
Chief winemaker: Chris Whitfort
Year of foundation: 1989
Tonnes crushed on average each year: 9
Location: Stanthorpe
Area: 7 ha

Soils: varied from decomposed granite over a podsolic base to light-heavy loams
Varieties planted: White—chardonnay, roussanne; Red—barbera, cabernet franc, cabernet sauvignon, chambourcin, merlot, shiraz
Leading wines: Catspaw Farm Chambourcin, Cabernet-Shiraz
Notes: No wines tasted. Cellar door sales: Thurs–Sun and public holidays 10am–5pm; daily during Qld school holidays. At other times by appointment.

Felsberg Winery NR

Townsends Road, Glen Aplin, Qld 4381
Ph 07 4683 4332, Fax 07 4683 4377,
Email felsberg@ozemail.com.au

Owners: Otto and Anne Haag
Chief winemaker: Otto Haag
Year of foundation: 1983
Tonnes crushed on average each year: 25
Location: Glen Aplin
Area: 8 ha
Soils: granitic, sandy loams free-draining but slightly acidic
Varieties planted: White—chardonnay, traminer, riesling; Red—cabernet sauvignon, merlot, shiraz
Leading wines: Felsberg Cabernet Sauvignon, Merlot, Chardonnay, Riesling
Notes: Felsberg is a wine estate, growing, making, cellaring and bottling wines made only from its own grapes. I have not recently tasted its wines. Cellar door sales: daily 9.30am–4.30pm.

Golden Grove Estate NR

Sundown Road, Ballandean, Qld 4382
Ph 07 4684 1291, Fax 07 4684 1247,
Email goldengrove@halenet.com.au

Owners: Sam and Grace Costanzo
Chief winemaker: Sam Costanzo and consultants

Year of foundation: 1958
Tonnes crushed on average each year: 200
Location: Ballandean
Area: 12 ha
Soils: decomposed granite and traprock loam, drip irrigation from Accommodation Creek
Varieties planted: White—chardonnay, sauvignon blanc, semillon, waltham cross; Red—cabernet sauvignon, merlot, muscat, shiraz
Leading wines: Golden Grove Estate, Chardonnay, Merlot
Notes: No wines tasted recently. Cellar door sales: 7 days 9am–5pm.

Granite Ridge Wines (formerly denlana Ferguson Estate Wines) NR

Sundown Road, Ballandean, Qld 4382
Ph 07 4684 1263, Fax 07 4684 1250

Owner/chief winemaker: Dennis Ferguson
Year of foundation: 1995
Tonnes crushed on average each year: 20
Location: Ballandean
Area: 2 ha consisting of Ballandean 1.2 ha and Stanthorpe 0.8 ha
Soils: Ballandean, granite based soils; Stanthorpe, deeper granitic soils
Varieties planted: White—chardonnay, pinot gris; Red—cabernet sauvignon, merlot, petit verdot, shiraz, tempranillo
Leading wines: Goldies Unwooded Chardonnay, First Oak Chard Granite Ridge Cabernet Sauvignon, Shiraz
Notes: No wines have been recently tasted, but Dennis Ferguson is pleased with his Cabernet Sauvignon and finds that his Unwooded Chardonnay is extremely popular. Cellar door sales: 9am–5pm daily.

Heritage Wines of Stanthorpe NR

Granite Belt Drive, formerly New
England Highway, Cottonvale, Qld 4375
Ph 07 4685 2197, Fax 07 4685 2112

Owners: Bryce and Paddy Kassulke
Chief winemaker: Jim Barnes
Year of foundation: 1992
Tonnes crushed on average each year: 55
Locations: Cottonvale and Mount Tamborine
Area: 4 ha
Soils: decomposed granite
Varieties planted: White—chardonnay;
Red—cabernet sauvignon, merlot, shiraz
Leading wines: Heritage Wines of Stanthorpe
Merlot, Roswall Shiraz, Semillon
Notes: This winery has a good reputation for
Shiraz, having won the Small Winemakers
Show Trophy for best Queensland Shiraz
recently. Cellar door sales: 7 days 9am–5pm.

Jester Hill R80

Mount Stirling Road, Glen Aplin,
Qld 4381
Ph 07 4683 4380, Fax 02 6622 3190

Owners: John and Genevieve Ashwell
Chief winemaker: Mark Ravenscroft (contract)
Year of foundation: 1993
Area: 5 ha
Soils: sandy loam with granite
Varieties planted: White—chardonnay,
sauvignon blanc, verdelho; Red—cabernet
sauvignon, merlot, shiraz
Leading wine: Jester Hill Shiraz
Notes: A new Granite Belt vineyard, making
promising Shiraz. Cellar door sales: Fri–Sun
10am–4pm.

Kominos Wines NR

New England Highway Severnlea,
Qld 4352
Ph 07 4683 4311, Fax 07 4683 4291,
Email kominoswines@flexi.net.au

Owners: Tony, Stephen and Penelope Comino
Chief winemaker: Tony Comino
Year of foundation: 1976
Tonnes crushed on average each year: 50
Location: Severnlea
Area: 12 ha
Soils: shallow granite soils
Varieties planted: White—chardonnay, chenin
blanc, riesling, sauvignon blanc, semillon;
Red—cabernet franc, cabernet sauvignon,
merlot, shiraz
Leading wines: Kominos Merlot, Shiraz,
Cabernet Sauvignon, Chardonnay
Notes: Nothing recently tasted but a good
show record, including a trophy for best red at
the Small Winemakers Show 1999. Cellar door
sales: Mon–Fri 8am–4.30pm, weekends
8.30am–5pm.

Mountview Wines NR

Mount Stirling Road, Glen Aplin,
Qld 4381
Ph 07 4683 4316, Fax 07 4683 4111

Owner: Pauline Stewart
Chief winemaker: contract
Year of foundation: 1990
Tonnes crushed on average each year: 15
Location: Glen Aplin
Area: 4 ha
Soils: crushed granite
Varieties planted: White—chardonnay,
sauvignon blanc, semillon; Red—cabernet
sauvignon, merlot, shiraz
Leading wines: Mountview Shiraz,
Cabernet-Merlot, Cerise (a sweet red),
Sparkling Wine Traditional Method
Notes: No wines recently tasted, but the
vineyard has had a good reputation for Shiraz.
Cellar door sales: Fri–Mon, during school and
public holidays 9.30am–4.30pm.

Old Caves Winery NR

New England Highway, Stanthorpe,
Qld 4380
Ph 07 4681 1494, Fax 07 4681 2722

Owners: David and Shirley Zanatta
Chief winemaker: David Zanatta
Year of foundation: 1980
Tonnes crushed on average each year: 30, of
which 25 are used for Old Caves wines
Location: Stanthorpe; (vineyard) Applethorpe
Area: 5 ha
Soils: sandy decomposed granite on clay
Varieties planted: White—chardonnay,
sauvignon blanc, viognier; Red—cabernet
sauvignon, shiraz
Leading wines: Old Caves 'Armchair' Port,
Light Red (Lambrusco style) Semillon-
Chardonnay
Notes: Nothing recently tasted. Cellar door
sales: Mon–Sat 10am–5pm, Sun 10am–4pm.

Ricca Wines NR

Ricca Road, Ballandean, Qld 4382
Ph 07 4684 1235

Owners: Adrian and Frances Tobin
Chief winemaker: for table wine (contract), for
traditional bulk wine Joe Ricca (consultant)
Year of foundation: 1960
Tonnes crushed on average each year: 43,
about 35 of which are used for Ricca wines
Location: Ballandean
Area: 9 ha
Soils: decomposed granite loam, well-drained,
varying into dark loam
Varieties planted: White—italia, semillon,
waltham cross; Red—muscat, purple
cornichon, shiraz
Leading wines: Ricca Shiraz, Semillon, bulk
wine
Notes: Joe Ricca sold his vineyard recently to
Adrian and Frances Tobin, who plan from 2001
vintage to place greater emphasis on Shiraz and
Semillon table wines, each of which will receive

bottle maturation before release. However, the
tradition of bulk winemaking will continue, if
only to satisfy the loyal following for such wine
built up over the years. There are no cellar door
sales. Sales by mail or phone order.

Robinsons Family Vineyards R85

Curtin Road, Ballandean, Qld 4382
Ph/Fax 07 4684 1216, Email
robinsonwine@hotmail.com

Owners: John and Heather Robinson
Chief winemaker: Craig Robinson
Year of foundation: 1969
Tonnes crushed on average each year: 50
Location: Ballandean; Lyra (vineyard)
Area: 12 ha consisting of Lyra 8.5 ha and
Ballandean 3.5 ha
Soils: Ballandean, infertile,shallow duplex soils;
Lyra, granitic sands over clay
Varieties planted: White—chardonnay,
gewurztraminer, sauvignon blanc;
Red—cabernet sauvignon, merlot, pinot noir,
shiraz, gamay
Leading wines: Robinsons Family Vineyards
Cabernet Sauvignon, Shiraz, Vintage Brut
(a sparkling white)
Notes: This vineyard has achieved great success
recently at the Sheraton Queensland Wine
Awards, winning Best Red for its Cabernet
Sauvignon and Best Sparkling with its
Non-Vintage Brut. Its Chardonnay is very good
also. Cellar door sales: 7 days 9am–5pm.

Severn Brae Estate NR

Lot 2 Back Creek Road, Severnlea,
Qld 4352
Ph 07 4683 5292, Fax 07 3391 3821

Owners: Bruce and Patrick Humphery-Smith
Chief winemaker: Bruce Humphery-Smith
Year of foundation: 1987
Tonnes crushed on average each year: 90, of
which about 30 are used for Severn Brae
Estate wines

Location: Severnlea
Area: 7 ha
Soils: granitic free-draining sandy loam
Varieties planted: White—chardonnay;
Red—merlot, sangiovese, shiraz, muscat
hamburgh
Leading wines: Severn Brae Estate Chardonnay,
Unwooded Chardonnay, Shiraz, Merlot
Notes: No wines tasted recently. Cellar door
sales: Mon–Fri 10am–4pm, weekends
10am–5pm.

Stanthorpe Wine Centre NR

Granite Belt Drive, Thulimbah, Qld 4376
Ph 07 4683 2011, Fax 07 4683 2600,
Email stanwine@halenet.com.au

Owners: Stanthorpe Wine Co.
Chief winemaker: contract
Year of foundation: 1998
Tonnes crushed on average each year: 20
Location: Thulimbah
Area: 5 ha
Soils: Granite Belt loam (a well-drained gritty
soil which is quite fertile)
Varieties planted: White—verdelho;
Red—cabernet sauvignon, merlot, petit verdot,
pinot noir, tempranillo, zinfandel
Leading wines: Stanthorpe Wine Co. Shiraz,
Pinot Noir
Notes: A wine company new to me, with
Shiraz as a leading wine. Cellar door sales:
daily 9.30am–5pm.

Stone Ridge Vineyards R85

35 Limberlost Road, Glen Aplin,
Qld 4381
Ph/Fax 07 4683 4211

Owners: Jim Lawrie and Anne Kennedy
Chief winemaker: Jim Lawrie
Year of foundation: 1981
Tonnes crushed on average each year: 20

Location: Glen Aplin
Area: 2 ha
Soils: decomposed granite, free-draining
Varieties planted: White—chardonnay,
semillon, marsanne, viognier; Red—cabernet
franc, cabernet sauvignon, malbec, merlot,
petit verdot, pinot noir, shiraz
Leading wines: Stone Ridge Shiraz,
Chardonnay, Viognier
Notes: Jim Lawrie and Anne Kennedy work
hard to make Stone Ridge one of the best
vineyards in this region. Their Marsanne and
Pinot Noir are very good. Cellar door sales:
7 days 10am–5pm appointments preferred
Mon–Fri.

Windermere Wines NR

(Cellar door sales) Summit Cellars,
Tourist Drive, The Summit, Qld 4377
Ph 07 4683 2055
(Winery) Watters Road, Ballandean,
Qld 4382
Ph/Fax 07 4684 1353

Owners: Julie and Wayne Beecham
Chief winemaker: Wayne Beecham
Year of foundation: 1994
Tonnes produced on average each year: 10
Locations: (winery and vineyard) Ballandean;
(cellar door sales) The Summit
Area: 3.85 ha
Soils: deep decomposed granite soils
Varieties planted: White—chardonnay,
sauvignon blanc, semillon; Red—cabernet
sauvignon, merlot, sangiovese, shiraz
Leading wines: Windermere Chardonnay,
Lilybrook Dry White (a blend)
Notes: At 970 m, Windermere is one of the
highest vineyards in the Granite Belt. At this
early stage its Chardonnay is performing
creditably, having won two bronze awards at
local wine shows. Cellar door sales at the
Summit during usual business hours.

SOUTH BURNETT REGION

The region was first explored in 1842 by Henry Stuart Russell who, in company with William Orton and an Aboriginal named Jemmy, was in search of country to graze his sheep. The party discovered several rivers and creeks, later to be named the Stuart, Boyne and Burnett Rivers and the Barambah and Barkers Creeks. Over a period of time, the general area became known as the Burnett and as its population grew, it evolved into three districts: the South, Central and North Burnett.

By the early twentieth century the South Burnett had been widely settled, with major towns at Kingaroy, Nanango, Wondai and Murgon. Initial pastoral activity concentrated on sheep farming, but this has long since been discontinued and today the region has broader-based primary industries including coal mining, cattle, pigs, forestry, peanuts, grains, fruits and a small but flourishing wine industry.

As usual, early settlers brought with them vinecuttings which they planted for household fruit, and a small table grape industry has existed in the region for many years. But there is no history of wine grape production until 1994 when, as a result of a government-commissioned report, the region was recommended as suitable for the production of wine grapes, although a few growers had anticipated the Macarthur Report and made their initial plantings in 1993. By 1999 there were 32 growers, whose plantings in the region were over 200 ha in total, with three wineries and six cellar door sales facilities.

Location: Kingaroy latitude 26°33'S, longitude 151°51'E, about 150 km north-west of Brisbane
Elevation: Kingaroy 442 m with the majority of the region between 300 and 600 m. Most vineyards are planted between 300–340 m
Topography and soils: The region dates from the early Devonian to the early Triassic period, many of its features being formed under the ocean. These features, made up of structural blocks, were formed by the deposition of transported volcanic material during the Devonian period and, aligned roughly parallel to the coastline, were later intruded by granitic rock. During the early to middle Triassic period, subsidence occurred between adjacent blocks, creating low points ('troughs') which accumulated thick layers of sediments and volcanic flows. The Esk trough folded during the middle Triassic period, causing the western areas to stabilise and the receding of the ocean to its present coastline. Further periods of volcanic activity resulted in the deposition of plateau basalts, especially in the Bunya Mountains in the south-west of the region. The most recent period of vulcanisation produced long basalt flows along the Barambah Creek.

Within the region, there is a broad range of soils suitable for viticulture: granitic red, sandy soils, alluvial soils on flood plains and terraces and basaltic soils resulting from ancient vulcanisation. Described in ascending order, they are light sands, varying to a variety of red soils of light clay through to brown and black clays. The red, brown and black soils have moderate to relatively high fertility and range in pH from 5–7.5.
Climate: Kingaroy Prince Street MJT 23.5°C, MAR 12.25°C, HDD 1891 (cut off at 19°C but otherwise not adjusted), AR 780 mm (Oct–Apr 588 mm), RH 72% (9am Jan), 53% (3pm Jan), AI na, SH est 8.

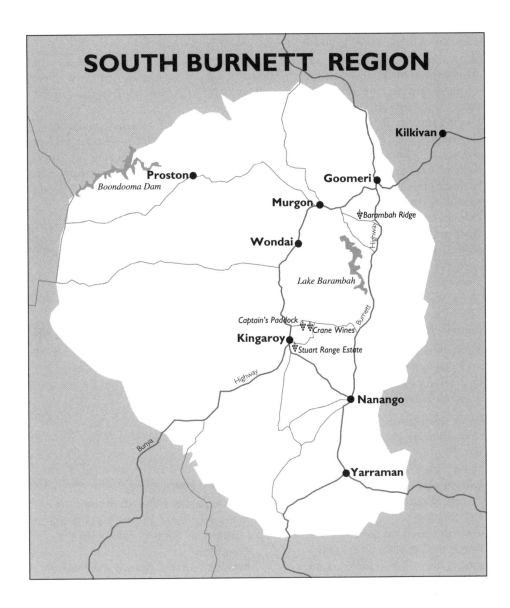

The South Burnett is undoubtedly a hot, humid, sub-tropical area with a rainfall occurring predominantly during the growing season. As in most such areas, there are also thunderstorms and scattered hailstorms during this time. Risk of hail damage in any given area has been estimated at once in every eight to ten years. While drought stress in such conditions would be a rare problem, such a climate does of course increase the risks of mildews and rots.

An irrigation scheme, facilitated by the construction of the Bjelke-Petersen Dam near Wondai and Murgon, operates along the Barkers and Barambah Creeks, whereby water from the dam is released to top up the creek systems from which irrigation water is drawn. All the water available in the system is currently allocated, although a planned extension of the scheme may alter the situation. Another irrigation scheme operates from the Boondooma Dam in the north-west of the region. Apart from these schemes, irrigation is confined to private bores, farm dams and 'trenching' to harvest surface water for such purposes.

Principal varieties: White—chardonnay, semillon; Red—shiraz, cabernet sauvignon

Harvest time and budburst: chardonnay budburst early September, harvest end of January; semillon budburst mid September, harvest end of first week of February; shiraz budburst late September to early October, harvest end of February; cabernet sauvignon budburst early October, harvest end of first week of March. These times are slightly variable according to seasons and elevation.

Principal wine styles: It is rather early in the region's history to prophesy what might be dominant wine styles and I have tasted comparatively few of the local wines, but in hot regions, full-bodied white styles are usually made with the most beneficial results. Certainly the early Stuart Range Chardonnays were promising enough.

Total area: 201 ha (1999)

Barambah Ridge   NR

79 Goschnicks Road, Redgate
via Murgan, Qld 4605
Ph 07 4168 4766, Fax 07 4168 4770,
Email sbw@esprov.com.au

Owner: South Burnett Wines Ltd
Chief winemaker: Charles Williams
Year of foundation: 1995
Tonnes crushed on average each year: 250, including some contract crushing
Location: Murgon
Area: 6.85 ha
Soils: grey-brown loam over clay
Varieties planted: White—chardonnay, semillon; Red—cabernet sauvignon, shiraz
Leading wines: Barambah Ridge Chardonnay (unwooded)
Notes: One of the 'older' wineyards in a very new region, Barambah Ridge has built up a good reputation for whites in a very short time. However I have not tasted any wines recently. Cellar door sales: 7 days 10am–5pm.

Captain's Paddock   NR

Crawford-Booie Road, Kingaroy, Qld 4610
Ph 07 4162 4534, Fax 07 4162 4767

Owners: Don and Judy McCallum
Chief winemaker: (contract)
Year of foundation: 1997
Tonnes crushed on average each year: 8
Location: Kingaroy
Area: 4 ha
Soils: red volcanic soils
Varieties planted: White—chardonnay; Red—merlot, shiraz
Leading wines: Captain's Paddock Shiraz, Chardonnay
Notes: This is a small vineyard whose vines are just coming into full bearing. No wines tasted. Cellar door sales and mail order from the above address.

Crane Wines   NR

Haydens Road, Booie, Qld 4610
Ph 07 4162 7647, Fax 07 4162 8381,
Email cranewines@bigpond.com

Owners: John and Sue Crane
Chief winemaker: John Crane

Year of foundation: 1992
Tonnes crushed on average each year: 10
(a further 50 tonnes are purchased from local
growers to fulfil Crane Wines' grape
requirements)
Location: Booie
Area: 4 ha
Soils: fertile free-draining red scrub soils over
basalt
Varieties planted: White—chardonnay,
sauvignon blanc, semillon; Red—cabernet
sauvignon, chambourcin, merlot, pinot noir,
shiraz
Leading wines: Crane Wines Chardonnay,
Shiraz
Notes: Crane Wines is the oldest winery in
this region. Regrettably, I have not tasted any
of its wines. Cellar door sales: daily
9am–4pm.

Stuart Range Estates **R83**

67 William St, Kingaroy, Qld 4610
Ph 07 4162 3711, Fax 07 4162 4811,
Email srewines@kingaroy.big.net.au

Owner: Kingaroy Wines Pty Ltd (a private
company consisting of 20 shareholders)
Chief winemaker: Charles Pregenzer
Year of foundation: 1997
Tonnes crushed on average each year: 200
Location: Kingaroy. No vineyards are owned,
the Company purchasing its fruit from five
local growers
Leading wines: Stuart Range Estates
Chardonnay, Goodger Chardonnay
Notes: Stuart Range Estates has won a
consistent array of silver and bronze medals for
its Chardonnays and Shiraz. These are arguably
the best wines of the region. Cellar door sales:
daily 9am–5pm.

NORTHERN TERRITORY ZONE

The Northern Territory is an unlikely area for viticulture, being hot and arid in its southern parts, and hot and humid in its tropical north. However, wine is made, though whether winemaking will ever be more than a tourist diversion, is hard to say.

Chateau Hornsby Wines ❧ NR

Petrick Road, Alice Springs, NT 0870
(10 km south-east of the town)
Ph 08 8955 5133, Fax 08 8955 5532

Owner: Denis Hornsby
Chief winemaker: Gordon Cook
Year of foundation: 1974
Tonnes crushed on average each year: 10
Location: Alice Springs
Area: 3 ha
Soils: coarse red sand high in iron oxide and,

Denis Hornsby adds, 'not much else'.
Irrigation, which of course is necessary, comes from a bore 100 m deep. The water is high in calcium and carbonates but 'is suitable for the job'.
Varieties planted: White—chardonnay, riesling, semillon; Red—cabernet sauvignon, shiraz
Leading wines: Chateau Hornsby Early Red (Shiraz), Shiraz
Notes: Australia's furthest winery from anywhere! Cellar door sales: 7 days 10am–5pm. There is also a restaurant.

❧ GLOSSARY

Baume (Be): a measure of sugar in grape juice, or unfermented sugar in fermenting musts or dessert or table wine

Biscay: a self-mulching, dark-coloured, cracking clay

Cytokinins: plant hormones formed in growing root tips. They ascend via the xylem system to upper plant parts and have two major functions: a) to promote cell multiplication in newly differentiating tissues; and b) to attract sugar and other nutrients to where they are in greatest concentration. Adequate cytokinins promote budburst, lateral branching, the development of leaves and fruiting structures and fruit-set. Cytokinin production and its transmission from the roots are encouraged by ample sunshine and leaf exposure and consequent ample sugar to the roots, as well as by a warm, well-aerated root environment.

Dr: red duplex (a soil classification)

Dy: yellow duplex (a soil classification)

Floraison: a French term meaning 'the flowering of the vine'.

Geographical Indication: the places of origin of Australian wine (i.e. the wine zones, regions and sub-regions)

Gibberellin: a plant hormone causing growth of its stem

Gout de terroir: a French term meaning literally 'the taste of the earth'. The distinctive taste given to certain wines by the vineyard soils in which they are grown, for example, the characteristic flinty taste of French Chablis or older Hunter River Shiraz, or perhaps the taste of Pemberton and Manjimup Pinot reds.

Hedging: the training of vines into a hedge by removing excessive foliage to aid aeration, sunlight penetration and ripening

Hotspots: areas of excessively hot fermentation within fermenting grape musts, especially applicable to pinot noir

Hundred: in South Australia, a part of a local government district, originally an administrative division of an English county, equivalent to a 'parish' in other Australian states

Leaf-plucking: the hand plucking of leaves from around bunches of grapes to aid ripening

Lyre: a trellising system shaped like a 'U' whereby vine-shoots are trained upwards between two pairs of foliage wires so that the fruiting zone of the vine is basal and the canopy walls are inclined slightly outwards

Must: the mixture of grape juice, skins and seeds that emerges from a grape crusher, which later becomes wine after fermentation

New World: winemaking countries outside Europe

Phylloxera: the vine louse, an aphid that eats the roots of vitis vinifera vines, ultimately causing their demise. It has proved resistant to all means of eradication and the only means of control is by replanting vitis vinifera cultivars on phylloxera-resistant root-stocks.

Pigeage: a French term describing the Burgundian practice of foot-stamping the must of pinor noir to even out its fermenting temperature by removing hot-spots.

A practice now commonly used in the New World for the production of superior Pinot Noir.

Scott-Henry: a trellising system originally developed in Oregon, USA named after its developers and further refined by Dr Richard Smart. It utilises two fruiting wires, one at 1 metre in height and the other at 1.15 metres. The shoots on the upper wire are trained upwards between two pairs of foliage wires and those on the bottom wire downwards generally using one foliage wire.

Traditional expression: a term describing how or when the wine is made, for example, Botrytis, late harvest, bottle-fermented

Veraison: the change of colour of grapes as they ripen, especially noticeable in red varieties, but occurring equally in whites

Vertical shoot positioning (VSP): a trellising system designed to train shoots into a narrow vertical canopy, increasingly common in cooler vineyard areas of Australia

❧ BIBLIOGRAPHY

Busby, James *A Treatise on the Culture of the Vine*, R. Howe Government Printer, Sydney, 1825 (as reprinted by David Ell Press, Sydney, 1979)

Coombe, B and Dry, P (eds) *Viticulture* vol. 1, Winetitles, Adelaide, 1988

Dunstan, D *Better Than Pommard*, Australian Scholarly Publishing and Museum of Victoria, Melbourne, 1994

Gladstones, J *Viticulture and Environment*, Winetitles, Adelaide, 1992

Jacqueline, L and Poulain, R *Wines and Vineyards of France*, Paul Hamlyn, London, 1962

Niewwenhuis, J *A Preliminary Assessment of Soil Groups for Wine Grape Production in the Ovens Valley*, Wangaratta Regional Development Corp, 1993

Smart, RE and Dry, P *Viticulture* vol. 2, Winetitles, Adelaide, 1988

Ward, E *Vineyards of Victoria*, 1862 (reprinted by Sullivans Cove, nd)

❧ ACKNOWLEDGEMENTS

In the preparation of this book, I acknowledge and have been extremely grateful for the cooperation of the many vignerons and winemakers who have given unstintingly of their time to respond to my letters, faxes and phone queries concerning their vineyards, wineries and winemaking. However, I would especially like to thank Ernie Sullivan, the secretary of the Geographical Indications Committee, for his generous assistance concerning applications made for regional and sub-regional status.

❦ INDEX OF WINERIES

❧ WINE TASTING NOTES